THE
LAST
MAFIOSO

THE LAST MAFIOSO

The Treacherous World of
Jimmy Fratianno

OVID DEMARIS

NYT
Times
BOOKS

Third printing, February 1981

Published by TIMES BOOKS, a division of
Quadrangle/The New York Times Book Co., Inc.,
Three Park Avenue, New York, N.Y. 10016

Published simultaneously in Canada by
Fitzhenry & Whiteside, Ltd., Toronto

Library of Congress Cataloging in Publication Data
Demaris, Ovid.
The last Mafioso.
Includes index.
1. Fratianno, Jimmy, 1913–
2. Crime and criminals—United States—Biography.
3. Mafia. I. Title.
HV6248.F68D45 1980 364.1'06 [B] 80–50926
ISBN 0–8129–0955–0

MANUFACTURED IN THE UNITED STATES OF AMERICA

For David and Donald
and
their lovely wives and children

AUTHOR'S NOTE

† † † †

JIMMY FRATIANNO HAD BEEN IN THE WITNESS PROTECTION PROGRAM seven months the first time we met to discuss the possibility of my writing this book based on his recollections. Protected by U.S. deputy marshals who stood guard outside the door, we talked privately for three hours, each taking the measure of the other. My interest was in determining the depth and scope of his experience, the soundness of his memory, the range of his knowledge, and the extent to which he could articulate his story. His success on all counts far exceeded my expectations. As added bonuses, I found him to be enormously energetic and surprisingly considerate and amicable. I came away with the conviction that his life story would make an extraordinary document.

Although this was my first personal contact with him, I had known him by reputation for a long time. Twenty years ago Los Angeles Police Captain James Hamilton had played a tape recording for me of a telephone conversation in which Jimmy had threatened to blow a man's head off, and I remember Hamilton saying with a grin, "And the son of a bitch really means it. This guy's the Mafia's top enforcer on the West Coast." Based on that tape recording and records of the investigation, I wrote a suspense novel entitled *The Extortioners.* A few years later, in a non-fiction book, *The Green Felt Jungle,* I named two of Jimmy's murder victims. It was based on police information and has since been confirmed in my conversations with Jimmy.

If Jimmy was aware of any of this as we talked that first time, he gave no indication of it. He mentioned having received a substantial offer for his story but when I expressed a preference for another publisher, he immediately turned to his attorney and said, "Forget them, we go with Ovid." That, as I was to learn in short order, was classic Jimmy. He is not one to agonize over decisions. His life is testament to that fact.

We began working together almost immediately. As the government moved him to various locations for appearances before grand juries and court trials, I followed to take advantage of every free moment he could spare me. Once determined to tell his story, there was no holding him back. His energy made

vii

it possible for me to interview him in grueling ten-hour stretches, for days on end, and the questioning was as relentless as I could make it.

I had done my homework. I had accumulated extensive background information, consisting of FBI and police surveillance reports covering the last thirty years of his life; court and police records; parole reports; prison records, with several psychological studies; and nearly two thousand pages of transcribed FBI wiretaps from several of Jimmy's telephones as well as those of his associates; plus just about everything written about him and his associates in newspapers, magazines, and books—everything I could lay hands on.

I hurled a barrage of questions at him, but Jimmy just leaned back in his chair, puffed on his big cigar, and took it all in stride. Nothing daunted him. Not even a malfunctioning tape recorder. When I told him one morning that we had to repeat a whole day's work, he shrugged and said, "It's just one of them things, Ovid. Let's get to it."

I warned him at the outset that if I caught him in a single lie, I would walk out and burn the tapes. His response was, "Ovid, forget about it. My life's in your hands." The way Jimmy saw it, his only chance of escaping the vengeance of the Mafia bosses who wanted him dead in the worst way was for the book to earn enough money for him to leave the country, taking with him his wife, step-daughter, and divorced mother-in-law. He understood that one lie could lead to the book being discredited and that was the last thing he wanted in this world.

The government had also issued its warning. One lie and all plea bargains were off, which meant that he would spend the remainder of his life behind bars, or could even face the death penalty for two murders in Cleveland and one in San Diego.

To my knowledge, and this has been verified by the FBI, this was the first time the government had ever allowed a key witness to talk freely with a writer prior to his giving testimony in upcoming trials. I bring this up primarily to show how much FBI agents and prosecutors had come to trust and respect his information. Jimmy has committed just about every crime in the book, but when he gets on the witness stand, juries believe him. He knows details no one else will talk about. Federal Strike Force Attorney James Henderson calls Jimmy a "spellbinder." Indeed, he is that and more.

His memory is absolutely phenomenal. Not only could he go back sixty years and come up with the names of teachers and school chums, but he could describe countless incidents in minute detail. I soon discovered that my job consisted of pressing the right buttons. Every time he repeated a story, and he repeated the important ones at least a dozen times over a two-year period, the details became richer, but the basic facts never deviated.

Besides the interminable face-to-face questioning sessions, we talked on the telephone almost every day during the entire two-year period it took me to research and write this book. In all that time, not once did I ever catch him in even a contradiction.

At this writing, in July 1980, Jimmy has served twenty months of two concurrent five-year sentences, much of that time in the "Valachi suite" at La Tuna federal penitentiary near El Paso, Texas. He is presently out on parole but will remain under government protection until he fulfills his remaining court obligations which are still considerable. The value of his testimony speaks for itself in the results it has achieved against his former associates, and is the subject of the Epilogue.

However novelistic the techniques I have used to portray his life and times, this is strictly a work of non-fiction, based entirely on factual material and from my experiences gained in a lifetime of investigating and studying the crime world. This is a true story about people with real names. Only one name has been changed ("Cindy"), but no identity has been altered. To help the reader keep track of the vast cast of characters in this book, I have added a Dramatis Personae in the Appendix. Of course, the dialogue is as Jimmy and others recall it, in some cases reconstructed.

In the interest of clarity, I have made a few minor deviations in the time sequence, and, for the purpose of exposition, it was necessary in rare instances to combine in some scenes several conversations into one or vice versa. But at no time were there any departures from the real, verifiable events. If nothing else, this book is the exact true account of the life and times of the "last Mafioso," Jimmy Fratianno, the Cosa Nostra's highest-ranking member ever to "turn."

If it reads like fiction, the credit belongs to the central character. Few novelists, in fact, possess the creative imagination to conceive a plot as fascinatingly intricate and suspenseful as the one woven by Jimmy Fratianno in the course of his extraordinary life.

To maintain objectivity in the presentation of the material, it was important that I retain complete editorial control of the material. Accordingly Jimmy Fratianno will not see these pages before publication.

In all, I tape recorded nearly two million words in my conversations with Jimmy, his friends, relatives, and others. Some of the sources have asked to remain anonymous. Other key contributors include James F. Ahearn, Assistant Special Agent in Charge of the San Francisco FBI office; Nathaniel H. Akerman, Assistant United States Attorney, Southern District of New York; Jack Anderson, columnist and author; Jack Armstrong, former FBI Special Agent, San Diego; Jack Barron, FBI Special Agent, Los Angeles; James P. Cantillon, Los Angeles lawyer who represented Jimmy and Johnny Roselli; Richard C. Chier, Los Angeles lawyer who represented Jimmy; "Cindy," Jimmy's former girlfriend; Duke Countis, former bookmaking agent for Jimmy, who now resides in Australia; Michael Ewing, investigator for the Select Committee on Assassinations, U.S. House of Representatives, Ninety-Fifth Congress; George Faris, a California trucking contractor; Hamilton P. Fox III, Special Attorney, U.S. Department of Justice, Washington; James D. Henderson, Special Attorney, head of the Federal Strike Force in Los Angeles;

Iva Lee Henry, archivist, California Department of Correction; Richard Huff-man, former Assistant California Attorney General; Ivan Markovics, Knights of Malta special ambassador to U.S., and his daughter, Eve; Dennis McDonald, Jimmy's lawyer; Donald "Bud" McPherson, Inspector with the U.S. Marshal Service, in charge of the Witness Protection Program in greater Los Angeles; Marion B. Phillips and Joel Taylor, investigators, California Attorney General's Office; Joseph Shimon, former District of Columbia Police Inspector involved in Operation Mongoose; and A. David Stutz, a San Diego lawyer and former IRS intelligence agent.

I am also indebted to several newsmen for background information: Lowell Bergman, Jim Drinkhall, Bill Hume, Mel Martin, Jack McFarren, John Rawlinson, Denny Walsh, John Winters. I owe a special debt to Michael Hamel-Green, who conducted the investigation for _Look_ in the Joseph Alioto libel lawsuit and whose files of printed material on Fratianno and associates were the most complete anywhere. I appreciate the patience and wisdom of my Editor Hugh Howard and the expertise of my Production Editor Rosalyn T. Badalamenti. And finally, I thank my wife Inez for the long hours devoted to transcribing tapes and typing this book from the original draft and for her assistance in innumerable ways.

This has been a remarkable adventure for me. After thirty years of being on the outside looking in—that is, writing about organized crime from secondary sources—I have now had the rare opportunity of being on the inside looking out. It was a unique experience and one I trust I have managed to convey in these pages.

CONTENTS

† † † †

PART V: THE HELLHOLE—1966

PART VI: LOOSE AS A MONGOOSE—1966–1970

PART VII: THE DEBACLE—1967–1970

PART VIII: SCAMMING THE JOINT—1970-1973

PART IX: INTERLUDE IN MIAMI—1974

PART X: THE ACTING BOSS—1975-1976

PART XI: SHOW BIZ—1975-1976

† *Contents* †

PART XII: SINATRA—1976

PART XIII: LAST FLASH OF POWER—1976–1977

PART XIV: THE CONTRACT—1977

Illustrations follow page 204.

THE
LAST
MAFIOSO

PROLOGUE:
THE MAKING OF
A MADE GUY

† † † †

IT HAD TAKEN HIM THIRTY-THREE YEARS TO ARRIVE AT THIS MOMENT.
Early that evening he was brought to a winery on South Figueroa Street and
now he waited in a small, dimly lit room for the final act to be played out.

Jimmy Fratianno prided himself on his ability to remain calm under stress,
but he could feel the excitement stirring through him. He locked the feeling
inside, not wanting to share it with the other four candidates. He could hear
the deep rumble of voices in the other room, the scraping of chairs, and he
knew that many awaited his entrance. Standing room only, he thought, trying
to lighten the feeling that was knotting his nerves.

Then the door opened and Johnny Roselli* beckoned to him. "It's time,"
he said.

They walked down a short hallway and stopped before a closed door. Roselli
squeezed his arm and smiled.

"Just a couple things, Jimmy. After you've taken the oath, go around the
circle and kiss everybody and introduce yourself. Then join hands with the
others. Are you ready?"

He nodded and Roselli opened the door. It was a large room and the
pungent odor of fermented grapes was stronger here. There must have been
fifty men in the room, many of whom he had met in the seventeen months he
had been in Los Angeles. They were gathered in a circle around a long table,
their faces grim, their eyes shadowed by the harsh lighting from bare overhang-
ing bulbs.

Roselli led Jimmy to the head of the table where Jack Dragna was standing,
a short, heavyset man with horn-rimmed glasses, who reminded Jimmy of a
banker. Tom Dragna, as usual in sports clothes, was on Jack's left and Momo
Adamo on his right.

"Jimmy, Jack Dragna's the boss of our family," Roselli said. "Momo

---

*See Appendix for Dramatis Personae. Brief biographical sketches of John Roselli and other
principals are to be found there.

3

Adamo's the underboss and Tom's the *consigliere.*"

Jack Dragna raised his hand and spoke to everyone in the room. "Everybody join hands," he said.

On the table in front of where Jimmy was standing was a revolver and a dagger crossing one another. The next time Jack spoke was in a confusing mixture of Sicilian and Italian. He spoke rapidly and Jimmy tried desperately to understand what was being said to him in front of all these people.

What he was able to make out went something like this: "We are gathered here this evening to make five new members: Jimmy Fratianno, Jimmy Regace, Charley Dippolito, Louie Piscopo, and Tom's son, Louie Dragna. Now, Jimmy, you are entering into the honored society of Cosa Nostra, which welcomes only men of great courage and loyalty.

"You come in alive and you go out dead. The gun and knife are the instruments by which you live and die.

"Cosa Nostra comes first above anything else in your life. Before family, before country, before God. When you are summoned, you must come even if your mother, or wife, or your children are on their death bed.

"There are three laws you must obey without question. You must never betray any of the secrets of this Cosa Nostra. You must never violate the wife or children of another member. You must never become involved with narcotics. The violation of any of these laws means death without trial or warning."

There was more but, thirty years later, this was what Jimmy Fratianno remembered. The rest of the ritual sermon was a blur.

The next thing Jimmy heard was Jack Dragna asking him to raise the index finger of his right hand. He wondered at the request until Jack pricked his finger with a pin. A small bubble of blood burst forth.

When he looked up, Roselli winked at him. Still speaking in his Sicilian–Italian dialect, Dragna said, "This drop of blood symbolizes your birth into our family. We're one until death."

He paused a moment and then stepped forward and kissed Jimmy on both cheeks. "Jimmy, you're now a made guy, an *amico nostra,* a *soldato* in our *famiglia.* Whenever you wish to introduce a member to another member he don't know, you say, '*Amico nostra.*' In English, you say, 'This is a friend of *ours.*' But whenever you introduce a member to someone who's not a member, you say, 'This is a friend of *mine.*'"

The ceremony was over. Jimmy turned and kissed Roselli. People began talking again and Jimmy was so excited that he could feel his legs tremble as he moved from man to man, kissing and shaking hands, being slapped on the back, hearing words of congratulation. He was now a member of an ancient and extremely exclusive society. It made him a special person, an inheritor of enormous power. It was something he had wanted as long as he could remember.

In a way, it was almost as though a carefully plotted script had delivered Aladena "Jimmy" Fratianno to that room. Born on November 14, 1913, in a small town near Naples, he was brought to the United States by his mother when he was four months old. His father, Antonio, was already in this country with relatives in Cleveland. In 1915, a daughter, Louise, was born, followed by another son, Warren, three years later.

Fratianno's background was classical American Mafioso. Aladena, as Jimmy was christened, was one of thousands of Italian immigrants living in the Murray Hill–Mayfield Road district then known as Little Italy but also called the Hill.

At the age of six, he had seen three men mowed down by machine-gun fire in front of Tony Milano's speakeasy and his reaction had been an awed, "Holy mother of Jesus!"

The conditions in Cleveland's Little Italy were not all that different from those in the old country. Except, of course, that now the Italians were a minority, confined to a ghetto by their language and manners. They labored long hours in menial, back-breaking work for minimal wages, their crafts for the most part forgotten in their desperate need to provide food and shelter for their large families.

Some, however, were self-employed and could hold their heads up with pride. Among them was Antonio Fratianno, who worked as a landscape contractor and was known as a serious, sober man, a good provider, but also as the absolute autocrat of his household.

Aladena's first memory, and one he never forgot, remembering it always with a pleasurable glow, was the horse and buggy his father had bought when Aladena was three years old. They lived on East 125th Street then, and he remembered how the neighbors had admired the buggy with the fringed canvas top. He loved that horse and buggy and the way the fringe would dance happily as the horse trotted down the street. He cried the day his father sold it, harder than he did when his father used the strap on him.

His father was strict and quick to punish. Although he was strict with Louise and Warren, he spared the rod with them, a fact not lost on Aladena, who grew even more resentful. The punishment gradually became a duel of willpower between two determined enemies. The harder he was beaten, the harder he became to handle. He grew obstinate and defiant, determined to have his own way and ready to defy all who contested him.

In school he was rowdy, getting into fights with other boys and teachers, until finally he was sent to Thomas Edison, which was known as a "bad boy" school. There he formed a life-long friendship with Louis "Babe" Triscaro, who later would become an important Teamsters official and the liaison between Jimmy Hoffa and the Cleveland Mafia.

Almost from the time he could walk, Aladena had been preoccupied with the importance of money. Besides having his own paper route at the age of six, he hawked newspapers at the No. 4 gate at the Fischer Body plant, and in front of the Hayden Theater evenings and weekends. At eleven he was working with his father, putting in a six-day week during summer vacations and all day Saturdays during the school year.

During this period he gained the cognomen that would stick to him for the rest of his life. There was a policeman who used to chase him whenever he stole fruit from sidewalk stands, which was often, and one day Aladena hit the policeman in the face with a rotten tomato. The policeman gave chase. People stopped to watch, and an older man said, "Look at that weasel run!" When making out his report, the policeman wrote down the nickname and it became part of his police record, following him wherever he went.

It was just prior to this incident, that he had started calling himself Jimmy —Aladena sounded too much like a "broad's name"—and the next thing he knew he was "Jimmy the Weasel." Although at sixteen he entered amateur boxing competition as Kid Weasel, winning the Collingwood Community Center trophy in the lightweight division, his friends never used the nickname, at least not to his face.

His first experience with bootlegging was at the age of twelve. He was a waiter in a speakeasy owned by a woman called Bessie. For nearly two years he worked part time for Bessie and saw so many drunks that it turned him against liquor. He would see men come in and drink their entire paychecks, money they needed for their families. At night in bed he would think, "God, people got to be crazy to get drunk." It was the money part that bothered him the most.

His behavior in school gradually improved and he transferred to Collingwood High School for the ninth grade, but a year later he caught cold, ignored it until it turned to pneumonia, and with a fever of 106 degrees lapsed into a coma. It was two weeks before he regained consciousness and when he did he found a priest giving him the last rites. As the priest touched his tongue with the Communion wafer, Jimmy opened his eyes and said, "I'm better." Then he slipped back into his coma for another week.

By the time he opened his eyes the second time, the pneumonia had turned into pleurisy, which had created an enormous deposit of pus in his left lung and pleural cavities. It got so thick it was pushing his heart against his right lung. When all efforts to remove it with a syringe failed, Dr. Victor Tanno decided that the only way to get at it was to remove a rib. Because of his weakened condition, ether was out of the question. They would use a local anesthetic, but as Dr. Tanno warned him, it would freeze the flesh but not the bone. With Jimmy strapped to a chair, facing the back of it, and held by his mother, Dr. Tanno made the incision in his back and began cutting into the rib.

The memory of that pain would be with him all the years of his life. Fifty years later he could still remember how he had screamed and cursed that doctor, could still feel the teeth-gnashing pain of the saw cutting into bone, a pain so intense he felt blinded, his brain on fire, every nerve end begging for mercy, and he could still feel his mother's arms around him, hear her cries as if they were coming from a great distance, echoing off the walls and pounding at his ears with his own cries and curses.

When the doctor finally cut through the rib and pulled it out, the pus shot out with explosive force. Dr. Tanno laughed and said, "Look, nurse, it's like an oil well erupting."

He never returned to school. Although his grades had been below average, he was extremely quick with numbers, a talent that he had already put to practical use. At the age of fourteen, while hawking newspapers at Fischer Body, he had become acquainted with Johnny Martin, a gambler who operated games at Mike's, a Greek restaurant across the street from the No. 4 gate. Martin, who had taken a liking to the boy, spent hours in a room above the restaurant teaching him all the cheating tricks he knew. He taught him how to shuffle cards, how to deal seconds, and how to mark them during a game by using a small piece of sandpaper hidden in the palm of the hand. Jimmy got so he could mark an entire deck in less than an hour. He learned to use shaded dice, to palm the third dice, to switch, and which numbers were winners and which losers.

By the age of seventeen he had become Martin's partner at Mike's, receiving an even cut of the winnings. Later Jimmy bought a portable crap table and began holding his own games at a friend's house. Booking the game and using shaded dice, he would clear three or four hundred dollars in a matter of a few hours. This money was a far richer reward for less effort than the paltry wage he received from his father for driving a truck each day.

At eighteen he was charged with raping a twenty-five-year old divorcee. Under cross-examination the woman confessed she had lied because she thought she could extort money from his father, and the case was dropped. But the charge of rape, like the nickname "Weasel," would become part of his police record, a blemish irrevocable for all time.

A few days before his nineteenth birthday, on a cold moonlit night, Jimmy and a friend went ice skating at Elysium Park. Jimmy could do just about anything on skates. He played hockey, was an agile figure skater, and could even dance on ice while wearing his long-bladed racers. This made him popular with the girls, which was all the incentive he needed to strut his stuff.

On this particular evening, he showed off for a girl who was with three other girls and five tough looking Polish boys. When he was leaving the Elysium, the five boys attacked him. The next thing he knew fists and feet were coming at him from all directions. He tried to fight back, but he was pounded into the ground. He was groggily crawling around on all fours when a heavy boot caught him square in the nose. Bone shattered, blood spurted out, and he flopped over on his back in time for the boot to catch the side of his nose. He rolled over on his stomach and tried to protect his face and head with his arms. He was vaguely aware of blows raining against his body but he was soon beyond pain.

He came to in a receiving hospital. The bridge of his nose was hopelessly crushed and they had to rebuild it with gristle taken from the lower part of his chest. After the operation, he was advised to return for plastic surgery when it had healed, but he never went back.

With the help of his friend, Anthony "Tony Dope" Delsanter, a husky six-footer, Jimmy went out looking for the Polish boys. He caught four of them, in the dark of night, when each was alone, and after knocking them to the ground, Jimmy had gone to work with a blackjack, breaking noses, knocking out teeth, fracturing jaws, and cracking skulls, even breaking the arm of the boy whose boot he suspected had broken his nose. All the boys required hospitalization and all needed many stitches in their heads. The fifth boy had moved away, but Jimmy continued looking for him for a whole year before he grudgingly acknowledged defeat.

For Jimmy, it was something that had to be done, a wrong that had to be righted, a vendetta in the best Italian tradition. While working the boys over with the blackjack, he had realized how easy it would be to kill. He had hit hard enough for that, he had thought at the time; it had not bothered him in the least. For Jimmy, it was an important realization.

When Jimmy was twenty, Jack Haffey, the boss of the 26th Ward, who worked as a state inspector on highway construction, confided to Jimmy that he had top political connections and if they worked together they could make some money. The first opportunity was a contract calling for 25,000 yards of fill for a reservoir. Jimmy's father had two trucks, and Jimmy suggested that he lease six more. The state was paying fifty cents a yard and, with sideboards, they could load two and a half yards in their one-and-a-half-yard trucks. His father was interested until Jimmy told him it would cost $500 to get the job.

"I don't want to get in no trouble," his father said.

"You ain't going to get in trouble," Jimmy replied. "This guy's a pal of the governor."

"I don't want to do nothing crooked."

"Ah, forget it," Jimmy cried. "I can't make no fucking money with you. I'll lease some trucks and do the job myself."

The next day he became his own boss. He leased eight trucks—and gave Haffey the $500 payoff. When the first truck arrived at the reservoir, Jimmy said, "Jack, measure this truck coming in. All my trucks are the same size."

Haffey looked the truck over. "What do you think, Jimmy?"

"Three and a half yards, Jack. We're stacking them up high."

From then on, Haffey wrote down three and a half yards, which meant that Jimmy was making fifty cents extra on each load. With eight trucks making six and seven trips a day, it meant that he was earning an extra $25 to $30 a day, besides the ten cents a yard broker's fee he was making from the truck owners.

About this time, Jimmy also started booking at the local racetracks and hanging around the clubhouse of the Italian–American Brotherhood (IAB) on Mayfield Road. Run by Tony Milano (who would later become the underboss of the Cleveland family), the IAB was the hangout for all the local big shots, who sat outside in the summer, talking quietly among themselves and watching people walk by.

"Big Al" Polizzi was the boss. There was Johnny DeMarco and "Johnny King" Angersola, with his brothers, Fred and George. Jimmy also got to know the leaders of the Jewish mob, known as the Cleveland Syndicate. These men —Louis "Lou Rhody" Rothkopf, Moe Dalitz, Morris Kleinman—operated gambling joints in Cleveland, as well as in Newport and Covington, Kentucky, all with the blessings of Big Al's Mayfield Road Gang. Others in the syndicate included Ruby Kolod, Sam Tucker, and, in later years, Lou Rhody's nephew, Bernard "Bernie" Rothkopf, who would grow up to become president of the MGM Grand Hotel in Las Vegas. They also were involved in Buckeye Enterprises, which controlled various gambling concessions, and was the hidden link between the Mayfield Road Gang and the Cleveland Syndicate.

Even as a young boy, Jimmy had suspected that there was some kind of a secret Italian organization that was more cohesive and powerful than the Jews or Irish with whom they worked, but in those days the words Mafia or Cosa Nostra were never used even on the Hill. The only reference to any crime organization ever mentioned was "The Combination." And it was The Combination which then controlled organized crime in Cleveland.

In 1934 Jimmy bought a two-year-old Marmon limousine and began chauffeuring customers from the East Side to the The Combination's gambling joints around Cleveland. Lou Rhody paid him seven dollars a load. Jimmy drove the limousine himself for a while and then hired a driver.

With money rolling in from the gambling, the chauffeuring and the trucking, he bought himself a new Chevrolet coupe and began having his clothes tailor-made. He wore a broad-brimmed Capone-style hat, alligator shoes, and carried a couple thousand dollars in his pocket. Life was sweet in the midst of the nation's worst depression.

With more leisure than he knew how to handle, he turned to golf and met Bill McSweeney, a big, tough Irishman who broke heads for the Teamsters union when he was not belting golf balls out of sight. McSweeney's boss was Tommy Lenahan, a man in constant need of head breakers because the Teamsters was a small, struggling union in those days.

Jimmy's first involvement with the union was in their effort to organize the parking lots in Cleveland. With the "Neanderthal" McSweeney and others at his side, five-foot-nine Jimmy, who weighed a hundred-fifty soaking wet, would march into parking lots and throw muriatic acid on cars while his partners slashed tires and broke windshields. The pay was fifteen dollars a day, plus ten dollars a day for every man Jimmy could induce to work for five dollars a day on his crew. During the Premier Aluminum strike, Jimmy had a crew of nine, recruited from the Hill, who fought against scabs and cops, both private and public, with lead pipes, baseball bats, blackjacks, and tire chains.

Jimmy's old friend from bad boy school, Babe Triscaro, was also cracking heads on the picket lines. From the Premier it was on to the knitting mills around Seventy-ninth Street and Euclid Avenue. And from there to the transportation drivers, with special instructions from Lenahan as to whose head to break.

By the end of 1935, after an exhausting four months of hand-to-hand combat on picket lines, Jimmy came into his own. He went to Florida with the rest of the big boys on the Hill. That was the year The Combination opened The Plantation, its first gambling casino in Miami. He bought a new Oldsmobile, a flashy wardrobe, had $2,500 cash in his pocket, and some expertise in bookmaking.

Johnny Martin had long ago explained the fundamentals which had proved profitable at the local racetracks. Hialeah would be no different. "Booking at the track," Johnny had told him, "is the easiest, safest way to gamble in the world. If you know what you're doing, you'll never lose a nickel. Just balance your book and never refuse a bet. Drop all the long-shots in the box—but when you go to the window don't let the bettor know. The reason they bet with you instead of going to the window themselves is that they don't want to reduce the odds. Get yourself a runner. And at night when you go to bed, pray that your bettors get their horses from the racing form and not from some fucking hot tips. Stay away from hot horses."

On his first day at Hialeah, Johnny King introduced him to "Lucky" Luciano, who looked pretty relaxed for a man who was then the subject of the hottest investigation in New York history. Two of Luciano's boys began giving Jimmy their action, going a hundred and a hundred, win and place, on each race, each selecting a different horse from the racing form. It could not have been more perfect. The meet was fifty-five days and in that time Jimmy took them for $24,000.

When he returned home, Jimmy started booking at the World Exposition, which had moved from Chicago to Cleveland. He made his headquarters in the midgets tent, most of whom were avid horse players. He liked their company, enjoyed their sense of humor, their ability to ignore the misfortune that had made them objects of curiosity. And they were good customers.

In the evening, Jimmy and his friends made the rounds of nightclubs, getting the best tables and hobnobbing with the owners, who showed their pleasure at meeting these rising Young Turks by introducing them to their friendly chorus girls. The friendliest girls, the ones who flattered their ego by never asking for money, were also introduced to James "Blackie" Licavoli, who was on the lam for the murder of Toledo beer baron Jackie Kennedy and his girlfriend. Blackie's cousin, Thomas "Yonnie" Licavoli, and four others were serving life terms for this crime, while five others involved in the murder had evaded justice by going into hiding. It was through Blackie Licavoli, when Licavoli went to Pittsburgh to stay with Mafia boss John LaRock (*nee* LaRocca), that Jimmy and Tony Dope met Frankie Valenti, who one day would be the Mafia boss of Rochester, New York, and would, in these early years, teach Jimmy a few tricks.

At the French Casino Jimmy first met his future wife. He walked into the place, took one look at the hatcheck girl, and immediately sent for the owner to be formally introduced. She was eighteen and her name was Jewel Switzer. She was Irish and German, with blonde hair and big blue eyes, not exactly the kind of girl Italian boys brought home to mother in those days. On August 1, 1936, they drove to Bowling Green and were married. Two months later she was pregnant.

In the summer of 1936 Jimmy and his Cleveland friends discovered that it was a lot quicker and far more profitable to rob gambling joints than to run their own crooked game. Tony Dope Delsanter, who had spent time in a reformatory, was ready for a fast score.

Their first job was a poker game. Jimmy and Tony Dope walked in without disguises, pulled out revolvers, and ordered the nine men in the room to strip down to their underwear and face the wall. They got $5,800 in cash and some jewelry.

The LaRock–Licavoli connection set up the next score. Frankie Valenti had a swanky gambling joint picked out: They went in fast, with their faces obscured by silk stockings, and Jimmy and Tony Dope, who carried sawed-off shotguns, jumped on top of crap tables and screamed, "This is a stickup, against the walls, motherfuckers," and two hundred people ran to obey their command. The take was $70,000.

It was the kind of easy score that encouraged them to try others. One was a customer of the Cleveland Trust Bank, which was just around the corner from the home of his parents on Earlwood Street. Every two weeks, this man, whom he had met at Mike's, used to draw $25,000 from his bank to cash checks at Fischer Body.

Jimmy had parked his brand new Buick, which was to be the crash car, on St. Clair Avenue, about a hundred yards away, but with an excellent view of the bank. A friend, Hipsy Cooper, in the getaway car, was about fifty yards ahead of him, and both were watching as Valenti and Tony Dope held up the man at gun point as he emerged from the bank and ran down the sidewalk toward the corner of Earlwood where Hipsy was supposed to pick them up. Except that he was not moving. Jimmy gunned the Buick, pulled up alongside Hipsy, and screamed at him to get going. But Hipsy appeared to be in a state of shock. Cursing and threatening dire retaliation, Jimmy knew that he had no alternative but to use his own car to help his friends escape. The theory of a crash car is to obstruct whatever pursuit there may be of the getaway car, regardless of the risk involved.

Jimmy skidded around the corner. He knew his friends, fleeing on foot, would head down the alley behind the bank to Blemheim, take a right, run up Blemheim about ten houses, jump a fence and dash through back yards to his house. Jimmy hit the alley, slammed on the brakes, and threw the Buick into a spinning skid, coming to a stop sideways so that it completely blocked the alley. Behind him was the man who had been robbed, standing on the running board of a car he had commandeered to give chase. And behind him was a police car, with siren blaring.

Jimmy jumped out of his car and started waving his arms in an hysterical fashion. "They've got guns," he cried. "They've got guns, I saw them, they're armed and dangerous, duck down, they've got guns and they're dangerous."

"Get the hell out of the way," the man on the running board screamed. "Let us through here."

"Oh, my God, this is terrible. They've got guns," Jimmy continued to cry, waving his arms like a man who has lost his senses.

"Get that car out of there," a policeman, hanging out the opened window of his car, shouted as he waved his hand, signaling Jimmy to move out.

Jimmy jumped into his car, spun the wheel around, threw it into reverse, and slammed on the brakes inches from the other car's front bumper. He threw up his arms in desperation, stalled the engine, turned the motor over with the ignition off, ground the gears, and finally roared out of the alley when he was sure that his friends had had ample time to reach his house.

They were sitting in the parlor, gulping steaming cups of coffee his mother had just served them, and they were livid. They wanted to kill Hipsy. "Where's the cocksucker?" Tony Dope wanted to know. "He left us there to die."

Valenti was angry but less emotional about it. "Where'd you get that *cretino?*"

"It's his first score," Jimmy said. "He panicked, froze at the wheel."

"I'm going to kill that prick," Dope promised.

"Fuck him," Jimmy said. "Let's cut it up three ways and forget him."

Jimmy's daughter Joanne was born on June 24, 1937, a beautiful, happy baby, but Jimmy had little time to spend with his family. Exactly one month later he pulled his last job for a while. The victim was Joe Deutsch, a layoff bookmaker who was too slow in paying off. When Jimmy called to ask why he had not been paid, Deutsch said, "Listen, punk, you'll get paid when I get good and ready to pay. No sooner, understand." Jimmy started screaming and Deutsch slammed the phone in his ear.

For the next few days, Jimmy was like a demented man. He told Tony Dope and McSweeney that he wanted to hurt Deutsch, and they suggested that they might as well get some money while they were at it. For a while they followed Deutsch as he made the rounds of his drops. Jimmy decided to use his Buick and Tony Dope stole some plates which they attached to the Buick's plates with clothes pins painted black.

They struck at nine-thirty on a Saturday night at the downtown intersection of Ninth and Superior, with people five rows deep along the sidewalks. McSweeney was behind the wheel of the Buick and Jimmy and Tony Dope were in the back seat, each armed with a .38 revolver. When the light turned red, they were right behind Deutsch's car. They jumped out of the Buick and came at Deutsch from both sides, with Jimmy on the driver's side. They opened the doors and Jimmy said, "Joe, move over. Don't make no dumb plays and you won't get hurt."

The moment Deutsch saw the guns, he began screaming for help. "Hit him in the fucking mouth," Jimmy told Tony Dope as he tried to shove and push Deutsch out of the way so he could squeeze in behind the steering wheel. He heard the dull thudding of Tony Dope's gun as it repeatedly smashed against Deutsch's head. Blood spurted on Jimmy's new gray gabardine suit and he screamed at Tony Dope, "Pull him away from me." The light turned green and he frantically shifted into gear. He meandered up side streets, getting away from the commercial district, until they were on a quiet residential street.

Deutsch was unconscious and Tony Dope had cleaned out his pockets. Jimmy pulled to the curb and McSweeney stopped behind them. While McSweeney removed the hot plates, Jimmy looked for a sewer to dump the plates and guns. But McSweeney had borrowed his gun from a friend and refused to throw it away. Instead he put it in the glove compartment, and with him behind the wheel, with Tony Dope at his side and Jimmy in the back seat, they decided to go to McSweeney's house for Jimmy and Tony Dope to clean up and to divide the sixteen hundred dollars found on Deutsch, which was a long way from the ten thousand they had expected.

"We nearly got in the shit," McSweeney said. "That sonovabitch screamed loud enough to wake the dead."

Jimmy laughed. "As long as he don't wake the cops."

Before he could finish the sentence they heard a siren. Seconds later a squad car pulled alongside and a policeman waved them to the curb.

They waited in the Buick as two policemen approached from both sides of their car. The officer on Tony Dope's side played a flashlight on Jimmy in the back seat.

"What happened to you, buddy?" he asked.

"I was in a little fight at the poolroom," he said, with a note of apology in his voice. "They're taking me home so I can clean up."

"Oh, yeah? Get out of the car, all of you."

What happened next was inevitable. They found McSweeney's gun and later they found Deutsch, who refused to identify his assailants, but the police lab matched the blood, and that was it.

The judge handed down ten-to-twenty-five-year prison sentences to all three. Jewel screamed when the verdict was pronounced and his mother and sister held onto each other and wept. There were tears in his brother Warren's eyes when Jimmy turned to wave to his family, refusing to walk to the railing to touch or speak to them. His father's eyes were dry as he stoically gazed at his son. He shook his head, once or twice, as if to say, "Why didn't you listen to me," but it was too late.

In 1937 the nation's second oldest penal institution was the Ohio State Penitentiary. Its forty-foot high gray stone wall covered four square blocks in downtown Columbus, an awesome, soul-chilling sight. Passing through its massive steel gates at the age of twenty-three, Jimmy knew he would have to spend some of the best years of his life behind that forbidding wall. For the first time in years, he felt weak and powerless, vulnerable in a world that could crush him like a bug.

All that he had to draw succor from was the advice an old con had given him: "Jimmy, remember one thing when you walk through that gate. Once you're in that joint, you're going to do that time. Nothing can stop that. So do good time. Learn how to relax. Forget your family, forget your friends on the outside. Pretend they don't even exist. Don't worry about nothing. Don't count the days, throw out the calendar. Sleep all you can and dream about sexy movie stars. When your pecker gets stiff in the night, think about Jean Harlow and whack it. Stay away from punks. There's nothing they can do for you that you can't do with your palm. Get involved in prison activities. Keep your nose clean but don't take no shit from nobody. Grab a club and break their fucking heads in a minute. That way nobody's ever going to fuck with you again. When you don't know what to think about, try to imagine what you're going to get for breakfast or dinner or supper. Get involved in team sports. Don't worry about cockroaches or bedbugs and rats.

"Face up to the reality of prison life. Don't talk to screws, you've got nothing to say to them. They've got nothing to do with what happens to you in there. Remember that it's the cons that run the prison. They're the clerks, they do all the paperwork, keep the files, assign the good jobs, the good cell blocks, they see that you get extra privileges. Screws don't do nothing but watch. Go to school, you won't learn nothing, but you'll get to see other cons, for that joint keeps everybody under lock and key twenty-four hours a day.

"It's a hard place and it's killed lots of good men, young and old, but it can't kill nobody that knows how to do good time. That, my boy, is the secret of surviving in that joint. Do one day at a time and let the outside world go fuck itself."

Jimmy never forgot that advice, and recites it verbatim forty years later. It served him well through the many years of time he would do.

He soon learned that it really was the cons who ruled the prison, and that the most important one at the Ohio Penetentiary was Blackie's cousin, Thomas "Yonnie" Licavoli. Yonnie got Jimmy a job in the kitchen, a prize assignment, and had him transferred from a cell block to a dormitory. For the three years that he was there, Yonnie was his protector.

In the spring of 1940, Jimmy's father brought him both good and bad news. The good news was that he had met a man who could get him transferred to the London Prison Farm for $1,500. The bad news was that Jewel, who had moved to Los Angeles with her parents, had divorced him. "She still loves you," his father said, "but they made her do it." Jimmy wanted to laugh— not that he was happy about the divorce, but because it was so unimportant at this point in his life.

There were no gray walls at the prison farm in London, Ohio. There was a cyclone fence, dormitories, freedom to talk, no marching to the dining hall, plenty of windows with no bars, and lots of fresh air and outdoor sports. From early spring to late fall, Jimmy spent most of his time playing softball. Warden William Amrine was a softball freak. He had an all-star team called Amrine's Angels which played games all over the state and the players lived in the honor dorm. Jimmy made Amrine's Angels his second year there. He was a good player, quick on the bases, slick with a glove, and the best line-drive hitter on the team. His batting average led the league for three consecutive years.

Not neglected, however, was his talent for gambling. Shooting craps on top of their bunk beds, without a backboard, Jimmy was soon an expert at a pad roll. By rolling the dice with the two sixes facing each other it was impossible to crap out on the first roll.

For a while Jimmy was the farm's fire chief and he used to sleep days. Late one afternoon he reported on sick call. Jimmy knew the doctor, who was a softball fan. He said, "Doc, this's probably going to sound awfully funny to you, but I think there's something wrong with me."

"What's the problem? Getting headaches."

"Doc, I had four wet dreams this afternoon. I took four showers and scored four times for sheets. That ain't normal."

"I never heard of that," the doctor said. "What have you been eating, for Christ's sake?"

"Well, doc, when I get off work, I have a quart of half-and-half, a couple eggs, you know, and some vanilla extract, and I stir it all up like a milk shake."

"My God," the doctor said. "I've got to try that. Four? Are you sure?"

"I usually get a couple, you know, but never four before."

"My advice is stop drinking that stuff until you get out of this place."

The solution, Jimmy decided, was a three-day pass, which he arranged by having his sister send a telegram that his mother was too ill to visit him. Deputy Warden Jay Young accompanied him to Cleveland. Jimmy gave him a $250 bonus, free and clear of all expenses. When word got around the prison, officials began competing with each other for the privilege of taking him home. In all he had five three-day passes.

Jimmy was released from the prison farm on Washington's Birthday 1945. A month earlier, he had found an opportunity to visit Yonnie Licavoli at the Ohio penitentiary and had told him of his plans to remarry Jewel and move to Los Angeles.

"Jimmy, if you go to Los Angeles, get in touch with Johnny Roselli," Yonnie had advised him. "He's in the federal joint at Leavenworth right now. He got caught in that movie extortion rap with some of the top guys in the Chicago outfit, but I hear they're working out some deal to spring them. When he gets out, he'll come to L.A., and you give him my regards. Tell him I'd appreciate it if he got you straightened out with the right people." It would be two and a half years before Jimmy would finally meet Johnny Roselli.

Following his release from the prison farm, he went back to pulling jobs with

Frank Valenti, trying to build up a nest egg for his California venture. To satisfy his parole officer, he managed canteens at three factories for Babe Triscaro, who was now the business agent for the trucker's local, with plush offices in the new Teamsters building.

Managing canteens looked like a legitimate job to Jimmy's parole officer, but it was a black market operation and a gold mine. He sold nylon hose, cigarettes, liquor, food and gas ration stamps—anything that was hard to get. He bought from hijackers, burglars, and hustlers, and sold at markups of two and three hundred percent. From time to time, to improve his markup, he would personally venture into the hijacking business, with the deals set up by Teamsters officials.

Jimmy and Jewel were remarried before moving to Los Angeles in June 1946. Unknown to Jewel, Jimmy had nearly ninety thousand dollars stashed in the trunk of his new Buick, the money he had been collecting to launch his California career.

His first large-scale operation in Los Angeles was as a bookmaker at the Chase Hotel in Santa Monica. He rented a three-room suite on the third floor and opened a cigar stand in the lobby. He formed a friendship with Salvatore "Dago Louie" Piscopo and gradually became friendly with the Dragnas and some of their associates. Over pizza and coffee at Mimi Tripoli's pizzeria on the Sunset Strip, and over some of the best Italian food in town at Naples, he met Giolama "Momo" Adamo, and his brother, Joe; Charles Dippolito and his son, Joe, who owned a vineyard in Cucamonga; Leo Moceri, who, like Blackie Licavoli years earlier, was on the lam from the Jackie Kennedy murder in Toledo; several Matrangas, Frank, Joe, Jasper, Leo, and Gaspare, who was not related to the other four and had once been the boss of Calumet City, Illinois, but now lived in Upland, California; Pete Milano, Tony's son; Frank "Bomp" Bompensiero, who was from San Diego and was in partnership with Jack Dragna in a couple of bars in that city, including the Gold Rail; Tony Mirabile, also from San Diego, who owned dozens of bars; James Iannone, who under the alias of Danny Wilson had acquired a reputation as a muscleman but was in fact terrified of violence; Louis Tom Dragna, who was Tom's son; Nick Licata and his son, Carlo; Frank DeSimone, who was an attorney; Sam Bruno and Biaggio Bonventre, both of whom always looked ready for action, and were; and Simone Scozzari, who years later would be caught at the Apalachin, New York, Mafia meeting with DeSimone and deported.

It was in September 1947 that Jimmy went to Dago Louie's house to meet Roselli. He found him to be a gentleman in every sense, which pleased Jimmy because he had heard so much about this man from Yonnie and Dago Louie. Jimmy noticed that the cut of Roselli's suit was far more conservative than anything he had ever worn. Everything was subtly color-coordinated and Jimmy resolved to discard his own wardrobe which looked flashy and cheap by comparison.

Looking at Roselli only confirmed that old saying about not being able to judge a book by its cover. Some of the toughest guys he had known had often appeared more gentlemanly than the rough-looking punks who fainted at the sight of blood. Here was Roselli, looking like a man of distinction in his conservatively tailored suit, his blue eyes gently amused as he spoke in soft, modulated tones. Who would have guessed that as a kid he had been tough enough to make it with Capone at a time when tough guys were dying like flies. Later when Capone went to prison, Roselli took his orders from the new Chicago boss, Frank Nitti. Roselli was then dispatched to California, where his job was to protect Nationwide, then the only horserace wire service in the country. He also was a "labor relations expert" in the motion picture industry, keeping an eye on Willie Bioff, who Nitti had placed in charge of the International Alliance of Theatrical Stage Employees and Motion Picture Operators. Then, in 1944, on the testimony of Bioff, the top hierarchy of the Chicago mob was convicted for extorting a million dollars from the movie industry and sentenced to ten-year prison terms. Then, following his release from Leavenworth Penetentiary on August 13, 1947, Roselli had rejoined Jack Dragna in Los Angeles.

At this very moment, Roselli and his Chicago cohorts were the subject of a congressional investigation that charged they had been prematurely released from prison in a scandal that cast suspicion on the Justice Department and the White House.

But here he was, a month later, talking pleasantly in Dago Louie's parlor. The contrast and subtlety of it made a deep impression on Jimmy. Having paid his dues, Roselli could sit back and live on his reputation. The organization would take care of him. He would never want for money or power. He had it made. That was what Jimmy wanted, what was missing from his life, what made him feel like he was standing still. He needed that feeling of accomplishment, to be separated from the multitude of hustlers he worked with every day, the punks of the world. Roselli was a gentleman, a man of respect, and Jimmy Fratianno was a hustler in search of an identity.

Later in the evening, Dago Louie excused himself and Jimmy had an opportunity to relay Yonnie's message about straightening him out with "the right people." When Roselli asked if he knew what Yonnie had meant, Jimmy said, "Johnny, I've been wanting this since I was a kid. I knew the Italians on the Hill had something special going for them, but it's so fucking hard to crack."

Roselli smiled. "That's right, Jimmy, and that's the way it should be. When you get the wrong guy in there, you've got to clip him. There's no pink slip in this thing."

Following the initiation ceremony at the winery, Jimmy and Roselli went to Dago Louie's house to celebrate. Roselli lifted his glass and offered a toast to the two men he had sponsored. *"Amici nostra,"* he said, "may we all live long and prosperous lives."

"I'll drink to that," Jimmy said, laughing happily. "Christ, that was really something tonight." He paused and looked at the two men. "You know, Johnny, this'll probably sound crazy, but for a while there I felt like I was in church."

Roselli nodded gravely.

"I felt like Jack was going to make me a fucking priest."

"Well, Father Fratianno," Dago Louie said, "how about a blessing?"

They laughed and both started asking Roselli questions at the same time.

"Hold it," he said. "Why don't I lay it out for you guys. You know, tell you what you should know about our thing." He paused and looked at them. "You are soldiers. In the old days they called you buttons. This is a special kind of army. It's made up of a boss, the commanding general; an underboss, who may or may not be important, depending on the family situation, but most times he's there to back the boss's play. The *consigliere*'s the adviser, the guy who's supposed to know all the ins and outs of the organization. Then there's *capiregime,* captains or skippers; and finally, *soldati* . . . See, it's really an army of captains and soldiers.

"But there's soldiers and then there's soldiers. It's like a democracy, some are more equal than others. Certain soldiers carry more respect than others. But any soldier, no matter who he is, carries the power of the organization with him wherever he goes in this country. And no other family can touch him without the approval of his boss. See, all families, no matter how big or how small, have separate but equal power. Oh, yes, going back to what Jack was saying about made guys. Whenever made guys get together to talk family business, everybody that's not made has to leave the room, no matter how much they're trusted.

"Now, the commission. It's made up of the bosses from ten families. The five New York families, Buffalo, Philadelphia, Cleveland, Detroit, and Chicago. The point is that these bosses don't have an ounce more power than any other boss. It makes no difference whether the boss is Tommy Lucchese, who's on the commission, or Jack Dragna, who's not. Their power is equal. The only purpose of the commission is to settle disputes that come up between different families. It has nothing to do with the business of individual families. If Jack wants to clip somebody in his family, or somebody else in his territory, he clips him. He don't need the commission's permission. This is his country and he runs it any damn way he sees fit. No other family can fuck with him here. If they do, then it's a problem for the commission.

"Let's say we have a problem with Colorado. Jack would go see Joe Batters (*nee* Anthony Accardo) in Chicago. He's the arbitrator for everything west of Chicago. He straightens it out. That's what the commission's all about. All bosses on the commission also have equal power. There's no boss of bosses, never has been. That's all bullshit. Some bosses, maybe because they are older and wiser, command more respect than others, but that's all.

"Now you also hear a lot of bullshit about being paid for hits. Forget it. That's against the rules. You kill when you're given a contract by your skipper or sometimes it might come directly from the boss. If you're given the contract, you've got to do the hit. Most soldiers are under skippers. And it stops right there. Take Bompensiero in San Diego. He's the skipper down there and he runs the show in that town. He takes orders directly from Jack, but his soldiers take their orders from him. If Bomp says you clip somebody, you do it. You don't ask no fucking questions. You'll never make money doing work for the family. That's just part of your responsibility as a member.

"But there's another angle to this. The fact that you're a member gives you an edge. You can go into various businesses and people will deal with you because of what you represent. See, you've got all this power. Nobody fucks with you. We're nationwide. We can get things done nobody else can. And that means you can make a pretty good living if you hustle."

PART I

† † † †

THE
MURDERING YEARS
1947–1953

1
THE ITALIAN ROPE TRICK
AND MICKEY COHEN

† † † †

FRANK NICCOLI PARKED HIS CAR IN FRONT OF JIMMY'S WESTCHES-
ter, California, home on Holy Cross Place, a quiet street that was even more
quiet on this 1949 Labor Day weekend.

He rang the doorbell and Jimmy answered it. "Glad you could make it,
Frank," he said, escorting him into the living room. "How about a beer?"

"Sounds great," Niccoli said.

Jimmy brought two bottles from the kitchen. "Need a glass?"

"No, that's fine," Niccoli said, taking a quick swig of cold beer.

Jimmy smiled. "How's Mickey [Cohen] these days?"

Niccoli shook his head. "It's a fucking nightmare. All the rats are deserting
the ship. I wish I knew what's going on. High Pockets's gone back to Cleveland, Jimmy Regace's gone with you, Dago Louie don't show up no more, and
we don't see much of you either."

"Well, I call him a couple times a week."

Niccoli looked toward the kitchen. "Where's the wife and kid?"

"Out of town for a few days, visiting friends in Toledo. That's why I invited
you here. Gives us a chance for a little private talk."

Jimmy glanced at his wristwatch. He didn't have much time to turn Niccoli
around. Unless he stepped outside and signaled the men to leave, they would
come in and that would be it for Frank Niccoli.

"Frankie, you know, I've been doing a lot of thinking about this bullshit
going on with Cohen and for the life of me I can't understand why you stick
with the guy. What's the attraction?"

"He has his faults," Niccoli said, "but we go back a long ways."

"So what? It ain't worth your life."

"Jimmy, I'm with Mickey, what can I tell you."

Jimmy stood up and angrily clapped his hands. "That's bullshit, Frankie.
Why don't you get out of town, you know, while your hide's still in one piece.
This guy's bad news. Everybody around him's dying like flies. I don't trust the
bastard."

Niccoli shifted nervously and emptied his beer. "Listen, Jimmy, you can save your breath. I'm with Mickey all the way."

"Frankie, you're not listening to me. Mickey's got big problems."

"I've talked it over with Mickey and I ain't leaving him. Look, if it comes to a war, I'm on his side. If I had to, I'd kill Big Al or Dragna or anybody else for Mickey."

Jimmy sat down. "Frankie, I don't know what the hell to tell you. You're Italian and he's a Jew. You're pretty fucking stupid to talk that way."

"It's the way I feel," Niccoli said, tilting the bottle up to his mouth to drain the last drop.

"Here, let me get you another one," Jimmy said. As Jimmy stood up, the doorbell rang. "What the hell," Jimmy said, crossing the room to open the door.

"Well, Joe Dip," Jimmy exclaimed in surprise, reaching out to shake hands with Joseph Dippolito. Built like a heavyweight wrestler, with a bull neck and barrel chest, and legs like tree stumps, Joe Dip filled the doorway. Taller but slimmer, Sam Bruno stood behind him. "Hey, Sam, come in," Jimmy said, turning to look at Niccoli. "What a surprise. You guys know Frankie Niccoli?"

Niccoli stood up. "I don't think I've had the pleasure," he said, extending his hand to Joe Dip.

They had left the door open, and Nick Licata and Carmen Carpinelli came in fast, just as Dippolito's grip tightened over Niccoli's hand. Before Niccoli realized what was happening, Dippolito had flipped him around and his powerful arms were locked across Niccoli's chest in a reverse bear hug.

Nick Licata pulled a rope out of his pocket and Jimmy said, "Give me the fucking thing." With the rope in his hand, he turned to Niccoli. "Frankie, your time's up," he said, looping the rope around Niccoli's neck and handing one end of it to Sam Bruno. Pulling against each other, exerting all their strength in this deadly tug-of-war, they quickly squeezed the life out of Frank Niccoli. He died with a look of surprised terror in his eyes.

"What the hell," Jimmy said, "the sonovabitch pissed on my new carpet."

"They always piss," Bruno said. "Sometimes they shit. Count yourself lucky."

Dippolito released his hold and Niccoli's limp body slipped to the floor, with Jimmy and Bruno going down with him, still pulling on the rope.

"You can let go," Dippolito said. "He's gone and he ain't coming back."

Bruno laughed harshly. "All right, you guys, let's get to work. Nick, you and Carmen strip him bare. Dip, drive your car into Jimmy's garage and bring the bags."

Dippolito returned with two large canvas mail bags. He handed a bag to Licata, and without saying a word, he grabbed Niccoli's naked corpse, which had been stripped of its clothes, doubled it over, stuffing it into the other mail bag with the ease of a strong child playing with a stuffed toy. Then tying the bag, he picked it up and carried it out the back door to the garage, dumping it into his car trunk. The others came out with Niccoli's personal effects in the other mail bag. Jimmy opened the garage door and Dippolito drove away with the body. It would be buried with a sack of lime in his Cucamonga vineyard, a burial ground for many other past and future victims of unsolved "disappearances."

The Niccoli hit had gone off smoothly but that was not the case when the family made moves against Niccoli's boss. Mickey Cohen was a flamboyant bookmaker whose antics never failed to make the front pages of local newspapers. Pint-sized and pudgy, with simian eyes, a flattened nose, and a twisting scar under his left eye, he reminded Jimmy of so many punks he had known on the street and in prison.

Except that Cohen was now big time. Early in 1947 he had moved his bookmaking operation from a paint store on Beverly Boulevard to a haberdashery at 8800 Sunset Boulevard, which was in an unincorporated part of Los Angeles that was under the exclusive aegis of the Sheriff's Office. Known as the Sunset Strip, it was an area populated by nightclubs and bookmakers. Here they only had to pay juice (police protection) to one law enforcement agency. In those days the juice was pretty much controlled by two men, Cohen and Jimmy Utley, and bookmakers paid either one $250 per phone per week for this protection.

At his new location, Mickey's boys sold overpriced shirts and ties instead of paint when not otherwise busy booking, collecting, or running errands for the boss. It was a two-story building, built at the top of a steep hill. Mickey ran his book on the first floor, which was below the street level. The second story was the haberdashery. He had surrounded himself with Jewish henchmen from New York and Italians from Cleveland.

The year 1946 had been a bad one for enemies of Mickey Cohen. A bookie competitor, Pauley Gibbons, was fatally shot as he entered his Beverly Hills apartment. Later, Gibbons' two partners, Benny "Meatball" Gamson and George Levinson, were killed in their Los Angeles apartment. Cohen was questioned and released. (Hooky Rothman, who Jimmy regarded as Cohen's toughest and smartest henchman, would later bitterly complain to Jimmy that he had killed Gamson and Levinson, and had received nothing for it.)

Mickey was living well with a fleet of fast expensive cars, equipped with secret compartments to hide the gains of his lucrative enterprises. He had moved his wife Lavonne and his dog Tuffy into a newly built $150,000 home in Brentwood, one of the area's classier neighborhoods, and had spent another $50,000 for furniture and interior decorations. He had a closet that ran the entire length of the bedroom, with at least two hundred suits lined up under fluorescent lights. There were built-in chests filled with hundreds of monogrammed silk shirts and underwear. Cohen knew what he liked.

Jack Dragna had asked for Jimmy's help in trying to pull some of the Italians away from Cohen, particularly Jimmy Regace. At first Jimmy had not understood the reason for Dragna's move against Cohen, other than he personally disliked him. Jimmy later discovered that Al Guasti, undersheriff of Los Angeles County, told Dragna if Cohen were out of the way, they could control most of the juice in the county, which he estimated at $80,000 a week. That was the kind of motivation Jimmy understood.

So Jimmy had started spending more time with Cohen, even attending his bagel-and-cream-cheese brunches on Sundays. It was at a Sunday brunch that he had first met Abe Benjamin, a bookmaker and gambler, who would become one of his closest associates for many years.

Abe Benjamin was a card shark who played at Mickey's cardroom on Beverly Boulevard. Jimmy had bought a piece of the joint and was using card cheaters whom he backed, taking half of their winnings. One of Jimmy's card cheaters was Joe Kaleel, whom Cohen had sent to Jimmy in the hope Kaleel would make enough money to repay Cohen his shylock loans.

One evening as Jimmy and Abe Benjamin were leaving the cardroom to take their wives to a UCLA–USC basketball game, Kaleel asked Jimmy to back him in a high stake game. "It's a twenty-dollar condition," he said. "I think we can make a good score."

"Okay," Jimmy said, motioning to the manager to advance the credit.

The next evening Jimmy was told that Kaleel had won $2,900. But later when Jimmy asked Kaleel for his half of the winnings, Kaleel said he had given the entire amount to Mickey.

Jimmy said, "Come outside, I want to talk to you."

They went out on the sidewalk and Jimmy said, "Where's my fucking money?"

"I've told you," Kaleel said. "I gave it to Mickey. I still owe him eight grand."

"So what's that got to do with me?" Jimmy asked.

"Well, I owe it to him, see," Kaleel maintained.

"Listen, don't go telling me no fucking stories. Show me the money. You're playing in these games with my money. So don't give me no story about what you owe Mickey."

"Hey, you muscling me?"

"Kaleel, I'm going to give you one more chance," Jimmy said. "Now if you don't want to pay me, or if you want to but you can't, just tell me. If you want to pay it in little installments, say so. Because if you decide you don't want to pay me, I'm going to hurt you. You understand?"

"Hey, you muscling me? You better cut it out or I'll tell Mickey."

Jimmy had a blackjack in his hip pocket. He reached for it and Kaleel started running up the middle of the street. He had not gone ten steps before Jimmy grabbed him by his collar with his left hand, and with his right brought the blackjack down on top of his head. Blood spurted. Jimmy hit him again before his limp body hit the street. Jimmy turned and went back inside the cardroom. He knew without looking that Kaleel was out cold. He could even be dead.

Two days later Jimmy received a telephone call from a perplexed Mickey Cohen.

"Jimmy, what'd you do, for Christ's sake?"

"What's the problem?" Jimmy asked.

"Have you gone crazy? Why'd you whack Kaleel?"

"Mickey, let me tell you something. That fucker owes me fourteen hundred and fifty dollars."

"You nearly killed him," Cohen said.

"Mickey, every time I see him I'm going to whack him over the head until I get my money."

"Hey, wait a minute. You know the guy's with me."

"Mickey, don't give me no stories."

"Okay, Jimmy, how about coming over first chance you get so we can talk this over?"

Jimmy waited four days and the first thing he saw when he walked in was Kaleel with his head wrapped up like he was wearing a turban.

"You got my money?" Jimmy asked, reaching into his right hip pocket.

Kaleel jumped back, his eyes going wild with fear. Jimmy's hand reappeared with a handkerchief. "What the fuck's wrong with this guy?" Jimmy asked.

Mickey sat behind his desk, flanked by his two top thugs, Neddie Herbert and Hooky Rothman. Jimmy sat down on a couch that faced the desk and crossed his legs. He pulled out a cigar and lit it, with Mickey watching his every movement.

"Jesus Christ, Jimmy," he said, after Jimmy had taken a few puffs on his cigar. "Look at this guy. You nearly killed him."

"Mickey, I'm going to tell you this one time. I don't interfere in your business, so don't interfere in mine."

"But Jimmy this guy owes me a lot of money."

"I don't give a shit, Mickey. That ain't got nothing to do with me. I ain't paying his debts."

"Okay, Jimmy, let's patch things up. Let him play over there and he'll pay you back as he goes along."

"That's fine. That's all the man had to say to me in the first place. But if he don't pay me, I'll hurt him again. You hear me, Kaleel?"

Mickey laughed nervously. "You're fucking crazy," he said.

"Listen, Mickey, where I come from we don't get fucked without getting kissed. You get my meaning."

Within a week the story was all over town and Jimmy Fratianno's reputation as a tough guy was established.

It was a warm evening and the men sitting on Jimmy's patio were enjoying a favorite pastime, weaving stories out of their past. The coals in the barbecue pit had turned white and small gusts of warm air stirred ashes into the air.

Jack Dragna had loosened his belt. He and his brother Tom sipped coffee, Frank Bompensiero and Leo Moceri drank beer, and Jimmy had lemonade.

All five had fresh cigars in their mouths, the ends glowing like fireflies when-ever they puffed on them. Their wives were inside, doing the dishes and wondering what their men were talking about out there in the darkness.

Being the gracious host, Jimmy had patiently given each their turn before taking over. "A while back," he said, keeping his tone casual, not wanting to tip his hand, "Mickey called me and said we're going to some ritzy home in Bel Air and for me to put on the dog.

"When we get to this place, we walk into this huge living room and there's maybe twenty people and the first thing I know Lou Holtz, who's the master of ceremony, grabs Mickey, you know, and Mickey gets up there and tells them people that he's going to hold a couple benefits. He promises to raise a million dollars for the Jews in Palestine. He says that Max Gould, who owns Slapsy Maxie's and Billy Gray's Band Box, will donate his clubs free and that invita-tions have gone out to the biggest people in Hollywood. I can't believe my ears.

"After his little speech, we start moving around the room and Mickey's rabbi introduces us to a guy called Menachem Begin, who's the boss of the Irgun, an underground outfit in Palestine. This guy's wearing a black armband and he tells us he's wanted back there for bombing a hotel that killed almost a hundred people. He's a fucking lamster. Anyway, he makes a speech, and after him just about everybody made a speech. It just goes on and on. After-wards these other guys from the Hagana, another underground outfit, start arguing with Begin about who's going to handle the money. So Mickey chirps in and it's agreed that his rabbi will handle the money and Mickey will buy guns and ammo and ship them over there.

"So a month later Mickey holds the first benefit at Slapsy Maxie's. The place's packed. I've never seen so many Jewish bookmakers in one place in my life. Abe Benjamin's there, Morey Orloff, Bernie Cohen, Square Sam . . . They're all there. Famous actors, producers, big shots in the community. It's a full house. The entertainers are Lou Holtz, Ben Blue, Martha Raye, Danny Thomas. Sitting at our table's the chief of police of Burbank and his wife, Mickey and Lavonne, Neddie Herbert and his wife, and me and Jewel. And I'm sitting next to Mickey.

"So this thing starts and Lou Holtz asks who's going to be first. Mickey raises his hand and says, 'Mickey Cohen, twenty-five thousand.' After that, forget about it. Everybody's pledging thousands. Even the bookmakers are pledging five and ten grand. They know Mickey's running the show and they're going to have to pay off.

"I see all this shit going on and I ain't going to pledge nothing. So Mickey kicks me and says, 'Pledge fifteen thousand.' I says, 'You're fucking nuts.' He says, 'Donate it and I'll take care of it.' I raise my hand, 'Jimmy Fratianno, fifteen thousand.' My wife nearly has a heart attack.

"By now I'm convinced it's a fucking scam, but to make a long story short, they got nearly eight hundred thousand. The next day I see Mickey and I says, 'What's this scam all about?' He says, 'Jimmy, this ain't no scam. This money's for the Jews.' I says, 'Mickey, don't give me this horseshit. There's no way you're going to let eight hundred grand slip through your fingers. Not in a million fucking years.' But he swears it's on the level and now I'm wondering how this guy's going to pull it off.

"There's a couple more benefits. Now we're talking about a million dollars. Somebody's holding this money but I don't know who. Every day I bring it up.

"Oh, God, is this guy a good actor. 'Jimmy,' he says, for the umpteenth time, 'this money's for the Jews. I'm Jewish, Jimmy. This's serious business. Them people are fighting for their homeland.' I says, 'Bullshit, Mickey, you ain't conning me.'

"Well, he's not copping out to nobody. I talk to Hooky Rothman and Neddie and he's giving them the same bullshit. So now three months go by and Mickey calls me one day and wants me to come over right away. I walk in and he throws a copy of *The Herald* across his desk and says, 'Jimmy, my God, what do you think of this?' His finger's pointing to this article about a ship loaded with guns and ammunition that sunk at sea. He's tapping his finger against the newspaper and looking at me with his hound-dog eyes, not a fucking expression on his face, and he keeps repeating, 'Oh, terrible, terrible. What a tragedy.' The story mentions no names. It don't say why it sank, the name of the ship, nothing. Just that a ship loaded with arms sunk somewhere in the fucking ocean. He says, 'Jimmy, the boat carrying the guns and ammunition for the Jews has sunk. A million fucking dollars has gone to the bottom of the ocean.'

"I think to myself, 'You cocksucker, I know your game.' See, he's got this broad at *The Herald,* Aggie Underwood. She's a big editor there, and this broad would walk on hot coals for Mickey. Prints any shit he gives her. The way I see it, Mickey called her and made up a story about buying guns and ammunition for the Jews with the million raised at the benefits and then told her the boat sank. A few unknown people died, some were saved, and she prints it on his sayso. I says, 'Mickey, congratulations. You've just pulled off the biggest, cleanest fucking score I've ever seen made.' And he looks at me, just squinting, you know, and for a split second there's this big shit-eating grin on his face. But he says, 'Jimmy, you've got me all wrong. The story's right here in the paper.' I says, 'Mickey, with your bullshit you better hold on to that paper, it might come in handy when you've got to wipe your mouth.' "

There were some soft chuckles but Jimmy could sense that his guests were more envious than amused. You had to give Mickey credit no matter how you felt about him. Every man there was wishing that he could have done half as well.

Tom Dragna was the first to speak. "Well, the sonovabitch won't get a chance to spend it."

"How're we set on that?" Jack asked. "Are we ready to go tomorrow?"

Bompensiero barked a laugh. His speech was gruff and abrupt. Never without a huge cigar in his mouth, he always sounded the same, whether he was joking, commenting on horses, women, the weather, or giving the gruesome details of a murder. Short and heavyset, he had the thick features of an aging pugilist. His gutteral nickname, "Bomp," suited him perfectly.

"Yeah," he said. "We've got the tools at Dago Louie's house. Mickey's family's going to be away for the night. The way I see it, we get the signal from Jimmy and we go in fast."

"What about you, Jimmy?" Jack asked. "You sure you want to go through with it?"

"Why not?" Jimmy said. "It's foolproof."

Bompensiero barked another laugh. "When I told Simone Scozzari [a soldier in the L.A. family] what Jimmy was doing he couldn't believe it. He just kept shaking his head. 'Imagine,' he said, 'taking your own wife and kid on a fucking hit.' "

On Wednesday evening, August 18, 1948, a year before the Niccoli murder, the Fratianno family was enjoying a friendly chat with Mickey Cohen in the downstairs office of his haberdashery. Also in the room were several of Cohen's tough guys, Hooky Rothman, Al Snyder, and Jimmy Rist. With Jimmy, Jewel, and Joanne seated on a couch facing his desk, Cohen was expounding on the merits of *Annie Get Your Gun.* He had seen the musical and thought it was the best to hit Los Angeles in years.

"Mickey, what's the tab?" Jimmy was anxious to leave.

Cohen waved his hand in a way that reminded Jimmy of pictures he had seen of the Pope blessing an audience. "Be my guests," he said. "They don't cost me nothing anyway. I can get all the free tickets I want. Best seats in the house, too. I've got you third row, center aisle."

Jimmy stood up and walked to the desk to pick up the tickets. "I guess we better hit the road. See you tomorrow."

On an impulse Jimmy extended his hand and Mickey took it, standing up to shake hands. "Well, thanks," Jimmy said.

"My pleasure," he said, waving to Jewel and Joanne as they moved toward the door.

The moment they came out Jimmy spotted Frank DeSimone standing on the far corner of Holloway Drive and Palm Avenue and he gave him the signal. They had taken less than a dozen steps up the sharp incline toward Sunset where their car was parked when he heard a door open behind him and he turned to see Hooky Rothman coming out.

At that exact moment Scozzari had pulled up and three men were jumping out of the car. Bompensiero, wearing dark glasses and a white Panama hat pulled low over his forehead, swung the sawed-off shotgun in front of Hooky's face and ordered, "Get back in there." Bruno and Biaggio ran around Hooky and into the office just as Hooky tried to hit the shotgun out of Bompensiero's hands. The explosion was deafening.

Jewel and Joanne screamed and began running in opposite directions. Jimmy, who had just seen Hooky's face blown away, stood there for a split second, not knowing whom to chase. From the corner of his eye, he saw Bompensiero step over Hooky's body and charge into the office, his body hunched over.

When they got back to the car, Jimmy saw Cohen run out the front door of his haberdashery and head toward an apartment building as swiftly as his short legs would take him. With wife and daughter screaming hysterically at his side, Jimmy stood there not wanting to believe his eyes. He felt ill. All that planning, Hooky dead, and there was Mickey running like a deer for cover. But it was to be only the first of many frustrating attempts on the life of Mickey Cohen.

It was not until he read the newspapers the next day that Jimmy learned that Cohen's life had been spared because seconds before the attack he had suddenly decided to wash his hands. In recent months, Jimmy had noticed that Cohen's fetish for cleanliness had become more compulsive and it occurred to him that this sudden urge to wash his hands had probably been precipitated by Jimmy's impulsive handshake on parting. Jimmy cursed himself and thought it best not to bring it up when he saw the Dragnas.

The newspapers reported that Al Snyder had been shot in the arm and Jimmy Rist nicked in the ear by a bullet. There was considerable theorizing, with one writer drawing a parallel to the 1931 murder of "Joe the Boss" Masseria in a Coney Island restaurant while Lucky Luciano had been in the washroom. It was a nice touch. The implication was that Mickey, who had earlier feuded with Hooky, had plotted his murder.

Life at the Chase Hotel went on as usual. Jimmy's bookmaking operation had inevitably led him into shylocking. The money was rolling in from the book-making, but the operation was bogging down because of Jimmy Regace, whom Jimmy had lured away from Mickey Cohen. Regace had absolutely no aptitude for figures. In desperation, Jimmy hired Irving "Slick" Shapiro, a young man from Toledo, to work the telephone and switched Regace to collecting.

Meanwhile, Jimmy was living it up. He had two mistresses ensconced in cozy *pieds-à-terre*. At night he roamed the Sunset Strip, frequenting the most exclusive nightspots: Ciro's and Mocambo, but his favorites were Slapsy Maxie's and the Band Box. Three nights a week he attended the prize fights. At the Ocean Park Arena he became acquainted with Harry Karl and Marie "The Body" MacDonald, an actress Karl would later marry. This friendship with Karl would prove significant in late December 1948, when it was diagnosed that Jimmy had a small tubercular spot on his right lung. The fast life had caught up with him.

Jimmy discussed his problem with Jack Joseph, a wealthy bookmaker, who was a close friend of Harry Karl. A millionaire shoe manufacturer, Karl was a generous contributor to the City of Hope, the well-known charity hospital.

"Jimmy," Joseph said, "this City of Hope's the best in the world, and you don't pay a dime."

"I'm sold," Jimmy said.

"I'll give Harry Karl a call right away."

In his first week at City of Hope, Jimmy was examined by eight doctors. Every test imaginable was performed, and he was finally called into the office of Dr. Harold Masters, who was in charge of his case.

"I'd say the verdict is quite promising, Mr. Fratianno. We caught it in time. As I see it, you have two options. A year of bed rest and proper diet, or an operation that will put you on your feet in three months."

"Doc, I can't spend a year in bed. I'd go nuts. What kind of operation are you talking about?"

"The infection is in the upper right lobe," Dr. Masters said. "To put it in layman's terms, what we need to do is drop the lobe down so you don't use it."

"What does that involve?"

Dr. Masters smiled. "Have you ever played Ping-Pong?"

"Sure."

"Well, we'll insert about thirty plastic balls, about the size of Ping-Pong balls, on top of the lung. This will depress it and prevent you from breathing through that lobe, giving it a chance to heal. That's about it. Fairly routine procedure."

The operation was successful and his stay at the hospital was more pleasant than he had anticipated. Jewel visited him three and four times a week. Jack and Tom Dragna, Dago Louie, and Bompensiero were weekly regulars. Leo Moceri, whose thick lips had earned him the nickname "Lips," spent the most time at the hospital.

They played pinocle and reminisced about the old days in Ohio, but while they talked, Mickey Cohen lurked in the backs of their minds. They thought out various assassination schemes.

In the course of these conversations, Moceri told Jimmy about the decade-old murder of Les Brunemann at the Roost Cafe in Redondo Beach. "Let me give you a piece of advice," Moceri said. "If you ever work with Bomp, get him out in front of you instead of behind you."

Jimmy was sitting up in bed. "Hey, I saw him blow Hooky's head off and run right into the office. He looked like a pretty good worker to me."

"It was Bomp's contract, and he blew it. Listen, Jimmy, Bruno and Biaggio didn't know Mickey from a lamp post, but Bomp did. They go in there and blast away at Al Snyder, thinking he's Mickey. Then they shoot him in the arm, for Christ's sake. While this's going on, Mickey's in the shitcan, standing on top of the sink. They didn't pump one slug through that door. Like a bunch of cowboys, they panicked and ran out instead of finishing the job."

"What're you going to do?" Jimmy said. "It's one of them things."

"Let me tell you about Brunemann," Leo said. "See, Jimmy, in those days Johnny Roselli was with Gene Normile and they controlled Nationwide, which was the only wire service coming into California. Brunemann was bootlegging it, and him and Johnny got into a beef. The word got out that Brunemann was going to hit Johnny. When Jack Dragna heard that, he gave Bomp the contract.

"The first time out, it was like this deal with Cohen, they only wounded Brunemann. Then Bomp heard that Brunemann was getting passes from the hospital and taking his nurse out to the Roost Cafe, the same joint they hit him the first time, and Bomp said, 'Okay, Leo, you take him this time and I'll cover you.' Now listen to this, Jimmy. I've got a forty-five automatic and the place's packed with people. I walk right up to his table and start pumping lead. Believe me, that sonovabitch's going to be dead for sure this time.

"Bomp's supposed to be by the door, watching my back to make sure nobody jumps me. I turn around and I see this football player, his name was Frank Greuzard, coming at me. Bomp's nowhere in sight. Now I'm either going to clip this Greuzard or he's going to knock me on my ass. So I blast him and run out, and there's Bomp already in the fucking car with Biaggio, waiting for me. That guy showed me his color, that's all I've got to say."

Moceri's thick lips were moist and his eyes had a wild glint. "Want to hear the payoff? The cops arrested some dago, Pete Pianezzi, and believe it or not, the sonovabitch was convicted and he's still serving time on that murder rap. Jack and Tom talk about it often. It's a bum beef."

"I hear Bomp went on the lam about then," Jimmy said.

"It was a year later," Moceri replied. "He clipped Phil Galuzo, another messy job. He grabbed the guy off the street, forced him into the car, beat the shit out of him, dumped him in the gutter, and shot him a half-dozen times. But Galuzo was in the hospital a week before he died. I gave Bomp some names in Detroit and they stashed him a couple years. Then he went to Tampa and stayed with Santo Trafficante. When he came back in 1941, I think the cops had three robbery warrants against him beside the murder charge, but the fix was in and they dropped everything."

It was while lying in bed that Jimmy came up with the idea of asking Cohen to bring a show to the hospital to entertain the patients. Jimmy began calling Cohen every day to discuss the show and finally a date was set.

The logistics were worked out in Jimmy's hospital room. It was decided that the best place to hit Cohen was the parking lot. Get him in a cross fire of shotguns and blast away. They could pull it off and be out of there in thirty seconds flat.

The day of the show arrived and Jimmy sat in a wheelchair by the window in his room, which overlooked the parking lot, and waited for Cohen to arrive. Whoever had the contract, they were doing a good job of hiding, because Jimmy could not detect any activity other than the normal flow of visitors entering and leaving the parking lot.

He spotted the two flashy blue Cadillacs. They slipped into parking slots and the doors opened. Dave Ogul and Neddie Herbert stepped out, looked around, and gave Mickey the signal. He came out, followed by Dave Barry, the comedian who was going to emcee the show. A bunch of pretty girls bounced out of the second Cadillac, accompanied by Harry Cooper, an investigator assigned by Attorney General Fred Howser, who was on Cohen's pad. Jimmy watched them until they disappeared into the hospital and then rang frantically for his male nurse to wheel him to the auditorium.

He was wheeled to a chair next to Cohen and he sat there throughout the show, making small talk, and wondering what had gone wrong. After the show, he was wheeled back to his room, but by the time he got to the window, the Cadillacs were gone. Dragna later told him they had not been able to set it up to his satisfaction and he had ruled it out.

It was also during Jimmy's hospitalization that Cohen became enmeshed in an incident that would gain him even greater notoriety, and, ironically, make life far more hazardous for his henchmen. It began when a 63-year-old widow refused to pay an inflated repair bill to Alfred Pearson, a radio repairman and noted gyp artist, who forced the city marshal to put her $4,000 home on the auction block, and then acquired the property for $26.50. When Cohen read about the widow's plight, he became so incensed that he dispatched seven of his toughest hoods to teach Pearson a lesson. While Pearson was being thrashed to within an inch of his life, with his right arm and skull being broken in the process, two rookie policemen inadvertently arrived on the scene and proceeded to arrest Neddie Herbert, Frank Niccoli, Dave Ogul, Happy Meltzer, Eli Lubin, Lou Schwartz, and Jimmy Rist.

As the seven men were being rounded up, an amateur photographer happened along, snapped a picture and hurried to the Los Angeles *Times* with his prize. The picture and story hit the front page the next day, and created a minor scandal. With Mickey facetiously dubbed Snow White and his hoodlums the Seven Dwarfs, it was reported that not only had the Seven Dwarfs been released at the Wilshire station, without their arrests being recorded, but their weapons had been returned to them as well. A number of policemen were suspended and a grand jury indicted Mickey and his boys on charges of conspiracy to assault with a deadly weapon, conspiracy to commit robbery, and conspiracy to obstruct the due administration of justice.

Bail was a total of $300,000 and Cohen put up his Brentwood home and all other tangible assets to provide bail for his men and himself. He followed this with the grand gesture of lifting the attachment on the widow's home and returning it to her along with a substantial cash gratuity. Los Angeles newspapers, particularly the Hearst press, were once again singing his praises.

In June 1949, a few weeks after his release from the hospital, Jimmy sat in the kitchen of Tom Dragna's house and watched him make what he called a bangalore torpedo, an army term for a bomb designed to destroy barbed wire barricades. Using a pipe five inches in diameter and fourteen inches long, he packed it solid with sticks of dynamite.

From time to time, he would look up at Jimmy and grin. "Don't worry, I *think* I know what I'm doing."

"What the hell," Jimmy would say. "If it blows, it blows. It's just one of them things."

Tom liked this response. He admired Jimmy's courage and boundless energy, his compulsive drive to hustle. His doctor had ordered him to take it easy and even forbidden him to drive a car, but here he was, ready to plant a bomb under Mickey's house because he was the only one who knew the layout well enough to assure its success.

They had been working on the plan for weeks. Tom's son, Louie, had become friendly with Happy Meltzer, one of the "Seven Dwarfs." Years earlier, Meltzer had branched out into narcotics and had gotten in trouble with the Lucchese family in New York. A contract was put out and Jack Dragna was notified, since Meltzer had run to L.A. Dragna put the contract in abeyance when Meltzer agreed to keep him posted on Cohen's movements.

Jimmy and the Dragnas had discussed every phase of the operation. Having already cased the property when Mickey and his wife Lavonne were away for an evening, Jimmy had found an air vent in a perfect location.

"All I've got to do is remove the screen, toss the bomb in there about seven feet," Jimmy said. "It'll be right under Mickey's bed."

"What about Lavonne?" Jack had asked.

"They don't sleep together," Jimmy said. "Hooky was telling me about Mickey. This guy never sleeps with a woman. He gets his prick sucked by whores, he likes whores, hands out a C-note and gets rid of them. At home he gives Lavonne a quick fuck and goes back to his own bed by himself. It's all cash and carry with this guy."

"How much space between the ground and the floor?" Tom asked.

"About eighteen inches."

The telephone rang and Jack picked it up. He listened a moment and hung up. "That was Louie," he said. "Mickey's on the town with Lavonne. We go tonight. Jimmy, get Regace to drive you over there to put the bomb in place. Then come back and Louie will take you out there around four when everybody's asleep. You can light the sonovabitch and let the pieces fly."

Tom uncoiled twenty-five feet of fuse and carefully connected it to the dynamite. "This will burn about fifteen minutes. Gives you plenty of time to get out of the neighborhood."

Regace parked the car right in front of Cohen's house. The property was unfenced. Jimmy removed his shoes and walked up the winding driveway, cutting across the lawn to the back of the house. He found the screen, flipped a few clips and it came loose. Holding the bomb in his right hand, he reached through the opening and gently tossed it onto the soft earth. With about fifteen feet of fuse sticking out through a hole in the screen, he replaced the screen and made his way back to the car.

Following Jack's instructions, Jimmy went back with Louie at four o'clock. According to Meltzer, the Cohens had returned home three hours earlier. All the lights were out in the house. Louie had dropped him off about a block and a half from the house. Again Jimmy removed his shoes. Once he reached Cohen's driveway, he crouched low and darted silently to the back of the house. He put a match to the fuse and it immediately started spitting fire. He watched it for a moment, fascinated by its spitting and hissing dance, like a snake caught on fire. Moments later he was back in the car and they were driving down San Vicente Boulevard toward Santa Monica. They stopped near the Riviera Country Club and waited for the sound of the explosion. It never came.

A few days later Neddie Herbert noticed a wire poking through a hole in the screen vent under Cohen's bedroom. The screen was removed and the bomb found. A defect in the fuse had extinguished it ten feet before it reached the dynamite.

The police, once informed of the discovery, decided to keep it secret while federal agents completed their investigation. The dynamite was traced to San Francisco, but when no federal violation was found, the case was turned over to the Los Angeles police. Mickey Cohen continued to live a charmed life.

Jimmy Regace knew he would be asked to kill someone, but so far Jack had not said anything to him. But Fratianno and Dragna had discussed it on several occasions.

"This guy ain't done no work yet," Jack had told Jimmy. "How do you think he'd handle himself on a hit?"

"I don't know," Jimmy said. "He was a little slow at figuring odds, so I had to move him to collecting, but I think he'd do okay on a hit if the setup was fairly simple and not too dangerous."

"Well, Happy Meltzer's still keeping us posted and you know Mickey's out on the town just about every night," Jack continued. "His favorite places are the Plymouth House and Sherry's. We've cased both places and Sherry's looks like a perfect setup. Right across Sunset from Sherry's is Bing Crosby's building, and next to it is a flight of cement steps that lead down an embankment to a vacant lot. That flight of stairs is a perfect spot. It's a good, dark hiding place.

"The next time Mickey goes to Sherry's, Happy will call Louie and we'll hit him with twelve-gauge shotguns when he comes out, which will probably be when the joint closes. By then the whole street should be deserted."

"Sounds perfect," Jimmy said to Dragna. "Who else's on the hit?"

"Jimmy, you take it easy. You're in no condition to be crouching on cement steps two, three hours waiting for him to go home. I've got Regace and this kid, Army [nee Arthur DiMaria], who's with the Cowboy [nee Benny Binion] in Vegas. He's a made guy and can handle himself pretty good. Scozzari will drive."

"What about that cop, Harry Cooper, from the State D.A.'s office? Won't he be with Mickey?"

"Fuck him," Jack said. "If he gets in the way, it's tough shit."

It had been a slow night at Sherry's until Mickey Cohen arrived with his entourage for their usual coffee and pastries before calling it a night. Included in the group was Niccoli and his girlfriend, Dee David; Neddie Herbert; Jimmy Rist; Eli Lubin; and Harry Cooper. Joining the group at Sherry's was Hollywood reporter Florabel Muir and her husband, Danny Morrison. The talk was light and carefree, nothing there for a good headline, which was Muir's prime interest in Cohen.

At 3:30 A.M. on July 20, 1949, the restaurant's manager, Barney Ruditsky, a former New York policeman, reminded his customers that it was closing time. As he would later explain, "Every night that Mickey Cohen came in, for the protection of my customers, I sort of watched the place and walked around outside and inside."

With his perfunctory inspection completed, he directed the parking lot attendants to bring Cohen's cars. The group formed a small knot on the sidewalk as they waited. At that moment, Police Sergeant Darryl Murray arrived on the scene, joining the group in idle conversation.

Just as one of Cohen's Cadillacs made its appearance, Regace and Army squeezed off eight salvos of lead slugs and beebees directly at the group which was conveniently outlined against the bright lights of the restaurant. Cooper took two slugs in the abdomen, Dee David was hit in the buttocks and groin, Herbert in the spine, and Cohen caught one in the right shoulder. Sergeant Murray ran to his police car to give chase to a sedan he thought might be carrying the gunmen, but lost it in the maze of side streets.

Cohen had dropped to one knee and was clawing at his bleeding shoulder. Beside him, Herbert was moaning, "My legs, my legs. I can't move my legs." He would die a week later from uremic poisoning. Cooper would hover on the critical list for ten days before recovering. His boss, Attorney General Fred Howser, took a salvo or two of political flak.

Asked to explain the presence of Cooper with Cohen, Howser said in a brief statement: "I assigned agent Cooper to guard Cohen after his attorney [Sam Rummel] came to me and said Cohen was in fear of his life. We had specific information as to the source which might attempt to assassinate Cohen. The circumstances will testify to the authority of the information. But we are not at liberty to divulge any other details at this time." Or at any other time, for that matter.

The corruption kettle heated up. Up in Sacramento, Governor Earl Warren appointed retired admiral William H. Standley to head the Commission on Organized Crime. "I wouldn't be surprised if the attempt on Cohen's life blows the tops off some things," Standley said. Meanwhile, District Attorney William Simpson was forging ahead with his special grand jury to examine charges of corruption in Los Angeles' finest. There was a flurry of early retirements and extended sick leaves.

Determined to solve the ambush at Sherry's, police hustled five prime suspects to headquarters for a grilling. The "chief suspect" was Joseph Messina, a barber. The others were Jimmy Tarantino, who with Frank Sinatra's financial backing had become editor–publisher of the scandal sheet, *Hollywood Nightlife;* Joe Tenner, a convicted panderer who also served time at San Quentin for a morals offense, and was currently working as an "advertising salesman" for *Nightlife;* Anthony Brancato and Anthony Trombino, two shakedown artists from Kansas City. All were released in a few days and the case was never solved. Meanwhile, terrified that he would be called for questioning, Regace went on the lam.

Jimmy's home in Westchester, a quiet middle-class development north of Los Angeles International Airport, was a typical Southern California house, three bedrooms and a swimming pool, all of it securely fenced in from its neighbors on adjoining subdivision lots. In the morning, Jimmy could be found reclining on a chaise longue by the pool, a cigar stuck in his mouth and a telephone glued to his ear.

He had moved his bookmaking operation from the Chase Hotel to his home after discovering that Slick Shapiro had embezzled at least twenty thousand dollars, having lost the money in card games. At first Jimmy had wanted to kill him. Shapiro had pleaded with tears in his eyes, no doubt remembering what had happened to Kaleel. "Jimmy, I just got deeper and deeper in the hole," he cried. "I'm sorry, but please give me a chance to pay it back." It was early evening and they were sitting by the pool, having a private conversation while Jewel and Shapiro's wife, Inez, were in the kitchen preparing dinner.

"Pay it back with what?" Jimmy demanded. "Look, Slick, you're fucking lucky that Jewel and Inez are close friends. That's your fucking rabbit's foot. But don't push your luck. Stealing my fucking money when I'm sick in bed, that's a low blow, you motherfucker. The best thing you can do right now is go back to Toledo. I don't want to see your thieving face and be reminded of what you did to me. Only a dirty motherfucker steals from his friends." A few days later the Shapiros moved back to Toledo.

With Jimmy working out of his home, there was a steady stream of visitors to the house, beginning at mid-morning and continuing until late evening. Besides the three Dragnas, there was Dago Louie, Johnny and Charley Bats, Angelo Polizzi, Sam Bruno, Pete Milano, Nick and Carlo Licata, Bompensiero, Moceri, and Carmen Carpinelli, whose brother was serving time with Yonnie on the Jackie Kennedy murder conviction. Occasionally, old friends from Cleveland would drop by, among them Tony Dope Delsanter and Babe Triscaro. It made Jimmy feel secure to keep in touch with his old friends. Through one of his customers, Ned Marin, who with Max Feldman owned Famous Artists, which handled the top talent in Hollywood, Jimmy could arrange tours of the studios for his friends.

As for Mickey Cohen, Jimmy attributed his survival to pure dumb luck. Both Regace and Army had sworn that Cohen had ducked the instant they squeezed off their first rounds. At that precise moment he had noticed a little scratch on the fender of his shiny Cadillac and had bent down to inspect it.

"This guy's lucky," Jimmy said to Jack and Tom Dragna. "I was talking to Johnny Roselli yesterday and he was telling me that Cohen reminds him of Bugs Moran in Chicago. Capone tried to kill him a dozen times. They never laid a glove on that guy and look at the troops Capone had working for him. Somehow or another, he was never where he was supposed to be, or some other thing went wrong. It's the same with Mickey."

"We had him set up at the Band Box one time," Tom said, "and he didn't show."

"The big problem," Jack said, "is that he's got cops around him all the time. You just can't walk in somewhere and blast him. His protection's too good. Besides he's on his guard now. Every time he goes somewhere, his mouthpiece, Sam Rummel, calls the cops and tells them where Mickey's going. Rummel's wired in downtown."

"Then let's clip *him,*" Jimmy suggested.

"I've got a better idea," Tom said. "Mickey put up his house as collateral for all that bail. Let's start burying some of those guys. Let's hit him in the pocketbook for a while. Let's see how fucking sound he is."

"Who's worth the most?" Jack asked.

"Niccoli," Jimmy said. "He's got Mickey on the hook for fifty grand."

"How close are you to this guy, Jimmy?"

"Pretty close. He was here just the other day. Brought Dee David over, you know, the broad that was shot in the cunt at Sherry's."

Jack asked, "What about Niccoli? Can you set him up?"

"No problem," Jimmy said. "Give me a week to work it out."

And that was how Frank Niccoli, another of Cohen's "Seven Dwarfs," got on Dragna's hit list.

The next Cohen henchman to make the list was Dave Ogul. On October 10, 1949, Happy Meltzer delivered the body of his good friend, Dave Ogul, as directed. Police reported that Ogul was last seen around six o'clock that evening at the corner of Sunset and Holloway Drive. Two days later his car was found abandoned in the Westwood section of Los Angeles, only a few miles from Cohen's haberdashery. Snow White was rapidly losing his Dwarfs.

Cohen complained to police that his enemies were playing a ghoulish game, killing then hiding the bodies of his bailed-out boys to drive him into bankruptcy. The remaining four defendants, Lubin, Rist, Schwartz, and Meltzer, were reportedly so terrified by the chain of events that they surrendered themselves at the county jail, demanding to be locked up until bail could be arranged through a less dangerous benefactor.

† † †

Tom Dragna decided to make another bomb. This time he attached *two* fuses to the thirty sticks of dynamite he packed into a piece of pipe.

Sam Bruno was picked to deliver what they hoped would be a final message. He was a sleeper. He had been with Dragna going on thirty years and had served time in San Quentin, yet no one in law enforcement seemed aware of his existence. Bruno operated a bar at Alvarado and Pico and kept a low profile, never associating in public with other Cosa Nostra members.

At 4:15 A.M. on February 6, 1950, Mickey Cohen was awakened by an alarm buzzer in his bedroom. Still groggy from sleep, he wandered into the bathroom and opened a window. He peered into the darkness and listened for any unusual sound. Everything appeared normal. As he closed the window, he thought he detected an acrid odor, but dismissed it as smoke coming from a nearby incinerator. Reassured that it was a false alarm, he got back into bed just as the bomb exploded.

For a blinding, ear-splitting moment, it felt like the house was rising off its foundation and when it settled back every window shattered, including the glass doors of his wardrobe closet. Three-hundred-dollar suits flew in all directions. Cohen had closed his eyes and when he opened them, there was a hole in his bedroom wall big enough for him to walk through erect. Mickey, his wife Lavonne, his dog Tuffy, and his maid were shaken but unharmed. The only injured person was a teen-age girl neighbor who was struck in the throat by a piece of flying glass.

The bomb had been placed directly under a heavy cement floor safe. The explosive force of the blast had been downward and sideways, instead of up. It dug a crater ten feet deep under the house and broke windows throughout the neighborhood. But Cohen's greatest concern was the damage to forty of his precious suits.

Cohen's lament to the army of cops swarming over his damaged house was, "How tough can things get? I wish I knew the sons of bitches that are doing this to me."

The police's response was, "How lucky can a guy get."

As usual, the persons responsible for the crime were not among those questioned and it remained unsolved.

Although it cost Cohen $75,000 in forfeited bail bonds, Snow White and the remaining Dwarfs were acquitted in the Pearson case.

Not long thereafter Sam Bruno, hidden behind a tree, aimed both barrels of a shotgun at Cohen while Cohen was driving home one night. One of the coolest heads and probably the best shot in the outfit, next to Tom Dragna, Bruno dealt horrendous damage to the Cadillac, but not a single beebee touched Cohen. His uncanny luck had everybody puzzled. It was beyond all understanding, beyond any odds ever dreamed up by a gambler, beyond human comprehension. There was something inhuman about it, something almost supernatural.

In November the Kefauver crime committee came to town and Cohen became the star attraction for a day. He gave them a lot of conversation but very little straight information. Jack Dragna and John Roselli went to Chicago to testify, and if their performances were less spectacular, their information was not any straighter. Jimmy Fratianno's name was not even mentioned in any of the hearings by any of the witnesses.

On December 11, 1950, Angelo Polizzi and Carlo Licata got their chance to make their bones. Armed with a Remington twelve-gauge double-barreled shotgun, and with its eighteen-inch sawed-off barrel resting in the crotch of a tree, Polizzi waited in the darkness for his victim. Carlo Licata, behind the wheel of the getaway car, was parked a few houses up the street. Parked a short distance away was Jimmy in the protection car. And roaming the area in his own car was Nick Licata, hovering around Carlo like a mother hen over a new-born chick. Every time he drove by, Jimmy swore silently to himself.

For reasons he could not explain, Jimmy had never liked Nick Licata, and the son was a carbon copy of the father. The rumor was that years ago Nick had left Detroit under a cloud. He had ingratiated himself with Jack Dragna and his problem had been straightened out.

Nick made another pass and Jimmy felt like ramming him broadside. Laurel Canyon Drive was quiet after midnight, and a car cruising around in circles was bound to alert some nervous neighbors, who in turn might well alert some equally nervous cops. This was Jimmy's operation and he would not tolerate any slip-ups.

But he worried for nothing. A few minutes later, he saw Cohen's lawyer, Sam Rummel, come up the street and drive into his driveway. Jimmy could not see what happened from where he was, but it was only seconds before he heard the loud bark of the shotgun. Carlo gunned his car and pulled away from the curb, squealed to a stop in front of Rummel's house, and burned more rubber leaving with Polizzi on the floor of the back seat.

Later Jimmy would read that Rummel was shot in the back as he climbed the front steps of his house. According to the police, he was shot from a distance of twenty-nine feet. The shotgun, left in the crotch of the tree, was traced to Riley, Kansas, where it had been stolen in 1913. That evening before coming home, Rummel had met in his office with two deputy sheriffs, but the reason for the meeting or the names of the officers were not disclosed. It was reported that Rummel was scheduled to appear before the grand jury, and this was thought to be the motive for his murder. Many suspects were questioned, but the crime remained unsolved.

The "problem" of Mickey Cohen was finally resolved by the Internal Revenue Service. Following a sensational trial, he was sentenced to five years in prison and fined $10,000. But it was too late to help Dragna. By then undersheriff Al Guasti had been kicked off the force in a corruption clean up.

2
CHASING
BUGSY SIEGEL'S DREAM

✝ ✝ ✝ ✝

ONCE BUGSY SIEGEL HAD REVEALED TO HIM THE WONDERS OF SKIM-
ming, Jimmy's dream had been to own a piece of a casino, a big enough piece
to get him into the counting room, with all that green stuff rolling in. To be
legit and admired, while at the same time scamming the shit out of everyone:
That was his idea of having your cake and eating it too.

It was back in May 1947 that Jimmy and Dago Louie had visited Benjamin
"Bugsy" Siegel at his "fabulous" Flamingo Hotel in Las Vegas. The hotel,
which had become an obsession with Siegel, was in serious financial trouble.
The cost, as initially proposed to his backers, had been set at $1.5 million, but
by the time it was completed it had soared to $5.5 million.

To add insult to injury, the casino opened without the hotel, and dropped
nearly $300,000 in the first two weeks of operation. In desperation, Siegel had
closed the doors, announcing that it would not open until the hotel was
completed. By this time his frustration was beyond control. He knew he was
on a collision course with his backers and he reverted to type, living up to his
cognomen of Bugsy. Instead of seeking a compromise, he surrounded himself
with a crew of tough hoods which explained his interest in Jimmy and Dago
Louie.

Although by May the casino had reopened and was beginning to show a
modest profit, Siegel appeared tense, the lines around his mouth deeper, his
eyes flicking nervously to a closed bedroom door as they talked in his penthouse suite. Jimmy and Dago Louie had dropped by for a drink at Bugsy's
invitation before going out to dinner, and it was obvious that there was
something more serious on his mind than casual conversation. He talked about
the Flamingo as though it were a work of art he had created with his bare
hands, and he was proud of his achievement, particularly in view of the
struggle it had involved, a fact he felt few people appreciated.

"You guys wouldn't believe what I've been through here," Bugsy said.
"Everything went wrong. Look at this living room, it's half the size it
should be. They had a concrete beam running straight across the middle

that was so low only a fucking midget could walk under it without braining himself. I told them to take it out, but they said it supported the whole building." Siegel shook his head to indicate the degree of his frustration. "Every prick that worked here was on overtime, twelve hours a day, seven days a week. I had to fly plasterers in from Los Angeles, San Francisco, Denver, Salt Lake City, and Christ knows where else. No wonder the cost went through the ceiling. Those cocksuckers in New York can't understand this.

"The hell with it." Siegel paused. "The joint's built and it's the most beautiful on earth. Now, the way I see it, there's a big future in this state for guys with me who get in on the ground floor. Since the war thousands of people have moved to the West Coast. It's a short drive from here to L.A., and I'm going to make this place the greatest vacation spot in the world. The Flamingo's just the beginning. And so's Las Vegas. There's Reno, there's Lake Tahoe, all fucking gold mines if you can create vacation spots where people with a little money can have good rooms, good food, good shows, swimming pools, tennis, golf, and all the gambling they want, and all the fucking broads they want. All that shit's legal in Nevada."

He paused, his eyes again flicking to the closed bedroom door. Inside, Jimmy knew, was Virginia Hill, a tempestuous redhead whose underworld friends and their cash had made her an international playgirl. "See, you make it a volume operation. Sure, you want the high-roller, but the big dough is with a lot of little square johns with a few hundred bucks to blow on a vacation."

"Jesus, Ben, this's a great layout," Jimmy said. "And you're right, it ain't a bad drive. You can do seventy, eighty all the way."

"That's right, Jimmy. Once you hit Nevada, you can do a hundred," Siegel added. "There's no speed limit. And don't forget, this's the divorce capital of the world. There's a big future here. I know it looks like a lot of sand right now, but look at the nice grass I've got. And right under this sand is the world's biggest water reservoir. This whole desert could be made into a paradise," he said, suddenly laughing. "Would you believe it, this whole area here is called Paradise Valley.

"Let me tell you something else. There's this old timer in Reno by the name of Bill Graham. Been here since Moses was a pup, and he's got the juice with Governor Pittman and Senator McCarren. Got them guys in his pocket, and that's no shit. Now that's really valuable. He can get anybody a gambling license. Forget your background, makes no difference." Siegel paused, his eyes suddenly amused. "Get the point I'm going to make."

"Shit yes," Jimmy said. "If he's got a lock on them guys it means he controls this thing. If he can get one guy a license, he can stop another guy from getting one."

"That's it, on the head, Jimmy. This Graham's my man. You know, I've got the wire service in this state and I've taken good care of him. Besides he's got good connections in Chicago and New York. We're buddies. We get our

friends in and keep the other jerks out. We control the show and we get a piece
of everything."

Jimmy's eyes were shining. "Jesus, a whole fucking state."

"You guys like the idea?"

"You kidding?" Jimmy said. "It's the world's greatest scam. What about
taxes?"

Siegel was grinning now and suddenly he looked a lot younger. "That's the
beauty of this business. The government don't know how much the tables take
in. You skim the shit out of it and then write off this other shit. It's a perfect
setup."

Siegel looked at the door and glanced at his watch. "Fucking broad," he
said. "Takes her a year to dress."

"Sometimes it's worth waiting," Dago Louie said.

Siegel smiled. "You've got a point there, Louie." He leaned forward and
rubbed his chin, his blue eyes studying the two men.

"I want to build an organization right here in Nevada," he said. "I need
some good men. I've talked to Jack about you guys and he had nothing but
good things to say." He paused and leaned back in his chair. "How about it,
you guys, are you interested?"

"Shit, yes," Dago Louie said. "What's the proposition?"

"How about you, Jimmy?"

"Well, Ben, I'm interested. I go along with what you say about the future
of this state. I'd like to get me a piece of a casino. Get in on the count."

"Why not," Siegel said. "You guys move out here, come to work for me,
and I guarantee you'll each get a piece of a casino."

"Any chance of getting a little piece of this place?"

Siegel smiled. "Jimmy, you wouldn't want a piece of this place. There's too
many ends going to people back East. Don't worry, there'll be other joints."

As if on cue, the bedroom door opened and a woman with flaming red hair
walked out in a silver lamé evening gown with a plunging neckline and mid-
thigh slits on both sides. The men stood up but she walked right by them, her
greenish-hazel eyes set straight ahead. "Skip the intro for later," Virginia Hill
said. "Let's get out of here, I'm fucking starving."

A few days later, Jimmy and Dago Louie met with Jack and Tom Dragna at
Mimi's and related Siegel's proposition enthusiastically. Jack was three years
younger than his brother, and at five-foot-five was an inch taller and probably
forty pounds heavier. Both were quiet, reserved men, with dark, searching
eyes, who always made Jimmy feel that they were giving him their undivided
attention.

"And the way I understand it," Jimmy concluded, "he's talked to you about
starting an outfit over there."

Jack nodded. "Yes, we've talked about it many times. But I'm going to tell
you something, just between us, you understand, this Benny's a dreamer."

"It looks to me like he's got a winner," Jimmy said. "How can he lose? He's got the juice, the skim. How can you beat it?"

"The problem is that he's done his dreaming with the wrong people's money," Jack explained. "The casino's still in the red. When you look at it from them other people's viewpoint, see, maybe it's in the red because he's skimming them, too. Forget about the government. See, they don't understand how a setup like that can lose money. Meanwhile, this guy's living it up and his broad spends money like it's going out of style. Blows fifteen, twenty grand on a party. Tips waiters five hundred bucks. The point, you guys, is that he's spending money that belongs to some pretty important people."

Jimmy glanced at Dago Louie and they both shook their heads. "Well, I guess that takes care of that deal," Jimmy said.

Jack shook his head. "It's too bad. He's a smart guy. Lots of brains, but somewhere along the line he forgot something important. There are some people you just can't fuck. There's one thing about this business you've got to keep in mind," he said, pausing a moment to give emphasis to his words. "Fucking with people's money is the fastest way to get clipped."

He paused again, his dark eyes appraising them. "I'm talking straight to you guys, but keep your mouths shut. In fact, Jimmy, I may need you to drive a car in a couple weeks."

"Any time, Jack," Jimmy said. "Just give me the word."

John "Frankie" Carbo was with Allen Smiley [*nee* Aaron Smehoff] at the City Club in Santa Monica the first time Jimmy met him. Heavyset, with a bull neck and thick shoulders, Carbo was a man in his late forties who looked like he could still handle himself. He talked with a Brooklyn accent and gave no indication of suffering from an inferiority complex. He entertained them with stories about Abe "Kid Twist" Reles and his Brownsville gang of killers known as Murder Inc.

In August 1940, Bugsy Siegel and Frankie Carbo had been indicted for the murder of Harry "Big Greenie" Greenberg. The case was delayed time and again, until finally the key witness, Reles, whose testimony had sent Louis "Lepke" Buchalter to the electric chair in New York, went flying out a window of the Half Moon Hotel in Coney Island while supposedly being held in protective custody. The case against Siegel was dropped and it later came out that Siegel had contributed $30,000 to the successful campaign of John Dockweiler, the Los Angeles District Attorney who had not pursued the case because he wanted to save the taxpapers the cost of an expensive trial.

"That Kid Twist almost nailed me and Benny on that Big Greenie murder," Carbo said. "It was close, let me tell you. They dropped Benny from the case and I got a hung jury; then Reles took his swan dive and the D.A. decided against a retrial." Carbo touched his brow and went, "Phew, I sweated bullets for a while. I sat in my cell and tried to figure out what else that goddamn stoolie knew about me. He was giving the D.A. corroboration and the way it looked he had been around just about every time Lepke or Albert put a contract on somebody."

Jimmy knew that the Albert was Anastasia, and it was obvious that Carbo was enjoying bragging about the hits he had made without actually admitting anything. Only later did he learn the reason for Carbo's visit to Los Angeles. It was on the afternoon of June 16, 1947, that Dago Louie had come to the Chase Hotel with a message that Jack Dragna wanted to see Jimmy at nine o'clock. That evening, when Jimmy arrived at Mimi's, Jack was alone at a table and he shook hands without getting up.

After a brief exchange of pleasantries, Jack got down to business. "Remember my mentioning a while back that I might need you to drive a car?"

Jimmy nodded. "Sure, Jack, any time."

"Do you know your way around Beverly Hills? Ever been on Linden Drive?"

"Sure, I know this town like the back of my hand."

"There's some people coming in and they may need a local driver," Jack explained. "They'll be here tomorrow, but I don't know how long it'll take them to set up. They probably won't need a driver, but if they do, I want someone reliable who knows the area. If I need you, Dago Louie will be in touch."

Four days later a killer hidden in the shadow of a rose-covered pergola had rested the barrel of a .30-caliber Army carbine on a crossbar of the latticework, sighted, and gently squeezed off the entire clip. Nine slugs slammed through a fourteen-inch pane of glass. Two of them tore apart the handsome face of Benjamin Siegel. He died instantly, his blood-soaked body slumping sideways on a chintz-covered sofa in the living room of Virginia Hill's pink Moorish mansion at 810 North Linden Drive. Seated at the other end of the sofa, directly in front of the undraped window, was a shaken but unharmed Allen Smiley. At the time of the murder Virginia Hill was in Paris.

Frankie Carbo had pulled the trigger for Meyer Lansky. The motive for the killing had been money.

"Benny got money from some pretty important Italians," Jack Dragna had explained, "but Meyer being the boss was held responsible for all that money."

"What's the deal with Carbo?"

"He's been with Meyer for years. Before that he was with Lepke. He's been with the Jews all his life. He's not the only Italian with Meyer. These guys are not straightened out yet. Most will never get straightened out. You can't trust them, been with the Jews too long. But Carbo's a good man. He's done plenty of work for Meyer, and Meyer's in with us on lots of things, but he's a Jew and can never be a real member. Italians all over the country use Meyer's guys for fronts. See, Jimmy, Meyer's got a Jewish family built along the same lines as our thing. But his family's all over the country. He's got guys like Lou Rhody and Dalitz, Doc Stacher, Gus

Greenbaum, sharp fucking guys, good businessmen, and they know better than try to fuck us."

After the enlightening conversation in Siegel's penthouse suite, Jimmy had made a point of meeting Bill Graham. Jimmy knew that to fulfill his dream of a casino, he needed Nevada contacts like Bill Graham. Roselli had arranged for them to meet at Naples in Los Angeles in the restaurant-owner's private office, where they could converse with complete freedom, safe from the prying eyes of policemen and parole officers.

A man of impressive dimension in cowboy boots and a ten-gallon Stetson, with pale blue eyes and a florid complexion, Bill Graham impressed Jimmy as the warmest and friendliest man he had ever met. And the man was an authentic pioneer, a legend from the days of the gold and silver strikes in Nevada.

Born in San Francisco, he had grown up in the "South of Market" area. After the silver strike of 1907, he came to Tonopah and opened his famous Big Casino at eighteen. During the Roaring Twenties, when Nevada was wide open, Graham and his lifelong partner James McKay operated The Willows, the most popular roadhouse in Reno. Later they acquired the Bank Club and built it into the biggest gambling casino in the country, with the financial assistance of Joseph "Doc" Stacher, a Meyer Lansky lieutenant from New Jersey, and Charley Fischetti, a cousin of Al Capone, and a *caporegime* in the Chicago Cosa Nostra.

If gambling was his first love, Graham's second love was prizefighting. In 1931 Graham and McKay had entered into a partnership with Jack Dempsey to promote a twenty-round match between Max Baer and Pulino Uzcudun in Reno. The following year, they again staged a twenty-round match, this time between Max Baer and King Levinsky. Besides promoting fights, Graham also sponsored promising boxers.

This was a man after Jimmy's own heart. As their friendship blossomed, Jimmy made many trips to Reno and Las Vegas to visit Graham and attend the fights with him. As far as Jimmy was concerned, Graham knew more about boxing than anybody in the business. He counted as his friends all the ranking boxers, promoters, and managers in the fight game over a forty-year period.

Beginning in late 1949, Jimmy had started spending more time in Las Vegas. He could see that Siegel's prophesy about a boom in Las Vegas was coming true.

Following Siegel's murder, Meyer Lansky had taken control of the Flamingo Hotel. To manage it, Lansky had picked Gus Greenbaum, an Arizona bookmaker who had handled the wire service in that state for the Chicago outfit. Greenbaum's first move was to enlarge the hotel from ninety-seven to over two hundred rooms. A fancy dresser and fast talker, Greenbaum was considered a sharp administrator and proved it in his first year at the Flamingo by not only taking the hotel out of the red, but by reporting a $4-million profit. What was skimmed was anybody's guess. As for Greenbaum, his failings were as considerable as his virtues. He was a voracious womanizer, a heavy drinker, who would later turn to drugs, and a degenerate gambler.

Following the enactment of a special tax stamp law for gamblers, which required they pay a percentage of their gross "illegal" income to the federal government, many of the wealthiest bookmakers in Los Angeles moved to Las Vegas, setting up shop in the various "carpet" joints on the Strip and "saw-dust" joints downtown. Hy Goldbaum took over Grace's Dress Shop at the Flamingo and turned it into a commission book. Dago Louie, Abe Benjamin, and Polack Mike had their own private telephones in Hy's place.

Jimmy followed in the spring of 1951. One of Jimmy's phones was an open line to Carmen Carpinelli in Los Angeles. Carpinelli had replaced Shapiro, when the latter had hurried back to Toledo, and ran Jimmy's L.A. business in his absence. Besides a steady stream of bettors coming and going throughout the day, there were always fifteen to twenty bookmakers in the room. They spent their day studying scratch sheets, watching the blackboard and listening to the loudspeaker as the broadcaster for the wire service in Chicago recreated the races as they were reported to him from scouts at tracks across the country. Because of the time differential between East and West, the action started at nine in the morning and went on until the last track closed on the West Coast.

Jimmy was staying at the Desert Inn, which had opened the previous spring, paying a discounted six dollars a day for his room and being comped for everything else. Although Wilbur Clark fronted the hotel, the operation was under the control of his Cleveland backers: Lou "Rhody" Rothkopf, Moe Dalitz, Morris Kleinman, Sam Tucker, and Ruby Kolod, who owned about equal shares. Tom McGinty and Bernie Rothkopf had smaller shares.

Every time Lou Rhody came to Las Vegas, which was no more frequently than necessary, he often had dinner with Jimmy and Jack Dragna. One evening Rhody told them that the casino had declared first-year profits of twelve million, but had skimmed thirty-six million, a morsel of intelligence that further whetted Jimmy's heightened appetite for his own place. He and the Dragnas—Tom had bought a ranch in Las Vegas—often discussed the possibility of buying into a casino. Jack encouraged Jimmy, but did little on his own toward the realization of this goal. In fact, during one dinner, Rhody had expressed his appreciation to Jimmy for having sent Wilbur Clark to them in Cleveland when he had run out of money in 1947, and came right out and said, "Listen, if you guys ever see anything you want to buy into out here and need two or three hundred grand, let me know."

Jimmy was pulling in thousands of dollars every week but much of it was being cut up too many different ways, too many ends going to deadheads. His goal, which he had expressed to Jack countless times, was to build up a kitty for their family which they could use to buy into a casino. But every time he accumulated a hundred or a hundred and fifty thousand, Jack and Tom asked that a quarter or a third of it be cut up among them for expenses. Jimmy felt like he was on a treadmill, pedaling like a maniac, but getting nowhere. Rhody's offer was the most encouraging news he had received in months. Later, however, he would learn that Jack had hit Rhody for a heavy loan, which no doubt ruled out Rhody's offer, for Jack never repaid any loan.

What Jimmy found particularly frustrating was that others seldom shared their earnings with the family. The day following the Desert Inn's opening in April 1950, Dago Louie had won a quarter of a million dollars at the tables, which he later parlayed through a series of scams into almost a million dollars, but he never cut it up with anybody. At one point, Jack and Tom intimated to Jimmy that Dago Louie was talking to intelligence officers in Los Angeles. But it was only a hunch and they wanted Jimmy to help them get proof.

"Jimmy, you're close to Dago Louie," Jack told him. "Try to find out something."

"I see him every day," Jimmy said. "He seems straight to me."

"Maybe he is and maybe he's not," Jack said, "but from now on I don't want you discussing family business with him. And that goes for your men. I want this guy kept in the cold until we can straighten out this problem." It would take fifteen years before Dragna's hunch was confirmed.

Four or five times a week, during slow periods in the day, Gus Greenbaum would come to the sports room and solicit a game of contract bridge. Jimmy would say, "Who wants to play?" Abe Benjamin and Polack Mike would volunteer. They would select partners by cutting the deck, but it was always the three of them against Greenbaum. Whoever played with Greenbaum always threw his hand in when the others passed. Greenbaum's losses averaged from eight to ten thousand a week, which the three partners shared equally.

Back in the summer of 1947, Jimmy and Chico Marx had met while Jimmy was booking and scamming at Del Mar, Bing Crosby's old "Where the Turf Meets the Surf" racetrack a few miles north of San Diego.

Jimmy and Mickey Cohen had formed a partnership with Jack Morton, a hustler who was a friend of Cary Grant. Each of the three put up $15,000, and Morton, who was the only one of the group with Turf Club privileges, handled the action of movie celebrities like Al Jolson, J. Carroll Naish, Cary Grant, Harry James, and Mike Todd, who was then the owner of the Del Mar track and a degenerate gambler. Mac "Killer" Gray, a gofer for George Raft, also brought Jimmy action from the Turf Club.

It was also at Del Mar that Jimmy got to meet an interesting group of card cheaters. There was Jack Morton and his brother, Moe; Allen Smiley; producer Bert Friedlow, who was married to Eleanor Parker; one of the Ritz Brothers (Jimmy could never get their names straight), who used to be Jack Morton's partner in gin rummy games, playing for two dollars a point, Hollywood, using elaborate sets of signals. But the two sharpest card cheaters were Chico and Zeppo Marx. Jimmy and Chico became close friends, and it was only natural they would get together in Las Vegas to cheat the house when the opportunity presented itself.

It was later that Jimmy went into partnership with Chico Marx to past-post the El Rancho race book. Through Izzy Bernstein, Jimmy established contact with a man who lived in a house that faced the finish line at the racetrack at the New Orleans Fairgrounds. Watching the race through binoculars, the man could see the horses coming down the stretch.

Jimmy knew that the wire service had its own man up a tree at the fairgrounds, as they had at tracks all over the country, and the man had a radio set or an open phone line to Chicago. As soon as a race was off, the wire service announcer would give the precise post time right to a fraction of a minute. In Chicago, however, the broadcaster might be in the midst of relaying the results of another race, giving the mutuel for win, place, and show horses, and the time of the next post. This could take as long as a minute and a half.

A minute before post time, Jimmy would call his man at the fairgrounds and then place a call for Chico through the El Rancho switchboard, which always transferred it to the sports room. The man behind the cage would say, "Hey, Chico, there's a call for you." And he would slip the phone through an opening in the grill. While Jimmy and Chico were having a friendly conversation, Jimmy was listening to the public address system and waiting for his man at the fairgrounds to give him the winners. Sometimes when a horse was five, six lengths ahead at the stretch, he would give the number of the horse to Chico and hang up both phones. Then turning to the bookmakers in his own sports room, he would say, "Who wants this bet, five and five?" which meant five hundred dollars each on win and place. During the Marx Brothers' three-week engagement at the El Rancho Opera House, Jimmy and Chico had split about $40,000 in winnings.

He was no closer to getting into the counting room of a casino, but he was enjoying himself and making a lot of money.

3
THE TWO TONYS

† † † †

IT HAPPENED ON A DAY WHEN JIMMY WAS IN LOS ANGELES. FIVE MEN, their faces covered with strips of red-flannel cloth, held up Hy Goldbaum's commission book in Las Vegas and fled with $3,500 in cash. Two of the robbers, Tony Trombino and Tony Brancato, were immediately recognized by Goldbaum, whose former book in Beverly Hills had been robbed so many times by this pair that it had become a bad joke. "Oh, not again," Goldbaum would sigh. "Please tell me you're kidding this time." But the two Tonys had no sense of humor when it came to money.

Arrest warrants were issued and a week later they were apprehended in San Francisco. Out on bail, they skipped to a hideout in Los Angeles. They were hard-case shakedown artists and freelance muscles, with police records totaling forty-six arrests and seventeen convictions, major crimes, from aggravated assault to rape, narcotics, armed robbery, burglary, and countless murder suspicions. Along the way they had made too many enemies.

A month later, Abe Benjamin told Jimmy that the two Tonys had pulled a fast one on Sam "The Girl" Lazes. They had collected $3,000 from him which he owed to a bookmaking syndicate, but had kept the money instead of paying off his bet, and were now coming back for more money. Lazes, who was called "The Girl" because of his loathing of violence, was an agent for Benjamin.

Jimmy met with Jack and Tom Dragna at Nick Licata's Five O'Clock Club.

"You know, Jimmy," Jack said, "these guys are no good. We've gotten a lot of bad reports on them. The way I see it, we've got to clip them. Set something up, will you."

Jimmy never batted an eye. Jack had just ordered him to kill two men with a calmness that he had to admire. It was a compliment to him, and it demonstrated that Jack trusted him implicitly.

Jimmy had Lazes arrange a meeting at the apartment of Sam London, a movie extra and one of Jimmy's agents. At two o'clock on the afternoon of August 6, 1951, Jimmy and Sam London were having tea when the two Tonys arrived at 1648 North Ogden Drive. As London led them into the living room, Jimmy stood up and came forward to shake hands. He was smiling and dressed casually in a sports shirt and slacks, with the shirt tucked in so they could see that he was not armed. London served them beer and left.

"Where's Lazes," Trombino asked. "That's the guy we came here to see. What's going on here?"

Jimmy gave him a hard look. "Listen, Tony," Jimmy said, directing his attention to Brancato, "you know, you're fooling with Sammy Lazes and he's a friend of Abe Benjamin who's a good friend of mine. Abe asked me to step into this thing and straighten it out. What the fuck you shaking him down for, he ain't got spit? He's just a two-bit agent."

"Well, Jimmy, we got this robbery case in Vegas and we need some money."

"Well, you ain't going to get it from Lazes. Listen, there's other ways to get money."

"Yeah, like what?" Trombino challenged.

Jimmy shrugged. "There's a card game on Broadway tonight and I think you guys could take it off for fifteen, twenty grand."

"Oh, yeah," Trombino snapped back, "then why ain't you taking it off?"

Jimmy stood up. "You guys want to listen to this proposition or do you want to crack wise? Look, I want you to stop leaning on Lazes, understand? So I'm going to tell you how to make a score. You interested?"

Brancato nodded. "What's the setup, Jimmy? If it's so easy why don't you take it off yourself?"

Jimmy smiled. "I ain't in that racket no more. I'll set it up for you, bring the tools, and I get a full cut."

"We need more than two guys?" Brancato said.

"I'll bring a good man and I'll drive. Listen, there may be thirty, forty grand in there. It's a high-stake game."

Brancato looked at Trombino. "Sounds good to me," he said.

Jimmy could see that Trombino was getting that eager look. "Yeah, why not? We need the fucking score," he said.

They were waiting for Jimmy at the Five O'Clock Club. Jack and Tom Dragna, Nick and Carlo Licata, and Nick's son-in-law, Frank Stellino, Charley "Bats" Battaglia, Angelo Polizzi, Leo Moceri, and Louie Dragna. To set up an alibi, Licata had planned a party for that evening, a fish-fry that would begin at seven and go until closing time.

Jack, Tom, Nick, and Jimmy went into a back room to finalize the plan. Jimmy gave them a full account of what had taken place. Jack said, "You've got to hit them the second you get in that car."

"I agree," Jimmy said, "but I'm going to be the first guy the cops come looking for. I was right there with them this afternoon. The best thing I can do is get myself an ironclad alibi while somebody else does the work."

Jack shook his head. "Jimmy, who else've we got?"

Jimmy said dryly. "Give it to Nick."

Licata looked unhappy. "Jesus, you know the guys better than anybody, Jimmy. If they see somebody else there, it ain't going to work."

Jimmy shrugged. It was still his contract, and Licata's reaction was no less than he had expected.

Jack smiled. "Take Charley Bats [Battaglia]. Angelo [Polizzi] will drive. We've got a car and plates. Who do you want for the protection car?"

"Leo," Jimmy said, without hesitation. "If some cop gets lucky, I want somebody with experience protecting my ass."

"Good choice," Jack said. "Now, we've got the tools, two thirty-eight revolvers, and Angelo's gone over the route. You hit them, get in the car, go to Stellino's house, change clothes, shower, leave your old clothes and tools with Frank. Frank and Carlo will get rid of everything."

Jimmy nodded. "This shouldn't take more than an hour."

The drive took Angelo about twenty minutes. He dropped off Jimmy and Charley Bats and parked down the street with the car heading toward Hollywood Boulevard.

Jimmy looked at Charley Bats and fingered the gun he carried in his waistband. He was still wearing the sports shirt and slacks, but now he had a cardigan sweater buttoned over the gun. The safety was off. All he had to do was yank it out and pull the trigger. He glanced at Charley Bats standing next to him and saw that his face was frozen as if set in wax.

It was Charley Bats's first job and there was no way to judge how he would react. He had come from Buffalo and was indebted to Jimmy because Jimmy had settled a beef for him. In a way, this was cowboy stuff—anything could happen. A cop could come around the corner at any time, or an innocent bystander could blunder along and get himself killed. But whatever emergency developed, they had to handle it. The thought that Leo Moceri was in the protection car gave Jimmy a sense of security.

He touched Charley's shoulder. "Relax. It'll be over in five seconds. Remember, when they pull up, you slide into the back seat first and wait until I'm in and the door's closed. Then cut loose. Hit the guy in front of you. Empty your gun. Then get out fast, walk across the street and Angelo will be there to pick us up. You've got it straight?"

Charley Bats nodded and reached nervously to touch the gun in his waistband.

"Is the safety off?"

"Yeah, sure."

Jimmy smiled. "Just don't shoot yourself in the balls. Hey, did I tell you about Polack Mike? You know, he got his balls shot off during the war. Poor sonovabitch can't fuck. Can you imagine never having a good piece of ass? It must be hell. All them horny broads in Vegas, just crying for it, and all he can do is look. What a rotten deal."

Charley Bats nudged him. "They're coming."

"I know," he said. "It's showtime." It was a flippant remark, but at the moment it was the way he felt. He had never felt looser, more certain of success. Not that he was looking forward to it, that he actually enjoyed killing. It was more like something unpleasant that had to be done, and the sooner it was over with the better. A guy did what he had to do. There was no sense in worrying about it, or brooding over it, or making a career out of planning it. You went in, did your work, and got the hell out. Then you went on to other things.

The car came to a stop in front of them and Charley Bats fumbled with the door handle. Jimmy reached over and pulled the door open and Charley climbed in, with Jimmy right behind him. Trombino was driving, which placed Charley behind him, and Jimmy behind Brancato.

It happened so quickly that not a single word was spoken. Jimmy slipped the gun out of his waistband, shoved it against Brancato's head, and pulled the trigger twice, the slugs smashing into the skull with tremendous force, jerking the body up on the seat, the head snapping forward,—the way heads had snapped forward when Jimmy had struck them with a baseball bat on the picket lines—then snapping back, as if on a string, the body slumping sideways against the door, the bloody head flopping lifelessly against a shoulder. A mist of blood and brain tissue rose from the body like a fine pink stream.

Turning his gun, Jimmy emptied it into Trombino, whose body jerked with the impact of each slug like a fish on the end of a short line.

Charley Bats groaned, frozen in his seat. Jimmy screamed, "Shoot, you motherfucker!"

Charley Bats groaned again and Jimmy grabbed him. "Shoot! What the hell you waiting for?"

The sound of Jimmy's voice seemed to jolt him out of it. He pulled his gun and fired one shot. Then he flung the door open and ran across the street to the getaway car, which was waiting with its lights out and motor running. Jimmy walked, his head still ringing from the gun blasts inside the car.

He tried to conceal his anger as Angelo drove them to Stellino's house. If he told Jack what had happened, Charley Bats would get clipped. Try as he would, he could not understand Charley's behavior. He had frozen like a schoolgirl and could have fouled up the whole operation. What if Jimmy's gun had jammed, they would both be dead right now. That thought made him so angry that he wanted to lash out with the gun, but he controlled himself by squeezing his thighs until he could feel his fingers cramping. It was a good thing his gun had been empty when he first saw Charley's gaping mouth or there might be three bodies in that car waiting for the coroner.

Once in the shower, with warm water splashing over his head, he decided to forget the incident. Charley Bats had been a good worker, not too bright, but steady and dependable for what was required of him. He could intimidate welshers into paying their shylock juice without having to break their legs. It was an efficient way to conduct business. In those days Jimmy usually had from a hundred to a hundred and fifty thousand dollars on the street, so what it finally came down to was a question of economics.

Jimmy knew that most Cosa Nostra members were incapable of doing this kind of work. There was something lacking in them, a something that was hard for him to understand, but still it was something he had grown to accept. "There ain't too many guys in our thing these days that can do this kind of work," Jack had told him. "In the old days, you had to prove yourself. Now it's all different. If you've got fifteen percent that are killers, you're lucky. Take Chicago, they've got maybe three hundred guys and if they've got thirty killers, that's tops. Most guys just ain't got the stomach for it. Know what I mean, they're squeamish. I can't figure them out."

Jimmy carefully shampooed his hair, and scrubbed under his fingernails with a brush to remove all traces of gunpowder. He had a pretty good idea of what was in store for him. After tonight he would not have to use the names of other people to establish his credentials. His reputation would be established for all time.

4
THE ARREST

† † † †

THERE WAS A HEAVY POUNDING ON THE DOOR AND JIMMY OPENED HIS
eyes. In the bed next to him, Jewel said, "My God, what's that pounding?
Sounds like an elephant out there."

"You better put a robe on," Jimmy said, slipping into a pair of boxer
shorts. The clothes Stellino had given him were neatly folded on a chair by
the bed.

"It's not even six yet," Jewel complained. "Oh, my God! There's a face in
the window! Jimmy, what's going on?"

"Honey, relax, it's probably just another roust. Nothing to worry about."

Jimmy's brother, Warren, who was living with them, ran into their bedroom. "Jimmy, the place's surrounded by cops. They're everywhere," he cried,
his face drained of color, his eyes wild with fear. Jimmy had bought Warren
a dump truck and he was working for one of the biggest swimming pool
contractors in Los Angeles.

Jimmy grabbed him by the shoulders and shook him. "It's nothing, Warren.
Don't get excited, leave it to me. Understand?"

"Okay, Jimmy, if you say so."

Jimmy unlocked the door and stepped aside as an army of policemen, in
plainclothes and uniforms, stampeded into the room. The arrest went off as
though Jimmy had written the script. The first thing they wanted was the
clothes he had left on the bedroom chair. They would be rushed to the lab and
checked for powder burns.

Standing righteously in his boxer shorts, with his hands on his hips, Jimmy
began shouting at the police. "What's this all about? Don't you know what
time it is? Hey, don't touch them clothes. You got a warrant?"

"We don't need a warrant," the lieutenant in charge shouted back. "We've
got you for murder, Fratianno. Two murders!"

Jewel screamed and fell back on the bed.

"Now look what you've done," Jimmy shouted. "I'm not leaving here until
I call my doctor."

"Make sure it's a doctor, not a lawyer," the lieutenant said, standing next to him while he made his call.

Instead of going downtown, Jimmy and Warren were brought to the Hollywood station and booked on suspicion of murder. From there they were taken to the Ambassador Hotel. Police Chief William H. Parker's men had secretly taken over an entire wing of the third floor to get away from a frantic press. The double murder was making headlines across the country and receiving broad coverage on television and radio.

On the following morning, Wednesday, August 8, Chief Parker told the press: "I believe we have the man who engineered the deal." Captain James Hamilton, standing next to Parker, said, "The chief means we have the triggerman or the mastermind behind the shootings." The alleged triggerman was identified as Jimmy "The Weasel" (the old appellation being resurrected) Fratianno, and the *International News Service* reported that the slayings were "tied to a smashed southern California bookie empire and the legal bookmaking industry in gay Las Vegas." Fratianno had become the "alleged successor of gambler Mickey Cohen."

It was disclosed that he had met with the two Tonys in Sam London's apartment on the afternoon of the murders. In a front page headline, the Los Angeles *Times* reported: GANG KILLER USED TWO GUNS, POLICE SAY. Sam Lazes and London were arrested and Captain Hamilton announced he had located a witness who "saw the killer's face." But Hamilton refused to reveal the witness's name "for obvious reasons." Parker declared that "the underworld went too far this time. This was a sloppy killing job. We will break this case soon and with it, other gangland killings."

The next day, Nick Licata was arrested and booked on suspicion of murder. Parker said that Licata was seized after volunteering an alibi for Fratianno. "Licata injected himself into the case when he placed himself with Fratianno," Parker said. "We know that Fratianno was at Licata's cafe after ten P.M. Monday, but he wasn't there between seven and ten. We think Licata is lying." In another press conference, Parker brought up the vengeance angle: The two Tonys had been questioned in connection with the murders of Siegel and others.

On the third floor of the Ambassador, Jimmy was brought into the presence of Parker and Hamilton. So far he had been held incommunicado and questioned by a battery of investigators. He had steadfastly refused to say anything until he was permitted to contact his attorney, a request that was repeatedly denied.

Jimmy looked at them and shook his head in disgust. "What's going on around here? I want my lawyer. What is this place, Russia? Don't I have no rights?"

Hamilton, a tall, muscular man with a look in his eyes that said he had seen one too many hoodlums in his life, impatiently waved Jimmy to a chair. "Let's cut the bullshit, Fratianno. You know why you're here."

"The hell I do," he protested. "I've been pushed around since Monday morning, but nobody's told me nothing."

Parker watched the two men, whose eyes had locked in hard stares. "Trombino and Brancato were murdered," Hamilton said.

Jimmy shrugged. "So what? What's that got to do with me?"

"You didn't even blink an eye when I told you that," Hamilton said.

"What do you want me to do, cry? So they got killed. Big fucking deal."

"Tough guy, aren't you?" Parker said.

"Is that why you've got me here?"

"Not even a blink, no change of expression at all," Hamilton continued.

"Come on," Jimmy shouted. "Are they my fucking brothers or something? People die every minute of the day. What do you want from me, tears every time?"

"Sorry, Fratianno, but it won't wash. We know you killed them. We've got an eyewitness. What do you think of that?"

"Your witness's full of shit, that's what I think."

"We'll see, Fratianno, who's full of shit. You think you're pretty clever, but we've known about you a long time. We know you're a Mafia hitman and behind a lot of the murders around here in recent years. If it's the last thing I do, I'm going to nail you, Fratianno. I'm going to take that smug look off your face and when they fry your ass at Quentin, I'll be there to wave good-bye."

At nine o'clock that evening, Jimmy and Warren were taken to 1648 North Ogden Drive. It was the first time since his arrest that he had seen Warren, but they were not allowed to talk to each other. They came out of the police car and Jimmy looked up and saw a woman standing before a lighted window in a second floor apartment that looked directly on the murder scene.

Hamilton gripped Warren's shoulder. "Okay, run across the street to that car over there."

"Fast or slow, or what?"

"Just trot," Hamilton said, giving him a little shove in the direction he wanted him to go.

Jimmy said nothing as Warren trotted across the street.

Hamilton turned to him. "It's your turn, Fratianno."

"Fuck you," he said. "I ain't going no place. You want me across the street, you'll have to carry me. I ain't moving from this spot."

Hamilton grinned. "Are you worried she'll identify you?"

"Are you kidding," he sneered. "Are you trying to tell me that a woman can stand in a lighted room and see what's happening on a dark street? I can see her, but she can't see me. Go up there and look yourself. What kind of bullshit are you trying to pull?"

Hamilton looked like he could have throttled him with pleasure. "Get in the car," he said, waving for Warren to join them.

"Look," Jimmy said, "I've got to see my doctor. I've got a bad lung and I feel out of breath."

"You'll see your doctor when I say you can," Hamilton snapped back. "Now sit back there and shut up."

The next day Dr. Harold Masters had Jimmy moved to the County Hospital and his ordeal was ended. He lay in bed all day long, smoking cigars, while policemen stood guard on the other side of the door. Finally, the day came for his appearance before the grand jury. Nothing in his experience had prepared him for the reception he received at City Hall. News photographers popped flashbulbs in his face and television and radio commentators pushed microphones at him from all directions. His hands were in handcuffs, but there was a cigar in his mouth, and a smile on his face. He looked like a man without a care in the world.

Instead of going directly to the grand jury, Jimmy was taken to the Homicide Division for more questioning. Warren was there and when Jimmy learned that he was being kept in the hole at Lincoln Heights Jail, he flew into a rage. "Listen here, captain," he said, storming into the office of the division captain, "I don't care what you do with me, but why put my brother in the fucking hole? This guy ain't never done nothing in his whole life. He ain't got no police record. Why don't you treat him like a human being?"

To Jimmy's surprise, the captain motioned to a detective and ordered that Warren be transferred to population. Warren agreed to take a polygraph test, but Jimmy flatly refused, and in his appearance before the grand jury, he took the Fifth Amendment on all questions.

On their way back to the Hollywood station for more questioning that afternoon, Jimmy struck a bargain with "Jumbo," the detective in charge of the detail. For fifty dollars and steak dinners, they stopped at a restaurant and Jimmy and Warren were permitted to call their mother in Cleveland. Jimmy's mother, who had been following the story on television, dissolved into tears when she heard his voice.

"Hey, Ma, don't cry. There's nothing to worry about."

"How's Warren?" she sobbed.

"He's fine. He's right here with me. Listen, Ma, this's just a stupid mistake, believe me. They arrested Warren because he's living with me and they arrested me because I was with those guys a few hours before they died. I promise you, we're going to be out of jail in a couple days. Look, Ma, it's just one of them things. Now you tell Pa and Louise not to worry about nothing. Okay, Ma, here's Warren." Afterwards, they enjoyed a steak dinner and a glass of wine.

Six days after the murders, all five suspects were released on writs of habeas corpus when police failed to submit sufficient evidence to warrant their arrest.

The grand jury continued for seven weeks. A waitress from the Five O'Clock Club testified that Jimmy was at the cafe from seven in the evening to one-thirty in the morning. A bartender and Nick Licata confirmed her testimony. Meanwhile, All Points Bulletins had gone out for the arrest of Angelo Polizzi and Charley Battaglia. Dago Louie was questioned. In fact, most of Jimmy's associates were swept up in the investigation.

The police probe finally disintegrated when, before the grand jury, the waitress accused two detectives of coming to her home and burning her with cigarettes in an attempt to make her change her testimony. The prosecuting attorney, Adolph Alexander, turned the matter over to the department's Internal Affairs Division. That ended the case, but not the surveillance Hamilton had set up at Jimmy's home. They worked two cars on three eight-hour shifts a day.

Jimmy, who was driving a new Oldsmobile 98, gave them such a hard time that they finally asked for a compromise. One of the detectives said, "Look, Jimmy, we know this is tough on you, but the captain will get our ass if we lose you. From now on, if you want to go someplace, tell us and we'll meet you there. Do your business and we'll pick you up at a designated place so that we can come back home together."

The episode, with its incredible media coverage, established Jimmy's notoriety. In his own world, he had become feared and respected, exactly what he had sought most in his life. The public, too, had learned of his existence.

5
CAPOREGIME

† † † †

EARLY IN 1952, THE LOS ANGELES COSA NOSTRA FAMILY WENT THROUGH another initiation rite. This time they met in a large storeroom at the Dippolito vineyard. Six men were made on that day: Angelo Polizzi, Charley "Bats" Battaglia, Carlo Licata, Joe Dippolito, Joe LiMandri, and Joe Adamo.

After the ceremony, when everybody had gathered around a long table to enjoy a glass of wine, Jack Dragna raised his hand and beckoned to Jimmy, pointing to an empty chair beside him.

"Jimmy, you sit up here," he said.

Jimmy felt stunned. All eyes were on him as he stood up and walked to the head of the table. Instinctively, he glanced at Nick Licata and saw the shocked expression on his face. There had been talk of a *caporegime* being appointed to supervise the new *soldati,* but Jimmy had never dreamed that it would be him. The speculation had been that Nick Licata, who was older and had been around a lot longer, would get it.

Jimmy sat next to Dragna, who again raised his hand, this time to ask for silence. "I'm making Jimmy Fratianno a *caporegime* . . . are there any objections?"

No one said a word. Dragna smiled and turned to shake hands with Jimmy. "Congratulations," he said.

Dragna raised his wine glass for everyone to see and said, *"Salute."* The others joined in and the room reverberated with their friendly toasts. When the noise quieted down, Nick Licata raised his hand and Dragna motioned for him to talk.

"I don't want to be under nobody," he said, his voice trembling with anger. "I just want to be under you like before."

"That's okay," Dragna said, "you can stay under me."

For a while, Jimmy had no clue why Jack Dragna had put out a contract on Frank Borgia in San Diego. Seated in Bompensiero's office at the Gold Rail, Jimmy was listening as Bomp went over the plan he had worked out for the hit. "I've got Tony Mirabile to set him up. He's his best friend. That way Frank won't suspect nothing. Tony will take him to Joe Adamo's house and we'll be there waiting for them. We get the rope around his neck and that's it."

The next evening, as they were driving to the Navy Club with Carlo Licata in the back seat, Bompensiero said, "Listen, Carlo, we want you to dig a hole."

Carlo said, "What?"

"I said we want you to dig a hole."

"My God, have you checked with Papa," he cried, his voice trembling with fear, invoking his father's protection.

Bomp looked at Jimmy and shook his head. "Have I checked with *Papa?* What the hell're we running here, a Sunday school?"

At eight o'clock the next evening, Jimmy and Bompensiero were standing on either side of the door when Tony Mirabile brought his best friend, Frank Borgia to Joe Adamo's house. Jimmy had the rope in his hands and as Bomp kicked the door shut, Mirabile wrapped his arms around Borgia just as Jimmy dropped the garrote over his head, handing the other end of the rope to Bompensiero. Within ten seconds, Borgia was sinking to his knees. Mirabile released him and he fell on his face, with Jimmy and Bompensiero dropping to the floor with him, lying beside him and holding the rope firm, squeezing out the last breath of life. Like all the other victims of the Italian rope trick, Frank Borgia died with a surprised expression on his face.

While Joe Adamo and Biaggio disposed of the body and clothing, Jimmy and Bompensiero went back to the Gold Rail. They sat in the office and enjoyed a cold beer and cigars.

"Borgia goes back a long time around here," Bompensiero said. "He was bootlegging with Jack and Tom back in the twenties, and did some work of his own in those days. Him and Jack used to be good friends. Frank made lots of money in recent years, but he was an old stingy Mustache Pete. It cost him his life."

"What's the story with this guy anyway?" Jimmy asked.

"Didn't you ask Jack?"

"He's the boss, that's good enough for me."

"Well, the story with Borgia was that he got into a beef with Gaspare Matranga, who was trying to shake him down for some money. Borgia refused and went to Jack, but, see, what he didn't know, the dumb sonovabitch, was that Jack was in with Gaspare on the shakedown. They were going to cut up the money. Borgia was really steamed up and when Jack saw he couldn't cool him down, he had him clipped."

"Jesus Christ," Jimmy said, and took another swallow of beer.

"See, Jack's cunning. He gets money from this guy and never tells nobody. With Jack, things are not always what you think they are." Bompensiero laughed his raspy laugh. "The hand's quicker than the eye. But when he deals seconds, they bury you."

Jimmy had returned to Las Vegas after the contract. A month later Jack Dragna flew into town and the two men rode back to Los Angeles in Jimmy's new Cadillac.

Dragna had something he wanted to discuss with Jimmy, who also had news for Dragna.

"I don't know how it happened," Jimmy said, "but the Cleveland family don't have a piece of the Desert Inn."

"Are you kidding?" Dragna asked.

"I met these two guys from Chicago, Marshall Caifano and Philly Alderisio, and they've been gambling on markers and are into the joint for at least two hundred grand. You think they'd pull this shit if Johnny Scalish had a piece of it? They'd get clipped so fast."

"I better have a little talk with Scalish," Jack said.

"Oh, Christ," Jimmy interrupted, "I've got to tell you about the night I saw Sinatra with Benny Macri, you know the guy that clipped the union organizer in New York and beat the rap. Sinatra's making this movie, *From Here to Eternity,* and I ran into them at the Desert Inn. Frank wants to go see his cousin, Ray Sinatra, who's playing at some other joint. I'd just gotten my new Caddy and Frank gets behind the wheel, he wants to drive that motherfucker.

"So he starts backing up at a hundred miles an hour and nearly clips that sheriff, Glen Jones. Well, shit, Frank jumps out of the car and starts calling Jones a motherfucker, and everything. That fucking Sinatra's crazy, you know. I says, 'Frank, leave it alone.'

"This whole time Jones's not saying a word. He can't figure out what's happening. Anyway, we leave but I'm thinking about Jones. I make excuses and I come right back to the D.I. and Jones's sitting in the cocktail lounge. I says, 'Glen, I'm sorry, but this fucking Sinatra's nuts.' He says, 'Jimmy, don't worry about it.'

"But a week later I go to L.A. and I'm not back in Vegas ten minutes before I'm picked up. After some bullshit they let me go and now I'm fucking mad. I suspect somebody at the Desert Inn's calling the cops to get me bounced out —I know Morris Kleinman's got juice with Glen Jones.

"I drive back to the D.I. like a madman and rush into the cocktail lounge and there's Kleinman standing in a corner, talking to Meyer Lansky. I go up to him and I don't even look at Meyer. I says, 'Let me tell you something, Morris. Every fucking time I come up here, ten minutes later I get picked up. Now, I'm telling you something, you better straighten me out with that fucking sheriff. I don't know who's doing it and I don't give a shit. You straighten it out. I'm talking to you like a man, Morris, and you better listen to me.' He says, 'I'll take care of it.'

"Then he says, 'Jimmy Fratianno, I want you to meet Meyer Lansky.' It's, 'Hi, how're you,' you know, and that's it. I'm so fucking steamed up, I walk out. What do I care about Meyer? That guy can't make me no fucking money."

They rode in silence for a few miles. Then Jimmy started chuckling. "We had fun with Jimmy Durante one night. Philly and me caught him with one of his girls. He has this little van and he travels with these three blondes that are in his show. So he's hugging and kissing this one, and we can see through a window, and he starts fucking her. This's around two in the morning. About noon the next day, we tell him we have problems and he says, 'What about?' And we say, 'A reporter was going to take your picture while you was fucking that broad last night and we slapped the guy in the mouth and broke his camera.' Jimmy's been going steady with Margie Little for years and he knows if this shit hits the paper she's going to kill him. He says, 'Oh, my God.' He's so deadpan, you know. 'What can we do?' We had him going for a while, but he's really a very sweet guy."

Again they rode in silence until Jack said, "You really like it out here, don't you?"

"I like the money. Once you've got a piece of a casino, you've got a license to steal. There's nothing like it in the whole world."

Dragna was smiling. "Well, Jimmy, it sounds pretty good. But there's something I want to talk to you about. The Teamsters' convention opens in L.A. at the end of the week and Joe Batters called me to ask us to lend Joey Glimco a hand while he's in town. Johnny Roselli thought you should take over since you know Babe Triscaro, who's very close to this Young Turk, Jimmy Hoffa, who's with Beck."

"Right, and I know about Glimco," Jimmy said. "That guy controls a whole bunch of unions, everything from chicken pluckers to cab drivers."

"He's a made guy and tonight Johnny Roselli will introduce you as *amico nostra*. This is a good opportunity to make some important contacts with the Teamsters. As you've said before, families in other cities run this thing and it's about time we get moving in L.A."

If ever anyone typified the Hollywood stereotype of the pint-sized "Little Caesar" of the underworld, it was Joey Glimco. A five-foot-four Sicilian, Glimco spoke broken English but his arithmetic was faultless. By 1952 his annual income from unions and related business interests was estimated at close to a million dollars.

A *caporegime* in the Chicago family, Glimco's police record was impressive even in those circles. Indicted for murder at the age of nineteen after a death-bed statement by the victim, he was later acquitted and went on to collect some thirty more arrests, mostly crimes of violence.

At the time of the 1952 Teamsters' convention, he controlled at least fifteen Teamsters locals in Chicago and was a powerful behind-the-scenes manipulator in the politics of the union's International. Because of his police record, he could never become a member of the executive board, but that was of little concern to him as long as he could exercise control in areas he coveted.

As for the convention itself, it was merely a formality, a public confirmation of a *fait accompli*. Babe Triscaro had explained to Jimmy that the decision to elect Dave Beck president had been made three months earlier at a private meeting of the executive board. The deal was that Jimmy Hoffa, who had been giving the incumbent president, Dan Tobin, a hard time, as Hoffa went about consolidating his strength with the Central and Southern Conference, had agreed to wait until 1957 to make his move. Beck would serve one five-year term and retire, leaving the field open to Hoffa, who in the interim would continue to broaden his power base. Hoffa would be elected an International vice president, and at thirty-nine would be the youngest ever elected to the executive board. Also to be elected to the board was Tom Hickey of New Jersey, a decision that was being contested by Glimco, who was supporting Johnny O'Rourke of New York.

Following his conversation with Triscaro, Jimmy had tried to enlighten his fellow *capo*, Glimco. They were driving to the Bel Air Hotel, where Jimmy had registered him under an alias because Glimco had wanted a secluded place to take his secretary, who was also his current mistress.

"Listen, Joey, you're bucking the organization," Jimmy said. "Hell, you ain't got a chance. Babe says it's cut and dry."

"I don't give a shit," Glimco said. "Johnny O'Rourke's my pal and we're backing him, and what happens happens."

"But you could use this opportunity to strengthen your position with the executive board."

Glimco laughed. "You don't get it, Jimmy. See, that Babe Triscaro, that pal of yours who's so close to Hoffa, well, he's under the thumb of the Cleveland family. Babe ain't a made guy, but that don't mean nothing, because, see, Hoffa knows that Babe's got an in with made guys. Listen, if you ain't got the made guys with you in the Teamsters you've got nothing. We're the guys who crack heads for them assholes, the guys who get things straightened out. So when Babe goes to the president of a local and says I want so-and-so to be the business agent of your local, the guy knows that's what the family wants. That Union guy ain't never going to meet Johnny Scalish or Tony Milano, but he knows they're calling the shots through Babe."

"Babe says Hoffa's going to be general president next time around," said Jimmy. "And he wants to get the two of you together."

"Great, Hoffa's a comer, all right, and I'll get him straightened out with Chicago, St. Louis, Pittsburgh, and New York, but he's got to come across with what we want in the next five years. That fucking Beck ain't worth shit. If Hoffa uses his head, he can run the show right now and make lots of friends around this country. What I'm saying is that the general president ain't all that important to us. As long as we control the locals, have some good thieves in there calling the shots, what more do we need? That's the fucking ballgame right there."

The next day, in the lobby of the Statler Hotel, which was headquarters for the convention, Jimmy introduced Glimco to Triscaro and was himself introduced to Hoffa and Bill Bufalino, one of Hoffa's attorneys. A Los Angeles Teamsters' official, Frank Matula, happened to be standing beside Hoffa at the time and Jimmy, who had been slighted by Matula in a previous encounter, blew his top. Pointing at Matula, he shouted, "I don't want to be seen with this piece of shit. This motherfucker didn't want to get involved when I needed his help. I even gave him Babe's card and he shit on it."

As Jimmy was talking, Matula silently slinked away and Triscaro put his arm around Jimmy's shoulder, trying to calm him down. Hoffa looked shocked but Glimco was grinning. Later he would tell Jimmy, "That's the way to handle them. Next time you come around, that prick will shake in his fucking boots. Them guys got to know we're the power."

Every night for the entire week of the convention, Jimmy took Glimco and parties of twelve to fifteen, which often included Hoffa and Triscaro, to Naples for dinner, picking up the tab. He cemented new contacts with made guys and Teamsters from Chicago, St. Louis, Pittsburgh, and New York.

For a year and a half, Louis "Russian Louie" Strauss walked in the shadow of death and never knew it—until it was too late. He was a hustler and gambler, a card and dice cheater, and sometimes, with the right opportunity, he was handsome enough to score as a gigolo.

One of his most lucrative conquests was Mickey Smith, who operated a licensed card room in the Barstow Hotel, which she owned. An aggressive business woman, she showered him with expensive gifts, including a five-carat diamond ring that would later catch the fancy of several of his pursuers. Her source of wealth was "Big Bill" Bonnelli, the head of the California Board of Equalization. For the sum of three thousand dollars, Mickey Smith could provide anybody with one of Big Bill's liquor licenses. In time she would become the star witness in a liquor license scandal that would send Big Bill into lifelong exile in Mexico.

Russian Louie had another benefactor who contributed to his lavish life-style. Here the motive was not love but fear. Russian Louie had information that was so threatening to the "rehabilitated" image of Benny "The Cowboy" Binion that it had turned the former Dallas kingpin of crime into a desperate blackmail victim. It was a fatal miscalculation for Russian Louie.

Binion took his problem to Nick Licata. Being a man of action, he wanted Russian Louie killed, the sooner the better, and he cared nothing about where or how it was carried out. Binion had known Jack Dragna many years, but he knew that it was best to take a problem to a trusted underling rather than directly to the boss.

Dragna's response, relayed by Licata, was "What do we get for this?" Binion took Licata to the front of his Horseshoe Club, which was in Las Vegas's downtown "Glitter Gulch" section, and pointed to a vacant lot across the street. The moment Russian Louie was dead, Binion would build a casino on that land and give Dragna a twenty-five percent interest.

Dragna gave the contract to Licata, but with a condition. Because of a Cosa Nostra commission ruling, Russian Louie could not be killed in Nevada, unless his body was disposed of in another state. There was another commission edict that forbade Cosa Nostra members from committing murder for profit, but Dragna explained this away by saying that he had already planned to kill him because he had cheated family members in card games. The Binion offer was simply an opportunity for a little bonus.

Licata fooled around with the contract eighteen months before Jack Dragna turned it over to Jimmy, who enlisted the help of Marshall Caifano, a close friend of Russian Louie. Jack Dragna got permission from the Chicago family for both Caifano and Philly Alderisio to assist on the hit.

On April 16, 1953, less than a week later, Caifano introduced Jimmy to Russian Louie, who happened to be in desperate need of cash after a disastrous night at the gaming tables. On the pretext that Jimmy would lend him $12,000 after he collected a debt from a friend in Upland, California, Russian Louie was enticed into Jimmy's Cadillac. The plan, as concocted by Jimmy and Caifano, was that they would then drive to Palm Springs and try to extort money from oilman Ray Ryan, who owned the El Mirador, a plush hostelry in that desert playground. Russian Louie was told that his role would be that of intermediary in the shakedown. But at the last moment, Caifano told Jimmy something important had come up and he sent Philly Alderisio in his place.

While Jimmy and Philly Alderisio waited outside Russian Louie's apartment for him to pick up a change of clothes, Jimmy asked Alderisio to drive and got in the back seat. When Russian Louie returned with a small overnight bag, he got in the front seat with Philly. The moment he got into the car, Jimmy saw that Mickey Smith's diamond ring was not on Louie's finger. Jimmy cursed silently. Caifano had wanted the ring and would have given Philly and Jimmy five thousand each as their share.

"Listen, I'm going to take a nap," Jimmy said.

The dark green convertible hurtled through the searing desert heat, the only sounds being the wind slapping at the canvas top. Jimmy stretched out and went to sleep. The sun was sinking behind the San Bernardino mountains when he awakened. He peered at his watch. Philly was making good time, which was important in establishing an alibi. He sat up and yawned noisily.

They rode on in silence until Philly pulled up in front of the house and killed the engine.

"Philly, go see if the guy's home," Jimmy said.

They waited for Philly about five minutes before Jimmy climbed out of the car. "Let me see what's holding that guy," he said, and walked to the front door and knocked. The door opened and Jimmy said in a voice loud enough for Russian Louie to hear him. "What's going on here? Oh, there you are. Okay, great. Hey, Louie, come on in. I want you to meet this guy."

Russian Louie jumped out of the car and hurried up the walk. "Age before beauty," Jimmy said, giving him a shove into the room.

Joe Dippolito reached out with one huge hand and whirled him around while Bompensiero dropped the garrote over his head, tossing one end of the rope to Jimmy. If Russian Louie had not been struggling so desperately to breathe, he would have been surprised at the number of men interested in his execution. Besides Philly, seated around the room were Angelo Polizzi, Charley Battaglia, Louie Dragna, and Gaspare Matranga.

He probably never even saw Dippolito and Bompensiero. It happened too quickly. He was murdered by experts and if someone else had been the victim, he might have admired their expertise. Several years earlier, he had beat the charge of having murdered Harry Sherwood, his partner in the Tahoe Village, a plush gambling casino on the Nevada–California border.

A couple months later Jimmy was questioned but denied ever knowing Russian Louie. Newspapers linked him, among others, to the disappearance, but the murder remained unsolved.

As a *capo,* Jimmy had responsibility for enforcing the territorial imperative of the family. So Jack Dragna turned to Jimmy when he decided to make a move against Meyer Lansky, to let Lansky know the L.A. family wanted a piece of his action.

Dragna had cleared it with "Tommy Brown" Lucchese in New York. Jimmy's first target was Moe "Little Moey" Sedway, who had been a gofer for Siegel in the old days and was now a trusted watchdog at the Flamingo who helped verify the count for Lansky.

Five feet tall, with a large nose and moist, close-set eyes, Little Moey strutted across the lobby of the Beverly–Wilshire Hotel in Los Angeles like a man convinced of his own importance. The doorman jumped to open the door and Little Moey went by him without a glance, his hand rising imperiously to hail a cab, ignoring the doorman's efforts to perform that duty on his behalf.

Suddenly someone grabbed him from behind, spinning him around, and he looked up into the angry glare of Jimmy Fratianno. From years of experience with Siegel, Little Moey instinctively raised his hands to protect his face, his wet eyes going wild with fear.

Jimmy's left hand held him by the nape of the neck. "Moey, I want to tell you something, you motherfucker," Jimmy snarled. "You better walk straight around Vegas because next time I'm going to blow your fucking head off."

The backhand came so quickly that Little Moey never saw it until he felt it crack across his mouth, jarring his head back, and he tasted blood as he struggled to maintain his balance.

"What's the matter with you?" he whimpered. "Leave me alone." And the tears started flowing down his cheeks, mixing with the blood at the corners of his mouth.

"Remember, you better walk straight, you cocksucker," Jimmy said, and before Little Moey could say anything, Jimmy turned around and walked away with Nick Licata. In the world they lived in the message was clear. Meyer Lansky would soon hear of Jimmy's warning.

To look at the record, Joseph "Doc" Stacher was a tough hood. His police record in Newark, New Jersey, showed several arrests for "atrocious assault and battery," plus robbery, burglary, larceny, bootlegging, hijacking, and murder investigations. An associate of Abner "Longy" Zwillman and a power in Newark politics, he was the man Lansky had picked to head the group that built the Sands Hotel in Las Vegas. He was also a partner of Bill Graham in the Bank Club in Reno, but at the moment that was of no consequence to Jimmy Fratianno.

Five days after the Sedway incident, Doc Stacher was caught between the two sets of double glass doors at the entrance to the Sands.

"Listen, you motherfucker," Jimmy said, shoving Stacher against the closed glass door, "I want to tell you something. You're around here high-rolling like a fucking big shot. You better do the right thing." Again Jimmy lashed out with a backhand across the mouth. Stacher was so stunned that he just stood there with his bleeding mouth gaping open. He blinked a few times and Jimmy could see the fear in his eyes. "You fucking Johnny-come-lately, you better walk straight around this town or next time I'll blow your fucking head off." Before Stacher could recover, Jimmy gave him three stiff punches to the stomach and walked out. Charley Bats was waiting outside and the two got into Jimmy's Caddy parked in front of the entrance.

"He didn't do nothing," Charley Bats said. "He just stood there and took it. I thought this guy's supposed to be tough."

"Tough with who?" Jimmy said, giving Charley Bats a punch on the arm. "He ain't tough with me. He knows I'm a made guy. He'd get clipped in a minute and he knows it. The Jews don't fuck with the Italians. They learned that lesson a long time ago."

Charley Bats laughed. "I guess that's why they treat you like a king in their joints. They respect you."

"Listen, I'd whack Meyer tomorrow if Jack gave me the word. And he'd stand there and take it like the rest of them."

It was only a matter of days before Meyer Lansky ran to Tommy Brown. "Listen, you've got Meyer all shook up," Dragna told Jimmy after Lucchese had called him. "Meyer says, 'What's the matter with that Weasel, is he nuts or what?' So Tommy says, 'What's the problem?' Meyer says, 'Well, this Weasel whacked Moey Sedway and now he's whacked Doc Stacher. He told them to walk straight or he'd blow their heads off. Listen, Tommy, these guys are in my fucking family. Who does this Weasel think he is anyway?' Tommy says, 'Well, you know, he's their top man over there. He's done a lot of work for the L.A. family and they're fucking starving out there.' Meyer says, 'Oh, they're putting the arm on us, so that's it?' Tommy says, 'Listen, Meyer, that's their country you're in, don't forget.' Now Meyer's really getting excited. 'That's open country,' he says. 'They've got no right to whack my people.' Tommy looks at him and says, 'What, you want to start a war? They've got to make a living. What do they care about open country. Vegas's in their backyard. Look, Jack Dragna and me are *paesan'* and I'm going to let you straighten it out. But don't make no fucking mistake you can't live with, understand?' That was it," Jack concluded.

"All right," Jimmy said. "We ought to hear pretty soon."

Jimmy felt more relaxed than he had in a long time. He enjoyed being a *capo*. The fact that Lansky had run to Tommy Brown showed him that important people were paying attention to him. Jimmy was convinced something good would come of this.

PART II

† † † †

THE 6½-YEAR
PHONE CALL
1954–1960

6
MEETING MADE GUYS

† † † †

JIMMY HEARD OF THE DEAL ON THE EVENING HE WAS TO LEAVE ON A six-week trip that would take him to the Kentucky Derby, the Marciano–Wolcott fight, and on to Detroit for the wedding of Carlo Licata to Josephine Tocco, a daughter of "Black Bill," with many side ventures penciled into the itinerary.

It started so innocently that later it would be almost impossible to figure out where it had gone wrong. It was a legitimate business deal, the kind Jimmy had scrupulously avoided because his hands were tied when he dealt with straight people. So many of his friends had landed in jail because they had used racket methods in straight deals that Jimmy had shied away from.

The problem came in the definition of "legitimate" and "straight." The deal looked legitimate, but how could anything be straight when the people involved were oil promoters. Or, more like it, oil swindlers. The parties concerned were the owners of the Terry Drilling Company, George C. Terry and Carl B. Riddell, and two former Cleveland friends, James B. Modica, a liquor store owner in Tarzana, and Dominic J. Raspona, who owned a liquor store in Burbank. Back in Cleveland, both Modica and Raspona had worked on the periphery of The Combination. Raspona had been a bouncer in a dance hall and Modica had bumped slot machines.

The proposition, as presented by Modica and Raspona at Jimmy's Encino home, appeared foolproof. For five thousand dollars, Jimmy could join them in the purchase of a two percent overriding royalty in a 435-acre leasehold located in Ventura County's Tapo Canyon which was being explored by the Terry Drilling Company. Even more enticing was the news that the first well drilled was producing a steady flow of oil. Finally there was the assurance by both Modica and Raspona that if the venture failed, they would personally return Jimmy's investment, even if it meant doing it with monthly payments from the income of their liquor stores.

Jimmy's initial response was negative, but after discussing it with Jewel, he pulled out his wallet and counted out twenty-five hundred dollars, stacking the large bills in Raspona's hand. "Okay," he said, "Jewel will draw the other twenty-five hundred from the bank but I want some legal papers on this thing." Then he went cross country.

Dark Star, a longshot, won the Kentucky Derby in 1953. The Chicago gang was there. Besides Caifano and Alderisio, there was Albert "Obie" Frabotta, a short, pudgy, balding man, who also worked directly under Tony "Joe Batters" Accardo. With them was Benny Hankin, a card cheater, who was there for the purpose of ripping off their millionaire host, a Colorado oil promoter known to Jimmy only as Postie. They spent a week in Louisville, reveling in the carnival atmosphere of the town, and then separated, with Postie, Alderisio, Caifano, Frabotta, and Benny Hankin taking a chartered flight to Milwaukee, which was Alderisio's home town—one of his nicknames was "Milwaukee Phil."

Jimmy was driven to the Ohio Penitentiary in Columbus for a visit with Yonnie Licavoli and from there went to visit Irving "Slick" Shapiro in Toledo. Shapiro was booking small from a cigar stand because he was afraid to step on the wrong toes. Jimmy, who was still hoping to collect the $20,000 Shapiro had stolen from him at the Chase Hotel, decided that the wedding was the perfect place to acquaint Shapiro with the people he needed to know for his business to prosper.

For Nick Licata, the wedding of his son to the daughter of the most respected *caporegime* in the Detroit family signified a long journey back to the filial womb. Many years before he had left Detroit in disgrace and only after a hearing at the Ambassador Hotel to determine his fate had Jack and Tom Dragna decided against the hit suggested by Joe Zerilli, boss of the Detroit family. By making it a suggestion rather than a request, Zerilli had placed the ultimate decision in the hands of the Los Angeles family.

For Carlo Licata, a handsome boy who was not in love with Josephine Tocco, the wedding was a medieval accommodation arrived at more out of fear than respect for his father. But the wedding reception was an unqualified success. Fifteen hundred guests sat down to an elaborate Italian feast in the ballroom of a downtown hotel. There was an orchestra and dancing and champagne for everyone. Outside the hotel, reporters, detectives from the gangster squad, and FBI agents hovered about with cameras at the ready.

Inside the ballroom, Jimmy worked hard at meeting family men from other cities, and the phrase *amico nostra* was whispered from one end of the room to the other. In the course of the festivities, he managed to introduce Shapiro to Dominic Corrado, the Detroit *caporegime* in charge of Toledo. Corrado's son, Pete, who was in business in Las Vegas, had installed the air conditioning in the Desert Inn, and Dominic himself was a frequent visitor in Las Vegas, having gone on the town with Jimmy numerous times.

"Dom," Jimmy said, "Slick used to be with me in Los Angeles and now he's doing a little booking in Toledo. He don't want to do nothing wrong. He wants to stay on the right side of the people there and I told him if he had any problem to see you, that you would tell him how to straighten himself out."

Corrado, who was enjoying the champagne, put one arm around Shapiro and pulled him roughly against him. "Don't worry, Jimmy, we'll take good care of this Jewish millionaire. Slick's no stranger in Toledo. We've been watching his operation, believe me, so it's a good thing you told me this. *Salute.*" He drained his champagne glass and staggered away.

Shapiro nodded weakly. "Jesus, Jimmy, I had a feeling they were on top of me. Thanks. This guy's the law in Toledo."

"I've introduced you to at least a dozen guys here today," Jimmy said. "Now go talk to them while I circulate some more."

Jimmy danced with the bride and when he brought her back he pulled Carlo aside and whispered, "Well, Carlo, your Papa looks like the fucking cat that ate the canary. There'll be no holding him down now."

Carlo shrugged. "He worked hard for this day, let him enjoy it."

Jimmy edged closer. "And you'll never have to dig no hole now," he said. "You've married royalty."

"You really think you're smart, don't you?" Carlo hissed. "Well, I ain't scared of you no more. So get away from me."

Jimmy's hand reached inside Carlo's tuxedo jacket and grabbed a handful of loose flesh below his rib cage. "Don't say nothing you'll live to regret. You're a piece of shit in my book, just like your old man."

Carlo's face twisted with pain. "Let go of me, please."

Jimmy slowly released his hold. "That's more like it. Don't ever talk to me like that again. I'll bury you, you little cocksucker."

Later Jimmy noticed that Carlo was friendly with Jackie Tocco and Tony Zerilli, both made guys about Carlo's age, and Jimmy wondered if they were as worthless as most of the kids who had inherited their membership.

Going through the receiving line, with the bride and groom flanked by Black Bill Tocco and Nick Licata, with Joe Zerilli and the underboss, John Priziola in the line, Jimmy handed the bride a white envelope that contained five hundred dollars in cash (no checks allowed) and jovially shook hands with Nick Licata as he loudly congratulated him on his son's good fortune. Licata was not fooled by Jimmy's feigned jollity, and both men knew it.

When Jimmy arrived at Chicago's Ambassador East the next day, Louie Dragna met him in the lobby and told him that Chicago detectives and FBI agents were watching the hotel for him, having learned of his impending visit either through a wiretap or from an informant. Dragna had registered him under the name of James Fisher.

That didn't stop him from traveling in the same circles. He was introduced to a made guy called Sam Mooney—nobody told him then that his real name was Sam Giancana, or that he was then Tony Accardo's top aide. Within three years, Giancana would be boss of the Chicago family. To Jimmy he appeared to be a quiet, thoughtful man, who listened more than he talked, and who seemed to command the respect of the others.

Many new faces tramped through Jimmy's room, and every time he was formally introduced to a made guy, Alderisio, who had not yet taken the oath, had to leave the room. He would smile and say, "It's all right, I know you guys want to talk about something private and I can't stay here." One of the more interesting made guys Jimmy would meet that day was Dominic Galiano, a close friend of Louie Dragna, who owned the Talk of the Town, a B-joint on the Northside. Over drinks that evening, Galiano would confide that in 1947 he had killed Nick DeJohn in San Francisco on orders from John Franzone, a Chicago *caporegime* who had tried to take over that California city. (Thirteen years later Galiano himself would be murdered in Chicago.)

7
EXTORTION

† † † †

THE LAST RAYS OF SUNLIGHT HAD FLICKERED OUT OVER THE HORIZON
and evening had settled in. Gathered at poolside at Jimmy's new Encino home
were the Dragnas (Jack, Tom, Louie), with their wives. They had polished off
an American-style barbecue, with hamburgers, hot dogs, potato salad, baked
beans, hard-boiled eggs, olives, tomatoes, cucumbers—the full treatment, including strawberry shortcake for dessert. With the women in the kitchen, the
men were talking at the far end of the patio.

When he returned from Chicago, Jimmy ran into a monumental problem.
The Terry Drilling Company had struck it rich in Tapo Canyon with eight
producing wells. Jimmy had read a story that estimated the value of the strike
at eighty million dollars. A quick calculation told him that their two percent
override was worth one point six million. Cut three ways, that was over a
half-million each on a nine-thousand-dollar investment. It was a fantastic deal,
except that Terry and Riddell of Terry Drilling were trying to back out of it.
And that was something Jimmy refused to tolerate.

"These two, Terry and Riddell, are playing duck," Jimmy told his guests.
"We've tried to arrange a meeting, to get this thing straightened out, but these
guys are being cute. The minute they struck oil, they gave Raspona my money
back, trying to pull a fast one. But I know all about these oil swindlers. They're
all thieves, but this Terry's real stupid if he thinks he can get away with this
shit. He picked on the wrong guy this time."

"How long has this been going on?" Jack asked.

"It started in April before I left, and I kept calling Jewel about whether she
had the deal drawn up by a lawyer, but she couldn't pin nobody down. Then
I'd call Raspona and he'd say he was working on it, using all the pressure he
could think of, but nothing was working with those guys."

"Well, have you talked with them?" Tom asked.

"No, but I'm going to. I've got a phone number where I can reach them
tonight."

"You better call from a pay phone," Jack said.

"Don't worry, I'm so fucking hot at this point, I don't want to talk in no wiretap. Listen, if you guys will excuse me, I'm going to call them right now."

By the time Jimmy got to the pay phone, he was so angry he could hardly wait for someone to answer.

A voice said "Hello," and Jimmy said, "Who's this?"

"Carl Riddell. Is this Jimmy Modica?"

"No, this's the other Jimmy. Somebody told me to call this number."

"Oh, yeah, I know, you're Jimmy Fratianno. Say, Jimmy, what's this all about? Let me ask you one question."

"You listen to me, understand? I want to be a man with you and a man with Terry. Now, this has gone far enough, believe me. We put up our fucking money, people are talking, now I ain't going to stand for it. I'm going to tell you another thing, as far as Terry's concerned, I don't give a fuck, people can go to the police all they want. The police ain't going to watch him twenty-four hours a day, three hundred and sixty-five days a year. You know that?"

"Yeah," said Riddell.

"The cocksucker that goes to the coppers about me, he's going to die. I'll tell you right now, Carl, I'm pretty fucking mad about this whole fucking thing. Now I want to be a man and I want that other cocksucker to be a man because his fucking money ain't going to do him no good when he's dead. Now you tell him. You put him on the phone with me, Carl. You tell Terry I want to talk to him. Will you put him on the phone?"

"I sure will, but first let me ask you one thing, Jimmy. Why are you so damn mad at me?"

"Well, I'll tell you, Carl. I know that you're in with Terry and I know that you've done a little talking about me, understand? Now I don't stand for no sonovabitch to do any talking about me."

"Well, that's where you're mistaken. I haven't talked about you. If somebody's told you that, he's a liar. My wife . . ."

"Let me talk to Terry for a minute," Jimmy interrupted.

"All right. Just a moment."

While waiting Jimmy opened the door. It was hot in the booth and he could feel the perspiration running down his back.

When Terry came on the line he said, "Yeah."

"Terry, let me tell you something. We're not going to get fucked on this thing, you know that, don't you?"

"I didn't know I had any deal with you." Terry sounded more defiant, his tone of voice tougher than Riddell.

"Well, I had a deal with Don [Raspona] and you had a deal with Don. Is that right?"

"I started a deal with Don and told him that the deal was off."

"You did tell him? Well, look, Terry, it's not off with me and I'm going to tell you one fucking thing. I don't give a fuck who knows it, coppers or no coppers. I'll blow your motherfucking head off. I'll tell you right now, you ain't fucking with no kids. Do you understand?"

"Well, I've never met you in my life."

"You ain't going to meet me, you don't have to meet me, Terry, because you ain't going to know me. I'm telling you, you better straighten this fucking thing out and straighten it out fast."

"What do you want from me?"

"I'm going to give you one fucking week to straighten it out. If you don't straighten it out in one fucking week, you cocksucker, you can have people following you the rest of your fucking life, but I'll still blow your fucking head off. All your fucking money ain't going to do you no fucking good."

"What am I supposed to do?"

"You, Carl, and Don straighten this fucking thing out and straighten it out fast. Get off the fucking line, I want to talk to Carl."

Jimmy again opened the door and wiped his brow with his hand.

"Yeah, Jimmy," Carl said.

"Carl, I told Terry I'm going to give him seven fucking days to straighten this thing out. I don't give a fuck who he goes to, you understand? I've been talked about enough as it is in this fucking town. I've had enough fucking heat, and I'm not going to get any fucking more. I've given him seven fucking days. Now, you get ahold of Terry and Don and straighten this thing out. Let's get together. All right?"

"I'll do the best I can."

"Okay."

"What else do you want me to do."

"That's all."

"Will you lay off my family?"

Jimmy's heart skipped a beat. Like a cornered beast, he instinctively knew he had fallen into a trap. Somehow he knew Hamilton was involved—he sensed the phone was tapped. He pulled open the door and took a deep breath.

Riddell said, "Hello, you still there?"

"Yeah, Carl. Will you do that for me?"

"I'll do the best I can."

"And I'll do everything for you."

"Okay, good-bye."

Jimmy heard the line go dead and his knees felt weak. He replaced the receiver and leaned against the phone, his left hand gripping the top of the coin slot for support. Deep down inside he knew he was in trouble. He had been suckered into making a bonehead play, and would bet his life that the man behind it was Captain James Hamilton. That man was possessed with the idea of putting him behind bars.

Hamilton often had him picked up for questioning. Once, Hamilton had sworn to send him back to prison. Jimmy had shouted back, "The only way you're going to send me back is by framing me. I'll tell you one thing, you frame me and both you and Chief Parker will die miserable deaths."

Hamilton had ordered him out of his office and it was then that Jimmy had noticed a thick manuscript with a red folder on Hamilton's desk. His name and those of Brancato, Trombino, and Licata were typed on the cover along with those of Hamilton and Jack Webb, a movie actor and producer of the then popular *Dragnet* television series. Jimmy had whirled on Hamilton. "You going to make a movie?" Hamilton had smiled. "Perhaps." Two years later Jimmy saw the movie while in prison. It was entitled *Dragnet* and much of the story was based upon the killing of the two Tonys.

Jimmy left the phone booth and got into his Cadillac. Hamilton had been relentless in making Jimmy's reputation known to police departments across the state. Jimmy was picked up on robbery investigations in Beverly Hills, on the Sunset Strip, in Los Angeles, and he had been kicked out of San Diego when he had gone to help Bompensiero set up an orange juice distributorship. His travel plans were made known to the police of every city he visited.

Back at his Encino home, Jimmy pulled Jack aside and told him of his suspicions. "Jack, I don't like it. I think the damn phone was tapped."

"Well, how do you figure that?"

"Jesus Christ, Jack, at the end of the conversation, when I've got it all straightened out, this Riddell says something about my not hurting his family. Who said anything about hurting kids? I've never hurt a kid or a woman in my life. That's when I realized that somebody else was telling this guy what to say. You know me, Jack. I've never threatened anybody's family."

"It looks bad, Jimmy. Those guys must've gone to the cops and put a recorder on that phone. That's why they asked Raspona to give you that phone number."

"Yeah," Jimmy said, "and the deal's down the drain."

"That's the least of the problem right now. I think you should go on the lam. Go to Joe Dips or to Joe LaMandri in San Diego. His wife's an old-timer. Let's see what's up."

Two hours after making the telephone call, Jimmy had packed a bag and left home. Jewel, who was used to his peripatetic habits, had sensed a special urgency this time, but had said nothing about it. He told her not to worry, that he would be back in a few days, and an hour later he was with his mistress in the Franklin Street apartment.

He spent the next day on the telephone, touching base with his men, making arrangements for conducting business by long distance telephone, setting times and places for the calls. It was during a conversation with Charley Bats that he learned that the Eggman was trying to reach him. One of Jimmy's shylock customers, the Eggman, who had an egg store on Fairfax, had paid eight thousand dollars in interest on a twenty-five-hundred-dollar loan and still owed fifteen hundred on the principal.

When Jimmy called him the next morning before he was to leave for Joe LaMandri's home in San Diego, the Eggman offered him a deal. He would pay back the principal in full if Jimmy would forgo the interest. Jimmy agreed and decided to swing over to Fairfax to pick up the money before heading for San Diego. That change in plan was to cost him his freedom for many years.

A patrol car spotted his green Cadillac convertible and pulled him to the curb. He was searched, handcuffed, and delivered to the county jail, where he was booked in the presence of a lieutenant from Hamilton's Intelligence Division.

"Jimmy, the boss wants me to tell you he's got you dead-bang this time."

Jimmy's apprehensions grew when he started reading some of Chief Parker's comments in the newspapers. On the day following his arrest, Parker had said, "Fratianno boasted: 'I'm the Weasel. I belong to a very powerful organization. You've read a lot about it in the papers.' " Parker had gone on to say that Fratianno had threatened that if Riddell and Terry failed to comply with his demand for a two percent overriding royalty, " 'my organization, which has headquarters in Denver, will get you no matter where you go.' "

These words, falsely attributed to him, made him appear ridiculous. Later he would learn that these words, and others even more ridiculous, had been spoken by Ray Lanese, a third cousin, who had impersonated Jimmy in a threatening call to Riddell and Terry. Although Riddell and Terry would refer to this telephone threat in their testimony, the recorded call would not be played for the jury. Jimmy was convinced that it was because Deputy District Attorney J. Miller Leavy knew that it was not Jimmy's voice.

While free on bond, Jimmy went back to work. For some time, Louie Dragna had been trying to get a foothold in the Los Angeles garment district. Jack Dragna had been meeting with John Dioguardi, better known in union circles as Johnny Dio, a made guy from New York who was business manager of the AFL United Automobile Workers and also boss of the Truckers' Association. An expert union organizer, in the tradition of sluggings, maimings, and killings, Dio had built an awesome reputation by his ruthless methods.

Early in November, Johnny Dio brought Sam Berger to the Roosevelt Hotel in Hollywood for a meeting with Jimmy and Louie Dragna. Berger was a close associate of David Dubinsky, president of the International Ladies Garment Workers Union (ILGWU), with 400,000 members, most of them in New York City. At that time much of New York's giant needle trade industry was controlled by Cosa Nostra members through respectable fronts.

"By controlling the unions, you can operate your own factory without having to worry about union pay scales and rules," Dio told them. "You get waivers on practically every point in the contract, while your competitors have to operate under strict union conditions. It gives you the edge you need in the market place. It used to be that this industry was all Jewish, but now the Italians are really getting into it. Guys like Joe Stretch [*nee* Joe Stracci] control big companies like Zimmet and Stracci.

"To really make money," Dio continued, "you've got to get into the manufacturing end of it, and to do that, you've got to get some leverage with the ILGWU, from the needle trade to the pressers and truckers, every phase of it."

"That's what I want," Louie Dragna said, "my own factory."

"Well, I'll tell you how to do it," Dio said. "Dubinsky's man out here is Sam Otto. What you've got to do is hurt this fucking guy and make him run to New York. When he talks to Dubinsky, Sam Berger will be there, and he will tell him to get ahold of one of you guys."

"Tell him to get ahold of me," Dragna said, "Jimmy's in the news right now."

"So I've noticed," Dio said. "But, listen, you've got to really hurt this Otto, put him in the hospital."

"What's the next step?" Dragna asked.

"Then wreck a couple of them factories," Dio said. "Let Dubinsky know you're going to go your own fucking way out here."

To do the number on Sam Otto, Jimmy and Louie Dragna picked Rocco Guiliano and Gene Burg (nee Jimenez), a husky UCLA football player. They cracked Otto's skull with a blackjack and kicked him in the stomach and ribs when he was down. Two days later, Jimmy called Otto at the hospital, and without identifying himself, delivered the threat that would send him running to New York the moment he was released from the hospital.

"Listen, you motherfucker, this was just a small sample of what's in store for you if you don't fly right," Jimmy said. "Next time we'll kill you, you cocksucker. So you better do the right thing."

On the evening of November 17, 1953, Guiliano, Burg, and Jimmy Regace, who had finally come out of hiding from the Neddie Herbert killing, went through Mike Silver's factory with crowbars, ripping out telephone lines, and smashing sewing machines and other equipment. As Regace stood guard over Silver in his office, one of the two employees present slipped unnoticed down the back stairs and hid in the parking lot, taking note of the license number of Burg's car when the three men drove away.

Burg and Guiliano were arrested and eventually got three-year prison terms. Regace was not identified. The plan worked out as predicted by Dio and Louie Dragna became a wealthy clothing manufacturer. Twenty-five years later, his Roberta Company would be grossing $10 million annually and the profit margin would be as high as Mexican slave labor could make it, with the pay scale averaging eighty-five cents an hour for women working in their homes. Dragna never had to worry about union interference.

Meanwhile, Jimmy's trial was still pending, and he was living from day to day.

8
IN LIMBO

† † † †

CELINE WALTERS WAS PART OF WHAT SYNDICATED COLUMNIST WALTER
Winchell called the "International Set." It included Pat Baine, once married
to Tommy Dorsey; Peggy Malley, a mistress of movie mogul Harry Cohn;
Shelley Winters; Zsa Zsa and Eva Gabor; and others, who moved around the
world like wealthy celebrities.

A blonde in her early twenties, Celine was the most gorgeous woman
Jimmy had ever seen. The first time he met her was at Peggy Malley's
Beverly Hills apartment. Louie Dragna had invited him and he dropped by
with singer Johnny Desmond, who was then headlining at Ciro's. Desmond, who was being groomed by the Chicago family, was a close friend of
Caifano and Alderisio, and hung around with them and Jimmy when he was
in Las Vegas.

Celine Walters had come in around two that morning to speak privately
with Peggy, and when the two women had gone into the bedroom, Jimmy had
told Dragna that he wanted to take her home. She had taken a cab to the
apartment and when she came out of the bedroom, Dragna suggested that
Jimmy drive her home. They dropped Desmond off at the Beverly Hills Hotel
and for the rest of the drive to her apartment in Hollywood, which she shared
with her mother, Jimmy was trying to formulate a seduction plan. This was
no pushover: She had an apartment on Fifth Avenue in New York and was
in town for television work and an audition for a movie role. Then, as Jimmy
was pulling up in front of her place, she casually let drop that she was engaged
to King Paul of Yugoslavia.

"Oh, wow," Jimmy said, with a friendly laugh, "I've never competed with
a king before. How old's this guy."

"He's very young and quite handsome."

"I'll tell you what," Jimmy said, "I'll settle for being a good friend. I'm
always moving back and forth between here and Vegas, and when I come to
town it would be nice to have dinner with a beautiful lady. Make those guys
at Chasen's and Perino's drool. I'll be on my best behavior at all times. No

83

passes, okay? I'm not a king, but I promise you that you'll be treated like a queen wherever we go."

"I think I'd like that," she said.

"All right then," Jimmy said, opening the car door on her side and bowing, his quick eye not missing the white flash of thighs as she stepped out. "This is Wednesday morning, how about dinner on Friday?"

"It's a date," she said, as he walked her to the front door.

"You've made my week," he said. "Give me your phone number and I'll call you to set a time."

At the door he shook her hand, giving it a little extra squeeze, and left without trying to kiss her. And that was the way he played it for the next six or seven weeks. They went to expensive restaurants, but they also spent a great deal of time honkytonking at drive-in hamburger joints, drive-in movies, fish and chips places at the beach, and Italian restaurants with sawdust on the floor. During this time, he was learning as much as he could about her. She had a four-year-old daughter, Scarlett, and her ex-husband was a dentist in Palm Springs.

Jimmy saw a picture of King Paul in his uniform with a chest full of medals. He looked like a teen-ager posing as a king in a school play. They had met while he was on a visit to the U.S. and he had fallen in love with her. Now he wrote to her and sent her gifts, but she hadn't seen him since.

Jimmy, more patient than he had ever been with any woman in his life, finally reaped his reward. It was a lovely evening and they had gone riding in the Hollywood Hills when suddenly they came upon a house on fire. They watched for a while as the firemen fought the flames and drove back to her apartment. Her mother was there with her boyfriend and after a cup of coffee Jimmy excused himself, saying he would call her the next day. Celine stood up and suggested they go see if the fire had been put out. But once in the car again, she asked him if he knew a place where they could spend the next two hours.

As Jimmy would later describe it, "I was like a fucking mad dog. When she asked me that, forget about it. I headed down Cahuenga like a shot to this motel this Italian guy from Chicago owns on Ventura Boulevard. We go in this room and I start ripping off my clothes. I'm telling you, I was a fucking wild man. And she's ripping off her clothes and this broad's so beautiful I nearly come just looking at her. Forget about it. I fucked her three times in two hours. This broad got hung up on me. She really fell in love with me. I know that. I was good with her, treated her like a lady, and she told me, 'You know, Jimmy, I never thought you could be this gentle. I heard all those terrible stories about you being a tough guy, and you're the gentlest soul in the world.'

"Zsa Zsa was going out with Rubirosa and he gave her a shiner and she was going around with a black patch over her eye. This Rubirosa was trying to fuck Celine but she wouldn't give him a tumble because Zsa Zsa was her best friend. But Rubirosa can't give her the royal treatment I give her in these joints. All this bowing and scraping, these broads eat it up. They like the best table, to be with somebody who's respected. That Rubirosa's a big shot, but he don't get this kind of reception."

At the stroke of twelve, the orchestra in the cocktail lounge at the Desert Inn played "Auld Lang Syne" to welcome the year 1954. Jimmy kissed Jewel. A moment later he had vanished into the wild melee of drunken celebrants. Celine Walters saw him coming and she jumped up and down, waving her arms, while Jimmy pushed and pulled his way through the solid wall of people separating them. She called encouragement, her voice lost in the din of the uproar and pandemonium of the moment, but finally they were in each other's arms, kissing and laughing, and Jimmy said, "You've got to be nuts to come to this town on New Year's Eve."

"I love it," she squealed.

"I'd rather be alone with you."

"That will have to wait until tomorrow," she said. "Scarlett's sleeping in my bed."

"I know and tomorrow I'll have a room right next to yours."

He kissed her again. "I've got to get back. See you later."

Jewel was at a long table reserved by the owners of the Desert Inn. Jack and Tom Dragna were there with their wives. Morris Kleinman was sitting next to Jewel and the moment he saw Jimmy, he said, "Where the fuck you been?"

Suddenly, Jimmy was furious. "Kleinman, let's take a walk. You come with me," Jimmy said, walking away from the table.

Kleinman stood up and staggered to where Jimmy was waiting for him. "What's up, Jimmy?"

Jimmy poked at Kleinman's chest with a stiff finger. "Morris, I'm going to tell you this just once, understand? Don't ever use that fucking word in front of my wife again."

"What word, Jimmy?" Kleinman asked, peering drunkenly at Jimmy.

"That's my wife, you cocksucker. Don't ever use that fucking word fuck in front of her."

"Oh, that. Well, shit, Jimmy, I'm sorry. I didn't realize I said it."

"Morris, you've got a dirty mouth when you're drunk. It's fuck this, fuck that, and I want you to cut out that fucking language in front of my wife."

"Okay, Jimmy, my apologies to you and your wife."

"Ah, shit," Jimmy said. "Let's get back to the table."

When Jack Dragna saw Jimmy returning to the table, he beckoned to him and the two men walked away, trying to find an empty space in that crowded room where they could talk privately.

"Here," Dragna said, pulling Jimmy against a wall near the reception desk. "This's as good as we'll do tonight."

"It's a fucking madhouse."

"Listen, Jimmy, Meyer has sent word that we can buy into the Flamingo for a hundred and twenty-five grand. What do you think about it?"

"It's what we've been waiting for," Jimmy said. "Let's grab it."

Dragna shook his head. "Jimmy, I forgot to tell you, but this friend of mine, Al Khoury, owns this piece of land across from the Flamingo and he's thinking of building a hotel-casino."

"But the Flamingo's a going business. Let's take it, it's a bird in the hand."

"Yeah, but in that joint we'd be in the hands of the Philistines. We'd have to take what they give us."

Jimmy could see that Jack was opposed to it, and he knew that in the end it would go his way, but he persisted anyway. "How do you know Khoury's joint will ever open? He wouldn't be the first guy not to finish what he's started in this town."

"Don't worry, he's going to finish it," Jack said. "And I've talked to Bill Graham and there's going to be no problem getting the license."

Jimmy nodded. "Bill can get anybody a license, but, Jack, I think we should take Meyer's deal. We've got the money for it and then we can still go with Khoury when he's ready."

"Oh, Christ, Jimmy, we can't swing both deals."

Jimmy shrugged. It made little difference to him. A few days after his arrest, he had been brought to Hamilton's office and a recording of his call was played back while Hamilton sat behind his desk, grinning at Jimmy, who sat there trying to grin back at him. Afterwards Jimmy had said, "Take out the swear words and what've you got?"

"We've got a prima facie case of extortion, with or without the obscenities, but we're not taking them out. That's the way it's going to be played for the jury."

At that moment, Jimmy had realized that he was going back to prison.

"Whatever you do's okay with me," Jimmy told Dragna.

"I think we'll take a pass on Meyer's deal and go for Khoury's," concluded Dragna.

The next day Jimmy sent Jewel back home, telling her he had business to attend to in Las Vegas. Johnny Bats, who was married to Jacqueline Fontaine, a singer who would later marry comedian Lenny Bruce, also sent his wife home. Jimmy wanted a third party with him when he was out in public with Celine Walters. If word got back to Jewel, he could always say she was Johnny Bats's girl.

Jimmy and Celine made love all night and slept late in the morning. Johnny Bats took Celine's daughter Scarlett to the pool area in the morning, and although it was winter, the child enjoyed playing in the heated water. After lunch Jimmy and Celine would come out and sit in the sunshine and exchange stories, which was always Jimmy's favorite pastime.

One day, out of the blue, Celine said, "You really are a tough mug, aren't you?" She smiled as she spoke.

"Don't be silly," Jimmy said. "I'm a bookmaker."

"But you don't gamble?"

"Never. Just suckers like Johnny Bats buck the house."

"Don't you bet when you're a bookmaker?"

"Hell, no, the bettor wages six to make five. All I've got to do is keep that book balanced. The only time I bet is when I've got a sure thing. Like a while back, you know what I mean, Morey Orloff and Abe Benjamin got the fix in with the Hollywood Stars." Jimmy paused. "That's a baseball team in the Pacific Coast League. Anyway, they got a pitcher, a catcher, the shortstop, and the center fielder. We're careful not to overdo it, but when the fix's in, we clean up. I get this bookmaker, Hymie Miller, to call Ike Hassen in Portland, Oregon, and say he knows this Joe Decklebaum who wants to layoff with him. So I call Ike, go into my Jewish routine, and I says, 'Ike, Joe Decklebaum here. Hymie tells me you're an honorable man.' I give him this bullshit about bookmakers being slow paying off and I'm looking for a place where I can pay or collect by check every Monday. We agree on two-thousand a position and I give him my address at the Chase Hotel. The manager gets my Decklebaum mail and holds it for me. Now I pull the same scam on Harry Pelsinger, who's got the sports book at the Flamingo, and Mike Shapiro in L. A.

"Well, when the baseball season ends, I start betting big on college and pro football. I'm getting some good inside shit on conditions of the teams, the quarterback, the weather, and I figure what can I lose? Now I've hit these guys for sixty-five, seventy grand each, and they're paying regularly every Monday. Then I hit a week, Celine, you wouldn't believe. I lose about fifteen grand on Saturday and about twenty-five on Sunday—that's to each one."

"My God," Celine said, "that's crazy."

"Wait a minute," Jimmy said. "I haven't given you the kicker yet. I get Hymie to call all three guys and say he's also looking for Decklebaum, who's into him for forty grand. Then to say he's got a guy here that knows him real good, say his name's Jimmy Fratianno and he's hired him to collect for him and suggest they do the same.

"Well, Celine, forget about it. I get all three of them on the pad for three hundred a week. I tell them, 'Don't worry, I'll get your money. You might not get it all at once, but you'll get it all in the end.'"

"Oh boy," Celine said. "You are really devious."

"Listen, I had them guys on the pad nearly four years. Every so often I'd call and say, 'Hey, Decklebaum just came across with some money and I'm splitting it four ways.' I'd send them a little check for fifteen hundred and tell them Decklebaum's doing real good and it looks like they're going to get their money with no problems. The way I worked it out, they got back about half of what they were paying me, which means I cleared about another hundred grand."

"That's wild," Celine laughed. "Really incredible. How do you think up things like that?"

"I don't know," Jimmy shrugged. "It just comes naturally."

In bed with Celine that night, the last time they would ever be together, they made love and Celine moaned the way Jimmy liked to hear a woman moan when he was giving her pleasure.

Afterwards they lay in bed and talked about the art of lovemaking. Celine was interested in Jimmy's preference for straight old-fashioned sex. She could not understand his reluctance toward oral sex.

"Well, I'll tell you," he said, lighting up a cigar and sitting up in bed. "In this town everybody wants to get his prick sucked. It's quick and sanitary, gets a guy back to the crap tables real quick. But that stuff tears you down. Take Charley Bats, Johnny's brother, a broad has to suck his prick for him to get it up. That guy's in bad shape."

"Haven't you ever had yours sucked?" she asked, her fingers gently massaging him.

Jimmy laughed. "Of course, but I never really liked it. I'll tell you why. A doctor once told me that if your prick gets hard naturally you can fuck twenty times and it won't hurt you. You can fuck as often as your prick comes up naturally, but if you've got to do tricks to force it up, that's a different story. Then you're exerting yourself and that can hurt you."

"Well, goodness, we wouldn't want that to happen tonight, would we?" she said, pressing her body against his.

In the morning they went down to the coffee shop for breakfast and after their first cup of coffee, Celine said, "I feel so sad. How serious is this trial?"

"I'm not going to kid you," Jimmy said. "At first we had a chance to show these oil men are swindlers. I had this guy, Jack Lewis, who told me Riddell and Terry were forced to press charges against me. Carl Riddell told him the cops had several charges against them for swindling people and the deal was they'd drop all charges if they'd help send me to jail. That's how bad Hamilton wants to frame me. So I told Frank DeSimone, he's Raspona's attorney, to tape record this Jack Lewis, but he wanted to use him in court instead, and now he's disappeared. The cops probably stashed him away. With that tape I'd be home free. Understand? So now if they don't find this Lewis, I ain't got no way of showing this's a frame."

Jimmy paused. "Want to hear something funny? I'm a thirty-second degree Mason and once, when Hamilton saw this little lapel pin I was wearing, he had a fit. I mean, he went off his rocker."

"Now you've got me curious," Celine said. "How did you manage that?"

"I knew this Negro potentate and we started selling memberships. Listen, lots of doctors, lawyers, and businessmen want to be Masons. Instead of having to learn all that junk, we'd give them the answers ahead of time. Save them months of studying." What Jimmy didn't tell Celine was that he had joined the Masons to make it easier to clip Joe Sica, a close friend of the Negro potentate's and a Cohen henchman who was getting most of the credit for the hits the Dragna family was making. Later, Sica had straightened himself out with Jack Dragna, but he was never trusted enough to become a family member.

She squeezed his hand. "I know it must be terribly frustrating, to feel so helpless at a time like this. Jimmy, I've read a lot about this case and I don't understand how you could have said some of those things on a telephone."

Jimmy shook his head. "I've thought about it, Celine, believe me. You know, my problem's I can't stand for anybody to beat me. That's my downfall. I let my emotions get the best of me. Call it my ego or my temper. Whatever you call it, it's my biggest problem. See, Celine, I should have sued them guys. We had a verbal agreement, that's a binding contract, but they were trying to pull a fast one and I just couldn't stand still for that, no way. I'm just not built that way."

The trial in Los Angeles, which lasted two months, went pretty much the way Jimmy had anticipated. It was all downhill, despite the efforts of his attorney, William B. Beirne. The prosecution, deftly handled by J. Miller Leavy, the District Attorney's top gun, made it known to the jury that the witnesses and their families were under twenty-four-hour police protection. Nearly two hours of unexpurgated recordings were played to a jury of eight women and four men. Jimmy lowered his head when his own voice reverberated through the courtroom, each obscenity hitting him like a sledgehammer blow over the head. He couldn't force himself to look at the jurors to assess their reactions.

The day the jury brought in a verdict of guilty for all three defendants, Jimmy vented his frustration and rage on Frank DeSimone for not having prerecorded Jack Lewis, who could have proved Jimmy had been framed. "You fucked me, you cocksucker," Jimmy hissed at DeSimone. "Someday I'm going to break your fucking head, you piece of shit."

DeSimone's reaction was one of fear and protested innocence. "How was I to know Lewis would skip town?" he pleaded.

"Don't talk to me or I'll whack you right here," Jimmy said, turning away. Little did he know that DeSimone would soon be boss of the L.A. family.

Jimmy looked at Jewel, who sat crumpled with a handkerchief to her nose, but he avoided her eyes. He shrugged and glanced at his brother, Warren, who sat there with a confused expression on his face. "Poor helpless bastard," Jimmy thought. "Who's going to take care of you now?" He wanted to smile at them, to show there was still hope, but it was impossible.

The sentence was pronounced by Superior Judge Ralph E. Pierson on April 7, 1954. Co-defendants Raspona and Modica, who had made dozens of threatening phone calls while Jimmy had been away, were fined two thousand dollars each and placed on five years' probation. Jimmy, who had made that one call, was sentenced to five to fifteen years in prison—it was later reduced on appeal to one to ten years.

Beirne gripped his arm, "Jimmy, it's only the first round. Tom Hiller's already preparing the appeal. At most you'll serve two, two and a half years."

For a wild moment, Jimmy looked at his watch, wondering if he had time to call Celine, but then he saw a deputy coming toward him, holding a pair of handcuffs, and he knew it was all over. He could kiss the good days good-bye. He stood there, with that sinking feeling in the pit of his stomach, knowing all too well what was ahead of him.

9
BEHIND BARS AGAIN

† † † †

THROUGH A GRIMY WINDOW OF THE OLD GRAY GOOSE, THE BUS THAT shuttled prisoners from the Chino Guidance Center to Folsom, Jimmy stared at the world passing by. How many of those people racing down the freeway to the comfort of their homes had ever spent a single day in prison? Did any of them realize how precarious a world they lived in? Of what could happen tomorrow? Did they know anything about the prison system? How the sociologists and psychologists talked of rehabilitation and how they made animals instead? Even the dumbest prisoners could con the so-called experts. They all talked like psychiatrists. They got religion, became docile, cooperative, anything to cut one minute off their time. Perhaps one in a thousand changed and when it happened it was not because of the system.

Of all the bad things he had done in his life, Jimmy remembered a special notation appended to his Case Summary report at Chino, which a clerk had shown him. It read: "Police records indicated Subject has been known to have a hand in narcotics selling on a large scale." Jimmy had wondered why the Los Angeles police found it necessary to invent this lie, but he had soon realized that it was one more thing to keep him behind bars without parole for as long as possible. It was Hamilton's handiwork, and there was no doubt in Jimmy's mind that it was this notation, among others, that had gotten him to the worst prison in the system.

Folsom was another world, a gray, foggy, dismal world, with thirty-foot walls and machine-gun turrets. Prisoners called it the end of the line. Jimmy's first thought when he saw it, the gray walls looming through the fog, was "How do I get out of here?"

After being processed and given a number, A-28624, Jimmy and the others were taken to the mess hall for a late supper. Everything was fine until he walked into his cell. His cellmate was an overt homosexual. Having been assigned the top bunk, Jimmy lost no time getting into it.

The cellmate had stripped down to his shorts and was delicately powdering himself in all the right places. "What's your name?" he asked, rolling his eyes at Jimmy. "What terrible crimes have you committed?"

Jimmy leaned forward on one elbow. "Listen, you cocksucker, you lay in your bunk and shut your fucking trap."

"Well, there's no need to get violent. I was just being social."

"Unless you're packing a fucking rod in those shorts, you better shut up. I want to get some sleep. Tomorrow one of us's getting out of this cell."

The next morning Jimmy went to the captain's office and his clerk was a burglar who had once patronized Jimmy's old card room. When Jimmy explained his problem, the clerk transferred him to another building and gave him some valuable advice. "If you want to bunk by yourself, go see Dr. Day, he's a good friend of Danny Wilson's. Tell him you're nervous, very excitable, and you can't cell with nobody. He'll put a little note on your jacket: 'Keep this man alone,' see."

Dr. Day was only too happy to assist a friend of Danny Wilson. From then on Jimmy celled alone in population, the best of all possible worlds in a maximum-security prison.

His first job was working as a gardener in the vegetable garden, which was one of the few opportunities at Folsom a prisoner had to be out in the fresh air. Although he was in population, he associated with very few prisoners. In a way he was a celebrity, but he kept his distance. It was his belief that ninety-nine percent of all convicts were lunatics, men beyond cure or redemption, regardless of what psychiatrists put down in their reports. All one had to do was talk to them and it soon became obvious that they had a screw loose. He felt superior to these men. He was the only made guy in Folsom. In fact, he and Bompensiero were the only made guys in the entire California prison system.

A few months after Jimmy's indictment, Bompensiero had been snagged in the Bill Bonelli liquor license bribery case, in which Russian Louie's old girlfriend, Mickey Smith, was the state's key witness. Convicted of bribery in the sale of a liquor license, Bompensiero was serving a three-to-fourteen-year sentence at San Quentin.

Sometimes in his bunk at night, Jimmy thought about Mickey Smith. She had bought him silk pajamas and he had felt pretty special in that big house of hers in Ojai, with the servants giving him royal treatment. But she was a sharp one. At the time she was sleeping with him, she had worked out a big score with Caifano, Alderisio, and Louie Dragna. She had told them that one of Bonelli's men in San Bernardino had about $80,000 stashed in his home. While she was out on the town with this official, the three men had burglarized his home and found the money hidden in a bedroom closet. The theft was never reported to the police. The money was cut up four ways and Jimmy only learned about it months later from Alderisio. Jimmy had often wondered why she had not cut him in on the score, but he was not resentful. She had protected him during the Bonelli trial. Jimmy had bought two liquor licenses from her, and at first Jimmy had thought, "Here I go again," but not once had she mentioned his name in court.

† † †

One of the few friends Jimmy had at Folsom was Jeff Jefferson, the leader of the black population at that prison. Doing time on a robbery conviction, which is considered a life term, Jefferson got involved in a hassle with another prisoner over his "old lady."

"Hey, Jimmy, what d'you think, man?" Jefferson told Jimmy one day. "This fucking Shiek Thompson's trying to make my old lady."

Shiek Thompson was the biggest, toughest black prisoner there. He was, in Jimmy's opinion, "an animal, a fucking ape."

"Jeff, what's wrong with you?" Jimmy said. "Are you crazy or what? Don't get involved with Shiek."

"I'm going to kill that motherfucker."

"Cool down, man. Think what you're doing. You've got some time in, why fuck up your parole over some punk. Get another broad."

"That cocksucker's giving her a little muscle."

"Forget about it, Jeff. It's not worth it."

They talked about it for a long time and finally Jimmy thought he had convinced Jefferson to get himself another punk. There was one called Hazel that Jefferson quite liked, but still Jimmy could see that he deeply resented Shiek's blatant interference. A few days later, Jefferson caught Shiek in the Education Building and stabbed him about twenty times with a six-inch shiv. Even with all the stab wounds, Shiek got up and ran to the hospital.

Shiek Thompson survived but Jefferson was automatically given the death penalty—the law at that time made the death penalty mandatory whenever a prisoner serving a life term drew blood in an altercation with another prisoner or guard. Jefferson became known as "Death Row Jeff" and later became famous as the founder of the Symbionese Liberation Army. Some twenty years later, Randolph Hearst would go to the Vacaville prison to plead with Death Row Jeff on his daughter's behalf, but by then it was far too late for anyone to help.

Jimmy spent nearly two years at Folsom before his transfer to Soledad was arranged in 1956 by Attorney Louis Tom Hiller through Assemblyman Lester A. McMillan. The price was twenty-five hundred dollars and worth every penny of it. Soledad was Jimmy's kind of prison. You could get out in the fresh air and play softball and basketball, you could run and exercise, play dominoes, chew the fat out in the sunlight, and keep yourself healthy, your body tuned up for the day you walked out of that joint, again a member of the human race.

Warden Lawrence Wilson was so impressed when Mark Anthony, a booking agent whose clients included Bob Hope, came to visit Jimmy at Soledad that he let them use his office. During the conversation, Wilson expressed the hope that Anthony would bring a show to Soledad. Jimmy thought it was a great idea and Anthony brought the Australian Jazz Quintet, and later two other shows, but not Bob Hope. Anthony, whose real name was Petercupo, had grown up on the Hill with Jimmy and they were lifelong friends.

In March 1956 Jimmy became Chairman of the Inmate Council and Vocational Clerk, a job he held for two years, receiving grades for his work of "above average" to "excellent."

On June 17, 1959, headlines in newspapers across the state labeled Jimmy the "Mafia's Executioner on the West Coast." The quote was from the testimony of Captain Hamilton before a state senate subcommittee investigating organized crime. "I have heard," Hamilton testified, "as high as sixteen deaths attributed to Fratianno." The publicity made Jimmy the most celebrated prisoner in California. Ordinarily, he would have relished the notoriety, but all it meant now was another denial of parole and one more year in prison before the next review. Jimmy was convinced that this was a calculated plan carried out by Hamilton. In 1957 he had been responsible for releasing the story that Frank DeSimone had visited him at Soledad just prior to his attending the Apalachin meeting where some sixty Mafiosi were arrested. Every year he had come up with something to discourage the parole board.

On December 11, 1959, Jimmy was moved to San Quentin for medical attention. Several keloids had to be removed from his chest, which required skin grafting. Jimmy arrived at San Quentin with a dozen boxes of cigars and the first prisoner he recognized was Frank Bompensiero, who was working in distribution.

It was like old home week. They shook hands and hugged and exchanged gossip. Bompensiero personally took him to the hospital, made sure he had a good bed, introduced him to nurses and orderlies, and that evening came up for a visit and a good cigar.

Soon the conversation turned to Red Sagunda, a Cleveland thug who had moved to San Diego. "Remember that sonovabitch?" Bompensiero asked, taking a deep puff on the cigar. He closed his eyes to indicate his state of bliss. "Me and Biaggio clipped the bastard and buried him while I was awaiting trial."

Jimmy puffed on his cigar. "You know, Bomp, we put too much emphasis on clipping guys and not enough on fucking broads. I've done lots of thinking about broads lately and my only regret's that I ain't fucked enough of them. I had my share, believe me, but still there was always too many other things going on. Broads came second to money in them days. But now I often think about broads and I want to kick my ass for being a jerk. All that money's down the drain. What good was it? Think of it, Bomp, I could have fucked twice as many broads."

He paused again, a wistful look coming into his eyes. "Remember the Chase Hotel? When I first went there, Buster Crabbe was using the hotel's swimming pool to rehearse an aquacade he was putting together for a nationwide tour. I looked out there and the broads, I couldn't believe my eyes. There were thirty contest winners from all over the country. I started cooking spaghetti and filling the refrigerator with goodies and these broads would come up there to eat. Before the show left I'd fucked seventeen of them."

Bompensiero barked his familiar laugh. "I remember your fucking parole officer."

Jimmy nodded. "Norm Jolly. He'd come in there and give Patti the eye."

"Hey, the broad that handled your cigar counter? She was stacked."

"Well, one day we're standing in the lobby and he's eyeballing her and I says, 'Want to give her a little fuck?' Oh, shit, he nearly came in his pants. Patti was a good kid and she went for it. Then I started giving him a C-note. Then when my time was up, he tried to extend my parole for another year. The dirty sonovabitch wanted to go on fucking Patti and collecting the C-notes."

"Well, you can't blame the guy for wanting to keep a good thing going," Bompensiero said.

A few nights later Bompensiero came to ask a favor. "Jimmy, you remember Chuck Cahan?"

"Remember him?" Jimmy shouted. "That stool pigeon paid Jack Whalen five grand to break my head. Jack came to me and we split the five Gs instead of my head." Both men laughed.

"Listen, Jimmy, this guy's been here about four years and he's doing bad time. And now that you're here he's scared shitless."

"That's the best news I've had all year."

"Come on, Jimmy, why don't you let bygones be bygones. This guy sleeps next to me on the West Block. He's working for the priest and he's got a parole date coming up. Give him a break. Talk to him."

"Why should I, for Christ's sake?" Jimmy asked.

"I'll tell you why. This guy can help you get out. He's got a good connection with the priest here."

Jimmy smiled. "Well, that's different."

The next evening Bompensiero brought Cahan to Jimmy's hospital room. Bompensiero had been right. Cahan was doing hard time. He had changed so much that Jimmy would not have recognized him if he had seen him in the yard. Hard time could destroy a man so quickly that it frightened Jimmy to think about it.

They shook hands and Jimmy offered him a cigar. They talked quietly for a while, about nothing in particular, and when he was ready to leave, Cahan said, "Thanks, Jimmy. I feel a lot better. If there's anything I can do for you. . . . you know, I work for the priest . . . just let me know."

"I want what everybody wants," Jimmy said. "Some good shit in my jacket to get me out of here."

When it came time for the Adult Authority's next review, the Catholic Chaplain, Father J. Dingberg, contributed the following observation in Jimmy's Parole Release Referral Report: "Although subject has been at this institution but a short while, at the time of this report, he has contacted the writer for help with various problems and demonstrated an interest in the fulfillment of his religious obligations. Accepts his circumstances in an intelligent manner and evidences a sincerity of purpose toward the future. When not confined in the hospital subject has attended Mass and in his contacts with the writer has demonstrated appreciation of all efforts made on his behalf."

PART III

† † † †

GOING LEGIT
1960–1964

10
A FREE MAN

† † † †

PAROLE WAS GRANTED ON JULY 14, 1960. ON THAT DATE, CARL I. ROG-gi, parole supervisor for the Sacramento District, wrote a report to the Department of Correction. It concluded with this evaluation:

"He is a very personable individual and makes a rather impressive appearance. The writer somewhat questions the ability of any officer, academically experienced in the field of social welfare, to adequately supervise an individual such as this. . . . This man will, no doubt, cause us considerable trouble and will require the strictest type of supervision that we can exercise at this or any other time. Any mismanagement of facts and circumstances could easily embarrass our good parole system. We must be guarded at all times."

As a further safeguard, Jimmy was restricted to the small northern California town of Redding. On December 9, 1960, an "Activities" report was submitted by Parole Agent Craig Wright:

"Shortly after the first of September this Parolee acquired a job where he has remained continuously employed with the Riley Trucking Company . . . in Redding. He works through the International Brotherhood of Teamsters, Chauffeurs and Warehousemen, Local 137, Mr. Duane Wemple, agent. The Parolee earns $10 per hour for the use of his truck and himself on jobs procured by Mr. Riley.

"The Parolee continues to maintain a stable residence program with his wife, Jewel Fratianno, known also as Jewel Farrell, at 188 Oleander Circle. . . . The home is comfortably furnished and attractive. . . .

"Agent in charge William Davis, FBI, advised the undersigned that this Parolee has made four telephone calls . . . to one Raulin Dorsey of Anderson, Calif. Subsequently Mr. Fratianno advised the undersigned, without knowing of the latter's interest in Mr. Dorsey, that Mr. Dorsey was a fellow truckdriver and friend of his.

"It was also learned that Mrs. Fratianno, a licensed Real Estate broker doing business under the name of Jewel Farrell, will begin employment with the Don Cram Real Estate Company . . . as a real estate salesman.

97

"The Parolee is disarmingly friendly with the parole agent and . . . persistently makes strong overtures in establishing something more than a strictly professional relationship with the agents with whom he is involved. The Parolee is exceedingly clever at this undertaking and one must be careful to avoid any positive identification. Aside from this propensity on Fratianno's part his parole function has been satisfactory and his plans would appear to be consistent with his capabilities, both economically and socially."

It took Jimmy less than nine hours to drive from Redding to Los Angeles, some six hundred miles through the heartland of California, passing through rich farm country and lush fields of grapevines, with long stretches of nothing but grayish sagebrush and tumbleweeds. All the while, he kept an eye on the rearview mirror for cops. He had sneaked out of Redding, evading the heavy surveillance that had been monitoring his every movement since his release on parole, and the last thing he wanted now was for his parole to be violated. Yet his foot grew heavier on the accelerator as his impatience mounted.

The only person who could help him now was Johnny Roselli, the one man he trusted in this world. The Los Angeles family had stolen the shylock money he had left on the street when he had gone to prison and now they wanted his life because they were afraid of him. The old boss he had trusted, Jack Dragna, was dead and the two men he most disliked, Frank DeSimone and Nick Licata, were now boss and underboss, respectively, and he knew that the feeling was more than mutual. They were trying to put a blanket on him.

The restaurant Roselli had selected was on the top floor of a new office building, one of the tallest on Wilshire Boulevard, and when the elevator doors opened, he was greeted by a smiling maitre d' in a form-fitting tuxedo.

"Good evening, Mr. Fratianno."

Jimmy immediately recognized him as a waiter he had known at Naples, his favorite restaurant in the old days. "Dominick, right?" he said, shaking hands.

"Yes, sir," the maitre d' laughed politely, pleased that he had been remembered. "Mr. Roselli is waiting. This way, please. I have a nice secluded table for you."

He did not see Roselli until they were standing right in front of the table. The two men embraced and kissed in the European manner. This custom was not practiced by any of the Mafia families except those in New York where they always hugged and kissed in greeting each other, a practice that did not appeal to Jimmy. Of course, with Johnny, after all these years, it was different.

"John, how are you?"

"Jesus Christ, long time, Jimmy."

They looked at each other, smiling and shaking hands. "Seven fucking years," Jimmy said, "but what can you do, it's one of them things."

"Come on, let's sit down," Roselli said, indicating where he wanted him to sit. "See, I had the waiter bring you a scotch on the rocks. I knew you'd be here at eight sharp."

Jimmy leaned back and sighed. "I had to break the world's land speed record to make it."

"What are you driving."

"A new Ford," Jimmy answered.

"No Cadillac yet?"

"Shit, I'm busted. Besides I can't afford to flash in that one-horse town. You should see the heat I'm getting."

Roselli sipped his martini, his blue eyes studying his companion. "I swear you look better than when you went up there."

"Listen, you don't age either."

Roselli smiled and Jimmy noticed that his teeth looked pretty good for a man in his mid-fifties. He had a nice tan and his hair was beginning to gray at the temples. Johnny was still a good-looking man.

"How's the wife and kid?" Roselli asked.

Jimmy shook his head. "Jewel's fine but the kid, Joanne . . . I hadn't been up Folsom three, four months before Jewel comes up there with Joanne and this little *pezzo di merda* she wants to marry. See, Johnny, I didn't know she was going with anyone. When I was home I was very strict with my daughter. I wouldn't let her go out with just anybody."

"So who's this kid. Is he Italian?"

"Johnny, listen to this. His name's Thomas Thomas. I mean, for Christ's sake, it's ridiculous. . . . Anyway, I gave them my blessings."

"What can you do?" Roselli said. "Today, girls fall in love. You can't stop it."

"I know, but she could have done better. She's a beautiful girl, my daughter. She always was a very sweet girl. One thing about my daughter, she always believed in me. Sometimes she'd come from school crying but she never said nothing to me about all that bullshit in the papers."

"That's good, Jimmy. That's the way it should be, you know, a man's family should stick by him."

"Yeah, and that's a hell of lot more than I can say about this other fucking family of ours."

"What's this all about between you and Nick Licata?"

"You know, Johnny, I had some problems even before Jack Dragna died in fifty-seven. When I went up to Folsom in fifty-four, I left over a hundred grand in shylock money on the street with my crew. I put Charley Battaglia in charge and told Louie Dragna to keep an eye on him. So what does Charley Bats do? He gives Jewel a hundred and fifty a week for about six months, then Louie sends word they lost everything, which is a lot of bullshit."

Roselli nodded, his eyes narrowing. "Jimmy, isn't there also something about Bats trying to rape Jewel."

"Right. Louie's little message came a couple months after Jewel told me about that. He's lucky I was in prison. I'd have blown his fucking head off in a minute. So I tell her to go see Jack and Tom Dragna, tell them what happened. She comes back a week later and says they talked to Charley and naturally he denied it. He knows the penalty. He says she's only making up stories to protect herself. Well, Johnny, you know my *wife*. There's no way that my wife, who's a nice-looking woman, would ever go for a piece of shit like this guy. He's like a fucking bulldog. So I have Jewel tell Jack to forget about everything until I get out. How the hell was I to know I'm going to do six and half years?

"Them guys are something else. They must think I'm an idiot. How do you go broke with a hundred grand on the street? They just cut up the money. So my wife had to get a job.

"Now, Johnny, I began thinking about this thing of ours. Look at the pieces of shit that's now running the family. I don't want nothing to do with them. When I think of all the money I've cut up with them guys . . . That's one thing about me, I've always cut up my money.

"Johnny, except for you, I've got no real friends in this thing. I thought how could I've been so dumb. All they ever used me for was to kill people, set people up, and I never got nothing for none of it. All them guys are looking out for number one. I could've gone my own way and been a millionaire."

He stopped and looked closely at Roselli, trying to gauge his reaction. Although he felt sure Johnny shared his feelings, he was still on dangerous ground. He could get clipped for talking that way. And, after all, he had not seen Johnny in seven years. Yet he trusted him enough to say what was on his mind. What the hell, he thought, he couldn't be in worse trouble anyway.

"Years ago, Jimmy, it was a different ball game," Roselli said. "Today there's too much greed and jealousy. The greed and jealousy of little men. No vision, no imagination. That's why I got myself transferred when Jack died. I wasn't about to work with assholes like DeSimone and Licata. No way. When DeSimone got himself elected boss in 1957, he came to me and said, 'Johnny, what do you think happened? They voted for me unanimously.' "

"Bullshit," Jimmy said. "This prick came to Soledad just after Jack died and asked me who should be boss and I told him you should be boss. He says, 'Well, you know, Johnny's the most logical guy.' He went to see Bomp at Quentin and Bomp told him the same thing. So where does he get off with this unanimous shit?"

"He never told me I was the most logical guy," Roselli said, an edge of sarcasm in his voice. "I knew he wanted to be boss. I could see everybody jockeying for position. Nobody ever asked me if I wanted to be boss.

"I didn't even vote, and when this asshole gave me that unanimous bullshit, I said, 'You know, Frank, as of now, I'm putting it on record. I'm getting transferred back to Chicago.' He said, 'You checked this out with Giancana?' I said, 'Yeah, I've talked to Sam.' He's never seen Sam. Shit, I knew Sam when he was driving for Jack McGurn."

"I heard Sam's now the boss," Jimmy said.

"Sam's the boss, but the man in Chicago's still Paul Ricca. Sam don't make any big moves without consulting Paul."

Jimmy smiled. "And Paul's your man."

"Oh, yeah, I knew Paul in the twenties, and we did time together in Leavenworth. He's been the man in Chicago since Capone went to prison. Forget [Frank] Nitti and Joe Batters. They listened to Paul, believe me."

"I met Sam in 1953 when I was in Chicago with Alderisio and Caifano," Jimmy said. "Nice guy. By the way, just the other day, Bill Graham came up to see me in Redding and told me that Sam's in the Cal–Neva Lodge with Sinatra, they've got twenty-five points."

"Yeah, the one at Tahoe. They're working out a deal to get another twelve points."

"Did you know that Graham built that place back in the thirties?"

Roselli smiled. "Old Bill had quite a run. He was Mr. Big a long time, but there's been a power switch in Nevada, from Reno to Las Vegas. Today it's the Dalitz crowd that has the clout."

"I'll bet Bill still can do things. But coming back to Sam, I think he was just a fucking soldier when I met him in fifty-three. They called him Mooney."

"In those days Sam worked directly under Joe Batters, who was boss, but like I say, he was taking his lead from Paul. But Sam was in a different category then. He never worked for a skipper, just like I used to work directly for Capone, or later in L.A. with Jack. All bosses like to have a crew of workers directly under them. Marshall Caifano, Philly Alderisio, Obie Frabotta, Jackie Cerone, seven, eight guys now work directly under Sam. It gives him a little more leverage, if anybody gets out of line. I never wanted to be a *capo*. You've got too many mouths to feed."

Jimmy shook his head knowingly. "You're telling me, I had fourteen guys in my crew, and I'm booking and shylocking and working all kinds of scams, but I'm cutting the money with a bunch of fucking deadheads."

The waiter, who was assigned exclusively to their table, cautiously approached when he saw Roselli turn his head in his direction. With a motion of his hand, Roselli indicated they wanted refills. After he had left, Roselli gave Jimmy a wry smile. "The whole time you've been gone, they've clipped *one* guy. Angelo Polizzi clipped him and dumped his body in a field out in Ontario."

"Oh, yeah," Jimmy said, breaking into a grin. "I know who you mean, the guy the Buffalo family was after. James Delmont."

"Peanuts [John] Tranalone set him up for Angelo. You know Peanuts, don't you?"

"Yeah, he's from Cleveland. In fact, Delmont and Peanuts were good friends before Delmont became a snitch. Hey, speaking of Delmont, want to hear something funny?" Jimmy asked. "When I came out of Soledad, they stuck me out in Redding. I start looking for a job, anything, you know, to get my parole officer off my back. His name's Carl Roggi and after a month or so, he tells me I've got to get a job or there's the possibility I'm going back to the joint on a technical violation. There's nothing around there but lumber mills and they ain't hiring nobody. This Roggi, see, is a devout Catholic, and I told him the story of how I'd received the last rites when I was a kid and while I still had the wafer in my mouth I came out of the coma. It was like a miracle. This Roggi was really impressed. He says, 'Fratianno, you've been in prison all these years. I have friends who are Trappist Monks in Vina, which is about forty miles south of here.' The monastery's called Our Lady of New Clairvaux. He says, 'Why don't you go there on a retreat for three or four days. Just stop everything and think of where you've been and where you're heading.'

"So, naturally, I don't want to be violated. I says, 'Well, I'd like that, Carl. I'll go down and spend three or four days.' This Roggi don't waste no time. He drives me down there the very next morning. There're two groups in this place, fathers and brothers. The fathers wear white robes, the brothers brown robes. The guests on retreat stay in a special house but you get up when they get up and go to like seven masses a day. All the fathers and brothers are really thin. They don't eat meat or drink milk and they eat so little it's amazing they stay alive.

"Now comes the funny part. I meet this Brother Adams and he knows Delmont. Delmont was there last year, hiding out, and this Brother Adams got to know him pretty good. It seems this Delmont told him all kinds of shit he shouldn't have talked about. Like he's involved in murders and shit up in Buffalo and there's a contract on him. He tells Brother Adams the Mafia's bigger than the FBI and the only place a guy's safe from the Mafia's in the House of God. But this Delmont's a hothead and he's constantly getting into beefs with other guests at the retreat and finally they kick his ass out of there."

"That's a hell of a coincidence," Roselli said. "Did Brother Adams straighten you out?"

Jimmy laughed. "They worked my ass off out in the field all day and nearly starved me to death, but still I ate more than they did. But I'll tell you something. The last mass is vespers, and it's beautiful. It's a feeling I can't explain. It puts chills in your body, Johnny. You see all them monks, thin as skeletons, maybe two hundred of them, marching into this chapel, and they kneel, go through this little ritual, and then they chant. Boy, can they chant. These are strange people and it kind of makes you realize that life's a funny thing. There're people there from all walks of life. There's a big criminal lawyer there from New Orleans, a lot of millionaires go there that are just sick of life. They devote their life to the Trappist Monks. There's got to be something to it, but I'll be damned if I can figure it out."

"That's depressing shit," Roselli said.

"They pray and work, that's it. No milk, no meat, no wine, no women, no TV, no radio, no nothing. Just pray and work."

Roselli smiled. "There's a kicker on Delmont. Remember Nick Simponis?

He's got that gambling joint in Cabazon? Well, Delmont tried to shake him down and Nick went to DeSimone, wanted the guy hit. So they clipped Delmont for Buffalo but Nick thought they'd done it for him and gave them a piece of his joint."

Jimmy laughed. "That reminds me of Russian Louie. Benny Binion wanted him clipped the worst way. I don't know what kind of handle Louie had on Binion, but when we clipped him Binion thought he was getting an exclusive. But see, Johnny, Jack [Dragna] was a thief, too. He fucked me. I clipped the guy and got nothing for it, but now I hear Jack hit Binion for two hundred grand and never said a word to me about it. Besides, he let the bastards steal my money and made my wife go to work. And that fucking Licata."

Jimmy's face darkened angrily. "About five, six weeks after I'm out, I'm still wondering about the money I left on the street and at that time I'm washing dishes at fucking Sambo's for ten bucks a day. I call Nick. I says, 'Nick, how're you?' this and that, we exchange greetings, and he says, 'How're you doing?' and I says, 'Well, not too good.' He says, 'What can I do for you?' 'Number one,' I says, 'I need some money.' He says, 'Well, uh,' and there's this long silence. I says, 'You know I left a lot of money over there when I went to jail. What happened to it?' He says, 'Jimmy, I think the money's gone.' "

"Jimmy, I'm with you all the way. In fact, I've got an envelope here for you. Philly Alderisio sent you a thousand, Tom Dragna fifteen hundred, and I put in twenty-five hundred. Now if you need more money, let me know."

Jimmy took the envelope and slipped it into his inside jacket pocket. "Thanks, Johnny, and give my thanks to Philly, but fuck Tom. Look it, Johnny, this comes from the heart. You're the best pal I've got. You're the only one who tried to help me. I know you're the one that got me transferred from Folsom to Soledad."

"Folsom's a snake pit," Roselli said. "I tried to get you to Chino, but Soledad was the best I could do."

"McMillan came to see me a couple times. Nice man. A real gentleman. In fact, he got hold of my folder and told me the kind of bullshit they had in it. No wonder the parole board turned me down each time I came before them. And I appreciate your sending that Teamsters official from San Francisco, Jack Goldberger, to see me. He's got good connections with the governor's office. He got a big lawyer to help me write a letter to Governor [Goodwin] Knight which Jack personally took to Knight, but that was before that fucking DeSimone got caught at Apalachin.

"Anyway, coming back to Nick, he says, 'Let me check and I'll get back to you next Wednesday morning at ten o'clock.' I says, 'Nick make sure it's ten o'clock because I don't want to be hanging around this phone booth too long. I've got heat here.' So the next week I wait by this phone and no call. I wait until eleven, no call. Now I'm really getting steamed.

"So I drive off, I go into town, and an hour later I call Nick's son-in-law, Frank Stellino. He says Nick told him he called me and a cop answered the phone. I says, 'What! Forget about it, he never called this fucking number because I waited an hour.' Stellino says, 'Well, that's what he told me. He said a cop answered the phone and said Nick could give him whatever message he had for you.' I says, 'Hold the fucking phone, you cocksucker. You tell him he ain't putting a fucking blanket on me. That's my game, you prick.' And I slammed the phone down hard enough to bust his eardrums. He's trying to say I'm a stool pigeon. That I've got cops answering my phone. He's trying to get me clipped."

Jimmy was breathing hard as he leaned back and clenched his fists. "That's when I called you, Johnny. I want to get transferred to Chicago. I don't want to stay with Los Angeles no more."

"Yeah," Roselli said, "I think you better. I'll go see Tommy Brown in New York. As you know, he's been very close to our family. I think it's a good idea to touch base with him before I whip into Chicago to see Sam and Paul. Don't worry, there won't be no problem. Both Tommy and Sam know the kind of work you did for Jack."

"You know something, Johnny. One time Jack and I are driving to Vegas, I think it's in fifty-two, and he says to me, 'Jimmy, of all the years I've been involved in this thing,' and Johnny, Jack's in this thing all his life—shit, I think he was made in nineteen-fourteen. So he says, 'Jimmy, I've never known anybody with your capability. You can do it all.' I've never forgotten that. Jack really liked me, but still, you know, he fucked me, see."

Roselli barely moved his hand to catch the waiter's eye. "Menus, please," he said softly, returning his attention to Jimmy. "Bomp also wants to get transferred. But I don't want to mess up your deal. I don't want Tommy and Sam to think the whole family's deserting the ship."

Jimmy gave him a grateful smile. "I really appreciate this, Johnny. I owe you a lot, from the old days, too. I know you got Jack to make me a skipper, which burned Nick's ass. Jack never made no move without checking with you. Don't worry, I remember."

"Jimmy, I did what was good for the family. Jack and I had a good working relationship. But in the last years of his life, Jack got a little too cautious. He liked his women and his booze and the fewer the hassles the better. He preferred a little cash in hand to a long-range plan."

Jimmy pounded the table. "Jesus, now you've put your finger on it. That's why we never got a joint in Vegas. First, you know, we had our problems trying to clip that Mickey Cohen. He had more lives than nine cats. Jack was really hot on that. But my main objective in them years was always to get a piece of a gambling joint, to get in on the fucking count. I knew that once we got a joint we'd make millions."

"You're not kidding," Roselli agreed, pausing a moment while the waiter handed them menus and a wine list. "Jimmy, Meyer Lansky and his group have skimmed more tax-free money than anybody in the world. Just in Vegas alone, the last ten years, from the Flamingo, the Sands, the Thunderbird, the

Riviera, they've skimmed three hundred million easy. That's not counting the millions taken in joints in New York, Florida, Kentucky, Louisiana, Arkansas. Or all those years in Cuba, and now the Bahamas, England, Beirut, and Christ knows where else. He's one fucking sharp Jew. But let me tell you something, Jimmy. He's lucky to be alive. You know, he really fucked Lucky [Luciano] when he was deported. Meyer sent him peanuts, Christ's sake, and the only reason he's alive today's because he's under the thumb of Jimmy Blue Eyes [*nee* Vincent Alo]. Meyer makes no move without clearing it with Jimmy Blue Eyes."

"I know, I met Jimmy in Vegas back in 1953," Jimmy recalled. "He's with the Genovese family."

"Yeah, but he's got a special situation. Kind of works with all the New York bosses and Chicago, which you know handles everything west of there except Vegas, which is still an open city, but Chicago has Florida, except Miami, which is also an open city. Down there, when Santo [Trafficante] wants to clear anything with the commission, he goes to Chicago. But the reason for Jimmy Blue Eyes's situation's that Meyer's an international institution. Now all these bosses have respect for Jimmy Blue Eyes and the guy's with Meyer every day, sticks to him like a Siamese twin."

"You've got to give the Jews credit," Jimmy said. "They started out as fronts for the Italians and now they've got millions they made through Italians. They were smart and declared some of that money to the government. See, a Jew makes a million, he declares two, three hundred grand. A fucking Italian makes a million, he declares ten grand. The Jews in Cleveland—Dalitz, Kleinman, Rhody—they were running all them gambling joints and they tell the Italians they've got to put so much money aside for taxes. After seven, eight years, they've made millions of dollars and declared twenty, thirty percent to the government. At that time taxes ain't that high, which means they're building operating capital. That's how guys like Dalitz got wealthy and respectable. That's why they can invest in Vegas.

"Now look at the Italians. They stash their money. They can't invest it without going through fucking fronts. Them Italians in Cleveland made millions and what good is it? They live like peasants. Everything's under the table. Even when they die, their heirs's got to hide the money. Why don't they declare some of it? Uncle Sam don't give a shit how you earn your money as long as you give him his cut."

"Listen to this, Jimmy. Remember when Chin [*nee* Vincent Gigante] took a shot at Frank Costello in fifty-seven, May second to be exact . . . I'll never forget that date. Well, the cops found a slip of paper in Frank C's pocket that had the figures of the Tropicana's gross receipts for its first three weeks of operation. That little slip of paper, Jimmy, cost me maybe five million bucks. I promoted that deal and got them the license. I had a piece of it, plus I was booking the show, which meant ten percent off the top, and the tab was a hundred, a hundred-fifty grand each week. Shit, since then, with the *Folies*

Bergère, the tab runs two, two-fifty every week. Well, the press got into it, digging up the story and throwing around names like Carlos Marcello [boss of the New Orleans family] and the next thing I knew the state got into it and killed the deal."

"How did you maneuver that?"

"After I transferred to Chicago, Sam asked me to concentrate on Vegas. They had plenty of cash to invest and they wanted to get into some of these gambling joints. Going back to Chicago's the best move I ever made," Roselli said, opening the menu. "I'm now the man in Vegas. I got the Stardust for Chicago."

"Holy shit," Jimmy cried. "I'd heard something about you being the man, you know, but I didn't know you had a piece of the Stardust. I hear it's the biggest money-maker in Vegas."

"It sure is, Jimmy. I'm pulling fifteen, twenty grand under the table every month. They're skimming the shit out of that joint. You have no idea how much cash goes through that counting room every day. You, your family, your uncles and cousins, all your relatives could live the rest of their lives in luxury with just what they pull out of there in a month. Jimmy, I've never seen so much money."

"Jesus Christ, Johnny, how did you pull it off? I remember when Tony Cornero was trying to promote that joint."

"Well, Tony died in fifty-five and Jake Factor, an old friend of Capone . . . shit, I used to see him when he came to the Lexington Hotel to see Al . . . took over and finished building the place. So I went to Sam and told him we could move into this joint. Listen, Jake owed Chicago a big one. Moe Dalitz wanted in on it and so it's a fifty-fifty deal."

"Did you clear it with Johnny Scalish in Cleveland?" Jimmy asked.

"Yeah, Moe's their man. But Scalish is fat enough with the Desert Inn. He was glad to do Chicago a good turn. Besides he's getting a small piece."

"So who's watching the store for Chicago in the Stardust?"

"Sam's got Johnny Drew, moved him in from Bill Graham's Bank Club in Reno and he sent Al Sachs and Bobby Stella to help him. Dalitz's got Yale Cohen to watch his end. But Sam's got a sleeper in there, Phil Ponti, a made guy from Chicago. A really sharp operator."

Jimmy laughed. "Christ, Yale Cohen brings back memories. I met him back in 1937 at the Ohio penitentiary."

Jimmy studied the menu a moment. "Don't they serve Italian dishes in this joint?"

Roselli burst out laughing. "Still the same, you and your pasta."

"What the hell, Johnny, I like it. I taught the cooks at Soledad how to make meat sauce and meatballs. Listen, I'd give my right arm for gnocchi ricotta with chicken cacciatore on the side the way Naples used to make it. Remember the lobster diablo? Got them from Maine. Baked them and put that fucking hot sauce on. Shit, that was a dish."

"Fuck the menu," Roselli said, tossing it on the table. "You want gnocchi, you get gnocchi. And some good dago red."

"Now you're talking, Johnny."

Roselli turned his head and the waiter approached the table. "Tony, my buddy, we're going to forget the menu tonight. We want gnocchi ricotta with chicken cacciatore. The best in town. If you can't make the best in town, I'm sure you know where to get it. And your best chianti." Roselli looked sharply at the waiter. "Any problem?"

"No, sir, Mr. Roselli, as long as you give us a little time."

Roselli nodded and returned his attention to Jimmy.

"You know, about five years ago, Chicago got that stoolie, Willie Bioff, who testified against us. He was hiding out in Phoenix and chumming around with Senator [Barry] Goldwater and Gus Greenbaum. I did forty-three months because of that stoolie."

"And they got Greenbaum and his wife a couple years later."

"That was Meyer's contract."

The waiter brought refills as if by instinct. *"Salute, amico."* They drank and leaned back, warmed by the drinks and the pleasure of one another's company. It had been a long time since either man had talked this freely with anyone.

"What're you grinning at?" Roselli asked, grinning back at him.

"Oh, I just feel good. It makes me happy to hear of your success. I heard things, this and that, but I had no idea how great it really was for you. You're on top of the world. That's really something. You don't only have the fucking Stardust, but you're the man in that fucking town."

"Everything's nice and cool, Jimmy. Nothing happens without my say so. I keep it low key. Nothing flashy. I settle beefs but everything's done in a gentlemanly manner. I tip good, I gamble here and there, lose five, ten grand, you know, just spreading the good will around, play lots of golf, eat good food, and see more cunts. Jimmy, I'm fucking all these broads, not chorus girls, but the stars. You've never seen nothing like it. This Vegas has more broads than anyplace I've ever seen."

"When I get off parole in three years, I'm coming down to see you, don't forget."

"Jimmy, you won't recognize the town. It's doubled in size the past seven years, maybe tripled. I tell you, it's fantastic. There's all kinds of new joints, like the Dunes, Tropicana, Riviera, New Frontier, Hacienda, Stardust. Christ, I can't think of them all. Remember how the airport was out in the boonies? Well, the strip's built up all the way to the airport. Then you ought to see downtown. It's wall-to-wall joints. The money's pouring in like there's no tomorrow. Like it's burning fucking holes in the suckers' pockets."

"Sonovabitch, and it's your town."

Roselli raised his hand. "It's a job, but I'm getting my cut. Jack died at the right time. I thank God DeSimone rigged that election. That's the best thing that ever happened to me. I'm salting some of this cash away and some day

I'm going to blow this whole fucking scene. I'm going to retire in luxury, get away some place where I don't have to talk to hoods, live like an ordinary human being for a change."

Jimmy grew serious. "Johnny, you know you can't retire from this thing. They tell you when you're made, 'You come in alive and you go out dead.' "

"Forget it, Jimmy. Lots of made guys fade away when they get in their fifties and sixties. They go to Florida and take it easy. Sure, you're still with the family, but they leave you alone. They're not going to ask me to do any work at my age. Believe me, I did my share of work in the old days. They may want some advice, or some small bullshit deal, but nothing I can't handle nice and easy."

"Sounds great, Johnny, I wish you all the luck in the world."

"Well, Jimmy, I've got a little more than luck going for me. You know, something came up and if it works out we'll have the fucking government by the ass. And we choke 'em." Johnny clenched his fists and banged them together.

Jimmy's eyes widened in surprise. "What are you talking about?"

Roselli lowered his voice and leaned toward Jimmy. "There's this former FBI guy I know, Robert Maheu, who's got a connection with the CIA, and the government wants us to clip Fidel Castro. What do you think of that?"

Jimmy shook his head like a boxer who has been dazed by a sharp jab. "Hey, Johnny, you know what the fuck you're doing? This's a dangerous thing."

"No, no, Jimmy. Listen, let me explain. Nobody knows about this except Sam and Santo [Trafficante]."

"And Maheu, the CIA, and, maybe, the fucking FBI. Did Giancana clear it with the commission?"

"I went to see Sam and we decided to go along with it on the q.t., see what happens."

"Hey, Johnny, if the commission finds out. . . . Johnny, this's against the rules."

"Jimmy, we don't have to tell nobody. If we pull it off, then we get the power. If somebody gets in trouble and they want a favor, we can get it for them. You understand. We'll have the fucking government by the ass."

"How did Santo get into it?"

"Well, you know, Santo has connections in Cuba. Worked there for years, knows lots of Cubans who'd like to do Castro in. Besides, you know, when Castro took over the government down there, he cost our thing a lot of money. So here's a chance to even up the score and get the government over a barrel. How do you like that for a contract?"

"Jesus, Johnny, you can't kill people for the fucking government. You can't even kill people for money. That's against the rules."

"Come on, Jimmy, we were just talking about the rules. Who pays any attention to them?"

"But this is different, Johnny. You're on dangerous ground. That's against our thing."

"Fuck the commission. Look, Sam's on the commission, he's taken the responsibility. I cleared it with him. So he tells Santo what he wants, Santo's in the clear. Now, if we don't pull it off, nobody's the wiser. If we do, then we've got the power.

"Well, well," Johnny said, smiling at Jimmy. "Here comes your gnocchi."

Jimmy's eyes lit up with anticipation. "Smells terrific," he said to the waiter, and then repeated the compliment when the maitre d' came up.

"Thank you, sir. Enjoy your dinner."

Jimmy took a bite and rolled his eyes. "Ah, shit, this is so fucking good I'm getting a hard-on."

"Speaking of hard-ons," Roselli said. "You should see Sam's new girl. Now talk about an ace in the hole. Her name is Judy Campbell and this broad is none other than Jack Kennedy's mistress."

"Jesus."

"This broad used to go with Sinatra and he got her to Kennedy." Roselli said. "Then a couple months later, when Sam was in Miami, Frankie introduced her to him."

"So this broad goes out with both of them . . . the next President of the United States and Giancana?"

Roselli laughed. "Yeah, what do you think of that, baby?"

"Who's this broad anyway? She must be some looker."

"Beautiful. Looks like Liz Taylor, but nicer, a real sweet kid. Comes from a good family, lots of class. In fact, Sam's fallen in love with her. Can you believe that? I think he's getting jealous of Kennedy. He's talking about buying her a house in Miami and settling down."

"Sam in love?" Jimmy asked incredulously. "You've got to be kidding."

"I don't know what's the matter with him," said Roselli. "Who the fuck falls in love with broads? You fuck them and pass them on to someone else. I was once married to a fucking actress. You remember June Lang, don't you? She was a nice kid, but love—Sam's mooning around like some fucking Andy Hardy."

They ate in silence for a while, enjoying their dinner, but Jimmy looked pensive. "You know, Johnny, on the way down here today I was thinking about my situation, trying to figure out how I got in this hole. I was thinking of all the years in stir and I thought I had to be out of my mind to ever get involved."

"You and me both. You know, Jimmy, I've been sour on this thing a long time. The best years of my life were when I was a producer with Brynie Foy. I liked being with those people. I knew half the movie people in this town on a first-name basis. Jack Warner, Harry Cohn, Sam Goldwyn, Joe Schenck, Clark Gable, George Raft, Jean Harlow, Gary Cooper. Shit, I even knew Charlie Chaplin. I knew them all and enjoyed their company.

"Jimmy, you don't know Brynie Foy, do you? He's a genius. He was at Warners for many years and he knows all the tricks in producing B-movies. He was known as the 'Keeper of the B's' at Warners.

"I really enjoyed working with guys like him. If I had known as a kid what I was getting into, I wouldn't have come close to this thing. The less I see of our guys the better I like it, you know. Except for you and Sam, most of my friends are out of the rackets. Like Vegas now, if anybody comes in from New York, or whatever, I don't see them in public. I don't want to be seen with them."

Jimmy clenched his right fist and held on to it with his left hand. "What the hell, Johnny, when you're a kid, what do you really know about life? If you'd gotten into movie producing before you got into this thing, you'd probably be famous today, a fucking millionaire. But when you're a kid, like when I was growing up on the Hill, all the poverty, and you see guys with sharp suits and Cadillacs and flashy broads, big diamond rings and stickpins, and you like that. You know, you want to be like that. Them guys had respect, but you really don't know what you're getting into. Johnny, I'd bet there's hundreds of guys in this thing of ours that wish they'd never got into it. Who needs it?"

11
TRUCKING TYCOON

† † † †

WHEN JEWEL RETURNED HOME FROM WORK ONE AFTERNOON SHE FOUND
Jimmy sitting at the kitchen table, the telephone glued to his ear, as of old,
with slips of notepaper piled high in front of him, and chewing on a dead cigar,
which meant he had been too busy to light it. He waved to her, indicating he
needed a light, and went on talking into the mouthpiece. Her first thought was
that he was booking again, and her second thought was how in the world could
he make any money at it in a hick town like Redding.

She leaned over with the match and he gave her an affectionate slap on the
rump. "Want some coffee?" she asked. He nodded and she went to the sink
to fill the percolator. She tried to listen, to figure out what he was up to, and
she soon realized that whatever it was, it had nothing to do with bookmaking.

By the time the coffee was ready, Jimmy had completed his last call, and
was sitting there grinning at her like he had in the old days after a big score.
Not that she had ever precisely known the details of the score, or its dimension,
only that he was pleased with himself for having put over a big one. All she
knew for certain was that somebody, somewhere, had gotten royally screwed.

Jimmy tilted his chair back and plunked his stocking feet on top of the table.
"Give me a kiss, hon," he said, "we're out of the woods."

"Do you realize you've got your feet on top of my kitchen table? My God,
Jimmy, we eat off this table."

"Be grateful I don't make you wash my feet," he said with a grin. "In the
old country, Italian wives wash their husbands' feet every night. And do you
think the mamas complain?"

"I'm no Italian mama," Jewel said. "The day you find a German wife
washing the feet of a dago husband will be a cold day in hell."

"Don't tell me about German wives," Jimmy said. "I know what they like
to wash." Jewel was standing next to him with a mug of steaming coffee in
her hand and he reached up between her thighs and pinched her.

"My God," she cried, jumping back, coffee splashing out of the mug, "you
want boiling coffee in your lap?"

III

He was puffing on the cigar and still grinning. "For Christ's sake, sit down, will you, and let me lay this out for you."

"Listen, Jimmy, with that look on your face, I'm worried already. That man Wright's going to violate you if you look cross-eyed at anyone."

Jimmy waved his hand impatiently and she sat down next to him. "Here's the setup," he said. "I quit working for the Riley Trucking Company four days ago. They kept shorting me every month."

"Oh, Jimmy! You scare the daylights out of me when you get that look on your face."

"What look? I'm just happy, that's all. Listen to this, I've talked to Duane Wemple at the union, and I've been on the phone calling truckers and contractors, and I'm going into business for myself. I've lined up about forty independent truckers who'll work for me if I get them jobs. That means I get five percent off the top on everything they make. Figure it out. Forty trucks making a hundred bucks a day each, so you're talking five times forty which is two hundred bucks a day. Then there's the fuel. I've just rented a garage with a gas pump and an eight thousand gallon tank. Shell filled it today at eleven cents a gallon. The tax is eight or nine cents more, which makes it about twenty cents a gallon and I sell it to my truckers for twenty-five cents. I'll sell them oil, tires, fan belts, anything they need, and mark it up five percent which is a good deal all around."

"Where do you get these truckers?"

"From Riley. I called them and asked if they'd work for me if I got any jobs, and they all said 'in a minute.' They don't want to work for Riley because he shorts them and thinks he's king shit. I'm telling you, Jewel, this can't miss.

"Here's what I want you to do. Tomorrow, you apply for a broker's license in your name and call an insurance company and get us a fifty-thousand-dollar bond. Forget about your job at the real estate office. You're going to be president of the Fratianno Trucking Company and we're going to run Riley's ass right out of business."

"I give up," Jewel said, refilling his coffee mug and leaning over to kiss his neck. "You're a whiz."

Jimmy moved so rapidly that only two weeks after he had left Riley, Jimmy's parole officer, Craig Wright was trying to apply the brakes. In his "Activities" report dated February 23, he wrote: "Fratianno appears to be sincerely optimistic over his ability to operate successfully as a trucking contractor in the Redding area, an optimism not altogether shared equally by his PA. In his termination of relationship with the Riley Trucking Co., his purchase without restoration of civil rights, of a 1959 Ford dump truck and subsequent negotiations to purchase a 1961 International dump truck, based on arguments of sound economic planning which do have merits, the Parolee has presented us with several *fait accompli*. . . . It is strongly felt, however, that future planning would indicate a retardation in the pace at which this Parolee appears to be assuming responsibility in order that that responsibility now assumed may be adequately assimilated. This will necessarily carry with it, the recommendation that any further request for additional purchases of vehicles to expand this operation be scrutinized with extreme care in terms of the dangers inherent in possible over-expansion."

Jimmy soon landed a job in Eureka with a contractor who needed twenty-five trucks. Before long he had independent truckers coming in from Sacramento, Red Bluff, Cottonwood, Marysville, Fresno, and as far away as Knoxville, Iowa. The owners of the Shinn Construction Company, who were friends of Dorsey, brought six trucks from Knoxville and began using the Fratianno decal. This so frightened and incensed Jimmy's ex-employers the Rileys that both father and son began complaining to the FBI, Sheriff Balma, the Public Utilities Commission, the Adult Parole Division, the Rotary Club —in fact, they complained to anyone who would listen to them.

Once he started unburdening himself, Charles Riley Jr. went all out. He told Wright that Jimmy had called Peanuts Danolfo at the Las Vegas Desert Inn for reservations for Riley Jr. and his wife over New Year's Eve and related how he had been accorded the "red carpet" treatment by both Danolfo and Yale Cohen at the Stardust. "Mr. Riley then went on to state that on an earlier occasion Mr. Fratianno had invited him to his home and there had shown him a 'scrap book' containing extensive newspaper reports and clippings of the Parolee's former criminal background and activities. [Jimmy would deny this.] Mr. Riley stated that he was convinced of Mr. Fratianno's 'connections' and had since grown very frightened of his potential."

The pressure mounted, and finally, a few days after Riley had brought his charges before the Adult Parole Division (APD) in Sacramento, District Supervisor Carl Roggi paid Jimmy a visit.

"I'm afraid I've got some bad news, Jimmy," Roggi said.

"Don't tell me the Rileys've been shooting off their mouths again."

Roggi smiled faintly. "The word is *still*. The upshot is that the APD wants you out of Redding."

Jimmy felt like he had been punched in the stomach. "What have I done?" he cried. "I've got a going business here."

"That's the problem, Jimmy. You're running the Rileys out of their business."

"Have I done anything wrong, anything illegal?"

"The Rileys are natives of this community and they're going around saying a gangster is running them out of business."

"Hold the phone. You're not going to run me out of town. Where are we, Russia? I've got rights, don't I?"

"Jimmy, you're on parole."

"Everything I'm doing's legitimate. If I do something wrong, then send me back to jail, but I'm not leaving. This is my wife's business, not mine."

"Give it up, Jimmy," Roggi said. "As long as you're on parole, the APD can tell you where you have to do your time. That's the law in California."

Jimmy turned away and when he again looked at Roggi there were tears in his eyes. "Christ's sake, Carl, you can't do this to me. For the first time in my life, I've got something legitimate going for me. The way it's going now, I can net fifty grand this year."

Once Jimmy realized that it was inevitable, he quickly adjusted to the move to his new locale, Sacramento, and lost little time in visiting the office of Lester McMillan.

The Rileys continued to complain. In an FBI report, Special Agent Herbert K. Mudd, Jr., wrote that Riley Sr. stated ". . . that Fratianno apparently had political influence, probably through the Teamsters, and that they also understood that California State Senator McMillan had been of assistance to Fratianno. Riley said that at about the same time their company was subjected to a Public Utilities Commission audit, followed by an Internal Revenue audit, and that subsequent to the action of these governmental agencies their business failed and the Rileys eventually went into bankruptcy [in 1962]. Riley said that though they have no proof, both he and his son feel that Fratianno, through political connections, was, in part, responsible for their business problems."

What Riley, the FBI, and the Adult Parole Division never knew was that Jimmy's connection with the Teamsters in Redding was Jack Goldberger in San Francisco. Jimmy believed that it was through his intercession with Babe Triscaro in Cleveland and with Bompensiero's contacts with the Detroit family, that Goldberger was made an International Organizer.

For Jimmy it was his way of showing his appreciation for what Goldberger had done for him while he had been in prison after Roselli had gotten them together. Then when Duane Wemple, at his union local, told Jimmy that he wanted a certain business agent retired so that he could appoint his own man, Goldberger was only too happy to grant Jimmy's request. For Jimmy, this kind of quid pro quo was perfectly legitimate. As he saw it, it was a necessary expedient, something that was routine in the operation of any successful business.

For a while Jewel remained in Redding, keeping in constant telephone communications with her husband in Sacramento. The transition took about a month. By the time Jewel joined him in Sacramento, he had leased a duplex in a residential neighborhood and was parking his trucks at a service station. Although he continued to drive a truck ten hours a day, his primary interest remained in establishing himself as a broker, but his experience in Redding had taught him to be more cautious in the way he went about it, to move more surreptitiously, and to keep a low profile. His new parole agent, Edward Poindexter, had told him that there was already considerable resistance to his presence in his new location.

As indicated in a report to the APD, Jimmy's future was uncertain at best: "[Police] Chief James Hicks has indicated to me that if a move is not effected by our agency he will take the matter into his own hands to see that Fratianno is forced to leave town by using a program of pressure and harassment."

Again, McMillan came to Jimmy's rescue. "Information has been received indicating that Assemblyman McMillan did contact Chief Hicks in this matter," Poindexter wrote, "and reportedly a rather heated discussion resulted. The Parole Agent was also informed that the Assemblyman had contacted APD headquarters in the interest of the Parolee."

All of Jimmy's drivers, contractors, and acquaintances were repeatedly interviewed by various law enforcement agencies, and yet Jimmy prospered, the climb more gradual this time, but nonetheless steadily rising. He worked on jobs in Clarksburg, Colusa, Stockton, Tracy, Lodi, Marysville, Arbuckle, and in February 1962, he got permission to buy a new home in Sacramento.

After Jimmy's daughter, Joanne, and her husband, Tommy Thomas, had moved to Sacramento and were taken into the business, Wilbur wrote: "Parolee and wife brought up idea of incorporation. In order to set up the corporation by end of fiscal year, it was decided that the Parolee would not be an officer. They will go ahead with the plan and Mrs. Fratianno will be president, their daughter, vice president. . . . The Parolee may not go in until he is off parole. . . . This is a non-stock corporation."

Wilbur was sympathetic to Warren's dependency on Jimmy. "Warren has been dependent on his family all his life," he wrote. "He relied on his father, who owned a trucking business in Cleveland to put him to work. When the parents got too old he began to look to the Parolee and his wife for support. . . . The Fratiannos have helped Warren financially . . . innumerable times. . . . Writer has talked to Warren a number of times and found him to be a pleasant person but not too overly intelligent. He does not appear to be anything more than just a truck driver. He is not too adept at managing his finances but would work out okay under direction."

Given enough time and freedom, it was inevitable that Jimmy would begin to maneuver. His first opportunity came in the summer of 1962 while working for Lawrence Magini, the prime contractor for the Occidental Petroleum Company. Taking his direction from one of the oil company's executives involved in its search for gas discoveries in northern California, Magini's job was to clear locations for oil rigs, dig sumps, and build gravel roads on top of existing land to get heavy equipment to the locations which were frequently miles away from any access road.

During lunch with the executive one day, Jimmy was surprised to hear him say he was thinking of firing Magini because he suspected he was too clever with the pencil.

"Jesus," Jimmy said, lowering his voice, "we can make some fucking money together."

The executive nodded but said nothing. "Make me your prime contractor and I'll push the pencil for both of us," Jimmy said. "Anything over and above what my trucks earn, we'll cut right down the middle. Let's say I've got six trucks working eight hours, you put down eight trucks working ten hours. Sometimes I can get gravel for nothing but I'll charge you two dollars a yard for the three, four thousand yards you need. That's six or eight thousand right there. What I'll do is run it through my books and pay tax on all that money and we'll split the difference. That way we've got nothing to worry about from nobody." In the next four years they would split nearly a quarter of a million dollars.

Jimmy had no problem with his finances. Early in 1963, he leased a large building for office and garage space at 6929 Power Inn Road, plus an adjoining lot for truck and equipment storage. Surplus space in the garage was subleased to a mechanic who would work on Jimmy's trucks in addition to his own work.

By the summer of 1963, Wilbur noted that Jimmy was "working as an estimator—i.e., makes contacts, clocks miles from job to nearest aggregate location, sizes up type of trucks and equipment necessary, and contacts truck drivers. He confers with his wife and she gives the bid. . . . The Internal Revenue people have just about completed their study of the Fratiannos' income statements and remarked that . . . the Fratiannos might have money coming back. . . . Parolee continues to keep busy and the business occupies most of his waking hours. . . . He is doing better than most parolees. Prognosis very good."

By early winter, Wilbur wrote: "Parolee and wife spent Labor Day at Lake Tahoe as guests of Bob LaBrucherie. They stayed at State Line. Parolee was given permission to go. Bob LaBrucherie owns the Diamond T Truck dealership in Stockton and is well known to this writer. . . . Business has been good and Mrs. Fratianno has been dispatching in the neighborhood of 50 trucks per day. . . ."

On a mild November evening three men sat outdoors close to the dying embers in a huge barbecue pit, the tips of their cigars little beacons in the darkness.

Encouraged by Bompensiero, Jimmy was in the process of selling Frank LaPorte, a Chicago *caporegime,* on the merits of the trucking business. After briefly describing his rapid success in the business, he had gone into some of the fringe benefits. He told about the kickback deal at Occidental Oil. "But everything goes on the books."

"Hey, Jimmy, tell Frank about the church deal," Bompensiero said.

"Well, Frank, I needed about ten thousand yards of dirt. They were putting up a building but the ground was too low. The code in Sacramento calls for it to be at the same level as the road. So I'm thinking where do I get this dirt. I'm getting about a dollar a yard, and I look across the street from this place and there before my eyes's an empty lot with dirt piled up about four feet above the street level. My first thought is, 'My God, who owns that?' Right next to this lot is St. Patrick's Orphanage. So I go talk to the Mother Superior and she tells me the church owns it. I go see the bishop and his secretary, Monseigneur Higgins, tells me the bishop's out of town. So I explain the situation to him and he says, 'Oh, incidentally, that used to be a cemetery years and years ago.' 'Father,' I says, 'if you ever want to build on that land you'll have to bring it down to road level and I can do that for you right now for nothing. Besides I'll really do a good job grading it and I'll give the church a donation. Also, father, if at any time you need my equipment for anything, it's on the house.' So he gives me the dirt.

"Frank, forget about it. I go in there with my equipment, I'm there with a red flag holding traffic. I'm working now, Frank. Instead of twenty trucks, all I need are two trucks and they're going like hotcakes. I've got this big loader, boom, boom, boom, we're moving that dirt, brother. We hit some bones and we keep going. But I'm looking in there for antiques. Two days and the job's over, ten grand just like that."

"How much fucking equipment have you got?" LaPorte asked.

"Frank," Jimmy replied, "I'm getting bigger all the time, but I've got to be careful with the parole people. They watch me like a hawk. I just bought five transfer units. I'm the first guy around Sacramento to have them. They call them slam-bangs. They can haul twenty-five tons, which means you can haul a lot cheaper than the guy with the single dump truck."

"How much did they set you back?" LaPorte asked.

"About thirty-three thousand each, but they didn't cost me nothing up front. I buy from a friend in Stockton and he fakes the down payment. He jacks up the price to thirty-eight thousand on paper and the bank thinks I paid five grand down."

Bompensiero barked his laugh. "This fucking Jimmy's got more stuff on the ball than Sandy Koufax. I told you, Frank, this guy's the world's greatest scammer."

"Take the Teamsters," said Jimmy, encouraged by Bompensiero's praise. "All my drivers are union guys. If they're not Teamsters I put them in there. But I don't pay the union a fucking nickel. When the business agents in Redding and Sacramento get after me, I says I'm paying it to headquarters in San Francisco. Now say you're one of my drivers and you get hurt in July. I shoot a check to the union in your name for the month of June . . . you know, date back the check. So now I call the union and tell them I want you taken care of. But I never pay nothing for the pension, health, welfare, vacation, all this extra bullshit. You've got any idea how much money I've saved? The only thing I pay is Workman's Comp. That you've got to pay."

"Right now, Frank," Jimmy continued, "I've got twelve trucks plus all that heavy equipment and I'm working forty, fifty other trucks on five percent commission. You should hear the talk. All the fucking truckers are jealous of me. I get the big jobs. Then I've got the Teamsters helping me. When a contractor comes in from out of town, the union guy gives him my business card."

Jimmy chuckled and leaned back in his chair. He enjoyed telling stories, especially when he was trying to sell something.

"Tell me, Jimmy," LaPorte said, "doing any booking or gambling, any shylocking? What's the situation in Sacramento?"

"Frank, I've been booking since I was a kid. I'm always booking, but now very small. I've got a half-dozen steady customers and I book at the fairgrounds when I have time. But that reminds me about this kid Price who owns a bar. This kid was in Folsom with me. Well, we fucked a few guys playing Red Dog. We rigged the bar with magnets, had them wired, and we could make the ace and the six come up anytime we wanted. We beat one guy for nine grand and this other guy, Bob Daggs, who owns a bunch of restaurants in town, we took him for about twenty-five grand. One time we're playing and this guy drops his keys on the bar and I grab them just before the magnet pulls them over. Them magnets were powerful sons of bitches."

"What about Jimmy Lanza [boss of the San Francisco family]?" LaPorte asked. "Can the guy do you some good?"

Jimmy laughed. "What has he ever done besides sell olive oil and insurance? Them guys in San Francisco and San Jose wouldn't last two minutes if some real workers moved into their towns. Maybe we ought to move in and take over both towns. Knock off a couple guys, scare the rest shitless."

Bompensiero chuckled. "Yeah, Jimmy, we could bring in some good men and rule the roost."

"Someday," Jimmy said, "I might just do that."

12
JIMMY'S NEW FAMILY

† † † †

ALTHOUGH HIS LEGITIMATE BUSINESS WAS THRIVING, MOB BUSINESS was never far from his thoughts. Not long after their dinner in Los Angeles, Roselli, using the code name Shamus, had telephoned to say that the weather was beautiful in New York and Chicago and that he had completed a most enjoyable and successful trip.

The weather in Los Angeles, however, as Jimmy would discover a short time later, was not quite as pleasant. One evening Louie Dragna, nephew of Jack Dragna, telephoned and asked Jimmy to call him back at a certain number, which meant that he should make the call from a pay phone.

"Jimmy, how are you?" Dragna said when Jimmy returned his call.

"I'm fine," Jimmy said. "What's on your mind?"

"Long time no see. When do you plan on coming down to see your old buddies?"

"Louie, cut the shit. You know I'm on parole. Now you didn't get me out to this fucking phone booth to bullshit. What do you want?"

"Well, we heard you got transferred," Dragna said, pausing a moment before going on. "How did you do it?"

"What do you mean, what're you getting at? I went to Chicago and did it."

"Nick [Licata] and Frank [DeSimone] say you didn't talk to them about it."

"Listen, Louie, they tried to put a blanket on me. I'm not telling them nothing."

"But how did you do it?"

"I just took care of it," Jimmy answered, his voice even. "I went back East and got transferred. Period."

"Well, now, come on, Jimmy, didn't Johnny take care of everything for you?"

Jimmy tried to control his temper. "Louie, you're trying to get Johnny in trouble. This guy was like an uncle to you all your fucking life. He's a friend of your father and your uncle, and now you're trying to fuck him for that piece of shit Licata. Let me tell you something, Louie, you're

119

lucky I'm on parole and stuck out here six hundred miles away."

"Wait a minute, Jimmy," Dragna said in a placating tone. "No need to get heated up. We just heard Johnny went to bat for you, that's all."

"Bullshit," Jimmy shouted, "you know it's against the rules. You're trying to put Johnny in the middle and I thought you was his fucking friend."

"Listen, Jimmy, Johnny's not one of us no more," Dragna said. "He got himself transferred to Chicago. We've got to look out for our own family."

"Yeah, well, I don't want nothing to do with your family. I went to see Sam, and if you don't believe me, call him, and I got myself transferred. Johnny had nothing to do with it. Now you take it from there, you two-faced cocksucker." Jimmy hung up and it would be a long time before he again heard from Louie Dragna.

One morning while Jimmy was in his new office, working on a bid for a road construction job, he received another telephone call from Johnny Roselli: "Shamus, here, call F at one o'clock." The line went dead and Jimmy smiled as he cradled the receiver. By a pre-arranged code, Roselli's message meant that he wanted Jimmy to call him in one hour at a special number at the Friars Club in Beverly Hills. When Jimmy returned the call from a pay phone, Roselli asked him to meet him at the Del Mar Hotel around noon on Saturday.

At four o'clock on Saturday morning, Jimmy drove out of Sacramento and headed south on Route 99. On long solitary trips Jimmy could hypnotize himself for protracted periods of time. That part of his brain that had nothing to do with the operation of the vehicle would go to sleep, so that he could cover great distances without any awareness of time or space, and come to with no conscious knowledge of the passage of time or the mileage covered, wondering if a certain town lay before or behind him.

Route 99 became Route 5 and he went through Burbank at mid-morning and stayed on Route 5, passing on the periphery of Los Angeles, which he now despised with a passion. For a fleeting moment, he wondered what his life would have been like if he had remained in Cleveland. His old friend Tony Dope Delsanter was now a made guy and running things in Warren for Johnny Scalish. He had recently done some work, clipping Mike Farah, who had fronted the Jungle Inn in Youngstown for Blackie Licavoli.

The next thing he knew he was in the lobby of the Del Mar Hotel and Roselli was walking toward him, handsome in an elegantly tailored dark gray suit, his hair stylishly barbered.

Taking him by the arm, Roselli led him outside toward one of the cottages. "You still driving a truck?"

"The APD thinks it builds character."

They stopped before a cottage and Roselli said, "I've got a surprise for you. Sam's in there, wants to meet you."

"Giancana?"

Roselli nodded and gave the door a couple quick raps. It swung open and

Roselli pulled Jimmy into the room. The door closed and Jimmy turned to see Giancana standing there with his back to it. There was a big smile on Giancana's face and they quickly embraced, kissing each other on the cheek, and stepping back to shake hands.

"Hey, remember me, we met ten years ago at the Ambassador, with Philly and Marshall?" Giancana said, holding on to Jimmy's hand. "Sonovabitch, you haven't aged a day."

"I remember it like it was yesterday," Jimmy said. "You was introduced as Sam Mooney. How's Marshall and Philly?"

"They send their regards. Listen, they've told me plenty about you."

"All good, I hope."

"Nothing but the best."

They walked into the living room and Johnny went to a small bar to mix drinks. Giancana sat down in an easy chair and Jimmy sat at the end of a sofa near Giancana. Roselli brought the drinks and held up his glass. "*Salute,*" he said.

Roselli sat down next to Jimmy. "Jimmy, I've been telling Sam about you for years. He knows what you've done for the L.A. family and he knows what fuck-ups are now running the show."

"Just stay away from those gonifs," Giancana said. "When you get off parole, go see Johnny in Vegas and he'll arrange something for you."

"I wouldn't bet on that," Roselli said. "Jimmy's going to make his fortune in the trucking business."

"Yeah, but I'm always available for work," Jimmy said. "I'm grateful to you for taking me in your family and I'm ready to do whatever I can whenever you need me."

Giancana nodded, his small dark eyes narrowing as he studied Jimmy. "Glad you're with us, Jimmy. From what Johnny tells me, you've never fucked up a job in your life. You should see some of the bunglers we've got in Chicago. It's good to have somebody you can trust and depend on. Believe me, a family never has too many good workers." He paused and curved his lips to indicate his disdain. "Some guys, you know, are squeamish like little girls. They look big and tough and the minute they see a drop of blood they faint dead away."

"Well, you'll never have to worry about me fainting," Jimmy said with a laugh.

"Okay, so we're talking man to man," Giancana said. "The three of us are workers, we've made our scores, and that's good for a family to have men like us. Without good workers we wouldn't last two minutes."

As Giancana talked, Jimmy took the opportunity to look him over. He was a sharp-looking man, well-groomed, but rather on the unattractive side. His small close-set eyes gave a pinched look to his swarthy face.

A moment later Giancana stood up and offered Jimmy his hand. "It was good of you to come, Jimmy. I appreciate it," he said, gripping Jimmy's hand firmly. "We've got something we might want you to handle," he said, glancing at Roselli. "Johnny will explain it to you."

They moved in silence like strangers to the parking lot and neither one spoke until they were seated in Jimmy's car.

"Let's take a ride along the coast," Roselli said.

Jimmy loved the ocean, the pounding of the surf, the sunlight turning the water into a sheet of blue glass, the good clean smell, but he had never found the time to enjoy it.

"Before I go into this thing, there's something I'd like you to know," Roselli said. "Sam and I go back a long way. We know how it was in Chicago in the old days. I knew Capone better than he did, but we both knew Frank Nitti very well, and let me tell you, this was one fabulous guy. When Capone got sent up, Frank took over the outfit and really consolidated all the rival gangs, stopped all the wars, and made room in the outfit for guys of all nationalities, but we Italians, you know, the made guys, called the shots. When Prohibition went out, we branched into other rackets. We not only got into unions, but we ran the politics in that city, and we had plenty of juice in Springfield. Frank deserves much of the credit for moving the outfit into these areas."

Roselli paused and lit a cigarette. He smiled and tapped Jimmy on the shoulder. "You probably think I've lost my marbles. What do you care about Frank Nitti? Shit, that's ancient history, right?"

"Hell, no, I'm interested in Capone and Nitti, all them guys. I used to read about them when I was just a kid coming up in Cleveland."

"Well, I might as well get to the point. Have you seen that TV show, *The Untouchables?*"

Jimmy shook his head. "A couple of times but I don't have time to watch that shit."

"Let me tell you something, Jimmy. Millions of people all over the world see this show every fucking week. It's even popular in Italy. And what they see is a bunch of Italian lunatics running around with machine guns, talking out of the corner of their mouths, slopping up spaghetti like a bunch of fucking pigs. They make Capone and Nitti look like bloodthirsty maniacs. The guys that write that shit don't know the first thing about the way things were in those days. Eliot Ness, my ass. The tax boys got Al, not Ness. And what did he ever have to do with Frank Nitti?"

"Ness was in Cleveland for a while and did nothing," Jimmy said, wondering what Roselli had in mind.

"You know, Mae Capone brought a million-dollar lawsuit against CBS when they came out with a two-part film on Ness's book. She lost the suit and then Desilu Productions got ABC to do a series, and since then its gone from bad to worse."

"Nobody pays attention to that shit," Jimmy said. "It's like a comic book, a joke. Who cares?"

"I'll tell you, Jimmy. Sam cares, Joe Batters cares, Paul Ricca cares, and I care."

"Oh, I understand that, but the public don't care. Besides, you know, it's not putting nobody in jail."

"Jimmy, what I'm about to tell you has been decided by our family. The top guys have voted a hit. I've already talked to Bomp about it. We're going to clip Desi Arnaz, the producer of this show."

Jimmy whistled through his teeth. "Is Bomp setting it up?"

"Not yet. You talk to him. We want it set up so that nobody knows where it comes from. We don't want any heat. We've got to do it right."

"This is going to take some time to set up and you know I'm on parole. I've got to be back in Sacramento tomorrow."

"Jimmy, we might not even use you. We've got two, maybe three guys coming in from Chicago. Talk to Bomp, make sure he's on the right track and go back home."

"Okay, but if you need me, Johnny, you call the day before and I'll whip right down here. Remember, I'm available any time."

"Thanks, Jimmy, I know I can always count on you. Now you better drive me back. Bomp will meet you at the Grant around four, he'll be in the grill."

"Sam will probably think we've got lost."

Roselli laughed. "Don't worry about Sam. He's got a broad stashed in another cottage."

In the years they had been on parole, Jimmy and Bomp had met in Sacramento only three times, but there had been numerous calls from pay phones in which they had kept each other posted on developments. In a way they thought of themselves as victims of a cruel fate. The death of Jack Dragna had delivered them into the hands of their enemies. Recognized as the family's best workers in the old days, they were now feared by the new leadership: Both had been reduced from *capiregime* to *soldati.*

The moment Jimmy came into the grill, he spotted Bompensiero and went to his table. They shook hands and exchanged pleasantries.

"It's like old times," Bompensiero said.

"What's it been, ten years since Russian Louie?"

"You know, Jimmy, I miss those fucking days. We were going places and doing things and having lots of fucking laughs. Jack was a great fucking boss. These *pezzi di merda* today, I don't even want to think about them."

"How're you set on this deal?" Jimmy asked, not wanting Bompensiero to get going on his pet hate. He could rant about it for hours.

"I've cased his house down here but I don't think he's in Del Mar right now. But Johnny wants him hit here, not in L.A., so we'll have to wait 'till he gets back. I figure we hit him at night, like the Rummel job. Boom, boom, and we're gone."

"How about tools?"

"I've got a couple thirty-eights stashed with my barber, but I want a couple of sawed-off shotguns. That way we can work in the dark with no problem."

"I'll get a couple from Bill Graham. He's got a hell of a connection. They're non-registered, clean, brand new. You can drop them at the scene and nobody's ever going to trace them."

"Trace them or not, this's a fucking tough nut to crack. You can't be hanging around his fucking house with tools for three, four hours at a time waiting for him to come home. You get caught with them tools it's back to the fucking joint. Frankly, Jimmy, we're going to have to be lucky to hit this guy."

"Take my advice, let the other guys hold the tools."

"If we can set it up and they send only two guys, then I might need you to drive. There's nobody here I trust for this job. I'll handle the crash car."

"Okay, so what else's new with you these days?"

Bompensiero shrugged. "Well, you know, I married Marie, Momo's [Adamo] widow. You know, after Momo shot her in the head and killed himself, she recovered. How's Jewel doing?"

Jimmy winced. "Don't ask. She argues with me about everything. When she gets home at night she sits down and has a couple of tall highballs before starting dinner. I'm starving and I've got to sit there and watch her guzzle that booze. She don't see me home very often. I've got a couple broads in town.

"See, Bomp, everything's in her name and she really thinks she's president of the company. The money's gone to her head. Before she never knew what money I had, but now she sees three, four hundred thousand in the account and it's too much for her."

"You don't love her no more, huh?"

Jimmy looked at that battered face with the small pig eyes and could hardly believe his ears. "Love her! Are you fucking crazy? I've never loved a broad in my life. What the fuck's love? Do you know?"

"How would I know," Bompensiero said. "I can't even get it up no more."

"I've told you before, you've gotten your joint copped so many times you've lost your juices. I warned you years ago. Believe me, I know what I'm talking about."

"I've often thought about that," Bompensiero said, "and maybe you're right."

Two weeks later Bompensiero called Jimmy to say that "the boys from out of town got disgusted and went back home so the deal [Desi Arnaz] is down the drain. They say they're coming back but I don't believe it."

"What're you going to do?" Jimmy asked.

"Sit tight. When I wanted a transfer, they shit on me, so let them take care of their own fucking problems. You blame me?"

"Bomp, you do what you think's right. If they ask me, I'll do it, but if you want my opinion, the man [Giancana] had a cross-hair that day and I think he's already forgotten about it."

That concluded the contract. Desi Arnaz never knew how close he came to getting clipped.

Sam Giancana was having problems of his own in the summer of 1963. He wanted to get away from the FBI, who had been hot on his tail for months, in the worst possible way. Although he had won a court injunction that limited FBI surveillance to a single carload of agents and stipulated that a disinterested foursome must be between him and the agents whenever he played golf, Giancana was still unhappy because the local police had taken up the slack.

So in mid-July he decided to take advantage of his investment in Sinatra's plush Cal–Neva Lodge on the shores of Lake Tahoe. Although Giancana's name was in the Gaming Control Board's "black book," which meant he was persona non grata in any Nevada gambling establishment, he had in the past moved pretty freely around Reno and Lake Tahoe. In fact, on several occasions, he had stayed at Bill Graham's home, and had never been recognized as he moved around town—at least, not by anyone who had any adverse interest in his presence.

While Giancana and Phyllis McGuire of the McGuire sisters were sunning themselves on the front porch of Chalet 50, with Sinatra in attendance, agents of the Control Board were lurking in the bushes. The upshot was headlines that would later force Sinatra to divest himself of his investments in Cal–Neva and the Las Vegas Sands.

The second time Jimmy saw Sam Giancana was at Bill Graham's house.

"How goes the trucking, Jimmy? The Teamsters treating you all right?"

Jimmy nodded. "In fact, Jack Goldberger just did me a hell of a favor. Steve Dorsa, who owns the Santa Clara Sand and Gravel Company, a big fucking trucking outfit, was having trouble with the Teamsters. They were trying to force the independent owner-operator drivers working for Dorsa to join the union. Now if he had to put those guys on the payroll and pay all the union benefits, he'd go broke. He never figured that shit in when he bid on jobs. Then there's social security, Workman's Comp—well, he just couldn't hack it.

"I met with him a few times, trying to work out an angle, and Dorsa's telling me he's thinking of getting out of the business, and he'd sell me twenty sets of trailers at five grand a set, which's a good price because this's new equipment. Well, I straightened his problem with one phone call to Goldberger and Dorsa was so tickled he gave me five grand."

Jimmy went on to explain that LaPorte had secured loans of $150,000 from the Mercantile National Bank and $75,000 from the Exchange National Bank in Chicago for the purchase of sixteen International trucks. Jimmy would keep eight of the trucks and the others would go to LaPorte's brothers-in-law, Tony

Franze and Jimmy Ross, who would let Jimmy work the trucks on a five percent commission.

"That's a pretty good deal," Giancana said. "It ain't costing you a red cent."

"Well, I've got the business and the know-how," Jimmy said. "Frank's going to make some money with me. And I'll be making the payments on my half."

Graham was proud of Jimmy's accomplishment. "Jimmy's entire investment in his company was five hundred bucks, the downpayment on his first truck. Now, with these new tractors and trailers, he'll have close to a half-million in equipment. Not bad for a guy on parole."

Giancana shook his head. "How'd you do it?"

Graham laughed. "Jimmy, tell Sam about the guy at Kaiser Engineer."

Jimmy passed cigars around. He lit up and waggled his finger at Pancho, a gofer for Graham. "Pancho's the one that set it up for me," he said. "But let me start at the beginning.

"Kaiser Engineer's building some dams on the American River near Auburn. There's like seven contractors but they use Kaiser as the prime. I used to go up there just about every day and bid on different jobs, and shit I was getting nowhere.

"This guy was the main one for my type of work. There was a little bar by his office, and he would drop in for a beer and I'd try to get some work from him. He kept promising but nothing came of it. Finally I says, 'I'm not going to ask you for no more work, but I'll tell you what we're going to do. This weekend I've got business in Reno, a little convention of trucking people, so why don't you come with me as my guest. We'll have some fun.' "

Jimmy winked at Pancho. "He calls his wife and she says he can go and I call Pancho here and tell him we're coming up for the weekend. I want the best rooms in the Mapes and I want two beautiful sons-of-bitches and I'll give them four hundred apiece. They've got to do everything, these broads. Well, shit, we check in the Mapes around noon on Saturday and go to Harrah's.

"I call Pancho and tell him to bring the first broad over at two o'clock. We have a sandwich, bullshit a while, and here comes Pancho with this French broad. She's a sweet sonovabitch. I pull her aside and I says, 'Honey, I want you to take this guy and fuck him on the ceiling if that's what he wants. Give him the works. I want him to come out crippled. Here's two hundred and there's another two hundred for you when you're through.' Christ, she's all happy this broad. We get back to the table and I says, 'I want you to take this young lady to your room and you two have some fun. This girl says she's stuck on you, so what else can I say?'

"He looks at this beautiful broad and you can tell he's never done nothing like this before. But forget about it, he's all excited, you know. They go up to the room and he's up there like four hours. He comes back down and just looking at him you know he's had the time of his life. Well, to make a long story short, the broad the next day is even prettier and he's up there five hours this time. He comes back and he's dragging now. All the way home, this guy keeps telling me what a great time he's had, the best in his whole life.

"The whole thing probably cost me twelve hundred. Well, three days later he calls me and says, 'Jimmy, I need twenty-five trucks for forty-five days around the clock.' I says to myself, 'Oh, fuck, twenty-four hours a day. The rate's ten dollars and seventeen cents an hour for a ten-wheeler. I've got eleven of my own trucks I can use which means I've got to hire fourteen. We decide to work them on twelve-hour shifts, which means they work eleven hours and get paid for twelve. 'Then I says, 'Well, what's the rate?' He says, 'How about fifteen an hour?' I almost fall off my chair. Now the fucking money's clicking in my head, right? That's nearly five dollars over the going rate. Forty-five days, twenty-four hours a day, twenty-five trucks. We're talking about thousands of dollars. I say, 'Why don't we make it fifteen-fifty an hour because I've got to pay my drivers eight dollars per diem up in them boondocks,' which is bullshit.

"Sam, my wife figured it out, and we made a hundred-thirty thousand on that job alone. That goes to show you what a little public relations and two broads can do for you."

Giancana laughed. "That's fantastic. Who would have thought there was this kind of money up here in the sticks."

"The fantastic thing about what Jimmy's doing is that it's legitimate," Graham said. "He's not jacking off with the books."

"I don't have to," Jimmy said. "But I'll tell you something, Sam. Sticks or no sticks, I'm getting plenty of heat. This place's worse than L.A. Let me tell you about this Sheriff Misterly. This motherfucker used a shotgun mike on me.

"These three burglars came to see me in Sacramento, Ray Ferritto, Skinny Velotta, and Bob Walch, and we're talking in front of this building and they're telling me about some jewelry store they want to take off. So Walch says, 'Hey, Jimmy, who's that pointing that shotgun mike at us?' I look and it's a deputy sheriff. He's about a hundred yards away and that thing's zeroed in on us. I says, 'Excuse me, fellows, I'll be right back.' I walk over to this cop and I see all this electronic gear in the back of his car. Now I'm really pissed. I says, 'Hey, asshole, what's your fucking name?' He just stares at me with his mouth open, I says, 'What right've you got to invade my privacy? You go back to your office and tell that punk you work for that I'm going to have him in court next week for violating my civil rights.' "

Jimmy shook his head. "You never saw nothing like it. Sheriff Misterly must have hit the ceiling because he's had guys on my tail day and night ever since. Let me tell you, they're earning their money."

"Called him a punk, eh?" Giancana smiled. "When you talk about heat, you're talking to a man who's been through the mill. I took the feds to court and won the fucking case but the appeals court stayed it. Still, you know, you've got to fight back or they'll suck your blood until you're nothing but a fucking corpse."

"The feds have been on my tail ever since I got out of the joint," Jimmy said. "There's one FBI prick who follows me around with a camera, taking pictures of me going into motels with broads. Then he shows them to my wife, trying to get her to talk. My wife knows nothing.

"So I happened to see him in a restaurant one night. I says, 'Hey, how would you like it if I took pictures of you with broads and showed them to your wife?' He's looking at me like he thinks maybe I'm going to take a bite out of him. I says, 'Look, just because you're in the FBI don't mean nobody can't whack you, you know.' He says, 'Now, just a minute, are you threatening a federal officer?' I says, 'Listen, take the fucking badge off and let's go outside and fight like men.' So he sputters something about my being out of line and I says, 'If I do something wrong, pinch me, but stay out of my goddamn personal life. If I want to fuck a broad, that's my business.' Now he's going to my contractors to see if I'm muscling them. He can't understand how I'm doing it. I'll gross at least a million this year and it burns his ass."

13
OUT OF THE YOKE

† † † †

AFTER THREE AND A HALF YEARS ON PAROLE, JIMMY WAS DISCHARGED on April 7, 1964. In his final report, Wilbur noted that "his case is notorious in the annals of the Adult Authority and with law enforcement throughout the state. Numerous allegations have been made against the Parolee and all have been checked out with the results showing the Parolee to be clean. . . . He has many good qualities and this has been brought out in many dealings with employees and with people he does business with. Unless some unforseen circumstance should arise, Parolee should continue as a successful business-man and a good citizen."

At last he was a free man. After ten years with his neck in the yoke of the Department of Correction, he could once again come and go as he pleased, talk and associate with whom he pleased, and could tell the rest of the world to kiss his ass. He was off to the races, running at breakneck speed, the juices that had kept him going in perpetual motion all of his life flowing freely again, unimpeded by official restraints, the sublimated aggressions and resulting frustrations that had kept him sitting up in bed at night could now be channeled into actions that would bring his trucking company the kind of success he envisioned. There was also the matter of his lifelong ambition to gain a foothold in a gambling casino.

It was ironic how easily freedom could obliterate the perspective he had gained in prison. Alone in his cell at night, he had wondered about the life he had chosen for himself and had tried to grasp the true meaning of his life. What it was all about, what had made him so different from other men?

Yet he was not interested in what the prison shrinks had to say about him. What they never understood was that his total lack of interest in their little tests invalidated their results. He cared nothing about their opinions. In fact, for a carton of cigarettes he could have had any test score he wanted—inmates graded the papers. To him it was all bullshit. It was like their talk about rehabilitation. Pipe dreams. Shrinks were freaks. He would never forget the shrink who asked whether he had ever wanted to have sex with his mother.

The question had been more shocking than a sudden slap in the face. A black rage had swept over him and he had jumped to his feet, trembling with anger, his clenched fist raised threateningly at the doctor. "You prick," he shouted, "I ought to bust your fucking head. How many times did you fuck your mother, you cocksucker?" Without waiting for a response, he had walked out of the room, never to return.

He was left to his own introspection. The shrinks used words like aggression and hostility, and he had looked them up in the library. Vaguely he could see where they applied to him. He was aggressive and he harbored certain hatreds. He equated love with pride and possession, and the death of others had little meaning for him. Murder was easy, but mostly a waste of time. To kill for greed or jealousy was an exercise in futility. Of all the murders that he knew about, he could not think of a single instance where something important had been gained by it. He had done the bidding of fools, which made him an even bigger fool. Yet he was ready to begin all over again for other more important fools. He had taken his vows and there was no turning back.

By the standards of the society that judged him, he knew he was not like other people. He was possessed by a drive for money and power that was beyond his control. Money and power were the motivating forces of his very existence. Without those juices flowing in his veins he would shrivel up and die. He had perceived that much about himself for a long time. In personal contests, he had to win. Defeat was intolerable. Yet most of the schemes he dreamed up and so relentlessly pursued ultimately failed. But they were impersonal and as such had little effect on him. It was "just one of them things" that was immediately forgotten as he rebounded toward other promising schemes. In a way, the schemes were like pinballs bouncing off rubber impediments, ringing a few bells, creating a brief flurry of excitement, before vanishing into a meaningless hole. Sometimes when the juices stopped flowing for a moment and he collapsed in fatigue, a crazy litany would spin through his head: Hustle, hustle, hustle; run, run, run; chase your fucking tail like a mad dog.

To hustle meant that he had to use all the means at his disposal. His reputation as a "Mafia enforcer" created a certain aura that was useful in his business. He could get away with things other men would never dare try. It gave him a license to swagger and freely speak his mind in the company of richer and far stronger men. They listened to him, accepted whatever he had to say with respect, for they knew that if they retaliated, there would be dreadful repercussions. A Mafia reputation, like the six-shooter of the old west, was an equalizer. It turned little men into big men. It was a powerful weapon to be handled with delicate skill. In his world, it brought him respect through fear, and that was real power.

The harmony at the Fratianno company and in the Fratianno household that had so impressed the parole agents had been disintegrating for a long time. Now, with Jimmy's freedom, it soon flew apart. The blow up came one night when Frank LaPorte and Harriet Posey were house guests.

Jimmy had warned Jewel on several occasions not to discuss business in front of guests. As was his habit, the Chicago *capo* and Harriet were in the kitchen cooking dinner. He was an excellent cook and could make the kind of Italian dishes that Jimmy loved and could not find in any Sacramento restaurant.

On this evening, after her second highball, Jewel started criticizing Jimmy for having advanced $3,500 to an independent trucker. "You can kiss that money good-bye," she said, her voice dripping with sarcasm. "I knew he was a deadbeat the minute I saw him."

"Let it lay," Jimmy cautioned.

"Mr. Wiseguy, you got taken by a little punk." As she talked, she was shaking her head disgustedly.

"You better shut up, you're drunk. If you want to talk about money, talk about the money I've earned for this business. Never mind the thirty-five hundred. How about the three hundred and fifty thousand that's in the bank. Talk about that, goddamnit."

"I'm president of this company and if you want to throw away your own money, that's fine, but don't go to Joanne and ask her to sign checks on the company."

"I'm telling you for the last time to stop your yapping."

She stood up and staggered toward the liquor cabinet with her empty glass. "This is my house and I'll talk all I want."

Jimmy raised his right hand threateningly and hit the glass out of her hand with his left. "Don't pick it up if you know what's good for you," he hissed. "I've never hit a woman, but there's always a first time. Go to bed. Get out of my fucking sight."

For the first time since he had known her, Jimmy saw fear in his wife's eyes. She turned slowly and walked out of the room, placing each foot carefully in front of the other like a drunk trying to walk a straight line.

Jimmy stepped into the kitchen and LaPorte and Harriet went on about their business of preparing dinner like nothing had happened. "Listen, Frank," Jimmy said, opening the back door for a breath of fresh air, "never take your wife or any fucking broad into your business. Don't ever make a president out of a fucking housekeeper."

A few days later Jewel filed for divorce, charging extreme cruelty, but they continued to work and live together whenever Jimmy was around, which was not all that often. However, the marriage was over. The arguments over business decisions and strategy continued, but mostly when they were alone.

Then one night, after a violent argument, Jewel locked herself into the bathroom and took an overdose of sleeping pills. Jimmy broke down the door and found her lying on the floor, with an empty pill container at her side. Jimmy would later describe the scene to Bompensiero. "So there she is on the fucking floor and that's all I need right now. I can see the fucking headlines.

With my luck, I'd probably get the fucking chair for murder. So I call the fire department and they rush her to the county hospital. I'm right in the truck with them, and I'm yelling at them to step on it, for Christ's sake. They get into emergency and pump her stomach. They tell me she's okay and I go back home. The next day I go to the hospital and they've got her in the psycho ward with all the crazies. You should see that fucking place. Gives you the willies just walking in there. Jewel's so scared she cops out to me she was bluffing, faked the whole thing. She wanted my sympathy or some goddamn thing. She's crying and half out of her head. She says she'll never do it again."

Meanwhile, Jimmy's brother Warren, who had been divorced for several years, fell in love with Carla Irene Reuveni. Jimmy took one look at her and pulled his brother aside.

"What're you doing with this fucking broad?" he asked.

Warren shrugged. "What the hell, Jimmy, I married her."

"You what? This broad's a fucking hooker."

"Well, I love the broad and she loves me—we got hitched."

"Ah, shit," Jimmy said, "you need a fucking keeper."

As a wedding gift, Jimmy bought them a house but kept the title in his and Jewel's name. For a while Warren had a bumpy ride trying to keep up with his wife, who went right on hustling.

With his release from parole, Jimmy started going to Las Vegas to see Roselli and other old friends. There was Abe Benjamin, Hy Goldbaum, Yale Cohen, Peanuts Danolfo, Al Sachs, Bernie Rothkopf—it seemed that he knew someone important in each of the casinos, whether downtown or on the strip.

His two greatest sources of information were Roselli and Bompensiero. Whereas Roselli spoke rather freely with Jimmy, there still were areas beyond which he would not venture and Jimmy knew better than to push. But with Bompensiero, who was a compulsive talker, there were few boundaries. Another fountain of information was Bill Graham, whose stories of the old days in Tonapah, Goldfield, and Reno were exciting and whose knowledge of political chicanery was inspiring.

Jimmy loved Las Vegas, loved the respect paid him as he moved from casino to casino, loved running into old friends and the way they looked at him, their interest in his well-being and genuine delight in his new-found freedom. It was good to have so many loyal friends, a blessing few men enjoyed.

There were others, of course, like Moe Dalitz who resented his presence but would never dare show it. The first time he ran into Dalitz after he came off parole, Jimmy was with Graham and Roselli. The old mobster was with actress Barbara Parkins, whose meteoric rise to stardom in the *Peyton Place* television series would earn her the title of queen of the Tournament of Champions, a yearly golfing event sponsored by the Desert Inn as a benefit for the Damon Runyon Cancer Fund, a philanthropic venture to benefit local hospitals, including the Dalitz-owned Sunrise Hospital.

Dalitz was at the owner's table and when he saw them approaching he stood up to introduce Barbara Parkins. Jimmy, who never had time to watch television, was so captivated by her beauty that he hardly heard a word Dalitz said. His first thought was that she had to be a hooker. Otherwise, what would a gorgeous broad like that be doing with an ugly old *shlepen* like Dalitz. He tried to sit next to her but was outmaneuvered by Roselli, who could have given Errol Flynn lessons at that game. Jimmy ended up sitting next to Dalitz, whose first words completely puzzled him.

"You know, I never got that money from Johnny Battaglia."

"What?" Jimmy said, not taking his eyes from the actress.

"Come on," Dalitz said, "let's take a walk. I want to talk to you."

"Oh, shit," Jimmy said.

They walked away from the table and Dalitz said, "I'm still holding his markers."

"Hey, what the fuck're you talking about?"

"Remember New Year's Eve nineteen-fifty-four? You okayed Johnny Battaglia's markers for forty-five hundred."

"Are you kidding? Why are you bringing up this shit now? That was a million years ago."

"But he ain't paid it yet."

Jimmy smiled. "You fucking cheapskate. You've got billions and you still remember forty-five hundred bucks. Get away from me. I wouldn't pay you if it was two bucks."

"Okay, but talk to him, will you? You know the guy. If he's got it, he should pay. That's only fair."

"Moe, next time I see him I'll tell him you need his money. That you're going fucking bankrupt around here."

Later, as they were walking out of the Desert Inn, Jimmy said, "Christ, Johnny, that's the most beautiful broad I ever saw."

Roselli slipped his arm around Jimmy's waist and squeezed a handful of flesh. "You think she's beautiful, you should have seen Judy Campbell a few years ago."

"Hey, by the way, whatever happened to her? I thought Sam was nuts about her."

"He was. The guy even proposed marriage but she turned him down and that's all she wrote. Sam ditched her, Kennedy got killed, the feds were all over her, and she fell head first into a bottle."

"What a shame," Jimmy said.

PART IV

✝ ✝ ✝ ✝

MY FRIEND, JOE
1964–1966

14
JOSEPH ALIOTO

† † † †

LONG BEFORE HE MET JOSEPH LAWRENCE ALIOTO, A WEALTHY SAN Francisco attorney, Jimmy had heard many good things about him. Although not a made guy, there were rumors of interesting links in his family tree. Bompensiero had told Jimmy that one of Alioto's grandfathers had been a made guy, and a cousin of Alioto's father, John Alioto, had been boss of the Milwaukee family until 1962, at which time he had relinquished the reins to his son-in-law, Frank Balistrieri.

Back in 1917, some twenty years after the large Alioto clan had immigrated from Palermo, Sicily, settling in Milwaukee and San Francisco, Mario Alioto, an uncle of Joseph Alioto, was fatally shot by the LaFata gang while driving a truck of the International Fish Company, founded by Giuseppe Alioto, the attorney's father. In those days the Mafia, or La Cosa Nostra, was better known as *Il Mano Negri,* the Black Hand. Mario's father-in-law, Gaetano Ingrassia, was also murdered by the LaFata gang.

Until his death in 1937, James Lanza's father, Francisco, who was then boss of that city's Cosa Nostra family, operated a restaurant at Fisherman's Wharf with Giuseppe Alioto.

As far as Jimmy was concerned, Joseph Alioto had impeccable credentials. A close friend of San Jose Mafia members Salvatore and Angelo Marino and San Francisco Mafia boss Jimmy Lanza, Alioto had represented an impressive gallery of underworld figures. When Mario Balistrieri had wanted to get married while on parole, he had sought the assistance of Joseph Alioto, and when the police were looking for Tony Lima in 1947, during the Nick DeJohn murder investigation, Alioto had called the prosecutor to say that he was representing Lima and would bring him in the following Monday. Lima never appeared.

Three years later Alioto would use a similar tactic with the Kefauver Senate Rackets Investigating Committee. First he failed to produce Emilio "Gam" Georgetti when he was subpoenaed to appear before the committee in San Francisco. Alioto, who was Georgetti's tax lawyer, also managed to delay for several months the opening of his client's books. Although Georgetti's accountant had charged massive payoffs to public officials, by the time the investigators finally got their hands on Georgetti's records, the accountant was dead and no references to payoffs were found.

Georgetti had parlayed legitimate business, official corruption, and vice operations into a multimillion-dollar empire. He was known as the "Gambling Czar" of San Mateo County, a bedroom community south of San Francisco.

True to the gangster code, Georgetti never liked paying taxes, and it took the oratorical skills of the young Alioto to keep the old Czar out of prison after he was convicted for income tax evasion in 1953. After Alioto argued that Georgetti would die if imprisoned, the judge fined him $20,000 and placed him on probation.

Not long after the trial, Alioto became a partner in Georgetti's Holly Meat Packing Company, and with Louis and Charles Figone, two of Georgetti's partners, founded the Castlewood Corporation, a land-speculation venture, on a $55,000 loan from Georgetti. When Holly was sold in 1955, Louis Figone founded the Regal Meat Packing Company with his share of the proceeds, and hired Alioto as the firm's attorney. By 1960, the year of Georgetti's death, Alioto's brother-in-law, Rudy Papale, was hired and in a few years became president of the Regal company.

According to Bompensiero, there were also Cosa Nostra connections on the family side of Alioto's wife, the former Angelina Genaro of Dallas. He had heard that her father, Lawrence Genaro, a made guy, was ordered murdered by Joe Piranio, predecessor of Joe Civello as boss of the Dallas family. Angelo Marino had also heard the story from Jimmy Lanza, a close friend of Joe Civello. True or false, Angelina, as he would later learn from Angelo Marino, had a hot Italian temper. Arriving home late one night, Joseph Alioto found Angelina waiting for him with a shotgun. Having long suspected her husband of philandering, she had retained the services of private investigators to follow her husband. Judging from the shotgun incident, their reports had not been negative. Terrified by the shotgun and his wife's state of mind, Alioto had run from his home to seek the assistance of Angelo Marino and Jimmy Lanza, pleading with them to intercede with Angelina on his behalf.

Angelo Marino, a *caporegime* in the San Jose family, was proud of his friendship with Joseph Alioto and Jimmy enjoyed ribbing him about it.

"This guy's smooth as cough syrup," Marino remarked as they were driving from San Jose to San Francisco on the morning of November 3, 1964. Jimmy had business to discuss with Jimmy Lanza in San Francisco and Marino was trying to convince him to see Alioto first.

"Sounds like a great bullshit artist to me," Jimmy said. "Never heard of the guy until you started bragging about him."

"Hey, Jimmy, would I shit you, pal?" Angelo said. "I've told you this guy's the world's greatest trust-busting lawyer."

"So what, for Christ's sake," Jimmy said, glancing at Angelo for his reaction. "All mouthpieces are thieves."

"Well, that's great, as long as the best thief's on your side," said Marino. "Who wants a straight arrow for a mouthpiece? But this guy's different. He's too big to fuck with piddling shit. He's not chasing no ambulances, believe me. Let me tell you something, the feds are looking into my taxes and I'm glad to have Joe Alioto on my side. A few years ago, when we wanted to expand the cheese company, Joe got us two hundred and forty-seven thousand dollars from the Small Business Administration—if you don't think that's something, just go take a look at my FBI file. Man, you've got to tip your hat to this guy."

Jimmy kept a straight face. "The only kind of loans I like are the ones I don't have to pay back. Can he get me one of those?"

"Aw, cut it out, will you. Seriously, you've got to meet this guy."

"I need another lawyer like I need another hole in my head," Jimmy responded.

"This guy's just opened a bank, the First San Francisco Bank, and if I was you I'd put my money in his bank."

"Now what the hell good would that do me?"

"Well, I'll tell you, Jimmy. When you want to buy more trucks, he'll give you a lower rate of interest on loans."

"Like what?"

"Like four percent simple interest."

"That's pretty good," Jimmy said.

"There's something else, too," Marino said. "Alioto's president of the Rice Growers Association."

Jimmy blinked a couple times and if his eyeballs had been wheels in a slot machine the jackpot would have been dollar signs lit up in neon. All the major rice growers in California belonged to this cooperative. The hauling contract, Jimmy rapidly calculated, was probably worth a million dollars a year. From that moment on, Jimmy Fratianno was indeed interested in meeting Joseph Alioto.

Two minutes into his first meeting with Alioto and Jimmy knew he was dealing with a formidable operator. Immaculately groomed, his bald head gleaming like polished mahogany, his whole being pulsated with a charismatic energy. There was no doubt that this man could be devastatingly effective in a courtroom. The timbre and melodious inflection of his voice made a listener hang onto his every word.

Somehow, and Jimmy could not quite decide how it had come about, Alioto had launched into an episodic account of his life. He told of his years with the Justice Department's anti-trust division in San Francisco, with a starting salary of $150 a month. He laughed softly at the thought of such an impossible salary, but went on to reassure his listeners that the experience had been invaluable.

Two years later, in private practice, he had earned his first big legal fee in an anti-trust case—$60,000. "Well, you know, it looked pretty big to me then, but nothing compared to what we're doing today." He paused, smiling, letting that sink in. "In fact, Jimmy, and I say this with due modesty, million-dollar fees are becoming rather routine."

"Christ, I never realized there was this kind of money in this anti-trust business," Jimmy said. "Joe, you know, maybe I should have been a lawyer. I know how to handle myself in a courtroom. A lawyer told me one time that I was a spellbinder. After hearing about this trust-busting, that's the line I'd go into. Million-dollar fees! That's big fucking money, Joe."

Jimmy was pleased that Alioto was working so hard to impress him. Sitting in that plush office, with the city some twenty stories below them, Alioto looked like a man who belonged in that setting. Under other circumstances, Jimmy would have been immediately suspicious of a man with that smooth an approach. Having been a scammer and con-man all of his life, Jimmy had no problem recognizing a snowjob when he heard one. Never in his life had he met a man who could say more words per minute than Alioto. They flowed out without the slightest hesitation, words on top of words, each clearly articulated, tumbling out automatically, as though there were no thought process involved, that everything he was saying had been carefully rehearsed for this performance. A special performance for Jimmy and Angelo, from a man who subliminally created the impression that he was graciously taking precious time out of his busy schedule to entertain them in a private audience.

Not once did Alioto inquire as to Jimmy's background or question the purpose of his visit. Marino had obviously briefed him, for there were no crass references to banking until Jimmy decided it was time to bring it up. Even fifteen years later, Jimmy recalled his surprise at how solicitous Alioto was of him.

"By the way, Joe, Angelo tells me you've got a new bank."

"Yes. It's been open just a few months, and doing quite nicely, I might add."

"Angelo just sprung that on me this morning, but I'm going to talk to my wife about it and see about transferring our business to your bank. He was telling me I could get a pretty good interest rate on loans."

"Yes, that's true. We're a new bank and naturally we're looking for business. The competition is pretty fierce out there."

"I would think so," Jimmy said. "There's a bank on every corner in this town."

"Well, Jimmy, we enjoy a good challenge, and we've got some competent people at the bank. Nick Rizzo, our president, and Joe Demers, one of our vice presidents, are both excellent men. When you're ready to do business with us, let me know and I'll personally call both men and advise them of your intentions. I assure you they will take excellent care of you. By the way," Alioto said, standing up and offering his hand to Jimmy, a definite cue that the final curtain was coming down, "our bank is just around the corner. If you have a moment, take a look at it."

Jimmy firmly gripped Alioto's hand. "I think we can do business together."

"Thank you, Jimmy," Alioto said, turning to shake hands with Marino. "And whenever you're in the neighborhood, please drop in and say hello. You're always welcome."

"Well, I don't know," Jimmy said. "You're a busy man. I wouldn't want to interrupt your business or anything."

"Nonsense. I think we can help each other." As he spoke, he was expertly steering them out of his office. They said good-bye, he smiled and waved, and closed the door.

From August 11, 1960, to July 12, 1965, the FBI monitored a concealed microphone in the office of James Lanza at 559 Washington Street in San Francisco. During the same period, and for far longer, of course, the FBI maintained physical surveillance of Jimmy Fratianno. Therefore it was no accident that on the morning of November 3, 1964, that special agents Richard Vitamanti and Herbert K. Mudd, Jr., would report that Jimmy and Angelo "had been in San Francisco at approximately ten a.m. that morning to keep an appointment with Joe Alioto, the attorney. It was noted that the garage [at 52 Lick Place] where the car was parked is located next door to 111 Sutter Street, the offices of Joe Alioto. The United States Attorney in San Francisco is presently reviewing the income tax evasion case of Angelo Marino as authorized by the Department of Justice."

Marino and Fratianno were then observed entering the office of James Lanza. In its report the FBI admits that "Trespass was involved in the installation of each electronic surveillance. . . . The following is a summary of the illegally obtained information: Fratianno enters [Lanza's office] and is greeted by the individuals present. [James Lanza] asks Fratianno if he is up in Sacramento now, and Fratianno says that he has a business up there. Lanza is heard saying, 'They don't take their eyes off you for a moment, they watch every move that everybody makes. . . .' "

At the beginning of each FBI report concerning Jimmy Fratianno, there is the following notation, "No information received indicating illegal activities on the part of Subject," and the warning: *FRATIANNO SHOULD BE CONSIDERED ARMED AND DANGEROUS IN VIEW OF HIS PAST ACTIVITIES.*

Not one to pass up an opportunity, Jimmy wasted no time in getting back to Alioto. The lawyer's remark that "I think we can help each other" was a clarion call to a man with Jimmy's finely tuned antenna.

In Jimmy's vernacular, he began dropping by Alioto's office to "bullshit" with him whenever business took him to San Francisco. He never made appointments and when Alioto was in another office on a different floor, or he had people in his office, Jimmy would take off without leaving a message.

When he did see Alioto, he made the visits short, fifteen or twenty minutes, but he used the time wisely, dropping hints and sending out feelers to see if he could make any money with this man. He was already far too busy to be wasting time with a deadhead. If he was going to get anywhere, it was important that he ingratiate himself by being pleasant and polite, and by appearing flattered by the attention paid him by this man who struck him as having a monumental ego. He recognized that they were both playing a game, each waiting for the other to make the right move.

When Jimmy explained about the twelve sets of bottom-dump trailers he was buying from Steve Dorsa the question of a loan came up. Alioto quickly placed a call to Nick Rizzo at the First San Francisco Bank and told him that Jimmy would be in for a loan. The loan was for $60,500, discounted at four percent simple interest. It was the first of five loans Jimmy would receive from Alioto's bank. Although Jimmy was not asked to furnish a financial statement, at the time of the loan the Fratianno Trucking Company had total assests of $534,393.15 and liabilities of $209,666.47, which gave it a net worth of $324,726.68. It would gross a million in 1964 and a million-four in 1965. It was a successful business, good enough to satisfy most men, but with Jimmy it was merely a means to other ends.

They were talking one day and Alioto said, "Jimmy, Angelo tells me you know some of the Teamsters officials here in San Francisco."

"Well, Joe, I know the biggest guy here."

"Who is that?"

"Jack Goldberger. This guy will do anything for me. In fact, you know, I got him made International Organizer. This old friend of mine from Cleveland, Babe Triscaro, we went to school together, is Hoffa's right hand man. I just called Babe . . . Goldberger was just a business agent then . . . Hoffa promoted him just like that. So the guy owes me, right?"

"I would think so," Alioto said. "Do you suppose there is any chance that Mr. Goldberger would deposit some of the union's pension money in our bank?"

"Joe, say the word and I'll bring him up here personally and you'll meet him. You guys talk it over among yourselves. I'll introduce you and take off. Whatever deals you guys make is your business."

"Thank you, Jimmy," Alioto said. "I would appreciate it."

"Look, Joe, it's like you said when we first met. We can help each other. Why not? We're businessmen. Give me a number where I can reach you in the next couple hours and I'll get back to you."

"Now, Jack, we can make a buck with this guy," Jimmy told Goldberger later that day. "You know this guy's fucking rich. He's a great money promoter, has all kinds of big deals cooking, and you can trust the guy a hundred percent."

"Oh, I know about Joe Alioto," Goldberger said. "I don't really know the man, but I know his reputation. He's strictly big time."

"Jack, would I fuck with anyone who ain't? Let me tell you something. Play your cards right and I'll bet you can even buy stock in his bank and make some real money. This guy can raise millions for huge projects. So treat him right, Jack. Whatever you can do for this guy, do it, understand? We'll make some money with him later."

Jimmy neglected to mention that the money he was planning on making later was with the Rice Growers Association. First, however, he had to find a respectable front, and second he had to come up with a gimmick, some kind of legitimate reason that would be strong enough to persuade the board of directors to dump their present trucking contractor in favor of Jimmy's front. He already had some ideas, but the details had still to be worked out.

A few days later, he brought Jack Goldberger to Alioto's office, introduced the two men, and chatted with them until he felt that the atmosphere was congenial enough for him to make his exit.

On another occasion, Jimmy brought Bompensiero to Alioto's office and was pleased at how quickly the two men warmed up to each other.

"We've never met, counselor," Bompensiero said, "but I know a million Aliotos in Milwaukee. That's my home town."

"My ancestors came to Milwaukee and San Francisco by the boatload."

"Shit, you can't drive a block in Milwaukee without seeing the Alioto name on some fucking sign. They're into everything. Which reminds me, you know, years ago I met your father, Giuseppe, when he had the restaurant on the wharf with Lanza. Must have been thirty years ago. Fine gentleman, your father, very well liked by everybody."

Alioto beamed. "How interesting. It really is a small world. Where do you make your home now?"

"San Diego, been there for years."

"Are you in business?"

"Yeah, meat packing, mostly exporting to Mexico. Angelo Marino told me about your Regal Meat Packing Company and introduced me to your brother-in-law, Rudy Papale. I've been trying to talk him into a lard deal for Mexico. You know, Joe, people in this country don't use lard, but south of the border it's a big item."

"My understanding of the situation," Alioto said, "is that it is illegal to import lard into Mexico without a government permit."

"Everything's illegal in Mexico without a government permit," Bompensiero laughed. "See, Joe, there's one word you've got to bear in mind whenever you deal with Mexico. It applies to everybody. The word's *mordida*. In English that means 'the bite.' Nothing moves in that fucking country without *mordida*. They've got an army of bagmen collecting the *mordida* for the big shots. A bagman down there's like somebody in the diplomatic service in this country. It's a perfectly honorable profession. The game for the gringo is to find the right bagman for whatever he's interested in. You want to export lard to Mexico, have Rudy come see me, I'll personally take him to Mexico City and introduce him to my man. We'll work out a deal, don't worry. Remember, Joe, there's big fucking money in this lard shit."

"Well, it's certainly something worth considering. Let me talk to Rudy about it and we'll get back to you."

"By the way, you know, that cousin of yours, Frank Alioto, the one that's got the Alioto restaurant at Fisherman's Wharf, well, would you believe it, his wife's my godchild. It sure's a small world, like you say, Joe."

"Bomp, tell Joe about meeting John Alioto in Milwaukee?" Jimmy said.

"I almost forgot," Bompensiero said. "What a sweet old guy, a real fine gentleman. His daughter, Antonia's married to an old friend of mine, Frank Balistrieri."

They talked a few minutes longer before Jimmy and Alioto stood up almost simultaneously. However subtly executed, Jimmy never appreciated being dismissed. They shook hands and Bomp said, "Don't forget about the lard deal. I can swing it for you."

"Oh, don't worry," Alioto said. "Rudy will be in touch with you or Angelo."

15
THE CASINO HUNT

† † † †

NINETEEN SIXTY-FIVE WOULD PROVE AN EXCITING YEAR, THE MOST promising so far. The trucking business was booming and his relationship with Frank LaPorte made it possible for Jimmy to expand his own fleet of trucks and trailers with minimal risk to himself.

Jimmy put Bompensiero on the payroll at a $150 a week and provided him with a leased automobile. One of his jobs was to ride up and down the highways to make sure the drivers kept moving at top speed. But mostly he was there as a companion for Frank LaPorte whenever he was in California and as a sounding board for Jimmy.

But Jimmy's primary goal that year would be to try to fulfill the old dream of owning a casino. The moment he was off parole, Jimmy started searching for a place in Reno or Lake Tahoe.

Whenever LaPorte was in town, they repaired to the Holiday Lodge, on the outskirts of Reno, where each room had its own private pool of mineral water. A man and wife team came to the rooms to give massages. For LaPorte, who was getting on in years, it was like finding his own fountain of youth. Jimmy had little time to waste soaking in smelly water, but on occasion he would humor LaPorte and go along. To watch Bompensiero and LaPorte, two fat men in a steaming tub, puffing on cigars and sweating bullets, struck him as ludicrous.

A chance at a casino arrived when Jimmy became reacquainted with Duke Countis. Fifteen years before, Countis had been one of his bookmaking agents. Now Countis and a friend, Johnny George, were looking for backers, preferably persons with money and tainted reputations in search of respectable fronts.

"Jimmy, we've got a great place staked out at Tahoe."

Countis and George were having a drink with Jimmy at the Mapes.

"How big a place," Jimmy asked.

"It's a money-maker," Countis assured him. "They've got four hundred slot machines that alone take in a half-million a month."

"So what's the name?"

Countis hesitated, glancing at George, who shrugged. "What the hell," George said, "we've got it locked up. It's the Crystal Bay, Jimmy."

"I know the joint," Jimmy said. "It's on the north side, across the street from the North Shore. Nice joint but it's just a casino. No hotel."

"There's land for a hotel," Countis said. "We could get three, four hundred rooms in a highrise, no problem."

"What's the bottom line?"

"Jimmy, believe me, it's a steal," Countis said. "The two old boys who own it must be in their eighties. They want to unload it and not carry any paper. So we've got to come up with cash, but shit it's only two million three."

"Is that firm?"

"Yeah, it is. They wanted two million eight, but we knocked it down what, fifteen, twenty percent?"

Jimmy whistled. "It's just what I've been looking for. It's perfect. We buy the joint, you guys get the license, and I've got the man who can swing it, no sweat, and then we get a Teamsters loan for the highrise, five, ten million. See, the Teamsters don't play around with penny-ante shit."

"Then you're interested?" Countis asked.

"Don't you move on this until I get back to you."

"You've got a live one?"

"You can say that again. I've got a guy with so much money you couldn't count it in a month. Hold tight till you hear from me."

Before going to Louigi's for dinner one evening, Frank LaPorte took Jimmy and Bompensiero to the Stardust and properly introduced them as made guys to Phil Ponti.

Later at dinner, LaPorte said, "Ain't that something? That's the only made guy working in a casino in the whole state of Nevada."

"Well, you know, Charley Fishetti had a piece of Bill Graham's Bank Club and I think he had a made guy in the joint for a while, but that was a long time ago," Jimmy said. "Hey, did I tell you guys about the time Bill came to Sacramento with Jack Dempsey and his young wife, a beautiful Italian girl from Rome? I took them out to dinner."

"Oh, Christ," Bompensiero said, "that was the greatest fighter of all time."

"That Graham knows a lot of important people," LaPorte said.

"Everybody. He's a good friend of Giancana."

"Speaking of Sam," Bompensiero said, "I see where the papers blame him for the disappearance of Joe Bonanno."

LaPorte laughed. "Newspapers never cease to amaze me. Can you imagine the commission kidnapping a boss or anybody else for that matter? You banish him or clip him but you don't kidnap him. Joe's taken a powder on the grand jury and the commission."

"Well, I can tell you that story," Bompensiero said. "I know the whole thing. Joe had his own kid, Bill, and Charley Bats fake the kidnapping. They grabbed him right on Park Avenue, it was dark and raining, and Charley Bats fired a shot to scare Joe's lawyer who nearly shit his pants."

"There's no question that Bonanno's in trouble," LaPorte said. "Sam was telling me Bonanno tried to put contracts on Gambino, Lucchese, and Steve Magaddino. He got Joe Magliocco involved and he gave the contracts to Joe Colombo. Well, Colombo went to Gambino, told him the whole story, and Magliocco went crawling on his knees to the commission. They banished him and he croaked of a heart attack." LaPorte laughed. "It will take more than that to kill Bonanno. Wherever he's hiding out, you can bet it's in the lap of luxury. He'll show up one of these days when the heat cools down."

They sipped wine, devoured pasta and meat sauce, puffed on cigars, and searched the darkest recesses of their brains for interesting shop talk. Jimmy waited until they were comfortably satiated with food and wine before bringing up the Crystal Bay. He provided backgrounds on Countis and George and went on to describe in lavish details the possibilities of the Crystal Bay, not neglecting to mention the Teamsters loan for a highrise in the immediate future.

"All we need is two point three million and we're in business," he concluded. "Do you know how long I've been waiting for this chance?"

LaPorte leaned back in his chair. "Jimmy, I can't get out front with the money. They'd check it out and nail me. It's against the law in this fucking state. With all the wiretap shit coming out of this town right now, with the feds bugging everybody, it wouldn't work."

"But that's up in Tahoe. The feds don't fuck around there much."

"I'll tell you what, Jimmy. Find a buyer, some straight guy, and I'll come up with the lease money."

"Always some hangup," he growled, mashing his cigar in the ashtray. Then he smiled and clapped his hands. "My friend, Joe, that's the baby. We get Alioto to buy it and we lease it from him."

"Holy shit," Bompensiero said. "Let's get Angelo in on this. He's very close to Alioto. They're like brothers."

"Okay," Jimmy said, "let me work it out."

Bompensiero started talking about his meeting with Alioto and Jimmy leaned back in his chair, his mind already working out the details of his approach. Suddenly he felt a sharp pain in his chest and he broke out in a cold sweat.

The room started spinning around and he grabbed the table for support. He wiped his face with his cloth napkin. Perhaps it was a heart attack? The pain was on the right side and he wondered about the location of his heart. The floor and ceiling were undulating and he felt like he was going to fall off his chair in a dead faint.

LaPorte and Bompensiero went on talking, unaware of his distress. Finally he heard a voice say, and for the life of him he could not distinguish whose it was, "Jimmy, what the hell's wrong with you?" Another voice said, "Holy Jesus, he looks like death warmed over."

"Get me to a hospital," Jimmy heard himself groan, "right away."

Jimmy was hospitalized for ten days and his condition was diagnosed as "Lucite ball collapse Right Upper Lobe."

Somewhere something went wrong with the FBI's physical surveillance. In a report dated March 25, 1965, Mudd wrote: "The Las Vegas Division by communication dated February 26, 1965, advised that Detective Nage Palmer, Las Vegas Police Department, advised SA R. Burns Toolson on February 26, 1965, that Subject was in Las Vegas on February 16, 1965, at which time he checked into Southern Nevada Memorial Hospital. This was apparently for an emergency and related to a previous TB condition suffered by Subject. He checked out of the hospital on February 25, 1965, and his present whereabouts are unknown. Authorities did not learn of Subject's presence in Las Vegas until after he checked out of the hospital, otherwise, they would have arrested him [for not registering] as an ex-convict when he was released . . . . Hospital authorities report his physical condition is not good."

Although still experiencing discomfort, Jimmy went back to work. The first item of business was the Crystal Bay.

Jimmy talked it over with Angelo Marino and the two of them went to see Alioto. After explaining the situation, Jimmy said, "We've got these two guys to front the joint for us. Good kids, clean reputations, no problem getting a license. Plus I've got the guy that can guarantee the license."

"You say they want two million three?" Alioto asked. "How many months of the year is it open?"

"Most of the year. That area's really building up fast in the winter with all that skiing," Jimmy said. "Pretty soon all them joints will be operating year-round."

"Who are the other people involved?"

"Just two others," Jimmy said. "There's Angelo's cousin, Frank Bompensiero, you know, he was up here with me one day. The guy from Milwaukee."

"Oh yes, I remember. He's in the meat packing business in San Diego."

"Right, and there's Frank LaPorte," Jimmy continued. "He's in the trucking business with me."

"I don't think I ever heard his name," Alioto said, glancing at Marino.

"He's from Chicago," Marino said. "This guy's got money. Owns a big ranch in Linden and a bunch of silver and gold mines in California and Nevada."

Jimmy stood up. "Listen, Joe, this is a good deal and I'd appreciate anything you can do for us."

"Let me look into it and talk to some people. I'll get back to you."

† † †

This time the FBI was on top of the situation. "The Los Angeles Office of communication dated May 11, 1965, advised SF T-8 secured information to indicate that James Fratianno had entered Cedars of Lebanon Hospital on March 24, 1965, and was discharged on April 2, 1965," Mudd reported. "Fratianno was operated on for the 'removal of 30 lucite spheres' . . . the surgery was performed by Dr. Harold Masters." This was followed by a listing of all the people Jimmy had telephoned from his hospital room.

For a while it looked as though Jimmy would wake up from his favorite dream and find himself in the counting room of not one but two casinos. While Alioto was considering the Crystal Bay, Jimmy became involved with the Tallyho. Built in 1958 at a cost of several million dollars, it had remained idle for some years because it had no casino and showrooms. Of Colonial architecture and located on thirty-five choice acres just north of the Tropicana and across the strip from the Dunes, the hotel had some three hundred rooms and thirty-two bungalow villas.

Jimmy first heard about the deal from Bompensiero. Eddie Nealis, a Los Angeles gambler, had sought Bompensiero's assistance when Pete Milano, the son of Tony Milano, associated with the Los Angeles family, tried to muscle in.

"Here's the setup," Bompensiero told Jimmy. "Eddie's promoting this thing and he's raising big bucks. He's got two hundred grand from Shirley MacLaine and her husband. He got another bundle from a banker in Iowa. He's got this contractor building the casino and showrooms for fifteen points. Shit, he's doing a fantastic job. This's the big one, if we play our cards right."

"Well, what's the deal?" Jimmy asked.

"There's this doctor who's got a pretty big chunk of money in the joint and Pete Milano's trying to take over his end for the L.A. family. Eddie got scared and came to me to straighten it out. I said I'd come to you. We straighten it out, you know, we get in on the ground floor."

Jimmy laughed. "That fucking worm Milano, I'll make him die of a heart attack."

"Yeah, but I've got to be careful with DeSimone and Licata. I'm still in the family. They know I'm with you and I hear things. I've still got friends in that outfit who tell me things. All they need is some little excuse to clip me. They know I've got friends in Detroit and that's kept them away, but I don't trust them for a minute."

Jimmy shook his head. "Bomp, what's wrong with you? Them guys couldn't clip a flea. Roselli tells me DeSimone's scared of his shadow, never goes out nights. The guy's gone bananas."

"Nick's the guy to watch. Anyway, I told Eddie we'd look into it."

"Okay, but first I've got to clear it with Johnny."

"He's a fucking flunky," Bompensiero said.

"Hey, Bomp, I've told you before, Johnny's my friend. He's the man in this town and don't you ever forget it."

The meeting with Pete Milano in La Jolla was a lot shorter than it was sweet.

"Look it, Pete," Jimmy said, "we ain't got no time to fuck around. We're interested in the Tallyho. Tell DeSimone, or whoever's behind this, to lay off Nealis. This is our joint. If you're in with the doctor, whatever the doctor's got, you grab him. Don't be coming to Eddie Nealis no more. Understand?"

Pete Milano was terrified. A few more words and he might have died of a heart attack, as Jimmy had predicted. "Don't worry, Jimmy, I'll pass the word along."

Jimmy reached out and patted him gently on the cheek. "That's a good boy, Pete. Give my regards to your Daddy."

That spring Jimmy bought a home in Las Vegas but kept his Sacramento address at 1945 Sixty-six Avenue as his legal residence. His Las Vegas home was at 336 Mallard Street, next door to the home of John Anthony [*nee* Petercupo], a brother of Mark Anthony and also a childhood friend from the Hill.

Meanwhile, Jimmy's trucking business was gradually moving south. He still had trucks working on the American River and in Sacramento, others were working on California highways near Ione, Donner Summit, Bishop, Marysville, and the south end of Lake Tahoe. Still others were in Utah, a few were engaged in the construction of Harrah's Club at Stateline, and he landed a road construction job fifty miles northeast of Las Vegas.

When advised by the FBI of Jimmy's background, contractors would reply that they found it difficult not doing business with Fratianno Trucking because Jimmy had the newest and best equipment available and his bids were always competitive. Although they could have added that they never had to worry about union trouble when Jimmy's trucks were on the job, Jimmy himself was having a hard time with William Carter, business agent of the Las Vegas local.

Yet Jimmy hadn't forgotten for a moment Alioto and the Crystal Bay, nor the Rice Growers Association. The first word he received from Alioto on the Crystal Bay sounded like good news. Angelo Marino called him in Las Vegas to say they were meeting with Alioto the next day. Alioto appeared enthusiastic and it was only a question of working out the terms.

Detained by his problem with Carter, Jimmy arranged to meet Bompensiero, LaPorte, Marino, and Countis after they had met with Alioto. When he arrived, the atmosphere was not as cheerful as Jimmy would have liked, and his sixth sense for disaster gave him that familiar sinking feeling.

"Let's have the bad news."

LaPorte shrugged. "Jimmy, I don't know about this guy Alioto. He drives a hard bargain."

"How's that?" Jimmy asked. "What's wrong with it?"

"Just a minute, Jimmy, let me explain," LaPorte said. "The guy will buy the joint but he wants twenty grand a month rent, with six months in advance. That's for the lease. So that's a hundred and forty grand right there before we even apply for the license. How long will that take?"

"No time at all," Jimmy answered. "Bill will push it right through. Maybe thirty days, depends on the kind of investigation the commission gets into."

"Okay, that's another twenty grand. If for some reason they turn thumbs down, that's a hundred and sixty grand down the drain."

"Frank, I don't understand it. I thought you liked the deal."

"I still do," LaPorte replied. "But listen, will you? Let me finish. Now we need bankroll money, right? Another two hundred grand? Then you need operating money, right? So where are we now? Half a million? Jimmy, that's a lot of money for a joint that don't have no rooms."

"But we're going to build rooms, Frank," Jimmy said, his voice getting shrill. "We'll get a Teamsters loan. You knew up front this was going to cost some fucking money."

LaPorte ignored him. "Then there's the option to buy. Listen to this, Jimmy. No matter how many payments we make, none apply to the principal. Not even the lease payment. It's still going to be two million three. What kind of a deal's that?"

"Frank, that's a good deal. I told Alioto this joint would double in price inside of three years. There's only so much prime land available around there. In all the years I've been in Nevada, I've never seen a joint go down in price."

LaPorte looked at the others and shook his head. "I think we ought to stick with the Tallyho. That Nealis's going to need money before he opens. He's so hardup now his shoes are squeaking."

Nobody said anything for a moment. Then Duke Countis stood up. "You guys are throwing away a lifetime opportunity. Well, I've got to find somebody else. Jimmy, you think Alioto would keep that offer open a while?"

Jimmy rubbed his face with both hands. "Duke, right now I don't know nothing. I feel like I've been kicked in the ass so hard my brain's rattling. Talk to Angelo, here. He'll check it out for you."

That evening Jimmy flew back to Las Vegas with LaPorte and Bompensiero. While they waited for their flight, they sat at the far end in the departing area, away from the other passengers, as was their custom.

"Listen, I didn't say nothing before because I knew I could straighten out this problem with the Teamsters," Jimmy said. "See, it's against union rules to bring drivers in from another state. But I never pay no attention to that bullshit. My California drivers are working in Utah and all over the northern part of Nevada. But this Bill Carter's a prick. He wanted me to use only his men on the job, and I told him to go fuck himself. So now we're at a standstill, so I says, let's compromise, we'll go fifty-fifty.

"He agrees to it and the next thing I know he's got all his men up there,"

Jimmy continued. "So I call George Mock, an old friend, he's the sixth or seventh International Vice President, and he comes up to Vegas to talk to this big fat idiot. Mock says, 'Look it, you've made a deal with Fratianno, how come you don't keep it?' So Carter starts giving him this bullshit about my breaking the rules, this and that, and Mock says, 'All right, you sonovabitch, but every dog has his day. Remember it the next time you want a fucking favor from the International.'

"So this morning, I've got all my men on the job and Carter sends this guy, who's built like a brick shithouse, out on the job with his men, see. So now I'm really steamed. I says, 'Get your fucking men out of here. Go back and tell that big motherfucker to come over here himself and I'll break his fucking legs.' This guy just stands there, don't know what to do, then takes off. So when I come to town to catch the plane, I call Carter and I says, 'Bill, this's your last chance. You want to go fifty-fifty, say so now, or go fuck yourself.' Let me tell you something, he sounded a lot friendlier this time. So we've got a deal."

"Did he say anything about union dues?" LaPorte asked.

"Shit no. I'm not even paying the union scale. I told you from the beginning, Frank, I've got friends in this union. Forget about it. Lousy business agents don't worry me."

LaPorte had been right about Eddie Nealis. Next it was his turn to run into money trouble. He said, "Jimmy, the casino's about finished but we ain't got the money for the tables. I need some cash fast."

"Get them on credit."

Nealis shook his head sadly. "I can't swing it. We're too much in hock as it is."

"Give them a small piece of the joint," Jimmy said. "As long as we're in the counting room, what difference does it make?"

"I ain't got no pieces left to give. I'm telling you, I'm in trouble. We're on the brink of folding right now," Nealis pleaded.

"Where's the money going?" Jimmy demanded.

"Jimmy, you got any idea how big a staff it takes to keep this joint going even when it's closed? I've got sixty Japanese broads coming in to start rehearsal for the show. There's the rent on the lease. Then there's maids, gardeners, pool men, the fucking utilities. . . . The phone bill alone runs in the thousands. Then I gave Al Bramlet twenty-five grand for the license."

"Are you crazy?" Jimmy shouted. "Bill Graham could get us the license for nothing."

Nealis raised his hand in an appeasing gesture. "Jimmy, listen to me, will you. Bramlet's the head of the culinary workers, the most powerful union in this state. He's got political clout coming out of his ears. He's guaranteed the license. No ifs, ands, or buts about it. Still, you know, for a little insurance, I gave Sheriff Lamb's cousin a couple of points. It can't hurt. But forget about

Graham, he's an old man, his time's passed. He can't swing nothing in this town no more."

"That's bullshit," Jimmy said, but there was resignation in his voice. "Compared to Bill Graham, Bramlet's a fucking amateur."

"Bramlet's capable. Don't worry, he knows all the right people."

"Now, Eddie, if something goes wrong, you tell me right away. Let's not blow this joint with the gaming commission."

"No way, Jimmy. All we've got to worry about is money. We need equipment. You can't run a gambling casino without tables. And this's going to be a big room, believe me."

Jimmy sighed. "How much do you need?"

"A couple hundred grand to tide us over to the end of the year," Nealis said. "We want to open the joint on New Year's Eve."

"Why don't you ask for the moon?" Jimmy asked.

"I need thirty-five right now to show good faith and we'll worry about the rest later."

"Let me think about it."

"You'd better make it quick," Nealis warned.

"Eddie, I've got to go to San Diego tomorrow."

"That's perfect," Nealis said. "The guy's in San Diego. You can personally deliver the money to him while you're there."

For Jimmy it was an event long anticipated. After many telephone calls and lengthy entreating, his father and mother had consented to visit him in California, and on July 30, 1965, Jimmy flew to Cleveland to pick them up. To be able to show them the success he had achieved in the legitimate business world made him walk as proud as a peacock. They were entertained royally in both Sacramento and Las Vegas.

After they had returned to Cleveland, Jimmy told Roselli about their visit. "You should've seen my mother, she's a born gambler that woman. She's nuts about the slots. She likes to gamble, my mother. I tried to take them to shows but they're old-fashioned people who like to stay home nights. They saw Billy, my brother's son, who they raised from the age of nine. He's like their own son. They saw him dealing craps at the Stardust and boy were they impressed.

"What the fuck, Johnny, I've been a headache to them all my life. So now they're happy it turned out this way." He laughed. "Like in the movies, a happy ending, eh?"

"I'll bet your dad was impressed with the size of your trucking business," Roselli said.

"Forget about it. When he saw all them trucks with the Fratianno decal, all that equipment, he went crazy he was so proud. You never saw such a proud man. I took him on some of the jobs. He couldn't get over it. Kept walking around and shaking his head, and he had to touch everything, the loader, the dozer, the grader, them transfers blew his mind. But, you know,

Johnny, I didn't bring it up—I could've reminded him, you know, that we could've done this together years ago. But I didn't want to embarrass him. He's an old man. What's the sense of dragging out that shit. But me and him could have made millions if he would've listened to me years ago."

Jimmy and Frank Bompensiero were sitting in the living room of Jimmy's Las Vegas house. Jewel was back in Sacramento.

Over a period of time, Jimmy had been noticing a change in Bompensiero's attitude toward Roselli. At first Jimmy had attributed this growing resentment to Roselli's failure to effect his transfer to Chicago. There was no question that Bompensiero was unhappy with his situation, being the bastard child of the Los Angeles family, but the problem was not of Roselli's making, even if he could have unmade it. In the old days there had been moments when Jimmy had suspected that Bompensiero was envious of Jimmy's friendship with Roselli, who had been the family's elder statesman, Don Giovanni, whose advisory role had been far too remote to please an old workhorse like Bompensiero.

"I know he's your asshole buddy," Bompensiero said, "but this fucking guy's never done nothing."

"Look, Bomp, Johnny's my friend, so do me a favor and keep your thoughts to yourself."

"What makes him such a hotshit, for Christ's sake?" Bompensiero's manner was even gruffer than usual. "Let me tell you something. This pal of yours fucked me good. He's cost me a piece of the fucking Frontier."

So finally it was out, Jimmy thought, the poison that had been eating away at Bompensiero. From years of experience, Jimmy knew that the best way to get at the bottom of Bomp's thoughts was to use a reverse tactic. "Look, Bomp, I told you I don't want to hear about it. I've got problems of my own."

"Wait a minute, will you. This's important. Detroit owes me something."

"I know, you clipped a guy for them a hundred years ago."

"Hey, take it easy. Let me tell you the facts here. Never mind this shit about a hundred years ago. Look, they came to me not long ago and asked me to clip this guy, and they hint about getting the Frontier and maybe I'm going to get some points.

"Remember Borgia?" Bompensiero continued, his face flushed. "He was having this feud with Matranga, and they both went to Jack with their problem and we clipped him. This was the same kind of deal. These two guys were having a feud and they went to Joe Zerilli, each wanting the other guy clipped. So Mike Polizzi came to see me and this was strictly between us, nothing to do with the L.A. family. They tell me who they want clipped but I've got to do the job alone.

"As it happens I know the guy. So one night I see him at a party and I pull him aside. I says, 'Look here, you've been having this problem and the old man's given me the contract. I'm going to clip this guy but I'm going to need your help.' Now this guy's all happy, see, and I tell him I've got a bad back and I need him to dig the hole. We go out to this fucking place I've picked out ahead of time and this guy starts digging the fucking hole. Works like a sonovabitch, this guy, sweating bullets. So finally he says, 'How's that? Deep enough.' I'm sitting down, resting, so I get up and I says, 'It's perfect.' He starts climbing out of the hole and I shoot the cocksucker in the back of the fucking head. Back down he goes in the hole and I fill it in."

As he talked, Bompensiero was chomping on his cigar, barking little laughs from time to time, obviously enjoying the memory, proud of having fooled the victim. Jimmy puffed on his own cigar and said nothing.

"So what happens?" Bompensiero asked, removing his heavy horned-rimmed glasses to clean them. "Detroit got the fucking Frontier. Tony Zerilli and Mike Polizzi, right. So I go see Mike and Tony and they give me this bullshit, all these fucking partners, this and that, and I end up with nothing."

"Bomp, why get mad at Johnny? If you feel they fucked you, clip them. That Tony Zerilli's a piece of shit. Him and Billy Giacalone are asshole buddies of Carlo Licata."

"Wait a minute," Bomp said. "Johnny's the fucking man in Vegas, right? I went to him, told him I was supposed to get some points. I didn't tell him why, you understand, and he said he'd look into it. Bullshit. The cocksucker ends up with the gift shop there. A fucking gold mine. If you want my opinion, I think he got points, too. Maurice Friedman, who owns the land, is Johnny's buddy, right? I think he gave Johnny a piece of his end."

Jimmy never found out who Bompensiero had killed or where the body was buried. It was a sore point with Bompensiero and Jimmy thought it wise to let the whole matter of Roselli and the Frontier lie.

For a time, Jimmy had hoped to buy Bill Graham's Golden Hotel in Reno, but on November 6, 1965, at the age of 76, Graham died and with him went another piece of Jimmy's dream. All he could look forward to now was the Tallyho, and that situation was not improving. Jimmy had invested the $35,-000, and when more money was needed, Angelo Marino invested an equal amount, and, finally, Frank LaPorte went in for a total of $150,000 in three installments.

It was a beautiful place and Jimmy would have loved nothing better than to strut around it like an owner. But that was impossible. He had to be extremely careful that his connection was not exposed. Whenever he met with Nealis it was in one of the back bungalows. At night sometimes he would park his car at the Dunes and walk across the strip, trying to appear casual to passersby as he inspected the progress of the construction, his head filled with images that made his heart sing. The casino was crowded with eager players gathered around all the tables. The orchestra was playing in the lounge but the sound that was real music to his ears was the cacophony of the casino itself—the whirring of slot machines, the smooth clicking of the roulette wheels, the dice bouncing against the cush-ioned backs of the crap tables, the cries of the players, the monotone voices of the dealers—a siren song.

After what seemed like an eternity, the casino was completed early in December, in plenty of time for its scheduled New Year's Eve opening gala. But on December 14, the gaming commission decided it needed another twenty days to complete its study of the owners. Ironically, it was the discovery of Sheriff Lamb's cousin on the list—he'd been added as illicit insurance that the license would be granted—that led to another postponement, this time of thirty days. By then Jimmy was beside himself.

Nealis was running around in circles, pleading for money with everyone he met, but it was all in vain. By March he had missed two payments on his lease, not to mention paychecks for the sixty Japanese girls, the rest of the staff, and the purveyors.

The next thing Jimmy knew, the authorities had padlocks on the place and Nealis was back in Los Angeles. Jimmy jumped into his car and drove to Nealis' house. By the time he walked into the living room, he was angry enough to strangle him with his bare hands.

"Jimmy, let's not even discuss it," Nealis said. "I've got a bad heart and my doctor tells me I shouldn't get excited."

"Fuck your doctor," Jimmy said. "Eddie, we've got two hundred and twenty thousand fucking dollars in that motherfucker, you know."

"Well, Jimmy, what can I tell you? We got taken. Milton Prell, that gambler from Oregon, had the inside track all along."

"What's that?"

"Yeah, he's got the joint, going to open next month. What can I tell you, we got fucked."

Jimmy sat down and looked at Nealis. Nealis was an old man and his dream, maybe his last one, was gone, too. "So what about our money?"

"Listen, I'm suing for four hundred thousand," Nealis said. "If I win you'll get your money."

"What about the bankroll money, the million on deposit?"

"Gone with the wind, Jimmy. I'm flat broke."

"You cocksucker, you never had that money. I ought to break your head."

"I wish you would, Jimmy. I'm tired, man, I could use a rest in the hospital."

Suddenly Jimmy was laughing. "Eddie, I was warned about you. I've only got myself to blame. Let me tell you something, you're one of the few guys that ever scammed me."

"I'm sorry about your thirty-five grand," Nealis said, and there were tears in his eyes.

Jimmy crossed his legs, leaned back in the chair, and stretched. "Forget it, Eddie. Besides it's thirty grand. Bomp and me had a little scam of our own going with the joint. Remember the big meat packing guy from San Francisco

Rudy Papale brought to the Tallyho and we gave him the meat contract for the joint?"

Eddie smiled. "Sure, I remember. I thought it was a scam, but I figured, what the hell, you're entitled."

"Bomp and me cut up ten grand on the deal. Papale, you know, is Alioto's brother-in-law. Bomp took him to Mexico City a while back to try to work out a lard deal for Baja California. See Bomp knows this Sammy Ybarra who's the head of a big hotel chain in Mexico. Somehow or other years ago Bomp saved this guy's kid from getting killed in Tijuana and they became good friends. Alioto was interested in that lard deal so Papale went to Mexico with Bomp. They paid all expenses, but Sammy couldn't work it out. So now they come back and when this meat packing guy in San Francisco hears we're not getting the license for the Tallyho, he starts screaming for his money back. I says, 'Say good-bye, baby, nobody gets no money back.' Eddie, that's the law. So forget about the thirty-five grand. It's all part of the fucking game. You win some, you lose some, life goes on."

16
THE RICE DEAL

† † † †

FOR SEVERAL YEARS, ONE OF JIMMY'S CLOSEST BUSINESS ASSOCIATES IN the Sacramento area was George Faris, the owner of Union Transportation and a breeder of race horses. Back in 1961, when Jimmy was trying to get started in Sacramento, Faris had dealt fairly with him, providing work on the Fresno freeway. From then on they had worked together on several construction jobs. In time their relationship had matured into a close friendship. In fact, Jimmy and Jewel had spent a New Year's Eve in Reno with George and his wife as guests of Bill Graham.

After months of thinking about the rice haul, Jimmy finally came up with what he felt was the right angle. First he needed a front, a partner with an impeccable reputation. No one fitted that role better than George Faris. They each owned about an equal amount of equipment, but Faris' office was a marvel of efficiency compared to the turmoil that always seemed to prevail at 6929 Power Inn Road.

When Faris heard Jimmy's proposal, he said, "Jimmy, if we get the rice haul we'll be set for life."

"First, George, we've got a couple of problems. Between us, we've got what, fifty, sixty pullers? But our trailers are no good for hauling rice."

"I know, but if we get the haul maybe we can buy Clark's trailers dirt cheap," Faris suggested. "What the hell, he won't have any need for them."

"I've done some checking on Clark Trucking," Jimmy said. "They've had the haul since 1956. Vern Clark died a few years ago and his partner Dick Cunha now runs the company."

"What are our chances, Jimmy?"

"Listen, George, I need something my friend Joe can take to the board. I plan to tell him we're going to save the rice growers fifty grand a year. You know somebody that don't want to save that kind of money?"

"But, Jimmy, I'm not sure we can save that much. I haven't studied it yet. How did you get that figure?"

"Shit, I just made it up, George, I'm giving the man an incentive, don't you understand? It's a con. You think I'm going to give them fifty thousand? You've got to be crazy. I'm giving Alioto a shot, that's all."

As was his custom, Jimmy dropped in on Alioto unannounced and began chatting about nothing in particular. He lit a cigar and smiled contentedly.

"Joe, I've done some research on this and I've got some good news for you."

Alioto perked up. "What's on your mind, Jimmy?"

"It's about the rice haul. I want it, Joe. The way I've got it figured out, I can save you fifty thousand dollars a year."

Alioto smiled. "Jimmy, that's impossible. The trucking is nothing."

"Joe, don't tell me it's nothing. I see these rice trucks moving day and night all year round practically. Clark Trucking's grossing over a million easy."

Alioto frowned. "That's hard to believe. Of course, I know nothing about that end of it. I leave that to the people who work with it on a daily basis."

"Let me explain something to you, Joe. Clark Trucking's getting PUC rates to haul one mile, two miles, and so on."

"What is wrong with that?"

"Joe, trust me, will you? I know what I'm talking about. If you get the PUC rate on short hauls you'll make a million dollars so fast it ain't funny. They've got rates for all kinds of hauls. Nobody else in the trucking business works by that book. That's why Clark's getting rich. They're probably netting two, three hundred thousand a year."

"My God, I had no idea it was this lucrative an operation."

"Joe, do me a favor. Check it out. First, though, let me explain that I've got a good legitimate front for this operation. George Faris of Union Transportation. This guy's a Stanford graduate and breeds thoroughbred horses at his Columbia Farm, which is the biggest in northern California. Everybody in Sacramento knows him. This guy's a real gentleman. Been around for years and respected by everybody. We're going into partnership on this deal but I'm keeping my name out of it, know what I mean? No need to raise a stink for nothing."

Alioto nodded gravely. "I will check it out, Jimmy, and you will be hearing from me."

Three weeks later Jimmy again met with Alioto. This time he brought George Faris along to demonstrate his good intentions. After the introduction, Alioto got right to the point. "Jimmy, you were right. I had no idea it was this big."

"Joe," Jimmy said, "I've talked this over with George. All I can tell you right now is that we're not going to fuck the rice growers. There's enough money in this for everybody. Clark's been too greedy. Ain't it funny to you nobody's checked into this before?"

"Jimmy," Alioto said, "I think you should go to the Rice Growers and talk to some of the people over there. Tell them I sent you."

"Who do I talk to?"

Alioto shrugged. "Why don't you have Mr. Faris talk to Bob Freeland or Fred Schoof. Whoever is directing that part of the operation. See what they have to say about it. Then get back to me and I will take it up before the next board meeting."

Having implicit faith in his ability as a negotiator, Jimmy decided to tackle the assignment himself. He walked around the mill where the trucks came in and after several inquiries was directed to a middle-aged man.

"Joe Alioto sent me to talk to you," Jimmy began, purposely avoiding an introduction. "I represent George Faris at Union Transportation and we're interested in taking over the rice haul from Clark Trucking."

The man looked at him as though he had lost his mind. "I beg your pardon?"

"We can save you fifty thousand dollars a year."

"But, my goodness, Clark has been doing our trucking for twenty years. We're perfectly satisfied with the arrangement."

"Hey!" Jimmy asked, "didn't you hear me? We can save you fifty thousand dollars a year. What's the difference if Clark had this haul forty years. I'm saving you fifty grand, don't that mean nothing to you?"

"Honestly, what is this all about? What is your name, sir?"

"My name's Mr. Fratianno and I'm representing Mr. George Faris of Union Transportation. I'm here speaking to you because Mr. Alioto's interested in saving fifty thousand a year. That's a lot of money, my friend."

It was almost a month before Jimmy again heard from Alioto. Angelo Marino called him to say that Alioto wanted to see him at his earliest convenience. When Jimmy walked into Alioto's office, the lawyer stood up and started pacing his office.

"Jimmy, I ran into a buzz saw at the board meeting," he said, not waiting for Jimmy to respond. "The minute I brought up the rice haul, Dick Cunha raised holy hell. He started screaming that Jimmy Fratianno, a gangster, was trying to take over his contract. So I told him to wait just one moment. I said, 'I'm sorry but I don't know anything about a Mr. Fratianno. I know George Faris and he's an honorable man. He says he can save us fifty thousand dollars a year and I think it is something worth discussing."

"Shit," Jimmy said, "I shouldn't have told that motherfucker my name."

Alioto waved his hand. "That's all right. Nothing's lost. We should let it cool off about six months. Stay away from them. Let me handle it, and we will get the haul. I think it is something worth waiting for, don't you?"

"Joe, I'm telling you, somebody's getting paid off."

"I hate to think so. Let's wait and see what develops."

It would be years before Jimmy would discover that the Rice Growers had just awarded Clark Trucking, which had been working on a yearly verbal agreement, a five-year contract.

PART V

✝ ✝ ✝ ✝

THE HELLHOLE
1966

17
EL CENTRO

† † † †

EL CENTRO, CALIFORNIA, BECAME JIMMY'S WATERLOO.

After five long years of building a successful trucking business, he destroyed it in less than six months. Not to mention what he did to himself in the bargain.

It began routinely enough. Another trucking broker, Fred ReCupido, asked Jimmy to join him as a sub-hauler for Miles and Sons, the prime contractor, in the moving of two and a half million tons of earth for the construction of a freeway bypass in El Centro.

A small farming community ten miles from the Mexican border, El Centro lies at the foot of the "lettuce belt" in California's Imperial Valley. Its climate is one of the most torrid in the nation. Jimmy, who had the snow removal contract for Highway 50 in the Lake Tahoe area, which is in the Sierra Nevada, thought he had worked in all kinds of climates, but there was nothing in his experience to prepare him for this dusty, fly-infested, scorching hellhole.

That was only for openers. After moving his equipment to El Centro, at a cost of about ten thousand dollars, he discovered that Miles and Sons was not paying the PUC rate of fourteen dollars an hour for truck and driver. Instead ReCupido had agreed to haul dirt for twenty-four cents a ton. The drivers received 30 percent of the gross earned, and to meet state and federal regulations requiring an hourly rate, the amount earned was then converted into hours. A truck and driver working ten hours would end up receiving pay for seven or eight hours. The first month on the job, Jimmy's company lost close to $15,000.

For the first time he lost money on a job, and he found it totally unacceptable. He took his problem to Dick Mason, the truck boss for Miles and Sons.

He went into Mason's office screaming. "Listen, here, goddamnit, what kind of tricks are you guys playing around here? I was promised the hourly rate when I took the job, not twenty-four cents a ton."

"Wait a minute," Mason said. "I never promised you an hourly rate."

"Fred ReCupido told me . . ."

"Hold it. I don't know what Fred told you, but if he promised you an hourly rate, he flat-out lied to you."

"Well, I don't give a shit who lied to who, I know I can't work here under them conditions."

"Please, Jimmy, let's grab some lunch and talk this over calmly like two civilized men."

Jimmy relented. They went to the Airport Inn and the air conditioning had a soothing effect on his nerves. They ordered drinks and lunch before continuing with the discussion.

Mason smiled. "Jimmy, think a moment, will you, and tell me how we could pay hourly rates on this kind of job. We'd go broke in a month. These guys just won't hustle."

"What're you talking about? The drivers are waiting fifteen, twenty minutes to get loaded. Christ, at some of the pits they're backed up a mile long, waiting in that heat. It must be a hundred-twenty in them cabs. What the fuck's it going to be like this summer?"

Mason nodded agreement. "That's another problem, Jimmy. The drivers are stopping for Cokes and beers, some are taking three hours to get laid, there's no way we can pay by the hour. This has got to be piece work."

"Get laid?" Jimmy snarled in disgust. "Where the fuck're they going to get laid in this fucking dump? Look, Dick, you're violating PUC regulations."

"Jimmy, everybody violates PUC regulations. How many times have you violated them?"

"Plenty of times, but never like this. I've never lost money before and I ain't planning on losing much more either."

"Jimmy, have you ever thought of selling your tractors to the drivers on conditional sale contracts?" Mason asked. "That way you can list them as owner-operator and get away from all that costly red tape, you know, unemployment, Workman's Comp, social security, union dues, pay scales, etcetera. It would really simplify your operation."

Jimmy nodded. "I've been thinking of doing that for a long time. Get the jobs, hire the pullers, and lease the trailers."

"Then do it. You can get the contract forms at Crossland's Office Supply. It's really the best way out for you. It also will save us a lot of office work if we can put down owner-operator on the certified payrolls we have to submit to Washington."

"It won't work," Jimmy said. "These assholes are always busted. And they're quitting right and left. They hate this town."

"Okay, tell your drivers that when this dirt haul is over I've got a gravel haul that will help you and them recoup all your losses. You can give me a bid on the whole thing, loading and hauling, and I'm sure you'll make up your losses."

"It's that big, eh?" Jimmy was already beginning to feel better.

"You bet, take my word for it. We're in a bind right now but we've got a good reputation with sub-haulers. You can't fuck people and survive in this business. Stick with us, Jimmy, and I guarantee you'll come out smelling like a rose."

The drivers were milling around in Jimmy's motel suite. There were cases of cold beer and they were guzzling it down as fast as Nick Diacogianis could pass the cans around. He called himself Nick the Greek and he had served time at Folsom with Jimmy. Upon his release from prison, he had come to Sacramento looking for a job. Jimmy had looked at him, a big, tough, half-witted and half-blind con with bifocals so thick that he looked like he was peering through a couple of crystal balls.

"Nick," Jimmy had asked, "what the hell can you do besides break bones?"

"Well, shit, Jimmy, I need a fucking job or they'll violate me."

That was something Jimmy understood all too well. He had sent him to one of LaPorte's gold mines to guard his equipment, and when the El Centro job had come along, he had brought him down as a kind of handyman, picking up the driver's freight tickets at night, getting parts for the mechanics, and seeing that the drivers got to work on time and stayed on the job. Jimmy's foreman was Kenneth Bentley, a first-rate mechanic, and his assistant was Ray Giarusso. Diacogianis and Giarusso would occasionally steal some of Jimmy's equipment when Jimmy wanted to collect tax-free money from the insurance policy so generously provided by Allen Dorfman, who handled the Teamsters' insurance. A night's work of stealing 150 tires and wheels, valued at $18,000, did nicely to keep Jimmy in pocket money.

Jimmy came into the room smoking a big cigar and Nick's booming voice brought the drivers to attention. Jimmy smiled and accepted a can of beer from Nick. "You boys enjoying yourselves?"

This was met by whistles and laughter. Jimmy raised his beer can in a salute and gulped some down, wiping his mouth with the back of his hand. Just one of the boys.

"Fellows," he said, "hold it down a minute, will you? I've got something important to say." He waited until he had their full attention before going on. "How would you guys like to own your own tractors, be owner-operators instead of just drivers?"

"Hey, you going out of business?" one driver asked.

Jimmy smiled. "Just that end of it. I want to get away from all the paperwork, the red tape bullshit. I'll still get the jobs but I'll lease my trailers to guys with pullers. On a job like this one we'd all make money instead of getting fucked."

"I don't get it," another driver said. "We're all busted. How can we buy a thirty-thousand-dollar rig?"

"Just a minute," Jimmy said. "Nick's going to pass out some conditional contracts. They're all filled out. All you've got to do is sign them. Right now all this does is make you a conditional buyer until you've got enough money for the down payment. Then we'll go to the bank and finance it. I'll get my equity, pay off the balance, and you become the registered owner."

James Garrett, a driver whom Jimmy had already pegged as a troublemaker, handed the contract back to him. "This is a trick," he said, "to fuck us out of our benefits."

Jimmy let the contract drop to the floor. "Hey, nobody has to sign this contract, but anyone that don't is going to be looking for another job in the morning. The way I figure it, we can deduct so much from your paycheck until you've got the down payment."

Garrett picked up the contract. "What does this mean," he asked, reading from the contract, "that the driver 'agrees to lease tractor exclusively to the Fratianno Trucking Company. Driver and tractor to be under complete control of Fratianno Trucking Company. Buyer agrees to work whenever and wherever jobs are offered by Fratianno Trucking company.' "

"It means what it says," Jimmy replied. "You think I'm going to sell you a puller on a conditional contract and have you take off with it before I get my fucking money? Listen, you don't want to sign, find another job. Besides you're always late to work."

All the drivers signed that night except Garrett who signed the next morning. Dick Mason was delighted. "This will simplify our bookkeeping," he told Jimmy on the telephone. "Now, you can start making money on this job."

Within two weeks all but two of the drivers who had signed the contract had quit and Jimmy had permanently discarded the idea. Miles and Sons, however, continued to list his drivers as "owner-operators" on its certified payrolls, even though Jimmy had informed them of the venture's failure and all his freight tickets turned over to Miles and Sons listed his men as drivers and his company as the owner. To simplify matters even further, Miles and Sons continued using the names of the original buyers months after they were gone. They submitted the same certified payroll week after week without any indication of the hectic turnover taking place. The payroll made out in Sacramento by Jewel and Joanne listed the men as drivers but computed their wages according to the "guidelines," which not only shortened a driver's number of hours worked but reduced his share of the $14 an hour pay scale to $3.78, far below union and PUC scales.

As always Jimmy had established his credentials with the local Teamsters official and had nothing to worry about from that end. As for the Public Utilities Commission, the entire apparatus appeared moribund, strangling in its own red tape. If they ever cracked down on contractors violating its regulations, all construction in the state would come to an immediate standstill.

During his brief visits to El Centro, never more than two days at a time, Jimmy shared a motel suite with Bompensiero and Diacogianis. Leo Moceri came for a visit and gave ReCupido ten thousand dollars to shylock at five percent interest per week. Jimmy was already lending money to his drivers at that same interest rate. With Jimmy, LaPorte, Bompensiero, and Moceri strutting around that small town, it was only a question of time before their presence would be discovered.

18
JEAN

† † † †

THE FIRST TIME HE SAW HER HE WAS IN THE SMALL WAITING ROOM AT the El Centro Airport. She was reading a magazine and her shoulder-length hair was a radiant gold under a bright blue straw hat.

The moment the announcement was made that the plane was ready for boarding, Jimmy grabbed her suitcase. "Miss, do you mind if I carry your bag?"

She looked at him and Jimmy caught a little spark of excitement in her hazel eyes. "It's too hot for a beautiful girl to be carrying her own bag," he said, leading her out the door and toward the plane.

"Thank you," she said, and there was a lovely lilt in her voice.

They went up the steps into the airplane and Jimmy said, "Excuse me, I'll put your bag under the seat. This window seat okay?"

"It's fine, thank you." She settled in and Jimmy sat next to her. He looked at her and smiled, the excitement building up inside him.

"Do you live here?" she asked.

Jimmy laughed. "You've got to be kidding. I live in Sacramento. I'm a building contractor and some of my trucks are working on the freeway here. And you, what's your excuse for being here?"

She smiled, her white teeth flashing in the sunlight slanting through the small Plexiglas window. "A friend of mine from San Diego had a party in Mexicali."

"Are you from San Diego?"

She gave him a slanted, amused look. "No. Los Angeles."

Jimmy scratched his head. "Well, that narrows it down some. Look, my name's Jimmy Fratianno and I just want to be friendly."

"I'm Jean Bodul and I thought I was being friendly."

"Hey, you're pretty quick, I like that in a broad . . ." he laughed, shaking his head. "You'll have to excuse me, I've been around truck drivers too long."

"It's all right. I'm not offended. I've heard that expression once or twice before."

"Thanks. You're okay. Look, Jean, I don't know anybody in Los Angeles and I come through here two, three times a week. To be truthful with you, sometimes I stay all night and I'm very lonesome. Now, Jean, you know, I don't want you to get the wrong impression, all I'm looking for is a little companionship, someone to share an evening with me, to talk, have a few laughs. Know what I mean, Jean?"

"I know exactly what you mean," she said, and there was an amused glint in her eyes. "You're crazy about my bright conversation."

"I sure am, Jean. I'm crazy about everything you've got. Look, Jean, I've got a couple hours to kill before I catch my plane to Vegas, why don't we grab something to eat and carry on this pleasant conversation."

"I'm sorry, but I've got a million things to do."

"Oh, come on, Jean, give a guy a break. What've you got to lose? The minute I start boring you, just get up and leave. Okay?"

She laughed, and to Jimmy it sounded like music. "All right, but you better behave."

In the airport restaurant, they ordered drinks and he lit his first cigar. He felt expansive in that familiar atmosphere.

"You go to Vegas much?" he asked.

"I've been there a few times, but I've been too busy lately. I'm a working mother. I'm divorced and have a five-year-old daughter to support."

Jimmy shook his head sadly. "A beautiful young girl like you shouldn't have to work. What's your line?"

Jimmy could see that she was flattered by his compliment. "I sell cosmetics to beauty shops and department stores."

"Where's your daughter?"

"She's with my mother in San Pedro. Her name's Annette and she's really a sweet kid."

"Ah, I'll bet you really love her. I'm crazy about kids, myself. They're so honest, you know, tell you exactly what they think, no bullshit. Everything's up front."

She looked at him, her bright eyes undecided for a moment, and Jimmy thought he could see a mental shrug. "Do you have trucks working in Las Vegas, too?" she asked.

"Yes, but that's not why I'm going there now," he said, removing the cigar from his mouth. He leaned forward. "This is between us, okay, our little secret, but I've got a little investment that's going to pay off big."

"Oh, boy, you're something else," she said, but she was smiling.

"Let me tell you about this invention," he said. "It's really fantastic. I've got this kid from Australia, sharp little engineer, a real genius, working it out. It's a horse-racing machine, sort of a cross between a pinball and slot machine. Must have a million little electrodes and stuff in there. Believe me, I know, I've had to pay for most of it."

"How does it work? I can't visualize it."

"It's just like going to the track. You can put up to ten dollars in the slot, pull the lever, and the horses run. You bet the same as you would at a track, work out a daily double, parlays, bet across the board, the works."

"Sounds really complicated. Is it finished?"

"No, but it's coming along great. He's been working on it two years. It's a model he's working on, but when we get this thing mass produced, forget about it, it's going to revolutionize gambling. It's going to work just like a slot machine, but tell me, what would you rather do, pull the handle on a slot or bet on a horse race? You've got any idea how many horse players there are in this country?"

She smiled. "You can see your ship coming in over the horizon?"

He leaned back in his chair and puffed vigorously on his cigar. "I wish you could see it. Some day when you come to Vegas, give me a call and I'll show it to you. You know, I've got a home in Vegas."

"I thought you said you lived in Sacramento."

"I've got homes in both places."

"That must be nice." She paused, as if undecided, then said, "Are you married?"

"We're getting divorced, but married, not married, don't make no difference to me. I run my life to suit myself and she does the same. It's a free world. Know what I mean, Jeannie?"

"You're coming through loud and clear," she said, reaching for her handbag. "This has been fun but I really must run."

Jimmy looked alarmed and she laughed. "It's nothing you've said. I do have loads of things to do."

"At least, give me your phone number so I can call you next time I'm in town. What've you got to lose?"

She quickly scribbled a number on a piece of paper and handed it to him. "Please, finish your drink and good luck with your invention."

And she was gone. He sat there wondering where he had gone wrong.

For two years, Jimmy's end of the horse-racing machine had been financed by the gambling winnings of Abe Benjamin, an old friend from his Los Angeles days. Through Jimmy's intercession with Yale Cohen and Al Sachs, Abe Benjamin and two accomplices were permitted to play cards at the Stardust. Teamed together in high-stake games of lowball poker against unwary gamblers, they were invincible. Half of Benjamin's earnings, after expenses (his room at the Stardust was at the low complimentary rate), were handed over to the engineer for salary, parts and rent for the workshop.

The machine had reached the stage where Jimmy felt it was time for Roselli's opinion. They met at the Desert Inn Country Club. Roselli's reserved table overlooked the eighteenth green. Between rounds of golf, steam baths, and the romancing of gorgeous showgirls, there was time for audiences with those worthy of his favors. That table gained enormous significance to insiders with an understanding of local machinations.

After Jimmy had explained the situation, Roselli said, "How much money have you sunk into this thing?"

Jimmy shrugged. "I don't know, Johnny, maybe a hundred grand. This guy's been working on it a couple years. By the way, Danny Wilson's the guy that brought this engineer to Abe and me. This kid from Youngstown, Freddy Fox, is the one who found the engineer. He's from Australia and a fucking genius with electronics. Johnny, this fucking machine does everything but tell jokes and tap dance."

They drove to the engineer's workshop and as Roselli inspected the machine, Jimmy knew he was impressed.

"Jimmy, if this horse-racing machine works out the way this guy described it, I think it could be one of the biggest money-makers in gambling history."

Jimmy smiled happily. "Goddamnit, Johnny, I knew I had something there. But who can we get to mass produce this thing when his model's ready?"

"No problem, Jimmy," Roselli said. "But let's wait until Sam's out of the Cook County Jail. He should be out in a few weeks. Let me explain something, Jimmy. I could take it to Joe Batters or Paul Ricca, but I'd rather go with Sam. We talk the same language."

"What've you got in mind?"

"Number one," Johnny explained, "the Chicago family controls Bally and has controlled it right from the beginning. I'm going back now to Capone and Nitti, when Bally, under another name, was making slots and pinballs for the outfit. Now Bally's the world's biggest manufacturer of slot machines and pinballs."

"We had their machines in Cleveland when I was a kid. I hear from Babe Triscaro that the Teamsters got big money in Bally and some of the union officials own stock in it."

"We could get Bally involved in both the financing and development of it."

Jimmy frowned. "Well, Johnny, they'd have to come up with a good deal. We don't want to get fucked on this thing."

"Don't worry, when the time comes for a deal I'll have my attorney, Jimmy Cantillon, make sure the fine print's okay. Remember his old man, Dick Cantillon? We used to meet in his office back in the old days when I was still on parole. Well, his kid turned out to be a pretty sharp mouthpiece. But for now, let's wait for Sam, then we'll put the pieces together."

The next time Jimmy was going to be in Los Angeles he called ahead to make a date with Jean Bodul, but found she had given him her mother's number. After several calls, he finally reached her. He was angry but he played it cool, and after some friendly persuasion, she agreed to dine with him the next evening.

Jimmy flew in from San Francisco, rented a blue Chevrolet at the airport, picked her up at her Gower Street apartment, which she shared with a girl friend, and drove directly to the Villa Capri on the Sunset Strip. For added insurance, Jimmy had called the owner, Patsy D'Amora, so he could alert the staff of his arrival. Patsy, the maitre d', the captain, the wine steward, and waiters started falling over each other the moment they walked in. By the time they reached their table, protected by a reserved card, Jean's eyes were big as saucers. It was, "Good evening, Mr. Fratianno, so nice to see you again, sir. Please, this way Mr. Fratianno. I hope this table is satisfactory, sir. Watch your step, Miss." And Patsy rubbing his hands and repeating, "What a pleasure." And so it went, with appropriate bowing and scraping, chair pulling, water glasses brought at a trot, matches flicking from out of nowhere the instant a cigarette came into sight.

"My God," she said, after the staff was out of earshot. "Who are you, Ally Kahn or Rubirosa?"

Jimmy shrugged. "Them guys don't get this kind of service."

"Who are you anyway? How come I've never heard your name before?"

Jimmy curled his lower lip in a deprecating expression. "I'm nobody."

She smiled. "Try telling that to these jokers jumping around here like they've got ants in their pants. I don't dare look in their direction, they'd probably trip and break a leg getting here."

"It's nothing," Jimmy said. "I've known Patsy for years. You want to see some real service, come to Vegas with me sometime. Ringside seat to any show you want, everything on the house."

"You're a mystery man, Jimmy Fratianno. I'm going to have to look you up in *Who's Who.*"

Jimmy laughed so hard he nearly swallowed his cigar.

A few weeks later, Jimmy moved Jean to a new apartment on Normandie Avenue. "Now, you're my girl," he said.

"Wait a minute, buster," Jean said. "Paying the rent don't give you exclusive rights to my life. I just got rid of my husband—and he was one jealous, possessive son of a bitch. I'm not going that route again. I'll pay my own rent, thank you."

Jimmy grabbed her roughly and kissed her. "Will you shut up?" he said. "All I ask is when I call for a date, I get priority."

"No last minute phone calls, you hear? I'm not going to sit around here all week waiting for the phone to ring. I've got my own life to live."

"Hey, Jeannie, enough already. I've got the picture, okay? Look, I'm going down to La Costa on business this afternoon. How about my dropping you at your mother's place so I can meet that kid of yours?"

"That's sweet," Jean said, hugging him. "I haven't seen Annette myself in a couple weeks. You'll love her."

Jean was right. Jimmy and Annette fell for each other in a big way.

"What's your name?" Annette asked him.

"My name's Jimbo, king of the dwarfs."

She giggled. "No, you're not."

"Hey, look here, Punkie—"

"My name's Annette."

"No it's not. It's Punkie. See, you remind me of the queen of the dwarfs. Ah, she was so beautiful and she was crazy in love with me." Jimmy paused and shook his head sadly. "Oh, Punkie, it was terrible. I really liked her, you know. She was so sweet but her husband was jealous. He didn't understand what we felt for each other."

"Did he beat her up bad?"

"Not on your life. I protected her. One time he caught me with my step ladder and he just about went crazy. He was jumping up and down. Boy, did he have a bad temper."

"Oh, my goodness," she cried, her big brown eyes filled with horror, "what happened?"

"See, Punkie, I carried this stepladder around in case the queen wanted to give me a little kiss, you know, from time to time."

"Couldn't you bend over?"

"Oh, Punkie, how could you think that? Kings don't bend over for nobody, not even queens. She'd climb the ladder and we could look deep into each other's eyes, and sometimes we kissed, and then sometimes she whispered secrets in my ear she didn't want her husband to hear."

"Was her name Punkie?"

"That's right. How did you know that? You know, she really loved that name."

"What was her husband's name?"

"Punko. See, they had this act in this circus, Punko and Punkie, and I used to live with them when they came to the fairgrounds in Cleveland. That's when I was a young man."

"Was you tall like now?"

"Oh, yes, but them little dwarfs liked to bet on the horse races and I would kind of hold their money for them. Make sure that the winners got paid off."

"Do you miss her now?"

"I did for a long time, you know, but now that I've met you, I feel like maybe fate's brought us together. Now I've got myself a new Punkie . . . if you don't mind my calling you that."

"Oh, no, it's okay, Jimbo. Call me Punkie all you want."

"That's my sweet little Punkie, come on, give old Jimbo a big kiss."

She reached up with her little arms and he bent over to kiss her. "Oh, oh," she cried. "You forgot your ladder."

"Punkie, I've got to tell you something. I hope you don't mind, but I'm not a king no more. I'm only a friend and friends, you know, don't mind bending to kiss nice little Punkies."

Roselli was coming toward him, he nodded in recognition, and hurried into the golf shop. Jimmy followed without speaking. Once outside they got into a golf cart and sped down a winding path.

Rancho La Costa, some thirty miles north of San Diego, was the realization of Moe Dalitz's dream. With the death of Lou Rhody, Dalitz had assumed leadership of the Cleveland group and had expanded their holdings in Las Vegas with multimillion-dollar loans from the Teamsters Central States, Southeast and Southwest Areas Pension Fund, with offices in Chicago. Dalitz's long-range plan at Rancho La Costa, also to be financed with Teamsters' millions, called for a luxurious complex that would include a deluxe resort hotel, a championship golf course and clubhouse, an AMA-approved health spa, convention facilities, all of it enclosed by palatial homes and condominiums—an ultra-private playground reserved for the rich and powerful.

For its sheer plush ambience, Rancho La Costa equaled anything in Las Vegas and Palm Springs. The heart of this vast adult playground was the Country Club with its high-ceilinged lobby, restaurants, bars and shops. Its large windows gave a panoramic view of the lush rolling fairways and the crystal blue water of the Olympic-sized swimming pool. It was strange to think that this dream world had its origins in the dirty streets of Cleveland all those many years ago, with Jimmy operating his own limousine service to bring suckers to Dalitz's crummy joints.

Roselli turned his head slightly as he drove the cart and winked at Jimmy. "Glad you could make it, buddy."

"My pleasure," Jimmy said. "Johnny, look at this place. Sometimes, Johnny, I feel like I want to clip them Jews. They made it on our fucking sweat and blood."

"Jimmy, let it go. It's no good spinning your wheels about something you can't change."

Roselli brought the cart to a stop in front of a new home with a sloping red-tiled roof and fancy iron grillwork at the windows. It was instant Spanish architecture, a California specialty.

"Some layout," Jimmy said.

Roselli laughed. "It beats the Cook County jail." It was Roselli's first hint that Jimmy was there to see Sam Giancana, who had served a year in the Cook County jail when he had refused to testify before a grand jury after he was granted immunity.

As they walked into the large living room, their footsteps were absorbed by the thick white carpeting. Giancana was there to greet them.

They sat in deep-cushioned chairs and at first Sam talked about the death of Bill Graham. "That guy was a real close friend," he said. "I'd have trusted him with my life. Now you can't say much more about a man."

"Yeah, and in his day this guy was a worker," Jimmy said. "He was telling me one time that he had Frankie Frost clip Mert Wertheimer in Reno. You know, the guy that had the Riverside Hotel."

Roselli laughed. "That brings up memories, right, Sam? Frankie's real name's Foster. Back in 1930, him and Ted Newbury clipped that Chicago

Tribune reporter Jake Lingle for Capone. There was more fucking heat on that one killing than for the St. Valentine's Day massacre."

Giancana smiled. "Jimmy, I hear Bill's wife got all his money."

"Ain't that something," Jimmy said. "She was over ninety, had been dying of cancer for years, and she outlived him."

"Speaking of money," Giancana said. "What ever happened to that guy in Reno with those hookers. Remember, you were working on some river building dams?"

"Oh, yeah," Jimmy said. "Listen to this, Sam. He gets transferred back East, New Jersey, I think, and one day I get this call from him. He says, 'Jimmy, do you happen to know anybody around here that knows any girls like the ones in Reno?' What do you think of that, for Christ's sake?"

"Jimmy, you've ruined that fucking guy," Giancana said. "See, he's going to be looking for that shit the rest of his life and never find it again."

After more conversation, Giancana finally got around to Jimmy's horseracing machine. "Johnny tells me it looks promising," he said. "I've given it some thought and I want my man at Bally, Lou Lederer, to have a look at it."

"Hey," Jimmy interrupted, "I know him."

"Yeah, you probably met him in Vegas," Giancana said. "Anyway, I want him to look your machine over and if it's as good as you guys say it is, then I think you should make a deal. But let Lou work it out. Whatever he says to you, remember, he's talking for our family. If you need development money, don't worry about it, Lou will take care of it."

It was a week later when they met in Cantillon's office to iron out the details. There was Jimmy, Abe Benjamin, Freddy Fox, Danny Wilson, Johnny Roselli, and Lou Lederer, who took charge of the meeting.

"I like your machine," he said. "I think it's something Bally could be interested in if it can be simplified. It's a little too complicated right now. You don't need all that extra shit like daily doubles and parlays. That's the kind of stuff that sends the price sky high when you get into mass production. Your engineer tells me he's having trouble getting parts and I told him we'd see he gets what he wants once we get this deal ironed out. When it comes time to mass produce this thing, we'll put up all the money and go fifty-fifty. But the model's got to be perfected first. What do you think?"

"Sounds great to me," Jimmy said.

Freddy Fox looked worried. "What's this I hear about you taking our engineer to Chicago for a while?"

"What's that?" Jimmy asked.

"Nothing to get excited about," Lederer said. "We think he should look over our layout, see how we put these machines together, and get an idea of the parts available. It'll save time in the long run."

"Hey, Lou, don't forget, we want this guy back."

"Of course, Jimmy," Lederer said. "I'd say a couple months at most."

"I don't like it," Freddy Fox said. "What's going to happen to our machine while he farts around Chicago? And who's going to pay him?"

"We are," Lederer said. "We're giving him five hundred a week."

Jimmy jumped up. "You crazy, we've been paying him two hundred. Now when he comes back he'll want five hundred."

"Listen, fellows, as Sam told you, leave it to me. It's going to work out to everybody's benefit. You couldn't be in better hands than Bally's."

19
"MAFIA IN VALLEY"

† † † †

NICK DIACOGIANIS LIKED HIS NEW JOB. HE WAS NOT CRAZY ABOUT THE heat and flies, but he enjoyed the responsibility Jimmy placed on his broad shoulders.

One of his duties was to see that the drivers were punctual in the morning, and the one consistent thorn in his side was James Garrett, the outspoken driver Jimmy had earlier pegged as a troublemaker. Some mornings Garrett would not show up before eight o'clock. When advised of the problem, Jimmy told Diacogianis to fire Garrett the next time he was late.

A few days later Bompensiero called Jimmy in Las Vegas to say that Diacogianis was in the El Centro jail.

Diacogianis was beside himself with worry when Jimmy saw him in the visitor's room. "Hey, Jimmy, you going to fire me?"

"No," Jimmy said. "Now just give me the fucking story."

"Well, see, Jimmy, this guy's late again and like you told me, I took his truck keys and he ran to the union hall, yelling threats and shit. So now I see him coming back with his hands in his pockets. You know, when they come at you with a shiv in the joint, their fucking hands are in their pockets to hide it, so I gave him a shot in the mouth, knocked him on his ass. He ain't mad no more. Now he's scared. He starts running and I'm right after him, but when I see he's going to the cops, I take off the other way." He paused and looked at Jimmy, a confused expression on his face. "Where the fuck do you hide in this town?"

"Nick, why didn't you just follow him inside the police station and tell them your side of the story instead of running away" Jimmy asked. "Now they're going to believe him instead of you."

"Shit, I don't know. I got scared, I guess. You know, with my record, who'd believe me?"

On July 7, 1966, the *Imperial Valley Press* published the most sensational story in El Centro history. The banner headline proclaimed:

Exclusive Story

MAFIA PRESENT
IN VALLEY

The Mafia is reaching it's tentacles into the Imperial Valley.

The Bump, the Weasel, and Nick the Greek have taken up residence in El Centro. They are operating Fratianno Trucking Lines, Inc., which is engaged in hauling dirt for the new freeway being constructed across the southern edge of the county. . . .

After lengthy and hyperbolic descriptions of the central characters and their past deeds, which described LaPorte as "perhaps the biggest man in the Mafia today," it reported that Jimmy's "firm had sold a 1965 International Harvester tractor-truck to driver James Garrett for $16,500. The payments were to be $477.91 a month. A percentage of the payment for each load of dirt transported was to be applied toward the monthly payments. . . . If the driver does not stand for 'complete control' he can lose his truck and all that he has put into it. Garrett was apparently thrashed by Diacogianis when he showed independence. . . . Four trucks have been repossessed in El Centro during the period." As for the threat to El Centro itself, "the Mafia follows a pattern when it moves into a new area. It uses a legitimate business cover and soon starts to obtain 'control.' One of the 'controls' the Mafia is seeking is that of 'all trucking operations from San Francisco south.' They have boasted of that. 'Control' is also sought in the area of local government. The Mafia has that in Calumet City, for example, and to a large degree in Las Vegas."

The most serious inaccuracy, and the one that Jimmy would never be able to shake off, concerned James Garrett's charge that drivers had allegedly made payments toward the purchase of his trucks. Not one penny was ever paid by a driver or withheld from a paycheck toward the purchase of a truck.

Within hours of the publication of the story, Imperial County District Attorney James E. Hamilton (no relation to Jimmy's old nemesis, the since deceased Captain James Hamilton of the Los Angeles Police Department) had launched an investigation, abetted by State Attorney General Thomas Lynch, who sent one of his top aides, Richard D. Huffman, to take charge of the probe.

In the next four years, as the blows came with paralyzing force, Roselli made sure that his personal attorney, James P. Cantillon, was at Jimmy's side.

On August 15, 1966, charges of criminal conspiracy to defraud employees and the state were filed against Miles and Sons and Fratianno Trucking, as corporations, and five individuals: Jimmy; Bompensiero; Diacogianis; Fred ReCupido, the subcontractor responsible for bringing Jimmy to El Centro; and Jimmy's foreman, Kenneth Bentley. Bail for Diacogianis, who was already serving ninety days for his attack on Garrett, was not possible. ReCupido and

Bentley were released on minimal bail; but for Jimmy and Bompensiero bail was set at $55,000 each.

For the twenty-two days it took Cantillon to get their bail reduced, they sweltered in the ancient El Centro jail. It was still too early to assess the effect this would have on his trucking company, but he knew that his work in El Centro was finished. On August 18, he sent word to his assistant foreman, Ray Giarusso, to remove all his equipment from Imperial County, and four days later State Labor Commissioner Sigmund Arywitz ordered the Public Works Director to stop payments to Miles and Sons, which meant that Jimmy would not be paid the $100,000 owed him for his last month's work. It was a stunning blow, particularly since he had already paid his drivers. A few weeks later Arywitz fined Fratianno Trucking $59,250 for labor law infractions, which was the largest fine ever assessed against a trucking company in California. The biggest up to that time had been $5,000.

Jimmy was fit to be tied. Back in 1953 Arywitz had been Sam Otto's flunky at the time Jimmy had made his move against the garment industry, the fruits of which Louie Dragna was now enjoying in Los Angeles. In Jimmy's mind, Arywitz had found a way to get back at him.

Sixty-six witnesses would testify during a preliminary hearing that would last nearly three months. Jimmy sat alone at the defendants' table with Cantillon and three other attorneys. The other defendants were seated behind him, leaving no doubt as to who was top honcho in that group.

The surprise came on September 26 when ReCupido took the stand as a state's witness, having been granted immunity from prosecution. Objections by Cantillon were overruled. Hamilton would later explain to newsmen that ReCupido could help him make a case against Fratianno, whom he charged had brought the Mafia to Imperial Valley.

The judge apparently agreed. He ruled that all defendants, except Bentley and ReCupido, be bound for trial. Defense counsels took their case to the Superior Court, asking it to determine if there was sufficient evidence to proceed.

On January 5, 1967, Superior Court Judge Victor Gillespie ordered the charges against Bompensiero dropped and Hamilton conceded that evidence of conspiracy was lacking. Suddenly Bompensiero was a free man. Outside the courtroom, photographers took pictures of Cantillon and Bompensiero shaking hands. What no one suspected at the time was that Bompensiero had made a deal with the FBI. His fear of prison and the persuasive manner of Special Agent Jack Armstrong had turned him into an FBI informant. It would eventually cost him his life, but for the ten years that he worked with Armstrong, Bompensiero gave him a liberal education in the operation of La Cosa Nostra, with particular emphasis on the movements of his best friend, Jimmy Fratianno.

Six weeks later, conspiracy charges against the remaining defendants were dismissed by Judge Gillespie, but this time Hamilton filed an appeal.

In his ruling, Gillespie said, "There is absolutely no evidence whatsoever in the 2,468-page transcript of the preliminary hearing that the documents prepared by either James Fratianno or Fratianno Trucking Lines, or any of the truck drivers, were prepared with intent of fraudulent or deceitful purposes." He noted that while there were indications that at least some of the PUC rules had been violated there was no evidence of a conspiracy. The violation of PUC regulations, however, left the road open for a case of conspiring to commit a misdemeanor, which in California is a felony. "But this court," said the judge, "questions whether it or any other court in the state, with the exception of the Supreme Court, can rule on the matter until a decision has been reached in a hearing before the commission."

For the moment Jimmy thought he was home free, but there were deeper rumblings on the horizon and his trucking firm was in shambles. Six banks were clamoring for payments which were now seven months in arrears. Desperate for money, Jimmy stole one of his older trucks, and with Giarusso's help, stripped it of its engine, transmission, differential, wheels, tires, and other "goodies," and buried the carcass after cutting it into sections with a torch. Reporting the truck as stolen to the insurance company, he collected $10,000.

Another effort to raise cash took him to Las Vegas. For six years a little burr in his brain had been scratching away at his peace of mind, the irritation growing until the compulsion to act finally became irresistible. Picked up at the Las Vegas airport by John Anthony, he was driven to the Desert Inn where he conferred with Roselli before going to Benny Binion's Horseshoe Club in downtown Las Vegas. They walked around the tables, pushing their way through the crowded room until Jimmy spotted the Cowboy coming out of the restaurant. Cautioning Anthony to stay back, Jimmy walked up and touched Binion on the arm.

"Hey, Benny, you know me?"

Binion nodded, his eyes expressionless as he studied him. "Yeah, I know you. How're you, Jimmy?"

"Well, Benny, I ain't too fucking good. You know, I did six and a half years and now I'm indicted again and they've got my money tied up."

"Well, what do you want from me?"

"Benny, let's not play games. Forget about what I want. I've got something coming from you. You know I'm the guy that did the fucking job on Russian Louie, don't you?"

"Yeah, I know it."

"So how come I don't get no money?"

"What do you need?"

"I want sixty thousand."

"You've got it, Jimmy. Give me a day to get it together."

"That's number one, Benny. Number two, we was supposed to get twenty-five percent of that Fremont joint. What happened to that deal?"

"Jimmy, don't you know what happened? Jack wanted cash instead. Just as well, cause I got fucked real good on that deal by Eddie Levinson." Binion's eyes hardened. "Someday I'm going to take care of that guy."

"Are you saying you want him clipped?"

Binion smiled. "You're right, but let's wait a while. If you're interested I'll get back to you."

"I'm interested in listening to the proposition," Jimmy said. "Okay, I'll be back tomorrow for the money."

There were two payments of thirty thousand each over a period of a week's time. Each time the money was stacked in two shoe boxes, and each time Jimmy went to John Anthony's house to count it. He divided it into four equal shares. He kept $15,000, gave $15,000 to Bompensiero, and $30,000 to Roselli to divide with Alderisio. Jimmy had not changed. His trucking business was in deep trouble, but he was still cutting up his money.

PART VI

† † † †

LOOSE AS
A MONGOOSE
1966–1970

20
HOWARD HUGHES MOVES IN

† † † †

THE BIG STORY IN LAS VEGAS DURING THIS PERIOD WAS HOWARD Hughes. His arrival on Thanksgiving Day, 1966, was like a miracle, something on the order of a divine blessing, for he came with the largest fortune in cash ever held by one man. Forced by the courts to sell his entire holdings in Trans World Airlines, his net profit was estimated as $470 million.

This bonanza presented the eccentric billionaire with an unprecedented tax situation. To avoid becoming subject to the Undistributed Profits Tax (a special tax on profits retained by corporations beyond the needs of the company), it was vital that the money be reinvested within two years. Another tax provision required that passive income—rents, dividends, capital gains, interests, etc.—amount to no more than twenty percent of gross income. No business generates a bigger gross more quickly than gambling. And there were other visible inducements. Nevada had no corporate or personal income tax, no inheritance tax, no franchise tax, no warehouse tax. The sales tax was only three percent and real estate taxes were limited to five percent by the state constitution. And there were invisible inducements.

It was not mere chance that had brought him directly to the Desert Inn. Occupying the entire ninth-floor penthouse and cloistered behind blackout draperies and armed-guarded steel doors, "the Spook of American capitalism," as *Fortune* once labeled him, was about to embark on an historic buying spree of local real estate.

As far as Johnny Roselli and his associates were concerned, his arrival could not have been more timely if they had arranged it themselves, which in a real sense they had. Real estate was in a tailspin, with thousands of foreclosures, and for nearly a year the gambling interests in Las Vegas and J. Edgar Hoover had been at loggerheads over the issue of the FBI's illegal bugging of casinos in an attempt to uncover skimming of gambling profits on behalf of hidden Mafia interests. To compound matters, Hoover had tried to shift the onus onto former Attorney General Robert F. Kennedy, a maneuver not calculated to soften the spotlight focused on Nevada's gangster-ridden image.

With Hughes' arrival, the Las Vegas publicity mill had gone into action. He was pictured as a social dragon slayer. Singlehandedly, he would retrieve the city from the clutches of the Mafia. Later, of course, as he acquired certain hotel properties, this myth would gain tremendous popularity in the national press. Nothing could have been further from the truth. No one knew this better than Robert Maheu, Hughes' alter-ego in Nevada, the same Robert Maheu who had conscripted Roselli into the CIA plot to kill Castro.

But playing to the press was just one of Maheu's many talents. His boss, he eagerly volunteered to newsmen, had selected Nevada because it was one of the last frontiers. It would provide Hughes with "A last opportunity to build a model city because of the sufficiency of raw land available in all directions." In fact, Hughes, Maheu added, had made that decision back in 1954, but "you understand, of course, that there's naturally a time lag between a decision of this magnitude and the implementation."

It sounded so wonderful. The avaricious lunatic, reclusing like a mole in the penthouse, was being transformed into a great humanitarian, the answer to all those unanswered prayers. The sly manipulator was now the magnanimous builder. It was such an easy con. The only building he would do in his four-year hiatus would be the pipe dreams that he and Maheu would build in each other's heads.

Johnny Roselli and his friends, however, were not interested in pipe dreams. There was a reality in Las Vegas that needed their immediate attention. In a way there was poetic justice in the great manipulator being manipulated by forces even more invisible than he was. It is doubtful that all the machinations will ever be untangled. The convolutions are mind-boggling. Yet some of the threads have shredded, leaving telltale marks, clues to a world few people rarely get to see.

The inspiration to bring Hughes to Las Vegas originated with Johnny Roselli, who secretly arranged for Hughes to take over the penthouse floor of the Desert Inn. But the task itself was accomplished by Maheu and two close friends: Las Vegas *Sun* publisher Hank Greenspun, who had started his newspaper career in that gambling city as Bugsy Siegel's press agent, and Washington Attorney Edward P. Morgan. Maheu and Morgan were former FBI agents, both having served between 1940 and 1947, Morgan as the expert on Communism and Maheu as a "brick agent" on espionage. Roselli, Morgan, Maheu, and Greenspun were close friends, and all four would make money during Howard Hughes's brief stay in Nevada.

It was in 1954 that Maheu's Washington-based consulting-lobbying firm— Robert A. Maheu Associates: "Consultants in Management Engineering, Civic and Public Relations"—first went on the Hughes payroll. Nine years later Hughes had become his sole client. A stocky, balding, soft-faced man with dark bulging eyes and sharply slanted brow, Bob Maheu was well paid for his services. His annual billing ran in the neighborhood of $500,000 and his salary was hidden somewhere in that figure. His official title in Las Vegas —Chief Executive Officer, Nevada Operations, Howard Hughes—was specifically designed to soothe the ruffled feathers of other key personnel in the corporate kingdom.

At first, however, Maheu was not worried about jealous rivals in Houston, the home of the Hughes Tool Company. As the billionaire's front man in multimillion-dollar deals, he was to become one of the most powerful figures in Nevada. It was obvious to him that among all the vassals of the manor, he alone was privy to the inner workings of the whole mammoth operation—only he knew what the feudal lord in the penthouse was thinking at any given moment, for the other vassals had been out of touch for years, a fact that made him feel indispensable. All requests for funds were routed through Houston, not for approval, but merely for disbursement. Although Maheu would never personally meet Hughes, he tried to create the impression that he was conferring face-to-face with him on a regular basis. All their communication, however, was by telephone and memoranda.

Each of the four men performed a different role. Invariably identified in the national press as a "crusading and outspoken editor," Hank Greenspun became the self-appointed protector of the man in the penthouse, baring his teeth to all who dared invade his privacy.

In praising Hughes in his front-page column, "Where I Stand," Greenspun overlooked the vexing problem of double taxation, noting that Hughes "doesn't even draw a salary from the company as its president, for all funds are used to better mankind . . . he has helped make our country secure from its enemies and its people secure from physical wants . . . he has conquered outer space and surely his self-effacement and humility entitle him to a little private space here on his own earth. . . ." In another column, he compared Hughes' "genius" with that of Isaac Newton.

His love letters in the guise of columns and editorials shocked many of his readers. They knew that Freedom of the Press was his battle cry—absolutely no one was safe from attack when he got to wielding that shibboleth. For years he had talked to them like a Dutch uncle, telling them whom to like and dislike, how to vote, and where to buy what. He was their voice of experience. Nothing was held back, no one was bigger than the Press—how many times had he pounded that tenet into their heads. Now suddenly their hard-bitten prophet was giddy as a schoolgirl in the presence of the Beatles. It was downright embarrassing.

Unknown to his readers, but what Maheu learned, was that Greenspun was in deep financial trouble. He needed a large bundle of cash and the only angel around with that kind of money was the "genius" in the penthouse, who on the advice of Maheu, had decided that the best way to control the local news media was to buy it out. Two men owned just about all the media there was in Las Vegas: the *Review-Journal* and KORK-TV, the local NBC affiliate, was owned by Don Reynolds, and Greenspun had the *Sun* and KLAS-TV. Since

Hughes was not interested in controlling a part of anything, it was Maheu's job to convince him that everything was for sale.

In a progress memo to Hughes, Maheu outlined an irresistible proposition. Greenspun was willing to sell his TV station immediately but was hesitant to part with his newspaper. But if Hughes bought Greenspun's Paradise Valley Country Club, Greenspun would give Hughes an option to purchase TV station KLAS and "allow us to place a manager of the station with complete authority." As for the opposition, Maheu wrote, "He [Greenspun] is staunch in his conviction that within 6 months, Reynolds will be ready to negotiate seriously for the sale of his media properties." In such an event, Greenspun "would allow us to set the policy for the *Sun* as well—even to the extent of placing our own man in that organization. He claims that each paper could realize a $1,000 per day saving if they used mutual printing presses." But Hughes had to act quickly before some of "your long range plans become generally known." As if that was not enough motivation, Maheu added, "Furthermore, as of today, I have assurance that we could acquire all the Reynolds' media properties with full acceptance from the F.C.C. without even the possibility of any trouble."

Hughes took the bait in one voracious gulp. He paid $2.6 million for Greenspun's golf course and $3.6 million for his television station. In 1971, after Hughes had left Las Vegas, Greenspun would tell Morley Safer in a CBS-TV interview that Hughes had bought his station because "He worked mostly in the small hours of the morning, after midnight, and he liked to watch television . . . until five and six, and the calls became so frequent: why don't I run westerns, aviation pictures, why don't I run *Wings* again, Jean Peters? I said why not buy it? Now he runs all night long, twenty-four hours a day, shows all the good movies." Greenspun laughed. "I'm very satisfied with the price. I don't know if he can get return on his money, but I'm happy. Fact is, I sold him a golf course, Paradise Valley; he gave me a good price. . . . It wasn't making much money. That's why I sold it to him cheap." Greenspun had another good laugh.

Roselli had his own concerns. After years of lucrative skimming, the Dalitz group was in serious trouble and anxious to unload its Nevada package. Dalitz himself was under federal indictment for income tax evasion and three others of his group were at various stages of federal criminal prosecutions. Allard Roen had pleaded guilty in a stock-fraud case and Johnny Drew at the Stardust was under indictment for tax evasion. It was the third case that had generated the panic toward the nearest exit.

In early 1960 Ruby Kolod, a member of the Dalitz group, and Israel "Ice-pick Willie" Alderman, a hitman whose specialty consisted of pressing an ice-pick into his victim's ear, had invested $78,000 in an oil venture with a Denver attorney, Robert Sunshine, and when it failed, they had dispatched Felix Alderisio and another Chicago persuader to Denver to "threaten to injure and/or murder" Sunshine and his family if he did not return their money forthwith. Terrified by the encounter, Sunshine had embezzled from two clients and when arrested had promptly confessed. Called into the case, the FBI was intrigued by Sunshine's description of the way Kolod had acquired the $78,000. He had merely walked into the Desert Inn counting room and taken the money right "off the top"—that is, before it was counted for tax purposes.

Some months later the Henderson Novelty Company was formed in Las Vegas. Describing itself as a "musical rental service," it leased twenty-five private telephone lines, the purpose of which would not be disclosed until FBI agent Dean Elson, testifying in the Sunshine case, admitted that for a period of fifteen months the FBI had monitored all conversations in the executive offices and private homes of Desert Inn officials. Other hotels with FBI-tapped phones included the Sands, Frontier, Dunes, and Fremont. The operation had been part of a massive electronic surveillance to expose illegal skimming.

But things were looking up. Hughes' freshly polished image was casting a new light on the old gambling camp.

21
ROSELLI ON THE HOOK

† † † †

THE DEAL FOR THE DESERT INN WAS FINALIZED AT $13.6 MILLION. ON THE surface it appeared as an ordinary transaction, but, as Roselli would explain to Jimmy, it was anything but ordinary.

Throughout this period, Roselli and Jimmy had few opportunities for any lengthy conversations, for each was tied up with his own affairs. But on this evening, it was a time for celebration. They met in a hotel room at the Desert Inn and both men removed their jackets and ties, slipped off their shoes, and with drinks and cigars, settled down for a long evening of catch-up talk.

Roselli puffed on the cigar and grinned at Jimmy. "I just split four hundred big ones with Sam [Giancana]," he said, his blue eyes watching for Jimmy's reaction.

Jimmy gasped.

"Let me lay this out for you," Roselli said with a proud smile. "We've roped Hughes into buying the D.I. Now it looks like he wants to buy out the whole town, if we let him. At first nobody wanted this kook out here. He's bad news. He'd bring bad publicity, but I knew better. He's just what we need, especially with Maheu running the show."

"I'm real glad for you, Johnny."

"We put one over on Dalitz, that cheap prick," Roselli continued. "He didn't know who was up there taking up the whole penthouse floor. He's going crazy. They'd installed new locks. You need a special key to get the elevator beyond the eighth floor, and he's told there're guys up there with machine guns guarding the firedoors. Moe's yelling that he ain't running a hotel, that those penthouse suites are for high-rollers, he's having a royal fit. Which gives me an idea. I says, 'Moe, evict the prick.' The deal, of course, is that Maheu's already working on the governor and telling him that Hughes is thinking of building a medical school at the university, all kinds of bullshit, and Greenspun's writing this beautiful shit about Hughes. Makes it sound like the Second Coming.

"As you know, Jimmy, we've got problems in Vegas. So I talk to Sam and he tells me to see Johnny Scalish in Cleveland, have him tell Moe [Dalitz] to sell the joint. Scalish wants out, he knows the feds are all over the place, and he's a fat cat anyway, wants to retire in Florida, not Leavenworth. Besides he's going to get a good cut of the deal, a pretty fair piece of change, and so he talks to Sam and says Chicago can take over the Dalitz group after the sale. While this is going on, Dalitz's trying to serve Hughes with an eviction notice and Maheu's getting Hughes all steamed up about buying the joint or getting thrown out."

Roselli paused for emphasis. "That's when I got Ed Morgan to represent Dalitz, which is a laugh because he's Maheu's asshole buddy. But Ed knows Moe. I used to get him comped at the D.I. when he came to town. I'd meet with him in private, but I had Jimmy Cantillon take him around town, show him a good time."

"I think Dalitz's nuts to sell that joint," Jimmy said. "It's a money maker. They must have taken two hundred million out of that place on skim alone."

"Jimmy, it's been rough in this town the past year and it's going to get rougher. The skimming days are coming to an end."

"Never," Jimmy said. "There's a million ways to skim if you put your mind to it. Get me in one of them joints and I'll show you how to do it."

Roselli laughed. "Jimmy, I'd like nothing better, but right now we've got the D.I. in good hands. Maheu's keeping Bernie [Rothkopf] and Peanuts [Danolfo] is going to be casino manager. What's even better, Sam and I get to split a finder's fee," and he paused, his eyes sparkling, "of eight hundred thousand dollars—under the fucking table."

Jimmy did a double take. "I thought you said it was four hundred."

"Right, but that's only half," Roselli said. "We get the rest later. He's got to accumulate it. Even for Moe, that's a good size chunk of tax-free money to pay out. Also, you know, Dalitz paid Morgan a hundred-fifty thousand above the table. Morgan's giving Greenspun and me a piece of his end."

"What a deal," Jimmy said, trying to keep the envy out of his voice. He raised his empty glass in a salute. "Congratulations, Johnny. Nobody deserves it more than you."

"Thanks, Jimmy. A little good luck now and then never hurt nobody."

Jimmy got up to refresh their drinks. "Tell me, will you, how come you know this guy Maheu?"

"Oh, Jesus, I've known him for years." Roselli laughed. "I haven't thought about this in a long time, but I must have met this guy maybe ten years ago. It's a hell of a story.

"Maheu was with the FBI during the war and then he set up this private eye outfit, gave it a real fancy name," Roselli began. "But he was a shamus. Even then he was doing jobs for the CIA. Anyway, Beldon Katleman at the El Rancho, that was before Caifano burned the joint down, wanted to divorce his wife and hired Maheu to get something on her. So Maheu came over here with Joe Shimon, who was a police inspector with the D.C. police in Washington. Beldon's wife was sharp, and she outfoxed them.

"So they were over here talking with Beldon and he says I've got another job for you guys. He introduces them to Milton Berle, who's playing the joint with Louie Prima and Keeley Smith. Now listen to this, Jimmy. Berle is about to make a comeback on TV, had a new show lined up, but the problem is that he's got this contract with Louie and Keeley, and he knows goddamn well if he goes on TV with them, they'll steal the show, which scares the shit out of Berle. So he wants out of the contract."

Roselli laughed softly, shaking his head. "Now this really kills me. One day Beldon sees this dealer with a black eye and the guy tells him he's fucking Keeley in the dressing room when suddenly he feels someone licking his balls. He jumps up and Louie punches him in the eye. Now Berle's got something to work with, right? After all, they're fucking sex degenerates. Besides that Berle says he's heard they smoke pot and if they were found with some of the stuff on them that would be enough to kill the contract, some type of morals clause. So Beldon and Berle hand Maheu two grand as a retainer and tell him they're in a hurry for results.

"Shimon, who's sharp as a tack, tells Maheu, 'You know what these bastards want for their money, don't you?' Maheu's all innocence, 'What do you mean?' Shimon says, 'They've paid you to plant stuff on Louie.'

"Maheu's shocked, 'Oh, I wouldn't do that.' Shimon says, 'Let me put feelers out the next few days and see what I come up with.' And that's when I met Joe Shimon and Bob Maheu. They got this little publicity gal I knew, Jean—her father was the famous admiral who took a bribe from Tony Martin to promote him in the Navy, remember that old story, and they kept him a seaman because he got caught at it—anyway she put me in touch with them. I said, 'Hell, no, Louie's clean.' They checked sources all over the country and came up empty. So Maheu sent Shimon to give Beldon and Uncle Milty the bad news.

"I remember going out for a drink with Shimon afterwards, and this guy's been a cop all his life and seen all kinds of bad shit, and he's shaking his head, really disgusted. 'Oh, the awful people you have to deal with in this business,' he says. 'It's terrible.' And, you know, Jimmy, the guy's right. I couldn't be a cop or private dick. They deal with the scum of the earth."

At a time when Roselli should have been sitting on top of his world, disaster struck in the shape of FBI agent Jack Barron. For forty-five years, Roselli had been living with a dangerous secret that was shared by only a handful of people.

Born in Esteria, Italy, Filippo Sacco was six years old in 1911 when his mother brought him to the United States to be reunited with his father, who had immigrated earlier and was living in East Boston. After the premature death of his father, his mother remarried and it was his stepfather who introduced Filippo to a life of crime. Strapped for money, the stepfather induced Filippo to burn down the family home and then grabbed the insurance money and ran. When the insurance company became suspicious, Filippo, who was in the seventh grade, left home, taking with him a picture of himself with his mother. He ended up with Al Capone in Chicago, where he learned all phases of the crime business and changed his name to John Roselli. He would later tell the Kefauver Committee that his birthplace was Chicago.

After leaving home he had cut all ties to his family. Through a trusted friend in Chicago, he had arranged to have money sent home on a regular basis. Then one day, Jack Barron, who had been dogging Roselli and Fratianno for years, showed Roselli a copy of the picture he had taken with him so many years ago. Roselli realized that one of the few people he had entrusted with his secret had betrayed him. Like most special agents assigned to organized crime, Barron was anxious to expand his informant network. The fact that FBI agent Jack Armstrong had Bompensiero in his clutches was added incentive. A high-level snitch could mean the difference between beating his brains out digging up gossip and rumors on the street and sitting smugly back like Armstrong with a pipeline leading directly into the upper echelons of the organization. His reports would also make Washington sit up and take notice.

Roselli was offered a choice of either cooperating or being deported back to Italy as an illegal alien, for Roselli a fate worse than death. He chose, instead, to consult with his old and dear friend, Joseph Shimon, who had been the District of Columbia Police's liaison to the CIA. Also conscripted into the CIA–Mafia plot, Shimon was now a private investigator in Washington. Among his clients were Attorneys Edward Bennett Williams and his associate Tom Wadden and, of course, Maheu.

Accompanied by Jimmy Cantillon, Roselli went back East. When Roselli told Shimon that Barron and the agent with him had assured him they were the only ones who knew about it and would protect him as long as he cooperated, Shimon's response was, "Horseshit. Those guys are lying to you. There's no solo flights in the FBI. Don't believe them. By now lots of people in the Bureau know about it."

After kicking it around for a few hours, they went to see Ed Morgan, who was all in favor of Roselli becoming an informant. Shimon, who was also a close friend of Sam Giancana, a client of Edward Bennett Williams, said, "Forget it. The first guy they want him to inform on is Sam, his best friend. There'd be no end to it." Turning to Roselli, he said, "You wouldn't last twenty minutes." Cantillon agreed with Shimon. "Johnny, they'll never let you off the hook."

Morgan thought that certain parameters could be set up to limit the scope of their demands. "I could help work that out for you. This reminds me of Longy Zwillman. This is confidential but he was my informant. I turned him."

"Oh, that's a swell example," Shimon said. "They hung that stool pigeon."

"Only after he got into tax trouble and started talking to too many people.

I don't know of a single informant the FBI ever lost. You'd be given a code number and your identity would be protected."

Roselli cut him short. "Look, Ed, number one, I'm not going to snitch on nobody; number two, I want some way to keep those guys off my back; number three, I want the name of the prick that turned me in."

After leaving Morgan's office, Roselli made arrangements to meet privately with James P. "Big Jim" O'Connell, who had been the CIA Support Chief for Operation Mongoose, the code name for the CIA–Mafia assassination plot against Castro. It was O'Connell, a former FBI agent, who had brought Maheu into the operation. Prior to this contact, the CIA, through Big Jim, had been paying Maheu's rent for a long time for cloak and dagger work in the Caribbean. Roselli also spoke to William King Harvey, his CIA case officer, another former FBI agent, who had manned the German desk during World War II, his office just down the hall from Edward P. Morgan's Communist desk.

For a man who valued his privacy, Roselli had decided on a daring move. He asked both CIA men to intercede on his behalf with the FBI. In other words, get them off his back. Roselli was a long way from having the government by the ass, as he had once hoped, but his grip, shaky as it was, had a hold on something with a definite value in that market place. The previous month Big Jim had helped Maheu duck an appearance before a Senate wiretapping investigating committee by merely telling Senator Edward Long not to call Maheu to testify as he had been "involved in CIA operations." In Roselli's case, Big Jim had Security Director Sheffield Edwards, also a member of Mongoose, inform the FBI that Roselli wanted to "keep square with the Bureau" but was afraid that the mob might kill him for talking.

It was unfortunate for Roselli that his request came at a time when J. Edgar Hoover was not speaking to the CIA. Barron kept right on coming, forcing Roselli to make a desperate move.

Ever since President Kennedy's assassination, the news media had abounded with conspiracy theories contrary to the findings of the Warren Commission. The accusing finger was often leveled at the Mafia, particularly at Carlos Marcello and Santo Trafficante, who were quoted as having made threats against the Kennedys because of their tough stance on organized crime. Edward Bennett Williams' client, Jimmy Hoffa, whose conviction was enroute to the Supreme Court, was also high on the list of suspects.

Roselli, who was privy to the innermost secrets of the Cosa Nostra Commission through his intimate relationship with Giancana, knew that the theories were, as he had expressed it to Jimmy, "more fucking bullshit."

In fact, about three weeks after the assassination, Roselli and Jimmy had met at Bill Graham's house. After making them comfortable, Graham had excused himself, and the two men had discussed the CIA–Mafia plot. After having read about Lee Harvey Oswald's contacts with Cuba, Jimmy had suspected Castro as being behind the assassination. What amazed him was that there had been nothing in the newspapers about the CIA–Cosa Nostra plot to kill Castro. But there was a great deal of speculation about the mob doing it. There was even talk of Hoffa being involved, which convinced Jimmy, as if he needed any more convincing, that nobody outside of their thing understood anything about its operation. Hoffa was a front, a shell, a tool, a device, but whatever one wanted to call it, he was not a threat to anyone, particularly to the President of the United States.

"You know, Johnny," he had said, "the more of this bullshit I read, the more I'm convinced that we've become fucking scapegoats for every unsolved crime committed in this country. What's this mob the papers are always talking about, for Christ's sake? It's against the fucking rules to kill a cop, so now we're going to kill the President. You know, Jack once told me we should have started clipping cops and Feebees [FBI agents] years ago. Personally, I think he was right."

Roselli sighed. "Jimmy, what're you going to do? I'll bet you any amount of money the CIA never tells the Warren Commission about their little deal with us."

"I hope not, or you'll be dragged right into the middle of this thing. You think maybe Castro is behind the hit?"

"No question in my mind," Roselli said. "But it's got nothing to do with us. I think he hit Kennedy because of the Bay of Pigs invasion. I don't think he's even aware of our deal."

"Why not?" Jimmy asked, puzzled. "You've been at it three, four years. Something's got to leak in that time."

Roselli's blue eyes hardened. "Jimmy, I'm going to tell you something you won't believe." He looked away, the muscles along his jawline tensing into rigid lines. "This whole thing has been a scam. Santo [Trafficante] never did nothing but bullshit everybody. All these fucking wild schemes the CIA dreamed up never got further than Santo. He just sat on it, conned everybody into thinking that guys were risking their lives sneaking into Cuba, having boats shot out from under them, all bullshit."

"Does Sam know this?"

"Yeah, he knows, but what can he do about it. We had an opportunity here that comes once in a lifetime. Could've had the government by the ass, and the sonovabitch did nothing."

"Did Sam get on Santo's ass?"

"Jimmy, Sam can't do nothing. Santo's a boss like him."

Jimmy looked worried. "I don't like it, Johnny. I told you that before. I think it's fucking dangerous. You're playing with fire."

Roselli shook his head. "All for nothing. What a terrible waste of a lifetime opportunity. Imagine, Jimmy, if we'd knocked off Castro. Think of the power —" he stopped and slapped the arm of his chair. "What's the sense of talking about it."

"Maybe if you had clipped him, Kennedy would still be alive."

"Listen, Jimmy, in this business, you can't win them all."

† † †

Considering the importance of what Roselli had told Jimmy, his new plan was a bold and dangerous stroke. Although Maheu, Shimon, and the CIA officials involved knew all there was to know about the conception of the various assassination schemes, none knew anything about the actual execution of any of them beyond what Roselli had reported. Roselli hoped that by exercising his imagination and creating new and dramatic incidents, he could get the FBI off his back.

Years later Joseph Shimon would tell Senator Frank Church's Intelligence Committee that as far as Maheu was concerned it was "Johnny's contract." As for Giancana, Shimon said that the Chicago Mafia boss had told him that "I'm not in it, and they [the CIA] are asking me for the names of some guys who used to work in casinos. . . . Maheu's conning the hell out of the CIA."

This, of course, was well understood by Roselli when he visited the Washington law offices of Welch and Morgan to talk again with Edward P. Morgan. By this time Roselli and Morgan were close personal friends. They'd worked together in the Hughes operation, and Morgan had enjoyed Johnny's hospitality and influence in Las Vegas.

As always on his visits to Washington, Shimon picked Roselli up at the airport. On their way to Morgan's office, Roselli told Shimon, "I'm going to lay it out for him and see what he can do with it. Do you think he knows anything about Mongoose?" Shimon was positive that Maheu had told Morgan everything. Roselli had smiled and said, "Not everything, Joe, you'll see."

Seated across from Morgan's desk, with Shimon at his side, Roselli decided to play it dumb and had so advised Shimon in advance. Assured by Morgan that whatever was said would be protected by the attorney-client privilege, Roselli took it from the top, with Maheu's initial contact at the Beverly Hills Brown Derby Restaurant on September 4, 1960. He described his eagerness to be of service to his country, "because I owe it a lot."

He recounted the bizarre schemes first hatched up by the CIA's Technical Service Division to destroy Castro's image. A box of Castro's favorite cigars were impregnated with a chemical that would produce temporary disorientation. The hope was that he would smoke one before making a speech. Then it was thallium salts, a powerful depilatory that would make Castro's beard fall out if it were dusted on his shoes. The hope this time was that the Cuban leader would travel to a foreign country and, like all good tourists, would leave his shoes outside the door of his hotel room to be shined.

But once Roselli was inducted into the plot, the CIA decided it might be easier and certainly far more permanent to kill Castro. The first scheme that occurred to them was a Capone-style ambush with machine guns blazing. Roselli quickly nixed that idea, pointing out that although popular in Chicago, this method would present a recruitment problem in Cuba. Instead Roselli suggested a slow-acting, painless poison that would allow the assassin time to escape.

It was back to the cigars, but this time they were impregnated with botulin, a toxin so potent that it would kill the moment it touched a person's lips. The cigars were delivered to Roselli, who passed them on to an "unidentified" person and that was the last anyone heard about them. Roselli wanted a nice, clean hit, preferably a poison that would disappear without a trace. The first batch of pills were rejected because they would not dissolve in water. A second batch, containing the botulin would dissolve in water but could not be used in boiling soups. The Technical Service finally came up with a liquid that would kill him in two or three days without leaving a trace.

There was a certain urgency to attain results that was not explained to Roselli. The price on Castro's head was placed at $150,000, which made it pretty high as contracts go in that business. What Roselli did not know at the time was that the CIA wanted the Cuban leader dead before the Bay of Pigs invasion scheduled for April 17, 1961.

Roselli told Morgan of his first meeting at the Fontainebleau Hotel in Miami with Big Jim O'Connell where everybody used code names. Big Jim was Jim Olds, Roselli was John Rawlston, Giancana was Sam Gold, who would be Rawlston's "back-up" or "key" man, and Santo Trafficante, introduced as just plain Joe, was to be Gold's "courier to Cuba and make arrangements there."

There had been no end to the excuses offered by Trafficante that Roselli had passed on to Maheu and Big Jim. Castro had stopped patronizing a particular restaurant where the poison was to be administered, or there had been a mixup in signals, or an official close to Castro was fired before he received the poison. By the fall of 1961, the CIA had instructed Roselli to maintain his Cuban contacts but not to deal with Maheu or Giancana, who were described as "untrustworthy" and "surplus."

There were more fiascos, with three-men assassination squads being dispatched to poison Che Guevera as well as Fidel and Raoul Castro. But William Harvey, as Mongoose director, was getting discouraged. "There's not much likelihood that this is going any place," he told Roselli, who could not have agreed more, but had maintained his silence, as he did now in Morgan's office. That would remain his secret, shared only with Giancana and Jimmy Fratianno. Trafficante's Cuban rebels had been a figment of his imagination. The poison the Technical Service had so laboriously concocted had been simply flushed down the drain.

As he talked about his experiences in Morgan's office, he presented a positive picture of a man totally dedicated to come to the aid of his country at the risk of his own life. On several occasions, he told Morgan with a straight face, boats had been shot out from under him by Cuban patrols. Yet with all that work and risk, he had paid his own hotel and travel expenses and had never once asked for even a nickel in recompense. All the money and paraphernalia (rifles, handguns, explosives, detonators, poison, radios, and boat radar) supplied by the CIA had been turned over to the anti-Castro Cuban agents Trafficante had enlisted for the operation.

Looking Morgan straight in the eye, he said, "It's the one thing in my life that I'm really proud of." He paused for dramatic effect and lowered his voice. "What I'm about to tell you is so secret that even the CIA don't know about it. One of our assassination teams was captured and tortured until they told all they knew about our operation which they said was ordered by the White House."

By now Morgan's six-foot-three frame was poised on the edge of his chair. "My God, Johnny, are you absolutely certain of this information?"

Roselli smiled wearily. "Oh, yes, I'm sure, don't worry about that. In fact, one of our highly placed operatives actually heard Castro say that if that was the way President Kennedy wanted to play it, well, he too could play that game. I have it from a top source that the team was turned around, you know, brainwashed, and sent back into our country to kill Kennedy."

"Jesus Christ, Johnny, any way of verifying any of this information?"

Roselli shook his head. "I've told you all I can, believe me, maybe more than I should have. This was told to me in strictest confidence and I will never violate that trust. This man today is still close to Castro and it would mean his life."

"How the hell long have you been sitting on this powder keg?" Morgan asked.

Roselli shrugged. "Listen, Ed, as far as I know, all phases of this operation were approved by Allen Dulles and President Eisenhower. Well, as you know, Dulles was a member of the Warren Commission and I don't remember hearing him say anything about it. Did you? And I don't remember Eisenhower coming forward either. So what was I supposed to think? Maybe President Johnson wanted to keep the lid on. Maybe he thought it'd be bad for the country to know about this operation—you know, the government of the United States involved with the so-called Mafia to kill the leader of a foreign country and then it boomerangs.

"In fact, that's why I'm here right now. Since I've gotten to know you, I realize that you have important government connections and you're on the inside of things, you know how the wheels turn in this town. Listen, this has been going around in my head for a long time. I just don't want to fuck up the works. Frankly, to be honest with you, and this is no bullshit, I feel it's my patriotic duty to get this out in the open. Except I can't get personally involved, you understand what I mean? Ed, believe me, my life's in the balance here. Look, I've given you the information. You decide what to do with it, but just keep me out of it. That's all I ask."

Morgan, the former national debating champ, the man who had risen to the number three position under J. Edgar Hoover in less than seven years, was literally speechless. He just sat there shaking his head, trying to digest this incredible information. He was looking at Roselli, a man he found extremely charming and personable and engaging, a diamond in the rough, so to speak, but powerful in a smooth way, a man who could get things done in a hurry in his own arena, an important man to know.

"No problem, Johnny, you're protected by the attorney-client privilege, but once this gets out, there is bound to be enormous pressure exerted by powerful forces to get to the bottom of it."

Roselli smiled, his blue eyes amused. "Well, I can't think of a more qualified person to deal with those forces. Welcome to the club."

On the way back to the airport, Shimon said, "While you were talking with Morgan, I was thinking of that first night at the Fontainebleau. That's the first time I met Sam Giancana. Oh, I knew who he was, you know, but I liked him right away. Remember we went out on the town and Frank Sinatra was kissing Sam's ass all over the place.

"Then we shook him, Sam and I, and we walked alone for a while and Sam looked at me and said, 'Tell me something, for Christ's sake. You're a cop, what are you doing with people like us?' How do you like that, Johnny? I said, 'Sam, I don't know what I'm doing but I like you.' And he just looked at me and said, 'I like you, too.'

"As you know, Johnny, like with you, we became close friends," Shimon went on. "Whenever he's in Washington he comes to the house and my wife thinks he's lovable. He's such great fun, with his wonderful sense of humor. Calls me all the time to see if I'm getting along all right. I've been to his home many times and once while I was there he got a call from a crooked cop, some lieutenant with the Chicago police department that was trying to get a job in one of the newly incorporated villages, wanted to be police chief there, and asked Sam to go to the front for him. I heard the entire conversation because Sam put it on the blower. When he hung up, Sam said, 'That rotten sonovabitch's been on the pad all his life. In my book, there's nothing worse than a crooked cop. I wouldn't wish that sonovabitch on decent people for all the tea in China.' Then he told me, 'You know, Joe, I've spent a lot of money to find out you were a straight cop.' Ain't that something, Johnny?"

Morgan sat at his desk a long time after Roselli and Shimon had left. Another close friend was Jack Anderson, who was then Drew Pearson's co-columnist. Anderson was also a close friend of Maheu and Greenspun—in fact, he owned an interest in the Las Vegas *Sun*.

Morgan's first move was to contact Harvey at the CIA, who described Roselli as a patriotic "hero" who had three or four boats shot out from under him by Cuban patrols as he tried to land assassination teams on the island.

The sequence of events that follows was set down by the Senate Intelligence Committee in its June 1976 report: "In late January of 1967, Washington *Post* Columnist Drew Pearson met with Chief Justice Earl Warren. Pearson told the Chief Justice that a Washington lawyer had told him that one of his clients said the United States had attempted to assassinate Fidel Castro in the early 1960's, and that Castro had decided to retaliate."

The report goes on to state that Warren referred the information to James J. Rowley, head of the Secret Service. In his testimony, Rowley said: "The way [Warren] approached it, was that he said he thought this was serious enough and so forth, but he wanted to get it off his hands. He felt that he had to— that it—had to be told to somebody, and that the Warren Commission was finished, and he wanted the thing pursued, I suppose, by ourselves or the FBI." On February 15, Rowley bucked it to J. Edgar Hoover, who decided that "no investigation will be conducted regarding the allegations made . . . to Chief Justice Warren."

The next move was up to Jack Anderson and Drew Pearson. Their column of March 3, 1967, read in part:

> President Johnson is sitting on a political H-bomb—an unconfirmed report that Senator Robert Kennedy (Dem. N.Y.) may have approved an assassination plot which then possibly backfired against his late brother. . . . This report may have started New Orleans' flamboyant District Attorney Jim Garrison on his investigation of the Kennedy assassination, but insiders believe he is following the wrong trail. . . . The CIA hatched a plot to knock off Castro. It would have been impossible for this to reach the levels it did, say insiders, without being taken up with the younger Kennedy. Indeed, one source insists that Bobby, eager to avenge the Bay of Pigs fiasco, played a key role in the planning. . . . Some insiders are convinced that Castro learned enough at least to believe that the CIA was seeking to kill him. With characteristic fury, he is reported to have cooked up a counterplot against President Kennedy.

Since the "plot to knock off Castro" was "hatched" during the Eisenhower Administration, seven months before the Bay of Pigs fiasco, it is hard to understand how "Bobby" could have "played a key role in the planning." In fact, according to the Intelligence Committee, Attorney General Kennedy heard about the CIA plot on May 14, 1962, when the CIA was trying to prevent the Justice Department from prosecuting Maheu for the wiretap attempt on the phone of Dan Rowan, which was instigated by Giancana who suspected that the *Laugh-in* comedian and Phyllis McGuire were having an affair. In a memo to Kennedy, Colonel Edwards stated that "At the time of the incident neither the Agency nor the undersigned knew of the proposed technical installation." Under the impression that the covert operation had been terminated, Kennedy angrily replied, "I trust that if you ever try to do business with organized crime again—with gangsters—you will let the Attorney General know." Yet the underworld phase of the operation was not terminated until January 1963, when Harvey told Roselli to "taper off his communications with the Cubans."

At any rate, the Pearson–Anderson column, loaded with the wisdom of its "insiders," was another super scoop. It made millions of people happy from coast to coast, not to mention Pearson's pal in the White House, who was surreptitiously escalating the Vietnam "police action." The day before the column was published, Senator Kennedy had proposed a controversial bombing-suspension that was publicly rebutted by General William C. Westmoreland—this was followed by intensified bombing of North Vietnam.

No doubt intrigued by Kennedy's alleged involvement in this nefarious plot, delighting in the sheer irony of it—that his scheming had led to his brother's assassination—President Johnson directed the FBI to interview the annonymous source. On the evening of March 30, Morgan was interviewed by two agents from the Washington Field Office, who had no prior knowledge of Operation Mongoose, which gives some indication as to what Hoover thought of Johnson's request.

The following quotes are verbatim excerpts from their blind memorandum summarizing the interview with Morgan. After asserting the attorney-client privilege and affirming that his clients had no direct or indirect involvement in the death of President Kennedy, Morgan "pointed out he represented substantial citizens, people who loved their country and had a high regard for the then President." He went on to "point out that if he were a government investigator assigned to unravel all facets of the assassination of President Kennedy he would first concern himself with reading the newspaper articles [there was a follow-up version to the Pearson–Anderson column in the Washington *Post* on March 7] dealing with the topic of a Castro plot." The stories "were on the right track in regard to the theory of the assassination."

Morgan shifted into high gear: "The project had as its purpose the assassination of Fidel Castro, Premier of Cuba. Elaborate plans involving many people were made. These plans included the infiltration of the Cuban Government and the placing of informants in key posts within Cuba. The project almost reached fruition when Castro became aware of it and arrested a number of suspects. By pressuring captured suspects he was able to learn the full details of the plots against him and decided 'if that was the way President Kennedy wanted it, he too could engage in the same tactics.' Castro thereafter employed teams of individuals who were dispatched to the United States for the purpose of assassinating President Kennedy. Mr. Morgan further explained that his clients, here noting that he, Morgan, was employed by more than one of those involved, obtained this information concerning Castro's dispatch of these assassins from 'feed back' furnished by sources in place close to Castro, who had been initially placed there in effecting the purpose of the original project. Continuing, he said his clients were aware of the identity of some of the individuals who came to the United States for this purpose and he understood that two such individuals were now in the state of New Jersey."

This information would have surprised Roselli no less than it did the two agents, who eight years later would testify to their confusion at the time of Morgan's recital.

"Mr. Morgan further noted that one of the clients he represented was a high type individual of the Catholic faith," the memo continued. "Morgan said he queried him as to why a person with his high ethical standard had ever become involved in such a project as the assassination of Fidel Castro. The client indicated that his conscience bothered him; however, the project was so highly patriotically motivated that this in his mind overrode personal, ethical or moral considerations. He further described how one client, when hearing the statement that Lee Harvey Oswald was the sole assassin of President Kennedy, 'laughs with tears in his eyes and shakes his head in apparent disagreement.' "

Roselli had made his move. Now he would see how good a hold he really had on the "governments' ass."

22
HOWARD HUGHES
MOVES OUT

† † † †

THEY MET AT THE TOWER OF PIZZA IN LAS VEGAS, AND ROSELLI WAS livid. His blue eyes turned to slate, he said between clenched teeth, "I know the name of the fucking snitch who told the Feebees my real name."

"Jesus Christ," Jimmy said, leaning forward so Roselli could lower his voice. "How'd you find out?"

"Ed Morgan told me," Roselli said. "Jimmy, this guy's got more connections in the bureau than Hoover."

"Well, come on, the suspense's killing me. Who was it?"

Roselli hissed the name. "Dago Louie. After all I've done for him, would you believe it?"

"Sure I would," Jimmy said. "Years ago Jack warned me about him. He thought way back then he was a snitch. What're you going to do?"

Roselli puffed on his cigar. "I want this one all legal. I went to Sam and he talked to DeSimone. See, with Louie being in the L.A. family, it's up to them to make the hit."

"They'll never do it," Jimmy said. "Not in a million years. Dago Louie's too fucking rich and he's in tight with DeSimone and Licata."

"Sam gave them the word. They've got to do it."

"Johnny, you're getting carried away. If you want this guy hit, you're going to have to do it yourself."

Roselli sighed. "The hell with it, we'll see. What's been happening with you?"

Jimmy was glad to change the subject. "Well, the Mercantile Bank in Chicago sued me and got a judgment for six hundred and seventy-five thousand. I didn't even appear in court. Can they get blood from a stone?"

"Jimmy, you need anything, just say the word."

"I'm all right, Johnny. But I've got to tell you, when things go wrong, there's no end to it. There's this guy, Carl Held, I bought a few trucks and trailers from him. Anyway, I loaned Carl fifteen grand so he could buy a liquor license and open a joint in the Capitol Towers Apartments in Sacramento, which is close to the Capitol and the federal building. Lots of legislators drop in for lunch or drinks. So he gives my wife a note, six percent interest, and that's over a year ago and he ain't paid a nickel back. It's one sad story after another with this guy.

"Then there's this other character, Frank Greenleaf, who owns one truck and comes to see me in Sacramento after my trouble in El Centro and wants to know if I need money. I says, 'Look, Frank, you add up what equity I've got in this equipment and give me half. We'll appraise the trucks, and if I owe twenty thousand on a truck that's worth thirty, you give me five. We'll go down the line with each piece of equipment. Then you pick up the loans and you've got fifty percent of my company.' I figured my equity was worth a quarter-million anyway. By then I'd been paying on the new trucks three years. It was good equipment. I had no crap. So I take the guy to San Francisco and introduce him to Joe Alioto and then we go to his bank and Joe Demers gives him a bunch of forms to fill out. I told Alioto before going to his bank that Greenleaf might go into partnership with me and if he does, he'll be on the papers for the loans. See, Johnny, I got about a hundred and five thousand from Alioto's bank and I've paid back about half of it."

"What did Alioto think about El Centro?"

"I explained it to him. He knows it's bullshit, but I'm still trying to get the rice haul, but now with this publicity we've got to wait a while longer before he goes to the board again.

"But you know what the kicker is?" Jimmy asked. "This guy Greenleaf can't fill out the forms—he ain't got a nickel to his name. He just thought he could walk in there and take over my equipment. He has to be an idiot." Jimmy was getting mad all over again just by talking about it.

Roselli puffed on his cigar and studied Jimmy through the smoke. "Cantillon tells me there's rumors the federal grand jury in San Diego might look into the El Centro deal."

Jimmy nodded. "Yeah, and with my luck, they'll probably indict me. After I beat that fucker Hamilton in El Centro, I thought I was home free. It's really weird, Johnny, with the fucking things I've done in my life, and they'll probably nail me for violating some PUC regulation that everybody in the business has been violating since the beginning of time."

"In our business, Jimmy, it's always the little things you've got to worry about. Don't ever spit on the sidewalk."

In the next three years, from 1967 to 1970, Howard Hughes would pump more than two hundred million dollars into Nevada in a frantic attempt to create his own gambling monopoly. Besides the Desert Inn, he acquired the Sands, Frontier, Castaways, and Landmark Tower, all hotel-casinos, and the Silver Slipper casino, in Las Vegas, and Harolds Club in Reno. To make sure that gamblers found their way to his hotels, he acquired AirWest, with its fleet of sixty jets serving seventy-three cities in eight western states, Canada, and

Mexico. He also picked up two private airfields, several hundred acres of raw land around each of the airfields, the large Vera Krupp ranch, and almost every major piece of undeveloped property along the Strip, not because he planned to build on the land but to stop others from doing so, to keep would-be competitors out of his domain.

His most crushing failure in Las Vegas was his attempt to acquire the Stardust. Hughes, through Maheu, agreed to pay $30.7 million, but when the Justice Department announced it would file an antitrust action to stop the sale, Hughes folded, his enthusiasm quickly fizzling out, spooked by the prospect of being subpoenaed (his Achilles' heel) by the government.

Six months later the Dalitz group sold the Stardust to the Parvin-Dohrmann Company for a paltry $15 million, the deal consummated in a matter of hours by Sidney Korshak, who collected a $500,000 finder's fee. Korshak's presence assured the participants of the Chicago family's seal of approval. Korshak's importance to Chicago was dramatically explained by the late Willie Bioff during the movie extortion trial in 1944. He told the Court that Charlie "Cherry Nose" Gioe, a top *capo* under Nitti, had once warned Bioff to "pay attention to Sid. He's our man. Remember, any message he may deliver to you is a message from us." There has never been any reason for anyone to dispute that assertion.

What was even more galling, Hughes' entire Nevada operation was slowly sinking into the red, an almost impossible development. Even with the tens of millions upon tens of millions being skimmed from casinos, the state's norm was a 15 to 20 percent return on invested capital. Hughes's return was only 6.15 percent in 1968 and sank to 1.63 percent in 1969. In 1970 the Hughes properties lost $10 million.

The loss was not because of inexperience. A good ninety percent of the old personnel had been retained. Both Carl Cohen and Jack Entratter, former owners, became senior vice-presidents at the Sands, with Cohen as casino manager. Mario Marino, a *caporegime* with Carlos Marcello's New Orleans family, became catering manager, and Charles "Babe" Baron, for years the Sands' official greeter, a Chicago family front, became a casino shift boss. Moe Dalitz became a member of Maheu's executive staff. Chester Simms, who operated the Flamingo casino while Meyer Lansky skimmed untold millions, was brought in by Maheu to run the Frontier casino.

Whatever Hughes may have thought of the ballyhoo that pictured him in a death struggle with the Mafia, he had to know that unsavory characters were being collected along with the casinos.

One of Maheu's closest advisors, aside from Giancana and Roselli, during most of this period was Dean Elson, who had been hired after he resigned from the local FBI office. Elson was the agent who had been in charge of the FBI electronic surveillance operation.

Another valuable asset to the Hughes forces was the addition of Ed Morgan's law firm to the already formidable legal battery. The firm's retainer was $100,000 a year.

A friend of Morgan's, Charles A. McNelis, was the attorney in the Justice Department's Organized Crime Section responsible for the income tax prosecution of Dalitz and Johnny Drew at the Stardust. Eventually, McNelis dropped the case against Drew and settled the Dalitz case when his accountant accepted responsibility and was fined a thousand dollars. When the dust cleared, Dalitz's accountant left on a six-month, expense-paid trip around the world. Sometime after leaving the Justice Department, McNelis joined the Morgan firm.

In all, Morgan received $750,000 from Dalitz, in the form of legal and finder's fees, and gave a substantial sum, reportedly $150,000, to Maheu, plus smaller amounts to Roselli and Greenspun. In a deposition a few years later, Dalitz attempted to explain the importance of Morgan's representation: "I felt Mr. Morgan would be an asset to us in Washington. We were having Internal Revenue investigations, we were having different departmental governmental matters that put us into the position where we thought we should have a lawyer in Washington."

A few minutes after eight o'clock on Thanksgiving evening 1970, almost exactly four years to the hour of his arrival in Las Vegas, the "Spook of American Capitalism" flew the coop. His vanishing act caused as many sensational headlines as his earlier ghostly apparition. After four years of grandiose promises, Howard Hughes left Las Vegas the way he found it, having created nothing more substantial than a media event.

Jimmy, age eighteen, before his nose was broken.

Jimmy, age sixteen, in his amateur boxing stance.

One of Amrine's Angels at London Prison Farm. Jimmy sent this photograph to Jewel and Joanne on May 1, 1941.

(Above) Jimmy's mother and father on their fiftieth wedding anniversary.

Jimmy in 1947, before Johnny Roselli gave him some much needed dressing tips.

One night's work: the bodies of Tony Brocanto and Tony Trombino.

*Jewel visited Jimmy
at Soledad on
Mother's Day, 1957.*

Jimmy and Jean at Bimbo's in 1966.

Bill Graham in 1965, the year before his death.

John Roselli (ca. 1940).

John Roselli in 1975 after testifying before a Senate committee on the CIA–Mafia plot to kill Castro.

This 55-gallon oil drum, found floating in Miami's Biscayne Bay, contained the body of John Roselli.

Frank "Bomp" Bompensiero in an FBI
picture (with file markings) taken in Palm
Springs

The pursuer: James F. Ahearn, Assistant
Special Agent in charge in the FBI's San
Francisco office.

Former San Francisco Mayor Joseph L.
Alioto, who has spent considerable time in
the past decade denying that he had been
"friendly" with Jimmy.

A few admirers in Frank Sinatra's dressing room at the Westchester Premier Theater in September 1976. Top row, from left: Paul Castellano, Gregory DePalma, Sinatra, Tommy Marson, Carlo Gambino, Jimmy, Salvatore Spatola. Bottom row, from left: Joseph Gambino and Richard Fusco.

Eve and Ivan Markovics in September 1976.

Jimmy with Eve Markovics and Dean Martin in May 1977.

"Gonna whack you!" Irving "Slick" Shapiro threatens an Albuquerque photographer. (Courtesy of the Albuquerque Journal.*)*

*William "Billy" Marchiondo
in a contemplative mood.
(Courtesy of the* Albuquerque Journal.*)*

SOME FACES, PAST AND PRESENT*

Anthony Accardo
(ca. 1965).

Joey Aiuppa
(ca. 1965).

Sal Amarena
(ca. 1973).

Charley "Bats" Battaglia
(ca. 1950).

Johnny "Bats" Battaglia
(ca. 1950).

Bennie Barrish.

Dominic Brooklier
(ca. 1977).

Marshall Caifano
(ca. 1950).

Marshall Caifano
(ca. 1979).

John "Frankie" Carbo
(1944).

Mickey Cohen
(ca. 1948).

John "Jackie" Cerone
(1962).

*See Dramatis Personae for biographical sketches.

Jack Dragna
(ca. 1946).

Tom Dragna
(ca. 1950).

Louis Tom Dragna
(ca. 1950).

Louis Tom Dragna
(ca. 1975).

"Tony Dope" Delsanter
(ca. 1970).

Frank DeSimone
(ca. 1950).

Charles Dippolito
(ca. 1950).

Joseph Dippolito
(ca. 1950).

Sam Giancana
(ca. 1971)

Joseph Kaleel
(ca. 1950).

Sidney R. Korshak
(photo credit: NBC)

Nick Licata
(ca. 1950).

*James "Blackie" Licavoli
(ca. 1977).*

*Jack LoCicero
(ca. 1970).*

*Angelo Marino
(ca. 1960).*

*Harold "Happy" Meltzer
(ca. 1950).*

*Leo Moceri
(ca. 1970).*

*Thomas Ricciardi
(ca. 1975).*

*Mike "Rizzi" Rizzitello
(ca. 1975).*

*Benny "Bugsy" Siegel
(ca. 1940).*

*Sam Sciortino
(ca. 1975).*

*Anthony "Tony" Spilotro
(ca. 1974).*

*Rudy Tham
(ca. 1970).*

*Frank "Funzi" Tieri
(ca. 1980).*

PART VII

✝ ✝ ✝ ✝

THE DEBACLE
1967–1970

23
A FAVOR FOR A FRIEND

† † † †

WHILE SO MANY PROSPERED, JIMMY AND ROSELLI FELL UPON HARD times.

The first blow came on October 20, 1967, when a federal grand jury indicted Roselli on one count of failing to register and be fingerprinted as an alien and five counts of failing to notify the Immigration and Naturalization Service of his address for the previous five years. At that moment, however, the possibility of being deported was the least of his worries.

Another federal grand jury was probing into charges that a ring of conspirators had used ceiling peepholes and electronic signaling devices attached to a player's leg to fleece wealthy members of the Beverly Hills Friars Club out of at least $400,000 in rigged gin-rummy games. The indictment, handed down in December 1967, included Roselli and four others: Maurice Friedman, Manuel "Ricky" Jacobs, Benjamin J. Teitelbaum, and T. Warner Richardson—both Richardson and Friedman were former owners of the Frontier. George Emerson Seach, an ex-convict, who had manned the peepholes, was given immunity as a government witness. The electronics engineer who had installed the cheating device was convicted on fifteen counts of perjury during the grand jury hearings.

As for Jimmy, the anticipated blow in San Diego came in November of that year when a federal grand jury issued a 28-count indictment against him, Jewel, and their trucking company. They were accused of conspiring with certain unnamed persons to defraud the government by withholding substantial amounts of money that should have been paid to drivers. Each count carried a penalty of five years' imprisonment and a $10,000 fine. Three months earlier the California Assembly had passed legislation exempting dump trucks used in public works from PUC regulations, but unfortunately for Jimmy it was not retroactive. Then on January 12, 1968, the Imperial Valley prosecutor won his appeal for a retrial of the El Centro case against Jimmy and Miles and Sons.

When Jimmy and Roselli met in Cantillon's office to discuss those events there was not much to celebrate. They looked at each other and slowly each started grinning. Roselli brushed back the silver hair along his temples and said, "Who's in the worst shit?"

Jimmy laughed. "It depends on how much you like Italy."

Roselli waved that aside. "That's a phony rap. My friend Joe Shimon spent four days in the basement of the Boston City Hall and came up with papers that show my mother remarried a naturalized Italian and when that happened in those days the entire family automatically became citizens. We've not said anything about it, just waiting to see how far they're going to push it."

"Fantastic. Home run first time at bat."

"Well, next time up ain't going to be that easy."

"Yeah, that Friars case sounds rough. What about Chicago? Getting any heat?"

"Oh, Jesus," Roselli said. "Ice's more like it. With Sam [Giancana] in Mexico, out of it completely now, Joe Batters' back in power. Jimmy, they've cut my balls off. I got them the Stardust and when I arranged the Desert Inn sale I got Scalish to let go of Dalitz and now Chicago's got all of him. So what do you think Batters does after I'm indicted in the Friars case? He calls me into Chicago to tell me that Phil Ponti's going to handle things for the time being and for me to stay away until I get straightened out." He paused, his eyes narrowing angrily. "Not only have they stripped me of my power but they've cut off my income. Do you have any idea how much money I was taking out of the Stardust every month? Well, fuck it, they can shove it up their ass. I've still got the gift shop."

"What kind of fucking bullshit are they pulling, after all you've done for them?"

"Jimmy, Joe Batters never liked me. We're about the same age. He may be a year younger, but he was jealous of my position with Capone. Ain't that incredible? Something that happened a million fucking years ago, and he's still got a hard-on. Us fucking Italians ain't human, Jimmy. We remember things too long, hold these grudges inside of us until they poison our minds."

Jimmy was nodding, a sad expression on his face. "I can't believe this, Johnny, after all you've done for Chicago, never caused them a moment's worry, ran that town like nobody ever will again. Have you talked to Sam about it?"

"Yeah, I just saw him at Joe Shimon's house. This guy's having a ball. Travels under his own passport. He's been to Europe, the Middle East, thinking of getting an apartment in Beirut, one in Paris, and planning a trip to Africa. As far as he's concerned, he never wants to go back to Chicago. He told me straight out he was through for good. 'My investments are sound,' he told me. 'I'm enjoying this new life. Let the cocksuckers back there knock each other off all they want, who cares?' Jimmy, I have to agree with him. I wish my investments were that sound, I'd take off too."

"No, you wouldn't, you'd be lost out there."

Roselli stood up and leaned over until his face was close to Jimmy's. "Listen, pal, I need a big one from you. You don't have to do it. I'll understand, believe me, with the problems you're having, but let me tell you something from the heart. I'm innocent in this Friars scam. Oh, I knew about it, knew it was going on, but I never got a nickel out of it. Jimmy, that's not my style.

"Now, Jimmy, Maurice Friedman's a good friend of mine. I don't know whether I can beat this rap or not, but I know damn well he can't, they've got him dead-bang with Seach's testimony."

Roselli paused, straightened up a moment, and again leaned forward, this time even closer, his voice so low Jimmy could barely hear him. "Jimmy, the most important thing you could ever do for me is clip Seach. Bury the mother-fucker deep."

Jimmy placed his hands on Roselli's shoulders and squeezed gently. "Johnny, you can stop worrying. I'll handle it personally. Just tell me where I can find him."

Roselli grabbed Jimmy in a bear hug. "Sonovabitch, I knew I could depend on you." He reached into his inside jacket pocket and brought out a white envelope. "Here's a couple thousand from Friedman for expenses. Go see Peanuts at the D.I. and Yale Cohen and Al Sachs at the Stardust. They know Seach, they'll point him out to you, give you his address in Vegas."

Jimmy stood up and Roselli grabbed his hand in both of his, his voice shaking with emotion as he said, *"S'abbenedica."*

For the thousandth time or more, or so it seemed, Jimmy was driving from Los Angeles to Las Vegas. He knew every inch of the way, every twist and turn and bump in the road, every gas station, roadside joint, billboard, every tortured Joshua rising from the desert floor like giant grotesque corpses left to dry in the wind.

He was thinking about Jewel, her confusion and anger over the El Centro debacle, her pride in what she felt she had accomplished undiminished. She blamed him. It was all his fault. If only he had listened to her, they would be millionaires instead of criminals. The divorce, long in abeyance, was rein-stated. Joanne was already divorced from Tommy Thomas, and Jimmy remembered her embarrassement at being forced to testify in El Centro. But she had spunk and he was proud of his daughter. She was a good kid, always had been, and he knew that he had made her life unpleasant and difficult, but it was just "one of them things." What could you do about it? Things happened and you had to roll with the punches or go bananas.

There was Annette, another good kid getting a rough ride. At least he tried to do things for her, bought her toys and clothes, played with her when he had a moment to spare. He had talked to Jean about it but she was too involved with her own life to spend much time with her daughter. That job was left to Jean's mother, but Annette resented being farmed out. She felt rejected by both her mother and her estranged father, who had remarried and had no time for her.

As for Jean, she worried about everything, went into wild rages in which she lost control of herself, screaming and throwing things, driving him from the house for two and three weeks at a time. For reasons he never could quite understand, he always returned to her. Yet he had other women on a regular basis, whether he was with her or not.

As for himself, he was flying in twenty directions at once, not enough of him left long enough in any direction to accomplish anything. But he had to make a buck, to hustle, to run, which meant fighting the odds, and when you got knocked down, picking yourself up, dusting yourself off, and going on as if nothing had happened. You could not think about it, dwell on it, or you were finished.

In recent months he had been involved in a number of "deals." There was "Fat Bob" Tegay and his Seven-Eleven Tours, which they had worked through the Paradise Bus Company. Their end was fifty percent of all the business they drummed up. For Jimmy it meant a few phone calls. They bused people in from San Francisco to Lake Tahoe and Reno and the hotels paid eight dollars per head. With forty people jammed in a bus, and with a half-dozen buses making the loop, they were clearing twelve hundred a day.

There was the deal with "Trigger Abe" Chapman, an alleged hit man from the old Murder Inc. gang, and two other partners. They had opened up a giant furniture mart in Sacramento. Jimmy got twenty-five percent of the deal for showing them how to get the furniture on consignment.

Then there was the deal with Dr. T. Sherron Jackson, a Baptist minister who was the head of the Baptist Foundation of America. Trigger Abe found out that Jackson needed a ninety-day delay in repaying a $1.4 million loan to a Toledo bank. Jackson promised $40,000 if they would secure the delay. Jimmy called Irving "Slick" Shapiro, who was now the owner of a successful restaurant and happened to know four of the bank's board members. The extension was granted, and when Jimmy went to collect his fee, Jackson offered to do him a favor as well. "Look around and see where you need a loan and my man Al Glazer will work it out that way." Jimmy borrowed $200,000 for the furniture mart and Glazer gave him $42,000 under the table, which he split with Bompensiero.

In the red-ink column of the ledger was the situation with his trucking company. One day he had been sitting on top of the world with a million dollar business, and the next thing he knew it was all down the drain. One lousy newspaper story. It was hard to believe.

The vultures had fallen on him, trying to repossess his equipment. As he had explained to Bompensiero, "I stripped my five best tractors, took out all the goodies, just left the bare cab standing but threw some junk in there. This guy from the Morris Plan's scratching his head and I says, 'Take this shit out of here, I'm tired of looking at it.' Bomp, I wish you could have seen it. There's no wheels, no engine, transmission, rear-end, brakes, not even a seat or dashboard in the cab.

"He says, 'Looks like vandals, maybe we can get the insurance in on this.'

I says, 'Forget it, no vandals, just lots of hard use. These trucks have had it.' Finally, after he calls his office, he says, 'This stuff's not worth moving. We'll sell you the cabs for fourteen hundred.' I says, 'You've got a deal.'

"That same day Ray Giarusso starts putting it all back together again. Now I've got some belly-dump trailers I bought with a loan from Alioto's bank. So I get together with the vice president in charge of credit and I give him a proposition. With the five tractors, Giarusso started Camillia City Transport and I tell this guy to transfer my indebtedness and trailers to Camillia or I'm going to cannibalize them to the point where there's nothing left but old iron. They bought the deal, which means I'm left with a little trucking company that Giarusso's going to run for a while. I've got to steer clear of it until these trials are over."

George Seach was in the Stardust casino with a group of friends the first time Jimmy saw him. He was pointed out by Yale Cohen, who had remained president of the Stardust after Dalitz sold it to Albert B. Parvin, president and major stockholder of the Parvin-Dohrmann Company, which also owned the Fremont and the Tallyho, renamed the Aladdin. A Chicagoan, Parvin had operated the Flamingo from 1955 to 1960, at which time he sold it to a Miami group headed by Morris Lansburgh, paying a finder's fee of $200,000 to Meyer Lansky. Except for Peanuts Danolfo moving over from the Desert Inn to the Stardust, with the title of vice president, there were few changes in top management. Al Sachs remained casino boss and Phil Ponti continued his vigil for the boys back in the Windy City.

"I need his address," Jimmy said, not taking his eyes from Seach.

Cohen nodded. "Give me an hour to make a few calls. Shouldn't be any problem. He's pretty well known around here. I just don't want to be obvious about it, if you know what I mean."

"Thanks," Jimmy said, and casually moved away, stopping at various tables to watch the action, but keeping an eye on Seach. A half hour later, Cohen sidled up to him and gave him the address, a side street off Flamingo Road. When Seach and his party left, Jimmy followed them to the Tropicana, and when they went into the cocktail lounge to see the show, Jimmy left to take a look at Seach's house.

Three days later Jimmy, Bompensiero, and Skinny Velotta got together. He had met with Bompensiero in the law library at Cantillon's office and had given him half of the expense money. "Look, Bomp, we clip this motherfucker, there's no telling how much we can get from Friedman. We can nail him for a ton of money. This guy's rich, believe me." Bompensiero's response had been, "Yeah, well, just make sure we get it this time, not Johnny."

While Bompensiero and Velotta went to case Seach's house, Jimmy remained in the motel room. They had checked into a small motel near the airport. For tools they had brought a length of rope and two .38 revolvers.

Although it had been a long time since he had done any work, Jimmy had no doubt as to his ability and courage to carry it off. What was different was his attitude. Somehow his heart was not in it. He had been used in the past and the money the Los Angeles family had stolen from him, and the lies Jack Dragna had told him, after all he had done for them, still rankled in his mind. The only good thing that had happened lately was the death of Frank DeSimone, who had succumbed to a heart attack. To no one's surprise, Nick Licata had succeeded him as boss; Licata, in Jimmy's opinion, was an even worse piece of shit. But this contract, of course, was for Johnny, his best friend, the only man in the world he could count on.

When Bompensiero and Velotta came back late in the afternoon, Jimmy sat up in bed and rubbed his eyes. He had fallen asleep and for a moment he felt disoriented.

Bompensiero flopped into a chair and grunted angrily. "The cocksucker ain't home. No car there, nothing. We drove around the fucking place a million times. Finally we knocked on the door—nothing! We'd have clipped him right there if he'd been home alone."

The next day Jimmy went with them. They drove around the block a few times and Jimmy parked a couple of streets over. He had hot plates on his car that Velotta had stolen in San Diego. Bompensiero and Velotta again walked to the house and knocked on the door and again there was no answer. They came back early in the evening and there were lights in the house but still no one came to the door.

They repeated this routine four days in a row before Jimmy decided to check with Yale Cohen to make sure they had the right house. Cohen came out of his office and Jimmy followed him without speaking until he stopped and whispered. "Jimmy, he's gone. I hear the FBI took him to Hawaii about a week ago."

All the way back to Los Angeles, Jimmy silently cursed himself for not having clipped him that first night. But by the time he met with Roselli in the law library at Jimmy Cantillon's office, he was convinced it was not his fault.

Roselli seemed to take the bad news in stride. "Well, thanks anyway, you gave it your best shot. It looks like I'm going to do the time."

"Is this Seach setting you up?"

"Jimmy, I cashed one of the checks . . . Ah, shit, it's too involved to get into. You know, I had a feeling they were going to stash that guy."

"Johnny, I saw him that one night, and he was with these people. I didn't have any tools to do the work. I guess they must have taken him the next morning. We're lucky they didn't have a detail watching the house. What I don't understand is them lights being on in the house that one night. What can I say, Johnny? It's one of them things."

24
AN IMPASSIONED PLEA

† † † †

IN LATE JUNE 1968, JIMMY AND JEWEL WERE CONVICTED IN SAN Diego federal court of one count of conspiracy and fifteen counts of filing false statements with the federal government. To assist in the prosecution, Richard Huffman, who had been involved in the El Centro prosecution, was appointed a special assistant to the United States Attorney in San Diego. A month later, before Federal District Judge Edward Schwartz pronounced sentence, Jimmy was given an opportunity to address the court.

"Your Honor," Jimmy began, "I keep asking myself what happened to the general contractor and the subcontractors, and all the executives working for them in El Centro, doing just what I was doing, why aren't they in this courtroom, sitting here at this table with me?" He paused and shook his head. "If they were here, Your Honor, they couldn't all sit at this table; they would fill this courtroom. None have been prosecuted individually, as persons, but just as companies. If I'm guilty of a crime, so are they, Your Honor. I know ignorance of the law is no excuse, but I never realized that what I was doing was a crime. My attorney in El Centro, Mr. Cantillon, who could not defend me here because he had a prior commitment, Your Honor, in El Centro, where I was acquitted for a crime similar to what I've been found guilty of in this court, he told the court there, Your Honor, that if everybody that's doing what I was doing were put in jail there wouldn't be one mile of freeway built in this state. Just a while back, Your Honor, the California Assembly passed a bill exempting dump truck operators doing public works from PUC regulations. But still, Your Honor, they're going to try me again in El Centro and I would like to tell you why they're doing this to me.

"Many years ago, Your Honor, there was a police captain in Los Angeles, his name was Hamilton, and he put it on my record that I was a Mafia hit man and that I had killed eighteen or nineteen people. He also put in my record that I was a big dealer in narcotics, and, Your Honor, I've never been involved in narcotics, I don't even know what that stuff looks like. All those things were lies. They even lied about my wife. Your Honor, if you look at my record, just one time have I ever been picked up for investigation on a murder charge, and I was exonerated. I was never picked up for narcotics. But this report keeps following me and everything in it is hearsay. I went to prison in 1954 on a one-to-ten and served six and a half years because of that report. After I came out, I was on parole three and a half years and they sent me to Redding.

"As a boy, Your Honor, I worked with my father, who was a trucking contractor, and I learned that business. In Redding I bought a truck with a five-hundred-dollar down payment and after nine months we got a broker's license and one of the truck brokers in Redding had me chased out because I was giving him some competition and I had to move to Sacramento and start all over again with my trucking business. Within two years I was grossing over a million dollars and not once was I ever picked up. And during all this time, Your Honor, they were watching me night and day. The IRS checked my books and found that I had overpaid them. Nobody could understand my success and they hated to see it. My parole officer, a fair man, said that I made a good attempt to rehabilitate myself but they just couldn't let me alone.

"And now they're after me again. Why they picked on me and indicted me for a felony, I'll never understand unless it's because of that report again. As I said, Your Honor, I was acquitted in El Centro. Judge Gillespie there found no evidence of conspiracy or any fraud or deceit but the state appealed anyway and I'm going to be tried again for the same thing, just me, Your Honor, nobody else. The United States Attorney here in this courtroom wants me to do ten years, and the man helping him, Mr. Huffman, is the same man who tried me in El Centro and will be trying me again for the same thing. It goes on and on and they won't be satisfied until I'm back in jail. If they had their way, I would spend the rest of my life behind bars because of that report.

"I tell you the truth, Your Honor, I can't believe what's happening to me in this court and in this state and this country. If you think, Your Honor, that I've committed any crime to deserve a jail sentence, then you send me to jail. Thank you, Your Honor."

"Thank you very much," Judge Schwartz said. "Anything further?"

"Your Honor, pardon me, but I beg you, Your Honor," and suddenly there were tears running down his cheeks and he swiped at them with his hands. "I don't care what you do to me, but please don't send my wife to prison. She's a good woman and has worked hard to help me rehabilitate myself, made a lot of sacrifices, and she loved this company, it was the first time we'd worked together and we made a success until all that trouble started and now, Your Honor, we're penniless. She's a good mother and grandmother. My wife, Your Honor, has never done a wrong thing in her life. She stood by me through all the years I was in prison and always believed in me. I beg—" He stopped, seemingly unable to control his emotions, and stood swaying unsteadily until his two attorneys grabbed his arms and helped him to his chair. His sobs could be heard throughout the courtroom. There was hardly a dry eye in the house. His performance, as he would later tell his friends, deserved an Oscar.

Judge Schwartz waited patiently until Jimmy had regained his composure before pronouncing sentence. Jewel and the trucking company were each fined $4,016. Jimmy was fined $10,000 and placed on three years' probation. When he walked out of the courtroom, his feet were barely touching the floor.

Until Hamilton had won the reversal in the El Centro case, it had looked like Jimmy Cantillon had saved Jimmy Fratianno from prison. However, Cantillon did win a change of venue from El Centro to Los Angeles.

One day Cantillon called Jimmy to his office and told him that Hamilton and Huffman were ready to make a deal.

After much discussion, he agreed to plead guilty to conspiracy to commit petty theft, which was a felony in California, but the maximum sentence was one to three years, and he was promised the prosecution would not object to probation.

On January 10, 1969, in the courtroom of Judge George M. Dell, Jimmy learned that plea bargaining was a dangerous game. Attached to the probation report was a seven-page summary of unsubstatiated allegations prepared by the LAPD Intelligence Division, which repeated the old charges of Captain Hamilton as a take-off point to soar into its own heady melodramatics.

"In the summer of 1966," the report stated, without offering a shred of evidence, "it was learned that subject Fratianno had a girl friend in San Pedro by the name of Jean Bodul, female, Caucasian. Investigation revealed that Bodul was a prostitute working out of the Hollywood area where she maintained an apartment for just that purpose. She was handling her customers through referral from a known pimp in the Hollywood area. Fratianno made frequent trips to the San Pedro area and was seen on many occasions in the company of Bodul." Whereas the old report had mentioned DeSimone's visiting Jimmy at Soledad prior to his attending the Apalachin meeting, this report went on to add that Mafia leaders from "all over the United States and Europe were present. It has been speculated that if Fratianno had not been in prison during the time the meeting was held, he surely would have been in attendance." The report mentioned the various attacks on Mickey Cohen and most of the murders of that period, plus many others, and somehow tried to imply that he was involved in a murder committed while he was in prison: "When [Julius] Petro was finally sent to Federal Prison for Bank Robbery some eight to ten years ago, the Cleveland authorities had him figured for at least three murders. While in prison, the authorities managed to come up with a witness to one of the murders that Petro committed. During the time Petro was awaiting trial on the murder charge, the State's prime (and only) witness was found shot to death. Petro was released from the charge, due to lack of sufficient evidence. Since that time, the Petros [with brother Mike] now living in the Valley have been frequent companions with Fratianno and his associates."

As if additional corroboration were needed, the report quoted a Los Angeles

Times story in which "Fratianno was identified as the 'Mafia's West Coast Executioner.'" Fratianno and Charley Battaglia "were mentioned as being connected with a $300,000 burglary of a large drug company in Los Angeles. There was not enough evidence to connect these suspects with the burglary; however, it was later rumored that subject was dealing in the sale of narcotics to legitimate drug firms." In conclusion, the report raised the bloody specter of Chicago: "More recently, the Mafia has made some definite efforts to infiltrate the Unions on a large scale. Chicago is living truth to this, with the numerous bombings and killings of Union members and officials. Fratianno and some of his associates have also followed this same pattern on the West Coast, making some effort to infiltrate the Unions. Thus far, we have not had the violence Chicago has seen, but the infiltration is without a doubt present."

Cantillon was so angry he could barely sit still while Judge Dell went through the legal ritual before pronouncing sentence.

When the judge asked the prosecution if they would recommend probation, both Huffman and Hamilton said no. "Well," Judge Dell said, "in light of this probation report . . ."

"Your Honor," Cantillon said, jumping to his feet, "I would like a ten-minute recess."

In the hallway outside the courtroom, Cantillon lashed out at Huffman and Hamilton. "What's going on? I thought we had a deal?"

Huffman shrugged. "I've got orders from my boss, Tom Lynch, not to say anything. Whatever Judge Dell does is fine."

"But that wasn't the deal. You agreed to tell the judge that you would not object to probation."

"Let me explain it to you," Huffman said. "Word has gotten back to Lynch that Fratianno is going around saying that he's got the Attorney General in his hip pocket."

"Hey, Dick, what are you guys pulling?" Jimmy cried. "That's a fucking frame. I ain't talked to nobody about this case. I don't even know Lynch. Who said that? Give me a name."

Huffman shook his head. "That's all I can tell you."

"I don't care about that," Cantillon said. "You violated our agreement when you submitted that Intelligence report to the probation officer. You know the judge can't grant probation with this inflammatory report. The newspapers would crucify him. You've automatically disqualified Fratianno from probation. You've pulled a dirty deal and you know it. It's like saying you won't object to probation and then picking up the phone and telling the probation officer that Jimmy's a rotten son-of-a-bitch. You've violated the spirit of the agreement."

Back in the courtroom, Cantillon asked to take the stand. Keeping his anger under control, he argued that the prosecution had violated their agreement by submitting the Intelligence report. Judge Dell listened patiently but Cantillon's words were falling on deaf ears. When Cantillon asked to withdraw the guilty plea, the judge replied that it was too late. Then he passed sentence. Jimmy stood there and heard the words that would again send him to prison, this time for one to three years. His trucking company was fined $5,000. Released on bond pending an appeal, he felt like a robot as he walked out of the courtroom.

On that same Friday, as a jetliner took off at Los Angeles International Airport, someone fired a bullet into the back of Julius Petro's head, the shot muffled by the noise of the aircraft. His body, slumped over the wheel of his convertible, was not discovered until Sunday night.

The next day Jimmy and Roselli got together in the law library at Cantillon's office. Five weeks earlier Roselli had faced disaster in a federal district court. Found guilty on forty-nine felony counts in the Friars Club case, he was sentenced to five years in prison, and was also out on bond pending an appeal.

"Would you believe it," Jimmy said, "I lived with them guys while I was going to court. Juli Petro and Skinny Velotta own an apartment house in Van Nuys. Petro lived there in one of the apartments but Velotta's renting a place in Glendale. I was using both places. Anyway about three days before Juli was killed, they burglarized Sears in Glendale. This Skinny walks right in there at night like he had a permit. He's one sharp burglar. So's Bob Walch and Ray Ferritto. But all three hated Juli. In fact, while I was staying at Skinny's place, I think about two weeks ago, in the middle of the night, Walch and Ferritto come in the apartment and Ray's leg's all fucked up. He tried to put a bomb in Juli's car and it backfired. I think the cap went off. Anyway, I heard Skinny saying, 'What the hell're you doing? You can't do it that way.' "

"What was the problem?" Roselli asked. "You think they hit Juli Petro at the airport?"

"Fuck, yes. One night I'm lying on the sofa at Skinny's place. They think I'm asleep. I hear them talking about this sports bookie, Sparky Monica, and they're saying that Juli was shaking him down. I think Sparky gave them some money to get Juli off his back."

"So what are you going to do now?" Roselli asked.

"I've got a good thing going with the Seventh Step Foundation in Phoenix. Let's hope I win that goddamn appeal."

"What's that?"

Jimmy frowned. "Ain't you heard of it? This kid, Bill Sands, started it. He wrote a couple books while he was in the joint, *My Shadow Ran Fast* and *The Seventh Step*. Then when he got out he started this foundation to help prisoners get their heads straight when they leave the joint and to help kids avoid getting into trouble. I'm trying to raise money with some benefits. I called Mark Anthony to get Bob Hope to do one, but he's booked solid for the next eighteen months. So maybe Sinatra will do one. Maybe Sammy Davis. Them guys around Frank. Why don't you see him for me? After all, you know him better than I do."

"Jimmy," Roselli began, "Frank and I are on the outs. Sinatra took Sam for a lot of money when he sold Cal–Neva. He's come across with some money, but don't worry, Sam's going to get the rest. Did you see Frank in Palm Springs?"

"No, he'd just left on a trip, but I've got him on the back burner. This's important to me, Johnny. I get ten percent of all money I raise. The guy that owns the sports arena in Phoenix will donate the place for the shows, so that could mean a lot of money, that place seats about fifteen thousand.

"We've got a lot of other plans for Seventh Step," Jimmy said. "I'm leaving for Chicago in the morning to meet with Philly Alderisio. He's got this huge five-story warehouse full of furniture and appliances, all stuff donated by stores and people. He's got straight guys fronting the deal. They write thousands of letters and advertise, asking for donations for foundations. The plan is to open discount stores all over Phoenix and later into California. We'll get some of Philly's merchandise. We get to keep forty-nine percent of all profits, which is a good deal since the merchandise's donated."

Roselli was smiling. "Jimmy, you know, the more you talk the more enthusiastic you get and the more angles you see."

"Johnny, this's a great scam if you're careful. The business people who donate will never have to worry about labor problems, or as Philly says, arson." Jimmy laughed. "But I've got another idea—by the way, I'm the public relations director for Seventh Step and my job's to keep feeding Joe Wallace with ideas. He's the national president. See, we can start furniture factories near prisons where the cons learn them skills. Pay them three, four bucks an hour, let them make a good living. But this's long-range stuff. If I can promote some money the sky's the limit. Joe Wallace told me I could write my own ticket. What if I bring in a half-million a year? I get ten percent, plus a salary, maybe a hundred grand, plus credit cards, plus leased car. As long as I'm bringing in big money, what's the difference. When you think of the benefits with Sinatra and Hope, the discount stores and furniture factories, a hundred grand a year's nothing. I could take two hundred and they wouldn't even miss it."

Undaunted by his continuing court problems, Jimmy, as always, was off on other new scams and schemes.

25
FOILED AGAIN BY
THE FOURTH ESTATE

† † † †

JIMMY TOSSED THE NEWSPAPER ON THE COFFEE TABLE AND FLOPPED
on the couch. "Here we go again," he said, reaching into his pocket for a
cigar. He had been back in Phoenix from his trip to Chicago a little over
a week.

Jean picked up the paper, her eyes widening when she saw Jimmy's picture
on the front page of the Arizona *Republic.* The headlines and lead paragraphs
read: " 'EXECUTIONER' Coast Hood Likely To Succeed 'Batts'—A high-
ranking Mafia member from California expected in Arizona soon may have
been tapped to succeed the imprisoned Charley 'Batts' Battaglia as boss of
Joseph Bonanno's crime family activities in the state. He is James 'Jimmy the
Weasel' Fratianno, a 55-year-old long-time syndicate member and former
associate of West Coast mobster Mickey Cohen." The story went on to explain
that since the incarceration of Battaglia at Leavenworth in 1968 on a ten-year
extortion conviction, "rumors were heard that a 'big man' was being imported
from out of state. Fratianno apparently is that man." The rest of the story was
a rehash of old news clippings.

"I'm going to call that reporter," Jean cried angrily. "When are they going
to leave us alone?"

Jimmy looked at her and said nothing. In a way, it was humorous how
wrong they could be. If the opportunity had presented itself, Jimmy would
have murdered Battaglia in a minute. Jimmy had not forgotten how Charley
Bats had stolen his shylock money and tried to rape Jewel while Jimmy was
in prison. As for Bonanno, he had never spoken to the man and never would.
Bonanno was persona non grata and no self-respecting *amico nostra* would
dare even acknowledge his existence.

"How can you just sit there with that cigar in your mouth and act like you
don't have a worry in the world?" Jean demanded, crumpling the paper before
throwing it on the floor. "Why do you let them get away with these lies? Sue
the bastards."

"Relax, will you. If I was to sue every newspaper that lies about me, I'd be spending all my time in court. Forget about it. You call the reporter, he's going to put it in the paper, then things will be twice as bad.''

An avalanche of black ink hit on March 19, 1969. It was El Centro all over again. When Seventh Step president Joe Wallace came back from a meeting with Phoenix City Manager Robert Coop and Police Chief Lawrence Wetzel, he was boiling mad.

"The sons of bitches," Wallace snarled. "How do you talk to square johns anyway? I told them, Jimmy, I said, 'The whole purpose of this organization is to welcome ex-convicts. I don't care if it's Al Capone. We can't turn ex-convicts away because they get headlines in the fucking newspapers.' Finally I said, 'Look, why talk to me? If you've got questions, ask Fratianno, face to face.' So we set up a meeting with everybody for next Wednesday.''

By everybody, as Jimmy would discover at City Hall on that appointed day, Wallace had meant the city council, city manager, police chief, the head of the Intelligence division, and other city leaders. The only person he recognized was Tom Yamuchi, his probation officer.

"To be blunt about it, Mr. Fratianno," Coop asked, "why are you here with the Seventh Step? What are you trying to accomplish in Phoenix?''

Dressed in a conservative business suit, with thin streaks of silver in his dark wavy hair, Jimmy created the appearance of a successful businessman as he stood up to speak. "Gentlemen, I appreciate this opportunity to explain my interest in the Seventh Step. Being an ex-convict, I'm qualified for the program, but that's not why I'm here. I don't need a handout. I'm here for only one reason and that's to help the Seventh Step become a self-supporting organization. My function here's to help raise money so we don't need public funds. I believe in this program. Having spent about fourteen years of my life in prisons, I know what it's like to be an ex-convict without a dollar in your pocket and no chance for a job.''

He paused and looked at Tom Yamuchi. "Mr. Yamuchi, do you give parolees money, food, clothes, and a place to live? Do you find jobs for them?''

"Well, we try to help them find a job," Yamuchi replied, "but we don't provide clothing, food, money, or lodging.''

"That's right," Jimmy said. "If you belong to the Seventh Step while you're in prison, when you come out we give you a couple suits, shirts and ties, shoes, give you some money, find a home that'll take you in until we find you a job. We work with employment agencies, the state employment office, and we call them up all the time, keep after them until we get results. Ninety-five percent of the guys coming out of prison are broke and don't know who to turn to. This is a good program and I don't see why you don't get behind it instead of causing problems.''

Chief Wetzel waved his hand. "Just a moment, here. What are you getting out of this? Aren't you here to make money?''

"Look, that's not why I'm here. That's not my purpose, to make a lot of money for myself. Sure, if I raise money I expect to collect my ten percent. But I believe in this program. What's wrong with trying to do something for ex-convicts? Believe me, if I didn't think this was a good program, I wouldn't be here. Furthermore, if I was only interested in money, I'd be either in Las Vegas or Beverly Hills. Ask anybody in the program, I go to the prison in Florence every Monday, we take four, five juveniles with us, let them see what it's like over there, get them back on the right track. I attend the meetings here every Tuesday. I work all week and I've been doing it for nearly five months now and I still haven't made five cents. So I don't think it's fair to imply that I'm here to get rich."

He talked for a half hour and answered questions for another half hour, mostly about his background, denying the murders and Mafia affiliation, going on to expound on the success of his trucking company and how he had been destroyed by lies in the El Centro newspaper and how it was starting all over again in Phoenix. The next day the city council canceled its $1,000 monthly contribution to the foundation.

In April, both Jimmy and Jean had to appear before a grand jury in Los Angeles that was investigating the death of Julius Petro. The headline in the Arizona *Republic* read: "Mafia Man Here Subpoenaed in Killing." Relying on "inside information," the story stated that "A source sitting in on the California investigation told the Arizona *Republic* there is a 'good possibility' that Petro died while chauffeuring Fratianno to the airport. 'Although we are convinced he is involved, he may be too high in underworld stature now to have been the man behind the gun,' the source added. . . . Another investigator confirmed that federal agents had been keeping a constant watch on Fratianno and Petro 'for several months' before the killing."

The fact that Ray Ferritto and Bob Walch were not subpoenaed told Jimmy something about the effectiveness of that "constant watch."

Early in June, Jimmy flew to Sacramento to pick up a new Jaguar XKE from his old friend, Chris Sarantis, at Oxford Motors. To avoid problems with his numerous creditors, the yellow convertible sports car was registered in the name of Nick Rizzo, who was Ray Giarusso's partner in the Camellia City Transport Company, which was part Jimmy's, born out of the ashes of his old company.

From there Jimmy drove to the Mapes Hotel in Reno where Jean was waiting for him. For a year now, ever since his divorce had become final, Jean had been after him to legalize their relationship. Finally, after a violent argument, he had agreed to get married. Tomorrow was to be the day, but the more he thought about it, the more certain he became it was a mistake.

By the time he reached the hotel, he had decided to call the marriage off. Their room was on the second floor and as Jimmy came out the elevator he thought, "Well, she can't kill herself if she jumps out the window."

Jean opened the door and kissed him. "Look at me," she said, pirouetting to show her new dress, her long golden tresses coiling softly around her white throat. "You like?"

"Nice, very nice, and you smell good. What's up?" He slipped out of his suit jacket and dropped it on the bed. "Wait till you see the Jag—it's a beauty. Jesus, that mother really goes."

She came to him but he sat down before she could put her arms around his neck. "Is that my wedding gift? That's really sweet of you."

Jimmy took a deep breath. "Honey, let's think about this marriage thing, you know. Let's not jump into it without first thinking it through. There's a good chance I might be going back to the joint."

"Oh, you son of a bitch," she cried. "Are you trying to back out?"

"Well, you know, all I say is let's think about it."

She stood before him, her feet planted apart, the mini-skirt length of her new dress riding up on her thighs. "I hope to God you're kidding."

Jimmy glanced at his jacket on the bed and wondered how he could retrieve it in the event he had to make a quick exit. "Honey, listen a minute, will you? Please sit down and let's think about this a minute."

"A minute?" she screamed. "I've been thinking about it for three years. You better cut this out. I don't think it's funny."

"I'm not trying to be funny. Honey, you know, I was just thinking about it on the way up here and it seems to me that maybe we're rushing into this thing without really thinking it over. I just don't want to make no mistake."

"Stop it," she warned. "I'm getting goddamn mad, mister."

"Oh, Jesus," Jimmy said. "You start calling me mister, I'm taking off. I don't want my head broken."

He jumped out of the chair and Jean ran to the dresser for a heavy ashtray, whirling around in time to see him grab his jacket and dash for the door. She flung it with all her strength and it crashed against the doorjamb above his head.

It was a beautiful day and he drove to Lake Tahoe with the top down.

Not until five o'clock in the morning did he think about Jean and decide to return to the hotel. The minute he walked into the lobby the night manager signaled to him and Jimmy followed him to his office.

"Mr. Fratianno, I'm afraid I have some rather unpleasant news for you," he said, the moment the door was closed. "Your fiancee is in jail. She, er, imbibed a little too much and just demolished the room."

"Hey, wait a minute, who called the cops?"

"I'm afraid it was out of our hands. The people in the next room called. You see, she was screaming and throwing things, even broke a window, and they thought she was being attacked, which is understandable. She raised quite a ruckus, I can tell you. The room is in complete shambles."

"Don't worry about it," Jimmy said, "I'll pay for the damages. Send me the bill."

When Jimmy went to pick up Jean, she had spent the night in the drunk tank with the lushes and crazies. She was disheveled, her face soiled, her new dress torn, her eyes red and swollen from hours of crying, her step unsteady as she came into the room.

She looked at Jimmy and said, "You dirty bastard," and fainted dead away.

Jimmy sat on the sofa in his Phoenix home, holding a small pillow over the fly of his blue boxer shorts. He had been awakened by Richard Carlson and Lance Brisson, who identified themselves as writers interested in doing a magazine story on his trucking company. They commiserated as he spoke of his "bum rap," that "all the trucking contractors in California did the same thing but I'm the only guy ever convicted for it. It's a precedent case."

They asked about the Seventh Step and he said the newspapers had again spoiled things for him. He emphasized that he held no official position. "I just go down there and do what I can to help. I talk to kids, they listen to an ex-con like me. I'm telling you this from the bottom of my heart, sincerely, the Seventh Step's a wonderful program, the best organization of its kind I know of, and Joe Wallace's doing a bang-up job as national president."

The moment the writers began inquiring about his relationship with Joseph Alioto, who was now mayor of San Francisco, Jimmy grew suspicious. "Look, I did my banking with the First San Francisco Bank. I think I saw Alioto once in my life. I don't know the man."

Carlson was not satisfied. "But of all the banks in Sacramento, why come to San Francisco, to this particular bank?"

"A friend of mine did his banking there and told me I could get a low interest rate on loans. It was a new bank and it needed customers."

Carlson looked at his notebook. "Let's see, there were five loans for a total of about a hundred and five thousand dollars. Is that correct?"

Jimmy patted the pillow. "Hey, wait a minute, what are you getting at? Let me tell you something, you put this guy Alioto in your story and he'll sue you for a hundred million dollars."

Carlson laughed. "Don't worry, this is not a story about Alioto."

"This's an important man. He was almost Humphrey's vice-presidential candidate last year. You remember, he made that nominating speech at the convention. From what I hear, he's a fucking sharp lawyer. And don't forget, there's talk he might be our next governor. You write about him, he'll sue you to the fucking grave."

Brisson nodded. "The only reason Dick asked about Alioto is because he happens to own that bank. And we hear that he knows Angelo Marino and Jimmy Lanza, who we understand are friends of yours."

"I wouldn't know them from a bale of hay," Jimmy said. "Look, let me show you guys something interesting."

Jimmy went into the bedroom and brought out a large metal box. "This's a beeper, found it under my Jag. The L.A. cops put it under there. Look at this thing, it's got six magnets and batteries a fucking foot long. I went to visit a friend in Saugus, I was sure nobody had followed me, and I'll be a sonovabitch if I don't spot a tail that night. How would you like it, in this free country of ours, to have fucking cops put beepers on your fucking cars? Listen, I've been framed and double-crossed all my life. If you know anything about the courts in California, you know they'll take a shot in the dark and fuck you on your reputation, even if it's a pack of lies."

Jimmy caught the next flight to San Francisco. The more he thought about it, the more convinced he became that the writers were primarily interested in Alioto. Somehow or other, they had heard about Jimmy's association with the mayor of San Francisco.

At the First San Francisco Bank, Jimmy asked Nick Rizzo to get Alioto on the telephone, saying he had an important message for him.

With Alioto on the line, Jimmy explained about the two writers visiting him in Phoenix. "I think these guys are after you, Joe," Jimmy said. "They knew about the five loans and the total amount. They even knew I still owe about fifty thousand. It looks like they've done a lot of research on this thing."

"Jimmy, I know about it. They called me the other day. Did you tell them anything?"

"Not a fucking word, Joe. I said I saw you only once in my life and that you had nothing to do with my trucking business. Look, Joe, I warned them, I told them you'd sue for a hundred million if they mentioned your name in the story."

"Well, there's definitely something in the wind. I have received word from other people. Did they say which magazine would publish the story?"

"I'm not sure, *Look* or *Life.* You know, Joe, they've both been doing stuff on organized crime lately. I don't like it, Joe."

"Let us not worry about it yet. But thank you, Jimmy. Why don't you keep in touch with Angelo in the event I need to communicate with you."

"Joe, anything I can do, just say the word."

When the article written by Carlson and Brisson appeared in *Look,* Jimmy was in the San Diego County Jail, completing the thirty days required after he had taken a pauper's oath to avoid paying the $10,000 fine previously imposed by Federal Judge Schwartz. He was still waiting for his appeal to run its course in his other court case.

Advance copies of the article, which was scheduled for release on September 9, were distributed to the press a week early by Governor Ronald Reagan's office.

With the heading, "THE WEB THAT LINKS SAN FRANCISCO'S MAYOR ALIOTO AND THE MAFIA," the lead paragraph read: "Mayor Joseph L. Alioto of San Francisco, the rising politician who came close to the Democratic nomination for the Vice Presidency in 1968, is enmeshed in a web of alliances with at least six leaders of La Cosa Nostra. He has provided them with bank loans, legal services, business counsel and opportunities, and the protective mantle of his respectability. In return, he has earned fees, profits, political support, and campaign contributions."

Next to Alioto's, the most prominent name in the story was Jimmy's. A primary source of information for Carlson and Brisson had been Tommy Thomas, Jimmy's former son-in-law.

Although much of what they wrote was basically accurate, there was a fatal flaw. The authors had referred to "a series of nighttime meetings at the Nut Tree, a restaurant along the highway between San Francisco and Sacramento. Among those present at one or more of the conferences, in addition to Alioto, were Fratianno, Bompensiero, Angelo Marino, LaPorte, and one of Jimmy Hoffa's top Teamsters representatives on the West Coast. Alioto's plan to organize a bank was a subject of intense discussion. After one meeting, Fratianno said he was 'excited' about the possibilities for the future because 'my man [Alioto]' would control the bank's board of directors." This was followed by a fairly accurate history of the loans, but the damage had been done.

The authors' only source for the Nut Tree meetings was Tommy Thomas, whose fanciful imagination had led the writers down the primrose path on several unverified anecdotes. Once Alioto read that paragraph he knew he had them. Like a house of cards, an exposé story cannot survive without all its underpinnings remaining intact. Knock one down and the whole structure collapses. The Nut Tree meetings never took place. Even before the magazine hit the newsstands, Alioto had filed a $12.5 million lawsuit and issued a sixty-nine-page refutation of the five-page article.

He "categorically and unequivocally" denied every Mafia-tainted allegation in the story: "I have met James Fratianno in my office with Jack Goldberger. . . . At the time of that meeting in either late 1964 or early 1965 I had no facts of knowledge concerning Fratianno's background, which was of no concern to me. The records of the First San Francisco Bank reflect loans being made to Fratianno during the year 1965, substantially all of which secured by what the bank officers regarded as adequate collateral. I had nothing to do with determining whether or not the loan should be made. It was made on the merits by bank officials. Mr. Fratianno also borrowed from other banks at or about the same time."

In describing the meeting with Goldberger and Fratianno, he said: "I had never seen or heard of Mr. Fratianno before that meeting. The appointment was made through regular office channels. Up to that time, I had known Mr. Jack Goldberger in connection with local, state, and federal elections. We had been on the same side most of the time, but it is noteworthy that in 1967, in my mayor's election, Mr. Goldberger supported my principal opponent, Mr. Dobbs." In another part of his refutation, in referring to the Goldberger–Fratianno meeting, he said it "was the only time I met or knowingly talked with Fratianno in my life." For the next ten years, during repeated court proceedings, he would steadfastly maintain this position. He would be just as adamant about not knowing Bompensiero, "I do not know and have never met Frank Bompensiero," or Frank LaPorte, "whoever he may be."

26
A FEW LAST MANEUVERS

† † † †

THEY PLAYED HEARTS AND TRIED TO THINK OF WAYS TO MAKE
money. Jimmy and Dave Rapken were in the basement office of the Galaxie
night club in the North Beach section of San Francisco. Since he'd been driven
out of Phoenix by the press, Jimmy had rented a house in Fremont, a small
town about forty miles south of San Francisco.

Rapken, who owned the Galaxie and Mr. D's restaurant, was in financial
trouble. Jimmy had known Rapken about two years, having been introduced
by Bob Tegay.

"How many people can you pack into Mr. D's?" Jimmy asked, biting his
lower lip as he studied his cards.

"About six hundred."

"We've got to come up with some kind of benefit or testimonial, some way
of filling the joint, a fund raiser of some type. We charge so much per head,
take out your expenses, and cut up the rest. Know what I mean, Dave?"

"Yeah, I follow you, but I can't think of nothing."

Just then there was a rap at the door and Bennie Barrish poked his head
in, his ugly moon-shaped face creased in a smile. "What're you doing, fellows?"

Jimmy looked at him and bells went off in his head. He had known Barrish
twenty-five years, back in the days when Barrish used to drive down from San
Francisco to visit Mickey Cohen. As a youth in Chicago in the early Thirties,
Barrish had been a fair to middling club fighter, at a time when Cohen was
also trying to make his mark in Chicago. The friendship between Barrish and
Cohen, formed then, would last a lifetime.

"Hey, Bennie, are you a humanitarian?" Jimmy asked.

"Shit yes," said Barrish, sitting down next to Jimmy and trying to read his
hand. "I'm a Godfather, been one for years."

Jimmy glared at him. "I know you're a comedian, but I'm being serious
here."

"But I am a Godfather," Barrish insisted, rubbing his battered nose. "It's an organization started by Monsignor Clement McKenna at St. Patrick's Parish. There's about four hundred of us and we try to raise money for the Orphan Asylum at St. Vincent's School for Boys in San Rafael."

"I'll be a sonovabitch," Jimmy said. "What do you do for them?"

"I sell tickets when they have benefit performances."

Jimmy shook his head. "You're a swindler, Bennie. Didn't nobody check your background?"

"Wait a minute. I never served a day in my life."

Jimmy looked him straight in the eye. "Don't shit me, Mickey Cohen told me about you. You got convicted for burglary back in the thirties."

"I never served time. I got four years' probation."

"Yeah, but what about that extortion rap with Jimmy Tarantino, when you was shaking down little store owners for Tarantino's scandal sheet right here in San Francisco?"

"Again probation," Barrish said, "just six months."

"What's this I hear about you having the balloon concession at Golden Gate park? You stealing from kids now?" Jimmy joked.

Barrish grinned. "I'm never there. It's worth a couple hundred a month for doing nothing."

"In that case," Jimmy said, standing up and holding his playing cards over Barrish's head. "I pronounce you Humanitarian of the Year."

"By Christ, Jimmy, you've got it," Rapken said. "We'll give Bennie a testimonial, have the mayor present him with a plaque, and Monsignor McKenna can give the invocation. Shoot the works."

"That's a good touch," Jimmy said. "We say it's for his work with the boys at St. Vincent's, you know, create the impression that somehow this will help them."

"What do you think, Bennie?" Rapken asked. "Want to be Humanitarian of the Year?"

Barrish, who was a liquor salesman for Juillard Alpha Liquor Co., thought it was a grand idea. "That should make my boss happy."

"All right, we need a sponsoring committee," Jimmy said, "and no fucking deadheads. We want people who can push tickets. Let's get some union people. Morry Weisberger at the Sailors Union, Jerry Posner and Ed Turner of the Marine Cooks and Stewards, Jack Goldberger; someone from the police, Captain Charlie Barca; a couple of attorneys, Nate Cohn and George Davis; some bookies, Peewee Ferrari. We want Bennie to feel at home."

"How do we get the mayor?" Barrish asked. "I know him good, want me to talk to him?"

"Sure, just don't mention my name."

Rapken laughed. "Alioto's got all the Fratianno he can handle right now. How about my P.R. gal, Deborah O'Brien, coordinating the whole thing? She's got a head on her shoulders, that gal."

"Beautiful," Jimmy said. "How much you want for the food and services, what's the nut?"

"Six bucks a head should do it. They'll pay for their own booze."

"Okay, let's charge twenty-five bucks a ticket and split the extra nineteen bucks three ways. With six hundred tickets, what's that, eleven grand? No big deal but you'll get some publicity out of it, Dave, and you, you schlemiel, you'll be famous for a day."

And that, quite simply, was how Jimmy Fratianno made Bennie Barrish Humanitarian of the Year in San Francisco.

As Jimmy said, "You take a swindler and clown like Bennie and make him a humanitarian. With all the stories in the papers about it, publicity, it just goes to show you how easy it is to con the public."

On Sunday evening, January 4, 1970, the night before the Barrish testimonial, Jimmy and Rapken again played hearts. This time they were at Rapken's penthouse apartment on Russian Hill, not far from his North Beach establishments, which had a spectacular view of the Bay. That fall Jimmy had spent many weekends at Rapken's penthouse, playing gin rummy with Assemblyman John Burton (later a congressman) and his brother Phil, whom Rapken had known as a boy. On Sundays they would watch football on television and Jimmy would do a little booking on Rapken's telephone, servicing a few old customers, but nothing extensive.

But on this Sunday night Jimmy had something else in mind. "I'm not coming to the testimonial tomorrow," he said.

Rapken looked up from his cards. "Why the hell not?"

Jimmy laughed. "Dave, I've been fucking a spy for the FBI. I met this broad in Hayward, in a bar, and I take her to Warren's apartment in Hayward, and I fuck her. I do this about three, four times and this broad falls for me and cops out she's working undercover for two FBI agents, Larry Sidener and Roy Howland. They're with this new Strike Force working here and in Sacramento and they've got grand juries looking into organized crime."

"What's this broad's name?" Rapken asked.

"Bonnie Covey. She shows me news clippings where she's sent a bunch of guys to the slammer. Now she's meeting with the feds two, three times a week and telling them I'm fucking her, that everything looks good, and they give her money. But I ain't telling her nothing. Forget about it. So one day she brings up this testimonial dinner. She says, 'Jimmy, you've got to do something for me, I've got to look good with them guys, show them I'm doing something for my money. Why don't you take me to the Barrish testimonial. You know, the FBI will be there taking pictures of everybody there. Mayor Alioto's going to be there and it would be great if you came. You know, the mayor's lawsuit's going to court in a couple months.' I'm listening to this broad and I can't believe my ears. I says, 'Why, sure, I'll be glad to take you.' She's got a long wait, this broad," Jimmy laughed.

"I don't blame you. They'll be enough interesting characters to keep the

Feebees busy. By the way," Rapken continued, "the ticket sale wasn't too good, about half of what we expected, your end will be about fifteen hundred."

Jimmy shrugged, "What the hell."

Angelo Marino was worried that his father would be called upon to testify in the Alioto–*Look* lawsuit.

"He's got a bad heart and he's getting a little soft in the head," Marino told Jimmy over lunch at a San Jose restaurant. "His mind kind of wanders and he's liable to say most anything under cross-examination. He met with Alioto just the other day and then comes home and tells me that Joe wants him, me, you, Jimmy Lanza, Bomp, and LaPorte to give depositions to back up his claims in the suit. He even suggested we file lawsuits of our own, but Jimmy, my reaction is that Pop's dreaming this shit.

"So I call Joe and he sends me a copy of his statement, denying all the shit in the magazine, but he said nothing about us filing lawsuits. Listen, after all, he's been our attorney for years. He got me out of the tax case when he got the FBI to admit they'd bugged me, and he stopped them from deporting my old man. As for you and Bomp and LaPorte, remember he don't know you period. But Bomp refused to deny knowing Rudy Papale. As he said, their trip to Mexico on that lard deal is probably on a million fucking FBI reports."

"Well, I'm not giving any deposition. Right now I've got my hands full with grand juries."

"Is that one still going on in Tucson?" Marino asked.

"I've already testified three times. They gave me immunity, you know, and I told them the truth. I know nothing about Charley Bats' plans to spring himself from Leavenworth with phony testimony and to divide Arizona along 'territorial lines,' for Christ's sake. Bats couldn't control a bunch of Boy Scouts. Now he's in his cell writing letters on prison stationery to avoid the censors, which he thinks this clerk in the joint is mailing out.

"He's writing to Joe Bonanno and Pete Notaro, Joe's bodyguard, and to some barber called Pancho, and all the letters are copied by the warden and given to the FBI," Jimmy said. "Bats wants some of the witnesses at his trial to change their testimony and he's threatening this Pancho that he'd better get with it or he'll find his head decorating a cactus. In another letter, he tells Pancho he'll keep breathing only as long as he does what he's told. The minute he slips up he stops breathing. He writes, 'You know the Bat so you know this is it.'

"Then it's my turn. I get off the plane in Tucson and I'm grabbed by a bunch of feds and one hands me this newspaper and there's my name. This Pancho's supposed to give me a contract on several people Charley wants killed. My fucking picture's on the front page. Everybody's there, Pete Licavoli, Joe Bonanno, Pete Notaro, but who's on the front page, me. They give me immunity and now they want to know whether it was Bonanno or Licavoli who offered me a hundred and fifty grand to kill a former FBI agent and a former police sergeant. I says, 'Ladies and gentlemen, the last time I spoke to Mr.

Licavoli was in 1952 and I've never spoken with Mr. Bonanno. As for Mr. Battaglia, I last saw him in 1954, at which time he stole a great deal of money from me, and if I never see or speak to him again it will be too soon.' That pretty much wrapped it up. But, you know, Angelo, all this bullshit wears you down after a while."

"I'll tell you a guy that's in trouble," Angelo said, grinning. "Your son-in-law, Tommy Thomas, who started all this shit. Alioto says he's going to put him in prison for twenty years if he shows his face in court. He gave a deposition and went into hiding. One way to get out of testifying, and Alioto told me this himself when I was going to be subpoanaed in Joe Cerrito's lawsuit against *Life,* and that's to claim health problems. Get a doctor to say you've got a bad heart. Any shit like that will get you off the hook in a civil case."

"I see where Joe dropped his bid for the governorship."

"Well, as he said, he's got his hands full running the city and prosecuting this lawsuit. He's going to kill *Look,* believe me. By the way, Jimmy, what's this I hear about your driving a truck again?"

He sighed. "Angelo, I'm on probation, I've got to have a legitimate job. I've got a piece of the furniture store and the trucks, but no one's supposed to know that. This old friend of mine, Merle Brown, owns Triple A Wreckers in Hayward. It's a wrecking yard and I drive the tow truck."

"Jesus Christ, how can you do it, Jimmy? With the money you've made and now back to driving a tow truck. Can't you work out some phony deal?"

"Listen, this ain't bad. Besides, Angelo, I'd do anything to stay out of the joint. If I have a solid workingman's job, it will help me when I go before Judge Dell. My appeal should be coming down any day now.

"But let me tell you about this little scam I've got going with this highway patrolman." Jimmy brightened. "Whenever he finds a car illegally parked, he red tags it and calls to give me the name, address, and phone number of the owner. Once the car is red tagged, the owner's got twenty-four hours to move it.

"I wait about twelve hours before I call the owner to explain the law. Usually they're old cars and have to be towed out. So I arrange to meet the owner at his car and I say, 'What do you want to do with this heap?' Most of the time they say, 'How much you give me for it?' I says, 'It ain't worth nothing. The steel mill'll only pay twenty bucks. It costs more than that to tow it there. If the city picks it up it'll cost you fifty.' Nine out of ten times, they give me the car and pink slip. Maybe I give them five bucks. I take it to the yard and they strip it, get all the goodies, even the fenders and doors. Then the carcass goes to the steel mill and they still pay twenty bucks for it."

At noontime on July 29, 1970, special agents Larry Sidener and Roy Howland sat in the back of a van and grinned happily as the voices of Carl Held, the bar owner who owed Jimmy $15,000, and Jimmy Fratianno were being recorded on a tape cassette. They had wired Held and instructed him on how to proceed during lunch at the Edgewater West in Oakland.

"Oh, boy, they're having screwdrivers," Sidener said. "Loosens the old tongue."

"Hey, wait, listen. Held's got him going about the loan."

"It's no good, Carl, I tell you. You took her fucking money. I'm not looking for myself like I told you. It's my old lady and I ain't given her a quarter and I keep telling you, Carl, but you make no attempt to do nothing."

"Well, I ain't got no fucking money. Where am I going to get any fucking money?"

"Carl, that don't matter. You can send her a hundred or fifty, whatever you can, but you never sent her a dime. You've got to make an attempt. How do you think it makes me feel? She blames me for giving you the money. That money's got to be paid back, Carl. I don't care what anybody says, or what you say. It's got to be paid back. I'm responsible. I gave you the address. If you'll just send her some money and show good faith."

"All right, I'll try."

"Listen to this con," Howland said. "This guy's beautiful."

"Yeah, but what's wrong with Held? He just missed a great opportunity."

"Give him time. A couple of those screwdrivers will loosen them up."

"What a sad song he sings. You hear that? He owes Cantillon twenty thousand. That shyster can kiss that money good-bye."

"Oh, boy, there it is, listen."

"You remember, Jimmy, maybe you were excited or something but remember the last time down here, last time you give me that big spiel that I'm going to fucking kill you, blow your fucking head off, kill you?"

"Carl, you're liable to do anything with something like that. Listen, Carl, let me tell you something. I'll run it down to you."

"We've got him. He didn't deny it, did he?"

"That was pretty cute. Oh, there's more."

"What about me, Jimmy? Am I going to go around and shoot everybody that gaffed me? You know how much I've been gaffed in my life?"

"Yeah, Carl, I've been gaffed plenty, but I keep telling you, this's my old lady you've gaffed. She's going to blow the fucking house in Vegas if she don't get some money."

"Can't you help her?"

"Carl, I've taken a pauper's oath, I'm fucking broke. The IRS's checking me out right now. I ain't got no fucking money. Period."

"They're having another drink. Good luck, Jimmy."

"These guys are big bullshitters."

"Geez, Jimmy, I'm down there in that goddamn lot and you say, shit, I'm going to put a fucking gun to your head. I mean, you know, Jimmy, I mean, shit, you know."

"Carl, look, you want to know the truth? Do you want to know the truth? I'm liable to like it, you know, Carl. If I thought you was fucking me, I'm liable

to do that. And I'll tell you one thing, boy, I'd never get caught if I did it. I got news for you. No way, but you've got me so fucking mad. Listen, dude, if it was my money I'd say fuck it. Carl, I can always hustle a man but not a woman and that's what you're doing. You just don't do that, Carl. I mean, Carl, look. You could write to her and send her a little something. Show her your good faith."

"That's it, we've got him cold. Want to wrap it up?"

"No, no, let's keep listening. Quick, listen."

"Well, Jimmy, you don't think for one minute that I'm going to pull a frame on you and her."

"Yeah, Carl, but who knows what you're up to."

"I mean, if there was, if there was a frame, I mean I could understand your being mad."

"No, Carl, I know there's no frame."

"That's what you think, baby. That Held's got some nerve, I'll say that for him."

"Here comes a little bonus, maybe."

"I read in the paper that Joe Torchia got knocked off in Sacramento."

"Yeah, Carl, and they tried to blame me, but I was in Reno. I went to see the Wayne Newton show. Oh, they tried to find me in the worst fucking way."

"Well, everybody was after that guy. Got any idea who did it?"

"I don't know. Nobody knows. That prick had the bookmaking locked up in that town. But he was a piece of shit. You should see the way he treated his wife, Jean, who's a pretty sonovabitch, treated her like dirt. Anyway, Sheriff Misterly knew we had a beef a while back. Torchy, I called him, fucked me out of twelve hundred at the fairgrounds. That guy was always chewing a fucking angle. So that night I caught up with him at the Carl Greer Inn, the card room back there. I walk in there and he's got two guys with him. I open the door and I says, 'Line up, you squirts.' I'm smiling but they know I mean business. I says, 'Give me my fucking twelve hundred, you motherfucker.' I grabbed the money right out of his fist. I says, 'What're you doing here, you little cocksucker?' I give him a push. I says, 'Don't fuck with me or I'll tear your fucking brains out.' He's turned white as a sheet, just standing there with his mouth open, and I says, 'You ain't got no guts, you suck. Listen, it's too late in life to mess with me, you know. I'll kill all three of you motherfuckers."

"Oh, damn, the cassette's stuck."

"They're having another drink. Jimmy's over his limit right now."

"Was Torchia's wife mixed up with anybody?"

"Carl, who do you think was fucking her? Sheriff Misterly."

"Boy, this guy's a fountain of information."

"Jimmy, I've got to go, have to drive up to Atascadero this afternoon."

"Why don't you drop me off at the wrecking yard."

27.
THE VERDICT

† † † †

THE HONORABLE GEORGE M. DELL STARTED TO SPEAK AND JAMES CANTIL-
lon stood up. "Please don't interrupt me. If you don't like it, wait until I'm
finished. It has been a traumatic day and you are a nice guy and you are nice
to my children, but if you had been in this Court all morning, I think you
would be a little edgy at this point, too."

Jimmy thought, "Oh, great, the fucking judge's got a cross-hair."

"After reading the probation report," the Judge continued, "the Court
denied probation and sentenced the defendant to the state prison for the term
prescribed by law. The defendant felt grieved by virtue of the breach of an
alleged plea bargain and by means of appeal attacked the proceedings subsequent to the entry of a plea.

"I have now considered the original and supplemental report as well as a
number of letters that have been transmitted to me which are in the Superior
Court file, including, but not limited to, a group of letters received this last
week from a George Faris, a Monsignor Cornelius Higgins of Sacramento, and
a J. L. Feller of the Early Engineering Corporation. . . . There may be some
others, but I had those before me immediately and I recall reading those as
well as a long and extremely eloquent letter from Mr. Fratianno which is
attached to the probation report.

"I will be happy to hear from counsel in a moment. I just want to be sure
the necessary preliminary formats are complied with.

"Does the defendant waive any further arraignment at this time?"

"He does, Your Honor."

"Is there any legal cause why the judgment of this Court previously rend-
ered but stayed during the execution of the appeal shouldn't be ordered into
full force and effect?"

"Well, there is no legal cause, Your Honor," Cantillon replied.

"I will be happy to hear from you then, as far as any other matters which
you and/or Mr. Fratianno would like to present at this time, including any
correction of the record if you feel that is necessary."

245

Cantillon spoke gravely and eloquently for a long time, reviewing the evidence and the history of the case. The judge reclined comfortably in his large leather chair, his eyes closed a great deal of the time. Cantillon spoke of the harassment by police officers and of the prosecution seeking vengeance, of the excessive bail in El Centro where "Mr. Fratianno reposed in the county jail for two or three weeks, which is equal to about six months in Los Angeles, and went through months of preliminary proceedings through the years. I think it is four years to the day next week on the fourteenth of August. He comes before the Court now lashed by the whip of economic disaster."

Judge Dell opened his eyes and smiled, showing that he appreciated an eloquent cliche. He closed his eyes again as Cantillon continued for a while longer, finally ending with, "If the Court did feel there was something to be accomplished other than vengeance, other than imposing upon Mr. Fratianno no punishment for some conduct on his part for which he hasn't already paid his debt to society, then I think that a county jail, a term of probation to run consecutively with the term of probation he is now serving with the federal government would more than amply satisfy whatever interests the People of the State of California have at these proceedings."

The People, in the form of District Attorney Hamilton, "oppose Mr. Cantillon's statement. If Mr. Cantillon is suggesting a reduction of this crime by sentence to a misdemeanor, we would oppose that."

Then it was up to Jimmy and he spoke for a very long time, his words more passionate than eloquent, and Judge Dell kept his eyes closed until he had finished.

"Mr. Cantillon, is there something you want to add?"

"No, Your Honor. I think Mr. Fratianno expressed generally my sentiments, perhaps a little more emotionally than I could. I feel much as he. I don't think anyone has ever done three hours in jail for a violation of any of these regulations or tariffs that comprise the nature of this whole offense, and I just think it would be completely unfair to impose a prison sentence on Mr. Fratianno."

Judge Dell thanked him and also spoke at some length before delivering his judgment. "I have considered the entire matter again and feel there is no basis for a change in the prior judgment of the Court. Probation is denied. It is the order of this Court that the judgment previously imposed and suspended during the pendency of the appeal now be carried into full force and effect. . . . The defendant is remanded into the custody of the sheriff for delivery into the custody of the Department of Corrections."

PART VIII

† † † †

SCAMMING
THE JOINT
1970–1973

28.
DOING GOOD TIME

† † † †

HE LAY ON HIS BUNK, SMOKING A CIGAR AND CONTEMPLATING SMOKE spirals lazily drifting up to the ceiling. Sunday, December 27, had dawned cold and gray at San Quentin, a maximum-security prison on the bay just north of San Francsico. The only good thing that had happened to him in the past four months were the eighteen boxes of cigars friends had sent him for Christmas.

A guard opened the steel door and he sat up. "Hey, Frat, they want you at R and R [Receiving and Release] on the double."

Jimmy walked at his leisurely pace, puffing on the cigar, his head held high. He had been at Q, as the prisoners called the prison, four months, ever since a federal grand jury in San Francisco had handed down a two-count indictment charging him with "express and implicit use of threats and violence and other criminal means" in his attempt to collect the $15,000 Carl Held owed him. That trial, set for January 4, 1971, had been shifted to Fresno because of the notoriety created in San Francisco by the *Look* article. The indictment, handed down only a few days after his conviction in Los Angeles, had come as a complete surprise. Jimmy had spent barely a week at the Southern Reception Guidance Center in Chino before federal marshals had yanked him to Q for the convenience of the United States Attorney prosecuting the case.

Now as he walked into R&R, he saw Robert LaRoche, a deputy U.S. marshal from Fresno whose sole claim to fame was that he drove a Mercedes Benz. LaRoche, who was speaking to his partner, looked up when Jimmy came into the room. "Okay, Fratianno, get dressed."

"Where're we going?"

"Just get dressed, don't worry about it."

As Jimmy changed into street clothes, he was certain they were going to take him to Fresno. "Well, am I coming back here?" he asked.

"Who knows?" LaRoche replied. "Okay, spread your legs while we get the irons on." Jimmy felt the weight of the manacles against his ankles but said nothing. "Okay, now your hands." The steel cuffs snapped on his wrists and

Jimmy's only thought was that he would miss the football games on television. "Can I bring my cigars with me?"

"One box, that's it. Now let's move it."

They went out the main gate and Jimmy could not believe his eyes. Four marshals stood by the wall with machine guns at the ready.

"What the fuck's happening here?" Jimmy asked. "Are they expecting a demonstration of some kind?"

LaRoche and his partner hustled him to the Mercedes, pushing him into the back seat. "Stay down," LaRoche warned, as he and his partner sat up front. They shot away from the curb with a burst of speed that left a cloud of blue smoke in their wake. Jimmy turned around and saw that the men with the machine guns were following in two cars.

"Listen, you guys are really going to screw up my football games."

"Don't cry on my shoulder, Fratianno," LaRoche said. "We're only following orders."

The traffic was light that early on Sunday morning. Jimmy leaned back in the seat and listened to their constant chatter over the radio. Finally, he sat up and said, "Holy, shit, there's a guy I know going down the other way. I think he spotted us."

"Them assholes," Jimmy would tell Roselli years later, "I picked up on it right away. I figured somebody had put something in my jacket about there being a contract out on me. And who do you think it was? Some FBI prick in Sacramento. Just made it up to make things rough for me. Anyway, you should've seen them guys when I said that. They got all pushed out of shape, I mean they were scared shitless."

The Mercedes accelerated to ninety and Jimmy leaned back and closed his eyes.

"Did you recognize the guy?" LaRoche asked.

"Yeah."

"Well, who was it?"

"My brother. Must've been on his way to visit me at Q."

"You wiseguy," LaRoche snarled. "We're risking our necks here to protect your life and you play jokes. Thanks a lot."

Instead of taking him to Fresno they continued south to the Visalia county jail. A half-hour later Jimmy was in the hole, dressed in a pair of cotton trousers, a short-sleeve cotton shirt, rubber thongs, and no socks. He spent eight days in an unheated, windowless cell, in an empty cellblock, shivering under a single blanket. The food was so bad that the putrid aroma was enough to make him retch. By the third day his fever was so high that he was pleading for a doctor, but instead they gave him a handful of APC pills, which are a combination of aspirin, phenacetin, and caffein, the standard analgesic administered in prisons.

By the time he appeared before Federal Judge M. D. Crocker, Jimmy was anxious to unload his burden. After the judge had reset the trial date to June

22, Jimmy, ignoring the young Public Defender assigned to his case, asked to address the court. Struggling to control his emotions, he described in vivid terms the nightmarish eight days he had spent in the Visalia jail.

"Your Honor, the man responsible for my treatment is Deputy Marshal LaRoche. He's the one who told them to put me in segregation. I have been treated worse than an animal. No animal could eat the swill they gave me, no animal could survive the conditions imposed on me the last eight days. Your Honor, no disrespect to you, but I'm not going nowhere with that man. If you want me to go with him, you'll have to kill me, because I'll fight it with my last ounce of strength. What happened to me was no accident, Your Honor. It was done on purpose, to make me suffer, perhaps to kill me. Believe me, I nearly died in that cell and they wouldn't even call a doctor. Your Honor, both my lungs are collapsed and that's on my record. I'm still sick, I've got a fever, and I ask this Court to send me forthwith to Chino where the Department of Correction first sent me after my conviction in Los Angeles. Thank you, Your Honor."

"Thank you, Mr. Fratianno," Judge Crocker replied. "I will ask the United States Marshal's office to investigate your complaint. Meanwhile, it is the order of this court that you be returned to the Chino State Prison until such time as your presence is required in this courtroom."

After the judge had left the courtroom, Jimmy turned on LaRoche: "You dirty motherfucking cocksucker, I ain't never going to forget you. Where do you get off treating me like a fucking animal, you fucking Nazi?"

While Jimmy was going through his evaluation period at the Southern Reception Guidance Center (SRGC), the Adult Authority informed him that his term had been fixed at three years and that no further parole consideration would be given to his case. Although this did not come as a total surprise, it did start him thinking along the lines of survival for the next three years. Then one day Raymond Procunier, the Director of the California Department of Correction, came to Chino and Jimmy made it a point to talk with him.

"I'm Mr. Fratianno," Jimmy said.

"Oh, Jimmy Fratianno. What's your problem?"

"Look, Mr. Procunier, what're you going to do with me? I got a one-to-three but the board says I've got to do the whole three. I've got six months in, so where're you going to send me for the next two and a half years?"

"Well, Jimmy, where would you like to go?"

"Well, sir, I'd like to stay here or go to Vacaville. I'm having problems with my lungs and I'd like to stay in Southern California."

"I don't see why not. Got any job in mind?"

"Yes, sir. I've got a chance to take over the maintenance crew at SRGC and I know I could do a good job. I know how to handle men."

Procunier excused himself and went to speak to the captain and associate warden who were waiting for him a short distance away. When he came back, he said, "All right, the job is yours, but write me a letter. Now don't worry, you'll stay here. Good luck."

Jimmy's good luck turned out better than Procunier could ever have imagined. The Held case was disposed of with a plea bargain, the sentence to run concurrent with and not longer than his present term. Apprised of the situation, the federal prosecutor in San Diego considered his guilty plea a violation of his probation in that case and Jimmy again found himself before Federal Judge Schwartz. Advising his attorneys that he wanted to speak on his own behalf, Jimmy was anxious to address the court. He asked the judge to read the transcript of the tape recording of his conversation with Carl Held before passing judgment. The judge agreed.

Several months later, Jimmy described to his new attorney, Richard C. Chier, the second hearing, where the judge made his decision known. "Dick, I wish you could've seen that prosecutor, Bob Risso, who really had a hard-on for me . . . him and that Jack Armstrong . . . when Schwartz told them he'd read the transcript five times and couldn't understand what I was doing in his courtroom. He says, 'Mr. Fratianno was only trying to collect money due his wife, who was destitute, and this man Held had been coached by the agents to put words in his mouth.' Shit, they were slamming pencils on the table, jamming stuff into their briefcases. They were fucking mad. They thought the judge didn't know what he was doing, but let me tell you something, this judge's an intelligent man. He don't care about newspapers. He judges cases on their merits. But you should've heard this Risso telling the judge, 'Your Honor, probation should be revoked immediately to protect society from James Fratianno.' Dick, the guy's nuts."

Having known Jimmy for years, Chier enjoyed the story. Before going into private practice he had been associated with James Cantillon and therefore knew a great deal about Jimmy's background.

"Speaking of cases and their merits," Chier said, "what's on your mind? What's this big deal you want to discuss?"

Jimmy moved closer and lowered his voice. "Like I told you on the phone the other day, I'm in charge of the maintenance crew here at SRGC."

"Congratulations, Jimmy. I always knew you had it in you to move up in the world."

Jimmy laughed. "Save the jokes and listen to me a minute. I've got a little scam going that might interest you. You see, Dick, I can help guys that come through SRGC with a Z number. They're here ninety days for evaluation. It's the counselors that decide whether they do time or get probation. In that ninety days they take a bunch of tests but they see a counselor only twice. Here's what I can do for you. Let's say you've got a client coming up here for evaluation. I can guarantee you an A-one report."

"Hey, Jimmy, you're losing me."

"Dick, it's simple. There's six counselors here, a psychiatrist and a psychologist. Here's the angle. Let's say you want a good report on a client coming up here. You send word to me, tell him someone's going to take care of him, but don't mention my name. This guy comes up on the bus with the others from the county jail. They teletype the list and I look it over every day. I see his name and when he gets in R and R, I go to control and tell the sergeant I want this guy on my crew. Boom, it's done. That means he's going to live in the honor dorm. He's going to have a nice private room, a desk, plus I have all eighteen cells in the bottom row where you can see the visitors. Best cells in the joint. That alone's worth the twelve hundred dollars I charge for a good report.

"Now I go to the inmate that assigns guys to the various counselors. I says, 'Look, give Joe Blow to Mr. Keegan or Mrs. Snyder, or whatever. Let's say he gets Mr. Keegan, then I put him to work for Mr. Keegan. You get it, now, Dick? That way his counselor sees him every day. Every so often I go see Keegan and ask how Joe Blow's doing. We talk and I says, 'You know, Mr. Keegan, this kid comes from a good family,' this and that, bullshit him. Every day I tell Joe Blow make sure you do this, make sure you do that, keep that office spanking clean, ask Mr. Keegan if there's anything else he wants, be polite. I coach him, see. By the end of the three months, forget about it, this guy's in solid with his counselor.

"Inmates type all reports and if I don't like what's in there I go back and have another talk with the counselor. The report goes to the court, right, and I call you on the phone and say everything's double george, you know. Dick, I'm telling you, so far I ain't lost one."

Chier was smiling. "Jimmy, you're one enterprising, resourceful guy. Jimmy Cantillon and I have talked about you many times and we both agree that you possess the ultimate street sense. How long you going to stay on this job?"

"I've got to be at SRGC a year before I can transfer to the correctional facility across the street."

"Jimmy, I like the deal," Chier concluded.

One day Jimmy received an unexpected visit from Dick Chier.

"What's up, Dick? Anything wrong?"

"No, in fact, it could be quite good. I got a call from the law firm representing *Look* in the Alioto lawsuit. As you know, Jimmy, the first trial ended in a hung jury, eight to four in favor of *Look,* but now Alioto's going for a new trial and *Look* wants to know if you'd be a witness for them. I promised to discuss it with you and get back to them. What do you think? Know anything that could help their defense?"

Jimmy laughed. "Are you kidding? Listen, Dick, I can get them off the hook, just like that," and he snapped his fingers. "Alioto's been lying his fucking head off, under oath. But what's in it for me?"

"They have made no overtures, no offer of money at this point. They have to be extremely careful not to taint your testimony in the event you have to take the stand. Perhaps you could help them in other ways. Give them names of witnesses who knew of your relationship with Alioto, some corroboration."

"It'll cost them two hundred grand. What the hell, Joe's suing for twelve-point-five million. It's a drop in the bucket."

"Jimmy, you're now waxing into the realm of fantasy. Your testimony wouldn't be worth the powder to blow it to hell if Alioto ever got wind of it."

"Let them pay you a consultant fee, and we'll cut it up. It's done every day."

Chier shrugged. "I don't know, Jimmy. Let me explore it and get back to you."

As soon as Chier left, Jimmy telephoned Benny Barrish in San Francisco.

"I've got a job for you," he said, the moment Barrish came on the line. He never identified himself when making calls, expecting whoever was at the other end to recognize his voice. "Go see Alioto and tell him *Look* offered me big money to testify for them. Tell Joe it might be good for him if I go along with it, string them along, get the money, then when I'm in court, I tell how they paid me to lie for them. The thing would backfire, blow them right out of the fucking courtroom."

Jimmy called Barrish every day until he finally had something to report.

"Oh, Christ, Jimmy," Barrish laughed. "Joe nearly shit his pants when I gave him the proposition."

"What'd he say?"

"He don't want to get involved with nothing like that. He says for you to stay away from *Look*. I'm telling you, Jimmy, you should've seen that man. He looked like he was going to have a fucking hemorrhage."

"Okay, tell Joe not to worry about it."

Although the parole board had rejected him, it went against his nature to accept any kind of final judgment. As soon as he was transferred to the correctional facility, Jimmy asked Francis Keegan to write to Henry W. Kerr, chairman of the Adult Authority. Keegan's letter was not successful but it shows how smoothly Jimmy had ingratiated himself at the SRGC. Dated March 29, 1972, the letter read:

Dear Sir:

Inmate James Fratianno has informed me that he intends to submit to the Adult Authority a request for a modification of his sentence and has asked that, as his former Counselor, I render to the parole board an evaluation of his conduct and work habits while he was a member of the Permanent Work Crew at the Southern Reception Guidance Center. I feel that this is a fair request and believe that the reviewing panel will accept the information contained herein in the same spirit in which it is submitted.

For a period of fifteen months Inmate Fratianno performed the duties of Hall Maintenance Man at SRGC and during that time was a member of my caseload. On this job he was responsible for the janitorial services performed in the interior of the Guidance Center building. He supervised a crew of inmates, usually about ten in number, in the accomplishment of the required work. Although not required to do so, Fratianno was frequently seen on the "business end" of a mop or broom setting a pace and example for those who worked with him. The floors, windows, restrooms, and offices at SRGC were never cleaner than when Fratianno was on this assignment. I feel he is to be commended for a job well done.

The manner in which Fratianno conducted himself while at SRGC earned him the respect of the institutional staff and his peer group. Without being obsequious, he was supportive of staff and completely cooperative. While Counselor for the Permanent Work Crew I received no complaint from any person about the behavior of this inmate.

Should the Adult Authority deem it appropriate to shorten the period of Fratianno's confinement, such action could be thoroughly justified by Subject's institutional adjustment, positive attitudes, conduct and work habits.

During his fifteen months at SRGC, Jimmy successfully processed nine clients for Los Angeles attorney Ron Minkin and four for Dick Chier.

His father had died prior to his incarceration in 1970, but until his mother's death in 1972, Jimmy called faithfully every week. She was living with his sister in Cleveland, who accepted his collect calls without his mother's knowledge. During every conversation, his mother would remind him of her age and ask when she could expect a visit from him, and each time he would say that he was involved in a big construction project and would be tied down for at least five or six months. In the last year of her life, he was calling her two and three times a week and she never once suspected that he was back in prison.

On Sunday evening, June 25, 1972, KPIX-TV in San Francisco broadcast a special report entitled "An Essay on the Mafia." Moderated by Nick Pileggi, a noted crime writer, the program featured Joseph Alioto as its guest. In a rather lengthy introduction, Pileggi was generous in his praise:

"Joe Alioto's the most popular Italian on the West Coast. But there were two unresolved lawsuits at this time. One had been brought by the Justice Department, just about the time the Mayor was ready to run for governor of California. Another he had brought against *Look* magazine." Apparently moved by his own words, Pileggi said, "Joe Alioto's the only mayor in America who can kiss a hand without embarrassment." Then Pileggi went on to explain about the lawsuit: "In 1969 *Look* magazine tried to tie him to the Mafia. *Look* leaped before it checked. It was a cheap shot that wounded the Mayor for eight months. But, because he's a millionaire lawyer who could fight back, Alioto took the magazine to court. The trial exonerated him of all ties to the Mafia. The citizens of San Francisco returned Joe Alioto to City Hall by an even wider majority than he had received in his first election."

"First of all," Alioto said, "*Look* magazine is nice, uh, is now broke, as you know. And Nick, it couldn't happen to a nicer magazine," Alioto laughed. "In any event, *Look,* uh, in 1969 people were saying that I might be running for governor of California. Now, at the same time, you know, my office was still doing the principal antitrust work on, against the cartels, against big business in the country. The year before I ran for mayor, we had more lawsuits in my office against cartels than the Department of Justice had . . . just the year before I ran for mayor.

"Uh, so, this combination of things, uh, got a lot of people to thinking that maybe they had to clip my wings. And so what do you do when you have a fellow with an Italian name? And if his father came from Sicily? First thing you do is to suggest he's a member of the Mafia or has some kind of Mafia suggestions. And this is what *Look* magazine did.

"Now, if you read the article closely, the . . . the . . . the . . . the evidence was very, very thin. But nobody reads those articles. They just see the pictures and diagrams of the Mayor of San Francisco enmeshed in a web of Mafia affiliations, or some silly thing like that.

"Now, it didn't matter, you know, that San Francisco was a famous city in the country, so far as Mafia affiliations were concerned. And everybody said that from J. Edgar Hoover down to the U.S. Attorney, the Chief of Police, the Attorney General of the State of California, the President's Crime Commission. Everybody said that, but it didn't matter. Here was a fellow with an Italian name, of a Sicilian ancestry, and so they published this article.

"It worked. It kept me out of that governor's race in 1970. And there are political analysts whom I respect who have looked back and said that, but for that *Look* magazine article, that I would have been the candidate and would have won in 1970.

"Now, I don't know, you know . . . 'All the words of tongue or pen/ The saddest are by . . .' or whatever that line goes. I don't care about that, I really don't. I am willing to pay that price. I'd rather be an Italian and pay that price, an Italian–American and pay that price, than not be an Italian–American and not have to pay that price.

"It's also necessary, Nick, to beat that kind of stuff."

(A few days later, *Look* attorneys persuaded the station to make this retraction: "Actually, there was no exoneration because the jury was unable to reach a verdict and a mistrial was declared.")

From the moment he first saw Lyn Roman, Jimmy began angling for some way to be alone with her. She was a singer and had come to Chino with B. B. King and Jimmy Witherspoon to do a show for the prisoners. As a member of the welcoming committee, Jimmy had escorted the performers to the dining hall for a steak dinner after the show, making sure that he sat next to her.

It was not long before he was telling her about his friendship with Mark Anthony, who had since become manager of Bob Hope Enterprises, suggesting that perhaps he could get her on one of Bob Hope's shows.

"You've got a fantastic voice," he said, his eyes irresistibly drawn to her generous bosom pressing against the sheer material of her dress. "I'll talk to Mark first thing in the morning. Give me your number and I'll call you."

She wrote her number on a napkin and looked up just as Jimmy was leaning forward to gaze down her neckline.

"Sorry about that," he said, "but it's been a long time since I've seen a beautiful girl."

"I was just thinking about that," she said. "What do you do about sex?"

"Dream about it," he said. "Unless you're a degenerate and fool around with guys, there ain't no sex in prison."

"How long's your sentence?"

"Three years and I'm about halfway through it."

"Poor you," she said, touching his hand. "That's awful."

"Tell you what, Lyn. You'll be my first date when I get out."

For months he talked with her on the telephone at least once a week and twice she came to visit him. Then the Tennis Club decided to have a banquet and Jimmy, realizing his opportunity, promised to bring them a fabulous show. Usually when an inmate made plans to bring in outside performers for a show, he was granted a nine-hour pass to complete arrangements. After discussing it with Mark Anthony, who agreed to bring a show, Jimmy got Warden Griggs to approve a nine-hour pass that included another prisoner and a member of the civilian personnel staff instead of a guard.

That night Jimmy called Mark Anthony to give him final instructions. "I'm coming out day after tomorrow," he said. "Like I told you, I'm going to have nine hours. What we've got to do is find some way to shake the two guys with me long enough for me to fuck that broad I was telling you about."

"You mean that black singer, Lyn Roman?"

"Hey, Mark, this broad's skin's lighter than yours. I've already talked to her and she's going to be waiting at a restaurant across the street from your office on Riverside Drive. Here's the way I see it. We'll come straight to your house in Toluca Lake, maybe have a cup of coffee."

"I'll tell you what, Jimmy. We'll have brunch, then I'll take you guys to Bob Hope's house. He's out of town, but I'll give you a little tour of the place. That should impress your friends. Give them a few little trinkets, money clips with Bob's profile, lighters, little souvenirs like that, and from there we'll go to NBC studios, and then to the office. It's all in the same vicinity."

"Okay, but I've got to shake those guys for a while," Jimmy said. "Maybe you can send them somewhere to see somebody about the show and I'll tell them I have to stay back to make calls, give them some bullshit."

"No problem," replied Anthony. "There is somebody they can see in Santa Monica."

"Great, that will give me at least two hours. With what I have in mind, I'll need every minute I can get."

"You horny bastard, Jimmy, you're going to spoil that little gal for life."

She came into the room and he started undressing before she could say a word.

"Hey, baby," she laughed, "you look like you're boiling over."

"Strip, honey, and we'll talk later. This first one's going to be quick as a fucking rabbit."

She started pulling her clothes off. "Not even a little kiss for openers?"

"Don't worry, sweetheart, you'll get all the kissing you want, but right now let's get it on real quick before I shoot myself."

"Oh, daddy, what a mean old gun you've got," she said, dropping her skirt and panties at the same time.

For a year, from May 1972 to April 1973, Jean stopped coming to Chino on visiting days. During that period, Jimmy heard that her drinking problem had worsened. She was living in Palm Springs, only a short drive from Chino, and the rumor was that she was involved with Zeppo Marx, whose own estranged wife, Barbara, had caught the roving eye of Frank Sinatra. In a pique of temper, Jimmy had removed her name from his list of approved visitors. Two weeks later he heard that Zeppo had struck her while she was sitting in her car in the driveway of the Tamarisk Country Club. Jean would later file a lawsuit, seeking $350,000 in damages, charging that Marx had beat her in the face and head, had pulled her hair and attempted to break her nose. Marx, who was in his seventies, would maintain that it had been nothing more than a shoving and pushing match, occurring when she had attempted to leave with his house key and oil company credit card. Five years later a jury would order Marx to pay $20,690 in damages.

Refusing to serve any more time than required by law, Jimmy walked out of Chino at one minute past midnight. The date was August 28, 1973, and the next fifty-two months would be the fastest and headiest of his life.

PART IX

✝ ✝ ✝ ✝

INTERLUDE
IN MIAMI
1974

29
BACK IN ACTION

† † † †

MIAMI BEACH IN NOVEMBER 1974 WAS JIMMY'S KIND OF TOWN. THIS was where the rich and powerful came to play in the winter. It was also a returning to the womb of his first youthful adventure.

He had been barely twenty-two that first time, a babe in the woods, but where had the thirty-nine years gone? The old song, "Moon Over Miami," kept spinning away somewhere in back of his head and from time to time he wondered about the lyric. He could hum parts of the tune but the words had vanished with the years.

The change since 1935 was startling. It was even more impressive than the Las Vegas Strip. The water made the difference, the surf lapping at the sandy beach. In 1935, he had come to book at Hialeah, but this time he was working on a multimillion-dollar deal and staying at the exclusive Jockey Club, with its two gleaming high rises of luxury condominiums occupied by millionaires, socialites, and celebrities—the board of governors included Perry Como, Pierre du Pont, and Fess Parker.

This was his fifth trip in three months. It had been a golden opportunity to spend time with Johnny Roselli, whom he had not seen in over four years. After his release from McNeil Island federal penitentiary, Roselli had moved in with his sister and brother-in-law, Edith and Joseph Daigle, who lived in a rambling, white brick home in Plantation, a small town some twenty miles north of Miami Beach. He was trying to fulfill his promise to retire, having come to the mob's favorite retirement haven.

"Hey, Jimmy," Roselli said over dinner one evening, "did you get a chance to talk to Abe Teitelbaum while you were in Chino?"

"You mean Capone's old attorney? Yeah. In fact he gave me a good tip. He told me about a special law where you can go bankrupt on back taxes. Shit, I owed the feds and the state about thirty grand, so when I got out Ray Giarusso introduced me to this kid, this lawyer in Hayward, Dennis McDonald, and he looked up that law and Abe was right. So now the slate's being wiped clean but I've got to watch my step, don't want to flash. Oh, listen, before I forget, I've got to tell you this story. Remember when Juli Petro was clipped at the airport in sixty-nine? I was going to court then and staying with them burglars. I told you then I thought Ray Ferritto had done it. Well, I hit the nail right on the head. Ray came to Chino on a burglary rap while I was there and I got him a good job at the Guidance Center." Jimmy laughed.

"They needed a locksmith and I told the lieutenant Ray was the best in the business. I always liked Ray and we'd bullshit, so one day he tells me he clipped Juli for Sparky [John G. Monica]. He says, 'This cocksucker promised me five grand and fifty percent of his sports book and he's never given me a dime.'

"Juli was muscling Sparky," Jimmy continued. "Ray told me how he killed him—Bob Walch drove the car and when they got to the airport Ray shot Juli in the back of the head. Then he took the next flight home to Erie. If you'll remember, they pulled me before the grand jury, but they didn't even question Ray.

"So Ray got in touch with Sparky. He wants Sparky to deliver on his promise, but Sparky tells him, 'You want anything from me, you talk to Tony Plate.' "

Roselli laughed. "I knew that was coming up. Sparky went broke a few years ago, and Tony Plate bankrolled him. Remember, Tony works here in Miami under (Aniello) Dellacroce (a *caporegime* in the Gambino family). They clipped Charley Calise a few months ago when they caught him snitching to the FBI."

"Well, I put it to Tony. I says, 'This Sparky's throwing your name around,' and he says, 'Well, I ain't got nothing to do with that guy no more.' I'm looking at him, you know, and I just know the cocksucker's lying. So I told Ray to lie low for a while and see what develops."

Roselli smiled. "Never a dull moment. What do you hear from your old friend, Joe?"

"Oh, Christ, when I got out of the joint I had Bennie Barrish go see him, tell him I'm busted and find some thing for me to do. Alioto says there's nothing available right now. He bullshits him, so I send Bennie back to get me a parking lot, lease it from the city, you know, anything. But the *Look* case's still going on and this guy's scared to death of me. He just brushes Bennie off with more bullshit."

"Why didn't you go see him yourself?" Roselli asked.

"I wouldn't want to be seen talking to him," Jimmy replied. "I don't want to hurt the guy. He's a prick, but still I don't want to fuck his case. Someday when this case's over, I'll get something, don't worry."

"You're entitled," Roselli said. "What's happening with you and Jean?"

Jimmy sighed. "Johnny, I don't know what to do about that broad. She's turning into a lush. Oh, Jesus, it's terrible. She gets violent and throws things, goes on rampages. I get out of there in a hurry. Then Punkie, who's only, you know, thirteen or so, gets mad at me for leaving her alone with Jean. But what am I supposed to do, hit her on the head to calm her down?

"She's got this obsession about getting hitched. I says, 'Let me get on my feet.' I don't know what I'm going to do. So she's staying with a girl friend at Murrieta Hot Springs. Then her grandmother left her four thousand and Jean says, 'Well, I'd like to buy a lot over there and put a trailer on it.' You know, Johnny, one of them big ones that's like a house.

"After a few months, I went down to Murrieta and met this Paul Axelrod. He's taking care of the place for Morris Shenker, who took over some fifty miles of land down there when Irving Kahn died."

"Well, you know, Jimmy, it was Shenker who got Kahn about two hundred million dollars from the Teamsters. Shenker went right to Hoffa for the money without going through any of the families. At that time he was one of Hoffa's top lawyers and on the finder's fees alone he must have made millions with Kahn. I hear he's turning most of that land back to the Teamsters, getting out from under a lot of bad deals. This guy's been getting away with murder for years."

Jimmy laughed. "Want to hear something funny? This kid Funzied [nee Alphonse D'Ambrosio] from the Joe Colombo family [in New York] was telling me that a few years ago, before Colombo got shot—I think it was not long after Shenker took over the Dunes—Funzied was playing baccarat with Colombo.

"They're partners, and Funzied's playing three hands and he's down a few thousand. He got the limit removed and he's betting five thousand on each hand. So now he tells the dealer not to touch the shoe and the fucking guy touches it anyway. Funzied throws a fit and demands to be paid on all three bets.

"So up they go to Shenker's office and he calls Tony Giordano [in St. Louis] and he flies in. They meet in Shenker's office, but Colombo's a boss and Giordano's a boss, so it's a standoff. Tony tells Shenker to pay Funzied and later he tells Colombo he's glad this came up. Now, he's going to nail this Shenker for more money. After all, Shenker's supposed to be his man and all Tony's getting's about fifty grand a year, fucking peanuts. Shenker makes that in a day."

"Don't forget Nick Civella [boss of the Kansas City family]," Johnny said. "He's also on Shenker's payroll. There's a little rivalry going on between Nick and Tony. Shenker pays them both off, but nobody gets a piece of his action. If there's any skimming at the Dunes, Shenker's doing it without Nick or Tony knowing about it. But he does favors for them. He funded the Aladdin, your old Tallyho, when Albert Parvin sold it, and got a half-million finder's fee."

"Christ," Jimmy said, a wistful look coming into his eyes, "I came so close to getting that joint. Which reminds me, Johnny, what happened with the Frontier? I hear they gave you immunity before the grand jury."

Roselli nodded. "I told them nothing, but Maurice Friedman copped out and testified. Tony Zerilli, Mike Polizzi, and Tony Giordano all got four years. The FBI had tape recordings, but you know me, Jimmy, I don't say much on the phone."

"I met Shenker at Murrieta. In fact, he gave us one of his townhouses for a few months. You know, comped it. I introduced him to Bomp and Louie Dragna and we bullshitted a few times, but you can't make no fucking money with this guy. Now this Axelrod's sharp, very clever in banking, and Shenker told me he was paying him a thousand bucks a week, but the guy's a gambling degenerate, that's why he keeps him away from Vegas. After he told me that, I thought I'd stay away from this Axelrod, which I did for a while."

Roselli waited for the waiter to refill their wineglasses. He took a sip and raised his eyebrows. "This Dom Perignon is smooth stuff. This was Judy Campbell's favorite bubble. Do you realize that was only a dozen years ago? Seems like a million."

"Lots of water under the bridge, all right," Jimmy agreed.

"Yeah, lots of shit slipping by, which reminds me, I see where the L.A. family's in the shit again."

"Yeah," Jimmy said, "but let me tell you what happened when I first got out of the joint and I get this call from Jimmy Regace, who's now calling himself Dominic Brooklier—now he's an Englishman, right?

"At that time he's the underboss. Licata's still alive. So they hear I'm in town and I meet with them at a restaurant on Sunset Plaza Drive. He comes in with Pete Milano and introduces him as a made guy. So Brooklier says, 'Pete's a *capo* now,' and I look at this piece of shit and I want to laugh in his face. It's a fucking disgrace. Brooklier says, 'I just got through talking to the old man and he wants to know what you're doing in town. He's made some inquiries and don't like what he hears.'

"Jesus Christ, I blew my fucking top. I says, 'Listen, motherfucker, I knew you when your name was Jimmy Regace and you was scared of your shadow. I saved your life, asshole, when I talked you away from Mickey Cohen.' He says, 'Why are you getting mad? I'm just passing on what Nick told me.' I says, 'What do I care what Nick Licata wants to know?'

"Now, Johnny, I hadn't seen Brooklier in a lot of years, and one time we were pretty close. I'm godfather to one of his boys, and when he was on the lam I used to send him money. But I look at him and he's the enemy; still I can tell he don't like what he's doing. But that don't cut no ice with me. He says, 'Well, Jimmy, I'm sorry, but Nick asked me to talk to you. He knows you went to Louie Dragna about Vic Werber. We're shaking him down and you've got no right to interfere in our action. You know the rules, you've got to check in with us before handling any action in our country.' Johnny, he had me. Vic's an old friend and he's in the clothing business like Louie. He does a little loansharking and he just asked me for a favor. I tried to get the heavies off Vic's back. But then Louie turns around and tells Nick."

Roselli nodded. "Louie's a prick. I found that out the hard way. I haven't talked to him in years. If I never see any of those guys again it'll be too soon, believe me. Jimmy, the way things are working out in L.A., you've got nothing to worry about. I don't know all the details, but from what I read in the papers they're all in the fucking shit."

Beginning with the conviction of Pete Milano and six others for running a floating gambling operation in the San Fernando Valley, using crooked wheels and loaded dice, there had been a number of indictments and convictions in the previous year. The gambling setup had lasted four months before customers complained to police. When the case came to trial in March 1974, two key witnesses, John Dubeck and his wife Frances Ann, were shotgunned to death in Las Vegas. That delayed the trial five months. Although other witnesses were intimidated by the murders and refused to testify against Milano, he was convicted and sentenced to four years.

The next legal blow nearly bagged the whole family. In July 1974 an even dozen were indicted by a federal grand jury on charges of conspiracy, racketeering, and extortion against bookmakers, loan sharks, and pornographers. Included in the dozen were Brooklier, Milano, Frank Stellino, and Samuel Sciortino, a first cousin of Gaspare "Bill" Sciortino, the underboss in Jimmy Lanza's San Francisco family. Three months later Nick Licata died of natural causes. He was 77 and described in one newspaper account as "a true 'Godfather' in every respect." When Jimmy read that, he had a good laugh.

Over drinks at the Jockey Club bar later in November of 1974, they discussed the chaos in Los Angeles. "After Nick died they had an election and Brooklier was made boss and Sciortino underboss," Jimmy said. "The *consigliere's* Tommy Palermo, whoever he is. I never met the guy."

"What about the Dubecks?" Roselli asked. "Any idea who clipped them? This whole thing has gone crazy. It's against the rules to clip guys in Vegas. That's been the law since Benny built the Flamingo. They're getting pretty loose."

"The only guy in the L.A. family capable of doing any work's Angelo Polizzi," Jimmy replied. "And I hear he's gone a little screwy and kind of stays away from the family. I don't know about this Sciortino. He looks like a fat piece of shit to me. But there's a new guy that's friendly with Pete and Brooklier. A big motherfucker by the name of Mike Rizzitello, calls himself Rizzi. He got out of the joint a couple years ago, served nine years for armed robbery and kidnapping. They knocked off the kidnapping charge but he's on lifetime parole.

"He's from New York and used to be with Crazy Joe Gallo. In fact, he clipped a couple guys for Gallo, one of them [John Guariglia] in a joint called the Hi-Fi Lounge in Brooklyn. Remember Tony the Sheik? He told me to stay away from Rizzi because he was going to get whacked, but Rizzi went back East and somehow straightened out the beef. But back in 1960, when they first went to the matresses, Crazy Joe made Rizzi, and he went around thinking he was an *amico nostra*. Well, shit, Gallo had no authority to make nobody. Now Rizzi's hanging around Brooklier and Milano. I think he wants to get made the right way this time."

"They're not going to make him," Roselli said. "They wouldn't know what to do with a real worker. They've gone from Dragna to DeSimone to Licata and now Brooklier. What's worse's, they've got no solid soldiers."

"I've been talking to them lately, getting friendly," Jimmy said. "I've got a few deals going and I don't want no static."

As always, they talked for hours, drinking lightly, smoking endless cigars. Jimmy noticed that Roselli was not smoking cigarettes and inquired about it.

"The doctor in the joint told me I have emphysema, so I thought I'd better quit."

"Oh, shit. Sorry to hear that, Johnny. You think you should be smoking cigars?"

"I don't inhale, just puff away, gives me something to suck on while we chew the fat."

"Listen, Johnny, I've been wanting to ask you. What's the story with Giancana?"

Roselli gritted his teeth and for the first time Jimmy noticed how much he had aged in four years. His features were becoming more delicate, more fragile looking, and his hair had turned almost snow white. With the tan, it was a striking contrast.

"Jimmy, let me give you a rundown on the Chicago situation, which in some ways is as bad as Los Angeles," Roselli began. "In July Sam got thrown out of Mexico in the middle of the night. They grabbed him out of his fucking bed and threw him on a plane. He got off the plane at O'Hare in his house slippers, carrying his bathrobe. The spics robbed him blind for eight years and then spat him out like a piece of grizzle they can't swallow. So now he's back in Chicago and there's nothing left for him there. Paul Ricca's dead. Philly Alderesio's dead, so's a bunch of other guys, including Dick Cain, who went around the world with Sam and was hit in Chicago six months before Sam was thrown out of Mexico.

"Joe Batters is back in power, but he leaves the daily hassles of being boss to Joe Aiuppa. Jackie Cerone's the underboss and Batters acts as *consigliere*. My situation with Batters is still piss poor. We never got along. As I've told you, there's jealousy going back to Capone's days, and there's nothing I can do about it. This guy's got me on his shitlist, period.

"Let me give you an example. A while back I grabbed Moe Dalitz and tried to get that four hundred thousand he still owed on the D.I. sale. I talked it over with Sam first and he said shake him, but the little cocksucker runs to Chicago and I get called in and told to lay off. See, Jimmy, they took him over. With Ricca dead and Sam finished, and I do mean washed up for good, I've lost my last connection in that family.

"I'm giving it to you straight, Jimmy. There's nothing you can do when bosses turn on you. That's the trouble with this thing of ours. We're sitting ducks. So I said to myself, fuck it, I'll retire. I've made my contribution, the least they can do is let me live the remaining years in peace, let somebody else do the work for a while. So that's why I'm down here in Miami."

"What's Giancana doing?" Jimmy asked.

"Sam's a sick man. His health's all shot to hell. They didn't only steal his money down there, they ruined his stomach."

"By the way, Johnny, while I was in the joint I read this column by Jack Anderson and he brings up all this shit about the CIA wanting to kill Castro and actually names you and Maheu as being part of it. He said you had a boat shot out from under you. Holy Christ, Johnny, where the fuck did he get that crazy story? I couldn't believe what I was reading."

"It's pretty involved, Jimmy, but to make it short, Joe Shimon set up a meeting with Anderson at Tom Wadden's house. I just sat there, didn't say one word. Shimon answered all the questions. I wanted an affidavit from Anderson to give the judge in the Friars case. I thought he'd give me credit for this service to the country." Roselli paused to relight his cigar. "Know what he said? 'I don't think Mr. Roselli's entitled to Brownie points if these allegations are a fact.' "

Jimmy shook his head. "Oh, hey, Johnny, listen to this. I met this guy, Sal Amarena. He's got this pizza joint in San Francisco right across from the Hilton, calls it Sal's Esspresso Caffe. I'll give you his phone number. He takes messages for me. It's a hangout for boosters, burglars, bookies—junkies come in there with shit you wouldn't believe. This guy Sal was in Cuba when Santo was locked up before Castro kicked him out. Sal's known Santo for years— Sal operated a restaurant in Havana—and one day I asked him what he thought of Anderson's column, and he says Castro used to come to his restaurant all the time and if Santo had wanted to have him killed in there it would have been so easy it wasn't funny. Santo knew Sal was there but he never made no move."

"Jimmy, I've told you, Santo sat on his ass and did nothing."

"By the way, did Joe Batters ever mention the column?" Jimmy asked.

"Not a word."

"Christ, that's a relief. Maybe he don't know about it."

"Oh, don't worry, he goddamn well knows," Roselli said. "What can he do about it? Sam and Santo were involved. I was just following orders."

One night Jimmy and Roselli went to Tony Roma's for dinner and Jimmy told him about his running into Mickey Cohen in San Francisco. "Talk about doing bad time," Jimmy said, wincing. "That first stretch for income tax evasion, I think he served three years, then he's out six, seven years and they nail him again, this time fifteen years and he serves ten. Not only that, but some con beats him over the head with a lead pipe and really fucks him up. He's paralyzed from the waist down. He hobbles around with two canes, takes him five minutes to go ten feet, but most of the time he's in a wheelchair. He's lucky he's got all his marbles."

"He's one hard guy to clip, that's all I've got to say," Roselli commented.

"When I think of it, I feel that's when our family started going downhill. If we'd have clipped him right off we could've concentrated on getting a joint in Vegas. Anyway, Bennie Barrish called me one day and invited me to the Press Club. Mickey was going to be the speaker. We walk in and Mickey spots me right away. Mickey says I look good, this and that, and we're talking like long lost buddies. So he says, 'You know, Jimmy, we've got to get together. After we're through here come with us to Paoli's.' He makes his speech, pure bullshit. He's saying nobody's got no shame no more, no respect, no pride, that's the whole trouble with society, and the fucking reporters eat it up."

"You've got to give Mickey credit," Roselli began. "For a shitty little punk, he conned a lot of important people. One time he even had that evangelist Billy Graham thinking he could convert him."

"Oh, they were asshole buddies," Jimmy said. "I remember them running around town, going to Palm Springs, with Mickey throwing them hundred dollar bills around like confetti. Let me tell you, he ain't changed. Oh, listen, do you realize you're breaking bread with an ordained minister?" Jimmy laughed. "This kid at Chino wrote to the World Church in Modesto saying that I've always wanted to be a preacher, and they sent me this fucking certificate in the mail."

Roselli laughed. "You missed your true calling. By the way, who's this Barrish?"

Jimmy shrugged. "Oh, he's an old asshole buddy of Mickey. He's one of my booking agents and does some collecting. Anyway, getting back to Paoli's, I'm sitting next to him. So here comes time to pay the check. There's a dozen people at this table and Mickey goes in his pocket and pulls out a roll of hundred-dollar bills, must have been ten grand there easy. I'm looking like this, leaning over a little, and he looks at me, this guy's funny, you know. He says, 'What're you looking at?' I says, 'I'm checking that roll out.' He laughs and I says, 'You look in pretty good shape. Still got some left from that million you stole from the Jews in Israel?' He says, 'What're you getting at?' I says, 'Forget it, Mickey. You're still a fucking good actor.' He turns away, but I can see that little shit-eating grin, same one he gave me the first time I nailed him on it. He peels off a bunch of them C-notes and leaves a couple for a tip.

"Now, the next time I see Mickey, Barrish calls to say he's at the Mark Hopkins and wants to see me. His suite's full of people when I walk in, but he waves me over to his chair, shakes hands, and introduces me to Barbara McNair, the black singer, and her husband Rick Manzi, who happens to be the nephew of Obie Frabotta [a soldier in the Chicago family]. We go out in the hall and I says, 'Obie, what're you doing with this Mickey? This guy's no fucking good.' He says, 'Rick bought a piece of Mickey's book.' I says, 'Obie, don't you know Mickey's been selling pieces of that book to everybody he can con.' He was selling it for four grand a point. Knowing Mickey, he probably sold two hundred points. Obie later got Rick's money back.

"After this introduction," Jimmy continued, "I became friendly with Barbara and Rick. They invited me to their home in Vegas, but this Rick's a weirdo, the guy's one of them kleptomaniacs. I went in a drugstore with him one time and he's boosting, just stuffing his fucking pockets. From then on we didn't do no more shopping together.

"Hey, guess who I met at Rick's house?" Jimmy paused, waiting for Roselli to respond.

"You going to give me a clue?"

"Yeah, this guy's just a little bigger than a breadbox, about five-foot-five, has curly hair, was a burglar working for Philly [Alderisio] before he went to the joint on that Denver rap."

"Don't bother. You mean that fucking little ant, Tony 'The Little Guy' Spilotro."

"That's the one. Rick told me Tony's got a piece of Barbara so he can show the government some fucking income. Rick's not made so he couldn't introduce us as made guys, but Spilotro fucking well knew who I was, believe me. In fact, he says he met me in sixty-nine when I went back to see Philly about the Seventh Step, but I don't remember him. Anyway, Bomp came up and made the introduction . . . hey, Bomp's getting pretty tight with this guy. Him and Chris Petti from San Diego.

"Johnny, I hear Spilotro's got your old job in Vegas, you know, arbitrating beefs like you did in the old days. If you want my opinion, he don't look too capable to me. He's doing things there you never did. He's shylocking, has a crew of burglars working the town, and he's keeping a sharp eye on Allen Glick. Now that's the big mystery. Who the fuck's this Glick?"

The situation appeared so complex, so convoluted with legal razzle-dazzle, that it confused the press and frustrated the Internal Revenue Service, the Securities and Exchange Commission, the Gaming Commission, the FBI, and everyone else that tried to unravel it.

It began when Albert Parvin, who had bought the Stardust from Moe Dalitz, ran into a public relations problem. The press discovered that Associate Supreme Court Justice William O. Douglas was president of Parvin's controversial foundation. This had so enraged Republican Minority Leader Gerald R. Ford that he had taken to the floor of the House of Representative to launch an impassioned attack that not only castigated Douglas but stripped Parvin naked of seventy years of carefully acquired respectability. Even before one Chicagoan was shot down, another was on the way to the rescue.

Educated at Harvard, with a law degree from the University of Pennsylvania, Delbert W. Coleman, by the age of 42, had gained control of the J. P. Seeburg Corporation, that old Chicago jukebox maker. By 1968 Coleman had acquired a reputation as a go-go conglomerator who knew how to inflate stock prices. At his side was Sidney Korshak, a Chicago transplant with underworld ties every bit as mysterious to police and the press as Meyer Lansky's. Korshak had earlier collected a $500,000 finder's fee from the sale of the Stardust to Parvin.

The deal with Parvin was executed with dispatch. Coleman agreed to purchase 300,000 shares, representing 22 percent of the outstanding stock of Parvin–Dohrmann, which then owned the Fremont, Stardust, and Aladdin, for a total price of $10.5 million, or $35 a share, slightly below the trading price of the previous month. On October 11, 1968, Parvin signed the agreement, pending approval of a license by the Gaming Commission, which meant that control of the company would not officially pass into Coleman's hands until the license was granted sometime in January 1969. Parvin took off for an extended African safari and Coleman and Korshak went to work.

In no time at all, they had boosted the company's stock from $35 to $141.50 a share. Employing a fancy version of the old boiler-room promotion, they parceled off 143,000 shares to pivotal figures in the market game like Bernie Cornfeld's FOF Propriety Fund in Switzerland. Of the $5 million they retrieved from this sale, they plowed $4 million right back into the market, buying shares through ninety open-market transactions in which they acquired more than 51,000 shares at prices ranging from $68 to $107 a share. These purchases, enhanced by the touting of the pivotal figures, created a false appearance of active trading in the stock on the American Stock Exchange.

Then it collapsed. Amex suspended trading and the SEC charged that Coleman and his associates never intended staying on with the company. After the stock was driven up to a price of about $150, the company was to be unloaded to a merger partner. By May 1970 the stock had plummeted to $12.50. Parvin reclaimed his company, changed the name to Recrion, and Korshak pocketed his finder's fee, another cool half million, for his efforts, not to mention what he made on the 12,500 shares he originally allotted to himself.

Recrion was in shambles. With Amex and SEC on its back, attention was focused on its stock situation rather than its gambling operation and the dubious characters still in the woodwork. Parvin sold the Aladdin (once the Tallyho) for $6 million, suffering a $4 million loss, to some of Morris Shenker's friends in St. Louis and Detroit, who paid Shenker the $500,000 finder's fee. The friends turned out to be top family members and their watchdog was Vito "Billy" Giacolone. Not long after the purchase, they borrowed $38 million from the Teamsters to dress up the place. In a few years, the Teamsters would have nearly $100 million invested in Jimmy's old Tallyho. As for Recrion, by the end of 1973 it had reduced its debt to $37 million.

Then Allen R. Glick, a thirty-two-year-old attorney from San Diego with four years of business experience, appeared on the scene and bought all the shares of Recrion, paying $44 per share, for a total of $62,750,000, all of it financed by the Teamsters Central States, Southeast and Southwest Areas Pension Fund. Glick's net worth, only a year before, had been $250,000. In 1972, he also became the largest stockholder in the Hacienda Hotel. A few months later Glick would receive other loans totalling $30-plus million from the Teamsters. It was a mystery that intrigued all who gazed upon its glittering surface. What lay underneath was rather routine for those who practiced this art of legerdemain.

"Oh, Christ," Roselli said, "what a merry-go-round we get on when we join this thing. Let me tell you about that Tony Spilotro. He's a watchdog for Joe Aiuppa. But this guy's an animal, a punk, with no class, no finesse. He don't know what's going on around Vegas except for what he's told. He's just a soldier, and nobody confides in a guy like that. He's Aiuppa's messenger boy, a tool, but I hear he's acting tough, throwing his weight around. But you can't play tough in that town and last. There're too many factions in there. Sure, I got things done, and I was feared, I suppose, which is necessary if you expect to get the job done, but you've got to keep a low profile."

"But he's also a worker," Jimmy said. "This guy's clipped some people."

"Oh, sure, if Aiuppa wants any work done in this end of the country, he gets Tony, tells him to go ahead and take care of it."

"Bomp likes him. Tony lets him do a little shylocking in Vegas. Bomp introduced him to Nick Simponis, who's a sharp card player, and now Nick and Spilotro are buddies, together every night gambling in them joints, and whatever they win, Tony gives Bomp his end."

"Now, as to Allen Glick." Roselli continued. "This guy don't know what's going on. He made a deal with Lefty [Frank] Rosenthal, who runs all of Glick's gambling operations. You know, Lefty'll never get a license. He's got a conviction for fixing a basketball game, and he's one hell of a handicapper. Used to put out the football line from Chicago. Don't forget, Yale Cohen and Phil Ponti are still at the Stardust. So's Bobby Stella."

"Who was Glick's connection for the loan? Al Baron?" Jimmy asked.

"Well, Al Baron now holds Dorfman's old fund position. His new title is Asset Manager, but Chicago got the money through Roy Williams, out of Kansas City, who's a seventh or eighth International Vice President."

"Next to Jackie Presser, he's the closest one to Frank Fitzsimmons," said Jimmy. "There's been talk about who'd replace Fitzsimmons, Williams or Presser, and my money's on Williams. He's got more clout. Our family in Cleveland controls Presser. But Williams's got Chicago, Kansas City, and St. Louis behind him, and that's pretty heavy juice."

"That's right. Chicago worked it through Nick Civella in Kansas City, who's got the tightest hold on Williams," Roselli said. "But this shit's unknown to Glick. All this guy knows is that Lefty came to him with a proposition and he bought it. And that's all they wanted him to know. Glick fronts it and Lefty runs it. Glick seldom comes to Vegas. All the skimming, and, believe me, Jimmy, they're skimming the shit out of those joints, is Lefty's responsibility. Glick's corporation is called Argent. They have to keep changing the name, but they're still Chicago's joints."

"In other words," Jimmy put in, "Tony Spilotro runs messages between

Chicago and Lefty. When they want Rosenthal to know something, they tell Spilotro, and Lefty knows it's coming from them.

"But, tell me, Johnny, who controls Andy Anderson in San Francisco? You know, he's an International Vice President."

"Sid Korshak. Why, you trying to work something in the Teamsters through Andy?"

"Yeah, I'm trying to straighten out Rudy Tham with the International." (Rudy Tham—*nee* Rudolph Tham Antonovich—was the head of Local 856, the second largest Teamsters local in the city. Its membership included freight checkers and vending machine employees. Tham was also a member of the Teamsters Joint Council #7. And for additional prestige, he was one of Alioto's three fire commissioners.)

"Well, you watch that fucking Korshak. He's Gussie Alex's man. Gussie's Greek, but he's as close to Joe Batters as you can get for an outsider. He's run the Loop for the family for years, but Chicago, you know, has had quite a bunch of outsiders doing big jobs. Gussie was brought into the outfit by Jake Guzik, and believe me, Jimmy, even Capone listened to Jake. So if you want to do anything with Anderson, my advice is talk to Korshak first, play it cool, then if he won't cooperate, talk to Aiuppa.

"One thing you've got to keep in mind with Korshak. He's made millions for Chicago and he's got plenty of clout in L.A. and Vegas. When Jack [Dragna] was alive, I talked to him many times about Korshak pulling this shit for Chicago, but Jack didn't want to fuck with him. Since then Sid's really burrowed in. He's real big with the movie colony, lives in a mansion in Bel Air, knows most of the big stars. His wife plays tennis with Dinah Shore, and he's been shacking up with Stella Stevens for years. He's a lawyer, grew up on the West Side in Chicago, and got to know a lot of made guys. He calls himself a labor-relations expert, but he's really a fixer. A union cooks up a strike and Sid arbitrates it. Instead of a payoff under the table, he gets a big legal fee, pays the taxes on it, and cuts it up. All nice and clean. This guy ain't never going to the joint, believe me. And he's also got a pretty good piece of the Riviera [in Las Vegas] but the skim goes back to Gussie Alex who cuts it up with the family. In other words, if you're going to fuck with this guy, you better watch your steps.

"By the way," Johnny added, "Jack Goldberger's been after me to talk to you. Says you're out to fuck him, trying to get Rudy Tham in a more important position."

"I can't make no money with that asshole Goldberger," Jimmy said. "He's one way—all for himself. When I first got out of Chino, I picked up a fast forty, fifty grand and I'm thinking what to do next, besides a little shylocking and booking, you know. I'm scheming, how am I going to make some money? So I get ahold of Rudy Tham and we go to dinner one night. Rudy's vice-president of the joint council, but he tells me he's in trouble with the International because he's a Hoffa man. Andy Anderson, who heads the Western Confer-

ence, won't even talk to him. Any assignment made in San Francisco that
Andy should give to Rudy, he either keeps or gives to Goldberger.

"So I says, 'Rudy, I've got to make some money. What're you doing with
your dental program?' He says, 'Well, nothing yet.' I says, 'Rudy, I think I
can straighten you out.'

"Johnny, I can see in his eyes he don't believe I can do it, but he says, 'If
you can do it I think it'd be great.' I says, 'Well, if I do it will you give me
your dental program?' He says, 'Jimmy, it's yours.' I know I can make ten
grand a month easy, for my end, with the dental program. I says, 'We'll work
it through Allen Dorfman.'

"See, Johnny, this comes under the Teamsters Health and Welfare Fund.
You pick the dentist and the union gives him a contract to do all the dental
work for the members of the locals signed up and their families. Dorfman's
company, Amalgamated Insurance Agency, processes all medical claims and
authorizes payment, which means he controls the whole thing. So now we can
play some games. Number one, the dentists kickback to certain people so many
dollars for each member signed up; and number two, Dorfman can submit
phony claims and nobody's the wiser. It's a sweet setup, believe me.

"But first I talked to Dorfman about a dental program in Warren, Ohio.
That's Tony Dope's town. So Allen thinks it's a good idea, but he says, 'You
know, Jimmy, I'm blackballed. There's nothing I can do over there. You
mention my name and you'll get nothing done. Cleveland's thrown out all my
insurance.' Now I'm thinking. I'd talked to Tony Dope about the dental plan
in Warren, and he was all for it, so I says, 'Let me find out what I can do. I
know the guy in Cleveland that can turn Jackie Presser around.' Well, Allen
knows that Jackie can straighten out anybody in the Teamsters, so it's a
question of whether I can straighten Presser out.

"I know I've got to go to Cleveland. Jackie Presser, or his old man, Bill,
don't make no moves without Johnny Scalish giving the okay. I talk to Jackie
and he says, 'Look, tell Jimmy I can't make no moves unless he clears it
through the family here.' So, anyway, now I've got Rudy *and* Allen to
straighten out.

"We're sitting and bullshitting, and Dorfman brings up this federal indictment against him for some pension fund scam he pulled in New Mexico. Now,
Allen's just served ten months on a kickback deal and he don't want to do no
more time. This thing in New Mexico's been pending since 1971 and it involves
Spilotro and Philly [Alderisio], who died in the meantime, and a whole bunch
of guys—oh, yeah, and Joey Lombardo. Now this Lombardo's a *capo* in
Chicago and he's always around Dorfman's office. He's the guy that takes
people from Allen's office to Aiuppa when they have to see the old man.

"So Allen brings up the time Joe Louis walked into the courtroom in
Washington when Hoffa was on trial for bribery and shakes hands with Hoffa.
All the blacks on the jury, and there must have been eight or nine of them,
see this and they acquit the sonovabitch in about two hours flat. So Allen's

thinking how great it would be if Muhammad Ali walked into the courtroom and shook his hand. I says, 'Allen, you're in luck, Dick Sadler lives up the street from me in Hayward, and he's George Foreman's former manager, maybe he can do you some good. He's known Ali a long time.'"

Roselli burst out laughing, then suddenly started coughing, caught in a violent paroxysm that turned his face purple and brought tears to his eyes. Bringing a napkin to his mouth, he turned his head away, helpless in the throes of spasms that shook his body. At first Jimmy thought he had swallowed something the wrong way, but the deep, husky cough told him that it was something far more serious. He quickly extinguished his cigar and waited patiently for the attack to pass.

Roselli tried to pass the coughing off lightly. "Jimmy, you've got to cut out this shit or you're going to kill me. Next time wait till I've swallowed my food before pulling one of them fucking rabbits out of your hat."

"How're you feeling?" Jimmy asked, not fooled by Roselli's offhand dismissal of his attack.

"I'm fine. Let's have a brandy and call it quits for the night. But before we go, what happened with Presser?"

"Straightening Dorfman was no problem. I went to see Presser with Tony Dope and told him Dorfman was going to start a dental program in Warren, and we want him to give us his blessings. That was the first step in straightening out Dorfman with the International.

"As for Rudy, it was not that easy. I went back to California, tried to get some idea how big this dental program was going to be, and went back to Cleveland to see Jackie Presser. I told him Rudy had promised me his dental program if I could straighten him out and Jackie said he'd check it out and let me know. So I go back to San Francisco and tell Rudy the wheels are turning.

"A few weeks later, Dope calls and I fly to Cleveland. Jackie Presser says they're reluctant to straighten this guy out because he's a Hoffa man and it looks like Hoffa's going to make a move. I says, 'Listen, that's bullshit. Sure, like everybody else, he was a Hoffa man when Hoffa was president, but now he's with Fitzsimmons a hundred percent.' Presser says, 'Will you take full responsibility for him?' I says, 'Yeah.' He says, 'Are you sure he'll do what you tell him?' I says, 'Absolutely.' In other words, they want to make sure somebody's got him in hand. If he starts going wild, they're coming to me, he's my man. If I can't handle him then it's no good. He does the wrong thing, I've got to clip the bastard. I know that's what Jackie's telling me, so we understand each other. This was the second big step in getting this thing worked out.

"When I get back I says, 'Rudy, I want to tell you something. Number one, the reason you're on the shit list's because you're a Hoffa man. That's got to stop. Number two, if they straighten you out and somewhere down the road you make the wrong move, I told them I'd take full responsibility for you. They asked me if I could handle you, make sure you don't go the other way, that you do what I tell you. You know, whether I can hold you down. I told them absolutely.' He says, 'Oh, there ain't no problem, you know. I ain't going to do nothing wrong anyhow.' I says, 'All I've got to tell you, Rudy, is that I gave them people my word. I'm responsible for you and if you fuck up they're coming to me, and, Rudy, then I'm coming to you. Are you sure you know what that means?' He says, 'Well, yeah, I understand. I've got to do the right thing.'

"Johnny, I'm still working on it. That fucking Andy Anderson's ignoring Presser and I'm meeting with Teamsters officials all over the place. I fly into Chicago to see Dorfman and now that I'm back talking with Obie Frabotta, I call him before coming in, you know, checking in with the family. I told Obie what I'm doing in Warren and I says, 'Tell the old man [Chicago Boss Joey Aiuppa] whatever I do he's got a piece of it.' When I get to Dorfman's office, Lombardo's always there. By the way, all them guys call Aiuppa Joey O'Brien."

"He's been going by that name for years," Johnny said. "Listen, Jimmy, Aiuppa's nothing. He's not a capable man to be running that family. I've known him forty years, never did nothing in his whole life but run clip joints in Cicero."

Jimmy nodded in agreement, then went back to his story. "So I get the word out I'd like to meet the old man, tell him what we're doing in Warren with Dorfman. This Lombardo picks me up and drives about thirty miles to this restaurant. It's around three in the afternoon and there's nobody in the joint. Lombardo makes a call and about ten minutes later in comes Aiuppa with Jackie Cerone.

"We go to a table in the back and Lombardo stays at the bar. We shake hands and I tell him I've been in the joint and I'm trying to make a buck, and he says, 'Well, Jimmy, I don't want nobody coming into this town unless they report here. Nobody! You do something in Chicago or with our people in Chicago, we've got to know about it.' I says, 'I told Obie whatever I make you get a piece of it. This dental program in Warren's no big deal but it looks pretty good.' He says, 'Yeah, Obie told me about it, but, Jimmy, whatever you make, you keep it. All I ask's you follow the rules.' "

"Sounds like it went pretty smooth," Johnny began. "But, remember, Jimmy, he's put you on notice. This's an old man and a stickler for the rules. You better walk straight around that cocksucker. Cover your ass."

Jimmy was quiet a moment, then sighed. "As far as Ali's concerned, they won't need him now. They blew this witness' head off with a shotgun right in front of his fucking wife and baby. I was talking to Joey Lombardo about it. This witness was the key one against him, so now it looks like the government's going to drop the charges on him. The other witness's scared shitless. Forget about it, them guys are home free. I hear the prosecution can't even bring up the fact this kid [Daniel] Seifert was clipped."

"The way I got it, the old man gave the contract to Spilotro. As you say, this guy's a worker. He was also up on murder charges with Mario and Sam DeStefano, but Sam's a loony. No telling what he'd do in court, and so Mario and Spilotro clipped him. Blew him away with a shotgun. Ironic as hell, because twenty years ago, Sam killed his own brother Mike when he became a junkie. Giancana gave him the contract."

"Well, what the fuck. If a guy's rotten, makes no difference who he is, you clip him. That's it. One of them things, right?"

That night in bed Jimmy thought about David Kaplan, a so-called international financier. It was Kaplan who had lured Jimmy to Florida on a multimillion-dollar deal. Kaplan had taken him into his luxurious home on Biscayne Bay, with its own boat and dock, had introduced Jimmy and Paul Axelrod to his family, even to his in-laws and prominent friends, lawyers, doctors, his rabbi; a former Miami judge, Hugh F. DuVal, a real aristocrat from an old Florida family; and a former senator, Richard Dolwig, who had spent some twenty-five years in the California Assembly.

What had intrigued Jimmy was the open way Kaplan operated. To Jimmy, a swindle was to be done on the q.t., but Kaplan had gone so far as to invite Jimmy and Axelrod to a Bas Mitzvah party for his daughter.

It was there that Axelrod had run into an old friend, David Gorwitz. After introducing him to Jimmy, Axelrod had asked if Kaplan's Eurovest company, based on a Grand Cayman Island, was a straight deal. Jimmy's eyes had widened when Gorwitz had replied, "We've got over three hundred million in securities and after this party we'll have five hundred million. Paul, take my word for it, you've got nothing to worry about."

The original figure quoted by Kaplan had been fifty million in securities which could be placed with "prime" banks as collateral for the issuance of letters of credit. To obtain a letter of credit, the borrower had to post an advance fee based on a schedule of $25,000 for each $1 million of financing requested. But, as Kaplan had quickly explained, it was all perfectly routine. The Aetna Life and Casualty Company would issue a policy insuring the monies advanced. The advance fee itself would be deposited in a trust account at a specified bank, to be promptly returned if the letter of credit was not issued as promised. In fact, former senator Dolwig was Eurovest's escrow holder.

Jimmy had listened but deep down he felt uneasy about it. Having been a hustler all of his life, he smelled a rat whenever a promoter asked for front money.

The deal had started when Barbara Barnato and Abe Chapman, who operated a brokerage firm known as International Trade and Finance (ITF) in San Francisco, had been approached by Paul Heck, an Oakland developer, who needed $30.5 million to build a Sheraton hotel on a nine-acre site near the Oakland Coliseum. With a moratorium still in effect on Teamsters loans, Barnato and Chapman had contacted Jimmy, who in turn had gone to Axelrod, Shenker's brilliant banking expert, who just happened to have a connection in Florida. For the loan, ITF would receive a ten percent participation in the hotel's profits, and a finder's fee of one and a half points. In a separate contract with Jimmy and Axelrod, ITF agreed to split all earnings down the middle.

Jimmy asked around as he worked out the details and developed his investors. Kaplan had told him he was tied into Meyer Lansky and Angelo Bruno, boss of the Philadelphia family. Jimmy learned that nobody had ever heard of Kaplan.

Jimmy decided it was time for him to make an exit, but first he had a private talk with Kaplan.

"Well, Jimmy, this is a pleasant surprise," Kaplan said, waving Jimmy into his home. "Why don't we have some coffee on the lanai?"

They went out and sat by the pool and a maid served coffee and rolls. "What're you doing up before noon? I thought swingers like you slept till mid-afternoon."

Jimmy fixed him with a hard stare. "Hey, Kaplan, let's cut the shit. I've already wasted too much fucking time listening to your bullshit. Let me tell you something, you cocksucker, you couldn't wipe Meyer Lansky's ass. So you're connected with Angelo Bruno? Well, it just so happens I know Angelo. Want to give him a call? Here, I've got his number right here."

Kaplan's face had turned ashen. "What's this all about, Jimmy?"

"I want to tell you something, and you better listen, understand? Do you know what the fuck you're doing on this thing? You're fucking with people that don't stand for getting fucked. I treated you as a friend, and you invited me into your home like I was a friend. Well, if you ain't honest with your friends, things can happen. You follow me? You've been talking about loans since I first got here. Who's getting loans? Give me *one* name, you asshole. You know, I've introduced you to some pretty good friends and they ain't going to stand getting fucked. Besides I'm responsible for them. You want my opinion, I'm going to be honest with you. I think this whole thing's a scam."

Kaplan waved his hands excitedly. "Well, you're entitled to think what you want, but I'm trying to do the right thing."

"Yeah, well, listen, motherfucker, you're talking to an expert. Anytime you get front money you're out to fuck somebody. Don't go telling me about front money, that's my business, asshole. I came here today to tell you I'm pulling out and I'm going to tell Heck to look elsewhere for his money."

Kaplan cleared his throat. "Didn't Heck tell you? The deal's been consummated. I thought he told you."

Jimmy smiled. "How much front money did Heck give you?"

"Sixty thousand and a warranty deed on property valued at a million. Of course, that's only as security for the six hundred and forty-five thousand he still owes in fees."

Jimmy was still smiling when he stood up. "Well, you better kiss this little paradise good-bye. You're going to the fucking joint. Drop me a line, I'll have some of my friends take good care of you."

(Eleven months later, Kaplan was convicted on twenty counts of fraud and sentenced to twenty separate ten-year prison terms, to run concurrently. Gorwitz was given eight years and Dolwig five years. For one of the few times in his life, Jimmy talked freely before a grand jury. Axelrod, an unindicted co-conspirator, turned state's witness.)

The next morning, Roselli drove Jimmy to the airport.

"So what're you going to do now?" Roselli asked.

Jimmy shrugged. "I don't know, Johnny. I've talked to Bomp and Leo Moceri." He paused, glancing sideways at Roselli. "Maybe we'll start our own family in San Francisco. When I came out of Chino, I saw Jimmy Lanza at Bay Meadows and we took a walk, you know, made sure nobody was following us. I told him I'm living in the Bay Area now and I've got to make a buck, to move around, and he told me to do what I want. He knows I belong to Chicago, but I wanted to check in with him, follow the rules."

Roselli turned to look at Jimmy. "How the fuck old are you?"

"Was sixty-one this month," Jimmy said.

"My God, ain't you tired of this shit?"

"Fuck no. I'm scheming, man. I can't waste no time. While I was in the joint this last time I gave this a lot of thought. Then this idea came to me. Who needs this bullshit . . . L.A. or Chicago. This way we've got our own family. We bring in four, five guys, make them ourselves. We make our moves against the unions, bookmakers, shylocks, burglars, pornographers, shake them down. Another thing, right now there's no heat up there, not like L.A. with the intelligence on your back all the time. I sit and bullshit with people at Sal's and nobody's watching us. There's nothing going on in that town. I mean, no organized crime. Just them three old men with Lanza."

"Where're you going to get the soldiers?"

"That's no problem. Ray Ferritto wants to get out of Erie. Jimmy Westfield, I don't remember his Italian name, he's the skipper there for the Pittsburgh family, don't want to make Ray. There's a whole bunch of guys in New York that never got made, they ain't made nobody in that town for years. Them guys would jump at a chance to get made in Frisco."

Roselli smiled. "Well, Jimmy, don't forget, this thing of ours is the world's most exclusive men's club." Roselli punched Jimmy on the arm. "So what's happening with Warren these days?"

"He's married again, his wife's got a good job managing a department store. Which's lucky for me because Warren's got a bad back and can't get around too good."

"Right, let's somebody else support him for a while."

"Well, Johnny, Warren's okay. He's worked hard, drove a truck all his life and he's always worried about money. Spends most of his time sitting around worrying about this and that."

"So he's not driving for you no more."

"Johnny, my trucking company's gone. I had them five new tractors and belly-dump trailers which I left with Ray Giarusso, but this guy's a thief. In fact, I even thought of clipping him. Then I thought, oh, Christ, this guy ain't worth it. I don't know, Johnny. I like his parents. Old-fashioned people, remind me of my mother and father. The old man talks Italian to me."

Roselli drove in silence for a long time before speaking. When he did he kept his eyes straight ahead. "Jimmy, don't take this wrong, but what hope is there for this thing of ours when hard rocks like you turn soft? This guy fucked you out of a hundred grand and you worry about his fucking parents. You're the last guy in the world I'd figure for this."

"Oh, Johnny, come on, don't worry. I can do some fucking work, but what good would it do to bury this cocksucker? Besides I went to see him and he gave me a few thousand. The problem's this guy don't know how to run a business. But, Johnny, don't worry about me. I ain't never going to get soft. Forget about it."

On the flight home, Jimmy thought about Roselli's words. His tone of voice had been sad, like somebody had died, and Jimmy wondered what Roselli would say if he knew that Jimmy had been talking to the FBI ever since he left Chino, not telling them anything important, but taking their money just the same.

Special agent Lowell "Larry" Lawrence, a thin, gangly, affable man, had gradually gained Jimmy's respect and confidence. They met in hotel rooms—casual meetings, where they discussed many things, but never, in Jimmy's opinion, anything that involved the family. Larry had been generous with the government's money for the little morsels of information handed out. Yet Larry seemed satisfied with the arrangement.

At first Jimmy had talked about himself, mentioning his bookmaking and shylocking in San Francisco, but as the months had slipped by and his frustration with the activities in Los Angeles mounted, Jimmy found himself discussing some of his pet peeves. He told Larry about their effort to muscle Vic Werber, that Brooklier's old alias was Jimmy Regace, and in a moment of anger had told Larry that Brooklier and a guy called Army had killed Neddie Herbert. Larry had not pressed him for details, perhaps because he knew it could never be proved in court.

Even as he had said it, Jimmy had known it was worthless information, and now in his window seat on the jetliner bound for San Francisco, he gazed out at the fleecy clouds drifting softly thousands of feet beneath him, and resolved to give the FBI only information that would serve his purpose in his effort to gain control of the San Francisco family. If he played his hand carefully, they could be very helpful. He liked that idea. The FBI, not only helping him, but paying him for doing in his enemies.

PART X

† † † †

THE ACTING BOSS
1975–1976

30
A STUNNING PROPOSITION

† † † †

IT WAS ANOTHER PLANE, SIX MONTHS LATER, THAT LANDED AT THE AIR-
port in Ontario, California, and taxied to the terminal. Jimmy looked out the
window and saw the bald head of Louie Dragna, with its white crown of hair,
and thought about how much the man had changed in the last twenty years.

He had been a tall, good-looking kid and now he looked like an entirely
different person. He was seven years younger than Jimmy and looked ten years
older. This was hard for Jimmy to understand, because Dragna had had such
an easy life, with everything handed to him on a silver platter. His company,
Roberta, was probably grossing close to ten million a year. Most of the work
was done by wetbacks in their homes at slave wages. He had Jimmy to thank
for that, for having worked it through Johnny Dio, getting him a pass with
the unions. They had broken Sam Otto's head and now Dragna was a millionaire. By right, Jimmy felt he deserved a piece of Roberta but he knew that was
hopeless.

Although he still didn't trust him, Jimmy's relationship with Dragna had
somewhat improved since his release from Chino. Still Jimmy wondered why
he had agreed to come to Ontario for a meeting with him. There had been an
edge of urgency in Dragna's voice and perhaps it had intrigued him. Whatever
the reason, it was an unusual request. After all, until this past year, he had not
seen Dragna in twenty years and had not spoken to him since 1960. There was
not much they had in common.

Dragna came forward to greet him as Jimmy came off the plane. They shook
hands and Dragna said, "Come on, Jimmy, let's grab a bite to eat."

At the restaurant, they ordered cocktails and talked a while about nothing
in particular until the food arrived. Methodically slicing his luncheon steak,
Dragna suddenly looked up as though a new thought had just occurred to him.

"Jimmy, I'm sure you know, Brooklier and Sciortino are going to prison in
a couple months."

"Yeah, I've read about it," Jimmy said. "Looks like they made pretty good
deals."

Dragna smiled. "Terrific. But, you know, the prosecution fucked up the case. In fact, Jimmy, your talking Vic Werber into putting all the blame on somebody else helped fuck it up."

Jimmy nodded. "Those guys were looking at ten years."

"Yeah, I suppose. But now Brooklier's getting twenty months and Sciortino eighteen."

Dragna chewed on his steak, a thoughtful expression coming into his eyes. "Jimmy, they've asked me to take over the family while they're away and I told them I'd do it only if you came in with me. You know, we'll run the family together." He paused and swallowed his steak. "They liked the idea. Are you interested?"

Jimmy's expression remained unchanged but his head was full of conflicting ideas. His first reaction was that Dragna was playing games with him, but then it began to make sense. Dragna was too busy with his clothing business to worry about running the family, and when you thought of it, who else did they have that was capable of being an acting boss?

"You mean we'll be acting bosses, share the responsibility?"

"Exactly, but you'll be carrying most of the load. I'm so busy now I don't know if I'm coming or going."

"Number one, Louie, I'd have to get Chicago's permission to transfer back to L.A."

Dragna waved his hand. "That won't be no problem. Just tell the old man we're going to be acting bosses while Brooklier's in jail."

"Number two, if I agree to go along, I'm staying put in San Francisco. I'm making a living up there and I'm not coming down here to make money for a bunch of deadheads. I'll set things up, start making some moves, but these guys here are going to do the work. This family's been laying dead for twenty years. It's about time we shake everybody up, including New York and Chicago. They've been getting away with murder around here for years."

"That's fine, Jimmy. You do what you want and I'll back you."

Jimmy looked at Dragna and felt the excitement of his own words. The moment seemed unreal. He felt like someone whose ears get plugged up by high altitude, like they were stuffed with cotton wadding. Then suddenly they cleared and he was amazed at the noise in the room, the clanking of silverware on plates, the hubbub of conversation, and it was as though he had not heard any of it until this moment.

In the meantime, Jean had finally left Murrieta Springs, bringing Annette with her to share his small one-bedroom apartment. Her drinking problem had worsened, climaxing one night when Jimmy arrived home to find Annette in tears. Jean had gotten drunk and run out of the house in her bare feet. Annette was terrified.

"Oh, Jimbo, she's going to kill herself," she cried.

"Now, now, Punkie, don't worry, I'll find her," Jimmy told her. "Nothing's going to happen. You go to bed and get some sleep, understand? You keep this up, you'll be an old woman before you're sixteen."

It was three o'clock before he found Jean on a deserted side street. He stopped the car and watched her in the glare of the headlights. She looked like a crazy woman, lurching around in circles in the middle of the street, falling to one knee, then crawling, struggling to get back on her feet, falling down again, repeating it over and over again until she finally rolled over on her back, her legs folding under her. He could see that her dress was torn and soiled with vomit. By the time he picked her up, she was unconscious.

He was filled with disgust and yet he felt sorry for her. She was as light as a feather in his arms. The booze was killing her. In a way, deep down, he felt responsible. She had stuck by him for nine years, and he placed great value on loyalty. Although love was not one of the emotions that moved him, he had been betrayed by so many in his life that he felt a deep sense of obligation for anyone who remained true to him. For many years, he had felt the same way about Jewel, and still did when he thought about her. But the problem with both Jewel and Jean was that they wanted to possess him, to own him, to make him toe the line. They wanted him home at night, like the nice little husbands who punch clocks at work and at home and never look at other women. That was not his style. He had moves to make, money to earn, friends to see, and all those other women to love.

Jimmy stayed home the next day, determined to have it out with Jean once and for all. He heard the bedroom door open but he continued talking on the telephone without turning his head. She came into the kitchen, poured herself a cup of coffee, and sat down across from him at the kitchen table. He was turned sideways, but from the corner of his eye he could see that she looked bedraggled, and for the first time he noticed the dark circles under her eyes that were heightened by the sickly pallor of her skin. Her hand trembled as she brought the cup to her lips. He wondered what had happened to this woman, who was younger than his daughter, and had been so beautiful at one time. She still looked good when she fixed herself up and stayed off the booze. He slammed the phone down and turned to look at her.

She glared back at him. "What are you staring at?" she demanded.

"Jesus Christ, I don't know, you tell me."

She looked away. "I know I look a mess."

"You don't only look a mess, you are a mess," he shouted angrily. "You passed out in the middle of the street. You're lucky I found you or you'd be in the morgue with a tag on your toe."

She lit a cigarette and started coughing. Angrily, she snuffed it out. "I made two decisions this morning," she said, looking directly at him. "First," and she took a deep breath, "I'm joining A.A."

"What? Are you nuts?" he cried, shocked at the idea she was an alcoholic. He had thought of her as a lush, but that word had a different connotation for him. "Hey, what's the matter with you this morning? You don't drink every day. You don't even drink in the daytime. Alcoholics are drunk all the time."

"Jimmy, I've given this a lot of thought and I know I can't do it by myself. I need professional help."

"Oh, honey, you can quit if you really put your mind to it."

She shook her head and lit another cigarette. "No, I can't," she said. She shook her head and swiped angrily at the tears she couldn't hold back. "Oh, shit," she groaned, "I look horrible enough without my eyes getting all red and puffy."

"Look, honey, you want to join that outfit, go ahead. If it's going to help, I'm all for it."

She dragged on the cigarette in silence for a long time and he waited—his instinct told him that she was about to pop the same old question that always caused a fight.

She reached in the pocket of her robe for a Kleenex and noisily blew her nose. "My second decision," she said, again looking directly at him, "is that we're getting married or we've had it. I mean it this time. I've got to put my life back together. So you make up your mind."

"Now, honey, let's take one thing at a time. Join A.A. and see how it goes. Then let's talk about getting hitched. What's the rush, there's plenty of time. Look, we've got Punkie in a good Catholic school . . ."

She slammed her hand against the table with such force that it sounded like a pistol shot. He marveled at the strength in that frail-looking woman. "Listen, mister, shit or get off the pot."

"Jesus Christ," Jimmy said, "if you're going to put it like that, how can I refuse?"

She looked at him, her lower jaw dropping.

"You join A.A., stay off the bottle one month, and we'll get hitched. That's a promise."

And he kept his word. They left Annette with the Giarussos and drove to Reno, again registering at the Mapes. They were married in one of the gingerbread chapels that specialize in quickie marriages. Everything in Nevada is designed to save time away from the tables. They spent that night in Reno and drove back the next day. Jean was happy but Jimmy was not all that certain he had made the right move. But there was that question of obligation and he was terribly fond of Punkie. What the hell, he kept telling himself, maybe it would all work out for the best in the end.

They rented a three-bedroom house at Moss Beach from the young lawyer in Hayward, Dennis McDonald, who had helped him file for bankruptcy and was very anxious to handle Jimmy's pending lawsuit against *Penthouse.* In its March 1975 issue, the magazine had printed an article that characterized Rancho La Costa as "The Hundred-Million-Dollar Resort with Criminal Clientele." Written by Lowell Bergman and Jeff Gerth, the story had concentrated on the "Dalitz mob—includes Dalitz, Allard Roen, Merv Adelson, and Irwin Molasky." It identified "The primary founders of La Costa" as "syndicate 'bluebloods.' Their roots were in Prohibition rum-running and bust-out gambling. The bulk of the financing for La Costa since its inception ten years ago has come from friends in the scandal-ridden Teamsters Central States Pension Fund. . . . Dalitz has been a prime mover in transforming organized crime into a financial powerhouse. . . . He and his partners at La Costa represent a major force in entertainment, television (Lorimar Productions, founded by Adelson and Molasky, among others, produces such shows as *The Blue Knight, The Waltons,* etc.), construction, laundries, and, of course, gambling." It was a hard-hitting article and the "Dalitz mob" struck back with a $630 million libel suit, orchestrated by a battery of top-notch attorneys, led by Louis Nizer.

As for Jimmy, the reference to him was purely gratuitous: "In 1967 . . . State agents were active in closing down the Baptist Foundation of America security fraud. Well-known mob figures began to have trouble. Jimmy 'the Weasel' Fratianno, an infamous hit man, found his movements closely watched." That was the extent of it. Jimmy, who had been called far worse things in his life, was taken by surprise when Roselli asked him to file a lawsuit.

"But, Johnny, what good will it do?" Jimmy had protested. "Why get involved in all that shit?"

Roselli nodded. "I know, and I agree with you, but Dalitz talked to Aiuppa and he just told me to pass it on to you. The old man says do it, you do it, right?"

"Right," Jimmy smiled. He didn't want Roselli to think he held him responsible in any way.

"Give it to Dick Chier and don't worry about the cost. Everything's going to be taken care of."

Later McDonald had persuaded Jimmy to turn the lawsuit over to him.

"Dennis, believe me, you ain't going to make a dime out of this deal," Jimmy had warned him. "It's going to be a royal waste of your time."

"Jimmy, don't worry about it," McDonald said. "For me, it's a fun case. Besides, I've got a plan. We can place you in a courtroom in Alameda County, where people are not particularly knowledgeable about the Mafia, and don't know who you are, and I think I can present an image, with your help, that can prove you've been defamed by this article. After all, you've never been convicted or even formally charged with a murder. Obviously, they're in no position to prove you murdered anyone."

"You mean, we push so far and then settle out of court."

"No, no. We go to trial. Jimmy, I haven't known you all that long, but I recognized early in our relationship that you have a certain charisma, and between us, I think we can convince a jury that you've never killed anyone and therefore the reference to 'infamous hit man' is defamatory. I find you, as an individual, to be polite, gracious, thoughtful, a fact that's completely incongruent with your reputation. I think a jury will agree with me."

"Well, in that case, let's sue the bastards for millions."

The day after his conversation with Louie Dragna, Jimmy boarded a plane for Cleveland. As the plane began its descent, Jimmy thought of Yonnie. The poor son of a bitch had come out of prison in 1972 and died the next year, just a few months after Jimmy was released from Chino. Jimmy had planned on seeing him, but there had been too many other pressing matters. Then it was too late. He wondered how many stamps Yonnie had finally collected during those thirty-seven years in prison. The collection was probably worth a fortune.

Tony Dope was waiting for him when he came into the terminal. They shook hands, greeting each other warmly, and walked to the baggage area.

"You're looking sharp," Tony Dope said. "Where did you get that fucking suit?"

"It's a Baroni," Jimmy said. "Five hundred smackers retail, sixty hot."

Tony Dope whistled. "Jimmy, you look like a fucking millionaire. How many stewardesses give you their phone numbers?"

Jimmy looked startled. "You know something, I've got so much on my mind I didn't even notice them."

"By the way, Leo's coming in tonight," Dope said, "so we'll have dinner together."

"Thanks, Dope. Oh, there's my bag. Let's go."

At dinner that evening with Moceri and Delsanter, Jimmy told them about Louie Dragna's proposal, and by the time he finished they were both grinning and Jimmy could see they were pleased for him. "I didn't tell him I was coming to Cleveland first. What do you think?"

"I think you should grab it," Leo said.

"I do too," Tony Dope agreed.

"I don't know," Jimmy said. "All my troubles've been in L.A. Why should I be a whore for twenty, thirty people? It's too late in life. I ain't forgotten how they stole my money."

"Yeah, but they're going to jail," Leo said. "You'll be in charge. Run the show your own way."

"The point, Jimmy," Tony Dope said, "is all them other people are gone. It's a new deal."

"Right. One last shot, Jimmy."

"Revamp the family, Jimmy," Tony Dope said. "Then put it to a vote when he comes out of the joint. A lot can happen in twenty months."

When Jimmy arrived at O'Hare International Airport, he was met by Obie Frabotta and they went directly to Allen Dorfman's office. Again Joey Lombardo took him to the restaurant out in the boonies. As before, Joey Aiuppa and Jackie Cerone arrived a few minutes later.

Aiuppa listened, his face expressionless, as Jimmy explained the situation in Los Angeles. In concluding his recital, Jimmy said, "I told them I had to get your blessings on this transfer."

Aiuppa nodded. "Go ahead, Jimmy. You can tell them you've got our blessings."

On the flight home, Jimmy could feel the excitement beginning to take hold. Leo was right. This was his last shot. It could be the beginning of a whole new life for him. It was an engraved invitation to take over the whole state. He could revamp the family, as Tony Dope had suggested, consolidate his position with Chicago and New York, show them he was a mover, that acting or not he was boss material, a man who could be decisive and make things happen.

He closed his eyes. How much of this could he tell Larry Lawrence? So far he had collected about fifteen thousand dollars from the FBI for imparting worthless information. The thing that amazed him was that they knew so much about the inner workings of the Los Angeles family. At times Lawrence seemed to know more than he did about what was happening in Los Angeles and San Diego. It became obvious to him that they had turned some important made guys down there, who were not playing games like he was, but were seriously informing, and perhaps responsible for the case against Brooklier and the others.

Lawrence had started hinting that Jimmy was taking them for ride. He realized they were comparing his information with that of the other informants. Now that he was taking over the Los Angeles family, he would have to watch his step. There was no question that Lawrence would soon hear about it. He knew he could not hide this fact from him. It was not that he needed the under-the-table money they were paying him, but being an informant had given him a certain freedom of movement. The FBI did not waste time surveilling their informants. This took the pressure off and gave him a protective cover to continue his illegal operations.

31
TAKING OVER

† † † †

HE WALKED INTO VIC WERBER'S PRIVATE OFFICE IN THE LOS ANGELES Clothing Mart and Dominic Brooklier stood up and they shook hands. Behind him stood Sam Sciortino, Pete Milano, and Louie Dragna. Werber left the room.

"Jimmy, it's good we're back together again," Brooklier said, holding on to Jimmy's hand. "This should've happened a long time ago."

"The old man gave me his blessings," Jimmy said. "I'll do the best I can, you know. If I can make some money while you're in prison, we'll see that your family gets a piece of it."

"I'd appreciate that, Jimmy."

"I told Louie I plan to make some moves, you know, shake up a few people that's taken over in our country."

Brooklier smiled. "I'm glad to hear that, Jimmy. I'm all for doing something with this porno shit New York's pulling on us."

Brooklier released his hand and Jimmy greeted the others. They sat down, with Brooklier behind Werber's desk. He was on his way to prison but he was still boss. "There's a couple things we'd like you to jump on right away. It means going to Cleveland, but you can kill two birds with one stone. You know this Reuben Sturman? He's got about fifty porno shops in this town. This guy's one of the biggest porno dealers in the United States."

"I know him," Jimmy said. "Lives in a fucking mansion in Shaker Heights. His protection's Terry Zappi with the Gambino family."

Brooklier nodded. "Well, a couple years ago, we sent someone to Cleveland to shake him up. Went into his office and smacked him around and he went running to Zappi, who hit him for two hundred grand to straighten it out. We cut up the money. Why don't you get Leo or Tony Dope to send somebody to shake him up? Let him run to Zappi again."

"Okay, I'll tell them," Jimmy said, "but Zappi's in trouble right now and staying out of the picture. This fucking guy's worth millions. The two guys now running all the porno for New York are Mickey Zaffarano, he's a *capo* with Lillo's [Carmine Galante] family, and a guy called Debe [Robert DiBernardo], who's not made but works for Zappi."

"I don't care who he goes to, they've still got to come to us to straighten it out. Then we get our end," Brooklier said. "Okay, now, while you're there . . . Well, listen, let Pete explain it."

Milano smiled, pleased to be included in the conversation. "There's a friend of ours here, somebody we made while you were gone. Dominic Longo. And he wants to be introduced as a made guy to Tony Randazzo."

"Who's Dominic Longo?"

"Jimmy, this guy's got a Toyota dealership in El Monte that's the biggest in the country. He's originally from Montreal and Tony knows a lot of made guys up there. Dominic wants the family guys in Montreal to know he's made.

"What's this Longo like?" Jimmy asked. "Has he done any fucking work?"

"He's solid," Brooklier said. "He did a piece of work with Peanuts Tranalone. They choked a guy, but they never made him in Montreal."

"Is he active with the family here?"

"Well, this Toyota agency keeps him pretty busy. But he's useful in other ways."

Milano laughed. "Yeah, Jimmy, he's rich, good for a little touch now and then."

"Sounds great," Jimmy said. "Will do, no problem."

Their next meeting was in a restaurant off Sunset in the Silver Lake area. Brooklier and Sciortino were there when he arrived and they had a cup of coffee while waiting for Pete Milano. He came in twenty minutes late.

"Holy shit, I was tailed," Milano said in a trembling voice, "but I lost them. That's why I'm late. How did it go in Cleveland?"

"Okay," Jimmy said, "Longo met Randazzo and I told Dope and Leo to have someone grab this Sturman."

"That's great, Jimmy," Brooklier said. "Let him run to New York, we'll get a chunk of money. The legal fees are eating us up alive. We got twenty grand from Moe Dalitz which we spent. And now we need nine grand for Harry Hall. This guy's got connections with the Justice Department, claims to know the Attorney General. He got Joe Dip's sentence reduced, and I hear he helped Tony Giordano in St. Louis."

"Hey, Dominic," Jimmy said, "Bomp's told me about this Hall. He just got out of the joint himself. This guy's going to scam you."

"We're getting a money-back guarantee. If he cuts our time to three months, we give him an additional fifteen grand. If he don't, he returns the nine. What can we lose?"

"You could get yourself fucked up."

"It's a shot," Sciortino said. "Look, go see Jackie Presser. This guy Hall's in partnership with Presser. He's with a P.R. outfit in Vegas. Got a million-three from Presser to improve the Teamsters' image."

"That's a good idea," Brooklier said. "See what Presser thinks of this guy. We'll get the money from Longo. He owes us one."

"Okay, give me a couple days. What about the rest of the porno shit around here?" Jimmy asked.

"We want to reverse this thing," Brooklier said. "Pete's been working with Mickey Fine. He's connected with the Colombo family but we're getting a third of his business. There's a bunch of porno guys around here that need straightening out. There's Willie Bittner [William Haimowitz], Jack [Jacob] Molinas, Mike Pinkus, and Teddy Gaswirth, who's with Zaffarano, and one of the biggest operators around here. Now Mickey Fine's got that Playmates series with Johnny Holmes, you know, the guy with a fourteen-inch prick. This guy's the biggest star in porno. Everybody wants this stud. The reels retail for twenty-five, thirty dollars and wholesale for seven-fifty. Mickey's got a connection where he buys them for five-fifty, sort of middlemans it, you know."

After lunch, on their way to the parking lot, Brooklier pulled Jimmy aside. "What's the situation with you and Bomp?"

"We're good friends."

Brooklier pursed his lips. "Well, you know, while we're gone, kind of straighten out this guy, will you? He's got no respect for nobody in this family. It's fuck this guy and fuck that guy. This guy's got to stop pulling his prick in public."

At three hundred pounds and balding, Jackie Presser looked grotesque. He sat there like a fat toad, with rolls of fat cascading from his neck to his crotch, his eyes buried in puffy discolored flesh. Although Jimmy knew him well, he found it hard to concentrate on Presser's words. People who were grossly overweight disgusted him.

"Forget about Harry Hall," Presser was saying. "He beat a rap in Chicago, possession of stolen securities, by admitting he was a snitch for the IRS. The guy's just no good, that's my opinion." He placed both hands on his desk and it looked like his arms had been amputated at the elbows.

"Thanks, Jackie, I'll pass it along. Dope sends his regards," Jimmy said, making sure that Presser knew that he was there with the approval of the Cleveland family. "Oh, listen, about Andy Anderson. He's still fucking Rudy Tham. This guy don't straighten out, we're going to hurt him, you understand, Jackie? I'm running the show out there while them guys are in the joint, and I'm not going to put up with no shit, forget about it."

"Hold on, Jimmy. I'm going to see Fitz [Fitzsimmons] at La Costa and work out some arrangement. It might take a little while because my father's seriously ill, but I'll get to it soon as I can."

"That's great, Jackie," Jimmy said, standing up. "I'm sorry to hear about your dad. Hope he gets better soon."

32
DEATH OF A GODFATHER

† † † †

JIMMY HAD NEVER SEEN ROSELLI IN SUCH AN AGITATED STATE. THEY were in the law library at Cantillon's office and Roselli was pacing the floor, his white hair disheveled as he kept running his fingers through it in nervous frustration.

"Oh, Jimmy, they fucking killed a dead man. Sam [Giancana] could barely climb a short flight of stairs. He'd been to Houston and Dr. DeBakey performed a cholecystostomy and he was bed-ridden three weeks. He went back to Chicago and a couple weeks later he was back in Houston with a blood clot. DeBakey worked on him, ordered him to stay in bed, but the Houston police started hounding him and five days later he sneaked out of the hospital, wearing a doctor's gown and leaving in a hospital supply van. The cops caught up with him at his hotel, and he sneaked out the back way. Jimmy, it probably sounds like he's being very active, but the fucking guy's shuffling along, barely able to walk. Gets back to Chicago I think on the seventeenth [June 1975] and two days later somebody puts seven slugs in his head. He was in his basement kitchen cooking himself a little snack before bedtime."

He stopped pacing and turned to look at Jimmy, his blue eyes hard as flint. "That motherfucking Aiuppa and that prick Batters. May their fucking souls burn in hell for a million eternities."

"What's this bullshit in the paper about Sam trying to get back into power in Chicago?" Jimmy asked.

Roselli threw his hands up in dispair. "Forget the newspapers. Sam was finished with that bullshit. He's like me, he'd had it up to his eyeballs. Who needs it?"

"Maybe it was because he was going to testify before that Senate committee [the Senate Intelligence Committee, chaired by Frank Church]."

"What could Sam tell them that I didn't know? I just testified, Jimmy, gave them the same bullshit I gave Ed Morgan and Jack Anderson a few years ago."

Jimmy felt like a cold hand was squeezing his heart. "Johnny, you're not on safe ground. This's a commission contract."

Roselli dropped listlessly into a chair. "Have I told you they've reduced the commission to six bosses: Chicago and the five New York families? They've dropped the oldtimers, like Maggadino, Scalish, Zerilli, and Bruno. Which means Chicago's got a lot more fucking power now. So, maybe, Aiuppa took it to the commission. Still, Jimmy, I'm telling you, the man was fucking dead on his feet. It's petty revenge. They hated Sam and they finally talked Butch [Dominic Blasi] into clipping him. I'd bet my last nickel Butch did it. Sam trusted him and this guy's a worker. One shot in the back of the head, one in the mouth, and five under the chin. That's how you repay a guy that's trusted you forty years. I'd like to cut his fucking balls off and shove them up his ass."

"Johnny, please, listen to me. When you guys got involved with the CIA, you broke the rules. Sam should have brought the proposition before the commission. He was the boss, he knew the rules. When he got subpoenaed, I'll bet Santo ran to Chicago and told them the whole story, got himself a pass."

Roselli stood up again. "Santo got on a boat and took off the minute the committee was formed. Jimmy, Santo's a close friend."

"Yeah, so was Butch."

Roselli stared into space. "I don't know, Jimmy. You could be right, it just gave them the excuse they needed to clip him. Now they've got to clip a few of the old-timers that remain loyal to Sam. They don't want those guys coming after them."

"Take my advice, Johnny, don't say too much about this hit on Sam. Don't let the word get around you're pissed." Jimmy stood up and crossed over to Roselli, putting his hand on his shoulder. "Johnny, if you're in trouble, tell me, I'll do everything I can to help. Maybe we can get you transferred back to L.A."

Roselli looked into his eyes and smiled. "Thanks, buddy, but I'll be all right."

"Johnny, I know you're wise to all the tricks, but they've got a long fucking memory, don't forget."

Jean dropped him off at First and Gaffey in San Pedro and Jimmy walked into a parking lot next to a liquor store and got into Louie Dragna's car.

The windows were rolled up and rock music was playing on the radio. "I talked to the old man," Dragna said, "and he tells me he's talked to you about Bomp."

"Well, I haven't had a chance to bring up the subject with Bomp," Jimmy replied, "but I'm going to see him in San Diego tonight."

Dragna stretched his lips, pulling them tightly against his teeth. "Well, Jimmy, Brooklier wants Bomp clipped. Wait, before you say anything. I know you think Bomp's a good friend of yours, but he's not, Jimmy. He's bad-rapping you all over the place. This guy's gone crackers."

"That's just his way. He don't mean no harm."

"Mean it or not, he's doing harm," Dragna said. "This guy's become dangerous. He's got a loose mouth. Just because he's older, been around longer, he's got no respect for nobody in this family. I know he talks about me. Talks about Dominic, Pete, talks about Roselli, your good friend."

Jimmy felt like punching Dragna right in the mouth. Now he knew why they had given him this job, had tricked him into transferring back from Chicago. He was the only man capable of handling this contract.

"Well, okay," Jimmy said, but he thought, "You dirty motherfucker, it'll be a cold day in hell before I do your fucking dirty work again."

"Of course, we don't expect you to do the actual hit yourself. As you say, you're a good friend, and he trusts you. So you set it up and let somebody else do the hit."

"Who?"

"Take your pick. There's Sal Pinelli, old Tony's kid, we made him. There's Jack LoCicero, you know him he's a soldier going back to Jack's [Dragna] days, and Mike Rizzi . . . I understand he's been up to see you in San Francisco."

"Yeah, he likes it up there."

"The old man's pretty anxious about this, so give it top priority."

"Louie," Jimmy said, shaking his head, "you don't set up a guy like Bomp in two minutes. It takes time, unless you're lucky."

Jimmy wanted to change the subject. "Dope called, they grabbed that porno guy Sturman, we should be hearing from New York anytime now. Then I've had a couple meetings with Pete's [Milano] crew. Frankly, they're a bunch of nickle-dime hustlers. This guy Pinkus owes Mickey Fine thirty-five grand, so I sent a couple of them to break this guy's head and they do nothing. I've got Rizzi working with LoCicero and the other day LoCicero calls and says, 'Jimmy, there's a guy here by the name of Tommy Ricciardi from New York that's looking for Mickey Fine. He says Mickey owes some guy in Providence eleven grand and he's got the contract to collect this money.' I says, 'Put him on the phone.' I says, 'Tommy, Mickey's our man. Right now he couldn't pay you two cents because he's broke. Secondly, when he does get some money, we're going to take it, you know.' So now he's coming on strong, saying he owes the money. He's going to get it, this and that, and I says, 'Hey, let's keep everything cool, you ain't going to get shit from this guy, so you better go back East and give them the fucking message. I don't know who sent you and I couldn't care less. Just leave this man alone. Put Jack back on the phone.' So Jack comes on the line and I says, 'You better talk to this guy. He's going to get hurt if he starts muscling Mickey.' "

"Getting any money?"

"Nothing so far," Jimmy said. In fact, he had received five thousand dollars from Willie Bittner for not collecting from Mike Pinkus, who was associated with Bittner, and eight thousand dollars from Mickey Fine for trying to collect the thirty-five thousand from Pinkus.

"You know, Louie, this fucking running back and forth's expensive. If nothing pans out, I'm going to come to you pretty soon."

"We'll work something out, but first chance you get, go see the old man at Terminal Island. I know it may not be too easy getting in there, but see if you can work something out."

"I've already got it figured. I've got it fixed up with this kid I know over there. I'm going as his uncle. It's a big open visiting room. Dominic will come out to see his wife and I'll talk to him."

"He's not feeling too hot, Jimmy. His heart's giving him trouble. He had a slight attack."

"Oh, yeah, well, that's a shame. Sorry to hear it."

Jimmy's godson, Johnny Brooklier, was pushing his father's wheelchair when Jimmy came into the visiting room at Terminal Island.

Brooklier's face was as gray as his hair. Talking seemed to require a great effort. "Thanks for coming," he said, turning to look at his son, who quickly walked away, going across the room to sit with his mother.

"You don't look too hot, Dominic."

"Oh, I feel better than I look," he said dryly. He closed his eyes and Jimmy took a close look at the creases in his face. He was an old man before his time. His problem was that he was a chronic worrier. When he opened his eyes, he looked directly at Jimmy for a long time without speaking. Then he said, "Louie talked to you about Bomp?"

"Oh, yeah, that's in the works."

Brooklier nodded. "Did you talk to Bomp about his mouth?"

"Fuck no, why put the guy on notice? Listen, this guy's going to be tough enough to clip."

"Jimmy, this's important to me. If you don't move on it, we'll have to take care of it when I get out. Either way, this guy's going to get clipped."

"Don't worry, his days are numbered."

The disappearance of Jimmy Hoffa on July 31, 1975, posed no mystery to Jimmy and Tony Dope Delsanter. "It took them guys long enough," Jimmy said, the first chance they had to discuss it. "I knew the guy. He was a good man, but he was hard of hearing. Detroit told him to cool it. Christ, they blackballed everybody that stuck to him. Still, you know, he kept right on coming, making his moves against Fitzsimmons."

Delsanter, who had close ties to the Detroit family, said, "Forget that bullshit in the newspapers about Tony Pro [Anthony Provenzano] or Chuckie O'Brien or Russ Bufalino. Detroit don't need no outside help to clip their own fucking guy. They owned this Hoffa. Period. Tony Giacalone was in tight with Hoffa and he's the one that set him up. Tony Zerilli and Mike Polizzi gave the order and that was all she wrote."

† † †

Jimmy and Mike Rizzi were sitting in Jimmy's favorite booth at Sal Amarena's pizza joint.

"Jimmy, I lost a lot of money today," Rizzi said, handing his newspaper to Jimmy. "Look at this. Somebody killed Jack Molinas."

The story said the killer had used a .22 caliber pistol, shooting Molinas through the head. A former Columbia University basketball star and disbarred lawyer, Molinas had once served five years for fixing basketball games.

In the news story, Los Angeles Police Chief Edward M. Davis was quoted as saying that the Molinas "firm owed a quarter of a million dollars to an organized crime-controlled film-processing facility specializing in obscene material. It is also a fact that Molinas' firm held a $500,000 life insurance policy on his life." The chief speculated that the policy was probably a factor in his death, the same way a similar policy had played a part in the slaying of his late associate, Bernard Gusoff. As business partners Molinas and Gusoff had held identical $500,000 life-insurance policies on each other: "The strange thing is that Gusoff was killed just sixteen days before the premium on that policy was scheduled to lapse," the Chief said. "Molinas collected and for a while we thought he was a good suspect. But now he's dead and the Gusoff killing [on November 15, 1974] is still unsolved."

"How'd you lose money? Were you shaking this guy?"

"No, no," Rizzi said, leaning close to Jimmy. "I hit Gusoff for Molinas and he gave me fifty grand. I figured there was more where that came from."

Jimmy raised his eyebrows. This was something he understood. "I wonder who clipped Molinas? I was going to have you talk to that guy, get some of his action. You know, a guy's got to be nuts to work out an insurance deal like that. A half-million bucks. Jesus Christ, most guys would kill their own mother for a lot less."

From then on Jimmy and Mike Rizzi began working closely together. Rizzi was a man after Jimmy's own heart.

Jimmy met Tommy Palermo, the *consigliere* of the Los Angeles family, when Louie Dragna said he had devised a plot to put Bompensiero off guard. The meeting was at a Denny's restaurant in San Pedro. Jimmy took one look at Palermo and thought, "Holy shit, this fucking family ain't for real." Palermo reminded him of Pete Milano, Carlo Licata, Sal Pinelli—they all looked alike, all little *pezzi di merda*.

Dragna was beaming, delighted with his scheme. "Jimmy, we're going to give Bomp a title to relax him. Make him *consigliere*. This way, you know, he won't suspect there's anything wrong."

"Hey, Louie, that's a great idea," Jimmy said. "It might quiet him down, too."

"I've talked it over with Tommy here and he's all in favor of it."

"Sure, why not," Palermo said. "It'll put his mind at ease."

Jimmy kept quiet. This could work in his favor. With Bompensiero as *consigliere,* they might turn it around even if Brooklier should survive his prison term.

Jimmy had already bypassed numerous opportunities to kill Bompensiero. Bompensiero visited him in San Francisco two and three times a month. They had been alone in hotel rooms, had driven on deserted roads. In fact, he could have taken him any place because Bompensiero trusted him.

"Why don't you give Bomp a call and tell him the good news," Dragna suggested. "Then let's see if we can get moving on this."

"He'll be tickled pink," Jimmy said.

"Yeah, I'm sure he feels he deserves it," Dragna said. "That's the beauty of it. He'll never suspect a thing until it happens. Jimmy, I've never forgotten how quickly it happened to Russian Louie. The fucking guy walked in Gaspare's house and you and Bomp moved so fast he was a goner in ten seconds."

Jimmy said, "Louie, you ought to try it yourself sometimes. In the old days, you know, you couldn't even be made without first having done some fucking work."

Dragna's face looked flush. "I suppose you think I've had a free ride," he said, with more whine than anger in his voice.

"Louie, don't take it personal. I'm just talking about the old days. Times have changed. Yeah, Louie, I'd say you've had a good ride, but you was the king's nephew, so to speak. You'd be a sucker not to take advantage of it."

By now Dragna's face was crimson. "You've got it wrong, Jimmy, I've earned everything I've got. I don't think it's fair . . ."

"Louie, for Christ's sake, forget about it. Why're you getting uptight? If you really feel like you want to do something, I'll set Bomp up and you clip him. I'll get you the gun. A twenty-two with a silencer. Better still, I'll get the fucking rope and we'll both pull on it.

"Louie, you know, you guys've been playing games in L.A. ever since Jack died, and you know it better than anybody. We need to make some workers in this family and retire the deadheads. Revamp this outfit. Louie, I don't have nothing against you. You've always been fair and square with me, and I'm going to be fair and square with you, but just give this some thought, will you? The families back East think we're a bunch of fucking clowns out here. I'd like to turn that around. What do you say?"

Dragna was slowly regaining his normal coloring. "Jimmy, I hear you loud and clear, but let's sleep on it awhile. Let's get this thing with Bomp settled first, then we'll get together and see what can be done to revive this family."

Jimmy hadn't been in command long, but he was already asserting himself, knowing full well that Dragna was weak.

PART XI

† † † †

SHOW BIZ
1975–1976

33
TOMMY MARSON

† † † †

SEVERAL INVESTIGATIVE TECHNIQUES HAVE BEEN TRIED AND EXHAUSTED during this investigation. Physical surveillance of the alleged conspirators is virtually impossible due to the unique location of Thomas Marson's [*nee* Thomas Marsonak Dolowski] house which, according to the confidential sources, is the hub of activity and a central meeting place. Marson's residence at 37820 Halper Lake Drive, Rancho Mirage, California, is located in an exclusive private security area accessible through a security gate operated by an individual key. The residence is surrounded by the Tamarisk Country Club which is open only to members and their guests.

In addition, the area has a private patrol service who are the employees of the residents and who warn the residents of any suspicious activity in the neighborhood. Special agents of the Federal Bureau of Investigation have attempted to physically surveil Marson's residence for approximately a year in an effort to obtain evidence of the criminal activities under investigation, and only rarely have these surveillances been productive.

Surveillance, in and of itself, even if highly successful, rarely succeeds in gathering evidence of the criminal activities under investigation. It is an investigative technique that is used to confirm meetings between alleged conspirators and often leaves the investigators to speculate as to the purpose of the meeting. It is also a technique to corroborate information obtained from confidential sources. However, if the confidential sources will not testify to the true nature of the surveilled meetings as they pertain to criminal activity, then they are of little value.

All of the confidential sources referred to herein have stated repeatedly that under no circumstances would they be willing to testify at any formal proceedings concerning the activity which is the subject of this affidavit. All of the sources have stated that they are afraid of the subjects listed herein and fear for their safety. . . .

> *—Excerpt from an FBI affidavit submitted to a federal court in*
> *support of a request to install wiretaps on two of Marson's*
> *telephones for a period of thirty days.*

A garden paradise within the garden paradise of Palm Springs, Rancho Mirage is a ten-square-mile walled desert oasis of green grass, palm trees, and palatial homes on three-acre-plus lots that are painted in colors to blend with the terrain. It proudly calls itself the "Playground of Presidents." Former President Gerald R. Ford lives here, a neighbor of ex-Vice President Spiro T. Agnew. The "Sunnyland" estate of Walter Annenberg, former ambassador to England and close friend of Richard M. Nixon, sits here, walled within the walled oasis.

Others besides heads of states and multimillionaire diplomats live in Rancho Mirage. There are movie gods and goddesses, captains of commerce and industry, nabobs of unions, kings and princes of organized crime. In fact, anyone with the price can make the scene.

Jimmy and Slick Shapiro registered at the Ingleside Inn, the latest in deluxe hostlery to enhance Palm Canyon Road. They took separate rooms and met in the bar for a drink. Shapiro, who still owed Jimmy $20,000 he had stolen from him back in the Fifties when he had managed Jimmy's bookmaking operation, had moved from Toledo to Las Vegas.

"Slick, you cocksucker. You're getting fat like a pig. Why don't you go on a diet?"

"You think I'm fat?" Shapiro said. "Wait till you see Tommy Marson. They call him 'Fatso' and he's ugly as sin but he don't give a shit. He's our age or older, and his wife Bobbi's about thirty, a real sweetheart, and they've got two little girls. Besides he's fucking loaded. His house in Rancho Mirage is right on the sixteenth fairway, must have set him back at least four hundred grand. He's a seven-iron shot from Frank's place, who by the way lives on Frank Sinatra Road. Jimmy, the people that live there, forget about it."

"So what's the story with this Tommy Marson?"

"Jimmy, this guy's a good hustler, good money maker, I think we can make some money with him. One thing about this Marson, Jimmy, he knows how your system works. He's heard about you taking over in L.A. and right now he needs your kind of leverage. He represents one million-four in the Westchester Premier Theater, four hundred of his own money, plus eight hundred from Marty Eisner and two hundred from a dentist in Toledo. This Eisner's a half-ass hood from Detroit. Tommy thinks the wiseguys in New York are going to fuck him."

"Where's that theater? Never even heard of it."

"It's in Tarrytown, New York, and it's one beautiful place. Cost maybe seven million, and they book all the big acts. It seats thirty-five hundred, but they're losing money. I'll let Tommy run it down for you."

Before Jimmy could respond, Shapiro said, "Here's Tommy now."

They both stood up and Shapiro made the introduction. They ordered another round of drinks and Marson beamed at Jimmy.

"Jesus, Jimmy, this's a real pleasure meeting you," he said. "I've heard about you for years, feel like I know you. In fact, I think we've got a lot of mutual acquaintances."

"That could be," Jimmy said. "Where you from?"

"New York, Scarsdale, but I've moved around. When I was younger, I did some work with Joe DiCarlo and Sammy Pierri in Buffalo. Then I did some burglarizing with a guy called Clooney, from Detroit. Hell of a peet man."

Jimmy laughed. "That's really something. I was in the joint in Ohio with him. In fact, the first job I pulled when I got out was in West Virginia and this fucking Clooney was beautiful. He blew the safe with soup, just made a little poof. Got forty-eight grand, real piece of cake."

Again Jimmy was reminded of the relatively small size of the world he lived in. Who would have thought he would be sitting here in Palm Springs with a millionaire who had gone on scores with guys he had known forty years ago?

"Hey, listen," Marson said. "If you guys are ready, let's go up to the house."

The bar at Marson's home was obviously his favorite room. And as Jimmy would notice as the night wore on, Tommy Marson was a pretty good drinker, could put away a lot of booze without showing it. Jimmy was introduced to Bobbi Marson and their two little girls and after a few drinks Marson took Jimmy and Shapiro to Jack London's for dinner.

After a few more drinks, Marson leaned toward Jimmy and said, "Earlier I was telling you about jobs I did as a kid, but I don't want you to get the impression I'm washed up, that I don't have the balls no more."

"It never occurred to me," Jimmy said.

Marson rubbed his face and Jimmy realized that the booze was getting to the man. He was drinking three to their one. His face was beginning to look a little numb and he was trying to stimulate circulation by rubbing it.

"I pulled a score right here in Palm Springs not too long ago," Marson said. "I got this kid George Pazula from Columbus, he owns pornography stores over there, and he brought this friend of his along. Can't remember his name. I found this score, laid out the deal, and we went in and snatched close to fifty grand in cash." He laughed. "A friend of mine's house."

"Them are the easiest to case," Jimmy said.

"Jimmy, I'm leveling with you, so you'll know the kind of square shooter I am. We've got a lot in common, understand, and I think we can help each other out and make some money. What do you say?"

"Sounds good to me," Jimmy said. "What's the deal?"

"Let's go back to the Ingleside, have another drink, and I'm going to cash in for the night. I'll come over tomorrow and lay the whole thing out for you."

Jimmy and Shapiro were lying in chaise longues by the pool, dressed in swim trunks, soaking up the sun.

"Well, good morning," a cheerful voice called. They turned and saw Marson coming toward them, followed by the lifeguard pulling a chaise longue and an armful of towels. Wearing baggy shorts that came down to his knees and a zippered terry cloth short-sleeve jacket, he reminded Jimmy of cartoons he had seen of people wearing barrels.

He sat down, groaning, and slipped off his leather sandals. "I barely made it home last night. Must have been something wrong with my stomach, the booze really hit me. Where's that waiter, I need a Bloody Mary."

He looked up and the waiter was there smiling at him. "My boy, easy on the blood and heavy on the fucking Mary. Bring it in one of them big glasses, double or triple, whatever. How about you guys, want anything?"

They both declined. The lifeguard brought an umbrella and Marson said, "Now, that's more like it. I can't take the fucking sun out here, turns me into a boiled lobster." He stretched and yawned. "Man, this's the life, right, Jimmy?"

The waiter brought the Bloody Mary and Shapiro signed the tab.

"So what's this deal in New York all about?" Jimmy asked. "Slick was telling me somebody's trying to fuck you out of a million-four."

Marson nodded and placed the drink on a small table beside his longue. "Jimmy, I was thinking about this on the way over here today and I think the best way to handle this is to tell you the whole story so you'll know what's involved and whether you can help. One thing I should tell you right up front, both the Gambino and Genovese families are involved, I mean the bosses themselves, so I don't know if you want to butt heads with powerhouses like them."

Jimmy raised an eyebrow. "Hey, Tommy, give me the story. If I can make some money with you, okay, we're in business. If I can't, fuck it."

"You get me out of this squeeze and you'll make some money, don't worry. Anyway, I told you I'm from Scarsdale. There's this guy, Greg [Gregory J.] DePalma, he was a neighbor of mine, and he's with the Gambino family, but I don't think he's made yet. But he's very close to Paulie Castellano, who's Gambino's cousin and brother-in-law and kind of running the family, because, you know, Carlo's an old man and pretty sick.

"The way I understand it, back in 1973, DePalma and another guy, Ritchie [Richard 'Nerves'] Fusco, started a landfill operation on sixteen acres of swamp land in Tarrytown. They got a stockbroker, Eliot Weisman, to front the deal. The idea was to fill this swamp with garbage and trash and then build a beautiful theater for live performances right on top of it, and it's only about thirty miles from Times Square."

Marson reached for the Bloody Mary and gulped down several large sips. "Well, the corporation filed a prospectus with the SEC for a public offering of three hundred thousand shares of its common stock, which they list at seven-fifty per share. You know, to make this offer attractive to the public, they name Alan King and Steve Lawrence and Eydie Gorme as major stockholders. Actually, they sold them thirty thousand shares each at a penny a share. So already they've headed for trouble. This's early in 1973 and they've got until June fourteenth to sell a minimum of two hundred and seventy-five thousand shares, or they've got to refund the money and take back their stock from the buyers. Of course, DePalma's and Fusco's names don't appear in the prospectus. Weisman's holding four hundred and fifty-five thousand shares for them in his name.

"Now comes the crunch. The deadline's coming up and they're in serious trouble. So they start maneuvering, paying monies to front phony purchases of stock, and the fucking stock's dropping down to a dollar a share. They're getting officers of corporations to buy stock with the corporation's money at inflated prices and giving them kickbacks, and then getting the kickbacks returned by having the corporations pay phony claims to fronts. By pushing the pencil, they pull it off. They opened in March, this year [1975], and started out with a bang. They get Diana Ross and pay her two hundred and thirty-five thousand. Can you believe that? You'd think they had a gambling casino there, paying Vegas scales. From then on other performers are using this for their yardstick.

"But that's only part of the problem. They start out with a construction cost overrun of two-point-five million. They've got shylock money in there, two hundred thousand from a guy called Mickey Coco [nee Murad Nersesian], a Syrian who'd like to be Italian, and another two-hundred grand from Nino [Anthony] Gaggi and the juice's one and a half points, six fucking grand a week. Then there's this president of an investment house in Buffalo, [Salvatore] Cannatella, who invested one-point-one million of the company's money, and he's pretty close to DePalma and moving in to take control of the operation.

"By now the nut's big enough to choke an elephant and those guys, Weisman, Ritchie Fusco, DePalma, Cannatella, and Christ knows who else, are skimming the shit out of the joint. They're skimming from the cash concessions, two restaurants in the place, bars, parking, T-shirts and souvenirs, selling comped tickets, scalping their own tickets, and selling tickets for sixty-one permanent seats and a hundred and thirty-six folding chairs that are not on the theater's seating chart. A lot of this skim money's being used just to keep them afloat."

Marson paused and gulped down half of his drink. "Now, see, Jimmy, when I got into this thing I didn't know any of this shit. Fucking DePalma scammed me. Hell, he even got Gambino himself to invest a hundred grand under the table. Then they had to put Louie Dome [nee Louis Pacella] on the payroll to get Sinatra for some concerts—this guy and Sinatra are like brothers. Frank will do about a week in April and again in September. Louie Dome's with Funzi Tieri, the Genovese family, so we're getting them involved too. But Sinatra's going to make some money for the joint. Some of them other acts really bomb. So what do you think?"

Jimmy laughed. "Looks like you fell into a snake pit. What do you expect from me?"

"Well, I'd like to bail out, get my money back, but if I can't do it right away, I want a bigger piece of the skim. Think you can help me?"

"What're you going to do with this money if you get it back?"

"I'd like to get the whole million-four back, but I'll settle for my four hundred."

"Okay, what're going to do with it?"

"Invest it in California. I want to get away from New York. I want to live in California, I want to stay in California, I want to die in California. I'll tell you what, Jimmy. Get my money back and we'll invest it and split the profits right down the middle. How's that for a deal?"

Jimmy sat bolt upright. "Listen, Tommy, it just so happens I know of a terrific investment. There's this guy I know who was left a lot of property in Westborough but his partner fucked him. He's taking him to court, but meanwhile he's got a hundred and twenty-five lots in Chapter Eleven, and they're assessed at eight thousand but they're worth twenty-five grand each. Houses over there sell for eighty up. You could build beautiful homes and clear twenty grand per unit. That's two and a half million bucks. That four hundred thousand would get them titles out of Chapter Eleven. Then we go to a bank and get a construction loan to build them houses. We've got to clear a million bucks on this deal easy."

"Goddamnit, Jimmy, I like the fucking idea," Marson said. "I like anything to do with building. That's the best racket going. Jimmy, you've got my word on it, if we get this money back, I'll go into this deal with you as equal partners."

34
A COUPLE OF BODIES

† † † †

THE 24-DAY-OLD TAMARA RAND MURDER CASE HAS BECOME AN ENIGMA for the San Diego Police Department.

The complexities of the crime are overwhelming.

This is no ordinary whodunit.

"What we have is one heck of an extremely complicated mystery," says Captain Kenneth O'Brien, chief of detectives.

There is something for everyone.

The bizarre nature of the slaying itself; the entangled business dealings of the victim; the possibility the crime has underworld connections.

Homicide officers have little else. No clear motive. No suspect . . . .

Mrs. Rand, 54, a wealthy real estate broker and investor, was slain in her swank Mission Hills home on Sunday November 9.

She was shot five times: once through the back, once in the head through the ear and three times under the chin.

Her extensive dealings with Las Vegas associates have some people pointing a guilty finger at Nevada and organized crime.

Police expected the scope of the case to broaden today when investigators traveled to Las Vegas to question La Jolla financier Allen R. Glick.

Glick and Mrs. Rand were interwoven in numerous business transactions.

Investigators have interviewed scores of persons since Mrs. Rand was found by her husband, Dr. Phillip Rand, sprawled on the kitchen floor—a cup of tea sitting untouched on a countertop.

She had returned from a day of work at her nearby Balboa Park area office and was getting ready for a dinner date with her husband. Sometime between 3 P.M. and 5:30 P.M. she was slain. Neighbors have told authorities they heard no shots. . . . The clues are scarce. Five empty .22 casings. Some unidentified fingerprints. Complex business deals. Lawsuits. . . .

[Glick] is a Nevada gambling baron and former business and social associate of Mrs. Rand. It was an association that ended on the rocks. Last May Mrs. Rand filed a $560,000 suit against the 33-year-old Glick, alleging fraud and misrepresentation in a land deal. . . . Police do have a memo taken from Mrs. Rand's business office that details her conversation with Glick in Las Vegas in early May. . . .

Police say they have "some indications" a threat against Mrs. Rand was made last May in Las Vegas.

—San Diego *Evening Tribune,* December 3, 1975.

"Jimmy, this broad was going to drag Glick through a lot of shit," Bompensiero said.

They were in the cocktail lounge at the San Francisco Hilton and Jimmy was pumping Bompensiero on the Rand murder.

"So you're still working, you cocksucker?" Jimmy said. "Where'd you get the silencer?"

"Hey, not so fast," Bomp said, chomping on his cigar. He acted insulted, but there was a gleam of pride in his eyes that Jimmy recognized from the old days. "No shit, now, Jimmy, I'm an innocent bystander. I just took Tony [Spilotro] and showed him her house."

"Don't bullshit me," Jimmy said. "He didn't do it alone."

Bomp barked a laugh. "I didn't say he did, did I? Don't forget, this Tony's got a crew."

"Yeah, but that's your country," Jimmy said. "He's got to come through you. Hey, by the way, I'm the boss. How come you don't clear it with me first? This *consigliere* job's gone to your fucking head."

"Look, Jimmy, forget about Rand. Me and Tony are cutting up some money. I've been to Chicago and Palm Springs with Tony to see Aiuppa a few times, you know. Shit, me and the old man, we really hit it off. We have a ball, talking about old times. He's one hell of a guy. He calls me the old man and laughs his head off."

"Do you know where he got the silencer?"

Bompensiero shook his head. "Tony was telling me they've got a bunch of them in Chicago."

"I know," Jimmy said. "Last time I was in Cleveland Blackie told me he saw Jackie Cerone and he told him they had a guy in Miami making them. He told Blackie anytime he wanted silencers or any other tools to just let him know."

Bomp took a swallow of beer, wiped the foam from his mouth, and replaced his cigar. "I'll bet Glick's scared shitless. They don't tell this guy nothing about the Rand hit, but he's no fucking idiot. Jimmy, the money they're stealing out of them joints, holy shit. They're skimming the slots. That Lefty [Rosenthal] is something else. This guy could teach Moe Dalitz some tricks."

Jimmy was sixty-two years old and this was his first trip to New York City. Although he knew many made guys there, having met them in other cities, he never had any great desire to visit the Big Apple.

Now, of course, it was different. He was coming to the city as an acting boss and for a specific purpose: to make money. Tommy Marson had invited him to attend a $500-a-plate testimonial for Frank Sinatra who had been named Entertainer of the Year by the Friars Club. The Premier Theater had bought a table for ten. As Marson had explained it, this was an opportunity for Jimmy to meet the people he would be dealing with in his effort to recover his investment.

They met in TWA's Ambassador Room in Los Angeles and took the mid-morning flight to New York. The wheels of the jetliner had barely left the runway before Marson had a drink in his hand. "Hey, Jimmy, I see where you got a little action in San Francisco the other day. They finally got that Joe Barboza. What's that, the first Mafia hit there since Nick De-John back in the forties? The papers say there was a quarter-million-dollar contract on him."

"Tommy, that's bullshit. The guys that clipped him didn't get two cents. You think this thing's run like fucking reward posters in the post office?"

"I hear he was a made guy with Ray Patriarca [boss of the New England family] and years ago testified against him. He was in that Witness Protection Program, but still they got him."

"For Christ's sake, Tommy, this Barboza wasn't even Italian. He's fucking Portuguese. Forget it, will you. He was a punk."

Jimmy knew more about Barboza's murder than he would ever admit to Marson. Released from prison on October 30, 1975, Barboza had immediately started shaking down pornographers and bookmakers in the Bay Area. In mid-January 1976, about a month before his murder, Carl Eckstein, a San Francisco bookmaker who had turned to pornography, had approached Jimmy at Sal's, pleading with Jimmy to protect him and his partner, Ted Sharliss, who were being bled dry by Barboza.

"Jimmy, I've tried to get this guy killed," Eckstein told him, "but everybody around here's scared of him. Ted's been trying to contact people back East, you know, there's this contract out on this guy, but how the fuck do you go about it? So here, Jimmy, I've got his new name and address written down on this piece of paper."

"What's wrong with you?" Jimmy snapped. "Get away from me."

"But Jimmy, I thought you'd know who to contact."

"I don't want to know nothing about this guy. Get out of here."

The moment Eckstein had left, Jimmy picked up the piece of paper Eckstein had left on the table and walked to another booth, motioning for Sinio Danielle to follow him outside. Danielle was a close friend of Frank Scibelli, a *caporegime* with the Genovese family. Scibelli lived in Springfield, Massachusetts, and had close ties with the Patriarca family.

"Here, put this in your pocket," Jimmy said, handing him the note. "It's got Barboza's address and new name on it."

"No shit, thanks a lot, Jimmy. I'll call Frank right away."

That was all there had been to it. After clearing the hit with Jimmy Lanza, as required by the rules, a crew was dispatched to take care of Barboza and the problem was solved with two shotgun blasts.

The stewardess brought Marson another drink. He raised his glass and said, "Here's to us, and to lots of fucking money." By the time they reached New York, Marson had briefed Jimmy on the three major partners in the Premier Theater.

As president, Eliot Weisman had engineered the stock fraud and was fronting the operation for Greg DePalma and Ritchie Fusco, who were neighbors in Scarsdale, an exclusive residential district north of the city. Except for $75,000 in stocks bought by his mother-in-law, Ruth Rosenberg, Weisman had no personal investment in the theater.

DePalma's background was that of a fence, specializing in jewelry, and as a shylock. He had a hidden interest in Fudgies, a bar-restaurant-discoteque in Yonkers. Fusco was a bookmaker and with his brother ran a gambling operation at the Pompei Social Club in Brooklyn, a club formerly run by their father, a *caporegime* in the Colombo family. With DePalma in charge of the concessions and security, and Fusco in charge of the box office, the two men were in complete control of all skimming at the theater. Marson referred to the skim as "grocery money." His wife, Bobbi, was on the theater's payroll at $500 a week in a "no-show" job.

Jimmy and Marson checked in at the Ramada Inn in Tarrytown and DePalma came to pick them up. It soon became obvious that Marson had done an equally thorough job of briefing DePalma on Jimmy. DePalma's home looked expensive and Jimmy thought, "Well, they're not fucking starving." Ritchie Fusco, who lived nearby, came over to greet Jimmy. Except for Marson's several references to Jimmy as "my man," business was not discussed.

Jimmy enjoyed himself at the Sinatra testimonial at the Waldorf-Astoria. It was an elaborate affair; the masters of ceremony were Howard Cosell and Ed McMahon. Guests included Governor Hugh Carey, Mayor Abraham Beame, and former Vice President Spiro Agnew. Back at DePalma's house later that evening, Jimmy agreed to return for Sinatra's concert in April.

35
"A PIECE OF THE PORNO"

† † † †

AT APPROXIMATELY 11:50 A.M., MARCH 7, 1976, WHILE AT MURRIETA HOT
Springs, Special Agent John A. Larson and wife observed Frank Bompensiero in
the lobby of the hotel. At 12:25 P.M. Bompensiero was met by Jimmie Fratianno
and Louis Tom Dragna. All three entered the restaurant where they remained
until 1:45 P.M. During this meeting portions of the conversation were overheard.
. . . Dragna mentioned possible involvement or interest in a "legal" deal concerning an entertainer. The Cow Palace and Sports Arena, and also Las Vegas were
mentioned. The price per ticket of $15.00 with a concession to the city and "clear
of $7.50" was mentioned. This conversation was not heard by SA Larson. At one
point, after Bompensiero had left the table and entered the men's room, Dragna
asked Fratianno what he wanted. Fratianno responded, "Just give me a piece of
the porno."

—Excerpt from an FBI surveillance report.

Whenever Jimmy, Bomp, and Dragna met they always had numerous projects to discuss. In that one hour and twenty-minute luncheon observed by SA
Larson, they discussed far more things than the FBI agent realized.

Jimmy's first question to Dragna was, "What the fuck happened with Sturman? New York contact you?"

"No, haven't heard a word from anybody. What's happening with you?"

"I've had a couple meetings with those guys, Mickey Fine and Mike Colella,
who's going to sell Mickey some of his reels and magazines at a good price.
I've got Jack LoCicero and Tommy Ricciardi working together, shaking down
a few places. Looks like Ricciardi's going to hang around here awhile. We got
our little difference straightened out. He's not too bright, but he's better than
some of the fuckups we've got in the family."

Bompensiero grunted angrily. "I've been telling Louie we should retire a
half-dozen deadheads but he don't want to hurt their feelings."

"What the hell, Bomp," Dragna said. "What harm are they doing? Let's
leave them alone."

Jimmy knew what Bompensiero had in mind. He wanted to eliminate their vote. The plan was to call for an election when Brooklier was released from prison.

"When you can't cut it no more you should get out," Bompensiero insisted.

"I know, we've been all over that. Let it lay, will you. Jimmy, what about Mickey Fine going to San Francisco?"

"He's starting operating up there a little, you know, see how it's going to work out. I told LoCicero to grab that other porno guy Gaswirth, shake him for at least twenty grand. What I don't understand's how come we ain't heard from New York on this fucking Sturman."

"Listen, I'll let you know the minute I hear," Dragna said.

"Hey, you want to hear something funny?" Bompensiero asked. "I read in a magazine where the Mafia's getting seventy percent of the porno racket in California which they estimate earns a hundred million dollars a year."

Jimmy laughed. "I'll tell you, them people are something else."

Bompensiero excused himself and the moment he was out of earshot, Dragna said. "He looks pretty relaxed, don't you think? This's working out great. In fact, I've got him and Sal [Pinelli] going out together to collect some money. If Sal gets a chance he's going to clip him."

Jimmy looked at Dragna and nearly laughed in his face. Sal had about as much chance of clipping Bompensiero as a baby had of clipping a rattlesnake in its crib.

"Sounds like a great idea," Jimmy said. "Be good experience for Sal. You believe me, Bomp's going to be one surprised sonovabitch."

"That's the way I figure it. With this new position, he's really loose."

When Bompensiero returned to the table, Jimmy said, "I've got another idea. This Marson was telling me that Sinatra's concerts in April are sold out and they're really scalping them fucking tickets. When I was with the Seventh Step in Phoenix in 1969, I was going to get Frank to do a benefit but I got busted before I could do anything about it. Do you realize they're paying this guy eight hundred grand for about ten performances, one fucking week?

"My idea's to get him to do a benefit for some Catholic organization, hold it in the Cow Palace, pack them in there like sardines, charge fifteen bucks and give the city seven-fifty. Then there's the concessions, sell T-shirts, little souvenirs, there's big money in that shit."

"What's Sinatra getting out of this?" Louie asked.

"Nothing," Jimmy said. "The guy's already got two hundred million, what does he need another two hundred grand for?"

"Sounds like a great idea," Dragna said. "How well do you know Frank?"

"I knew him years ago, but it's been a long time since I've seen him. I'll probably see him when I go to the concerts next month. If the opportunity comes up, I'll ask him, but I don't want to push it. I want it to happen kind of natural, know what I mean?"

They drank and ate and talked on like businessmen having a pleasant lunch. Few besides SA Larson would suspect they were anything but successful businessmen.

As they were walking out to the parking lot, Dragna turned to Jimmy. "How's Johnny Roselli? It's been a long time since we've talked. You know, we were close one time, he was like an uncle to me, and we used to play golf. Shit, he taught me the game. His testimony before that Senate committee really surprised the shit out of me. Jimmy, next time you see him, tell him I'd like to bury the hatchet. Let's get together for lunch. Tell him, will you?"

"Be glad to, Louie," Jimmy said. They shook hands and went their separate way, the two acting bosses living in separate worlds.

36
SIDNEY KORSHAK

† † † †

THROUGHOUT THIS PERIOD JIMMY WAS STILL TRYING TO STRAIGHTEN out Rudy Tham. As promised by Jackie Presser, Tham had met at La Costa with Fitzsimmons, Presser, and Andy Anderson. Although it appeared that the problem had been solved, Anderson continued to ignore Tham.

Jimmy had paid Jackie Presser another visit in Cleveland.

"This guy's still playing it the hard way," Jimmy said. "Tham's bitching to me every day and I'm getting damn tired of it. You can't blame Rudy. He's been toeing the line. Remember when you called me a while back, when they gave Hoffa this testimonial at the Fairmont and you didn't want Rudy to attend? Well, the guy went to Mexico so nobody'd see him in town. Rudy's a hundred percent behind Fitzsimmons."

Presser waved his short arms. "What can I tell you? This Anderson's a cocksucker. Fitz don't lay the law down to this guy."

"Why not?"

"The way I hear it, they cut up some money a few years back, got a kickback or payoff somewhere, so Andy's got something on Fitz. But the funny thing's they're now kind of on the outs because Fitz heard Andy got a payoff from the farmers in the Delano area. They wanted Chavez out of there. Andy and Jack Goldberger got Sid Korshak to work it out. So there's a little friction between Andy and Fitz, but still, you know, he ain't going to put the clamp on this guy."

"Okay, I'll put the clamp on him. You better believe it."

"Wait, Jimmy, before you do anything, go see Sid Korshak. Andy's his man. You believe me, Jimmy, this Korshak can take care of the whole thing with one phone call. You know Korshak?"

"I know who he is, but we've never met. But he's heard of me."

"This's the smoothest sonovabitch in the business. There's nothing he can't fix. He's the highest-paid lawyer in the country and he don't even have an office. This guy don't even own a briefcase. Keeps everything in his head. A million's a lousy year for him. Forget Meyer Lansky, the cops are after him, but this Sid's remained legitimate. His clients include companies like Schenley, Diners' Club, the Dodgers, the Chargers, the Knicks, the Rangers, hotel chains like Hilton and Hyatt, Seeburg, National General, racetracks all over the place, probably a hundred top corporations. He's a pal of Lew Wasserman at MCA, Kirk Kerkorian at MGM, Charlie Bluhdorn at Gulf & Western which owns Paramount Pictures. In fact, when that producer Bob Evans wanted Al Pacino for his movie *The Godfather,* it was Sid that got him released from his exclusive contract at MGM. There's nothing he can't do in business, politics, unions. He's one incredible operator."

One of the few visible assets of Sidney Roy Korshak was the Bistro in Beverly Hills. Seated at a corner table, flanked by two telephones, he welcomed his friends for private chats that were constantly interrupted by beautiful women who came to give him a kiss and cheerful greeting. The telephones kept ringing but when he had important calls to make he preferred a telephone booth, usually arriving with a paper bag full of coins.

The maitre d' looked up from his reservation book and smiled at Jimmy who was scanning the room.

"Yes, sir, do you have a reservation?"

"Tell Sid Jimmy's here."

"Oh, yes sir, he's expecting you. This way, please."

"No, no, tell him to come out here."

The maitre d' hurried away and Jimmy watched him as he approached Korshak's table and leaned forward to whisper his message. Korshak stood up, excused himself from his two guests, and strode toward Jimmy, a tall, ruggedly handsome man in his mid-sixties, impeccably tailored and groomed.

They shook hands and Korshak said, "Would you like a drink or a bite of lunch?"

"Nothing," Jimmy said. "Let's step outside."

They went out and sat on a small bench. Jimmy took out a cigar and slowly unwrapped it before looking at Korshak.

"I assume you know who I am?" he said, lighting the cigar and taking a few puffs.

"Yes, when Rudy Tham called for the appointment, he told me you were his friend."

"Well, Sid, I'm a little more than his friend. Rudy's my man. I got him straightened out with the International and I've put a lot of fucking time and money into this and that Andy Anderson's got a hard-on for Rudy and don't treat him right."

"Is this the nature of your problem?"

"Wait, Sid, let me draw a picture for you, lay it all out so there's no misunderstanding. Have I ever asked you for anything before?"

Korshak was getting a worried look on his usually expressionless face. "Not that I can recall."

"Let me tell you something, Sid. This's our fucking country. You understand that? Chicago's got nothing to do with our country. You know, Sid, we've never come to you before, but now there's a new program and you've got to do what we want. There's been lots of changes around here. Some of our guys are doing time and we've got to make some money so that we can take care of them. Now, while they're in jail, I'm more or less handling things around here, calling the shots."

"Jimmy, what can I do to help you?"

"You tell Andy to take care of Rudy, give him what is rightly his. This Andy's got the twelve western states, for Christ's sake. If he wants to fuck around, let him do it with some other guys. Rudy's the boss in San Francisco and Andy's taking his power and giving it to somebody else. I want you to talk to Andy and straighten this out."

"Jimmy, Andy is his own man. I'll be glad to mention this to him, but I can't tell him what to do."

"Sid, don't give me no con. I don't want no fucking story. I've talked to you like a gentleman. I want you to do it, no maybes about it, understand? It's got to be done. If we don't get it done one way, we'll get it done another."

"Jimmy, I'll do the best I can, believe me. But, please, don't call me on the telephone."

"I'll have Rudy call you, that's legal, you're a union consultant. But, look, Sid, I don't want to have to come back down here to see you. I expect you to do the right thing."

Jimmy stood up and Korshak leaped to his feet. "Don't worry. I'll talk to Andy and get it straightened out."

When nothing happened in the next two weeks, Jimmy called Obie Frabotta and flew to Chicago to see Aiuppa.

Jimmy complained about his problem with Andy Anderson and his meeting with Korshak.

"Yeah, I heard you talked to him," Aiuppa said, smiling. "Look, Jimmy, do me a favor. If you ever need anything from Sid, come to us. Let us do it. You know, the less you see of him the better. We don't want to put heat on the guy."

"I understand, Joey, but I talked to him like a gentleman. The man gave me his word and did nothing about it. You know he's in our fucking country."

Aiuppa continued smiling. "Let me explain something, Jimmy. Sid's a traveling man. He's in everybody's country, but he's our man, been our man his whole life. So, you know, it makes no difference where he hangs his hat. Get my meaning?"

Jimmy nodded. "But what am I supposed to do when the guy won't move when we need a favor? See, nobody in California's ever done nothing about this guy. He moves around there like he's got a fucking permit."

Aiuppa laughed. "Jimmy, you're not listening, he's got a permit. We gave him one, understand?"

The lines around Jimmy's mouth had hardened. "So what're we supposed to do in California when this Andy jacks us off and Sid won't move to help? Sit on our fucking thumbs?"

"Look, I've told you, come to us, let us take care of it. Don't put any heat on Sid. We've spent a lot of time keeping this guy clean. He can't be seen in public with guys like us. We have our own ways of contacting him and it's worked pretty good for a long time."

The lines around Jimmy's mouth softened. "Sorry, Joey, if I came on a little strong, but I need this favor. I'll leave Sid alone, but if he don't do the right thing, we're going to hurt this Andy."

"That's your business," Aiuppa said, "but for the time being, let us talk to Sid. Now, how about ordering some lunch and relaxing?"

Jimmy's patience was wearing thin. Nothing had happened. The next time he went to see Sid Korshak, he brought Mike Rizzi along to the Bistro. Again they sat on the little bench outside the restaurant.

"Sid, Mike's my man here," Jimmy said. "If you need anything, any favor, get ahold of him." Jimmy gave him Rizzi's phone number and settled down for the serious work at hand. "Andy still ain't done a thing. What's the deal anyway?"

Korshak nodded sadly. "I talked to him but frankly something's happened between us. He's just not listening to me."

"Did Chicago talk to you or what?"

"No."

Jimmy looked hard at him. "Hey, Sid, they were supposed to talk to you. You mean to tell me Gussie Alex didn't relay a message from the old man?"

"Nothing," Korshak said.

"Sid, this has got to be done."

"I understand but what can I do if the man won't listen to me? He don't even return my calls. We're kind of on the outs."

"Then the guy's going to get hurt," Jimmy warned. "I told you last time, Sid, I don't want no stories. As far as I'm concerned, that's bullshit. You know this fucking Andy better than I know my own brother."

"Jimmy, I don't want to argue with you. I'll talk to him again. What else can I do?"

"Look, we don't want to take this into our own hands. We're not asking for the moon. All we want's for him to give Rudy what he's entitled to. And by Christ Rudy's going to get it, one way or the other."

He was registered at Caesars Palace, and his old friend from Youngstown, Ohio, Mike Vallardo, boss of the blackjack table, had comped him, as usual. About 2 o'clock in the morning, while Jimmy and Vallardo were in the casino talking, Jimmy noticed two beautiful young women walking toward them. One had a little gold key on a chain around her neck and, as she walked by, Jimmy stepped in front of her.

"Pardon me, Miss, but that key fascinates me. Is that the key to your heart?"

She looked kind of startled. "Yes, it is."

"Gee, I'd like to be part of it."

She laughed nervously. "Well, that's nice, but . . ."

"Please, just a moment. I'm Jimmy and this's Mike. Can we buy you girls a drink and discuss this fascinating key?"

She looked at her girl friend for a signal. "I don't know, I guess so. I'm Candi and she's Ronda."

They went into the cocktail lounge and Jimmy said, "There's no way you're going to get away from me." He reached to touch the gold key. "I'm going to take this gold key and unlock your heart and keep it all to myself. I'm going to be part of this key from now on."

An hour later, Candi was in his bed. The next morning, when the telephone awakened him, she was gone, but had left a cheerful note with her phone number.

He picked up the receiver and it was Tony Spilotro. "Jimmy, did I wake you up?"

"Yeah. What time is it?"

"Eleven. Man, you lead some life."

"What's doing, Tony?"

"I have to talk to you. Can I come up?"

Jimmy took a quick shower, leaving the door ajar. When he came out of the bathroom, Spilotro was sitting in a chair, his legs crossed, his foot swinging impatiently, looking cocky as ever.

"What's up?"

Spilotro grinned. "The old man wants to see you and Mike Rizzi."

Jimmy groaned. "Oh, shit, what's wrong now?"

"Don't ask me. Jackie called and said it's very important."

"Okay, I'll get Mike and we'll shoot up there. I'll call Dorfman's office, let them know when I'll be in."

Spilotro stood up. "Great. Well, buddy, have a good trip."

When Jimmy and Mike Rizzi arrived at the restaurant with Joey Lombardo, Jackie Cerone was already there. A stickler for protocol now that he was acting boss, Jimmy took Cerone aside and introduced Rizzi as "a friend of *mine.*"

"Jackie, you know, Mike's not a made guy." Jimmy said. "Be sure to tell the old man."

"Yeah, okay. Listen, Joe Batters [Tony Accardo] is also coming over."

Aiuppa was the first to arrive and Jimmy introduced him to Rizzi as "a friend of mine," and they went back and sat at their table. A few minutes later Joe Batters came in and Aiuppa introduced Rizzi to Batters as *amico nostra.*

"Wait a minute, hold the phone," Jimmy said. Turning to Mike, he said, "Go to the bar."

Aiuppa looked at Jimmy as though he had lost his mind. "What the fuck's going on?"

"Joey, Mike's not a made guy. He's proposed but we ain't gotten around to making him yet. I told Spilotro and Jackie to tell you this."

"Wait a minute," Cerone said. "Why tell Spilotro? He's nothing but a fucking soldier. You've got no right telling that guy nothing."

Aiuppa raised his hand. "That's okay. No harm done, the guy's going to get made. Call him back here."

Jimmy smiled and stood up. He had made his point. He signalled Rizzi to return to the table.

After he had sat down, Aiuppa said, "I understand you went to see Sid by yourself?"

Rizzi shrugged. "I just happened to run into him."

"How's that possible? Didn't you go to his restaurant?"

"Well, I was in Beverly Hills, driving by, and I thought I'd stop and say hello to him. Listen, I didn't grab him, I talked to him like a gentleman."

Aiuppa turned to Jimmy. "I hear you and Mike also went to see Sid a while back. I told you last time, we don't allow nobody in the family to talk to this guy. We don't want no fucking heat on him."

"Joey, he's in our country and won't raise a finger to help us. He bullshits me about being on the outs with Andy. You said you'd talk to him, but he says nobody from Chicago talked to him."

"Let's calm down," Joe Batters said. "Jimmy, Sid's been with Gussie over thirty years and Gussie's with us. Sid's a good provider for our family and we don't want nobody to fuck with him."

"But, Joe, all we did is talk to the man. We need a fucking favor."

"I appreciate your problem, but we don't want him to be seen with nobody. I can't make it no plainer than that. He's off limits. That's it, Jimmy."

Before Jimmy could respond, Aiuppa said, "What about the dead fish? Who put the dead fish in his mailbox?"

Jimmy looked like he couldn't believe his ears. "That's ridiculous! We don't pull dumb shit like that in our family. Look, I went to talk to the man, that's it. That's bullshit. If he said that, he's lying, or he's got some enemy I don't know nothing about."

Joe Batters said. "Jimmy, look into it, see if you can find out who did it. We don't want nobody muscling this guy."

"Joe, believe me, we respect the guy on that account, that he's with you people. But by the same token we need a little help with this Andy and I'm just trying to find out why he won't help us. If he can't help, we're going to grab Andy."

Batters smiled. "I know how you feel, Jimmy. Do what you've got to do but keep it under control. If Sid's having problems with him, your grabbing Andy might make it worse. Let us talk to Gussie and see what can be worked out."

† † †

Later on the plane, Jimmy was still steaming. "Turning this thing around ain't going to be no picnic," he told Rizzi. "Everybody's in California. They ain't got no right being in our country but they're in so solid, first thing you know California's going to be an open state. We're going to have to do something but I'll be fucked if I know what right now."

The Teamsters building in Burlingame looked like a prison. "Look at this place," Jimmy told Mike Rizzi, "fucking steel bars, electric doors, probably bullet-proof glass. Now watch this."

Jimmy looked at the girl behind the glass partition and smiled. "Honey, we're with Jim Muniz's Local Seventy, having a little meeting here today. Push the button, we're already late."

He flashed the membership card Muniz had given him and the door buzzed. Jimmy winked at Rizzi as they quickly went in. A secretary walked by and Jimmy said, "Miss, we're here to see Andy Anderson."

"Do you have an appointment?"

"Yes, we do."

"May I have your names?"

"Just friends."

She excused herself and they followed her down the hallway to Anderson's office. The door was open and Jimmy said, "Thank you, Miss. Andy, I'm Jimmy Fratianno and this's Mike Rizzi."

Anderson stood up and from the expression on his face Jimmy could tell that their sudden apparition had frightened him. "I beg your pardon?"

"We've never met, Andy, is that right? But you've heard of me?"

"Yes, I have. Will you sit down?"

They sat in chairs flanking his desk. "We're here to ask a favor of you. You know Rudy Tham?"

"Of course."

"Well, you know he's my man, like you're Sid's man. You follow me?"

"No, I don't."

"Oh, yes, you do, Andy. Now, for some fucking reason I can't understand, you're avoiding him. I thought that meeting at La Costa I had Jackie Presser set up had done the trick, but I see you've gone back on your word. You've got a cross-hair and I want to know what it is, understand. No bullshit, let's put it out in the open."

"Well, Jimmy, Tham talks about me every chance he gets, goes around bad-mouthing me all the time. How can I work with a guy like that?"

"That's a fucking lie," Jimmy said, raising his voice. He looked at Mike and indicated with a gesture that he wanted the door closed. Anderson's eyes shifted nervously to Rizzi as he jumped up and closed the door.

"Want me to lock it, Jimmy?"

Jimmy leaned forward in his chair, looking hard at Anderson, as though he were considering the suggestion. "Naw, it's okay. Andy, I want you to be straight with me, no bullshit now. I want you to give Rudy what he's legally entitled to. You know, it gives him a little recognition when he handles these little problems that belong to him."

"I'm not lying to you, Jimmy. That's what I've been told by a lot of people."

"Look, forget about it, it's not happening. Sure, Rudy might complain now and then that you're bypassing him, which is a common thing for a guy to do when he knows somebody's fucking him. I want you to get together with him and let him assume his rightful responsibilities. Andy, you've got twelve states to handle. Rudy's only got San Francisco. All problems in this town are supposed to go to him. Andy, I'm talking to you like a gentleman, right? Rudy's got the blessings of the International, all he needs is your blessing and that's it."

Anderson cleared his throat. "All right, Jimmy, tell Rudy to call me and we'll straighten it out."

Jimmy stood up. "Andy, you do it. We don't want to come back here a second time. I've been fucking around with this as long as I'm going to. It's been a fucking pain in the ass, so you do the right thing and we're square. You go your way and I'll go mine."

Anderson stood up and they shook hands. Jimmy started for the door and stopped. "By the way, what's the problem between you and Sid?"

Anderson looked puzzled. "There's no problem. Why?"

"Nothing, Andy, nothing at all." Jimmy smiled. Somehow he knew the message had finally gotten through to Anderson. Chicago had listened to him.

37
MAKING MIKE

† † † †

JIMMY STAYED AT THE RYE TOWN HILTON INN FOR ELEVEN DAYS. MUCH of his time was spent at the Premier Theater but he was not interested in seeing a single show. He spent his time in the theater's bars and restaurants meeting made guys who came from the five New York City families and from other parts of the country.

He became fast friends with "Louie Beans" Fucceri, a soldier in "Tony Ducks" Corallo's family—his brother, Vinnie Beans, was a *caporegime* in the same family. Louie Beans introduced Jimmy as *amico nostra* to countless made guys, who in turn introduced him to others, including "sleepers" like Andrew Russo, a *caporegime* in the Colombo family, who was involved in movie productions with a famous Hollywood producer. There was "Jimmy Nap" Napoli who had taken care of the skim at Caesars Palace for the Genovese family but was not yet a made guy. His immediate superior had been "Fat Tony" Salerno, a Genovese *caporegime*, who later became *consigliere*. Fat Tony's man in Caesars counting room was Jerome Zarowitz.

Caesars, which opened in 1966, was built by a group headed by Nathan Jacobson, described in a *Wall Street Journal* story on May 23, 1969, as "a Baltimore insurance executive widely respected as one of the 'new breed' of honest, orthodox businessmen who are brightening the Las Vegas image." In the next paragraph of the same *Journal* article, the author, Steven M. Lovelady, noted that ". . . the manager of the Caesars Palace casino is Jerome Zarowitz, whose background includes a conviction in the 1950's on a federal charge of fixing football games for gambling purposes." The new breed, even on the surface, was a strange combination. Jimmy Nap told Jimmy tens of millions of dollars had been skimmed in less than a decade.

Jimmy had dinner with Anthony "Abbie Shots" Abbattemarco and Alphonse "Alley Boy" Persico, underboss and *consigliere* respectively of the Colombo family. (Shot in the head in 1971 by one of Crazy Joe Gallo's former prison inmates at an Italian unity day rally, Joseph Colombo remained in a semicomatose condition, the leadership of the family passing to Thomas

DiBello. Ten months later Crazy Joe's rebellion had come to an end in a fusillade of bullets at Umberto's Clam House.)

What Alley Boy and Abbie Shots wanted to know was whether Mike Rizzi had been made in California.

"Not yet," Jimmy said, "but I've proposed him."

"You better make him," Abbie Shots said, "or we'll bring him back out here and make him in our family. He's a fucking good man."

Although Rudy Tham had introduced Jimmy to "Benny Eggs" Mangano in San Francisco, it was at the theater that Alphonse "Funzied" D'Ambrosio introduced them as *amici nostra*. Mangano told Jimmy he had a clothing store at 137 Varick Street, Resource Sales Corporation, and invited Jimmy to come over the next day and he would introduce him to Frank "Funzi" Tieri, the boss of the Genovese family.

"Listen," Jimmy said, "how can I get in touch with Fat Tony [Salerno]?"

"Come over around two tomorrow and he'll be there."

The next day, Fat Tony was there as promised. With the formal introduction out of the way, Jimmy told him he was carrying a message of good will from Tony Dope Delsanter, who expressed his regrets at having missed Fat Tony on his last visit to New York and was looking forward to seeing him in Florida next winter. Jimmy and Fat Tony talked for a while and then Mangano took him to a dumpy little cafe, a greasy spoon about a five-minute walk from his store. There was a small counter with stools and a few tiny tables.

Except for an old Italian behind the counter, Funzi Tieri was the only one in the place. He sat at one of the tables with his hat and topcoat on. He was the boss of the second largest family in the country, the first being the Gambino family, and he looked like a retired old man wearing his Sunday best.

Mangano made the introduction and excused himself, telling Jimmy he would see him back at the store. The counterman brought them coffee and disappeared into the kitchen.

"The boss and underboss are in jail and me and Louie Dragna are running things until they come out," Jimmy said.

Tieri nodded approvingly and when he spoke, it was with a strained hoarseness. "That's the way it should be, guys helping each other out. We have some bosses in prison here, too. It happens and when it does it's good to have someone step in that can carry on."

"But I live in San Francisco, which means a lot of running back and forth," Jimmy said. "But they're not going to be in the joint that long, not worth moving down there, besides I have business interests up there."

"Well, it's good that you do what you can. The family comes first. You got good people to help you?"

Jimmy shrugged. "Well, not too many, really. We've got a lot of old people who are kind of retired, never see them."

"Some people don't take care of themselves," Tieri said, who looked in excellent physical condition for a man of seventy-two who had overcome throat cancer. "You look in good shape. How old are you?"

Jimmy smiled. "Sixty-two and feel like twenty-two."

"I can see you're a man who don't abuse himself. By the way, who's this guy 'the Weasel' out there in California?"

The question took Jimmy totally by surprise. "What, why, well, that's me."

"That's you, the Weasel?" Tieri said, the answer taking him by almost as much surprise. "Well, what're you doing with Joe Bonanno?"

"What do you mean, what I am doing with Joe Bonanno? I don't even know the guy."

"Well, we got a report you went to see him in Tucson two weeks ago."

Jimmy struggled to control his temper and language. "You've got a wrong report because it wasn't me. I never even met the guy, never saw him in my whole life, wouldn't know him if he walked in this room right now."

"Well, somebody in your family's been seeing him."

"That's right and I think it's the same guy that made this wrong report. It's Frank Bompensiero. He's been tight with Bonanno for years."

"That's against the rules," Tieri said. "Nobody's supposed to talk to this guy. He's out. This's a commission ruling."

"I know that, Funzi, and I've told this guy not to fuck with this Bonanno."

"Well, now that you're acting boss you better clean up your family. This Bonanno's a leper. Anybody that touches him gets poisoned, *capito?*"

Jean, who had come to New York with Jimmy, was staying with her brother and his wife, and Jimmy got them tickets for Sinatra's closing performance at the Premier Theater. After the show, there was a private party in the East Dining Room. A special chef was brought in to prepare all of Sinatra's favorite dishes.

Seated at the head table with Sinatra and his fiancee, Barbara Marx, were Billy Martin and Frank Howard of the New York Yankees; actor Telly Savalas; Sinatra's constant companion, Jilly Rizzo; his attorney, Milton "Mickey" Rudin; and the man responsible for Sinatra's being there in the first place, "Louie Dome" Pacella.

Halfway through the dinner, Jean nudged him. "Have you noticed how Frank keeps staring at you?"

"Yeah, I caught it," Jimmy laughed. "From the look on his face, he knows he's seen me somewhere but he ain't figured it out yet."

Louie Dome, who had been introduced to Jimmy at the theater, noticed Sinatra's perplexed glances and later brought him over to Jimmy's table.

"Frank, this is Jimmy Fratianno."

Jimmy stood up, introduced Jean, then said, "I look familiar to you, you think you remember me from someplace?"

Sinatra smiled, "Yeah, but I can't place you, damnit. That bugs me. I know it was a long time ago."

"Like almost thirty years," Jimmy said. "Remember the testimonial for Jimmy Tarantino? We were both at Mickey Cohen's table."

That had been back in 1947. Tarantino had edited a scandalmongering sheet called *Hollywood Nightlife* that had the entire film colony intimidated. Financed by Sinatra, Tarantino, a former cab driver from Orange, New Jersey, was practically illiterate, but had managed to skate on the thin ice of extortion quite a long time before ending up in prison.

There was a flash of recognition in Sinatra's eyes. "Yeah, yeah, I remember. That sure as hell was a long time ago."

"Then remember that time in Vegas when you drove my Cadillac, Eddie or Benny Macri was with you, and you nearly hit Sheriff Glen Jones."

"Oh, God, I think we nearly got busted, right?"

"You mean me, not you. I had just gotten straightened out with that thief. I left you at that joint where your cousin Ray's band was playing and went back to the D.I. to talk to Jones."

Sinatra was nodding, "Yes, yes, I remember. Well, how've you been? Living in New York now?"

"Hell, no. I just came for the concert. Been here all week."

Sinatra laughed. "Well, you're some kind of fan."

"No, well, yeah . . . See, I'm here with Tommy Marson, he's one of the owners of the theater. Lives right next to you in Rancho Mirage. In fact, he's sitting right there." Jimmy turned and signaled for Marson to join them. After the introduction and a few words, Sinatra said, "Well, Jimmy, it was good seeing you again. Coming back in September?"

"Yes, I am."

"Come by the dressing room and say hello. Let's not wait another thirty years."

Jimmy, Rizzi, Dragna, and Bompensiero met again in the hotel's restaurant at Murrieta Hot Springs on the evening of June 6, 1976.

They ordered coffee and Jimmy said, "Well, how're we going to do this?"

"Why don't we have Bomp say the words," Dragna said. "He can do it in Sicilian."

"You mean I can do it in half-ass Sicilian like your uncle Jack and almost as fast," Bompensiero said, winking at Rizzi.

"Bomp's kidding," Jimmy said, "but this's a serious matter, a big step in your life. Remember, Louie, how we waited in that room until Johnny came to get us. Sonovabitch, you believe me, that was some moment.

"I'm sorry, Mike, you're going to get a quickie deal," Jimmy said. "It's kind of like a kid going to college four years and getting his diploma in the mail instead of going to graduation. Since you're not going to understand a word Bomp says, he talks Sicilian like I talk Chinese, I'm going to tell you a few things you've got to know, this way it's going to mean more to you than this guy rattling off a lot of strange words.

"The way Jack Dragna said it to me, you're joining this thing of ours, you know, an honored society, and you've got to be brave and loyal. You come in alive and you go out dead. That's what the gun and knife are all about. Them're the tools by which you live and die. This thing of ours, Cosa Nostra, comes before anything else, your wife and kids, your country, even God. When you're called, you've got to come even if your mother's dying."

Jimmy paused to light a cigar. "Now, what I'm telling you's secret, so you can't tell nobody that's not a member any of this shit, or any other secret, like becoming a snitch. You can't violate the wife or family of another member and you can't deal in dope. If you do any of them things, the penalty's death. Bomp, you've got anything to add? You, Louie?"

"Only that from now on," Louie said, "when you want to introduce one made guy to another made guy, you say *amico nostra,* or this is a friend of *ours.* If he's not made, then you say, friend of *mine.*"

"Okay, so where're we going to do it?" Bomp asked.

Jimmy shrugged. "Let's do it in the car, find some deserted spot and park. We don't have a gun and knife, but I brought a pin."

Dragna drove and Rizzi sat in front with him, with Jimmy and Bompensiero in the back. A few miles out of Murrieta, Dragna swung onto a dirt road and stopped when they were out of sight of the highway. They held hands while Bompensiero quickly rattled out the strange-sounding liturgy, the cigar clamped tightly in a corner of his mouth. With Jimmy also puffing on his cigar, and with the windows closed, the car was quickly filling with smoke.

Bompensiero said, "That's it, now for the blood."

"Mike, give me your right hand, the trigger finger."

Jimmy punctured the skin and squeezed until he saw blood. "Mike, this drop of blood's a symbol of your birth into our family. We're all as one until death." He paused and smiled. "That's it, Mike, now we kiss and the four of us hold hands. You're now one of us. Congratulations, *amico nostra.*"

They kissed and held hands and Dragna opened a window. "Let's get moving," he said. "I need some fucking fresh air."

38
"DEEP SIX FOR JOHNNY"

† † † †

A FEW DAYS AFTER MIKE RIZZI'S INITIATION, JIMMY, KEEPING HIS promise to Louie Dragna, got him and Johnny Roselli together for lunch. They talked at each other for an hour, polite but cool, neither saying anything that would soothe old wounds. At one point Roselli inquired about Dago Louie and Dragna told him he was almost totally blind, an old man living out his remaining years in seclusion. They talked about golf but there were no reminiscences of the days when they had played together. Johnny said that he was living a quiet life, playing golf a few times a week, watching television at night, and reading by the pool in the daytime. His swinging days were behind him. Jimmy calculated that Roselli was probably seventy-one but still looked trim and physically fit.

One day, Jimmy and Roselli went driving in the Santa Monica mountains, which overlooked the sprawling city on one side and the equally sprawling San Fernando valley on the other. It was a beautiful day, with only a thin shroud of smog hanging low over the land. Up in the mountains the air was fresh, the warm June sun cooled by a gentle breeze.

Although not much had been written in the newspapers about the CIA–Mafia plot in recent months, the subject was very much on Jimmy's mind.

"What's happening with Washington?" he said. "Are they still after you?"

Roselli chuckled. "They had me up at the Carroll Arms Hotel, Bobby Baker's old stomping ground, for a secret session and I really fixed their fucking wagon. All hot, you know, about who killed Kennedy. Sometimes I'd like to tell them the mob did it, just to see the expression on their stupid faces. You know, we're supposed to be idiots, right? We hire a psycho like Oswald to kill the President and then we get a blabbermouth, two-bit punk like Ruby to shut him up. We wouldn't trust those jerks to hit a fucking dog.

"Anyway, they start questioning me about this bullshit I'd told Morgan years ago. You know, Castro retaliating against Kennedy because of our attempts on his life. I said, 'I have no recollection of receiving or passing on such information.'

327

"Well, Jimmy," he said, laughing, "it's not my fault if Morgan has a vivid imagination. I've also been dropping by Jack Anderson's office and we're getting pretty chummy, having lunch and dinner together. Nice guy, but he's always trying to pump me, but he's cool about it."

"Johnny, it's not what you don't tell them guys that worries me," Jimmy said. "You've got to touch bases, go to Chicago and tell them what you're doing, let them know it's just fun and games."

"What the fuck," Johnny said. "I'm not saying anything. Why go there and get a lot of bullshit shoveled at me? Either way, I'm on their shit list. And that's something I've got to talk to you about. Somebody's got to shut Bomp's big yap. He's really trying to bury me. He's filling Spilotro's head full of bullshit, says I gave secret testimony to the grand jury in the Frontier case that turned Friedman into a witness against Tony Zerilli, Mike Polizzi, and Tony Giordano, which is plain, unadulterated bullshit. What's this fucking guy's problem?"

Jimmy decided it was time to tell Roselli. "Johnny, it goes back to when you got the gift shop at the Frontier. See, Bomp did some work for Detroit and he was expecting to get a piece of the Frontier. He thinks you fucked him out of it."

"Oh, Jimmy, what a treacherous world we live in. All I did is help Joe Breen get the gift shop and he was grateful enough to cut me in for a piece of it. So I net fifty, sixty grand a year out of it, big fucking deal."

Jimmy was still worried about the assassination committee. "The problem, Johnny, is that Chicago don't know what you're saying to the committee. Maybe Aiuppa and Batters figure if you talk to them, then you'd talk to grand juries. Don't forget, they've already started clipping guys close to Sam."

Roselli pondered this a moment, gazing out at the scenery as they drove. The wind was ruffling his hair, which seemed as light and silky as a baby's. That was what old age did to people, Jimmy thought, it turned them into babies again.

"Jimmy, let me think out loud for a minute. I'd like your reaction to this idea. You remember Joe Shimon, don't you? He was with us on the Castro plot, former Washington police inspector.

"We've talked about Sam's murder, the three of us were close, and he thinks Santo [Trafficante] made a deal with Castro. Remember when Santo was jailed and they grabbed his money when Castro came into power, then suddenly he was released with all his money? Shimon thinks he's a Castro agent spying on Cubans in Florida. Sam shared that suspicion. That's why Santo sat on his ass and did nothing with all that shit we gave him. He was probably reporting everything to Castro's agents, and Miami's full of them.

"I still see Santo, we have dinner or lunch every now and then. He thought his name would never surface in the hearings, which is stupid. But if he was playing both ends against the middle, he had plenty to worry about. Those Cubans, either side, would cut his balls off if they thought he double-crossed them. They don't give a shit about the Mafia down there. I remember Sam telling me when he got his subpoena. He said, 'Santo's shitting his pants, but you can't keep his name out of it. I introduced the guy to the CIA, for Christ's sake. Everybody knows it. Maheu, Shimon, you, the whole FBI and CIA. This Santo's crazy to think we can stop his name from surfacing.' "

"Don't let this cocksucker set you up," Jimmy said. "Watch yourself."

"Jimmy, right now my problem is Bomp. This guy's got telephonitis. Like with Santo, I've got no proof, but I've got a feeling about this prick. I think he's a snitch. Him and Dago Louie are in the same fucking boat."

"Johnny, don't worry about Bomp," Jimmy said, pausing for emphasis. "It's in the works. Brooklier put the contract out. We're just waiting for the proper spot."

"Well, that's the best fucking news I've had all year."

"It might take a little while, this guy's cagey," Jimmy said. "He goes home every afternoon, around three or four o'clock, and he never leaves the house at night. But I'll tell you something, him and Spilotro clipped that broad, Tamara Rand, that was giving Glick all that heat."

"I had a pretty good idea that little ant was involved, but I didn't know about Bomp."

"Oh, he denies it, but not too hard, you know what I mean. Says all he did was show Tony where she lived. One thing about Bomp, he's capable of it."

Roselli was registered at the Beverly Hilton, and one night he dined at the hotel's Trader Vic's restaurant with Jimmy, Allen Smiley, and Mike Rizzi, who had been anxious to meet Roselli after all the praise Jimmy had heaped upon him. Smiley and Roselli were old friends, but Roselli never discussed family business in front of Smiley. Their conversation was always pleasantly challenging—current news, movies, books, sports, women—and Jimmy always enjoyed their friendly bantering.

On this evening, however, he was too busy wrestling with his conscience to pay much attention to the conversation. Months ago he'd heard from Peanuts Tranalone that there was a contract out on Roselli. Tranalone was close to Trafficante and knew all the made guys in his Tampa family. This was probably the straight dope, but how could he tell Roselli without getting Tranalone in trouble? He just couldn't say it was a rumor because Roselli would insist on knowing the source, which was only natural, for how else could he judge its accuracy? So Jimmy had said nothing and had been agonizing over it ever since.

Later that evening, when he was alone with Roselli in the lobby, Jimmy tried to warn him.

"Johnny, what we talked about the other day, about Bomp poisoning Chicago and your testifying before that committee—be careful, will you? You're right, this thing of ours's treacherous. You never know when you're going to make the hit list. Remember what I told you. Don't let Trafficante or Cerone set you up. Be fucking careful."

"Jimmy, Jimmy, not again," Roselli said. "Will you stop worrying? I'm all right. Everything's under control."

"Johnny, you've got some money. Why don't you go to Europe for a while?"

Roselli gave him a searching look. "What's this all about? Have you heard something?"

Jimmy shook his head. "No, but I'm just worried about it. I hate that Aiuppa. He's a snake. And so's Batters."

Roselli smiled. "You know something, Jimmy? I've never realized it before, but you're a worrier. Is this something you're acquiring in old age, or was it always there and I never noticed it before?"

Jimmy forced a laugh. "Okay, you win. I give up. You can handle yourself without my stupid advice."

They stopped before an elevator and Jimmy was so moved by the turmoil in his mind that he grabbed Roselli and emotionally kissed him on both cheeks. Pulling away, he said, "Why don't you come to New York for Frank's concert in September? We'd have a ball."

"Thanks, but I'll take a rain check. If there's one thing I can do without right now is meet a lot of made guys."

The elevator doors opened and Roselli stepped in, turning to smile at Jimmy before the doors closed. "Don't forget about Bomp. It's the first good idea Brooklier ever had. It'd be a shame to waste it."

The doors closed and Jimmy slowly walked away. There was a cold, hard knot in his chest that seemed to impair his breathing. He stopped, looked back at the elevator, at a bank of house telephones, then turned away and quickly left the hotel.

On July 16 Roselli dined with Santo Trafficante at the Landings Restaurant in Fort Lauderdale. Early one afternoon, twelve days later, he left his sister's home to run an errand and never returned. His car was later found at Miami International Airport, parked where he usually left it when he went on trips, a newspaper partially opened on the front seat, leaving the impression that he had rushed at the last moment to catch his flight.

Jimmy knew these details long before they became public knowledge. What he had feared had happened and he was convinced Roselli's body would never be found. Yet on August 7 fishermen became suspicious when they spotted a 55-gallon oil drum, with holes punched through it, floating in Biscayne Bay. Heavy chains were coiled around the container to weigh it down, but the gases caused by the decomposing body had given the drum enough buoyancy to float it to the surface.

It was a grisly sight and only a partial fingerprint enabled the FBI to identify the grotesquely swollen corpse as belonging to Roselli. It was "Deep Six for Johnny," as *Time* titled it's full-page story on his murder, concluding that

"Roselli was one of a breed that is dying off—usually by murder."

The medical examiner reported that Roselli had been asphyxiated by someone holding a washcloth over his mouth and nose, a rather simple feat considering the serious nature of his emphysema and frail condition. There were stab wounds in his chest and abdomen but he was presumably dead at the time they were inflicted. Then his legs were sawed off and his torso hoisted into the drum, with his legs stuffed in with it. Although no news story Jimmy read mentioned the real reason for cutting off the legs, he guessed that it was because Roselli had been killed almost as soon as he had reached his destination, and by the time they got around to stuffing him into the barrel rigor mortis had set in, making it impossible for the killers to fold the limbs as desired.

It had been a sloppy job, from beginning to end, and looking at it from a professional standpoint, Jimmy felt it was exactly what one could expect from a family bossed by a creep like Aiuppa.

39
GANG WAR

† † † †

GANG WAR HAD BROKEN OUT IN CLEVELAND AND THE FBI WAS TRYING
to stay on top of it. The details were set forth in an affidavit:

> This . . . sets forth probable cause to believe that James T. Licavoli, also known
> as Jack White; James T. Fratianno, also known as "Weasel"; John P. Calandra;
> Angelo Lonardo; Ronald Carabbia; Pasquale J. Cisternino, also known as "But-
> chie"; Thomas James Sinito; Raymond W. Ferritto; Alfred S. Calabrese, also
> known as "Allie"; and others as yet unknown, are associated in fact in an enter-
> prise as defined in Title 18, United States Code, Section 1961 (4), the activities of
> which affect interstate commerce, to wit: a group associated in fact to control
> loan-sharking and other criminal activities in Northern Ohio and to commit
> various criminal acts, including murder, threats involving murder, and conspiracy
> to murder, and participating directly and indirectly in the conduct of the enter-
> prise's affairs through a pattern of racketeering activity, including threats involv-
> ing aggravated murder and felonious assault. . . . Confidential Source #1 advised
> he learned through statements made by Leo Moceri . . . [that] John Nardi had
> five criminal associates who were killing people by putting bombs in their cars.
> John Nardi appeared to be making a play for leadership in the Cleveland orga-
> nized crime family. . . . Confidential Source #1 advised that . . . Tony Delsanter
> was avoiding as many people as possible. Confidential Source #1 advised that
> during the course of a conversation with James Licavoli . . . he learned that four
> Cleveland family members, who were not further identified, had alligned them-
> selves with the "Irish mob" headed by Danny Greene. James Licavoli . . . de-
> scribed Danny Greene and his associates as a tightly knit group who were utilizing
> explosives and other sophisticated weapons to attempt to gain control of criminal
> activities in Cleveland. James Licavoli . . . further stated that he and Tony
> Delsanter are now convinced that they have to kill Danny Greene if they hope
> to retain power.

On August 22, 1976, another old friend disappeared. After receiving a call from
Tony Dope Delsanter, Jimmy took the next flight to Cleveland. That evening
they talked late into the night. Delsanter explained that Leo Moceri's car had

been found in the parking lot of the Holiday Inn outside of Akron and there was blood in the car. There was no doubt in Tony Dope's mind that it was the work of the Greene–Nardi gang.

"Nardi's the fucking brains behind it," Tony Dope said. "This guy's gone crazy since Johnny Scalish died. You know, he was never made and it really pissed him off. The way I hear it, they took Leo out first because he was a fucking good worker, a tough sonovabitch, and he's the one they feared the most. So now we've got a war on our hands."

"This's the second close friend I've lost in two weeks," Jimmy said. "What're you going to do?"

"We're mobilizing, Jimmy," Dope continued. "They asked for it and they're going to get it, don't worry. Leo and me, you know," he paused and Jimmy realized he was close to tears, "we go back a lot of years. It's like with you and me, Jimmy, he was a brother. But, listen, Blackie's got an idea. He's going to New York to talk to Paulie Castellano [acting boss of the Gambino family]. See, this guy's got a big meat packing plant in Jersey, and Greene and Nardi go up there sometimes. Set it up to kill them right there, freeze and bury them."

"You're going to have to make some soldiers," Jimmy said. "How long since you've made anybody?"

"Oh, shit, that Scalish made nobody for years and years. We need some young guys, new blood, some good workers."

"Why the fuck don't you make some? Know any good men?"

"Yeah, a couple. I've talked it over with Blackie." Delsanter laughed and shook his head. "Know something, we talked about that with Leo just a few days ago, and none of us remember the ritual, it's been that long since we've had a ceremony around here."

"Well, you find the guys and I'll come over and help you. We just made Rizzi a couple months ago."

"Hey, Jimmy, with all the problems around here I haven't had a chance to extend my condolences on Johnny Roselli. I know you guys were close. It's a fucking shame. That prick Aiuppa."

"You want to hear something, Dope? I was in Chicago just a few days ago to talk to Aiuppa. He starts going like this, waving his little finger in a circle, like he's trying to remember something, you know, and he says, 'By the way, do you remember that guy, what the fuck's his name, you know, the guy they found in a barrel in Florida?' And he's looking me right in the eye and I'm looking right back at him. 'Oh, yeah,' I says, 'what's his name. I know the guy.' Now, his hand's moving faster and he says, 'You know, he got clipped down there, used to be a friend of Sam. Don't you remember his name?' 'Oh,' I says, 'you mean Johnny Roselli?' 'Yeah, yeah,' he says, 'Johnny Roselli. What do you think of that?'

"Now, Dope, he wants to see my reaction. If my reaction's wrong, you know, they're ready to clip me right there. I says, 'Well, Joey, it's one of them things, so he's dead.' Like it was nothing to me, right? The cocksucker knows we were close. So he's still looking at me and he says, 'You know, of course, I'm on the commission?' "

"Rubbing it in, the dirty prick," Tony Dope added.

"This motherfucker ain't all that popular in Chicago," Jimmy said. "I know Marshall Caifano hates his guts. I had dinner with him one night and he's hot at Aiuppa and Cerone because they don't have Ray Ryan number one on their hit parade. Back in sixty-four, Ryan testified against Caifano, said he tried to extort sixty grand from him. Caifano got ten years. So he's hot and wants this Ray Ryan clipped but Aiuppa's sitting on it. Marshall's pretty bitter about it. He says, 'I can't sleep nights. It's on my mind all the time.' He's determined. I wouldn't give two cents for Ryan's chances.

"But I don't get it about Nardi," Jimmy continued. "He's got a good job with the Teamsters and he's a bright guy. You remember, Dope, back in 1946, I opened a book with Nardi at the corner of Murray Hill and Mayfield Road? Peanuts Danolfo was our doorman. I always liked Nardi, but you're right. Something's gone wrong with his head. He knows he can't buck this outfit. He's going to get fucking killed."

"I can't figure it out," Dope said. "He's got a crew, they've killed four, five guys, but nobody in the family until Leo. They took out the sparkplug first off."

"You can get some help in here from Chicago or New York, from any family in the country," said Jimmy. "All you've got to do is ask. You can go to New York and bring back twenty guys. Listen, Dope, I'm going to be in New York next month and I'll bring it up with Funzi [Tieri]."

"Yeah, okay, but don't ask for help yet. I've talked it over with Blackie and we'd like to take care of our own family. Don't look good to ask for help, you know."

"How about Ray Ferritto?" Jimmy said. "He's a good man. Want me to give him a call, get him over here?"

"You know, Jimmy, he's a good friend of Ronnie Carabbia. Known him twenty years. In fact, we had Ray at Mosquito Lake for one of our Fourth of July bashes. Yeah, give him a call. I'd like to talk to him."

The meeting with Delsanter and Ferritto was at Cherry's Restaurant in Warren. At first Jimmy told Ferritto he was going to New York in late September and would talk to Paul Castellano about Tony Plate and Sparky Monica, then he briefly mentioned the situation in Cleveland before excusing himself.

"You two guys got business to take care of," Jimmy said. "I'll see you later."

Jimmy's casualness belied the seriousness of the gang war that was taking lives and challenging the supremacy of the Cleveland family in its own territory.

PART XII

✝ ✝ ✝ ✝

SINATRA
1976

40
THE KNIGHTS OF MALTA

† † † †

THEY WERE HAVING A DRINK IN THE COCKTAIL LOUNGE OF THE SAN Francisco Hilton when Rudy Tham said, "Hey, Jimmy, how would you like to have dinner with Miss Australia tonight?"

"Great!"

"And her father."

"You asshole."

"No, I'm serious. This guy, Ivan Markovics, is a Hungarian who sneaked into Australia during the war. Then he got in trouble in Australia. Now's he's in Germany and a big man in the Knights of Malta. His daughter represented Australia in the Miss Amber pageant in Santo Domingo, came in second or third, beautiful broad, but a real lady, you know."

"I've heard of the Knights of Malta," Jimmy said, frowning, trying to recall what he knew about it.

"Oh, listen, this's a very exclusive order," Tham said. "In fact, I just got in myself."

"I guess this guy can make anybody he wants?" Jimmy asked.

"Are you kidding, all applications have to be approved by a committee in Rome. But if he sponsors you, and you pay his expenses, he'll go to Rome and push it through himself. Besides his expenses you've got to donate at least ten grand, but still you've got to be worthy to get in."

"Bullshit, not if you're in it, buddy. Sounds like a high-class scam."

"Jimmy, this's on the level. Lots of famous people belong to this order, kings and presidents, royalty all over Europe. You ask Ivan tonight, he'll give you a rundown on it. Pretty fucking impressive, let me tell you."

"Rudy, any outfit that would have you in it can't be that high class. Which reminds me, now that Andy's talking to you, what about the dental program? I've talked to Allen [Dorfman] and he's ready to roll on it whenever you give the word."

Rudy suddenly looked worried. "Jimmy, we've got to wait. It's too soon. We've got to wait for new contracts."

Jimmy leaned forward until their noses were almost touching. "How would you like to go visit Hoffa?"

Rudy fell back in shock. "Hey, come on, Jimmy, we're buddies. Don't talk like that. Give me a break, will you. It'll work out. Just be patient."

"Patient, my ass," Jimmy said. "With all the fucking time and money I've spent on straightening you out, you better come through for me."

The more Ivan Markovics talked about the Knights of Malta, the more convinced Jimmy became that this was high-class con he could use to his own advantage. Somehow, and he could feel the idea beginning to take form in the back of his head, there was the possibility for a high-powered scam.

A tall, heavyset man in his late sixties, Markovics spoke with a thick accent that reminded Jimmy of Otto Preminger. In fact, he kind of looked like Preminger. He would later tell a story about Bianca Jagger mistaking him for a producer. "I was in London, sitting in this club, and the girl on the other side was bowing her head and smiling on me. I lunch with a couple friends of mine and when I go out the woman says, 'Hello, how are you?' I sit down and talk with her and she had mistaken me for the producer. I didn't know who was she and I find out it was Bianca Jagger. She told me I looked and sounded like a producer. I told her, 'No, I'm just an ordinary poor little doctor.' She looked so disappointed."

Markovics was talking about the Knights of Malta, explaining that he had offices in the United Nations Plaza and his title was Ambassador for Special Missions.

"Who's the head man of this outfit?" Jimmy asked, trying to cut through to the heart of it.

"Every country has his own chapter. There's one in Italy, France, England, Germany, all over, and the one here in America is a hundred years old. All the chapters are independent, you see."

"But what's this about going to Rome to make somebody?"

"Yes, well, Prince Petrucci, he's the Prince of Italy, the head of the Italian chapter."

"Who's the top man?" Jimmy asked. "Is it the Pope or something?"

"The Pope, actually, has nothing to do with it, but the Prince works with cardinals, and when we have the investiture, he comes over and brings a couple of cardinals, makes it quite a ceremony, you see."

"It's really terribly impressive," Eve said. "Other members come and they wear these beautiful silk robes, red with a white Maltese Cross."

Jimmy loved her voice. It was soft and with just a slight British accent. "Do you have to be Catholic?"

"The Knights of Malta has two kinds of chapters, you see," Markovics replied. "The Military Order, strictly for Catholic, and the Ecumenical Order without any religious background. You see, I'm involved in the Ecumenical Chapter here in America, only, but I don't call it Ecumenical, but the Knights of Malta, it's all the same thing, you see. The formal title of it is the Sovereign Order of the Hospitallers of Saint John of Jerusalem. It started out as a military-religious brotherhood of knights to protect merchants and pilgrims going back and forth to the Holy Land in the days of the Crusades. They built a chapel and two hospitals close to the Holy Sepulcher. Ever since then the sole purpose of the Knights of Malta has been to help the sick and the poor and we build hospitals all over the world, you see. And lately we've established the Knights of Malta's World Peace Student Exchange to help kids study in different countries, you see, to exchange ideas and further peace. These are all good things, don't you think?"

"Yeah, that's terrific," Jimmy said. "It sounds like something one can be proud to belong to."

"That is it exactly, you see. For a thousand years the Knights of Malta has been one of the most exclusive social orders in the world. And the Maltese Cross, which is given for outstanding accomplishment in various fields and service to humanity, is one of the most prestigious awards in the world. In a thousand years, only seven hundred people have received it, you see. At first, you know, it was given only to Catholic members of royalty, but now it's become democratic, right? Your President Eisenhower received it."

"How many members in the United States?" Jimmy asked.

"About three, four hundred," Markovics said. "But I don't know the American organization so well, you know. I just come here to look it over."

"You need money?"

"Yes, we most certainly do."

"Well," Jimmy said, an idea taking shape, "maybe we can get somebody to do a benefit for you."

"Oh, that would be splendid," Eve said, smiling at her father. "Who do you have in mind?"

"Well, you need a superstar, someone that can pull in people with money, someone like Sinatra."

"Oh, how marvelous. Do you know him?" Eve asked.

"Yeah, sure. He's a good friend of mine. Listen, you going to be in New York later this month?"

"Yes, we will probably be there for about a month, getting things organized," Markovics said. "Do you really think he'd do a benefit for us?"

Jimmy laughed. "Let's take it step by step. First we get Frank in the Knights of Malta, but we don't say nothing about no benefit until he's a member. Then we put it to him."

Ivan and Eve looked at each other and smiled. Jimmy leaned back in his chair and took out a cigar. He was smiling but numbers were clicking through his head at blinding speed. Sinatra would do the benefit at the Premier Theater. Two days, four performances, with about two hundred unrecorded seats at fifty dollars a seat: That was ten thousand dollars. A thousand scalped tickets, the best seats in the house, going anywhere from fifty to a hundred dollars above cost: That was about seventy-five thousand. All the other stuff, the programs, the T-shirts, at least three thousand per performance. Multiply everything by four and you got about four hundred thousand dollars, split three ways: one-third to DePalma for the theater, one-third to Louie Dome, one-third to Jimmy. Louie Dome was included for insurance, to make sure Sinatra fulfilled his obligation. Besides, Louie was Frank's good friend, which automatically earned him a cut.

The party moved to a North Beach nightclub and Jimmy danced with Eve. He told her she looked gorgeous and she told him she wanted to marry a millionaire. He told her he would find someone for her and she told him he had to be good-looking.

"Too bad about Frank," Jimmy said, holding her close, dancing cheek to cheek, "he just got married a few weeks ago."

"Is he really a close friend of yours?" Eve asked.

"You believe me, honey, I'll take you right in his dressing room at the theater and introduce you."

"Oh, God, I can't believe this is happening."

"Believe it, believe it," Jimmy assured her. "You've got my word on it. I'll pick you up in a limo and take you there in style. You'll have the best seats in the joint."

"I'm going to have to pinch myself."

"I hope you don't bruise easily."

41
BITING THE BIG APPLE

† † † †

CARLO GAMBINO SAT AT THE HEAD OF THE TABLE, A GAUNT OLD MAN with a nose that reminded Jimmy of the beak of birds he had seen in movies, the kind that perched on branches, waiting for someone to die. He was only seventy-four but many years of illness had ravaged his body. Yet, mentally, he was what he looked like, a tough old bird, for twenty years the titular head of the largest Cosa Nostra family in the country, having ascended to power in 1957 with the murder of Albert Anastasia. But his days were numbered. Within two weeks he would be dead.

Seated at the table with him were Paul Castellano, Gregory DePalma, Thomas Marson, Richard Fusco, Joseph Gambino, a nephew, and Jimmy Fratianno. They had finished dinner and were lingering over coffee when someone walked up to the table and spoke to Gambino.

The old man raised his hand and all conversations immediately stopped. "All right," he said, "now we go see Frank."

Sinatra, who had removed his jacket and tie, welcomed Gambino with a kiss and hug. Jimmy was right behind him. "Hey, Frank, great seeing you again," he said, kissing him on the cheek as they hugged.

"So you did come back," Sinatra said.

Jimmy lowered his voice. "A little later, Frank, there's something very important I've got to talk to you about. Can you spare a few minutes?"

"Oh, absolutely."

After Sinatra had greeted everyone, a photographer came into the room and they all lined up for a group picture, with DePalma and Marson flanking Sinatra. Someone cracked a joke and everybody laughed as the shutter clicked. Gambino's eyes closed at that instant and the pleased expression on his face was not unlike the one the mortician would soon create for his loved ones.

Marson, DePalma, and Fusco stayed behind when the others left, waiting to see how Jimmy would score with Sinatra.

"Frank, have you ever thought about joining the Knights of Malta?"

The question seemed to take Sinatra by surprise. "Yes, yes I have. Why?"

"Well, Frank, the top man here in New York is a good friend of mine. This's really a fantastic organization. This guy's an ambassador with the United Nations. He was telling me that kings and princes, all big important people belong to it. They knight you and you become a Sir, like Sir Francis, and you get a diplomatic passport, so when you travel nobody can fool with your luggage . . . Well, they can, but they don't when they see this red passport."

"Jesus," Sinatra said. "I've been trying to get into the Knights for fifteen years. My mother's a devout Catholic and I know this would mean so much to her."

"Yeah, well, you know," said Jimmy. "When they have the investiture, the Prince of Italy comes over with a couple of cardinals and they have this mass and other Knights come, wearing their beautiful red silk robes. It's really a fantastic ceremony. I'll tell you what, Frank. I'll bring this ambassador here tomorrow night."

Funzi Tieri was seated at the little table and stood up when Jimmy came to his table and they kissed in the traditional fashion. The counterman brought them coffee and again disappeared into the kitchen. After dispensing with the amenities, Jimmy told him about the situation in Cleveland.

"Tell Jack [Licavoli] if he needs any help to let me know," Funzi said.

"Thanks," Jimmy said, "I will, but right now, they want to handle their own problem. I gave them a good man [Ray Ferritto] and on my way out here I stopped in Cleveland and we made two guys."

Jimmy paused and chuckled softly. "This's really funny, Funzi. It's been such a long time since they've made anybody over there nobody remembered the ritual. I had to go over there and do it in English for them. I can't do it in Italian. We were in the fucking basement of this restaurant, the Roman Gardens, and there was myself, Jack, Tony Delsanter, who's the *consigliere,* and the new underboss, Angelo Lonardo."

"Did you make good men?"

"Yeah, I think so. Tony Liberatore. When he was a kid, I think he killed a couple cops during a robbery, he was only seventeen, and he did like twenty years, but now he's got a big job with the county. The other guy's John Calandra. I've known both guys for years. But they need to make more soldiers if they want to stop that Irish gang."

Funzi nodded gravely. "It's been a long time since we've made anybody in New York. Since the Apalachin meeting we've been careful. You've got to protect yourself against worms who turn against you. Too many guys today will betray their family for one reason or another. Times have changed. Well, you give Jack my regards and my offer stands. Now, listen, we're having a sitdown here tomorrow and it concerns someone in your country. Can you make it at about this time tomorrow?"

"No problem, Funzi. I'll be here."

† † †

Eve Markovics saw Jimmy enter the lobby of the Warwick Hotel and she stood up. "Daddy, here he comes," she said with a flutter of relieved excitement. "Don't you look elegant," she said to Jimmy as he kissed her cheek.

"And you look gorgeous," he said, holding her at arm's length to admire her white silk jersey dress with the princess waistline. Her father, with the gold medals hanging from a red silk ribbon around his neck, looked like a king going to his coronation. "Well, what about me, Jimmy?" he asked, reaching to shake Jimmy's hand. "Don't I look gorgeous?"

"I've never been out with royalty before," Jimmy said. "I'm glad I've got a limo."

The limousine, provided through the courtesy of Louie Beans, who owned a limousine service, was naturally being comped like most of the good things Jimmy enjoyed in life.

"Oh, I'm so thrilled," Eve said, as the long sleek automobile glided softly through downtown traffic and headed north toward Tarrytown. "I've never seen Sinatra perform in person before. I'm really looking forward to it."

"I've never seen him either," Jimmy said, resting his feet on the jumpseat and lighting up a cigar.

"How could that be possible? You're there every night, you said."

Jimmy laughed. "I just go there to shoot the bull with the guys. It's funny because all my friends bring their wives . . . send them in, you know . . . and wait outside in the bars or restaurants for them to come out."

"That's atrocious, must be terribly embarrassing for Frank. What does he think about that?"

"Nothing, he knows we don't care about stuff like that. We've got business to discuss. See, my friend, Tommy Marson, who you'll meet tonight, is one of the owners of that theater. I'm here to protect his investment."

"Oh, I get it," Eve said. "You're a business consultant. I've wondered about your occupation."

Jimmy smiled. "Yeah, something like that."

"Do you have any of your own money in the theater?" Markovics asked.

"No, I never invest my own money in schemes like that."

"That's fascinating," Eve said. "You work on a fee basis?"

"Well, let me put it this way," he said. "I invest my time and what do you call it, expertise, for a certain percentage of the operation."

They both looked at him with new respect. "Maybe I should try to get you in the Knights of Malta," Markovics said. "You must be a very rich man."

"Don't worry about getting new members," Jimmy said, "I'll find all the new members you need."

After the performance that evening, Jimmy escorted Eve and her father backstage. The dressing room was crowded with well-wishers and Jimmy called out, "Hey, Frank, over here. I want you to meet these dear friends of mine."

Sinatra, who had removed his jacket and was in the process of loosening his tie and shirt, came right over and he and Jimmy kissed and hugged. With his wife Barbara hovering in the background, Sinatra shook hands with Eve. She would later tell Jimmy, "Damnit, I was dying to kiss him but I didn't dare. I could sort of feel Barbara's eyes on me."

Ivan tried to describe the Knights of Malta but there were so many people in the room, most of them converging on Sinatra, that he finally gave up and Sinatra invited them to join him for dinner at Twenty-One after the show on Thursday. Ivan gave him an application form to fill out and Sinatra promised to bring it back on Thursday with a couple of good photographs.

After they left the dressing room, Eve said, "Dinner at Twenty-One. I'm still pinching myself to make sure it's really happening. Are you coming too, Jimmy?"

"Of course," Jimmy said. "Listen, we're a team."

Jimmy and Funzi Tieri embraced and then Jimmy introduced Mike Rizzi.

"Glad you could make it," Tieri said. "Come with me, the boys are waiting."

They went out a side door and down a narrow hallway to another door. Tieri gave two sharp raps and the door swung open. It was a small room, perhaps twelve by fifteen feet, and the only furniture was a long table with eight or nine folding chairs.

"My underboss Eli [nee Carmine Zeccardi], this's Fat Tony [Salerno] my *consigliere,* and Chin [nee Vincent Gigante]. This's Jim Fratianno, the acting boss in Los Angeles, and Mike Rizzi."

"Mike's my skipper in L.A.," Jimmy said.

They shook hands and sat down at the table. A bodyguard, not introduced, remained seated against the wall, directly behind Tieri.

Chin, Jimmy remembered, was the one who had taken the shot at Frank Costello that had cost Roselli the Tropicana. In the intervening years Gigante had acquired a couple more chins and his nose, which had been splattered by a brutal blow many years ago, looked like it had been haphazardly pasted on his face.

"The reason for this sitdown," Tieri said to Jimmy, "concerns somebody in your country. Chin will lay it out for you."

"This guy, Joe [Joseph Spencer] Ullo stuck me for a bundle of shylock and skipped out to California. So we sent this guy, Gazut [nee Vincent Calderazzo], to collect and now Gazut's missing. So we figure Ullo probably thought this guy was going to clip him and he hit him first and buried him."

"Now we vote," Tieri said. "I say, hit."

Salerno said, "Hit."

Zeccardi said, "Hit."

Gigante said, "Hit."

"That's it," Tieri said. "Send somebody out there right away."

Jimmy said, "Listen, Funzi, if you need any help, all you've got to do is ask. I'll give Chin Mike's number, he can call him any time."

"Thanks for coming," Tieri said. "This wraps it up."

(It would be seven months before two informants would lead police to the desert grave of Vincent Calderazzo. Already serving a five-year prison sentence for loansharking, Joseph Ullo would later be charged with the murders of Calderazzo and Jacob Molinas. The trials were still pending at this writing.)

Another sitdown, this one with the Gambino family, was held at midafternoon in the banquet room of a Brooklyn restaurant. Its purpose was to straighten out the Tony Plate–Sparky Monica situation. Jimmy had arranged for it.

Present were acting boss Paul Castellano, acting underboss "Jimmy Brown" Failla, and *consigliere* Joe Gallo—no relation to the late Crazy Joe Gallo. Mike Rizzi accompanied Jimmy, who looked upon the sitdown more as an exercise in power than a matter of grave importance. It provided him with his first opportunity to flex his muscles as a boss and to convey a message to the New York families that a new regime had come into power in California.

They ordered drinks and something to eat, chatted amiably for a few minutes, with Jimmy explaining the new setup in California.

"Look," Jimmy said, getting down to cases, "we've got a problem with Tony Plate and this Sparky Monica. As far as I'm concerned this Tony Plate has no right fucking around with a guy in our country."

"Look, Jimmy," Joe Gallo said, "Tony and this Sparky go back a lot of years. When Sparky went busted eight, nine years ago, Tony bankrolled him."

"I don't care about that," Jimmy said. "If Sparky owes him money, he can pay him back. That's not what I'm talking about. Sparky's going around saying Tony's his man, practically told Mike here to go fuck himself. Well, that just ain't going to happen. We've got a new ball game in California. Me and Louie Dragna are going to stick by the rules. I can't come into New York and do something illegal unless I get permission, am I right?"

Castellano nodded. "That's right, Jimmy."

"The same goes for Tony Plate. He ain't got no right doing anything with this guy. 'Cause number one, this guy's got an obligation to a very dear friend of mine, a very serious obligation, and Sparky's got no right leaning on Tony Plate for protection. This Sparky's going to do the right thing or he's going to get fucking hurt. What we do in California is our own business. We don't come to New York to protect New York guys from other New York guys, that's against the rules. And we don't expect New York guys to do it in California. That's strictly out of bounds."

"The trouble with Tony and Sparky is that they're old pals," Failla said. "They're not really looking at it that way."

"Well, then, Sparky should have gone to Tony when he wanted this favor from my friend Ray Ferritto. He promised him fifty percent of his business, that's how desperate he was, and now he sits back and says fuck you, Tony Plate's my man. Well, I say Tony Plate better stay in his own fucking country if he knows what's good for him. As a matter of fact, you know, I dropped by Chicago to talk this over with the old man but he was out of town. If we can't straighten it out here, I want him to take it to the commission."

"Jimmy, there's no need for that," Castellano said. "We'll talk to Tony and have him come see you in California. After all, you're right. Nobody has any right to go out in your country and do anything without your permission."

"Paulie, we're going to grab a lot of guys in our country who got no right being there. Guys from all over the country are running around like they've got a fucking permit. If they tried that in Chicago or New York they'd get clipped so fast they wouldn't know what happened to them. Our problem for years has been we've had no boss with muscle. When Jack Dragna died, the family fell apart. Well, we've got a new ball game now and we're going to stay on top of things."

"Jimmy, I'm a hundred percent with you," Castellano said. "Don't worry, Tony's going to straighten this shit out real fast."

Having said his piece, Jimmy enjoyed his lunch. He could see that his words had gained him new respect in the eyes of these men who ran their own family with an iron fist.

(Castellano kept his word. Tony Plate had come to California and relinquished all rights to Sparky Monica. Mike Rizzi had collected five thousand dollars from Monica, sending three thousand to Jimmy in San Francisco, keeping a thousand, and giving a thousand to Brooklier's wife. Jimmy had given Ferritto a thousand and told him he was free to move in and take over the fifty percent of Sparky's business he had been promised, after he had completed his work in Cleveland.)

On the drive back to Tarrytown that afternoon, Rizzi was curious as to why Jimmy had not brought up the pornography problem.

"In a case like that, Mike, you don't have to tell them a fucking thing. All you do is break a few heads and let them run to New York and stew in their own juice. See, if you bring it up they're just going to deny it. They know they're out of bounds. They're not going to admit it. That way we let the porno dealers know that New York can't protect them, that they've got to deal with us in our own country."

"Well, have you heard Bomp talk about this Forex outfit?

"Mike, that's an entirely different deal. Bomp says they're independents in the porno business, selling to South America, but I told him I didn't want no part of the deal. Who're them fucking guys? Tony Zappi don't know them. Gaswirth and Bittner don't know them. Them guys come out of nowhere. I don't like it. Bomp says they're making a hundred grand a year, this and that. I says, 'Great, you grab them. I've got my own fucking things to worry about. And keep my name out of it.'"

"Well, he came to me, too," Mike said. "I got LoCicero and Ricciardi checking it out."

"Mike, you're walking into a blind alley, but that's your business," Jimmy said. "I don't want no part of it and I'm going to tell you what I told Bomp, keep my name out of it. If them guys are legit, they'll burn you. Fucking around with straight people's the fastest way to the joint I know of."

"How can they be legit?" Mike asked.

"Semifucking legit, not connected with no family, understand? They'll burn your ass. Bomp should know better. Listen, it's your neck, you want to stick it out, go ahead," Jimmy warned. "Just remember what I told you when somebody chops it off."

It is said that the Rainbow Room, on the sixty-fifth floor of Rockefeller Plaza, offers a view of the entire world, almost. It was Mike Rizzi's night and many old friends from the Colombo and other families had turned out to greet him. Jimmy counted fifteen made guys at their table alone. The Brooklyn hierarchy was there: Boss Tommy DiBello, underboss Anthony "Abbie Shots" Abbattemarco, *consigliere* Alphonse "Alley Boy" Persico. There was Andrew Russo, Alphonse "Funzied" D'Ambrosio, but there was also Benny Eggs, Louie and Vinnie Beans, Terry Zappi, Frankie "Redshirt" Felice from Angelo Bruno's Philadelphia family, and Russell Bufalino, boss of the Pittston family.

On this evening, Bufalino had his own problem. After being introduced as *amico nostra* to Jimmy, he pulled him aside and explained his predicament in hoarse whispers.

"They tell me you're the acting boss in L.A. but that you live in Frisco. Is that right?"

Bufalino's eyes bothered Jimmy. They had a tendency to rotate to opposite corners, giving Jimmy the uneasy feeling they were looking around him instead of at him.

"Well, I commute back and forth."

"Are you acquainted with Walnut Creek? Know where it is?" Bufalino asked.

"Yeah, it's about twenty miles east of Oakland."

"How big is this burg?"

"I don't know," Jimmy said. "Thirty, forty thousand, but it's strictly residential."

Bufalino sighed with relief. "Listen, Jimmy, I need a favor. This's very important. I've got a case coming up and this fink's trying to nail me. See, the cocksucker owed a friend of mine twenty-five Gs, fenced some diamonds, so I thought I'd talk to this prick and I got pretty hot and threatened to whack him myself. So this fucking guy's recording this shit and now they've got me fucking indicted for extortion. Ain't that great?"

"Oh, Christ," Jimmy said, "I've been that route myself. Cost me six and a half fucking years. How can I help you?"

"Jimmy, I thought you'd never ask," Bufalino smiled and one eye did a quick flip to the opposite corner. Their movements seemed beyond his control. "This guy's now in the government witness program and they've changed his fucking name and moved him out, but I know where he's hiding."

"Don't tell me it's Walnut Creek?"

"That's it, that's where the motherfucker's holed out. His name's Jack Napoli, but he's changed it to Naples, or something like that, but this guy, Jimmy, will stick out like a sore thumb in that small town. He's real tall, with blond hair and he's opening up a pork store in Walnut Creek."

"I guess you want him clipped?"

Bufalino patted Jimmy's shoulder. "Clipped and fucking buried. I don't want that cocksucker to surface until Judgment Day, and then only after I've made my appearance."

Jimmy laughed. "No problem, Russ, I'll handle it myself. If he's there, I'll find him, set him up, and you can send out a crew." With another pat on the shoulder from Bufalino, Jimmy walked back to his table.

Everybody was moving around, table hopping.

"Hey, Jimmy, over here," Abbie Shots called. "You enjoying yourself?"

"Having a ball," Jimmy said. "I didn't know this character here had so many important friends."

Abbie Shots laughed. "Rizzi's a good Brooklyn boy. I don't know what he's doing in California. Why don't you kick his ass out of there, send him back here to us?"

"Not a chance," Jimmy said. "He's my main man in L.A. now."

"Okay, listen, both you guys are invited to my daughter's wedding reception Sunday night. This's going to be a real fucking Mustache Pete wedding, man. We're blowing the works. All five families will have their own tables and there'll be separate tables for families from all parts of the country, even a table for California, how's that? Come see how we put on the dog here in New York. Did you see that fucking movie, *The Godfather*? Well, this wedding's going to make that look like a picnic. Maybe four hundred made guys in the place. I'll show you that all them stories in the newspapers about the families here fighting each other's a lot of fucking bullshit."

Abbie Shots' speech was getting slurred and his face was flushed but his eyes were shining brightly, alert to everything going on around him. "Now, you going to come?"

"Can I bring some friends?" Jimmy asked.

"Bring anybody you want. The more the merrier."

"Where's this going to be?"

"On Staten Island," Abbie Shots said. "Mike knows where, but it's going to be first class all the way. Even Funzwall [Funzi Tieri] is coming."

Alley Boy came up and grabbed Jimmy by the arm. "Excuse me, Abbie, I've got somebody here that wants to meet this guy."

"Be my guest, but don't forget, Jimmy, you come now."

Alley Boy was pulling on his arm and Jimmy jokingly waved good-bye as he was physically hauled away. "Hey, Jimmy, I've got old man Guiccione here, Bob Guiccione's father, the guy that owns *Penthouse* magazine. Says he wants to meet you. After I heard about your lawsuit, I told him you was here and he got all excited. Play your cards right and we can make some money with this guy. That fucking Dalitz at La Costa's pulling their balls off."

Anthony Guiccione, who was with a flashy centerfold type, excused himself and walked away with Jimmy and Alley Boy. After the introduction, Guiccione said, that they felt bad about the story and wanted to make it right with him.

"It's kind of late for that kind of shit," Jimmy said. "You've already taken my deposition. Now it's our turn. My attorney wants to push it all the way, but we're reasonable men."

"Jimmy, we'd like to do what's right with you."

"Fine. Get ahold of Alley Boy and work out something."

After they had left Guiccione's table, Jimmy told Alley Boy they would cut up whatever he could get out of the magazine. Although he didn't let on, Jimmy had already instructed his attorney, Dennis McDonald, to drop the suit.

In the days he spent in New York, Jimmy became involved in several deals. There was a straight artichoke deal with Terry Zappi and Freddie "Redshirt" Felice, whom Jimmy would introduce to the Parra Brothers, the largest growers in the country, with 5,000 acres in the Castroville–Watsonville area north of Salinas, California.

Jimmy also decided to open a clothing store in San Francisco. He met made guys who specialized in hijacked clothing; others, like DePalma's brother-in-law, owned or worked in warehouses where boxed merchandise was stored for shipment. They would open the boxes and steal three or four items from each container. Jimmy could buy the goods for pennies on the dollar.

The proposition was so appealing that Jimmy invested fifteen thousand of his own money in opening a store on lower Mission Street, in a predominately Mexican neighborhood. Rudy Tham and Marson each invested five thousand. "Clothes Out" would turn out to be a profitable business, and provided Jimmy with another convenient hangout besides Sal's. On the sidewalk directly across the street was a pay phone which he would put to good and constant use.

Jimmy and his party arrived at the 21 Club ahead of Sinatra, who had to drive in from Tarrytown after his performance that evening. While they had a drink in the small room adjacent to the main dining room, the maitre d', who looked Italian, kept bouncing over to see how they were bearing up. After an hour, Jimmy was beginning to look impatient. Eve and Ivan Markovics seemed quite contented and Tommy Marson loved the place. The moment he had walked in, he had spotted Jackie Onassis at one of the tables along the wall.

"That's a pretty dap guy with her," Jimmy observed.

"I wonder who it is," Marson said. "You think I ought to ask the maitre d'?"

"Who cares?" Jimmy said. "What difference does it make?"

The maitre d' came over again. He leaned forward and lowered his voice. "Oh, we had quite a little scene here this evening," he said. "Rona Barrett, you know, the movie columnist, got terribly upset when she heard that Sinatra was coming in."

"I don't blame her," Marson said. "Frank hates her guts and don't mind telling the world about it in pretty fancy language."

"Well, thank God, she had the presence of mind to make a graceful departure."

Around eleven-thirty, Frank and Barbara arrived with a half-dozen other people and were seated at the large table right up front, the most conspicious table in the main room. It was obvious to Jimmy that they wanted everyone coming in to see who was there. Why not, Jimmy thought, this was the place where celebrities came to look at celebrities. For Jimmy, who judged all places by Las Vegas and Miami standards, it was just another small, overcrowded, overpriced, overrated New York joint.

Jimmy sat on Frank's right and Ivan on his left and Jimmy smiled as he heard Ivan rattle off the wonders of the Knights of Malta. Sinatra had brought the completed application form and two passport-sized photographs. There was no question that Sinatra was already sold on the idea of becoming a Knight, but Ivan kept the sales pitch going anyway.

At one point in the evening when Barbara went to the ladies room, Sinatra turned to Jimmy. "Look at her," he said, indicating Jackie Onassis, "she's been gunning me all night." Jimmy looked up and Jackie's gaze shifted back to her escort.

Later Jimmy went to sit with Jilly Rizzo and Marson who were at a different table.

"Have you noticed how Jackie's been gunning Frank?" Jimmy asked.

"You kidding, she can't take her eyes off him," Rizzo said. "She and Frank were going at it pretty hot and heavy for a while. She was nuts about him, but Frank never stuck to nobody very long in them days.

"See, Frank says that Jackie wanted to marry him, but he dropped her like a hot potato. To him she's just another broad, right? He's already had what he wanted, right, so what's he going to do with her now that she wants to get married? You know what I mean? He said, 'See you later, baby, bye-bye.' "

"Barbara's a different story, I guess," Jimmy said.

"Oh, yeah. Frank's a changed man. He don't fuck around no more. They're together all the time. She don't let him out of her sight for a fucking minute."

"I noticed that," Jimmy said. "You've got to give Frank credit. I sure couldn't stick to just one broad, forget about it. Variety, that's the spice of life, and I'll never get too old for that, never."

Jimmy was fit to be tied. They were in the East Dining Room for the private party after the final performance of Sinatra's second concert and Tommy Marson had just informed him that Sinatra's lawyer, Mickey Rudin, was telling Sinatra that Ivan Markovics was a con man and that the Knights of Malta deal was nothing but a big scam.

"So he doesn't want to approve the five thousand Ivan needs for his expenses to Rome to push this thing through himself," Marson said. "The sonovabitch's really bending Frank's ear. I saw Rudin in the bar earlier tonight talking to Markovics."

"It's Ivan's accent," Jimmy said. "The guy sounds like he just got off the fucking boat. Well, fuck that Rudin."

"What're you going to do?" DePalma asked.

"Listen, Greg, we'll pay for Ivan's expenses, take it out of the fucking skim. Don't worry, we'll get it back a thousand times when Frank does the benefit."

DePalma looked at Marson and Ritchie Fusco for approval. "Okay, Jimmy, we'll put up the fucking money."

Jimmy stood up. "I'll straighten out this cocksucker."

Jimmy walked up to Rudin, who was sitting on Sinatra's right, and tapped him on the shoulder. "Mickey, come here, I want to talk to you."

They walked a few feet away from the table and Jimmy stuck a stiff index finger into Rudin's chest. "Listen, cocksucker, let me tell you something, you fucking prick. Why're you calling this Markovics a fucking con man? Do you know what the fuck you're talking about, you motherfucker?"

"Just a moment . . ."

"Shut your fucking trap, you cocksucker. I'm going to tell you something, this ain't no scam and this guy's no phony. Furthermore, we don't want your fucking money. Shove it up your ass,"

"Hey, really, Jimmy, it's a misunderstanding, I didn't mean it that way."

"Fuck, you didn't, you prick," Jimmy said. "I don't stand for no motherfucker talking about my friends. I don't run around with phonies. And I certainly would never try to con Frank out of a dime, you dumb cocksucker. I never pull scams on my friends. Now, Mickey, you better listen to me, I don't stand for nobody talking about me and my friends. Now get the fuck away from me."

On the night of the wedding reception, Jimmy and Mike Rizzi picked up the Markovicses in a limousine and rode to Staten Island in style.

It was the most elaborate Mafia wedding reception Jimmy had ever seen. There must have been eight hundred guests in a huge barn of a place, with long tables decorated with flowers and candles, champagne in silver buckets, linen tablecloths, waiters in tuxedoes, with an orchestra playing and people everywhere kissing each other, with the laughter audible over the music. It was so unreal, it reminded Eve Markovics of a movie set. Jimmy was everywhere, kissing and paying his respects to made guys who outnumbered all other guests. Except for Tony Ducks Corrallo, all the New York bosses were there, with their underbosses, *consiglieri, capiregime,* and hundreds of *soldati.*

There were course after course of delicious Italian dishes, with champagne toasts to the bride and the groom, and the bride's mother and father, the groom's mother and father. Then the bride and groom did their initial waltz around the dance floor, then it was the father's turn with the bride. Later the bride and groom walked to all the tables, kissing and shaking hands, and collecting white envelopes filled with money. Jimmy had one of the best times of his life.

42
SIR FRANCIS

† † † †

IN HIS LOS ANGELES OFFICE, MICKEY RUDIN CAME ON THE LINE AND Jimmy said, "Hey, I've got great news for Frank. Tell him he's been approved by the Knights of Malta."

"That's wonderful, Jimmy," Rudin said. "Look, I'll connect you with Frank and you tell him. I know Frank's going to be thrilled and it's going to mean so much to Dolly [Natalie Sinatra]. Just hold on now, Jimmy, he's on the other line."

"Hello, Jimmy, I hear you've got good news."

"Frank, congratulations, you've made it."

"Jesus, that's great, Jimmy."

"Look, Frank, Ivan's coming to Tommy's place at Rancho Mirage, and he's bringing the scroll, medals, flag, all that stuff, and he wants to make final arrangements for the investiture. You want to come to Tommy's place or do you want us to come to your place?"

"Jimmy, why don't I just skip over there when you're ready for me. In case my mother should be over at my house, I'm trying to keep it a surprise. Coordinate the time with Jilly, okay?" Sinatra asked.

"Fine, we'll set it up for early next week. See you then, and again congratulations."

Bobbi Marson ran into the bar, her face flushed with excitement. "Frank's coming, he's walking over, be here any minute now."

Jilly Rizzo sidled up to Jimmy. "Look at this gang, what's going on?"

"I know, I know," Jimmy said, looking over the assembled guests. Besides Markovics, Bompensiero had brought his attorney, Nick DePento, Joe Stead, Chris Petti, and a Dick somebody that Jimmy had never met before. "I told Bomp he was crazy, but they wanted a chance to see Frank. What the fuck, it won't bother Frank. He's used to having people around him."

"I know, Jimmy, but I don't like for guys to take advantage like that."

Jimmy smiled. "Jilly, why don't you go tell Bomp your problem. Kick his ass."

Jilly laughed. "Very funny. I better go meet Frank, brief him on the setup."

When Sinatra walked in with Jilly, Jimmy was the first to greet him with a kiss and hug, with the others lining up to politely shake his hand.

Ivan Markovics, resplendent in his red silk robe with the white Maltese Cross and the medals hanging from the silk ribbon around his neck, was an imposing figure as he presented Sinatra with an ancient scroll with the Latin words embroidered in gold, a red silk box with gold medals, a red flag with the white Maltese Cross, and a red passport also with the Maltese Cross.

"Now, Mr. Sinatra, I must warn you," Markovics said in jest. "This is not a diplomatic passport, it will not get you through United States customs with millions in hot diamonds, but it is very much respected in European countries."

"Now, you tell me," Sinatra said, winking at Jimmy. "This pal of yours over there told me I'd have diplomatic immunity."

"I think he meant diplomatic courtesy. As you know, I personally went to Rome and spoke with Prince Petrucci and according to your wishes, the Prince will be accompanied by two cardinals from the Vatican. They will bring a special Papal blessing for you and your mother."

"Excuse me," Bompensiero said, "but while you're over there in Rome, could you get a Papal blessing for my mother who died in nineteen sixty-six? Her name was Maria Anna."

"Of course," Markovics said. "I will see to it personally. I'll have it mailed directly to your home."

"Thanks a lot," Bompensiero said, "I really appreciate that."

Markovics returned his attention to Sinatra. "It looks quite promising that Prince Bernhard of Holland will also attend if we can arrange for his transportation. And there are many prominent members in the United States who would like to personally welcome you into the Order on the day of your investiture if transportation can be arranged for them."

"That's no problem," Sinatra said. "I'll have a plane for them at LaGuardia and arrangements will be made for their stay at the Canyon here in Palm Springs. Can we do it in December?"

"We better think in terms of January or February, get a firm date that will be agreeable to the princes and the cardinals. I've got to organize all these people, send out invitations. It all takes time, but believe me it will be worth it. It's going to be the most fantastic affair imaginable, something deserving of a man of your exalted station in life."

"Well, well," Sinatra smiled, "recognition at last."

After the ceremony, Jimmy took Sinatra by the arm and gently led him to a bedroom. "Listen, Frank, can you spare me a minute, there's something important I've got to talk to you about."

"Of course."

"Bomp's coming with us."

"That's fine."

They went into the bedroom and Bompensiero closed the door. "Look, Frank, first I want to apologize for getting hot at Mickey when he said Ivan was a phony. You know, Frank, we never fuck our friends, you know what I mean?"

Sinatra nodded but remained silent.

"We're honorable with our friends. So when I heard what he'd told you I got pretty hot.

"Look, Frank, our family's in trouble. We've got people in jail and we've got to make some money, know what I mean?"

"Certainly. What can I do to help?"

"Number one, Frank, the Knights ain't got no money. The guy that was there before ripped off the place for a million or so and now Ivan's here trying to get it back on its feet. The answer to both the Knights and our family could be solved if you did a benefit. Two days, four performances. I've talked to Greg DePalma and you could do them at the Premier Theater. You know, add a couple days to your next concert there. We've got a good system working over there, we're with the right people, you know. You understand what I mean, Frank?"

"Oh, absolutely," Sinatra said. "My pleasure, Jimmy. Have Greg work out a schedule with Mickey. Now, Jimmy, when you want to talk to me, work through Mickey, he's my buffer, but if he bullshits you, go to Jilly and I'll straighten Mickey out. That way I don't have to fuck around with business details."

"Frank, I hear you loud and clear. No problem, we'll set it up for sometime next year, whatever's convenient for you, Frank, and thanks a fucking million. The family will appreciate it, believe me, and if ever there's anything we can do for you, just say the word and you've got it."

It was only a matter of days before Sinatra said the word through Jilly Rizzo. Jimmy was at Marson's house and when Jilly came over they went for a walk. Jimmy recalls Jilly coming right to the point.

"Jimmy, Frank has asked me to speak to you about a jerk that used to work for him as a security guy. A real fucking animal. Hit a guy in the mouth one time and broke his jaw and collarbone with one punch. He's about six feet, two-thirty, and he's got this big handlebar mustache. His name's Andy Celamtano, but everybody calls him Banjo. This guy's a horse player, a degenerate, always at the track. Wherever the bangtails are running, this Banjo's there. Anyway, Frank fired him and this guy's had a hard-on for Frank ever since. He's been spouting off some bullshit to them scandal sheets they sell in grocery stores."

"Sue the bastard," Jimmy said.

"Jimmy, it's a royal waste of time. If Frank sued every time some prick wrote some bullshit about him, he'd be spending his life in courtrooms. Now we hear this Banjo's writing a book about Frank and we want this guy stopped once and for all. Know what I mean?"

"You want the guy clipped? Just say the word and the motherfucker's good as buried."

"No, not right now. Just hurt this guy real bad. Break his legs, put the cocksucker in the hospital. Work him over real good and let's see if he gets the message."

"Where does he live?"

"That's the problem, I don't know. Burbank or Glendale, but he ain't in the book. The best place to look for this guy's at racetracks. You can't miss him."

"Tell Frank we'll do it, but it might take some time," Jimmy said. Jimmy thought of the fruitless week he had spent in Walnut Creek looking for pork stores and a blond giant who by now could be thousands of miles away. He'd tried to find the witness Russ Bufalino had asked him to, but had failed. This time, however, he had an advantage: Celamtano was not anticipating an attack.

In Jimmy's world there was nothing unusual about Sinatra's request. All kinds of people wanted some work done. There was Al Baron, former assets manager of the Teamsters pension fund, who had gone to Slick Shapiro to find someone to kill Foy Bryant, the owner of a cemetery who had told a grand jury that he had paid Baron $200,000 to obtain a $1.3 million loan. Baron gave Shapiro a $2,500 retainer and then changed his mind. When he asked for his money back, Jimmy told Shapiro to tell him to go "fuck himself."

A builder in Westborough, with whom Jimmy and Tommy Marson had thought of doing business, had wanted a measure of revenge against his partner who had cheated him out of the land he had inherited from his family. His first request was to get his partner's home burglarized. "This guy's got two safes in his home," he had told Jimmy. "There's bound to be thirty, forty thousand dollars in there, plus jewelry, but all I want are the deeds he stole from me with a power of attorney I'd given him."

Although Jimmy had sympathized, he was quick to inform him that he was not in that line of work. At the time they were in Phil Maita's office at his Easy Street theater and Jimmy said, "Maybe Phil can find somebody." Maita had agreed to arrange it and as they were leaving Maita's office the builder turned to Jimmy and said, "I'd like to get back at this guy. You know, get even with him." He had stopped walking and lowered his voice. "You know, Jimmy, I'd give ten thousand dollars to get this guy put to sleep."

Jimmy shook his head in disgust and started walking toward his car. The builder caught up with him. "I mean it, Jimmy, name your price." Jimmy had whirled around. "Don't even talk to me about that kind of shit. I don't even know who you are. You've got a lot of nerve talking like that to me." The builder had apologized.

Maita had sent three burglars to crack the two safes and they had come up empty. When Jimmy reminded the builder of his obligation to the burglars, he promised to make it up to them. "Give them a piece of land, let them build a house," Jimmy said. "Those guys risked going to jail for twenty years for nothing. It's the least you can do."

Rick Manzi had a problem of his own. He thought Harry Margolis, a tax shelter expert, had hustled Barbara McNair for a cool million dollars and he wanted Margolis whacked if they lost their lawsuit against him. But on December 15, 1976, long before the case would go to trial, Manzi was found shot to death in his Las Vegas home. The murder remains unsolved.

Then there was the dentist from Toledo, who was having marital problems. He told Shapiro he wanted his wife killed but he also experienced a change of heart.

Another contretemps involved Oscar Bonavena and Joe Conforte. Once the world's fifth-ranked heavyweight contender, Bonavena at 33 was rapidly falling off the ladder of contention when he hooked up with Sally Conforte, who at 59 was grossly overweight and had been a madam since the age of seventeen. At the time she fell in love with Bonavena, Sally and Joe were jointly involved in the completion of their new million-dollar whorehouse on the outskirts of Reno. Called the Mustang Ranch, it was built along the lines of a prison, with seven wings of cinder block cell-like trick rooms shooting out like spokes from the enormous hub of the reception room where as many as fifty girls gathered in a chorus line whenever a customer wanted to make a selection. There was a ten-foot fence topped with barbed wire and a wrought iron gate that was electrically controlled by an armed guard. Overlooking the entire spread were two 24-foot gun towers. It would soon become known as a pleasure fortress.

When Jimmy came into his favorite hangout, Sal's, one day, Sal Amarena sat down next to him and said, "Jimmy, you won't believe what just happened here. Oscar Bonavena was in here today with Sally Conforte. She introduces this guy to me as her lover and takes off to do some shopping."

"That must have been exciting."

"Wait a minute, this Bonavena can barely speak English and he's sitting there, eating a fucking pizza, and looking at me like he's trying to make up his mind about something important. Then he says, 'How much it cost to get Joe Conforte killed dead?' I told him I didn't know but I'd check around."

A few days later, Jimmy received a frantic call from Joe Conforte who wanted Jimmy to fly to Reno to discuss an urgent matter. Jimmy took the next flight and Conforte picked him up at the airport.

"I want to show you my new joint," he said, "I've got a million bucks in this place. It's got everything. You can even fuck in a Jacuzzi."

"I hope you didn't drag me all the way up here to show me a fucking whorehouse," Jimmy said.

Conforte looked at him. "How's your nerve?"

"What're you talking about? Do I look like I've got fucking palsy or something?"

"Well, I've a little piece of work I'd like done. How do you feel about icing a woman? Did you ever ice one before?"

"Joe, don't come up with them questions. What are you, a prosecutor? Are you talking about Sally?"

"Let's say it's Sally. Now I'm not saying it is, you understand, I'm just trying to get a ballpark figure. Would ten thousand do it?"

"Let's lay it out in the open," Jimmy replied. "If it's Sally, it's going to be one hundred grand. Think it over and let me know and I'll let you know."

"I'd like to have it done in South America. She's going on a trip with Bonavena."

"Forget South America. We can do it right here, bury her and nobody'll ever find her."

"Well, let me think about it. A hundred is your rock bottom figure?"

"Yeah, but I wouldn't wait too long if I was you. Somebody else might get the same idea about you, know what I mean?"

Less than two weeks later, Oscar Bonavena was dead, shot through the heart at the Mustang Ranch at six o'clock in the morning. He and Sally had been barred from the whorehouse by Conforte and as Bonavena was angrily walking back to his car, having been refused admission, someone called "Freeze!" and a shot was fired from the rear gun tower. Bonavena's body was shipped home to Buenos Aires, Sally returned to the Mustang Ranch, and the guard who shot Bonavena took up writing and singing country music.

PART XIII

† † † †

LAST FLASH
OF POWER
1976–1977

43
BROOKLIER RETURNS

† † † †

ALTHOUGH DOMINIC BROOKLIER WAS RELEASED FROM PRISON ON OC-
tober 28, 1976, it was not until late November that he requested to see Jimmy.
The meeting was at the law offices of Brooklier's son, Anthony, and Jimmy
brought Mike Rizzi with him to introduce him as *amico nostra.*

If anything, Brooklier looked more frail than he had at Terminal Island. He
looked tired and his movements were slow and deliberate. It was hard for
Jimmy to picture that old man as the young Jimmy Regace he had known
thirty years ago. He had changed more than his name. His speech, his manner-
isms, the strange look in his eyes when he asked questions had been acquired
since those days. This was a different man, a stranger.

After speaking a few words with Rizzi, Brooklier took Jimmy to another
room for a private discussion. Jimmy told him about Sinatra agreeing to do
a benefit for the Knights of Malta.

"Whatever we make on the skim, I'll cut you in for your end," Jimmy
promised.

"Yeah, Louie [Dragna] was telling me about that deal, sounds real good.
What about this guy Sinatra wants whacked? Got somebody looking for him?"

"Yeah, Mike's got his name and description but he's having trouble finding
him. This guy could have moved and you can't spend your life going to
racetracks looking for a guy with a handlebar mustache. But he's got some
feelers out in Burbank and Glendale. Maybe something will turn up."

"Let's find him," Brooklier said. "If we can do this favor for Sinatra there's
no telling what kind of money we can make with this guy."

Jimmy nodded. "You know, Dom, when I think about it, I wonder what
kind of favors Giancana did for Frank. They were close for years. After all,
you know, I don't know Frank all that good, and still he comes right away
and wants this favor in return for a favor. Makes you wonder, you know."

"You think he knows the benefit's a scam?" Brooklier asked.

"Dom, Frank's no fucking dummy. I told him our family needed to make
some fucking money. I don't have to give him a blueprint. But I know one

361

thing, Frank will take money under the table. Both Marson and DePalma told me they gave him fifty grand in cash, under the fucking table, after the April concert. They gave it to him while he was playing at Caesars Palace and Mickey Rudin heard about it and blew his top. This Rudin watches Frank like a hawk. Anyway, I don't know what happened. Last I heard they were dickering over it. What do I care, right? I've got my own problems."

"Oh, before I forget," Brooklier said, "I want you to tell Jilly Rizzo that Sam Sciortino's like you, without coming out and telling him that he belongs to the family. Sam's ready to get back in action as the underboss, so maybe he'll want to deal directly with Jilly on this Banjo deal. Besides, you know, Sam's got a house in Palm Springs and spends lots of time over there. Now, in about five or six weeks, I want you to take Sam and me over to Marson's house. We want to meet this guy."

Jimmy wanted to change the direction of the conversation. "By the way, how about making Mike a *caporegime*?"

"Sure. Louie was telling me he's a good man. Go ahead, tell him he's got it. Now what's happening with Bomp?"

"Well, I've got him kind of straightened out," Jimmy said. "He's not shooting off his mouth like he used to."

"That's not what I mean," Brooklier replied. "How do you get in touch with Bomp?"

"That's what I was telling Louie. Bomp goes home every day around three or four o'clock and never leaves the house at night. So we talk pretty often. I call him at his house and say I'll call him in ten minutes and he goes to the pay phone down the street."

"Who else contacts him this way?"

"Louie, Mike, Spilotro, and maybe Chris Petti. Him and Bomp are tight."

"Okay, you forget about Bomp, we'll take care of it. For the time being, just go on as you've been doing while I get back on my feet. It's been a rough sixteen months."

44
BOMP GETS BUMPED

† † † †

THERE IS PROBABLE CAUSE TO BELIEVE THAT THOMAS MARSON . . . ALAD-
ena T. Fratianno . . . Irving Shapiro . . . William Marchiondo; Jackie Presser;
Daniel Levine; Anthony John Spilotro . . . Alfred J. Pilotto . . . and others as yet
unknown, have been and are now committing offenses against the United States;
that is to say: being employed by or associated with . . . the Alfa Chemical
Corporation of Nevada . . . engaged in . . . a pattern of racketeering activity.
. . .

A confidential source, who for the purpose of this affidavit shall be referred to
as Source One, told Special Agent Jack D. Armstrong . . . that a small commercial
detergent factory was in the process of being set up in Las Vegas to supply cleaning
detergents to Las Vegas hotels.

Pilotto and Spilotro told Source One that the cleaning company was to be
"fronted" by Irving Shapiro and that money for the company was going to be
furnished by Thomas Marson . . . and from a loan from the Central States
Teamster Pension Fund.

[They] told Source One that the Teamsters loan would be arranged because they
"controlled" Jackie Presser. . . . [and] further told Source One that the chemical
company would easily get contracts to supply cleaning detergents to many Las
Vegas Hotels which are the recipients of loans from the . . . Teamsters Pension
Fund by threatening the hotels to either call these outstanding loans or threats
of "labor problems" at the hotels. . . .

Source Two, in conversation with Thomas Marson during early December 1976,
had learned that Marson had been in contact with William Marchiondo, an
Albuquerque, New Mexico attorney with close connections with the Governor of
New Mexico [Jerry] Apodaca, and Marson was attempting through Marchiondo
to obtain contracts to supply cleaning detergents to public buildings in New
Mexico. Marson explained to Source Two that this would require some sort of
kickback to the Governor and Marchiondo. . . . Fratianno told Source One that
. . . Marchiondo . . . is the "bag man" for . . . Apodaca.

For the ten years he was Jack Armstrong's ubiquitous Source One, Frank
Bompensiero enjoyed the best of both worlds. On the one hand he was permit-

ted to pursue his criminal career with impunity, and on the other he could use
the government to malign or dispose of his competitors and enemies. It was
an ideal arrangement, but in the end, however, he would become expendable
when the opportunity to catch bigger fish presented itself. On January 31, 1977,
he had ten days left to live.

To judge from the above FBI affidavit, Bompensiero was not always infallible
when he spoke on matters of criminal conspiracy. Whether this was due to lack
of information, clever distortion, or SA Armstrong's tendency to embellish is
of no particular importance except, of course, to those gratuitously included
in reports who futilely proclaim their innocence.

The original founders of Alfa Chemical were Irving Shapiro, Al Baron,
Tony Spilotro, Kin Adams, and Jimmy Fratianno. Each controlled twenty
percent of the company. Shapiro, Baron, and Spilotro invested $20,000 each
for their participation; Adams invested the chemical formulas; and Jimmy
invested his persuasive salesmanship. As he had done so often through the
years, Jimmy cut Bompensiero in for half of his end.

Jackie Presser never had any involvement with Alfa Chemical and Jimmy
never met Daniel Levine. The charge that the "chemical company would easily
get contracts to supply cleaning detergents to many Las Vegas Hotels which
are the recipients of loans from the . . . Teamsters Pension Fund by threatening
the hotels to either call these outstanding loans or threats of 'labor problems'
at the hotels" was either Bompensiero's or Armstrong's way of dramatizing
a fairly routine operation. Instead of threatening to recall loans, an assumption
that implies that Teamsters loans were somehow delinquent, Jimmy merely
picked up the telephone and talked to old friends.

For example, he called Morris Shenker at the Dunes and said, "Look,
Morrie, we're starting a new company, Alfa Chemical, and we're manufacturing our own cleaning detergents. Now I'm going to send Irving Shapiro over
there to see you and you direct him to the guy that handles that for you over
there. I'd appreciate your cooperation."

To Shapiro, Jimmy said, "Now, Slick, Shenker don't care about this shit.
He's going to send you to the man that does. He's going to say to this guy,
'Do what you can for this man, he's a good friend of mine.' Now what you've
got to remember is that all them guys are getting greased off when they buy
shit for the hotels. Nobody's going to switch from one outfit to another if he's
going to lose grease. So grease them. Don't fuck around, put your fucking
cards on the table right off the bat."

That was all there was to it. He made similar calls to Bernie Rothkopf at
the MGM Grand; to Jimmy Tamer at the Aladdin; to Henry Lewin, a close
friend of Rudy Tham, at the Hilton, whom Jimmy would get into the Knights
of Malta; to Benny Binion at the Horseshoe. As for the Stardust, Fremont,
Hacienda, and Marina, Spilotro got those through Lefty Rosenthal.

Early in the fall of 1976, Al Baron sold his interest in Alfa to Tommy

Marson, and later on in the year, when Proctor & Gamble started making noises, Spilotro bowed out, giving his percentage to Marson and Shapiro. Aside from the phone calls, Alfa Chemical was of little concern to Jimmy— it was just one more deal in a bulky portfolio.

One day while at his clothing store Jimmy received a call from Mike Rizzi. "Jimmy," he said, "I'll call you in three minutes." This was the signal for Jimmy to go to the pay phone across the street from his store. By the time he got there it was ringing.

"What's doing, Mike?"

"Jimmy, not too good. I've just been given a subpoena on that Forex deal to appear before the grand jury. You know the two guys that were running that porno outfit. Well, they're fucking FBI agents."

"What!" Jimmy screamed. "Are you sure?"

"Am I sure? They're the same guys that gave me the subpoena. They showed me their credentials and thought it was real fucking funny."

"Oh, I had a feeling about that outfit. Did you ever mention my name to them guys?"

"Jimmy," Rizzi said, "I only saw them once. But, Jimmy, I'm with you, I had this feeling about that outfit, from the very beginning I thought they were cops."

"Well, why didn't you back off?"

"I did, for Christ's sake. I even told LoCicero and Ricciardi that I thought they were cops, but they're so hungry for money . . . Well, they dragged me in there one fucking time. But what I want to know is where did that Bomp get the lead on that outfit? It was his fucking tip."

"Yeah, that's a fucking good question," said Jimmy. "Let's see if I can find the answer. I'll get back to you. Meanwhile, just take the Fifth and sit tight."

What Jimmy would not discover for a long time was that the inspiration for the FBI's creation of Forex had been the Murrieta Hot Springs luncheon observed by Special Agent John Larson and his wife. Jimmy's alleged remark of "Just give me a piece of the porno" to Dragna had been the catalyst.

Special Agents Jack Armstrong and Jack Barron, who had spent a good part of their careers chronicling the misadventures of Jimmy Fratianno, were so anxious to trap him that they were willing to sacrifice Bompensiero. They questioned Bompensiero and he confirmed Jimmy's interest in shaking down pornographers. After setting up Forex, they told Bompensiero that the FBI was interested in a new company called Forex, that it was making a lot of money selling pornography to Mexico and South America. They then suggested that he bring it to Jimmy's attention. They walked him out on a limb and sawed it off.

Now it was Jimmy on the phone and he was hot.

"What the fuck's the matter?" Bompensiero asked.

"Listen, asshole, who's the fucking guy that told you about Forex?"

"What do you mean?" Bomp asked.

"I mean what the fuck're you doing?"

"What the hell you talking about?"

"Bomp, that fucking Forex was an FBI undercover operation."

There was dead silence for a moment. "You kidding?"

"Where did you get the fucking tip? Who told you about this outfit?"

"Jesus Christ, Jimmy, you've got to be kidding."

"Bomp! Stop fucking stalling. Give me a fucking answer."

"Jimmy, it's just a guy down here that owns a porno store. Let me check this out and I'll get right back to you."

Two days later Bompensiero called Jimmy at Sal's.

"Jimmy, know the guy you was asking about, Bye-Bye Blackbird?"

"Bye-Bye Blackbird?"

"Yeah. Bye-Bye Blackbird."

It hit Jimmy like a bolt of lightning. For the first time in all those years, he understood what Roselli and Brooklier had meant when they called Bompensiero a wrong guy. He was a snitch and he had set them up. This "Bye-Bye Blackbird" was a last desperate shot and Jimmy knew that the last thing he wanted to do at that moment was to put Bompensiero on notice that he was wise to him.

"Okay, Bomp, I get you. You better cover your tracks. If it was a setup, they'll be looking for this cocksucker."

"Everything's cool, Jimmy."

"Okay, take care. Talk to you later."

No sooner was Bompensiero off the line than Jimmy was calling Bennie Benjamin in San Diego to ask him to check around to see if anybody had been reported as missing. But Jimmy knew it was a lie, that you didn't clip anybody in two days' time, especially someone supposedly working with the FBI. But there was something else that nagged at Jimmy, and that was Bompensiero's genuine surprise at hearing that Forex was an FBI operation. There was something there he just couldn't put his finger on, and it bothered him. Whatever his doubts before, he knew now that Bompensiero was a dead man.

Jimmy walked into Marson's garage as an acting boss and walked out a few minutes later as just another soldier. Brooklier sat in Marson's golf cart, while Mike Rizzi and Sam Sciortino stood nearby. Before Brooklier even spoke, Jimmy knew what he was going to say.

"Well, Jimmy, I'm feeling pretty good, so we're taking back control of the family. We appreciate what you did for us and we'll continue cutting up the money on the deals you've got going with Marson and the Sinatra benefit."

Jimmy took it without flinching.

"What effect do you think Sinatra's mother dying in that plane crash will have on this Knights of Malta benefit?" Brooklier asked.

"Well, he's cancelled the investiture," Jimmy said. "He was only doing it to please her. Christ, I've flown in that same Lear jet many times between Vegas and Palm Springs. Slick's a good friend of the owner. In fact, Tony Dope was in Vegas that day waiting to take that plane back to Palm Springs. It's a shame, that Dolly really had it good, big house right next to Frank's. Well, it's one of them fucking things, right?"

"Speaking about one of them fucking things, it looks like this grand jury is starting another federal investigation," Brooklier said. "They're going beyond that Forex deal."

"They had me up there. Somebody, either Ricciardi or LoCicero, mentioned my name to those undercover feds, but I took the Fifth," Jimmy said. "They had Bomp up there, too."

"Yeah, well, we're going to clip that cocksucker. This has gone far enough." Brooklier stepped out of the golf cart. "Well, Jimmy, again thanks for your help. Let's keep in touch."

Sciortino walked out of the garage without saying anything and Jimmy felt like he wanted to grab the handiest blunt instrument and pound him over the head with it. He shook hands with Brooklier and they walked outside. Sciortino was already behind the wheel of his silver Cadillac Seville. Jimmy stood there while they drove away, trying to control the anger building inside of him.

The touch of Rizzi's hand on his shoulder startled him. He had forgotten that he was there. "For whatever it's worth, Jimmy, I think you should be the boss. You've got more on the ball then all them guys put together and then some."

"Thanks, Mike. Look, I'll see you in the house in a minute."

"Okay, Jimmy, but I think it's a fucking rotten deal."

He walked away and Jimmy took out a cigar and lit it. Let them play the big shot all they wanted, let them scrounge around for a few measly bucks, in the end they were nothing but a bunch of losers. They had used him and thrown him out without even making him a skipper.

But he didn't need a title. Johnny Roselli never had a title but had been respected by people who recognized his ability and accomplishments. He achieved a status that went beyond a mere title. Jimmy felt he could do the same. A lot of good people respected him and even the New York bosses treated him as an equal. Jimmy resolved to maintain that status. He had no choice if he hoped to protect Marson's investment in the Premier Theater and share in the Sinatra benefit. They were in Los Angeles and he was in San Francisco. Let them go their way and he would go his.

Around seven o'clock one evening a few days later, while Jimmy was at Sal's, he received a call from Tommy Ricciardi.

"Jimmy, how're you, buddy, long time no see."

"Yeah, what's doing, Tommy?"

"Jimmy, I'm in San Diego. Are you going to call Bomp tonight?"

Jimmy hesitated. "Yeah, in about fifteen minutes."

"Okay, thanks, buddy, see you."

Jimmy went back to his booth and angrily crushed his cigar in the ashtray. So in the end they were using him for the setup and there was nothing he could do about it. Bomp had telephoned him earlier in the day to arrange for this call. Their timing, he had to admit, was pretty good.

Ten minutes later he walked across the street to the Hilton and used one of the pay phones in the lobby.

Bompensiero's voice came on the line and Jimmy said, "Hey, what's doing?"

"What's this I hear about Brooklier taking over? Where does that leave us?"

"I don't know about you, Bomp, but it leaves me fucking relieved. The more I think about it the happier I am to be away from them fuckups."

"You think Palermo's going to get back as *consigliere*?" Bomp asked.

"Bomp, if you want to know the truth, I don't give a shit, okay?"

"Yeah, okay, fuck it."

Jimmy wondered if they would shoot him in the booth, while they were talking, or wait until he was walking back to his apartment building. This was probably the last time he would hear his voice.

"Jimmy, I've got to get going, it's cold out here."

"Okay, good night, Bomp. Take care."

Jimmy went into the cocktail lounge and had a drink at the bar alone, something he seldom enjoyed doing. He liked being with people, talking business or telling stories, just bullshitting with the boys. He could visualize Bompensiero returning home, his squat body hunched over against the cold, the cigar stuck in a corner of his mouth, his eyes behind the horn-rimmed glasses warily peering in all directions as he hurried to the security and warmth of his home.

Jimmy was distracted for a moment by the thought that Bompensiero went home between three and four every day, spending all his evenings watching television with his wife. Jimmy couldn't visualize that kind of a life for himself. In fact, his latest conquest, Cindy, was one of the most beautiful girls he had ever known and she was crazy about him. She was insatiable and had told Jimmy that he was the only man who could truly satisfy her, that even her husband, a husky longshoreman less than half Jimmy's age, could not compare with Jimmy. It was the kind of compliment that kept a man going at full speed regardless of age. Meanwhile, Jimmy had bought a condominium at the Biltmore in Palm Springs for Jean and Annette. Geographical separation was the only thing that could save their marriage. Jimmy felt sorry for Jean. He knew she was lonely, but he had no desire to change his lifestyle. At least she had Annette and Jimmy saw to it that they were financially secure.

A half hour later, Jimmy dialed Bompensiero's home phone and when he heard his gruff voice he quickly broke the connection.

† † †

On Thursday evening, February 10, while Jimmy and Skinny Velotta were enjoying *cioppino* at Count Montefusco's restaurant, Sal Amarena burst through the door and ran to their table. "Guess what I just heard on the radio. They just hit Bomp in San Diego."

Velotta said, "Holy shit, are you sure?"

"What do you mean, am I sure? You think I'd be here if I wasn't sure? What do you think, Jimmy?"

Jimmy reached over and broke off a piece of Italian bread to sop up some of the sauce. "What do you mean, what do I think? If you say he's dead, he's dead. It's one of them fucking things. Sit down and have some wine."

SAN DIEGO MAFIA CHIEF,
A REPUTED INFORMER,
SLAIN

Frank (Bomp) Bompensiero, the 71-year-old Mafia chieftain who was shot to death near his San Diego home Thursday night, had been an FBI informant for the last 10 years of his half-century crime career, law enforcement intelligence sources said Friday.

Bompensiero, a long-time associate of top organized crime figures and rumored candidate for overlordship of West Coast gangdom since the death of Los Angeles Mafia kingpin Nick Licata in 1974, was gunned down near his expensive Pacific Beach apartment where he had lived for the last four years under the name of "Frank Gavin."

Police said the killer, probably using a silencer-equipped automatic pistol, pumped four .22-caliber bullets into Bompensiero's head as he returned from making his nightly series of phone calls from a pay phone booth he used because he believed his home phone was tapped. . . .

—San Diego *Union,* February 11, 1977.

45
"BILLY" MARCHIONDO'S DREAM

† † † †

WILLIAM "BILLY" MARCHIONDO HAD A DREAM TO END ALL DREAMS, and the man he chose to help him realize his dream was Jimmy Fratianno. Of course, when it came to dreams of casinos, Jimmy was the man to talk to.

Described in the FBI's affidavit on Alfa Chemical as a "bag man" for New Mexico Governor Jerry Apodaca, "Billy" Marchiondo, as his friends called him, was a wealthy and prominent criminal lawyer who was more of a king maker in his sparsely populated state than a bag man.

Until Billy was introduced to Jimmy Fratianno, his closest Mafia-type friend was Jimmy "Nap" Napoli. Prior to making the introduction, Tommy Marson had carefully briefed Marchiondo on Jimmy's acting-boss status with the Los Angeles family. Marson was proud of his man, and was quick to acquaint special friends with Jimmy's lofty role in the underworld.

Following their initial meeting in the late fall of 1976, Jimmy and Billy became fast friends, each measuring the other in terms of what could be derived from their relationship. This required lengthy conversations over drinks, and Marchiondo, like Marson, was a serious drinker, easily downing three and four drinks to Jimmy's one.

Billy was also a serious gambler, especially when he was drinking. "Goddamn," Jimmy would tell Marson after one incredible night at Caesars Palace, "this Billy gets drunk and goes crazy. He's got a line of credit there that won't quit. You never see money changing hands. He just keeps on signing fucking markers. Shooting craps the other night he got ahead about a hundred twenty-five grand, then lost it plus another seventy-five, then came back and won fifty. Most of the time he don't know what he's doing, for Christ's sake."

Yet, in many ways, they spoke a common language. They were connoisseurs of the art of quid pro quo. They had known instinctively that they could make money with each other.

In early December 1976, Jimmy had gone to Albuquerque for a visit with his friend Billy. At Marchiondo's office that afternoon, the lawyer gave Jimmy a demonstration of his political power in his home state. When a phone call came in from former Senator Joseph M. Montoya, Marchiondo put him on the "blower" so Jimmy could hear both ends of the conversation. Montoya was calling to ask whether Governor Jerry Apodaca had already picked someone for a judicial vacancy that had just been created.

"Jerry's coming in on Wednesday for lunch and I'll ask him," Marchiondo said.

"Well, Billy, if you don't mind, I'd rather see you move on this right away. No telling what can happen between now and Wednesday."

"Okay, Joe, let me ring him and I'll get back to you."

Marchiondo pushed the button cutting off the connection and shrugged. "Excuse me, Jimmy, this will only take a minute."

He dialed and when the governor's voice came on the blower, Marchiondo said, "Jerry, just got a call from Joe Montoya wanting to know if you've selected anyone yet for that judicial appointment."

"No, I haven't, Billy. Does Joe have someone special in mind?"

"Look, Jerry, don't move on this until I see you on Wednesday. Take care, buddy, I've got to ring off. I've got somebody in here waiting for me."

Marchiondo called Montoya and told him to sit tight, that he would get back to him before the day was out so they could discuss his candidate.

Marchiondo smiled at Jimmy. "This guy [Apodaca] owes me a big one but I've never asked for it. I haven't needed it yet."

"What about Alfa Chemical?" Jimmy asked. "You going to ask him to tie us into the state with Alfa?"

"Jimmy, that's nothing. Know what I mean? I'm talking about something only a governor can give you. Something really important. Right now I don't know what the fuck it could be but when the time comes I'll know."

It was while having drinks at Pojo's that first evening that Marchiondo unveiled his magnificent dream.

"Jimmy, remember how Bugsy Siegel got money from various families to build the Flamingo? We talked about it last time I saw you in Vegas."

"Sure, but I told you Benny fucked with the money and you can't do that with them people," Jimmy said.

"I know, Jimmy, but listen to this idea of mine. I own a large tract of land across from the Tropicana . . . I'm in this with Johnny George . . . and by the way he was telling me about the Crystal Bay and Alioto. Well, why can't we get several families together on one fantastic hotel-casino? I figure we could do it for a hundred twenty-five million. A thousand rooms, great fucking casino, huge showroom, with the latest and best of everything. In my opinion, the only way you're going to make a dent in that town today's by going in there with the biggest and the bestest. The days of breaking in small are gone forever."

"It's a great idea," Jimmy said, his eyes widening with anticipation, "but the big problem's my people don't put money into joints. They come in and give you protection for their end."

"Come on, Jimmy, I know for a fact that the Genovese family had money in Caesars Palace. How about Detroit in the Frontier and the Aladdin, Kansas City in the Tropicana, Chicago in the Stardust and Freemont? Shit, there's so many of them."

"Billy, you can hide a million here and there, but a hundred twenty-five million? How're you going to hide that kind of money? You're an attorney, you're supposed to be smart, tell me how the fuck to hide it?"

Marchiondo smiled. "Jimmy, don't worry. Get me the money and I'll show you how it's done. Look at Kirk Kerkorian at the MGM Grand. Where did he get his millions? I'll tell you, loans from foreign banks. All right, how much of that money was laundered mob loot? Maybe none of it, but the point is clear, that's one perfectly safe way of doing it. Get money in and out of any tax-haven bank and you can take your secret to the grave. It's really no big deal. It's done every day."

"Another way's for the families to get the money through the Teamsters," Jimmy said.

"Right, like Shenker and Glick and Dalitz, a whole bunch of guys. Jimmy can you get me to represent the Teamsters?"

Jimmy nodded. "I'll bring it up to Jackie Presser. Introduce you to him and you take it from there."

Marchiondo was getting excited. "My understanding, Jimmy, and if I'm off limits here, you tell me, but I'm told you've got solid gold connections with most of the big families . . . like Chicago, Cleveland, Detroit, New York, and they're the ones with the money."

Jimmy nodded thoughtfully. "There's truth to it but I ain't going to elaborate on it."

"Jesus, why not take this proposition right to the commission. Lay it all out for them."

"What have you got on paper? I'll tell you what, Billy. Give me a package, all the plans and figures, the works, and I'll get it to the right people. But, you know, you don't get millions from them people with a fucking fairy tale."

Marchiondo reached over to touch Jimmy's shoulder. "Hey, that's great. This is my big dream. I've had this dream a long time but I never knew anybody like you, Jimmy, that could carry out that end of it. I'll get you the package, but it'll take a few months. Meanwhile, if you get the opportunity, send out feelers."

"Listen, Billy, I know of a place that's up for sale right now in Jackpot, Nevada. You can get it for two-point-five million and it's a money-maker."

"Where the hell's that?"

"It's on Highway Ninety-three as you drive north from Wells, Nevada, toward Twin Falls, Idaho."

"That's nowhere. Jimmy, I can get five million from Dick Bokum anytime

I want. He's the richest sonovabitch in New Mexico. But I'm saving him for a big one."

"That's the story of my life," Jimmy said. "Nobody wants a bird in the hand, it's always two in the bush that always die before you get to them."

Marchiondo laughed. "Jimmy, you want a bird in the hand, I'll give you one. I'm on the board of Bokum Resources and I've got what you call insider information. I'm going to give you a surefire tip. If you want a short-term investment with a guaranteed high profit, buy some Bokum stock right now. It will jump to seventy, eighty dollars in a couple months. Being on the board, I can't buy it for you, and this stock can only be bought by New Mexico residents, but if you want to invest, or can get a friend to do it, I'll show you how it's done."

"Hey, that's great," Jimmy said. "I know this guy Joe Durtz from Houston who owes me one."

"Have him call me, Jimmy. Tell him to invest up to ten thousand and I'll show him how to do it. You've got my word on it, you'll make a quick profit." (Joe Durtz bought 800 shares at $10 per share and within a few months the stock had jumped to $31. Jimmy told him to sell and Joe Durtz sent him $12,000 in cash by parcel post, having kept the extra $4,800 for tax purposes. As for Billy's dream of a spectacular casino, it never materialized.)

In its affidavit on Alfa Chemical, the FBI alleged that in a telephone conversation between Marson and Shapiro on March 25, 1977, Shapiro "told Marson that Governor Apodaca was flying in that night on a private plane with three other people and that he, Shapiro, was going to pick him up at the airport at 7:45 P.M. Shapiro told Marson that he was having the Governor's party 'comped' at Caesars Palace and into the Shirley MacLaine show. . . . Marson told Shapiro to handle the matter with the Governor as tactfully as possible."

The next morning Shapiro told Marson that he had the Governor's party nicely settled into Caesars Palace and was planning on talking business with Apodaca that evening. "Shapiro told Marson that Billy told him that the state paint contracts will run out in May and that the state uses 100,000 gallons of this paint every six months and that they could make a profit of $2.00 a gallon every six months. Marson told Shapiro to 'water it down and make $4.00 a gallon.'

The next afternoon Shapiro reported to Marson that he "had taken good care of the Governor for the last two days and 'everything is all set now. . . .' Shapiro told Marson that he . . . worked on the paint deal when he took the Governor to cocktails and later when he took the Governor's party to lunch. Shapiro told Marson that he had asked the Governor if there had been some sort of mix-up over there because it had been such a long time. Shapiro then told Marson that the Governor said that evidently Billy didn't do what he was supposed to do."

46
TWO FACTIONS

† † † †

THE SILVER CADILLAC SEVILLE STOPPED IN FRONT OF THE BILTMORE IN
Palm Springs and Sam Sciortino waved impatiently to Jimmy who was standing there with Jean. The power window rolled down and Scortino called, "Get
in, Jimmy."

"Where's Brooklier? I thought we're supposed to meet."

"Come on with me, leave your wife here. We're going for a ride."

Jimmy felt Jean grow rigid at his side and he pulled her away from the car.
"Jimmy, please, don't go, I don't trust him."

Jimmy smiled. "You've got to be kidding. That piece of shit. I'll tear his
eyeballs out if he gives me one wrong look. Take it easy, I'll be back in an
hour."

In the car with Sciortino, Jimmy said, "What's up?"

"Listen, you know we eliminated Bomp and there's more to come."

"What do you mean, there's more to come?"

"You'll see," Sciortino said.

They rode in silence to a condominium owned by a cousin of Sciortino.
Brooklier, who was sitting on a sofa, merely looked up when Jimmy came into
the room. With him was Dominic Longo, the El Monte Toyota dealer.

"Will you guys excuse us," Brooklier said, still not acknowledging Jimmy.
Jimmy took a chair next to the sofa. After they were alone, Brooklier turned
and looked long and hard at Jimmy but remained silent.

"What's up?" Jimmy said. "Are we going to play games?"

"Jimmy, I want to hear it from you."

"What do you want to hear?"

"I understand there's two factions," Brooklier said.

"What the fuck you getting at?" Jimmy asked.

"I hear you've got a crew of your own."

"Hey, let me tell you something, Jimmy . . . Dominic, or whatever your
name is today. While you were in the joint, I came here to try to do some good.
I went and grabbed a few people, tried to make some money for this family.

Do you remember I saved your life when I pulled you away from Mickey Cohen? What's this bullshit all about? Who's starting it? What the fuck do you mean two factions?"

"Jimmy, you've got a bad mouth, like Bomp, you know."

Jimmy could barely force himself to remain in his chair. "If anybody's got a bad mouth, it's Sciortino. Where'd you find that prick, anyway? He's been poisoning your mind about me. Look, if I've got a complaint I'll tell it straight to you. And you do the same with me. Don't go telling me about two factions. Don't try that Nick Licata shit on me. I've had that treatment once before and that's enough. Look, I transferred from Chicago to help you guys when Louie asked me. There's nothing in L.A. I want. I hate that town. It's all yours, *Dominic.* You're welcome to it."

"Your living in San Francisco makes no difference," Brooklier said. "You're still a soldier in my family. You understand that, I'm the boss?"

"I don't want to fight you. Say what you've got to say and let me get out of here. And one last thing, what's Sciortino getting at when he says, 'We eliminated Bomp and there's more to come?' "

"Tell those guys to come in."

Jimmy went to the door and waved to Longo and Sciortino who both hurried into the house. "Now that they're here, Jimmy, I'll tell you what Sam meant," Brooklier said. "There ain't going to be no more bullshit around this family like there's been in the past. Anybody that don't chalk the line's going to get hit in the head." He paused for effect and then turning both thumbs down, he said, "I made the call when Bomp got hit. That's the way it's going to be from now on. Cut and dry. No more bullshit."

Sciortino was grinning. "By the way, Jimmy, we want you to get ahold of Chris Petti and tell him that LoCicero's going to San Diego to take over whatever Bomp had going down there. We hear Petti's tight with Spilotro and they're running around Adamo and LaMandri like they ain't even there."

Jimmy smiled. He could have told them that Adamo and LaMandri were weak sisters and rich enough not to want to bump heads with Spilotro and his crew. Instead he said, "Sure, I'll talk to Petti. Want me to talk to Tony?"

Brooklier shook his head. "Just get the word to Petti. That should do it."

That evening Jimmy had a good laugh and good news at Marson's house.

"Jimmy, I saw something at Frank's [Sinatra] house the other day that really floored me," Marson began. "You know, Vinnie [Albanese] is buying Frank's mother's house so he can be even closer to his idol. Now he's going to be right next door. We were at Frank's, doing a little drinking, and this fucking Vinnie drops to his knees in front of Frank's chair and starts kissing Frank's hand, like he's a fucking God or something.

"Holy shit," Jimmy said. "I wouldn't do that for the fucking Pope."

"As you know, Jimmy," Marson said, "Frank and I have become pretty friendly since he's joined the Knights of Malta. And I always know when he's home, he flies the Knights of Malta flag. It's really funny. Vinnie idolizes Frank and now that he's seen Frank's flag, he wants to join the Knights. I told him it'd cost ten grand. So we'll give Ivan five for his expenses and cut up the other five. I'm thinking of going into business with Vinnie."

"Wait a minute, Tommy," Jimmy said. "What about our real estate deal with my builder friend in Westborough?"

"Jimmy, forget him. You're with me; whatever deal I go into, we're partners. In fact, Vinnie wants to take Frank's boy in with us. Junior's not singing no more and Frank wants to get him into business. So I told Frank, get him with Vinnie, he's buying a lot of land around Rancho Mirage and builders always need cash. Jimmy, believe me, this comes from the heart. When we start building around here, we're going to build you a deluxe house, one of them free jobs. I've already talked to Vinnie about it. I'd like to have you right here in Rancho Mirage with me. It's time you started enjoying life."

Although the alleged criminal conspiracy in the Alfa Chemical investigation resulted in no indictments, the initial wiretap on Marson's phone produced such a volume of perplexing revelations that it led to a plethora of wiretaps, including the business and home phones of Gregory DePalma in New York and four of Jimmy's phones in San Francisco, including the pay phone across the street from his clothing store. Transcriptions of the tapes ran into thousands of pages, a great deal of it fatuous nonsense, but some sections are of particular interest to this story. Quite often the conversations were purposely vague and last names were seldom used. In the case of Jimmy, he was variously referred to as "Doc," "Doctor," "Doctor Schwartz," "Schwartz," and sometimes as "The Croaker." A few abridged excerpts follow:

—9:02 P.M., 4/10/77—MARSON: "Here, say hello to the doctor. Go ahead." JIMMY: "Hi, pal." DEPALMA: "Hey, buddy, Happy Easter." [They have a veiled discussion about the importance of seeing Mickey Rudin to set up a date for the Knights of Malta benefit.] JIMMY: "Here, say hello to Billy." MARCHIONDO: "How come every time I call you're out?" DEPALMA: "I got you the message though where he was, right?" MARCHIONDO: "You're the champion. How's that joint doing?" DEPALMA: "Struggling away there." MARCHIONDO: "You know I got some good people up there that you know. They tell me you guys are putting that show [Knights of Malta benefit] on for them. I'll talk to Tommy about it here. Anyway, I'll be looking forward to seeing you come to New Mexico." DEPALMA: "Yes, as soon as I get a chance."

—2:32 P.M., 4/11/77—JIMMY: "Hello." BROOKLIER: "Hi, how are you?" JIMMY: "All right. What's doing?" BROOKLIER: "Oh, not too much. Listen, you know that guy I talked to you about the other day, B.B. [Benny Binion] up in Vegas? . . . I want you to take Jack [LoCicero] and go to this guy and tell him, you know, we got problems down here. . . . And we need help." [It was a halting, awkward conversation. Brooklier wanted Jimmy to grab Binion and shake him down for more money and Jimmy displayed little enthusiasm for the idea.] BROOKLIER: "You know we need help and you, you guys can help us. So what the hell do you want us to say?" JIMMY: "Well, why take what's his name. I . . . I think . . ." BROOKLIER: "Because, I'll tell you why. This way, after that if, if for any reason we have to go, I can send him." JIMMY: "The only thing you know, the guy's been whacked so many times." BROOKLIER: "Oh, yeah, but not by us." JIMMY: "Well, sure the old man [Jack Dragna]." BROOK-LIER: "Oh, that was . . . You're talking about a hundred years ago."

—8:21 P.M., 4/15/77—MARCHIONDO: "What're you doing?" MARSON: "I'm watching the kids in the pool. They're diving in with the dog." MARCHIONDO: "This Dean Martin and Frank Sinatra show starts when?" MARSON: "May seventeenth and finishes the twenty-seventh." MARCHIONDO: "Can you get me twenty tickets? I want to pay for them." MARSON: "Well, that don't make no difference, Billy, because, hell, they're just all gone. Don't forget, we give each family three hundred. You know what I'm talking about? And there's five of them over there. Frank takes five hundred a night. I'll get you something, Billy. What night you want to be there?" MARCH-IONDO: "Okay, get me four or five for opening night."

—11:43 A.M., 4/16/77—DEPALMA: "That Lola Falana, I had a great big party here, must have had fifty fucking broads. I had them fucking bombed with champagne and brandy. She was paralyzed. I had her dancing on her butt all fucking night long." MARSON: "Who went with you?" DEPALMA: "That fucking ball breaker came, that fucking priest had to come stick his nose in. I had a broad with her skirt up. The priest's shaking his head, 'Greg, that's not nice.' " [Marson inquired as to the whereabouts of DePalma's wife Terri.] DEPALMA: "I got home before four-thirty bombed. Fuck, and her manicurist was in there, and I know I'm getting ratted out there." MARSON: "So how's Lola doing?" DEPALMA: "Terrible. I gave a thousand tickets away for tonight. This is a bomb."

47
ON THE FRONT PAGE

† † † †

IT WAS A COVER STORY IN THE MAY 16, 1977, *TIME* MAGAZINE, WITH THE title: THE MAFIA/Big, Bad And Booming. Jimmy blinked twice when he saw his name in the lead paragraph: "New Orleans Mafia Boss Carlos Marcello has doubled his force of bodyguards and shipped his family to a safe haven out of state. New York Don Aniello Dellacroce confuses his enemies by sometimes having a look-alike impersonate him in public. James ("the Weasel") Fratianno, a high-level mobster in San Francisco, rarely goes anywhere without two hulking companions. Other Mafia chieftains start their cars by remote control just in case bombs are wired to the ignitions."

Jimmy couldn't believe his eyes. The gist of the story was that the Mafia was in a state of unrest since the death of "Don Carlo Gambino, who as *capo di tutti capi* had brought a measure of peace to the nation's Mafia families through guile, diplomacy and strong-arm discipline."

Jimmy smiled. How they liked that boss-of-all-bosses bullshit: "The Mafia is overseen nationally—but loosely—by the commission, a dozen or so dons who usually, but not always, defer to the dominant boss in New York because he controls the most men and rackets. He may not get his hand kissed as often as Marlon Brando and Al Pacino did in the *Godfather* films, but he is first among equals. Since Gambino's death, two New York dons have been competing for his crown as *capo di tutti capi.*" The competitors were identified as Carmine Galante, boss of the old Bonanno family, and Aniello Dellacroce, described as the new boss of the Gambino family.

Both Galante and Dellacroce were freshly out of prison. Dellacroce was the underboss and Paul Castellano was the new boss of the Gambino family, and Nick Marangello had been running the Bonanno family for years while Galante was in and out of prison. As for the commission, itself, it had long ago been reduced to six members: the bosses of the Chicago and the five New York City families.

Jimmy quickly skimmed through the story to see what else it had to say about him:

Fratianno, 62, is believed by police to have made up to 16 hits as the Mob's West Coast executioner. When the Gambino and Chicago mobsters decided in 1975 to move into the West, they tapped Fratianno as their point man. With their blessing, he recruited Rizzitello, now 50, a handsome stickup artist, who migrated to Los Angeles in the early 1960's because he wanted an easy racket and respect that he had never got from the hoodlums back home. Both were a long time coming, but now he is rising quickly in influence and power. Says a West Coast lawman: Rizzitello helped the Mafia take over 80% of the $100 million-a-year Los Angeles pornography business. . . .

Jimmy thought, "Wait until Brooklier sees this shit." Brooklier's name was not even mentioned. Skimming along, Jimmy's eye caught this observation about Spilotro and himself: "Spilotro, who operates from his modest, $55,000 stucco house, also watches over the Chicago Mob's investments in Las Vegas casinos and controls loansharking, narcotics and prostitution along the Strip. Says a Justice Department official: 'Spilotro takes a cut of all illegal activities of any consequence.' He spends much of his time traveling by private jet on Mob business in California, where he has helped Fratianno and Rizzitello guide new Mob involvements in narcotics trafficking, bookmaking, loansharking and extortion from legitimate businessmen as well as from illegal Mexican immigrants who work in garment-manufacturing firms owned by the mobsters."

At one time Jimmy would have enjoyed the publicity, phony as it was, but now was a bad time for it. He knew it would only inflame the already envious Brooklier and Sciortino. They might even convince themselves that he was actually involved with New York and Chicago in a conspiracy against them.

It sounded to him like the writer had repeated every lunatic notion ever dreamed up about their thing and dumped it into this one story. Here he was, hanging by the skin of his teeth, hustling every minute of the day and night just to stay afloat, and Brooklier and Sciortino were so desperate for money that all they could think of doing was to shake down Binion for a murder committed twenty-four years ago and paid in full many times since. Spilotro was nothing but a strong-arm errand boy. The thought that he could control loansharking, narcotics, and prostitution along the Strip was mind-boggling. It would be like trying to control three tidal waves with a machine gun. As for Mike Rizzi, he was so hard up for money he had robbed his own office supply business and was once more headed for prison.

Jimmy stopped in Cleveland on his way to see Sinatra's third concert in New York. He and Tony Dope met at "Blackie" Licavoli's house and from there the three of them walked over to the Roman Gardens.

"Do you realize it's been nine months since Leo [Moceri] disappeared," Jimmy said, "and them guys [John Nardi and Daniel Greene] are still walking around? What's the story anyway?"

Licavoli looked at Delsanter and they both smiled. "Well, Jimmy, we expect a development here pretty quick."

"Greene or Nardi?"

"Nardi," Delsanter said. "Let me run it down for you real fast. First of all, Butchie [Pasquale Cisternino] fucking up the first attempt on Nardi last September when he tried to mow him down from a moving car, for Christ's sake, really made our work a lot tougher. Ferritto got all excited but he's calmed down since. Now it's Butchie that's really hot. Nardi put the word out that all five guys that took shots at him 'are going to go.' Not long after that Nardi had a bomb put in Allie's [Alfred Calabrese] Lincoln and when Frank Pircio went to use the car he was blown to pieces. Then they blew up Gene's [Ciasullo] house."

"Hey, let me tell him this one," Licavoli said. "Last month they tried to put a bomb in [John] Delzoppo's Oldsmobile and Enos Crnic blew himself up doing it. We know that Henry Grecco made the package, packed enough shit in there to put the Olds into orbit."

"Butchie's taking all this personally," Delsanter said. "But, see, this Butchie knows how to make a remote-control bomb."

Licavoli leaned closer to Jimmy and lowered his voice. "Butchie's worked out a real cutie-pie scheme. He's got a car loaded with dynamite and he's going to park it right next to where Nardi parks his car at his Teamsters office. When he comes out to get into his car, all Butchie's got to do is push this little remote-control switch, it works like one of them gadgets you use to change channels on TV, and that fucking Nardi's going to the moon in little pieces."

"You mean it's already set to go?" Jimmy asked.

Licavoli smiled. "Yeah. Jimmy, you better get out of town before you're hit with a ton of heat."

"If there's one thing I don't need right now is more heat."

"Listen, did I tell you about that fucking Aiuppa?" Licavoli asked. "He told his people to have nothing to do with us until this shit's cleaned up. The miserable cocksucker."

It was four o'clock in the afternoon and Jimmy and Mike Rizzi were having a drink at some joint in New York when Tommy Ricciardi came in with his wife and another couple.

Rizzi touched Jimmy's arm. "If you don't mind, I'd like to bring Tommy over and introduce him to you as *amico nostra*. Brooklier made him a couple months ago."

"Sure, good idea," Jimmy said.

Jimmy was smiling but now he knew exactly what had happened. The moment the introduction was over, Jimmy grabbed Ricciardi's arm and pulled him to the side.

"Hey, Tommy, why did you call me that night about Bomp?"

"I wanted a trial run before the hit."

"Who was with you?"

"Jack LoCicero. You know, that fucking Bomp, he shit his pants when he saw me with the piece. He tried to give me a tough time."

Jimmy smiled. "How tough a time can a guy with four slugs in his head give you?"

Back at the bar, after Ricciardi had rejoined his party, Jimmy said, "So that's why they made that jerkoff. The shit never stops."

"Jimmy, believe me, I knew nothing about the hit," Rizzi said. "They told me nothing. I knew it was coming. Brooklier made it plain enough at Marson's garage that day, but I didn't know when. You want to know something funny? This Ricciardi's got a pacemaker. Some hit man, right?"

Jimmy shrugged. "It don't take no strength to squeeze a trigger. Just balls."

Again they kissed and hugged when they met in the greasy spoon cafe. They sat at the same little table and the old man was still wearing his coat and hat. Funzi Tieri looked exactly the same as the last time. Since the sitdown when they had voted the contract on Joseph Ullo, Tieri's underboss, Eli Zeccardi, had disappeared and the talk was that he had been kidnapped by an Irish gang demanding a $200,000 ransom, which was not paid. Since then Tieri's soldiers had supposedly caught and killed the four or five Irishmen involved. There was another story that said Tieri had ordered the murder of Zeccardi and had invented the Irish story. As Jimmy so well knew, treachery went with the territory.

After politely inquiring about each other's health, Jimmy got right down to cases: "Funzi, we've got a little problem here."

"What is it, Jimmy?"

"Well, you know, I talked to you about my man, Tommy Marson, and the one-point-four million he represents in the theater. Now that they've gone into Chapter Eleven he's really getting worried. He thinks he's going to lose his money. Last October I talked to Fat Dom [Alongi] about it to make sure this guy's money's protected and I helped Fat Dom when he wanted Sal [Cannatella] to take charge. Now I'd like for you to reassure me you'll talk to Fat Dom to make sure my man don't blow his fucking investment."

"Jimmy, no problem. You tell your man he's got nothing to worry about. How's everything in California?"

"Oh, just fine."

"I see where you cleaned up your family," Tieri said.

"What do you mean?"

"Well, that Bompensiero guy that was fucking around with Bonanno got hit."

"Oh, right," Jimmy laughed. "It took some doing. Them old-timers, you know, are wise to all the tricks."

Tieri nodded. "Been to Cleveland lately?"

Jimmy grinned. "Yeah, I just got the hell out of there in the nick of time."

"Pretty clever how they blew up that Nardi. Give my best to Blackie next time you see him. You know, I respect a man that can take care of his own family."

Marson looked anxious. "What did the old man say?"

DePalma, Marson, and Jimmy were having a drink in the West Lounge at the Premier Theater. "Everything's cool," Jimmy said. "He says you've got nothing to worry about."

"So what's the latest on the Knights of Malta benefit? Are you getting anywhere with that prick Rudin?" DePalma asked.

"You've got to know how to handle this Mickey," Jimmy said. "I saw him at Tahoe. Frank played Harrar's in March, and I went up there with Rudy Tham. This Mickey starts telling me that everybody tries to go around him. He says, 'It's funny, Jimmy, when they go to Frank he always consults me. A guy would do better coming to me first, save a lot of time.' So Rudy and I had a couple broads and we went upstairs and shook hands with Frank and he asked us if we wanted to have dinner and I told him we'd eaten already. We chatted a few minutes and then I talked to Mickey about a date for the benefit. He says, 'Jimmy, why don't we have something else instead of a show.' I'm looking at this fucking guy like he's lost his mind. I says, 'I would rather do a show at the Premier Theater.' He says, 'Well, let's think about it.'

"Mickey gives me sixteen tickets for Frank's performance at the Circle Star Theater, which Frank did in April, and now I get together with the owner of the Circle Star, Donjo [Medlevine], a guy I met in Chicago back in fifty-two with Caifano. In them days, Donjo owned the Chez Paree. Now he's one of the biggest guys in the theater business. In fact, he's got the Music Hall here in New York. So we're talking and he says, 'Frank's coming to the Music Hall in January, why not do two extra days for the Knights right there.' I go see Mickey and I says, 'Look, if we can't do it at the Premier, let's do it at the Music Hall.' He says, 'That's fine. Let's think about it.' Then I get this phone call from Louie Dome, he's with Frank at Caesars and he wants to know how July at the Premier sounds. By now I'm so confused I don't know what's coming off."

"Them fucking guys," DePalma said, "are up and down like honeymoon pricks, goddamn yo-yos or something. I don't trust none of them. Mark my word, we're going to get fucked on this deal."

Jimmy nodded and thought of Jilly Rizzo who kept after him on Celamtano. Jimmy was getting tired of saying they were still looking for him. It made him feel like he wasn't holding up his end of the bargain. Finally, at Tahoe, Jimmy had told Jilly that since he lived in San Francisco, he had turned the contract over to Sciortino.

—6:12 P.M., 5/19/77—DEPALMA: "You should've seen the nice time I had with him [Sinatra] last night. Just all alone. No Louie, no nobody, pal. Him, Barbara, and Jilly. Period. And I didn't even push myself on to go, you know what I mean?" ELIOT WEISMAN: "Well, it's good that you did go." DEPALMA: "Forget about it, I'm out with him tonight." WEISMAN: "Yeah. Where you going?" DEPALMA: "Maybe Sergio's tonight. I'm going to meet him and Dean. He wants me to take Dean out. He says, 'Greg, you've got to get him out of his fucking shell.'" WEISMAN: "You're going to be taking a chance taking them over to that joint. The other guy [Louie Dome] will go crazy." DEPALMA: "What the fuck do I care. I told Louie I went with them to Gregory's last night." WEISMAN: "What did he say?" DEPALMA: "'What do I give a fuck. Let him go where he wants.' That was his answer. Believe me, I was talking to Frank all about the joint last night. If we could get some financing. About seven and a half million dollars. He says, 'We'll talk a little bit. Me and you.' I said, 'It's hard to talk. To sit down with you. There's so many people breaking your balls.' I says, 'I ain't looking to break your balls, but you don't know what I'm going through over there.' He says, 'I got the gist of it in the dressing room.' He says, 'You must be responsible for ninety percent of the money here.' I says, 'Oh, yeah, easy, believe me.' He says, 'Let's sit down and talk a little bit.' You see, if the other guy [Mickey Rudin] wasn't involved with him, you know what I mean? I could jockey this guy into position, like, forget about it, because I'll tell you one thing, Eliot, he's the classiest guy you'll ever meet, this cocksucker." WEISMAN: "True." DEPALMA: "He's a fucking sweetheart. I'm supposed to play golf tomorrow with Dean Martin. But he's drunk as a fucking log. He wanted to play today. He can't. So he wanted to play the other day, forget about it. Frank says, 'Wait, let's wait until next week. I'll take him with me and you. We got to get him out of his shell.'" WEISMAN: "What's wrong with this guy?" DEPALMA: "The broad. He's flipped out over the broad. He's gone, this guy. He's fucking gone. He came in the dressing room, he says, 'Hey Greg, what's the password?' I says, 'What password?' He says, 'Don't you know the password?' I says, 'No.' He says, 'It's swordfish tonight.' This is a sick fuck."

—10:35 A.M., 5/20/77—DEPALMA: "He's [Louie Dome] a cocksucker." MARSON: "Why, certainly. He's so fucking jealous. Listen, if they play golf, split Frank and Dean. Let me play. I don't want to play with fucking [comedian] Pat Henry." DEPALMA: "Tom, everything you play by ear here. When we get there, we'll make all the arrangements." MARSON: "Let me play with one of them guys. I can do some good there, 'cause this fucking joint you know ain't going to last. You know that. You told me Frank's ready to move. Right?" DEPALMA: "Yeah." MARSON: "Well, sure, we could make a ton of money out there with Frank. Ah, boy, I mean, we come out there, Greg, what the fuck, eh, Jesus Christ, I've got that big builder, Vinnie Albanese, he wants to open a nice joint in Vegas. Plush. We'll make some fucking scores, you know. Let me get the fuck back to California, Palm Springs, San Diego. If you don't like Palm Springs, you'd love San Diego." DEPALMA: "He [Sinatra] told me last night that Mickey's coming in Tuesday and he wants to put his money right up. He says, 'I'm going to straighten that out with Mickey and Tom when Mickey gets in.' I'm telling you, Tom. I spoke about you more than I spoke about anything. I says, 'They think he's a dumb Polack.' I says, 'Frank, this guy made more fucking money by accident than we could've made on purpose.' I says, 'Well, not you really because you've got the voice, but put a guy on the street like him, forget about it.' I says, 'And then if you give him five dollars or five million, you could go home, go to bed, don't even worry about a quarter with him.' " MARSON: "Well, that's right. Which is the truth."

—6:48 P.M., 5/20/77—DEPALMA: "We only played nine holes." WEISMAN: "What do you expect?" DEPALMA: "When I went this morning to pick up Dean, Frank was in the fucking hallway. He says, 'You can't do that and give him anybody to play with. I've got to play with him.' But he should of stayed home." WEISMAN: "Why?" DEPALMA: "He's awful. Both of them are awful." WEISMAN: "I thought Dean Martin was supposed to be pretty good." DEPALMA: "Ah, he's fucked up. This guy's on pills. Forget about it. He's got the shakes. His fucking head's gone. He played horrible. Frank, on the fifth hole, he says, 'Let me tell you something, if you'—I made three pars in a row—'if you make one more fucking par, or if you beat us, you guys [DePalma and Fusco] will go on the stage tonight and we'll play the lounge.' So I says to him, 'Do you see that bullseye? Hit the ball over the bullseye.' He hit a fucking house." WEISMAN: "Who did?" DEPALMA: "Dean Martin. Frank says, 'Oh, oh.' But Frank can't play at all. Dean, you could see at one time he could play. He started the last two, three holes, he parred. But the guy is junked up though. Definitely, definitely." WEISMAN: "He sure as hell looks it." DEPALMA: "Definitely. I don't know, I can't figure it. I feel so sorry for him, fuck it. I'm going over to the joint. You coming over?" WEISMAN: "Yeah." DEPALMA: "I'll see you there. We'll talk a little bit, alone."

For the second time in a month, Jimmy made *Time.*

Mixing Business and Pleasure

"When I look out through your windows," crooned Frank Sinatra, "you make me young again, even tho' I'm very old." Ol' Blue Eyes' rendition of *I Write the Songs* brought his audience to its feet last week at the Westchester Premier Theater in suburban Tarrytown, N.Y. So did Co-star Dean Martin's antics.

The twelve-day run was virtually a sellout, but not all eyes were on Frankie and Dean. A few were on the audience which included top Mafiosi from New York and other parts of the country. Among them were Jimmy ("the Weasel") Frantianno of San Francisco, Mike Rizzitello of Los Angeles, Tony Spilotro of Las Vegas, Russell Bufalino of Scranton, Pa., and several associates of Philadelphia Boss Angelo Bruno.

What had brought the Mob chiefs together was a series of powwows with New York City Mafia bosses about the new Mob power structure. (TIME cover, May 16.) TIME has learned that the Western gangsters reported on the progress they have made in expanding their rackets. . . .

En route to New York, Fratianno stopped off to visit Mob friends in Cleveland. That same day, John Nardi, 61, who was feuding with Young Turks in that city, was torn apart by a bomb as he started his car. . . .

—*Time,* May 30, 1977

There was no end to it, Jimmy thought. At this point it had ceased to be amusing. Yet, when he thought of Blackie and Tony Dope as "Young Turks," he had to smile. As for Spilotro, who had never been to the Premier Theater, he wondered if Aiuppa would smile when he thought his errand boy had made a trip without his permission.

The San Francisco *Examiner* followed it up with a picture and a banner headline in lower case, all above the logo and taking up about one-third of the page:

is he S.F. mob boss?

There is an organization called the Law Enforcement Intelligence Unit that helps some 40 cooperating police organizations around the country keep tabs on known mobsters. There are LEIU files on [18,000] thousands of alleged crime figures.

LEIU file No. 1 belongs to James Fratianno of San Francisco, known as "Jimmy the Weasel."

Insiders have told the *Examiner* that Topic A [in New York] was drugs—how to divide nationwide drug distribution.

For San Francisco law enforcement agencies the question now is: What is Jimmy Fratianno up to?

There was more. There was the usual reference to the "16 hits." Yet with all that great surveillance, the "police aren't sure exactly where he does live. But they know he is running his clothing store and although they suspect it is a front for narcotics or some other illegal operations they have been unable to pinpoint illegal activity."

This was followed by a lengthy two-parter in the Berkeley *Barb*. The headline of the first story was "Jimmy the Weasel": Profiling the Mob's Elusive S.F. Point Man."

In the midst of all this hoopla, Billy Marchiondo came to San Francisco on two separate dates, June 7 and 13, to visit with his good friend, the now nationally renowned Jimmy Fratianno.

Marchiondo checked into the Holiday Inn in Chinatown and Jimmy picked up the tab. That first evening they dined at the Imperial Palace, one of the city's fanciest Chinese restaurants, and the Teamsters union, through the generosity of Rudy Tham, paid the bill.

Waxing eloquent on the merits of his Star-Glo briquettes, which he was planning on incorporating in Nevada in a few weeks, Marchiondo told Jimmy that Marson had promised to invest $20,000 and that Shapiro was taking Marchiondo to Chicago to raise $200,000.

"You getter get in on this thing," Marchiondo told Jimmy. "All you've got to do with these briquettes is to put a match to them. No more messing around with lighter fluid. We'll cream the competition. It'll revolutionize home barbecuing."

"I'm already in," Jimmy said. "I've got a piece of Tommy's end. We're partners in everything. That's my main man."

"All right, Jimmy, that's great."

Jimmy puffed on his cigar and his expression turned reflective. "Tell me something, Billy, you're a fucking lawyer. What's a point man?"

Marchiondo laughed. "Now, Jimmy, if you were a cowboy, I could tell you."

"Well, tell me."

"When you've got a trail herd, you've got two cowboys riding point up front on each side. They're the guides, setting the course. They're supposed to know where they're going. I guess that's you, Jimmy."

It was Dennis McDonald's opinion that people's reputations usually exceeded them. Although he had read the stories about Jimmy, he remained convinced that Jimmy was a harmless human being incapable of harming anyone. He admired Jimmy's intellect and ability to maneuver, to put deals and people together; his amazing memory and shrewd calculating mind fascinated him to the point where the evil reputation became a troubling enigma. The two were totally incongruent in his mind.

He enjoyed Jimmy's company, particularly when they went to Las Vegas. Here Jimmy reigned supreme. He was treated like a visiting shah, except that they weren't after his money. Everything was on the house. Jimmy's suite at Ceasars Palace was always filled with people paying homage. On this day, there were Tommy Marson, Slick Shapiro, Mickey Fine, Mike Vallardo, Freddy Fox, and the way they were behaving toward Jimmy was incredible. They seemed to idolize him.

When McDonald came into the room, Jimmy was telling them about his last encounter with Joseph Alioto.

"I was at his cousin's restaurant, Frank Alioto's, over at Fisherman's Wharf, with a bunch of guys and I'm parked in the lot across the street. So who do I see as I'm going to my car?" He paused and puffed on his cigar. "Joe and his Boston debutante. I says, 'Joe, what's doing?' He says, 'Jimmy, how are you?' He opens the door and she gets in the car. So I grab him. Now we're face to face, and I says, 'Joe, what the fuck you going to do for me? What's your story?' Now he's trying to slip by me and I'm just standing there. He says, 'Jimmy, some other time. I'm with this lady and I have to go now.' I says, 'Just one fucking minute, you cocksucker. I could have buried you in that lawsuit and I didn't say a fucking word to nobody. What are you going to do for me? Let's have it in the open.' He says, 'Jimmy, I'm still suing *Look,* please stay away from me. You know, I'm engaged to be married, please give me a break,' and he scoots around me like a fucking rabbit, scared to death. I says, 'Joe, you've got a billion dollars but you're nothing but a cheap prick. Go on, get the fuck out of here.'

"I ain't seen him since, but I had a real funny incident at the TWA Ambassador Room in Frisco. I was going somewhere and I dropped by to say hello to Irene Valley, who runs it, and I rap on the door and this other gal opens it.

She tells me it's Irene's day off, so I says, 'Tell Irene that Jimmy Fratianno was here and I'll catch her on my way back.' I come back the next day and Irene says, 'Do you have any idea of the excitement you caused here yesterday? Joe Alioto was sitting in the corner over there and when he heard your name he got absolutely frantic. He demanded to know what flight you were on, and she didn't know, of course, and he started calling all over the place to see if you were on his flight, and he kept saying he wasn't going on the same plane with you.' So Irene says, 'What in the world have you done to that poor man?' I says, 'Irene, forget it, I think the guy's got a screw loose since he met this Boston debutante.' "

At dinner that evening, Jimmy and McDonald were joined by Candi and Ronda, Mickey Fine, and Howard Cook, a small-time hustler Jimmy had met at Chino. The conversation was light and pleasant. At one point, Jimmy reached in his pocket and brought out a diamond-studded wristwatch which he casually handed to Candi, who squealed with delight. It was a $500 watch which Jimmy had picked up at Sal's for $40. Candi and Ronda were so beautiful that McDonald had first thought they were showgirls, but later learned they were models, whatever that meant in Las Vegas.

Around eleven-thirty Jimmy asked if anyone wanted to see a show and Candi said she would like to see Dean Martin at the MGM Grand. Jimmy asked for a telephone to be brought to their table, took out a little address book, dialed a number, and said, "Hey, Carl [Cohen], what's doing? I'm bringing a party of six to see the show. Okay, see you."

And they were off in two cabs for the MGM Grand, where Jimmy, who led them directly to the front of a long line of people waiting to see the midnight show, was immediately recognized and courteously escorted to one of the best tables in the house. Although Jimmy left some money for a tip, no bill was presented.

Except for one bad moment, that was the way it went for the weekend. Wherever they went, everything was free, and the best was none to good for Jimmy. It was an impressive performance. That bad moment came when McDonald found himself in a warehouse on the outskirts of town with Jimmy, Freddy Fox, and three other men, and was shown a horse-racing machine. This was a new solid-state electronic version of the earlier model that had been designed by the engineer that had gone to Bally for six months and had never returned.

In the meantime Freddy Fox had gotten two New York investors to put up a hundred thousand dollars in the development of a new machine, and when a dispute had arisen over the ownership of the machine, the investors had taken the model and put it in storage. Fox had told Jimmy that he had stolen enough parts to build another one, and now that it was built, they formed a corporation and Jimmy received 200,000 shares. That was when McDonald discovered why he was in that warehouse. Jimmy asked him to act as nominee for his shares. Since a gambling device has to be licensed, it was necessary for Jimmy to hide his ownership.

McDonald looked at Jimmy and Freddy Fox and the three strangers, hard-looking men, and suddenly realized that he was faced with a serious decision. It was obvious that Jimmy had told them that McDonald was his attorney, had probably described him in glowing terms, and McDonald knew that his response would place Jimmy in an embarrassing position, but he had no alternative. It was a traumatic moment when he said, "I'm sorry, Jimmy, but there's no way I can involve myself with this machine and hold shares in my name for anybody."

He waited for the explosion which never came. Jimmy said, "Well, that's fine, Dennis. I'll put them in somebody's else name." They returned to the hotel and to the great relief of McDonald, Jimmy never again mentioned the incident.

From the way Jimmy was conducting himself, it was impossible to tell that he had been stripped of his authority. Like his friend Johnny Roselli, Jimmy felt that power had nothing to do with a title.

PART XIV

† † † †

THE CONTRACT
1977

48
THE DOUBLE CROSS

† † † †

AGAIN, "TONY DOPE" DELSANTER, JAMES "BLACKIE" LICAVOLI, AND JIM-my met at the Roman Gardens in Cleveland. Delsanter looked at Licavoli and said, "Jimmy, Brooklier has started some shit on you. He sent Dominic Longo and Sam Sciortino to Detroit to say you're going around the country misrepre-senting yourself. They went to Detroit and then Carlo Licata and Jackie Tocco came to see us."

"Them cocksuckers knew better than to come directly to us," Licavoli said. "They know how close you are to this family. I told them it was bullshit, that we knew the whole story, that you was acting boss while Brooklier was in the joint. But, listen, Jimmy, them guys are up to something, laying the ground-work. I know they also went to Chicago."

"This's crazy," Jimmy said. "It's them stories in *Time*. Fucking jealous cocksuckers."

"Jimmy, they denied Brooklier made you acting boss," Delsanter said. "They said Louie Dragna was the acting boss and all he asked you to do was shake down a few porno guys."

"So what're the cocksuckers up to?" Jimmy asked.

"I don't know," Licavoli said, "but it don't sound good. Something's hap-pening. My advice is you better straighten it out fast. Look, Jimmy, I want to do what I can to help, so you go to Brooklier and have him call me. I want him to say it to my face, then I'll go to Chicago and Detroit and straighten it out."

But back in California, Jimmy was unable to reach Brooklier.

On June 24, 1977, for the first time in over a decade, each of the five New York families initiated ten new members. Among the fifty were Jimmy Napoli and Gregory DePalma.

—7:28 P.M., 7/8/77—DEPALMA: "You know this is between me and you. Don't say nothing. This guy [Jimmy] ain't what he's going around saying he is, you know."

MARSON: "Oh, I know that. They changed it." DEPALMA: "They changed my ass. They got . . ." MARSON: "No, they did. I knew it a long time ago." DEPALMA: "Don't even, don't say nothing. Boy, I tell you, you know, this guy had better watch himself." MARSON: "I was . . . I know that. Ah . . ." DEPALMA: "I don't even know if he had the right to do that thing with that Mike [Rizzi]." MARSON: "Yeah, yeah, yeah. Yeah, they were all here." DEPALMA: "They were all there, you know, the other day, all the guys from Chicago [Aiuppa and Cerone]. The top guys." MARSON: "I know, but at that he was . . ." DEPALMA: "Well, don't even say nothing that I said anything." MARSON: "No, you kidding. What's the matter with you?"

—2.43 P.M., 7/13/77—JIMMY: "You were crying poverty and now you're in La Jolla for a month. Well, God bless you. What's doing?" MARSON: "Nothing. I know you were in New Mexico." JIMMY: "That's right. I told you I was going. You talked to Billy [Marchiondo]?" MARSON: "Well, he called me about a week ago." [There follows a discussion of Jimmy's Palm Springs condominium and the possibility that he will move the location of his clothing store.] MARSON: "Say, I'm going to tell you something, but Greg told me not to tell you. You know, the people in Chicago, you know?" JIMMY: "What about it?" MARSON: "Well, that you misrepresent, you know what I mean?" JIMMY: "Who told them?" MARSON: "That you're not the [he spells it out] B-O-S-S wise, which I knew, you know." JIMMY: "Well, who told him that?" MARSON: "The guys from Chicago were in there.

—4:02 P.M., 7/14/77—JIMMY: "What's doing?" DEPALMA: "How're you?" JIMMY: "Listen, I talked to what's his name, you know. Whoever told you that is full of shit. There was another fucking rumor in Detroit. I had to straighten that out. You know what I'm talking about?" DEPALMA: "Yeah." JIMMY: "Just tell them they're full of shit. They better check their fucking information." DEPALMA: "Well, I tell you, there were some guys in from Chicago. They said it to Paul [Castellano]." JIMMY: "Well, you tell Paul what I said. What happened, see, some guy went back there and I had to straighten it out. I was pretty hot, you know." DEPALMA: "Yeah." JIMMY: "And when I see you, I'll explain to you something else. Things are, you know, pretty bad." DEPALMA: "Yeah." JIMMY: "We got to, you know, forget about it." DEPALMA: "All right." JIMMY: "And you tell Paul that." DEPALMA: "I will certainly take care of it." JIMMY: "You know, they're lying. They ain't supposed to talk like that. You know I'm thirty some years in there, you understand. I had to go back to Cleveland to straighten it out. So now what do I have to do, go all over the world? You know, this is ridiculous."

—12:02 P.M., 7/15/77—MARSON: "I had company yesterday and they scared the shit out of my wife and my kids and, ah, they stopped, and I was getting my car greased and oil changed." JIMMY: "Uh-huh." MARSON: "They wanted to talk to me, so they start with the shit, that, this and that. They know all about the meetings at my house and this and that, they're telling me. They give me the dates and they know who the trigger guy is and then I says, 'Listen, why are you telling me all this? Why don't you go arrest them? The people you're mentioning, half of them I don't know. I was raised in Detroit and around Ohio.' I says, 'I know Jimmy for forty years.' Ah, well, they're going to the grand jury, you're going to the can and then they start telling me Mike Rizzi shoved down two FBI guys. I broke out laughing." [Jimmy chuckles.] MARSON:

"So, to make a long story short, they say, 'We're going to take you to the grand jury, your wife,' and all that shit. I says, 'Well, I can't stop you from doing what you ought to do. All I know is that they come over, have a few drinks and eat, and they don't tell me their business.' I says, 'You're welcome to come over and eat and drink any time you want.' Then he gives me his card, Mel Flohr, FBI in L.A. I ain't worried about me. I'm just worrying about Bobbi, you know. She says, 'What'll I tell them,' I says, 'Tell them the truth. I introduced you to all kinds of people.' But, ah, the fucking heat, the kids, my kid, Tammy, nine years old, 'Daddy, daddy, what'd the FBI want?' You know." [Jimmy keeps chuckling.] MARSON: "Fucking embarrassed me."

—4:56 P.M., 7/17/77—"Good afternoon, Caesars Palace." JIMMY: "Mike Vallardo please." VALLARDO: "Hello." JIMMY: "What's doing?" VALLARDO: "Oh, not too much. How've you been?" JIMMY: "Oh, so-so, you know. Just coasting along." VALLARDO: "Where are you, at a pay station?" JIMMY: "Yeah. Hey, listen, there's a guy from New Mexico, that lawyer, Billy Marchiondo." VALLARDO: "Yeah, he's here." JIMMY: "All right, listen, his partner, Val Torres, wants to come there the twenty-second, twenty-third, and twenty-fourth, him and his wife." VALLARDO: "Let me get a pencil. Here's someone who wants to say hello." DELSANTER: "What're you going to do?" [They talk Italian for a while.] JIMMY: "What the hell you doing there?" DELSANTER: "I just came for three days, going right back, I snuck over." JIMMY: "You got your girl there?" DELSANTER: "My girl's here, yeah," [Jimmy says something in Italian.] DELSANTER: "Took a long time, Jim. I'm catching up now." JIMMY: "Well, that's good. How's the keister?" DELSANTER: [Says something in Italian] "I've got to go [to the hospital] one more time. The doctor says it's [hemorrhoids] looking good." JIMMY: "Boy, that's good." DELSANTER: "Boy, it burns. But it must be doing all right. I'm getting along. I'm losing a lot of weight. What are you going to do?" JIMMY: "I'm going to try to come back for the fifteenth." DELSANTER: "I'm going to Chicago, you know, about the tenth." JIMMY: "The same old shit happened over there. Somebody from Chicago went to New York. The same bullshit you told me about. I'm going to bring [Brooklier] back with me, you know, maybe next month. We're going to New York and stop where you're at, you know. I'm going to stop this bullshit." DELSANTER: "Cocksuckers." JIMMY: [Sciortino's] a cousin of Carlo [Licata]." DELSANTER: "That's where the whole shit starts." JIMMY: "I don't know [Jackie Tocco]." DELSANTER: "What the hell, he's just as bad as the other kid [Carlo]. Stay the way you are, go by the old guys and that's it. What the hell, you ain't got no problem, have you?" JIMMY: "No, nothing. But, Tony, you know, it kind of hurts you. I've been in this thing some thirty years and this guy wants to just throw it down the drain. He wants to get credit, which is all right, you know, I don't give a shit." [Jimmy then talks to Marchiondo.] JIMMY: "Listen, Billy, there's a guy there, he's like my fucking brother. Ah, shit, you've got to meet this guy. He and I went to the can in thirty-seven together." MARCHIONDO: "Well, he's not around me, they let me talk by myself." [They discuss various business deals they are engaged in.] MARCHIONDO: "Well, I want to know, 'cause you know me very well." JIMMY: "Billy, forget about it. I know you like the rest of my life." MARCHIONDO: "Right." JIMMY: "I love you." MARCHIONDO: "Jimmy, I should have been born the same time you guys." JIMMY: "Right." MARCHIONDO: "But the problem's there's too many people try to get smart, try to get cute." JIMMY: "I know it."

—11:27 A.M., 7/18/77—JIMMY: "Rudy, honey." THAM: "What's doing?" JIMMY: "Ivan [Marcovics] called me. They got the whole thing set up for September. He's been trying to get ahold of you and you were out of town. I've got it all set up. They talked to the monsignor. They talked to the archbishop and the other guy under him. Everything's all set, they're going to do it in September. Now, Ivan's going to come out here. So I called Bob Chew [a Chinese businessman] and told him, 'Bob, they're going to have it in September if you come up with the fucking money. If you don't come up with your fucking money, you're not going in it.' " THAM: "Yeah." JIMMY: "You know what I mean? So now you've got to see Ivan. He don't know how in the fuck you guys want to do it. I talked to one of the main guys, from a foreign country and he happened to be in New York." THAM: "He's the guy who makes the speeches, the con man. He's the guy that handles the sword." JIMMY: "Oh, yeah. Well, anyhow, he says he can bring a few dignitaries in like a big rabbi. You know, somebody that don't belong to the order." THAM: "We don't want a rabbi!" JIMMY: "Well, wait a minute. Dress it up! A big, ah, rabbi, a big Protestant, you know. He knows how to dress it up." THAM: "I know this guy's a con man. JIMMY: "Yeah, well, this is it. They don't know how far you want to go. So if there's five or six you can get [Prince] Petrucci and the cardinal to come here. All you've got to do is pay the nut. Now, here's what the guy said, the archbishop. He says, 'God forbid if I happen to be someplace.' His understudy will take it. One of them will be here. The thing now, this fucking Chew, I told him. I says, 'Don't send no checks over there.' Rudy, you get the checks in your hand yourself."

He looked ten years younger, the heavy lines in his face having been smoothed out to give him the gentle expression of someone having a pleasant dream. Jimmy leaned forward and kissed the cold brow. He straightened up for one final look at the face he knew so well, at this man who had been his lifelong friend. They had stolen together as kids, had gone to prison together, had dated girls together, had eaten, drunk, talked, joked, laughed together, and now it was over forever. He would have trusted him with his life and would have risked his own for him. The bond they had shared had finally been broken by death, but the warmth of their friendship would be with him to his own final breath.

How quickly it had come. Only three weeks ago Tony Dope Delsanter had been at Caesars Palace when Jimmy had phoned to talk to Mike Vallardo. From there Delsanter had returned to Florida to be operated on for hemorrhoids and had succumbed to a massive heart attack. Jimmy first heard of his death from Mark Anthony. His body was flown to Warren and Jimmy was there when it arrived. His spacious home at 373 Central Parkway was filled with friends and relatives. His young girl friend and his stepson, a pilot, greeted everyone solemnly as they came to eat and drink and express their admiration for the deceased.

Jimmy and Blackie Licavoli stood together in the backyard and talked about their mutual friend.

"I'll tell you a real strange thing, Jimmy. You remember Mary? She was just a plain girl, you know, no flash, but real nice, and Tony Dope really loved that woman. They got along great until the day she died."

"Everybody loved Mary. She was good people," Jimmy said.

"Jimmy, listen to this," Licavoli continued. "Just about a month before he died, it's a funny thing, I was talking to Dope and suddenly he starts telling me about this dream he had the night before. Hell, you know, we never discussed dreams before. He says he has this dream about Mary, he's talking with her and can see her really clear, and she's young but he don't know what he is. He says to her, 'Honey, you wait for me, I'll be with you pretty soon.' Then he wakes up. What do you think about that, Jimmy? Ain't that strange? A month later he really goes to join her. I can't explain it, can you?"

Jimmy shook his head. "It's one of them coincidences. Maybe, you know, in his mind he knew he had not long to go. But I didn't know he had a bad heart. I knew he had the piles, but shit you don't die from that."

"Well, the old pump failed during the operation."

Licavoli reached into a pocket, brought out a sheet of paper, and carefully unfolded it. "Here, Jimmy, take a look at this."

Jimmy blinked and looked back up at Licavoli. "Where'd you get this?"

It was page two of a San Diego airtel to the Director of the FBI dated November 4, 1976, and captioned, "ROSKIL; OOJ, OO: Miami." It went on to say. "For further purposes of identification, this is serial 1005 in San Diego file 137-1088."

"What the hell," Jimmy said, "this's about Bomp's trip to Chicago with Spilotro. That's when he met Aiuppa. What he must have done is tell the FBI about his trip, that's how it got into this report. Bomp snitched for ten years."

Licavoli took the paper out of Jimmy's hand. "Okay, that's what I thought it was. Listen, Jimmy, we've got a connection in the FBI office here through some broad."

"Fantastic," Jimmy said. "Does this broad have access to all kinds of shit?"

Licavoli nodded. "We know there's four stool pigeons and we've got the names of two of them. Tony Hughes and Curly Montana. And we've got the code numbers of the other two and she's trying to get their names."

"You think she will?" Jimmy asked, trying to sound casual. "Who's this broad?"

"She's a clerk and she's got her ways of getting shit. See, the FBI gives all them stoolies code numbers which they use in reports but there's a list in each office that gives the names with the code numbers and what they've been paid."

"I know," Jimmy said. "But this's from San Diego and its about Chicago. What's it doing here in Cleveland?"

"That shit floats all over the place. Do you have any idea how many stoolies have been clipped in the past few years? Look at [John] DiGillo in New Jersey. He had a broad sneaking out FBI documents in her fucking girdle and she gave him the names of the two stoolies that were going to testify against him. They both got clipped."

"They caught that broad though," Jimmy said. "Remember the names of those guys?"

"Yeah, I read a story on it. One was Vince Capone and the other some fucking Chink called [Frank] Chin. But don't worry, we're being careful with our broad."

At the mortuary that evening, as the mourners knelt during the rosary, Jimmy never heard a word the priest said. His mind was in turmoil.

The woman in the FBI office was a threat to him. He remembered how Roselli had gotten the name of Dago Louie from a former FBI official. This was a loose organization. He had never told them anything of importance but still they had paid him $16,000. There had to be records of everything he said and every penny they paid him. Since he was from Cleveland and visited here often, it was only reasonable to assume that the Cleveland office had a complete jacket on him and it was only a question of time before that woman got to it. He was having enough trouble trying to straighten himself out without having this dropped on him.

If that happened, he would either have to kill them all or leave the country. And that brought up another problem: money. He needed to make a big score —at least, three, four hundred thousand dollars, maybe a half-million. If he pooled all of his present resources, he probably could raise a hundred thousand. The merchandise in his store was worth about twenty-five, thirty thousand and he had over sixty thousand on the street, but there was no easy way of converting any of it into ready cash.

The brutal truth was that he was stranded. Even if he could cash in everything, including his jewelry and Cadillac, his present net worth was just not enough. How long would he last in a foreign country with that kind of money? What he needed was a bundle big enough for him to live on the deposit interest paid by a foreign bank. Then he could lie back and relax, stop hustling for the first time in his life.

But where could he get that kind of money? There was only one way to make a big score, clean and quick, and that was dope. But how did one go about getting any at a good price? He would have to move cautiously, because now he was going against his own oath. It was ironic when you thought about it. The one thing he had been accused of doing all his life and had never touched could now be the one thing that could save his life if he didn't get himself straightened out pretty damn quick. But even if he could get back into the good graces of Brooklier, there was still the problem of how to go get rid of that woman in the FBI office.

The idea came to him while he was flying back to San Francisco and he mulled it over for three days before acting on it. But first, before burning his last bridge, he tried one more time to reach Brooklier through his son, Anthony, a Los Angeles attorney. Although he had known him since Tony was a baby,

Jimmy felt like he was talking to a stranger. Try as he would, he could not make him understand the importance of his meeting with his father. It was obvious that Tony was acting on his father's instructions.

"Hey, listen, Tony, I'm telling you I've got to talk to your dad. It's really important."

"Jimmy, dad's not feeling well. He's not seeing anybody. As soon as he feels better, he'll be in touch."

"Yeah, well, maybe then it'll be too late."

"I'm sorry, I can't help that."

"Okay," Jimmy said. "Just remember I've tried."

Although Larry Lawrence had retired from the FBI, Jimmy decided to bring his problem to him. Using a pay phone at the Hilton, Jimmy called Lawrence and without preamble told him that the Cleveland family had a connection in the local FBI office.

"Oh, my God, Jimmy, you've got to be kidding," Lawrence said.

"Hey, Larry, believe me, this broad's giving them valuable information. I'll give you the names of two of the snitches, Tony Hughes and Curly Montana. You check it out. But, for Christ's sake, Larry, you've got to promise to keep my fucking name out of this. My sister lives in that town. I'm giving you the information, but that's as far as it goes with me. Don't tell nobody I told you this. Keep it under your hat. Just say you got an anonymous tip."

"Jimmy, you call me tomorrow. I've got to move on this right now."

The dial tone came on and Jimmy was immediately sorry that he had made the call. The excitement in Lawrence's voice told him that this was something far bigger than he had imagined. He sat there with the receiver in his hand and stared unseeingly at people in the lobby. He had made a terrible mistake. He had not thought it through. This could raise a real stink, especially if Hughes and Montana were clipped. At any rate, the FBI would not rest until they had ferreted out the woman, plugging the leak and saving him from one fate while exposing him to another. Either way he was a loser.

49
THE PURSUER

† † † †

UNTIL FEBRUARY 1977, WHEN HE BECAME THE ASSISTANT SPECIAL AGENT in Charge (ASAC) of the San Francisco field office at the age of thirty-six, James F. Ahearn had spent most of his fourteen years with the Bureau as a "street" agent, developing informants among homosexuals, prostitutes, pimps, and junkies in some of the toughest neighborhoods of Detroit, New York, and Washington. He worked the "heavy" squad, robbery and burglary, and the data he gathered from his informants often proved invaluable in the area of organized crime. It was in the dingy bars of those cities that he received his real education as an agent and as a human being who could have compassion for the shattered lives of those who lived where he worked.

Jim Ahearn's father had been a New York City policeman nineteen and a half years, dying of cancer six months before he would have qualified for his retirement pay. A proud and jovial man to the end, he had remained a patrolman, passing up several opportunities to get into detective work because too many of the people in it were dirty. Fellow patrolmen would come to visit and their camaraderie and pride in their work made a lasting impression on the boy. He was nine years old when his father died but he knew what he wanted to do with the rest of his life.

Yet in 1956, during his third year at Bishop Loughlin High School in Queens, he was expelled for poor scholarship. At the time he was involved in gang activities and fighting had become a means of survival. It was the era of black leather jackets and ducktail haircuts. Everybody he knew was drifting, living for the moment, with no thought given to the future.

Then one day, as he was walking home, he was attacked by a gang of drunken kids, including some of his own friends, and was nearly killed. Police officers, who happened upon the scene, took him to the hospital. He had multiple bruises and contusions, including a broken arm, cracked ribs, two black eyes, broken teeth, and internal injuries. For a while he was on the critical list. During those long days of lying in a hospital bed, he resolved to change the direction of his life.

With the guidance of the family priest, he enrolled in Archbishop Molloy High School and began concentrating on his studies. But he had not forgotten the friends who had turned on him. Using his fists, on a one-to-one basis, he methodically got around to all of them, breaking their teeth and blacking their eyes, letting them know what it felt like to be on the receiving end. As his father's son, it would have gone against the grain to take a beating without retaliation.

From high school he attended St. John's University in Queens and worked nights as an FBI investigative clerk in the New York field office. From that moment on, there never was any doubt as to the branch of law enforcement he would devote his life to. He was married to his neighborhood sweetheart while he was in agent training school, but his real marriage was with the Bureau. The long hours at the work he loved finally destroyed the other marriage. But his ex-wife remained in San Francisco and he kept in close touch with his three sons.

Tall and heavyset, with blond hair and mustache, and with a nose broken enough times to give it character, Jim Ahearn's handsome features belied the toughness acquired in those years of working the street. By the time he met Jimmy Fratianno, Ahearn was determined to make him his prize catch. He had seen Jimmy's picture on surveillance photos, had heard his voice on wiretaps, had read endless transcripts until he felt he really knew his man. He had studied Lawrence's "Informant" file on Jimmy and knew he had a worthy adversary, which made the challenge all the more fascinating. There was no doubt in his mind that it was a game, a deadly serious one, but a game none the less, with the good guys trying to get the bad guys off the street.

As he waited in a hotel room with SA Charles "Chuck" Hiner for Jimmy to arrive, Ahearn said, "I've reread his file and I think it was a mistake to stop talking to this guy. He needed to be redirected, somebody to get him by the balls and say, 'Hey, we want solid information, not this drivel.' Now, maybe, we'll get a chance to do just that. And this time we'll squeeze until he cries uncle, but let's keep smiling while we're doing it."

"This really comes out of left field," Hiner said. "What is he up to? Why would he want to get the Cleveland family in trouble?"

"Chuck, he wants that leak plugged before it gets to him, but let's see what he has to say about it."

There was a knock at the door and Hiner opened it. Jimmy came in, shook hands with Hiner, whom he had met with Lawrence, and looked closely at Ahearn.

"This is my boss, Jim Ahearn," Hiner said.

"Are you the top man?" Jimmy asked, as they shook hands. "I told Larry I wanted to see the top guy."

"I'm the second banana," Ahearn said. "My boss, Charles ["Roy"] McKinnon, is out of town, and from what I understand from Larry, you want immediate action on this."

"What do you mean by that?" Jimmy said, looking from Ahearn to Hiner. "I just passed some information to Larry I thought he'd like to know. But, listen, I gave Larry the information, not the FBI, he's retired. I told him I wanted to be kept out of it. If you want to investigate, go ahead, but just keep me out of it."

Ahearn smiled. "If what you say is true, this is serious business. We don't want our informants killed. If there's a leak in the Cleveland family we want to plug it fast. To do that, Jimmy, we're going to need your help."

"Now just a fucking minute," Jimmy said. "My sister lives in Cleveland and Licavoli has helped my brother-in-law, nothing illegal, you understand, but still he owes him, you know. Listen, let me tell you, there's no way I'm going to put heat on my sister and her husband. That's one of the conditions under which I told Larry. Find out who it is but keep me out of it."

Ahearn sat down. "Jimmy, let's get one thing straight right off the bat. Larry's in no position to make deals. Besides, you know, you can't tell somebody something of this magnitude and then stipulate conditions. To be perfectly honest with you, Jimmy, you're the one who opened the bag, and like it or not you're going to have to help us catch that cat you let loose. We'll protect you and your family all we can. Now there's several ways to do this. For example, there's the Witness Protection Program."

"Hey, wait, what the fuck you talking about?" Jimmy said. "What's happening here? All I did was call Larry and tell him there's a leak in the office. Period. Do what you've got to do but leave me out of it."

Ahearn pinched his nose and stared at Jimmy through slits. "Jimmy, let's back up a minute. There's something here that puzzles me. If you're worried about your sister and brother-in-law, and I suppose Licavoli wouldn't be too happy with you either if he found out you had given us this information, why did you tell Larry? What was the motivation?"

"Hey, what's this motivation shit?" Jimmy asked.

"Did you notice if Licavoli was watching for your reaction when he showed you the report and told you about the informants?"

Jimmy laughed. "Shit, you're playing fucking games with me."

Ahearn kept smiling. "I'll tell you what, whatever your reason for your telling Larry, let's let it lie for the time being and direct our attention to the problem itself. You may think I'm playing games, but I'm going to ask you to go back to Cleveland and try to get more information. My question as to Licavoli's behavior was to make sure he wasn't checking you out. I wouldn't want to place you in a dangerous situation."

Jimmy shook his head. "All I know is that somebody got the information from a broad."

"Jimmy, I'll tell you what, we've got to sit down and work out a plan to get you back there for more information. Right now the Cleveland office thinks it's bullshit. They don't believe it. Let's make believers out of them. The sooner we yank that woman out of there the better it's going to be for everybody. Meanwhile, we'd like to start talking to you again on a regular basis. Can you find some excuse for going back this soon?"

Jimmy nodded. "Yeah, in fact, I'm taking a guy over there to introduce him to Jackie Presser."

"Are you going to see Licavoli?"

"Why sure. I can't talk to Presser without Blackie's permission. But now there's something I want up front. Whatever happens in Cleveland, grand jury or whatever, I've got to be kept out of it. There's no way I'm going to hurt my sister and her family."

"Jimmy, we'll protect you all we can, but from now on you've got to level with us. No more bullshit. Your secret's going to be between the three of us. No other agent will approach you. There's a lot of stuff we want to know about Cleveland . . ."

Jimmy stood up. "Hey, I've got to run, there's somebody waiting for me. But I'll tell you right now, if you're talking about Nardi and the bullshit going on out there, I know nothing about it."

As he said these words, Jimmy was convinced they were true. He had scrupulously avoided any envolvement. Aside from bringing in Ferrito, and receiving an occasional progress report, he had kept hands off. It was not like the old days, where he would have been right in the middle of it, doing more than his share of the killing.

Milton Holt, a labor consultant in Los Angeles, had a client in Philadelphia with a labor problem who needed a favor from Jackie Presser. Jimmy's fee for the audience with Presser was $5,000, plus expenses.

—5:48 P.M., 8/23/77—JIMMY: "What's doing?" CARABBIA: "All right." JIMMY: "Listen, I'm going to be in tomorrow night at five-ten. CARABBIA: "All right." JIMMY: "Get ahold of that friend, you know?" CARABBIA: "Yeah, well, he'll be there." JIMMY: "The dark guy [Licavoli], will he be there?" CARABBIA: "Yeah." JIMMY: "All right, we'll be there. I want to go right to his house, you understand?" CARABBIA: "Right." JIMMY: "Okay, I'm going to have somebody with me. Where's our friend from Erie [Ferritto]?" CARABBIA: "He'll be with me tomorrow." JIMMY: "Okay, then we'll get ahold of you sometime tomorrow night."

Jimmy arrived in Cleveland with Mike Rizzi and Milton Holt and that evening had dinner at a restaurant in Mentor, Ohio, with Licavoli, Calandra, and Lish. It was late in the evening before Jimmy had a chance to speak privately with Licavoli.

"So what's happening with Greene?"

Licavoli smiled. "Jimmy, we've got a tap on his phone. We know every fucking move he makes. It's only a question of time before we nail him."

"That's great," Jimmy said. "By the way, have you found out anything from that broad?"

"We ain't heard nothing. Might take a little time. She's got to be careful how she goes about it."

"What about this broad?" Jimmy said. "You think she could get information from L.A.? We've got somebody there that's informing."

"I don't think so, unless it's got some connection with Cleveland."

"That's really something about Tony Hughes and Curly Montana."

Licavoli shook his head. "Jimmy, sometimes, you know, I think this fucking outfit of ours is like the old Communist party in this country. It's getting so there's more fucking spies in it than members."

Jim Ahearn spent two days in a Cleveland hotel room waiting to hear from Jimmy, who made hurried calls to say that nothing new was developing. It was frustrating not being able to do anything, but by now Ahearn was convinced that Jimmy's interest in plugging the leak was certainly as great as his own. His life could well depend on it.

From Cleveland, Jimmy and Mike Rizzi went to New York and spent five days scrounging around the city trying to find a narcotics connection. Jimmy approached a number of made guys, including Greg DePalma, and told them he had a friend that was interested in scoring big on cocaine or heroin and would pay good money as long as it was high grade. They all denied knowing any connections. Before leaving he had discussed it with Marson and was told that Mike Fusco, of *French Connection* fame, was out of the business.

After his talk with DePalma, Jimmy turned to Rizzi. "What's going on? This fucking city's full of this shit and nobody knows nothing."

Rizzi had talked to friends in the Colombo family with the same result. "Well, Jimmy, like you told me when I was made, it's against the rules."

"I know, I know," Jimmy said, "but the rules are broken all the time."

"The way I see it, Jimmy, the families here deal with it like they do porno. They shake down dealers but don't touch none of that shit. What about them Mexican friends of yours in California?"

"Mike, you've got to buy it right if you're going to make some fucking money. Their stuff's garbage, cut forty times. See, if you can buy a kilo of high-grade junk or coke, let's say for thirty grand, you can clear a hundred grand on every kilo. Now, see, Skinny knows guys that can handle all we can get."

"Which is zilch, right?"

—11:00 A.M., 8/28/77—SAL AMARENA: "Hello." EVE MARKOVICS: "Hello, Sal?" AMARENA: "Yeah." EVE: "Hi, it's Eve. AMARENA: "How are you?" EVE: "Fine, thanks. How are you?" AMARENA: "All right, hon." JIMMY: "What's up, Sal?" AMARENA: "Ah, you finally did it, huh?" JIMMY: "What happened?" AMARENA: "Nothing, I ain't heard from nobody. Listen, you know, ah, Lou Scott,

Roger Scott's wife?" JIMMY: "What about her?" AMARENA: "She's flying into New York tonight. So I give her your number." JIMMY: "What do you mean?" AMARENA: "Well, she just wants to say hello, you know, I told her you'd, you'd like that, all right?" JIMMY: "Well, I'm going to be busy." AMARENA: "So, if you're not home, you're not home, that's all. You know, I just thought that would be nice." JIMMY: "Yeah, right." AMARENA: "So, how's Eve there?" JIMMY: "Very good, okay." AMARENA: "Yeah?" JIMMY: "Talk to you later."

—1:21 P.M., 8/28/77—AMARENA: "Hello." JIMMY: "Where's Skinny at?" AMARENA: "Right here." JIMMY: "Let me talk to that guy." VELOTTA: "Where you been?" JIMMY: "What do you mean, where I've been?" VELOTTA: "Hey, what am I going to do with that [football] line now Monday? Who do I get it from?" JIMMY: "Well, that, ah, Bennie [Barrish] is supposed to call you." [Jimmy wants to know if certain checks have come in and Velotta tells him of people trying to reach him. Then Jimmy gives Velotta false hope.] VELOTTA: "So how's everything going?" JIMMY: "Ah, all right, you know. Looks pretty good. I've got to get results, you know."

—2:00 P.M., 9/9/77—AMARENA: "Operator, I'm trying to call Albuquerque. This is an emergency. The number is five O five two four three one four O O." OPERATOR: "All right, you want to deposit two-fifteen for three minutes, please." AMARENA: "Hello, Billy? Billy?" MARCHIONDO: "Yeah, Sal, how are you?" AMARENA: "Fine, how are you?" MARCHIONDO: "Fine, Sal. I mailed you your [unintelligible]." AMARENA: "Did you send me one of the ones you had made?" MARCHIONDO: "Naw, because see they only gave me a couple. I want you to look at them, but you'll get one. It's solid eighteen karat gold." AMARENA: "Beautiful, love you, Billy. When you coming up?" MARCHIONDO: "Well, I can't come up. I've got to go into Vegas tomorrow night." AMARENA: "Well, shoot over here. We got some nice company here. Here's Jimmy." JIMMY: "Hello, what's doing? You get the sausage?" MARCH-IONDO: "Yeah, came in yesterday. Thank you." JIMMY: "Hey, don't forget now, when the Miami Dolphins play you're going to come over here. See, I got it arranged so you're going to sit with this guy [Edward DiBartola, owner of the Forty-Niners]." MARCHIONDO: "Well, I want to talk with this guy, but that's a bad time for me to leave." JIMMY: "That's when they play. How's the briquettes coming?" MARCH-IONDO: "Terrific. Sold all we could make." JIMMY: "You know, Sinatra's coming to Harrar's on the twenty-fifth. Now do you want me to connect to him about it?" MARCHIONDO: "He got two cases. Tommy Marson asked for two cases, we sent two cases to Frank Sinatra. So why don't you ask him, 'How do you like my briquettes?' Or whatever you want to say." JIMMY: "Well, I'm going to say, 'How do you like the briquettes?' I ain't going to tell him . . . you know, you're with me." OPERATOR: "You're now at the end of three minutes." JIMMY: "See, if you come for the game on the twenty-fifth, maybe on the twenty-sixth we could go up there [Harrar's]." MARCHIONDO: "Not a bad idea." JIMMY: "Well, let me arrange it and then I'll call. How about the property in Palm Springs? MARCHIONDO: "This guy that bought the property from Shenker, Bob Terry, I met with him and he has agreed to give us access to the property. So we made application to lease the property immediately behind that from the Indians, from the Bureau of Land Management." JIMMY: "Yeah, yeah!" MARCHIONDO: "And that's between us and him. And if we get that then we'll have about a hundred and seventy acres." JIMMY. "Oh, my God!"

MARCHIONDO: "Then we'll have to do something." JIMMY: "Let's not wait too long, Billy."

However intriguing the phone calls were, Ahern steered clear of them in his questioning. Jimmy was opening up on the Los Angeles family and giving him an education. It wasn't long before Ahearn sensed that Jimmy was in serious trouble and that Brooklier was the only one who could straighten him out.

By now Jimmy had closed his clothing store, turning over his inventory, valued at about $30,000, to Ray Giarusso's brother, Gino, who was opening a store in Anaheim. Jimmy spent most of his time at Sal's. The only contact he had with the Los Angeles family was Mike Rizzi, who made frequent trips to San Francisco.

On a visit in September, Rizzi told him that Brooklier wanted Jimmy to move to San Diego and take over Bompensiero's former operation.

"He's got to be crazy," Jimmy said. "No way am I leaving this town."

"Jimmy, here's what I heard. Jimmy Lanza blew his top when you got all that publicity and he sent his underboss, Bill Sciortino, who's a cousin of Sam, to say he wanted you out of town because you're bringing too much heat."

"Have you been talking to that cocksucker?"

"Jimmy, I ain't seen Brooklier in two months. Sciortino's running the show, or at least he's relaying Brooklier's orders. Know what he had me do? See, a while ago Brooklier and Sciortino met with Aiuppa, Batters, and Cerone. I don't know if they went to Chicago or met them in Palm Springs."

"You mean more shit on me?" Jimmy asked.

"Well, maybe that, too, but Chicago wanted a little pressure put on Moe Dalitz, who hasn't been coming across the way he's supposed to," Rizzi said. "So the idea was for me to grab him and he'd run to Chicago for protection. So I go to the Las Vegas Country Club, he's there every day playing cards. I grab him. I says, 'Hey, motherfucker, you ain't doing the right thing, understand? We're all done fucking around with you. We want a million dollars and you know who to contact.' This guy nearly shit his pants. I just turned around and walked out. Now, Jimmy, I'm telling you, between this Dalitz and that Binion, you've got something like a hundred and ninety-five years. Fucking unbelievable."

"Mike, you keep on top of it because Brooklier and those guys will get their end and never tell you a thing. I know how they work. They can't tell me they got nothing from those porno guys, Sturman and Gaswirth. Thieves. Well, I've got a piece of the Dalitz action. If they get anything from him, I'm coming down there and demand my cut."

"Jimmy, I wouldn't advise it," Rizzi said. "They're really down on you."

"Who gives a fuck. Tell me, who in that fucking town's going to do anything? LoCicero? Pinelli? Longo? Adamo? LaMandri? Polizzi? That fat piece of shit, Sciortino? Mike, the only guy in that family that can do some work is you."

"Well, Jimmy, you know, you've got nothing to worry about from me. I'm with you. But you've got to remember they're pretty tight with Chicago."

Jimmy grinned. "I know that, Mike. Listen, I got word just the other day from Marty Allen [a Los Angeles gambler] that he heard from Johnny George at the Dunes there was a contract on me. So Johnny's pretty friendly with Spilotro and maybe that's where he got it."

"You're pretty cool about it," Rizzi said.

"Mike, it's a rumor, and it ain't the first one. A porno guy here called me a few weeks ago and told me he heard the same thing from Phil Maita. See, Phil's grandfather's a made guy and maybe he heard Lanza say he don't want me around no more and maybe he told Phil if he don't get out of here he's going to get clipped. So what do you want me to do, go hide somewhere? Don't worry, I know this game. You're talking to an expert."

"If you say so, Jimmy."

"Mike, them guys are on an ego trip. My mistake was in getting transferred back from Chicago to L.A. I could have accomplished the same thing if I'd stayed with Chicago. Now I'm stuck with them bastards.

"Now here's what I want you to do, Mike. Try to get to Brooklier and tell him I've got to have a sitdown with him. We've got to iron this thing out. If you can't get to him, I want you to go see Russell Bufalino in Pittston. He's a good friend of ours and he's been around a long time. This guy's smart. Ask him for advice. Tell him the whole story and ask him what we should do about it."

"Okay, Jimmy, I'll try Brooklier first, as you say," Rizzi promised. "If that don't work, I'll go see Bufalino, but I just don't know when I can get away."

"Jesus, don't wait too long." Jimmy said. "Look, Mike, you're the last fucking friend I've got left that can do something in this fucking outfit. Don't let me down."

That evening Jimmy met with Ahearn, who would later write in his report that "Fratianno told the source [Ahearn] that he believes a strong possibility exists that a contract, in fact, has been issued but felt that if this had occurred it would not be known outside of the actual 'made' members of the LCN [La Cosa Nostra]. The source also learned that a contract of this type would have to be approved by the Chicago LCN 'Family,' specifically Joey Aiuppa, and that if the contract was to be carried out it would undoubtedly be handled by Chicago LCN members since pratically no one in the Los Angeles LCN 'Family' is capable of handling a contract of this type. Fratianno speculated to the source that while he trusts Rizzitello implicitly and believes he is the only one really on his side, the possibility does exist that Rizzitello could be used to set him up for a 'hit.' The source learned that Fratianno would be attempting to arrange a sitdown with Brooklier and attempt to get the matter resolved."

† † †

Over a cup of coffee at Sal's on October 12, Jimmy glanced at the front page of the *Examiner* and did a double take. The San Jose family had finally done some work but true to form they had botched it up. A man and his son, Orlando and Peter Catelli, had been found in the trunk of a Cadillac, alleged victims of a gangland slaying, except that the father was alive and talking his head off to the cops. The grisly details led to the arrest of Angelo Marino's son, Salvatore, and three others, but Angelo, not having forgotton Alioto's sagacious advice on how to thwart the legal system, had conveniently suffered a heart attack and had been hospitalized instead of questioned and jailed.

It would be nearly three years before Angelo would be well enough to stand trial and hear Orlando tell his story to a jury. The order for their murder had been given by Angelo while he sat behind his desk in the trailer office of the cheese factory. Angelo had told Orlando to take a knife off his desk and kill his son, Peter, who had tried to extort $100,000 from Angelo. When Orlando refused, saying he could not kill his own blood, Angelo, who was called Don Marino by the others, told him that he could kill him and "go home and eat my supper and it wouldn't bother me at all."

The five men took a vote and decided to "blow him away." It was while he was kneeling beside the body of his dead son, shot in the head by Salvatore, that Orlando felt a tremendous blow on his own head that sent him pitching forward on his face. He decided to play dead and when they kicked him he grunted and faked a death throe. Weighing 270, it took three men to lift him into the trunk and moments later his son's body was dumped on top of him. "Take a piece with you," Salvatore told the driver, "I think one of these guys is still alive." But an hour later the driver abandoned the car and Catelli banged on the trunk lid with a hammer until he was rescued.

For a moment Jimmy forgot his own problems. It had been years since he had seen or talked to Angelo. He smiled when he thought what Bomp's reaction would be to this story. He remembered Bomp telling him about the only contract Angelo had ever been asked to execute. He had delayed long enough for the government to deport the intended victim.

50.
CALLING IN THE TROOPS

† † † †

I. E. MICHAEL KAHOE, SPECIAL AGENT, FEDERAL BUREAU OF INVESTIGA-tion, hereinafter referred to as the FBI, being duly sworn, deposes and states as follows:

. . . Monday or Tuesday, the first week in October, 1977 . . . Ferritto was taken to a boat [at Mosquito Lake] believed to belong to a doctor where he met with James Licavoli, John Cisternino, and Angelo Lonardo. . . . A tape recording taken from the Greene wiretap was played and it was noted that Greene was to have a dental appointment . . . on Thursday, October 6, 1977. Ferritto agreed to attempt to kill Greene if he kept his dental appointment. . . . Wednesday, October 5, 1977, Ferritto drove the 1973 blue Plymouth previously furnished him by Pasquale Cisternino and Alfred Calabrese to Cleveland . . . where he was met by Cisternino and taken to an apartment. . . . Cisternino assembled a bomb in the presence of Ferritto and explained in a step-by-step procedure how the "package" would be detonated by a remote control switch. Ferritto and Cisternino left the apartment and Cisternino showed Ferritto a Chevrolet Nova which had the door altered by someone who had welded a thick metal box in the door. Cisternino explained that this would work as a blast director. . . . The bomb package was carried in a shopping bag, and Cisternino drove the Nova and led Ferritto and the Plymouth to the parking area of the office building which housed Greene's dentist.

The Chevrolet Nova was parked nearby, and Cisternino and Ferritto watched for Greene to enter the parking area. . . . Ferritto drove the Nova and parked it in an adjacent spot to the automobile Greene had been observed exiting. Cisternino and Ferritto loaded the bomb package into the welded box in the door of the Nova and armed the bomb. . . .

Ferritto then drove the 1973 blue Plymouth adjacent to a telephone booth where Cisternino pretended to be using the telephone. . . . When Greene was observed approaching his car, Cisternino entered the back seat of the 1973 Plymouth and Ferritto slowly pulled out into traffic. As Greene entered his automobile, Cisternino detonated the bomb contained in the door of the Nova by activating the remote control switch [that killed Greene]. . . .

(The only problem with the above affidavit was that it had the wrong man pulling the switch. The bomb was made by Cisternino, but it was Carabbia who detonated it. Asked in court six months later why at one time he had told the FBI it was Cisternino, Ferritto said that he was angry at Cisternino for furnishing him with a car that could easily be traced by police. "I felt that when Cisternino gave me the blue Plymouth he put me on 'Front Street.' ")

On October 18, 1977, Ray Ryan finally made Number One on Marshall Caifano's hit parade: *MILLIONAIRE KILLED AS BOMB DESTROYS HIS CAR IN INDIANA.* The AP story, datelined Evansville, Indiana, stated that Ray was killed "when a bomb of large dimensions demolished his automobile in the parking lot of a health spa." Ryan, it said, "acquired his wealth in the oil business and later owned a resort in Palm Springs and a gambling casino in Las Vegas. He also had joint ownership with film actor William Holden in the Mt. Kenya Safari Club in Africa."

Throughout October the pressure kept mounting. At one point Jimmy asked Louie Dragna to straighten out the problem but Dragna feigned ignorance. "Jimmy, I'll try to talk to Brooklier, but I've got problems of my own. The FBI's watching me all the time."

"Louie, you dirty motherfucker, you're in on the fucking play."

"Jimmy, don't get excited," Dragna said. "I'll do what I can."

"Louie, you're going to live to regret this fucking day. Now you believe me, you prick." Jimmy had slammed the phone down and sat in the phone booth a long time trying to get himself back under control. Later that day he again called Tony Brooklier.

"I still haven't heard from your dad," Jimmy said. "Tony, this's serious. You understand what I'm trying to tell you. This problem better get straightened out pretty quick or your dad's going to find himself before a fucking grand jury."

"A grand jury? What are you talking about?"

"I can't make it no plainer, Tony," Jimmy said. "You just tell him that. I'm all done playing games."

"Jimmy, I don't know what you're talking about, but I'll tell him."

"Tony, you're a fucking lawyer, try to guess what I'm talking about. You tell him I'm not calling no more. You've got my number. Your dad's cutting off his nose to spite his face and he's going to end up with his nose up his ass."

Rudy Tham was in trouble. A grand jury was investigating the alleged embezzlement of union funds to pay travel, hotel, and restaurant bills for himself, family, and friends, many of them organized crime figures. For years whenever Jimmy traveled to other cities, or friends visited San Francisco, or when he needed a hotel room for an assignation, he would call Rudy who would have his son-in-law, Joseph Hurley, the business agent for Local 856, make a reservation at the low Teamsters rate. Jimmy would sign for the bill and later reimburse Tham, who often paid the bill out of union funds and pocketed the money.

They were at Sal's and Tham was pleading with Jimmy. "They're subpoenaing Mike [Rizzi] and, Jimmy, you've got to tell this guy to say he was coming up here on union business."

Jimmy looked at him as if he had lost his mind. "Are you fucking insane? What're you trying to do, put him in the middle? I'm not going to tell him to perjure himself. For Christ's sake, Rudy, no jury in the world would believe that for a second. I'm going to tell him to take the Fifth, which I'm going to do."

"I hear they're going to call Marchiondo."

"That's no problem, he can claim lawyer-client privilege, and who can prove otherwise?"

Tham shook his head. "It looks bad."

"You asshole, why did you pocket the money? You know, Rudy, you're too fucking greedy. That's your fucking problem."

Jimmy was still looking for a narcotics deal. Finally it looked like Jimmy was going to make it. A friend of Ray Giarusso in Walnut Creek, Mike Buster, had a connection with customs in Taiwan and was planning on smuggling $400,000 worth of Thai sticks into the country if he could get a connection. The plan was to hide them in a furniture shipment. When Jimmy had all the facts, he went to see an old friend, a business manager of a Teamsters local, whose Teamsters unloaded container ships and moved the containers to bonded warehouses for inspection by customs. Jimmy's end of the deal would net him about $200,000, not as much as he wanted for his vanishing act, but it would have to do. He would cash whatever other assets he could and be gone in a flash.

Jimmy told him everything except how much money was involved. "This guy has extra seals. So the way I see it, we get Ray a job with your local unloading them container ships. This shit's coming in a container full of rattan furniture. Ray will pick it up at the dock and drive it to a warehouse where we unload it, reseal the container, and he drives it to the bonded warehouse. Simple fucking operation."

The business manager laughed. "Simple for you, maybe, but how do I get Ray a job here? I've got a list as long as my arm of my own people out of work. They have priority. It's going to take some time to sneak him in."

"I understand, but don't take too long. This guy could get himself another connection. We can make a good score with no risk to nobody."

"Jimmy, believe me, I'm with you. I'll do what I can. Have Ray stay in touch. At least, he's already a Teamster which is one problem out of the way."

Mike Rizzi brought disappointing news from Russell Bufalino. Jimmy had considered him a friend, and would have set up that witness with the pork store in Walnut Creek if he could have found him, but now, as he listened to Rizzi, he realized that Bufalino was also part of the play.

"Russ sends his regards," Rizzi was saying, "and he's sorry to hear about our problem."

"Our problem?" Jimmy asked.

"Well, I told him I was with you. Well, he knows that, you know. His advice, and this guy's got a lot of experience, is for us to go to Chicago and have it out before Aiuppa. I'll back you up, tell him, you know, these guys are twisting the truth. What do you think, Jimmy?"

"I think it stinks," Jimmy said. "Number one, it ain't going to do no good going to Chicago. Number two, they've got nothing to do with the internal problems of our family. He's trying to lay a trap. I thought he'd say fight your way out. Which you're supposed to do anyhow. I knew that but I wanted to hear it from him too."

"Jimmy, I'm sorry, but that's what the man said."

"Let's get something straight, something Russ knows goddamn well," Jimmy said. "I can't go to Chicago or no place else and undo what Brooklier's done. He's the fucking boss. He's an idiot but he's equal to all them other idiots. Nobody's going to side with me. Not even Blackie, for Christ's sake, not until he hears something from Brooklier. The rule in this thing of ours is to fight your own family battles. You settle it right with the family. I'm surprised Russ didn't tell you that, he knows the fucking rules, if you don't." Jimmy paused and looked hard at Rizzi. At this point Jimmy was thinking that Bufalino had probably told Rizzi that this had gone too far for anyone to help and he would be wise to give his allegiance to Brooklier.

"What'd you mean a while ago when you said he was trying to lay a trap?" Rizzi asked.

"Fuck it, Mike, I'm just disgusted with the whole setup."

Late one evening a few days later, Jimmy received a call at his Moss Beach home from Marshall Caifano, whose favorite alias was Johnny Marshall.

"Jimmy, baby, how you doing? Long time no see."

"Hey, Johnny, where you calling from?"

"Chicago. Listen, Jimmy, how soon can you come in here, it's important?"

"What? What do you mean, how soon can I come in?" Jimmy asked.

"Jimmy, I want you to talk to the old man."

"What about?"

"I want you to tell him you'll introduce me to the Cowboy," Caifano said.

"Why do I got to talk to Aiuppa? Why don't you go see Binion yourself?"

"Well, Jimmy, you know the guy. Tell the old man you'll introduce me."

"Johnny, I don't know what the fuck you're talking about," Jimmy said. "You know the Cowboy better than I do. What's this bullshit all about? Furthermore, if you want to talk to me, and it's so important, why don't you come out here?"

"Jimmy, what's the matter with you?" Caifano asked. "I thought we were friends."

"Johnny, don't bullshit me. Let me tell you something. If you want to see me, and it's so fucking important, come over here and I'll meet you at the airport."

"Jimmy, I don't understand what you're getting at."

Jimmy laughed. "I'm not getting through to you, that's for sure. Look, John, first of all you should've gone through the routine. Go to my boss and tell him to tell me to come back there."

"What if I sent you the fare?"

"John, forget about it. You want to see me, come here and we'll meet at the airport or in Palm Springs. I'm not going back there."

"Okay, Jimmy, see you later."

Jimmy slammed the phone down and thought, "Not if I see you first, you cocksucker. This's my fucking racket, I'm the fucking expert. Nobody's going to bury me in Chicago."

Jimmy sat by the phone a long time. The way he figured it, Brooklier must have asked Chicago for help and they had given Caifano a shot at him. Now logically they would turn it over to Tony Spilotro, telling him to do whatever he could to help Los Angeles, which was a good play for Chicago, giving them greater access to Southern California. A family that was too weak to kill one of its own members was too weak to protect its country.

He lay awake a long time that night and the next morning he knew what he had to do. Since he didn't have the money to escape, he had two alternatives: kill them or go into the witness program, as Ahearn had suggested. Either way, he was going to get them. Before he was finished, they would either be rotting in the ground or in prison.

Once Jimmy had decided on a course of action, it took him a few days to locate Champ Reynoso, a member of the Mexican Mafia he had met at Chino. They met in a bar in Oakland and Jimmy told him his plan.

"Champ, I've got to clip a couple guys and I need some help."

"Jesus, Jimmy, no problem, man. I've got a crew here, all top guys."

"All I want is you and one more guy. Keep it under your hat," Jimmy instructed. "There's going to be some heat on this so we've got to do it right."

"Jimmy, anything you say," Reynoso agreed. "Man, for you, Jimmy, I do it for nothing but I need expense money. I'm broke."

"Look, don't worry, you'll get expenses, and if we clip them fuckers, you've got a piece of what I do. I don't know if we'll make any money, I can't promise you a million dollars."

"Forget it, man, we can do you a favor, no problem. What's the score?"

"Two guys, maybe three," Jimmy said. "The first prick lives in Palm Springs, in the Sunset District. Here, I've got his name and address written down. Copy it. This guy's five-seven, five-eight, about two hundred pounds, looks like a little bull."

"How do you say his name?" Reynoso asked.

"Sciortino. Here's four hundred for expenses. Go to Palm Springs and check this guy out. Watch his house and see how we can nail him. This guy goes first, but I've got to get the other lined up before we make the hit. When this guy goes it's going to scare the shit out of the other guy. After we clip this guy, we'll go to my condo in the Springs. That fucking town's like an island. There's only one road leading in and out of that town. So we'll spend a couple days at my condo and leave one at a time."

"That's great, man, you've really figured this thing out. What about tools?"

"Don't worry about tools, I'll supply them. What I'd like to do is choke the cocksucker."

Reynoso laughed. "I'll bring a piece of rope, man."

"Okay, Champ, remember, only one other guy."

Reynoso stuck the money in his shirt pocket. "Thanks a lot, man. I'll call you at Sal's when I get back."

"Okay, but stay away from his joint. We'll meet right here."

On his drive back to San Francisco, Jimmy tried to figure out a way of discovering Brooklier's address. He knew he was living with one of his sons in Anaheim. When Brooklier had first come out of prison, Jimmy reached him through Tony who had told him to call a pay phone at a certain time. The first three digits of the number were the same as the number for Gino Giarusso's store in Anaheim, which meant that it was in that general vicinity. Chances were Brooklier lived close to the pay phone and was probably still using it. At this point Jimmy could have used Rizzi's help but he no longer trusted him. Somehow he had to find the location of that pay phone. His plan was to clip him right there, the way they had clipped Bompensiero, but in the daytime so that he could see it was coming from him.

51
RACE AGAINST TIME

† † † †

FOR JIM AHEARN IT WAS NOW A RACE AGAINST TIME. HE KNEW THAT JIM-my's life was in the balance. He had to turn him before they killed him. After Jimmy had told him about Caifano's phone call, Ahearn had done some serious thinking and had decided it was time to take a good shot at turning him all the way around. What he had to do was convince Jimmy that the Witness Protection Program was his last haven. There was a treasury of information locked in that brain and the challenge was to find the key to it.

The problem was that the tempo of Jimmy's activities had not slowed down. He was still working on countless deals as though nothing had changed. Yet Ahearn was doing his damndest to generate fear by telling him that he was hearing from various sources that there definitely was a contract out on him and it was only a question of time before they got him. During those sessions, Jimmy would get bitter when he talked about Brooklier and Sciortino, but on the whole he remained maddeningly under control.

As the weeks had gone by, Ahearn felt that a bond of respect was developing between them. He was beginning to like this guy, who could be so pleasant one moment and so obstreperous the next. This was a complex human being: He was uneducated but intelligent enough to talk with you on just about any level you chose; he could talk like a hood or like a gentleman, like a punk or a lawyer.

There was no question that Jimmy would make a fascinating psychological study. He had a sharp mind and an extraordinary memory. There was no doubt that he was an accomplished liar, could probably con the proverbial birds out of the trees, and yet so far, based on what Ahearn could corroborate with the wiretaps, Jimmy was being truthful with him.

From years of experience, Ahearn had developed a sense about the people he dealt with in his work. His first reaction when confronted by a hoodlum with Jimmy's background was to take everything with a large grain of salt. It took a continuing period of interrogation to alter that impression, but once altered Ahearn would thereafter have to be convinced that his confidence had been misplaced. When Jimmy continued to insist that he knew nothing about the bombing murders in Cleveland, Ahearn began to believe him. And when his counterpart in Cleveland, ASAC Joseph Griffin, argued that Jimmy was involved, Ahearn defended him. He realized, of course, that Jimmy was fiercely loyal to his sister and would do just about anything to protect her. He was strangely sensitive in this respect, his Achilles' heel, a weakness his enemies could effectively use against him if they only knew about it.

Using his code name, Frank Cost, Ahearn called Jimmy at Sal's on the afternoon of October 28 and told him he had to see him right away.

"Hey, that's impossible," Jimmy replied. "I can't meet you today."

"Jimmy, you've got to meet me. I'll see you at the usual place at six. You be there."

Chuck Hiner opened the door and Jimmy came in with his usual cocky walk. Ahearn nearly fell off his chair when he saw him. Jimmy was wearing a brown pin-striped suit, gleaming alligator shoes, a black shirt, and the gaudiest tie Ahearn had ever seen.

"Who are you, Al Capone?"

Jimmy smiled. "I'm going to the Hookers' Ball. That's a society event in this town. It draws all the big celebrities."

Ahearn struggled to maintain a grave expression. "Jimmy, sit down, will you. I'm sorry I had to insist on this meeting but I've just received a report from our Los Angeles office that I think you should know about."

Jimmy sat down and lit a cigar. "I know exactly what you're going to say. There's a contract out on me, right?"

"There's more to it, Jimmy. You know, we have some pretty good sources down there. What I'm going to tell you is not a rumor. We know who's got the contract on you."

Jimmy stopped puffing on the cigar. "Yeah, who?"

"Let me ask you a couple questions first, all right?"

"Go ahead."

"Have you heard from Mike Rizzitello lately?" Ahearn asked.

Jimmy nodded. "Yeah, I've had a couple calls from him."

"What did he have to say?"

"Same old bullshit. He thinks they've got an informer down there."

"Did he tell you who?"

"He don't know but he thinks it could be LoCicero," Jimmy said.

"All right, Jimmy, I'm glad you told me this because it fits right into what I'm going to tell you." Ahearn paused. "First of all, I don't know who's informing in Los Angeles but I know they've got a couple of excellent sources."

"What do you mean you don't know?" Jimmy asked. "Can't you find out?"

"Jimmy, it's the same as with you. You're my source, I'm protecting you. I'm not about to tell Jack Barron or Jack Armstrong that you're talking to me, and they're not going to tell me who's talking to them. But I get the reports and the word is that Mike Rizzitello's got the contract on you. No question about it, Jimmy."

Jimmy shrugged. "Maybe, but I ain't going to worry about it."

Ahearn looked at Hiner. They had rehearsed this ahead of time. It was strictly a shot in the dark. At this point Ahearn had resolved to use any means that would propel Jimmy into the Witness Protection Program. He had decided to pull out all the stops. The plan was to devise a scenario that would increase the pressure on Jimmy until his nerves cracked. Since Rizzitello was Jimmy's last link to the Los Angeles family, Ahearn decided to make him his bête noire.

"Chuck, why don't you tell Jimmy what surveillance has come up with."

"Well, Jimmy," said Hiner, "we've got a few cars kind of checking your place out from time to time, making sure no one's lurking about. Well, twice in the past week they spotted Rizzitello prowling around there in a rented car. I think he spotted us both times and left."

Jimmy sat there, the cigar a few inches from his lips, as though he had been injected with a paralyzing drug. His face, which had been animated when he had first walked into the room, now looked drawn and tired, and for the first time since he had known him, Ahearn thought he looked his age. Jimmy blinked a few times, jammed the cigar back into his mouth, and stood up.

"Hey, I've got to split, I've got people waiting for me."

"Have a good time tonight, Jimmy," Ahearn said, resisting the admonition to be careful. There was a limit to how thick you could lay it on. "Stay in touch."

"Yeah, sure, Jim, see you."

Jimmy went with Skinny Velotta and two girls to the Hookers' Ball. In recent days, Velotta had moved into the guest bedroom at Jimmy's Moss Beach home.

Conceived by San Francisco's most eloquent hooker, Margo St. James, the Hookers' Ball was held in the Civic Auditorium. It was a costume affair and the crowd that night was estimated at eight thousand. That was the night that the city's police chief was photographed with his arms around two comely hookers, grinning fiendishly for the camera. It was a gala affair and despite Ahearn's grim message, Jimmy had a good time.

On November 11, 1977, Jimmy made a brief appearance before the grand jury investigating Rudy Tham. As always, he took the Fifth Amendment, and refused to talk to reporters. The front-page headline in the *Examiner* was GRAND JURY CALLS CRIME FIGURE.

Later that day Jimmy received a frantic call from Ron Carabbia who was in danger of losing his junkets to the Tropicana in Las Vegas. Asked to do what he could, Jimmy called Joe Agosto, an executive at the hotel-casino and the producer of the *Follies Bergere* show, the one started years ago by Johnny

Roselli. Jimmy had known Agosto a long time. In fact, at one time Jimmy had tried to help his group obtain a $150 million loan from the Teamsters to add a thousand more rooms. That was before Deil Gustafson had sold control of the hotel to the Doumani brothers who in turn sold it to Mitzi Stauffer Briggs. Her accountant had come to Jimmy when they suspected that the casino manager and pit bosses were stealing huge amounts of money. Jimmy had explained the various cheating schemes that could be used by people operating the casino, particularly when the owner knew nothing about the gambling business. In the process, Jimmy had saved the jobs of two pit bosses who were friends of Alphonse "Funzied" D'Ambrosio, who always came away a big winner when he visited the Tropicana.

As to Carabbia's request, Agosto told Jimmy that everybody concerned had decided to stop junkets.

"Jimmy, you tell Ronnie it's nothing personal and if we get back in the business we'll go to him again."

"Okay, Joe. How's everything else going?"

"Jimmy, I plan to get up to San Francisco in a few weeks. I'd like to talk to you. It's very important."

"Okay, Joe, any time, just give me a call."

At nine o'clock on Sunday evening, November 13, as Jimmy was dressing for an evening on the town, the telephone rang as he was knotting his tie. He picked up the phone and said, "Yeah."

"Jimmy, how are you?"

It was Mike Rizzi. "Fine, what's doing?"

"Listen, Jimmy, can you get to a pay phone right away? It's very important that I talk to you."

"Mike, I can't go to no pay phone."

"Why, what's the matter? This's important, Jimmy."

"Look, Mike, I'm in my fucking pajamas."

"Well, put some clothes on, it's real important."

"Mike, I've seen cars around my house. It ain't a good idea to go out right now. Can't it wait until tomorrow?"

"I'd rather tell you right now."

"Mike, forget about it. I'll talk to you tomorrow."

"Okay, buddy, if that's the way you want it."

Jimmy broke the connection and dialed a number. "Cindy, what's doing? Listen, hon, I'll maybe be a half hour late."

Cindy was only twenty-five when Dennis McDonald first introduced her to Jimmy after she had expressed a desire to meet him. To look at Cindy is to be dazzled by physical beauty that hides the crippling scars of a brutal childhood. At seventeen she was married to an immature youth who thought that lovemaking was sacred and that only one position had been sanctified by God.

She became pregnant, had a son, a divorce, and a new marriage with a husky longshoreman who was "sexually fulfilling but intellectually boring." The first time Jimmy took her to bed, he made love to her five times in three hours.

She fell hopelessly in love with him. She found him to be "very attentive, very gentle, and very loving, and from that first time we always had super sex. You wouldn't believe it, but for a man of sixty-four or sixty-five, it's amazing. He's the most virile man I've ever met in my life. He kisses, he fondles, he's very oral, he's a very loving person. He's not selfish sexually at all. Or brutal or kinky. I really adore him. He's very special to me. He can just come and get it up and come again and get it up and there just doesn't seem to be any end to it."

After they had been going together a few months, Cindy told Jimmy something about her childhood: "At night when my mother was at work as a waitress, my stepfather would wake me up and say 'come out here and rub my feet while I watch TV.' And he'd take out his penis and say 'give it a kiss for daddy.' He'd get drunk and choke my brothers and beat them really bad, but he never beat me. I was daddy's little pet. I'd rub his feet and suck his penis and he'd tell me what a good girl I was. I remember one time he said he had a surprise for me, and he had a mattress in the bushes. I feel embarrassed to say it, but it's really true, you know. He said he got it so I could take a nap. He'd remove my clothes and finger me while I sucked him." The story had so infuriated Jimmy that she had resolved not to say any more about her childhood.

On this evening, the last time they would be together, they drove around for hours. Cindy knew that Jimmy was trying to shake any cars that might be following them. In recent weeks there always seemed to be cars following them. Jimmy had told her it was the FBI and one night after they had left Swiss Louie's Restaurant, where they had enjoyed a leisurely dinner with Billy Marchiondo and a group of friends, the FBI had again tailed them. The next day a couple of agents had come to see her, offering her money to spy on Jimmy, to tell them ahead of time where they were going, and she had told them where they personally could go.

They finally ended up at a motel in Burlingame. They went upstairs to their room and the telephone rang almost immediately. Jimmy answered it, listened a moment, and slammed the receiver down.

"That was your husband," he said.

"What are you talking about?"

"That was your husband. He must have followed us out here. It had to be him, he asked for you."

Cindy sat on the bed and stared incredulously at Jimmy. "That's nonsense. My husband's not that kind of person."

Jimmy shrugged. "Well, hon, whoever it was said, 'We know you have Cindy in there and you better let her out.' "

Cindy jumped up from the bed, her eyes growing frantic. "Oh, God, how could that be? How could anybody know we're here?"

"Hey, calm down," Jimmy said, going to her, and the telephone rang again.

"Let me answer it," Cindy said, lunging for the instrument.

"Is Jimmy there?' a man's voice inquired.

"Who's this?"

"Is Jimmy there? Listen, I know he's there."

"If you don't tell me who you are I'm going to hang up on you."

"Yeah, well, you tell Jimmy that if he sticks his dick in you we're going to cut it off."

Suddenly Cindy was more angry than afraid. "Get fucked, you jerk," she shouted and hung up.

She looked at Jimmy and tried to smile. "I guess that wasn't very ladylike, but this is so bizarre."

"Come on, hon, let's go down and have a drink."

She had two drinks while he had one. She told him what the man had said and she was surprised at how calmly he was taking it. They went back upstairs and Cindy called home and spoke to her husband. Then Jimmy made a few calls and afterward they made love. Everything was fine again. Later, while Jimmy was sitting up in bed, puffing on his cigar, Cindy said, "You better not let anybody cut that off. It would definitely cramp your style."

The next day Jimmy met Ahearn and told him about Rizzi's call.

"What did he want?" Ahearn asked.

Jimmy hesitated. "Ah, some bullshit about my going to a pay phone. He had something important to tell me."

"Did you go?" Ahearn asked.

"Are you kidding?"

"Well, I know you didn't, Jimmy."

"Hey, Jim, they must've found somebody else to make the hit. He called from L.A.," Jimmy said.

Ahearn shook his head. "Jimmy, sometimes you surprise me. How do you know he was in Los Angeles?"

"He told . . ." Jimmy stopped, his eyes widening.

"That's right, Jimmy. He was spotted in a phone booth around nine o'clock no farther than a quarter-mile from your house."

"I'll be a dirty sonovabitch."

"Jimmy, I don't want to push," Ahearn said. "But I want you to give serious thought to the Witness Protection Program. You play ball with us, give us what we want, and we think that's a lot, and we'll protect you. If you can make some cases, we'll give you immunity."

"What kind of cases could I make?" Jimmy asked.

"How about Bompensiero for openers?"

"Hey, Jim, you're too much. I've got to get moving. Thanks for the tip."

"Think about what I've told you," Ahearn said, shaking hands with Jimmy. "It could save your life. I'm serious, I worry about you. You're not using your head. They've got a contract on you, Jimmy. How are you going to get around that if Brooklier won't even talk to you?"

"Hey, I've got to go. See you."

And he was gone.

That evening when Jimmy and Velotta arrived at the Moss Beach house, they drew the heavy drapes and blocked the kitchen windows with newspapers and masking tape. He had bought tools from Sal Amarena, who conducted a brisk trade in weapons. There were a pump shotgun and three automatics, two .38's and one .25, which he began carrying in the outside right-hand pocket of his suit jacket. Whether in a booth at Sal's or walking down the street, Jimmy was always ready for a shoot-out. There were no hedges around his house and the garage door was operated by remote control. He felt he was ready for any eventuality.

Jimmy and Champ Reynoso were in the same Oakland bar. "You cased it pretty good?"

"Hey, man, I can tell you when that guy takes a shit," Reynoso said. "I've got Rodriguez with me and, man, we can make this hit ourselves, no problem. We don't need the condo, just hit the cocksucker and hit the road. By the time they know what's happened, we're halfway home."

Jimmy nodded. "Number one, Champ, I want to do it. You understand, I want that motherfucker to look me in the eye when I put the rope around his fucking neck. What this guy did to me, forget about it. Number two, halfway home ain't good enough if they put out roadblocks. Number three, I'm still trying to get an address for the other guy. This has got to be coordinated. We clip this guy, wait a couple days, and clip the other, boom-boom. By then I might have another guy to hit, but I know where he lives."

"Hey, man, we need some wheels for the hit," Reynoso said.

"Okay, let me look around. I'll pick up something when I get the other guy lined up. Stay cool, Champ, I'll be in touch."

On his way back to San Francisco Jimmy had a brainstorm. He knew how he could find the location of Brooklier's pay phone. All he had to do was call the number from time to time and one day somebody walking by would answer it and he could ask whoever it was for the location, and then he'd have Brooklier set up, too. The moment he got back to Sal's, he dialed the number and kept dialing for several days, until other problems took precedence.

52.
THE "LITTLE GUY'S" CONTRACT

† † † †

ONE EVENING IN LATE NOVEMBER JIMMY AND DENNIS MCDONALD HAD dinner at Antonio's in Hayward. Since Jimmy had insisted on seeing him that evening, McDonald wondered what was on Jimmy's mind. At the moment he seemed his normal relaxed self as he ate his veal parmesan.

Then Jimmy looked up and said, "Dennis, I've just been indicted on an extortion rap in Los Angeles."

"Jimmy, how do you know? Is there a warrant out for you?"

"No problem, Dennis. An FBI guy I know came around and told me about it so they wouldn't have to arrest me. I want you to surrender me early in the morning."

McDonald was stunned. He couldn't imagine Jimmy having that kind of relationship with an FBI agent. It was inconceivable, totally contrary to his image of Jimmy. Yet he was hesitant to question him about it, deciding that Jimmy would tell him in his own sweet time. He decided to stick to the problem at hand. "What can you tell me about the indictment?"

"Dennis, believe me, it's a bum rap. Some guys I know tried to shake down a porno outfit [Forex] that was an undercover FBI operation."

"Oh, my God," McDonald said, "I can't believe what I'm hearing."

Jimmy laughed. "Dennis, believe me, it's bullshit. I never saw them people. I don't know them but maybe somebody mentioned my name. What can I tell you, that's all I know."

Although Jimmy appeared under control, there was something different in the tone of his voice, something that signaled a greater urgency than the problem created by the indictment.

Two weeks earlier McDonald had stopped at Sal's to have a cup of coffee with Jimmy and he had looked drawn and tired, giving McDonald the impression that he was under enormous pressure. He had looked at McDonald through the cigar smoke and said, "Dennis, life is very treacherous. You never know what's going to happen. I don't know how long I can keep this juggling act going." Then he had brightened up, but McDonald could see that it had taken quite an effort.

"This veal's terrible," Jimmy said, pushing his plate away. "What kind of Italian restaurant is this, anyway?"

"Why don't you order something else?"

"I'm not hungry. Besides, I've got to run. I've got a date."

"Cindy?"

Jimmy smiled. "No, some new broad."

Rudy Tham came up with Jimmy's bail for the Forex extortion rap, and McDonald, who had to surrender Jimmy in Los Angeles the following Monday, had another surprise coming when he suggested they make airline reservations for a Sunday flight.

"I don't want to spend the night in Los Angeles," Jimmy said, "It's too dangerous. In fact, I don't want to fly on a commercial plane."

They were walking down the courthouse steps and McDonald took Jimmy by the arm. "Jimmy, is there something you've forgotten to tell me, something I should know for my own safety?"

Jimmy pulled his arm out of McDonald's grip. "It has nothing to do with you, Dennis."

"Well, what do you want me to do?" McDonald asked.

"Dennis, you'll think of something. I'll call you tomorrow."

"If you won't go commercial, we'll have to charter a private plane."

Jimmy smiled. "I knew you'd think of something."

Early Sunday morning McDonald was awakened by the telephone. He reached for it on the nightstand and heard Jimmy's voice.

"Have you looked outside yet?"

McDonald yawned. "Jimmy, not really, you woke me out of a sound sleep."

"It's fucking fogged in," Jimmy said. "It can last for days. How can we fly down there in one of them little planes in this shit? What are you trying to do, get me killed?"

"Jimmy, not really, since I'm going to be right there with you. Relax, will you, come over and we'll watch the ball games."

"What kind of plane have you chartered?"

"It's a Cessna three-ten, a big, safe plane or I wouldn't be on it," McDonald replied.

"Let's go to Burbank instead of LAX."

"That's fine, it's even closer. Now, you come over and we'll have a nice, relaxing day."

They watched three football games and Jimmy enjoyed himself. His love of sports was insatiable. McDonald, who had played football in high school, was impressed with Jimmy's intimate knowledge of the finer nuances of the game and with his ability to pick winners.

After dinner that evening, with a log burning in the fireplace, they played checkers. McDonald, who fancied himself an excellent player, was trounced soundly, to the delight of his girl friend, Sharon, who really liked Jimmy. They were laughing, having a good time, when Jimmy said, "Dennis, you must remember, I spent seventeen years in the joint learning this game."

Sharon stopped laughing. "Jimmy, I don't understand it," she said. "You're such a bright individual, you have so much ability, it's really sad that you got involved in the things you did and have had to live the kind of life you have. I don't mean that I believe everything they say about you in the newspapers . . . I hope you know what I mean."

Jimmy looked at her and smiled. "I know what you mean, hon, and I'm sorry too for the decisions I made a long time ago. I shouldn't've gotten involved in the things I did, but what're you going to do? It's one of them things." He paused and looked gravely at Dennis. "As I told you the other day, we live in a treacherous world. People you think that're close to you, ain't; people you think you can trust, you can't. You can live your whole life before you find that out. Dennis, believe me, you don't meet many people in your life you can trust or be close to. Most of the people I thought I could trust are dead. There's no one to replace them."

As he listened to him, all McDonald could think of was, "My God, the king is about to topple off his throne."

They made a brief court appearance in Los Angeles the next morning and had to wait several hours to be assigned to a judge. At the first opportunity, Jimmy went up to Mike Rizzi, and, looking him straight in the eye, asked what had been so important the night he had asked him to go to a pay phone.

"Oh, yeah. What do you think happened?" Rizzi said. "You remember that investigator I introduced you to that was working for Rudy Tham's lawyer? This guy used to be a cop in New York and had good contacts with the FBI. Well, he was in Vegas and this FBI guy told him that Spilotro's got a contract on both of us."

"That's no fucking news," Jimmy said. "That's no reason to get me to a phone booth at night. It could have waited till the next day. In fact, it's waited this long. I tried to call you a half dozen times and you never called me back."

"I'm sorry about that, Jimmy. I had to go out of town."

"Oh, yeah, well, let's forget about it."

McDonald had moved away when they started talking. He had met Rizzi in San Francisco and had known immediately that Rizzi was one man who could rob him without a gun. He was physically menacing and McDonald was certain that his heart was made of granite.

By talking to the other attorneys and defendants, McDonald had learned that Jimmy's involvement was peripheral at best. Yet, not being a criminal attorney, he suggested to Jimmy that he call his good friend Billy Marchiondo, who had attained an impressive reputation in that field.

Jimmy immediately telephoned Marchiondo, who already knew about the case. "Jimmy, whenever you need me I'll come in and represent you at no cost," Marchiondo told him. "Furthermore, the Little Guy [Spilotro] is holding ten thousand dollars he wants you to have to tide you over this rough spot." Jimmy hung up and thought, "Yeah, I'll bet!"

The next day McDonald sent Marchiondo a letter with a copy of the indictment and Marchiondo called him to say that he was looking forward to working with him on the case. He wanted McDonald to make some of the less important appearances and promised to have his researchers help prepare the defense. In the ensuing days they planned some initial strategy on the discovery they wanted and on a motion to dismiss, and if that failed on a motion to separate Jimmy's case from the other defendants. At no time was there any discussion of fees and McDonald assumed that he also was volunteering his services.

53
END OF THE LINE

† † † †

A FEW NIGHTS AFTER RETURNING FROM LOS ANGELES, JIMMY AND VEL-
otta were on their way home when they spotted a tail as they neared Moss
Beach.

"Keep your eyes on those headlights," Jimmy said, jamming his foot down
on the accelerator, the big Caddy leaping forward as he swung down a side
street.

"They're still with us," Velotta said. "I just caught it in the street light when
it made the turn. It's the same red and white T-bird we've spotted before."

"Okay, hold on," Jimmy said, hitting the brakes and swinging the steering
wheel, throwing the car into a spinning, tire-burning skid. The next moment
they were heading in the opposite direction, straight for the Thunderbird.
"Let's see who's a fucking chicken," Jimmy said, through clenched teeth.

At the last moment the Thunderbird swung to the right into another side
street and Jimmy went skidding by sideways, the heavy car rocking almost out
of control.

"Holy shit," Velotta cried, "are you crazy? I'm glad they had the sense to
swing right. You'd have killed us all."

"Skinny, I gave them the option," Jimmy said. "Let's go home."

The next morning Jimmy was still asleep when Velotta called him from his
dry cleaning store. He had bought the business for $28,000 and had insured
it for $90,000. His plan was to burn it down after a few months and collect
the insurance.

Velotta said he wanted to see him right away and from the tone of his voice
Jimmy knew it was important. He got dressed and hurried to the store.

"Jimmy, guess what, that T-bird tailed me this morning," Velotta said.
"Listen to this, I got off the freeway and went down a one-way street and
stopped. I tried to block them but the street was too wide. Just the same I
jumped out and there's two guys and they're wearing baseball caps. They pull
their caps down to hide their face and whip right by me, missed me by a
fucking coat of paint. But I got the license number."

Jimmy slapped Velotta on the back. "Okay, Skinny, that's good going. I'll call Bennie [Barrish] and find out who it belongs to. This guy's got more friends in the PD than the mayor."

An hour later Jimmy called Ahearn and arranged for a meeting.

Jimmy walked into the hotel room and Jim Ahearn said, "I hear you had a little excitement last night."

"You know about it?"

Ahearn smiled. "It was kind of funny. A couple of my surveillance guys were sort of escorting you home . . . you know how I feel about your safety . . . when they spotted this tail on you."

"A red and white T-bird."

"Yes."

"Did they get the license?" Jimmy asked.

"Yes."

"Did you check it out?"

"Yes."

"Know who it was?"

"Yes."

Jimmy laughed. "Okay, you tell me."

"Do you know who it was?" Ahearn asked.

"Yes."

Ahearn leaned back in his chair. "Then you know that Joey Hansen is one of Spilotro's boys."

"One of his jewel thieves."

"There's more to it, Jimmy. He's also got a reputation as a killer. If I were you, I wouldn't minimize his presence on the scene."

"Don't worry, I don't," Jimmy said.

"The point I want to make, Jimmy, and I know you're probably tired of hearing it, but there's a limit to the protection we can give you out there on the street. These guys appear pretty damn determined."

"Jim, I appreciate it, but I never asked for your protection. This's my battle. I'm the only guy that can straighten it out. I know what I'm doing."

"Oh, sure," Ahearn said, "famous last words."

The next day, after Velotta had left for work, Jimmy called a moving company and had his furniture put into storage. He piled his clothes into the trunk of his car and drove to a three-room furnished apartment on Nob Hill he had rented an hour after Barrish had told him that the Thunderbird belonged to Joey Hansen. He was determined to keep his new address secret from everybody. Later, he thought, he might give it to Ahearn, but for the moment all he wanted to do was sit there and figure a way out of his troubles.

He sat in the small living room and stared at the wall in front of him. It was Saturday and the television was on but he stared at the blank wall above it.

One phrase kept echoing through his head: "This is the end of the line." What could he do to reverse his situation? His own friends, guys he had known for thirty years, were trying to kill him. And for nothing. What had he done to them? How had he harmed them? What possessed them anyway?

He sat there, shaking his head, bewildered by his predicament. For the first time he was really thinking about it. It was all going down the drain. In a way he was lucky to be involved with a bunch of bunglers. How many men had been clipped without ever realizing it was coming? At least the bunglers had given him advance warning. If this had happened in an eastern city he would have been killed and buried long ago.

Instead he was in this small apartment, hiding out like public enemy number one, with not one friend left he could trust. How had he arrived here? Where had he gone wrong? If only Johnny Roselli had become the boss when Dragna died. They would all be rich now. The man had been brilliant, capable of making millions. Los Angeles was a rich city and they had starved in it. Las Vegas was just across the street and they had starved. The Los Angeles family never had a boss that knew how to maneuver, how to make real money. All Jack Dragna had ever cared about was to make enough money to keep himself in booze and broads. The rest of the bosses had been jokes. But it was all down the drain. There were three made guys left in San Francisco, useless old men, even worse in San Jose. In the eastern cities the bosses and *capiregime* had all the money and the soldiers did all the dirty work and had nothing to show for it. Greed and jealousy were the malignancies that were destroying their thing from within. The senseless killings. They were forcing their own people to turn on them, becoming informants, because it was the only way they could save themselves or strike back.

Big shots were going to jail every day—they didn't know whom to trust anymore. The Strike Forces and FBI were getting a handle on it, their modern surveillance techniques were more widespread, their knowledge of the Mafia's inner workings more definitive, their informant network now penetrating all the families. If they couldn't get you for one crime, they got you for another; either way they took you off the street. The conviction rate of Mafiosi in recent years was staggering.

The big money today, except for families that had pieces of Las Vegas casinos, was in legitimate business. Louie Dragna and Dominic Longo were getting rich with legitimate businesses while the rest of the family went around shaking down pornographers. Most pornographers, and bookmakers, for that matter, were Jewish and the only way the families could extract anything from them was to shake them down. Paul Castellano probably made more money with his meat business than he did with shylocking. Prostitution and narcotics were freelance rackets and to his knowledge always had been. Nobody could ever convince him that Luciano had ever been involved with whorehouses. That had been an even greater disgrace in those days than today. Regardless of what the newspapers said, a made guy had his code of honor. Only creeps lived off women. The millions involved in prostitution were not going to families—that he knew for certain.

The only big steady money he had ever made was with his trucking company. If they had left him alone he would be a rich and respected man today. All the missed opportunities that had slipped through his fingers. He thought of all the money he had made. If only he had kept it instead of sharing it with dead heads. At some point, he could have gone into a legitimate venture. His problem was that he had been too quick to share his earnings with others. What had he received in return?

Johnny Roselli had been so right: "Who needs this thing of ours?" In the end they had killed him, a harmless old man who had not been a threat to anyone. Forget this nonsense about his having been an informer. Never in a million years. His downfall had been jealousy. With Giancana out of the way, there was no one to save him from whatever had been eating away at Joe Batters for fifty years, some slight suffered in the days of Capone that even Johnny had forgotten.

Every time things had started going right for him, disaster had inevitably struck. It had happened in 1953 and 1969 and it was happening now. All the big deals with Marson and Albanese and Marchiondo, the Sinatra benefit for the Knights of Malta, the Thai sticks. What if Brooklier had died in prison? What if he had been a free man when Jack Dragna died? Everything would have been different. What if he had never gone into this thing in the first place?

Marchiondo had told him the Little Guy was holding $10,000 for him. How was he supposed to collect it? He had called Slick Shapiro several times but there had been no answer. Velotta was afraid to go to Las Vegas to collect it. In fact, Velotta was one inch away from switching sides. Ray Ferritto was in custody for the murder of Danny Greene, and Blackie Licavoli, the last guy in Cleveland that he trusted, had a plant in the FBI office that at any moment could reveal his role as an informant. Brooklier and Sciortino had corrupted Detroit, Chicago, and New York, and who knew how far it had spread.

If he succeeded in killing Sciortino and Brooklier, would anything change? He knew he had made enemies of Aiuppa, Batters, and Cerone. What about Funzi Tieri, Paul Castellano, Russ Bufalino, Alley Boy, Abbie Shots? Had they too been alienated? For all he knew there was probably a commission contract on him. Which meant that it was out of Brooklier's hands. It was final. There was no way out. How long could he hide in this room? The word had probably spread throughout the underworld. Still, there would be some gratification in taking Sciortino and Brooklier with him. He could ally himself with the Mexican Mafia, he had many friends in it, and that was the future in California. They were plentiful and had guts. All they needed was leadership. It was something worth thinking about, a last resort. Somehow, no matter what happened, he would get back at Sciortino and Brooklier and Dragna. They would pay for what they had done to him. Of that he was certain.

† † †

Jim Ahearn spent a nervous weekend. Only moments after Jimmy had called to say that he was moving and would be in touch later, Ahearn heard from ASAC Joseph Griffin in Cleveland that Ferritto had confessed and implicated everybody in the Greene murder, including Jimmy. Griffin asked Ahearn to serve the murder warrant.

"Look, Joe, it's fine," Ahearn said. "If I've been bullshitted, I've been bullshitted, it's okay with me."

Ahearn sat waiting by the phone until Sunday night. When it rang, Jimmy said, "Hi, what's doing?"

"Not much, Jimmy. How's it going with you? How's the new apartment?"

"Huh, what can I say, it's three little rooms."

Ahearn thought that was still bigger than that prison cell awaiting him. "Is Jean with you?"

"No, she's gone to her folks in San Pedro. She don't even know where I'm at."

"Well, look, it's important we get together."

"I can't meet you now."

"Let's do it tomorrow for sure. Jimmy, this is your life we're talking about."

"Well, what's up?"

"Jimmy, I can't talk on the phone."

"Oh, Christ, I was planning on taking it easy for a few days. You know, let things cool off."

"Jimmy, things aren't going to cool off. If you don't give a shit about your life, I do. Now you meet me at the Holiday Inn by the airport. Just dial the desk and ask for Frank Cost. Two o'clock, okay?"

There was a long pause and deep sigh. "I just hope this ain't more bullshit."

"Believe me, Jimmy. This time it's for real."

When Jimmy knocked on the door of Room 222 at 2:40 P.M. the next day, the trap was set. Two agents were hiding in the bathroom and Ahearn's boss, Roy McKinnon, and another agent were in an adjoining room. Ahearn had two primary concerns. One, that Jimmy was probably packing a gun and in a desperate moment might try to use it, and two, that he might have a heart attack when told he was being arrested for two murders in Cleveland.

Ahearn opened the door and Jimmy came in. They shook hands and Ahearn steered him to a chair that placed him with his back to the doors of the bathroom and adjoining room. Again he was wearing his brown pin-striped suit, with the black shirt and gaudy tie.

"Going to another Hookers' Ball?" Ahearn asked, smiling.

Jimmy shrugged. "It's the only clean shirt I could find."

"How's Jean feeling?"

"A little on edge. She was over and we stayed in a motel. So naturally she's suspicious that something's up. What can I do?"

"She doesn't know your new address?"

"Nobody knows it. I'm going to give it to you but nobody else." He paused and looked at the floor. "You're the only guy I trust right now."

"Well, Jimmy, trust is a two-way street." Ahearn stood up and walked to Jimmy's chair. "I'm disappointed in you. I thought you were shooting straight with me."

Jimmy looked up. "What do you mean? I never lied to you. That's the God's truth."

"I wish I could believe that," Ahearn said, resting his left hand on Jimmy's right shoulder, ready to pin it with his fist if Jimmy made any sudden move. The signal for the other agents to close in was the moment Ahearn started reading him his rights. With his other hand he reached into his pocket and handed Jimmy a sheet of paper. "Jimmy, know what this is?"

Jimmy looked at the paper and up at Ahearn, a confused look on his face. "What is it?" He held it as though he thought it might burn his fingers.

"It's your rights, Jimmy. You're under arrest for murder."

At that moment the other four agents rushed into the room, pulled him to his feet, cuffed him with his hands behind his back, and physically took him into custody as they would any other prisoner. Jimmy's glasses slipped down his nose as they quickly searched his person. He offered no resistance. The expression on his face was one of total astonishment. His eyes kept blinking and for a moment Ahearn thought he was going to have that heart attack. It was apparent that he was struggling to maintain his composure. Yet his teeth were clenched firmly on his cigar, which became his immediate concern.

"How the fuck can I smoke this cigar with my hands behind my back?"

An agent took the cigar from his mouth, dropped it in an ashtray, and pushed the horn-rimmed glasses back up his nose.

"What the fuck's going on? What the fuck's this? I don't get it. How could you do this to me? I thought you was my friend."

"Hey, man, you really let me down," Ahearn said. "So just cut this tough-guy shit."

"But, Jim, honestly, I never lied to you."

"Jimmy, we're talking about murder and it's more than one murder."

Jimmy's eyes widened and Ahearn noticed that his glasses were becoming a little foggy. The expression in his eyes, as Ahearn read it, was how much do they know and which murders are they talking about? "I don't know what the fuck you're talking about."

"I'm talking about Cleveland. Think about it, I'll be back in a minute," Ahearn said, going into the adjoining room with McKinnon to discuss the procedure to be followed at this point.

Chuck Hiner read Jimmy his rights. Jimmy waited until he had finished, then asked to speak privately with Ahearn.

Ahearn came back into the room and they stepped aside to a corner.

Jimmy said, "Look, I've got a little thing in the car."

"What do you mean, a little thing?"

"Well, you know, something to take care of myself."

"Jimmy, tell me what it is and specifically where."

"It's a little Bauer automatic and it's behind the fold-down armrest by the driver's seat."

"Okay, I'll send somebody down to get it."

"Hey, Jim, I've got a box of cigars on the front seat, have him bring them up, will you?"

Ahearn smiled. "Sure, Jimmy, as you know, we don't go in for torture."

"Thanks, but listen, I never lied to you. I really mean that." And at that moment Jimmy was convinced he was telling the truth.

"Jimmy, Ray Ferritto has made a full confession, implicating everybody, including you. Now we're going downtown to the Federal Building and I want you to think this over. You want to call your lawyer to meet us there?"

"Not right away."

"What about your car? What do you want us to do with it?"

"I want Skinny Velotta to take it to Jean."

In his office in the Federal Building, Ahearn again read Jimmy his rights. The handcuffs had been removed and Jimmy was permitted to smoke his cigar. This seemed to restore his confidence in Ahearn, which was precisely what the agent had anticipated. They were back again on a friendly basis. Jimmy had requested the private audience.

"Listen, Jimmy, we've called Dennis McDonald and he's on his way over here. You know, I want your cooperation but I still want to protect your rights. I think we ought to wait until he gets here before we go any further with this questioning."

"Forget about it, Jim. I know what I'm doing."

"Well, okay, but I want you to sign this other form. Anything you say may and probably will be used against you. As long as you understand that you're waiving your rights."

Jimmy leaned forward and signed it. "Look, I'd like to help you, but what could I testify to? I wasn't in Cleveland when Nardi and Greene were killed. All I know's hearsay. I can't corroborate anything. Sure, I know Ray, known him for years, but Ron Carabbia's known him a lot longer than me."

"I don't have to explain the law to you. You don't have to make the bomb or pull the switch to be charged with murder one. All you've got to be is part of the conspiracy and Cleveland says they've got it locked tight."

"Well, I'm telling you they don't. So we'll find out, right?"

"I hope you're right. What I'd like is for you to help us here in California."

"Like what? I told you I was doing a little booking and shylocking. That's no big deal."

"What about Bompensiero's murder? I'll bet you could tell us that whole story."

Jimmy grinned. "What do you know about it?"

Ahearn's phone buzzed and he picked it up, listened a moment, and looked at Jimmy. "McDonald's here. Want to see him?"

"No, no, not now. Let's talk some more."

Ahearn hung up and leaned back in his chair. "I know who killed Bomp." Ahearn would later tell McKinnon that he was lying through his ass. "Ricciardi, Brooklier, Sciortino, and Rizzitello."

Jimmy's face remained impassive. "Not bad, you got three out of four."

"Okay, Jimmy, now we're finally getting somewhere."

At that moment Jimmy knew that he was going to get precisely what he wanted: safety and revenge. "Brooklier got Bomp to the phone, Ricciardi made the hit, LoCicero drove the car, Sciortino and Dragna and myself were in on the contract. Took nearly two years to clip that guy."

"How much detail can you give me, Jimmy?"

"Everything you'll ever need to put the whole bunch away for a long time."

"Oh, Christ," Ahearn said. "The entire Los Angeles heirarchy?"

"Yeah," Jimmy said, "and that's only for openers. But I want immunity and protection. And I don't want to serve no fucking time."

At this point Ahearn was not interested in negotiating anything. All he knew was that the hump was broken. He had himself a hell of a case. And Jimmy, for his own safety, was off the street. Only time could tell how good a collar he had made. Neither realized at that moment how big a step they had taken. Jimmy, according to FBI records, would become the first made guy ever to testify in open court against other made guys. An invisible link had been broken, something dark and mysterious had been released, exposed to the light of day, and for the first time the public would be given a close look at something that had been hidden within the corpus of society far too long.

Jimmy Fratianno was the classical American Mafioso, born of another time and place that could never again be duplicated. Others would replace him but his particular breed was rapidly becoming extinct. Quintessentially, he truly was *The Last Mafioso.*

EPILOGUE:
GETTING EVEN
AND OTHER DESTINIES

† † † †

AS I WRITE THESE WORDS SOME TWO YEARS LATER, JIMMY FRATIANNO has already testified before several grand juries and court trials, proving without question that James Ahearn's "collar" was indeed a good one.

—Before returning Jimmy's Cadillac to Jean, Frank "Skinny" Velotta stole all five new radial tires, replacing them with worn-out casings. This act of petty treachery so incensed Jimmy that he told James Ahearn about Velotta's plan to torch his Oakland dry cleaning place (Select Cleaners) which he had insured for $90,000. A few months later, true to his word, Select Cleaners went up in flames, but the FBI waited until Velotta had collected $60,000 from the insurance company before charging him with mail fraud—the use of the U.S. mail to receive fraudulent insurance payments. The stealing of Jimmy's tires cost Velotta six months in prison and two years' probation—not to mention the $60,000 he had to return to the insurance company.

—Jimmy's first major test as a government witness came in the fall of 1978 during the Westchester Premier Theater trial in Manhattan Federal Court. The subject of sensational headlines, the first trial lasted several weeks and ended in a hung jury, but eventually the case resulted in the following dispositions for the ten defendants accused of violating security laws and looting the theater into bankruptcy: Eliot Weisman, six years in prison; Gregory DePalma, four and a half years; Richard Fusco, two and a half years; Louis "Louie Dome" Pacella, two years; Salvatore J. Cannatella, one year and one day; Thomas Marson, one year and one day. Murad Nersesian and Anthony Gaggi were acquitted, and Leonard Horwitz was convicted but a new trial was ordered. At this writing, Laurence I. Goodman is awaiting trial.

—Only weeks after Jimmy went into the Witness Protection Program, the FBI plugged its leak in the Cleveland office. Geraldine Rabinowitz, an FBI file clerk, and her husband, Jeffrey, an automobile salesman, pleaded guilty to two counts each of accepting bribes totaling $15,900 from Kenneth Ciarcia. They were sentenced to five years in prison.

—Jimmy was excused from testifying in the Cleveland trial for the bomb slaying of Daniel Greene. Although Ray Ferritto testified that James Licavoli hired him to kill Greene, only Ronald Carabbia and Pasquale Cisternino were convicted. Licavoli, Angelo Lonardo, and Thomas Sinito were acquitted. "This devastates the prosecution's contention that there is a Mafia," said defense lawyer Elmer Giuliani. "Organized crime is a myth that exists in the minds of the FBI and local police authorities," said Licavoli's lawyer, James R. Willis. Charges against a sixth defendant, Alfred Calabrese, were dismissed by the judge when the prosecution rested. In a second trial on the same charges, Thomas Lanci and Kenneth Ciarcia were convicted and John P. Calandra was acquitted. Anthony D. Liberatore and Carmen Marconi avoided prosecution by becoming fugitives.

—In May 1979, a federal grand jury handed down an indictment based on the Racketeering Influence and Corrupt Organizations (RICO) statute, charging conspiracy to bribe Geraldine Rabinowitz. Indicted were Licavoli, Liberatore, Calandra, Lanci, and Ciarcia, who later pleaded guilty to three bribery charges in the case. This time Jimmy testified against his former Cleveland associates, but again Licavoli and Calandra were acquitted by a Cleveland jury. Liberatore and Lanci were convicted—sentencing is pending at this writing. (To date no one has been tried for the murder of John Nardi.)

—It was Jimmy's testimony before a Fort Lauderdale federal grand jury that led to the indictment of Aniello Dellacroce and Tony Plate on RICO charges, including the 1974 murder of Charles Calise. For reasons perhaps best known to Dellacroce, Tony Plate promptly disappeared. Jimmy was scheduled to be the key witness but when U.S. deputy marshals failed to produce him on time, the judge refused to grant a recess, forcing the government to rest its case, which ended in a hung jury and a mistrial. A new trial is pending at this writing.

—While in Florida, Jimmy made an appearance in West Palm Beach federal court. Marshall Caifano, who earlier had been convicted of possessing and transporting stolen securities valued at $4 million, was awaiting sentencing under the Special Offenders Act, which empowered the judge to add ten years to the maximum sentence of fifteen years possible for the fraud conviction if it could be shown that Caifano was a "special dangerous offender." On the witness stand, Jimmy recalled Caifano's role in the murder of Russian Louie, and the judge handed down a twenty-year prison term. The Fort Lauderdale *News and Sun–Sentinel* observed that "Fratianno's testimony about the day-to-day workings of La Cosa Nostra and its strict rules of conduct gave law enforcement authorities who attended the hearing a rare peek inside the criminal organization."

—In Las Vegas, the casino empire of Allen Glick came tumbling down when agents from the Nevada Gaming Control Board's audit division discovered that $7,200 in quarters had been placed in the Stardust's auxiliary vault without being recorded in Argent's books. A search of another section of the vault produced $3,500 also unrecorded. Searches at the Fremont revealed similar unrecorded caches. After a lengthy investigation, the agents estimated that the skimming of the slot machines at both casinos amounted to nearly $12 million. The skimming was accomplished by rigging the scales to underweigh the coins. Jay Vandermark, whom Lefty Rosenthal had placed in charge of the operation, fled to Mazatlan, Mexico, where he hid out under an assumed name until investigators dispatched his son Jeffrey with an offer of immunity from prosecution in return for his cooperation. Shortly after Vandermark's return from Mexico, his son was murdered and he once again fled from Las Vegas, this time to Costa Ricca, where recently obtained evidence indicates that he also has been murdered.

A raid by fifty FBI agents swept down on the homes, offices, and cars of Tony Spilotro, Glick, and others. The agents came up with a dozen guns, radios to monitor police frequencies, secret police reports on the activities of the Chicago family in Las Vegas, loansharking records, and nearly $200,000 in cash at the home of Spilotro's brother, John, the money bundled in Dunes casino wrappers.

The Gaming Control Board filed complaints that Glick, as sole owner of Argent Corp., had failed to prevent a slot machine skimming operation and recommended the revocation of his licenses and a $12 million fine. The Gaming Commission revoked Glick's casino licenses but reduced the fine to $500,000. The commission then approved Allan D. Sachs as the new owner of the Stardust and Fremont casinos over the objections of its own enforcement arm, the Gaming Control Board, whose agents had interviewed Jimmy at great length and were thoroughly briefed not only on Sachs' connections with the Chicago family but also on his lifelong links to Yale Cohen and Bobby Stella and their own connections to Chicago. Back in the 1950's, both Sachs and Stella had been stickmen-dealers in Cicero and South Chicago gambling joints operated by the mob, and had been brought to Las Vegas by Johnny Drew, who could trace his own mob affiliations to the days of Al Capone.

As for Glick, he expected to net close to $70 million, before taxes, for the sale of his casinos to Sachs, his former employee, who took over the whole operation without using any of his own money. Sachs assumed a $92 million Teamsters loan, gave Glick a 12-year $66 million noninterest-bearing promisory note, and borrowed $4 million from the Valley Bank as front money which he repaid in a few months from receipts of the two casinos now controlled by his holding company, Trans–Sterling Inc. Sachs' partner, Herb Tobman, was a long-time associate of Moe Dalitz who, on orders from Chicago, was building the Sundance, heralded to be the largest hotel–casino in downtown Las Vegas. Dalitz financed it through the Nevada State Teachers Association and once completed it would be managed by Sachs' Trans–Sterling Inc.

—In March 1979, the Gaming Commission ordered that the Aladdin (Jimmy's old Tallyho) be sold after its top executives were convicted on federal charges of allowing hidden unlicensed organized crime figures to wield control over the hotel. Rushing to the rescue, with Sid Korshak at his side, was Delbert W. Coleman, the old go-go conglomerator, who had brought the Parvin–Dohrmann company to its knees with his boiler-room stock manipulation in 1969. Coleman's bid of $105 million for the newly enlarged and refurbished hotel, financed by the Teamsters fund, was about 2,000 percent above what Shenker's Detroit and St. Louis friends had paid for it in 1971. The Gaming Commission rejected the offer after the Gaming Control Board expressed skepticism that the deal between the hidden Aladdin owners and Colemen was "an arm's length transaction." At this writing, singer Wayne Newton was trying to buy the hotel.

—The trial in San Francisco federal court lasted twenty-one days and a jury of nine women and three men found Rudy Tham guilty on fifteen felony embezzlement counts and four misdemeanor charges involving the misuse of Teamsters funds. Twelve of the felony counts were for picking up Jimmy's hotel and restaurant tabs. On hearing the verdict, Tham angrily exclaimed: "They believed an admitted criminal . . . a guy who's admitted killing nine people and they listened to him." Strike Force prosecutor John Emerson told the press it was a "significant verdict and there can be no doubt now of Jimmy Fratianno's credibility." Tham was sentenced to six months in federal prison and fined $50,000. If the conviction is upheld on appeal, Tham would automatically be barred from holding union office for five years.

—According to the death certificate, Andrew "Banjo" Celamtano died of a heart attack on October 8, 1977. Jimmy was not aware of Celamtano's death, nor were the FBI or Los Angeles police at the time they questioned Jimmy about it. When Mike Rizzitello was arrested by Los Angeles FBI agents in January 1978, they found a note on his person with Celamtano's name on it. Puzzled by the name, they questioned Jimmy about it, who told them of Rizzo's request to have Celamtano's legs broken. A report was made, but no further action was taken. When I asked James D. Henderson, chief of the Los Angeles Federal Strike Force, about their lack of interest, he explained that Jimmy was a precious resource that could easily be burned out. "With Jimmy you've got a hundred cases you could work on, but you've got to pick your best five or six shots," Henderson said. "You don't screw around with guys like Jilly Rizzo when you've got a chance to put bosses in prison. Those are once-in-a-lifetime chances. With an informant-type of witness, overexposure is a terminal disease."

—In April 1980, a federal grand jury in Manhattan began looking into charges that Frank Sinatra had received $50,000 "under the table" in skimmed cash for the first series of concerts at the Premier Theater. When asked before the grand jury whether he knew "an individual named Frank Sinatra," "Louie Dome" Pacella refused to reply despite a grant of immunity from prosecution. He was cited for contempt and another year was added to his two-year sentence.

—In May 1980, Princess Grace of Monaco, Cary Grant, Gregory Peck, and sixteen hundred others met in Los Angeles to honor Frank Sinatra as Variety Clubs International Humanitarian of the Year. Past winners have included Albert Schweitzer, Jonas Salk, and Winston Churchill. Earlier in the year, Sinatra's application to the Nevada Gaming Commission for a license to become a "key employee" of Caesars Palace, working in public relations and promotion, had bogged down when both state and federal investigators reported that Sinatra had not only been seen in the company of Eugene Cimorelli but had exerted pressure to get Cimorelli a job as a casino host at Caesars Palace. Hotel executives had first refused to hire Cimorelli when they learned from the Gaming Control Board that Cimorelli was making frequent trips to Chicago with Tony Spilotro to meet with Joey Aiuppa and other Chicago family members.

—After four trials in his libel lawsuit against *Look* magazine, Joseph L. Alioto was awarded $350,000 in damages. However, Alioto's courtroom charisma failed him when a Wyoming cattleman, Courtenay Davis, sued the former mayor and his lawyer son, Joseph M., for breach of contract, negligence, fraud, and misrepresentation. In 1968 Davis and several other cattlemen had hired the Alioto law firm to bring an antitrust action against the A&P food chain for conspiring to fix beef prices. A federal grand jury returned a $32.7 million verdict, and the attorneys were awarded $3.2 million in fees, but upon appeal a settlement was reached for $10 million, under which A&P agreed to pay $1 million immediately and $1.65 million a year from 1975 to 1980. In the spring of 1980, Davis charged in his complaint that he was not informed about the settlement with A&P and that the Aliotos had refused to give him an accounting of the monies. After a day and a half of deliberation, the jury was unanimous in its decision. Under the verdict, Alioto, his son, and their law firm must pay $1,350,000 in compensatory damages. Punitive damages of $1.5 million were assessed against Joseph M. and $700,000 against Joseph L., for a total of $3.55 million.

—Fifteen-year-old Carlos Washington and two friends decided to take a "joy ride" in a car owned by one of the boys' mother. Surprised by police while they were pushing the car without lights down the street, Carlos ran behind an apartment building and leaped over a cinder block wall. A moment later there was a shotgun blast and Carlos lay mortally wounded. The officer who shot Carlos had been assigned to protect Mrs. Reta Wolkin, mother of the estranged wife of John "Sparky" Monica, who was awaiting trial for the 1969 murder of Julius Petro. The trial was pending at this writing.

—Pete Pianezzi, 77, served 13 years in Folsom Prison for the 1937 murder of Les Brunemann. Following Jimmy's disclosure that Leo Moceri was Brunemann's killer, Governor Jerry Brown asked the Community Release Board to conduct a preliminary inquiry on the "threshold question" of whether the new information warrants a full-scale investigation. Since Strike Force prosecutors would not permit Jimmy to appear before the CRB until he had fulfilled all his courtroom obligations, the CRB's decision remains in abeyance.

—In September 1978, Alvin Baron was convicted and sentenced to two years in prison and fined $5,000 by a federal judge for accepting $200,000 in kickbacks to arrange a $1.3 million cemetery loan. The key witness against Baron was Foy Bryant, owner of Mt. Vernon Memorial Park, Fair Oaks, California, the man Baron had once wanted killed.

—Jimmy's failure to find the tall, blond witness operating a pork store in Walnut Creek would eventually cost Russell Bufalino four years in prison. Bufalino, who had threatened the witness because he owed $25,000 to a diamond fence associated with him, told the court: "If you had to deal with an animal like that, Judge, you'd have done the same damn thing."

—On July 12, 1980, Angelo Marino was found guilty of second-degree murder in the slaying of Peter Catelli, and of attempted murder of Catelli's father, Orlando. Marino was in a Los Angeles hospital when the jury brought in the verdict. The trial, delayed and disrupted by Marino's recurring medical problems, was transferred to Los Angeles at the defense's request. Angelo was hospitalized three times for heart problems and his son, Salvatore, was severed as a defendant midway in the trial when two of his attorneys suffered heart ailments. Sentencing was pending at this writing.

—In July 1980, a Senate Judiciary subcommittee report criticized the Justice Department for what it called its failure to prosecute and punish organized crime for its role in the heroin traffic. The narcotics trade, valued at $44.6 billion to $63.4 billion, was being processed and marketed by Sicilian Mafia families with branches in the United States, the report said, replacing the old "French connection." And on it goes, round and round . . .

—Acting on Jimmy's information, it took James Ahearn two and a half years to crack the Thai stick deal, but the score was well worth the effort. The Thai stick turned out to be 15 pounds of 92 percent pure cocaine and the country of origin Peru instead of Thailand. Smuggled into two shipments of rattan furniture for Mike Buster's Walnut Creek store, the cocaine's wholesale value was estimated at well over $2 million—the street value was anybody's guess. Although Buster and four others were indicted, no case was made against Ray Giarusso and the Teamsters official.

—At first it appeared that the Los Angeles Federal Strike Force would move quickly against the local Mafia hierarchy. On February 28, 1978, following Jimmy's appearance before the federal grand jury, a six-count indictment was handed down against Dominic Brooklier, Samuel Sciortino, Louis Tom Dragna, Thomas Ricciardi, Jack LoCicero, and Michael Rizzitello. They were charged with racketeering, extortion, obstruction of justice, and conspiracy, which included the killing of Frank Bompensiero, all crimes covered by the RICO statute. "This is the first time in history that the entire leadership of a major Mafia family has been indicted," the Los Angeles *Times* reported. But it would be a long time before any of them stood trial.

Twenty-six months and three indictments later, the first two indictments having been dismissed because an insufficient number of grand jurors had heard all the evidence, the five remaining defendants (Ricciardi had since died during heart surgery) were again awaiting trial on the same RICO charges and Jimmy was again getting ready to testify against them.

Strike Force prosecutor James D. Henderson was getting apprehensive about his star witness. Having served twenty months in "Valachi's Suite" at La Tuna federal penitentiary near El Paso, Texas, Jimmy was out on parole and pretty much on his own. The longer the defense delayed the trial, the greater were the odds that he would be killed before he testified in Los Angeles.

There was no doubt in Henderson's mind that the Mafia Commission contract on Jimmy's life had top priority. To add to Henderson's anxiety, Jimmy's testimony in June 1980, before a New York federal grand jury, had led to a four-count indictment of Frank "Funzi" Tieri, who became the first boss ever accused by a federal grand jury of running a Cosa Nostra crime family, which was engaged in "various criminal activities," including murder, loansharking, extortion, interstate transportation of stolen property, and bankruptcy fraud. Jimmy's name was not mentioned in the news stories, but one allegation told Tieri all he needed to know. It stated that in 1976, in his capacity as a Mafia boss, Tieri and others had voted to murder Joseph Spencer Ullo. That was the sitdown Jimmy had been invited to witness. Without Jimmy's testimony, there would be no case in New York, or anywhere else for that matter. He was the man who could make it happen, the spellbinder who had nothing to lose and everything to gain by telling the truth.

After a lifetime of lying and deceit, Jimmy was enjoying his new role as a fearless and forthright witness. The dark, threatening glances from his former associates in the dock only added to his pleasure. He could tell from the look in their eyes that they knew he had found a way of getting even and there was nothing they could do about it. This was a vendetta in the best Mafia tradition. They would rot in prison and if in the distant future he must die for it, he was ready for that too. It would be an honorable death.

APPENDIX: DRAMATIS PERSONAE*

† † † †

ABBATTEMARCO, ANTHONY ("Abbie Shots")—underboss of New York City Colombo family.

ACCARDO, ANTHONY "TONY" ("Joe Batters")—former bodyguard of Al Capone; suspected as one of the gunmen in the St. Valentine's Day Massacre; boss of Chicago family, 1943–56; *consigliere* of Chicago family.

ADAMO, JOSEPH—brother of Momo Adamo; *capo* in Los Angeles family, supervising activities in San Diego.

ADAMO, MOMO—underboss in Jack Dragna's Los Angeles family; committed suicide.

AHEARN, JAMES F.—Assistant Special Agent in Charge (ASAC) of FBI's San Francisco office.

AIUPPA, JOSEPH ("Joey O'Brien")—boss of Chicago family.

ALBANESE, VINNIE—San Diego builder; friend of Tommy Marson and Frank Sinatra.

ALDERISIO, FELIX "PHILLY" "MILWAUKEE PHIL"—soldier in Chicago family; friend of Fratianno; deceased.

ALEX, GUS "Gussie"—protégé of late Jake "Greasy Thumb" Guzik, non-Italian associate of Chicago family; has vast business interests in Loop; works as liaison between Chicago family and Los Angeles attorney Sid Korshak.

ALIOTO, JOHN—former boss of Milwaukee family.

ALIOTO, JOSEPH L.—noted anti-trust lawyer; was mayor of San Francisco from 1968–76.

ALLEY BOY—*see* Persico, Alphonse.

ALO, VINCENT ("Jimmy Blue Eyes")—*capo* in New York City Genovese family; has spent his life as watchdog over Meyer Lansky.

ALONGI, DOMINIC "FAT DOM"—*capo* in New York City Genovese family.

AMARENA, SALVATORE "SAL"—owner of Sal's Esspresso Caffe in San Francisco.

ANTHONY, MARK (*nee* Petercupo)—native of Cleveland; manager of Bob Hope Enterprises; lifelong friend of Fratianno.

APODACA, JERRY—governor of New Mexico; close friend of William Marchiondo.

ARMSTRONG, JACK—FBI special agent in San Diego.

BARON, ALVIN "AL"—former Assets Manager of Teamsters Central States, Southeast and Southwest Areas Pension Fund.

---

*Information complete as of January 1978.

439

BARRISH, BENNIE—San Francisco bookmaking agent and shylock collector for Fratianno.

BARRON, JACK—FBI special agent in Los Angeles.

BATTAGLIA, CHARLES ("Charley Bats")—formerly from Buffalo; soldier in Los Angeles family in 1950's; later changed allegiance to Joseph Bonanno in Arizona; brother of Johnny "Bats" Battaglia.

BATTERS, JOE—*see* Accardo, Anthony.

BEANS, LOUIS—*see* Fucceri, Louis.

BENNY EGGS—*see* Mangano, Benjamin.

BIAGGIO—*see* Bonventre, Biaggio.

BINION, BENNY "COWBOY"—Dallas crime kingpin who moved to Las Vegas in 1940's; owns Horseshoe Club.

BLACKIE—*see* Licavoli, James.

BLASI, DOMINIC "BUTCH"—former chauffeur and bodyguard of Sam Giancana.

BOMPENSIERO, FRANK "BOMP" ("Frank Gavin")—member of Los Angeles family; was *capo* in charge of San Diego until incarcerated in 1955; demoted to soldier upon release; became Los Angeles *consigliere* in 1976; murdered.

BONANNO, JOSEPH—one of original founders of the five New York City families following murder of Salvatore Maranzano in 1931; deposed by commission in 1964; exiled to Arizona and declared persona non grata. Boss Carmine "Lillo" Galante incarcerated; Bonanno family under leadership of acting boss Nick Marangello.

BONVENTRE, BIAGGIO—soldier in Jack Dragna's Los Angeles family.

BROOKLIER, DOMINIC (*nee* Brucceleri; "Jimmy Regace")—former inmate, with Fratianno, at Ohio penitentiary; worked as booking agent and collector for Fratianno in late 1940's and early 1950's; elected boss of Los Angeles family in 1974.

BROWN, TOMMY—*see* Lucchese, Gaetano.

BRUNO, SAM—soldier in Jack Dragna's Los Angeles family.

BUFALINO, RUSSELL—boss of Pittston, Pennsylvania, family.

CAIFANO, MARSHALL ("Johnny Marshall")—soldier in Chicago family.

CALANDRA, JOHN—soldier in Cleveland family.

CAMPBELL, JUDITH "JUDY"—former girl friend of both President John F. Kennedy and Sam Giancana; introduced to both men by Frank Sinatra.

CANNATELLA, SALVATORE—Buffalo businessman; became involved with Westchester Premier Theater.

CANTILLON, JAMES—Los Angeles criminal attorney; close friend of John Roselli.

CARABBIA, RONALD "RONNIE"—associated with Cleveland family.

CARBO, JOHN "FRANKIE"—formerly with Murder Inc.; was later enforcer for Meyer Lansky; deceased.

CASTELLANO, PAUL "PAULIE"—boss of New York City Gambino family; succeeded Carlo Gambino in 1976.

CELAMTANO, ANDREW "BANJO"—former bodyguard of Frank Sinatra.

CERONE, JOHN "JACKIE THE LACKEY"—underboss of Chicago family.

CERRITO, JOSEPH—boss of San Jose, California, family; deceased.

CHAPMAN, ABRAHAM "TRIGGER ABE"—allegedly former member of Brooklyn Murder Inc. gang; San Francisco hustler and con man.

CHARLEY BATS—*see* Battaglia, Charles.

CISTERNINO, PASQUALE "BUTCHIE"—associated with Cleveland family.

CIVELLA, NICHOLAS "NICK"—boss of Kansas City family.

CIVELLO, JOSEPH—boss of Dallas family.

COHEN, CARL—executive with Sands hotel; later moved to MGM Grand.

COHEN, MICHAEL "MICKEY"—notorious Los Angeles bookmaker in late 1940's and early 1950's; deceased.

COHEN, YALE—executive with Stardust hotel; former inmate with Fratianno at Ohio penitentiary.

COLOMBO, JOSEPH—former boss of New York City Profaci family; changed name to Colombo family; shot in head in 1971; was comatose until death in 1977. Boss is Thomas DiBello.

CONFORTE, JOSEPH—owner of Mustang Ranch brothel on outskirts of Reno.

COOPER, HARRY—investigator with California's Attorney General's Office, assigned to protect Mickey Cohen in late 1940's and early 1950's.

CORALLO, ANTHONY "TONY DUCKS"—acting boss of New York City Lucchese family.

COSTELLO, FRANK "FRANK C." (*nee* Francesco Saveria)—former boss of New York City Genovese family; once popularly known as "Prime Minister" of organized crime; survived shot in head in 1957, but forced into retirement; was longtime associate of Lucky Luciano, who was original founder of Genovese family; deceased.

COWBOY—*see* Binion, Benny.

DAGO LOUIE—*see* Piscopo, Salvatore.

DALITZ, MORRIS B. "MOE"—former member of Mayfield Road gang and Cleveland Combination; came to Las Vegas in late 1940's with his group; became majority owners of Desert Inn and Stardust hotels, and of Rancho La Costa in Carlsbad, California.

D'AMBROSIO, ALPHONSE "FUNZIED"—soldier in New York City Colombo family.

DANOLFO, NICHOLAS "PEANUTS"—former doorman for Fratianno bookie joint in Cleveland; later executive with Desert Inn and Stardust hotels.

DELLACROCE, ANIELLO—underboss of New York City Gambino family.

DELSANTER, ANTHONY "TONY DOPE"—lifelong friend of Fratianno; member of Cleveland family; became *consigliere* in 1975; deceased.

DELUCIA, FELICE ("Paul Ricca")—elder statesman of Chicago family; highly respected for his sage advice; deceased.

DEPALMA, GREGORY "GREG"—in charge of concessions and security at Westchester Premier Theater; became soldier in New York City Gambino family in June 1977.

DESIMONE, FRANK—boss of Los Angeles family from 1957 until his death in 1968.

DIBELLO, THOMAS—boss of New York City Colombo family.

DIPPOLITO, CHARLES AND JOSEPH, father and son, respectively, "Dip"—owned vineyard in Cucamonga; both soldiers in Los Angeles family; both deceased.

DORFMAN, ALLEN—through his father, Paul "Red" Dorfman, a union organizer and early backer of Jimmy Hoffa closely allied with Chicago family, Allen Dorfman came naturally to power within the Teamsters, capturing control in the late 1950's of the union's Central States pension fund. Controlled by the Chicago family, he was the first to arrange huge mob-connected pension fund loans.

DRAGNA, JACK—boss of Los Angeles family until his death in 1957.

DRAGNA, LOUIS TOM "LOUIE"—son of Tom Dragna, soldier in Los Angeles family;

owns Roberta, a large dress manufacturing company.

DRAGNA, THOMAS "TOM"—father of Louis Dragna; *consigliere* of Los Angeles family until 1957.

FARIS, GEORGE—Sacramento, California, trucker; breeder of thoroughbred race horses; friend of Fratianno.

FAT DOM—*see* Alongi, Dominic.

FAT TONY—*see* Salerno, Anthony.

FERRITTO, RAYMOND "RAY"—professional burglar from Erie, Pennsylvania; involved with Cleveland family.

FINE, MICKEY (*nee* Feinberg)—involved in Los Angeles pornography.

FITZSIMMONS, FRANK "FITZ"—president of Teamsters union.

FRABOTTA, OBIE—soldier in Chicago family.

FRANK C.—*see* Costello, Frank.

FRATIANNO, WARREN—brother of Jimmy.

FRATIANNO, WILLIAM "BILLY"—son of Warren Fratianno.

FREIDMAN, MAURICE—owned land of Frontier hotel; involved in Friars Club fraud case; friend of John Roselli.

FUCCERI, LOUIS "LOUIE BEANS"—soldier in New York City Lucchese family.

FUNZI—*see* Tieri, Frank.

FUNZIED—*see* D'Ambrosio, Alphonse.

FUSCO, RICHARD "RITCHIE," "NERVES"—in charge of tickets at Westchester Premier Theater.

GALANTE, CARMINE "LILLO"—boss of New York City Bonanno family; serving prison term for drug trafficking; acting boss is Nick Marangello.

GALLO, JOSEPH "CRAZY JOE"—started "war" with New York City Profaci family when certain promises made to him and his brother Larry were not kept after they killed Albert Anastasia; many died, including "Crazy Joe" and Joseph Colombo.

GALLO, JOSEPH—*consigliere* in New York City Gambino family; no relation to "Crazy Joe" Gallo.

GAMBINO, CARLO—boss of New York City family founded by Philip and Vincent Mangano in 1931; both murdered in 1951 on orders of Albert Anastasia, who assumed leadership and was, himself, murdered in 1957, at which time Gambino became boss; deceased 1976. Boss is Paul Castellano; largest family in United States.

GENOVESE, VITO—in 1957 assumed leadership of New York City family originally founded in 1931 by Lucky Luciano, and bossed for twelve years by Frank Costello after Luciano was deported to Italy in 1945; Genovese died in prison in 1969; boss is Frank "Funzi" Tieri.

GIACALONE, ANTHONY "TONY"—*capo* in Detroit family.

GIACALONE, VITO "BILLY"—brother of Tony; soldier in Detroit family; known as enforcer and leg-breaker.

GIANCANA, SAM "MOONEY"—boss of Chicago family from 1956 until late 1960's when self-exiled in Mexico; murdered.

GIARUSSO, RAYMOND—worked for Fratianno's trucking company.

GIORDANO, ANTHONY "TONY"—boss of St. Louis family.

GLICK, ALLEN—in 1974, with approximately $95 million in loans from Teamsters pension fund, Glick, a young San Diego businessman, gained control of Stardust, Fremont, Hacienda, and Marina hotels in Las Vegas.

GLIMCO, JOSEPH "JOEY"—*capo* in Chicago family; boss of several Teamsters locals.

GOLDBAUM, HY—Los Angeles bookmaker who moved to Las Vegas; opened a sports book at Flamingo; later became executive at Stardust hotel.

GOLDBERGER, JACK—San Francisco Teamsters official.

GRAHAM, WILLIAM "BILL"—for many years a recognized political power in Nevada, operating out of Reno; responsible for providing many mob fronts with gambling licenses; deceased.

GREENBAUM, GUS—formerly from Arizona; brought to Las Vegas by Meyer Lansky to operate Flamingo hotel after murder of Bugsy Siegel; murdered.

GREENE, DANIEL "DANNY"—head of Cleveland Irish gang; associated with John Nardi; murdered.

GREENSPUN, HANK—publisher of Las Vegas *Sun*.

GUASTI, AL—undersheriff of Los Angeles County in 1940's and early 1950's.

HAMILTON, JAMES—District Attorney in El Centro in 1960's.

HAMILTON, JAMES E.—captain in charge of Los Angeles Police Department's intelligence unit in 1950's; deceased.

HILLER, LOUIS "TOM"—Los Angeles attorney; close friend of Louie Dragna.

HOFFA, JAMES RIDDLE "JIMMY"—Teamsters president from 1955 until incarcerated in 1967; succeeded to presidency by Frank Fitzsimmons; missing, presumed murdered.

IANNONE, JAMES ("Danny Wilson")—soldier in Los Angeles family.

JIMMY BLUE EYES—*see* Alo, Vincent.

KAHN, IRVING—San Diego builder; secured nearly $200 million in loans from Teamsters pension fund through Morris Shenker; deceased.

KLEINMAN, MORRIS—member of Dalitz's Desert Inn group.

KOLOD, RUBY—member of Dalitz's Desert Inn group.

KORSHAK, SIDNEY "SID"—attorney specializing in labor law; described in California's Attorney General's report as "the key link between organized crime and big business." His link to Chicago family is Gus Alex.

LANSKY, MEYER—teamed with Bugsy Siegel in early 1920's as freelance assassins; formed own family, consisting mostly of Jewish fronts for Mafiosi in legitimate business.

LANZA, JAMES "JIMMY"—boss of San Francisco family.

LAPORTE, FRANK—Chicago *capo* in charge of rackets in Calumet City, Illinois; invested in Fratianno's trucking company; deceased.

LAROCK, JOHN (*nee* Sebastian LaRocca)—boss of Pittsburgh family.

LEPKE (*nee* Louis Buchalter)—Jewish gangster who took over New York City garment district in 1930's and early 1940's, using services of Murder Inc. to dispose of enemies and competitors; executed in Sing Sing electric chair.

LIBERATORE, ANTHONY "TONY"—soldier in Cleveland family.

LICATA, CARLO—son of Nick; formerly a soldier in Los Angeles family; married "Black Bill" Tocco's daughter; now with Detroit family.

LICATA, NICHOLAS "NICK"—boss of Los Angeles family from 1968 until his death in 1974.

LICAVOLI, JAMES "BLACKIE" ("Jack White")—boss of Cleveland family.

LICAVOLI, PETE—brother of Yonnie; Detroit *capo;* lives on his Grace Ranch in Tucson, Arizona.

LICAVOLI, THOMAS "YONNIE"—brother of Pete; spent 37 years in Ohio penitentiary for murders of bootlegger Jackie Kennedy and his girl friend; deceased.

LILLO—*see* Galante, Carmine.

LoCICERO, GIOCCHINO "JACK"—soldier in Los Angeles family.

LOMBARDO, JOEY "THE CLOWN"—*capo* in Chicago family; watched over Allen Dorfman.

LONARDO, ANGELO "BIG ANGE"—underboss of Cleveland family.

LONGO, DOMINIC—soldier in Los Angeles family; owns Toyota agency in El Monte.

LOUIE DOME—*see* Pacella, Louis.

LUCCHESE, GAETANO ("Tommy 'Three-Finger' Brown")—boss of New York City family founded by Gaetano Gagliano in 1931; deceased in 1967. Boss is Carmine Tramunti, now incarcerated; acting boss is Anthony Corallo.

LUCIANO, LUCKY (*nee* Salvatore Lucania)—founder of one of the original five New York City families; incarcerated in 1936; deported to Italy in 1946; deceased. Family presently known as Genovese family.

MAGADDINO, STEFANO "STEVE"—boss of Buffalo family.

MAHEU, ROBERT—former FBI special agent; owned "private eye" agency that worked for CIA; was liaison between CIA and Mafia in plot to assassinate Fidel Castro; became chief executive officer of Howard Hughes' Las Vegas operation in 1966; fired by Hughes in 1970.

MAITA, PHIL—operator of Easy Street, a porno theater in Redwood, California; grandson of Filippo Maita, a soldier in San Francisco family.

MANGANO, BENJAMIN "BENNY EGGS"—soldier in New York City Genovese family.

MANZI, RICK—husband of Barbara McNair; nephew of Obie Frabotta; friend of Fratianno; murdered.

MARANGELLO, NICHOLAS "NICK"—acting boss of New York City Bonanno family.

MARCELLO, CARLOS—boss of New Orleans family.

MARCHIONDO, WILLIAM "BILLY"—criminal lawyer in Albuquerque, New Mexico.

MARINO, ANGELO—*capo* in San Jose family; owns California Cheese Co., founded by his father, Salvatore, a former member of Pittsburgh family.

MARKOVICS, EVE—daughter of Ivan; beauty contest winner; friend of Fratianno.

MARKOVICS, IVAN—United States representative for Knights of Malta, with offices at United Nations Plaza and title of Ambassador for Special Missions.

MARSON, TOMMY (*nee* Thomas Marsonak Dolowski)—Palm Springs promoter with large investment in Westchester Premier Theater.

MATRANGA, GASPARE—former *capo* in Chicago family; later moved to Upland, California.

McDONALD, DENNIS—lawyer in Hayward, California; represented Fratianno in 1970's.

McMILLAN, LESTER—California assemblyman; accepted $2,500 bribe to get Fratianno transferred from Folsom to Soledad prison.

MELTZER, HAROLD "HAPPY" ("Herbert Fried")—strongarm thug for Mickey Cohen; spied on Cohen for Dragna family.

MILANO, ANTHONY "TONY"—father of Pete Milano, *capo* in Los Angeles family; brother of Frank Milano, former boss of Cleveland family; underboss of Cleveland family until retirement in 1975.

MILANO, PETER—son of Tony Milano; *capo* in Los Angeles family.

MOCERI, LEO "LIPS" ("John Stevens")—soldier in Cleveland family; on lam in California for years, on same murder charge as Yonnie Licavoli; became underboss of Cleveland family in 1975; missing, presumed murdered.

MONICA, JOHN "SPARKY"—one of the biggest sports bookmakers in Los Angeles, with movie colony clientele.

MORGAN, EDWARD P.—former FBI executive; Washington superlawyer; friend of Robert Maheu and John Roselli.

NAPOLI, JAMES "JIMMY NAP"—soldier in New York City Genovese family.

NARDI, JOHN—Cleveland Teamsters official; former bookmaking partner of Fratianno; started "war" against Cleveland family in 1976; murdered.

NEALIS, EDWARD "EDDIE"—Los Angeles gambler who tried to buy Las Vegas Tallyho hotel.

O'CONNELL, JAMES P. "BIG JIM"—CIA agent in charge of CIA–Mafia Mongoose Operation to assassinate Fidel Castro.

OGUL, DAVE—associated with Mickey Cohen; murdered.

PACELLA, LOUIS "LOUIE DOME"—soldier in New York City Genovese family; close friend of Frank Sinatra.

PALERMO, THOMAS "TOMMY"—*consigliere* in Los Angeles family.

PAPALE, RUDY—brother-in-law of Joseph L. Alioto; president of Regal Meat Packing Co.

PATRIARCA, RAYMOND "RAY"—boss of New England family.

PEANUTS—*see* Tranalone, John.

PERSICO, ALPHONSE "ALLEY BOY"—*consigliere* in New York City Colombo family.

PETTI, CHRIS (*nee* Poulos)—strongarm thug in San Diego, associated with Bompensiero and Spilotro.

PINELLI, SALVATORE "SAL"—soldier in Los Angeles family.

PISCOPO, SALVATORE "DAGO LOUIE"—soldier in Los Angeles family; friend of Fratianno in late 1940's and early 1950's.

PLATE, ANTHONY "TONY"—soldier in New York City Gambino family; operates in Miami under direction of Aniello Dellacroce.

POLIZZI, ALFRED "BIG AL"—former boss of Cleveland family.

POLIZZI, ANGELO—formerly from Buffalo; soldier in Los Angeles family.

POLIZZI, MICHAEL "MIKE"—underboss of Detroit family.

PONTI, PHIL—Chicago soldier working as executive with Stardust hotel.

PRESSER, JACKIE—Teamsters International Vice President; Cleveland family's link to the union.

PROFACI, JOSEPH—founder of one of the five New York City families in 1931; deceased in 1962; name of family now changed to Colombo.

RANDAZZO, ANTHONY "TONY"—native of Cleveland; underboss of Tampa family.

REGACE, JIMMY—*see* Brooklier, Dominic.

RHODY, LOU—*see* Rothkopf, Louis.

RICCA, PAUL—*see* DeLucia, Felice.

RICCIARDI, THOMAS "TOMMY"—soldier in Los Angeles family.

RIZZI, MIKE—*see* Rizzitello, Michael.

RIZZITELLO, MICHAEL ("Mike Rizzi")—formerly with "Crazy Joe" Gallo; *capo* in Los Angeles family.

RIZZO, JILLY—gofer for Frank Sinatra.

ROSELLI, JOHN "JOHNNY" (*nee* Filippo Sacco)—began Mafia career with Capone in Chicago; later moved to Los Angeles; was Chicago family coordinator in Las

Vegas during late 1950's and 1960's; close friend of Fratianno; murdered.

ROSENTHAL, FRANK "LEFTY"—Chicago family's front man in Allen Glick's Las Vegas hotels.

ROTHKOPF, BERNARD "BERNIE"—nephew of Louis Rothkopf; former member of Moe Dalitz's Las Vegas group; president of Las Vegas MGM Grand.

ROTHKOPF, LOUIS ("Lou Rhody")—former boss of Mayfield Road gang; member of Cleveland Combination; associate of Dalitz in Desert Inn hotel; deceased.

RUDIN, MILTON "MICKEY"—attorney for Frank Sinatra.

RUMMEL, SAMUEL—attorney for Mickey Cohen who provided police protection; murdered.

RUSSIAN LOUIE—*see* Strauss, Louis.

RYAN, RAY—oilman and gambler; murdered.

SACHS, AL—executive with Stardust and Fremont hotels.

SALERNO, ANTHONY "FAT TONY"—*consigliere* in New York City Genovese family.

SANTO—*see* Trafficante, Santo.

SCALISH, JOHN—boss of Cleveland family from 1953 to 1975; deceased.

SCIORTINO, GASPARE "BILL"—underboss of San Francisco family.

SCIORTINO, SAMUEL "SAM"—underboss of Los Angeles family.

SHAPIRO, IRVING "SLICK"—Toledo bookmaker and scammer; moved to Las Vegas in 1975; associated with Tommy Marson; longtime friend of Fratianno.

SHENKER, MORRIS—former attorney of Jimmy Hoffa; majority owner of Dunes hotel.

SHIMON, JOSEPH—former District of Columbia police inspector; became involved in CIA–Mafia plot to kill Castro; friend of John Roselli and Sam Giancana.

SICA, JOSEPH—strongarm thug for Mickey Cohen; never a member of Los Angeles family.

SIEGEL, BENJAMIN "BUGSY"—New York City mobster and partner of Meyer Lansky; built Flamingo hotel; murdered.

SIMPONIS, NICK—former owner of gambling casino in Cabazon, California; associated with Los Angeles family members.

SMILEY, ALLEN (*nee* Aaron Smeoff)—friend of Bugsy Siegal and John Roselli; gambler with close tie to Los Angeles family.

SPILOTRO, ANTHONY "THE ANT," "LITTLE GUY"—soldier in Chicago family; replaced John Roselli as Chicago family coordinator in Las Vegas.

STACHER, JOSEPH "DOC"—member of Meyer Lansky's group; in charge of building Sands hotel; later deported; deceased.

STELLINO, FRANK—son-in-law of Nick Licata; member of Los Angeles family.

STRAUSS, LOUIS "RUSSIAN LOUIE"—gambler and blackmailer; murdered.

STURMAN, REUBEN—Cleveland pornographer with national distribution.

THAM, RUDY (*nee* Rudolph Tham Antonovich)—San Francisco Teamsters official; friend of Fratianno.

TIERI, FRANK "FUNZI"—boss of New York City Genovese family.

TOCCO, WILLIAM "BLACK BILL"—*capo* in Detroit family; deceased.

TONY DOPE—*see* Delsanter, Anthony.

TRAFFICANTE, SANTO—boss of Tampa, Florida, family.

TRAMUNTI, CARMINE—boss of New York City Lucchese family; incarcerated; acting boss is Anthony Corallo.

TRANALONE, JOHN "PEANUTS"—soldier in Buffalo family; operates in Miami, has travel agency.

TRIPOLI, MIMI—soldier in Los Angeles family; owner of Mimi's pizzeria.

TRISCARO, LOUIS "BABE"—Cleveland Teamsters official; link between Cleveland family and James Hoffa; deceased.

ULLO, JOSEPH SPENCER—soldier in New York City Genovese family; skipped to Los Angeles when unable to repay shylock loan.

VALACHI, JOSEPH—first made guy to reveal Mafia secrets; testified before congressional committee (hearings were televised in 1963); deceased.

VALENTI, FRANK—boss of Rochester family.

VALLARDO, MIKE—native of Youngstown, Ohio; casino manager at Caesars Palace; friend of Fratianno.

VELOTTA, FRANK "SKINNY"—professional burglar; associate of Fratianno.

WADDEN, THOMAS—Washington attorney; formerly associated with Edward Bennett Williams.

WEISMAN, ELIOT—president of Westchester Premier Theater.

WERBER, VIC—Los Angeles bookmaker and shylock; involved in garment industry.

WILLIAMS, ROY—Teamsters International Vice President; linked to Mafia families in Kansas City, St. Louis, and Chicago.

WILSON, DANNY—*see* Iannone, James.

YONNIE—*see* Licavoli, Thomas.

ZAFFARANO, MICKEY—*capo* in New York City Bonanno family; involved in pornography.

ZAPPI, ETTORE "TERRY"—*capo* in New York City Gambino family; involved in pornography.

ZERILLI, ANTHONY "TONY"—boss of Detroit family.

ZERILLI, JOSEPH—patriarch of Detroit family; deceased.

INDEX

† † † †